THE ANGLO-SAXON LIBRARY

THE ANGLO-SAXON LIBRARY

Michael Lapidge

OXFORD
UNIVERSITY PRESS

OXFORD
UNIVERSITY PRESS

Great Clarendon Street, Oxford OX2 6DP

Oxford University Press is a department of the University of Oxford.
It furthers the University's objective of excellence in research, scholarship,
and education by publishing worldwide in

Oxford New York

Auckland Cape Town Dar es Salaam Hong Kong Karachi
Kuala Lumpur Madrid Melbourne Mexico City Nairobi
New Delhi Shanghai Taipei Toronto

With offices in

Argentina Austria Brazil Chile Czech Republic France Greece
Guatemala Hungary Italy Japan Poland Portugal Singapore
South Korea Switzerland Thailand Turkey Ukraine Vietnam

Oxford is a registered trade mark of Oxford University Press
in the UK and in certain other countries

Published in the United States
by Oxford University Press Inc., New York

First published 2006
First published in paperback 2008

British Library Cataloguing in Publication Data
Data available

Library of Congress Cataloging in Publication Data
Data available
ISBN 978-0-19-926722-4 (Hbk.)
978-0-19-923969-6 (Pbk.)

1 3 5 7 9 10 8 6 4 2

Typeset by Anne Joshua, Oxford
Printed in Great Britain
on acid-free paper by
Biddles Ltd., King's Lynn, Norfolk

To Helmut Gneuss

Preface

THE core of the present book derives from three lectures delivered as the E. A. Lowe Lectures in Palaeography to the University of Oxford in Hilary term 2002. The lectures were delivered in the Examination Schools, but were hosted by Corpus Christi College, and I am extremely grateful to the President of Corpus, Sir Tim Lankester, and the Fellows of Corpus for their warm hospitality on those occasions. During my brief period of residence in Corpus I derived great pleasure from discussing libraries, ancient and modern, with the Fellows of Corpus most concerned with these matters, in particular Ewen Bowie, Stephen Harrison, David Rundle, and Michael Winterbottom. Members of the audience also made many helpful suggestions, and I should like to acknowledge the comments of Lesley Abrams, John Blair, Henry Chadwick, David Ganz, Stephen Harrison, Barbara Harvey, Simon Keynes, Henry Mayr-Harting, Richard Sharpe, James Willoughby, and Michael Winterbottom.

At an early point it was suggested by Oxford friends and colleagues that the lectures might be published in the form of a book, and I am very grateful to the Oxford University Press, and to Ruth Parr in particular, for their continuing interest in the project. In preparing the text for publication, I have retained the structure and often the wording of the original lectures, so that Chapters 1–3 are based on the first lecture, Chapter 4 on the second, and Chapter 5 on the third. The text of the lectures has been fully annotated. It was felt by the Press and its readers that the text of the lectures might be too slight to be viable as a monograph, and I was invited by Ruth Parr to consider whether I might 'usefully add a chapter or chapters on any other aspects of the subject'. The result of Ruth's invitation is that I have added five Appendices relevant to the discussion, as well as the 'Catalogue of classical and patristic authors and works composed before AD 700 and known in Anglo-Saxon England'. This 'Catalogue', which now forms a substantial part of the book and is intended as a replacement for Ogilvy's *Books Known to the English 597–1066*, has taken far longer to compile than I originally anticipated, and explains why the Lowe Lectures see publication several years after they were first delivered.

The research which underlies the 'Catalogue' was mostly done during teaching terms at the University of Notre Dame. It would be difficult to imagine a more convenient library anywhere in the world for this kind of research than the library of the Medieval Institute there, where computer terminals with access to all relevant electronic databases are placed adjacent to the principal series of patristic texts (CSEL, CCSL, PL, etc.) and reference works. I also received unstinting help from two of the Institute's Librarians, David Jenkins and Linda Major. Various friends and colleagues, British and North American, have been generous with advice and information: Harry Hine, Simon Keynes, Leslie Lockett, Tom Noble, Michael Reeve, Richard Sharpe, Dan Sheerin, Stephanie West, and Michael Winterbottom. Both David Ganz and Rosalind Love kindly made available to me papers then unpublished on aspects of Anglo-Saxon books and libraries. At the copy-editing stage Bonnie Blackburn brought her formidable learning and clear vision to bear on an unruly typescript, and succeeded in making the presentation much more user-friendly. And it is always a pleasure for an author to be the beneficiary of Anne Joshua's typesetting skills. Finally, Helmut Gneuss is a friend and colleague who has always generously shared information on Anglo-Saxon manuscripts and fragments as they came to his notice, and I dedicate this book to him in gratitude for thirty years' help and support.

M.L.

15 January 2005

Contents

Abbreviations

BAV	Biblioteca Apostolica Vaticana (Vatican City)
BCLL	M. Lapidge and R. Sharpe, *A Bibliography of Celtic-Latin Literature, 400–1200* (Dublin, 1985) [cited by item number]
BHL	[Bollandists], *Bibliotheca Hagiographica Latina*, 2 vols. (Brussels, 1898–1901, with *Supplementum* by H. Fros, 1986) [cited by item number]
Biblical Commentaries	B. Bischoff and M. Lapidge, *Biblical Commentaries from the Canterbury School of Theodore and Hadrian* (CSASE, 10; Cambridge, 1994)
Bischoff, *MS*	B. Bischoff, *Mittelalterliche Studien*, 3 vols. (Stuttgart, 1966–81)
BL	The British Library (London)
BM	Bibliothèque municipale
BNF	Bibliothèque Nationale de France (Paris)
BodL	The Bodleian Library (Oxford)
'Booklists'	M. Lapidge, 'Surviving Booklists from Anglo-Saxon England', in M. Lapidge and H. Gneuss (eds.), *Learning and Literature in Anglo-Saxon England: Studies Presented to Peter Clemoes* (Cambridge, 1985), 33–89; repr. in *Anglo-Saxon Manuscripts: Basic Readings*, ed. M. P. Richards (New York and London, 1994), 87–167
BSB	Bayerische Staatsbibliothek (Munich)
BTL	Bibliotheca Teubneriana Latina Database (CETE-DOC)
CBMLC	Corpus of British Medieval Library Catalogues (London)
CCSL	Corpus Christianorum, Series Latina (Turnhout)
CCC	Corpus Christi College (Cambridge or Oxford)
CCCM	Corpus Christianorum, Continuatio mediaevalis (Turnhout)
CIT	citation of a classical or late antique Latin work by an

Anglo-Saxon author, as listed in Appendix E [cited by author's name and item number]

CL   Cathedral Library

CLA   E. A. Lowe, *Codices Latini Antiquiores*, 11 vols. and Supplement (Oxford, 1934–71; 2nd edn. of vol. ii, 1972) [cited by volume and item number]

CLCLT   CETEDOC Library of Christian Latin Texts (database) (Turnhout)

Comm.   *Commentarius*

CPG   *Clavis Patrum Graecorum*, ed. M. Geerard, 5 vols. (Turnhout, 1983–7, with *Supplementum*, 1998)

CPL   *Clavis Patrum Latinorum*, ed. E. Dekkers and A. Gaar (3rd edn., Steenbrugge, 1995) [cited by item number]

CSASE   Cambridge Studies in Anglo-Saxon England (Cambridge)

CSEL   Corpus Scriptorum Ecclesiasticorum Latinorum (Vienna)

CSLMA   *Clavis Scriptorum Latinorum Medii Aevi: Auctores Galliae, 735–987*, ed. M.-H. Jullien and F. Perelman (Turnhout, 1994– ; in progress [vol. ii (1999) is devoted solely to the writings of Alcuin]) [cited by item number, with page references given in parentheses]

DACL   *Dictionnaire d'archéologie chrétienne et de liturgie*, ed. F. Cabrol and H. Leclercq, 15 vols. in 30 (Paris, 1907–53)

EETS   Early English Text Society

Ep(p).   *Epistula(e)*

GL   *Grammatici Latini*, ed. H. Keil, 8 vols. (Leipzig, 1857–80). Index by F. Boettner, vii. 579–668.

Gneuss   H. Gneuss, *Handlist of Anglo-Saxon Manuscripts: A List of Manuscripts and Manuscript Fragments Written or Owned in England up to 1100* (Medieval and Renaissance Texts and Studies, 241; Tempe, Ariz., 2001) [cited by item number]

Hom.   *Homilia(e)*

ICL   D. Schaller and E. Könsgen, *Initia Carminum*

	Latinorum saeculo undecimo Antiquiorum (Göttingen, 1977) [cited by item number]
ICVR	*Inscriptiones Christianae Vrbis Romae*, ed. G. B. De Rossi, 2 vols. (Rome, 1861–88)
INV(i)	the inventories of Latin books from Anglo-Saxon libraries (excluding biblical and liturgical books) printed in Appendix A [cited by inventory and item number]
INV(ii)	the eighth-century inventories of books from the area of the Anglo-Saxon mission in Germany, printed in Appendix B [cited by inventory and item number]
Kaster	R. A. Kaster, 'Prosopography', in his *Guardians of Language: The Grammarian and Society in Late Antiquity* (Berkeley and Los Angeles, 1988), 233–440 [cited by item number of author]
Lapidge, *ALL*	M. Lapidge, *Anglo-Latin Literature, 600–899* (London, 1996) [i]; *Anglo-Latin Literature, 900–1066* (London, 1993) [ii]
Libri Sancti Kyliani	B. Bischoff and J. Hofmann, *Libri Sancti Kyliani: Die Würzburger Schreibschule und die Dombibliothek im VIII. und IX. Jahrhundert* (Würzburg, 1952)
LLA	*Handbuch der lateinischen Literatur der Antike*, ed. R. Herzog and P. L. Schmidt (Handbuch der Altertumswissenschaft, 8; Munich, 1989– ; in progress: those published are I. *Die archaische Literatur: Von den Anfängen bis Sullas Tod*, ed. W. Suerbaum (2002); IV. *Die Literatur des Umbruchs: Von der römischen zur christlichen Literatur, 117 bis 284 N. Chr.*, ed. K. Sallmann (1997); and V. *Restauration und Erneuerung: Die lateinische Literatur von 284 bis 374 N. Chr.*, ed. R. Herzog (1989)) [cited by author number]
MBKDS	*Mittelalterliche Bibliothekskataloge Deutschlands und der Schweiz*, ed. P. Lehmann et al., 4 vols. in 11 parts (Munich, 1918–89)
MGH	Monumenta Germaniae Historica
— AA	— Auctores Antiquissimi
— Epist.	— Epistolae (in Quarto)
— PLAC	— Poetae Latini Aevi Carolini

MSS(i)	manuscripts written or owned in England up to 1100, as listed in Gneuss
MSS(ii)	surviving eighth-century manuscripts from the area of the Anglo-Saxon mission in Germany, listed in Appendix C [cited by item number]
NLS	National Library of Scotland (Edinburgh)
NLW	National Library of Wales (Aberystwyth)
ÖNB	Österreichische Nationalbibliothek (Vienna)
PL	Patrologia Latina, ed. J. P. Migne, 221 vols. (Paris, 1844–64)
PLD	Patrologia Latina Database
Poetria Nova	*Poetria Nova. A CD-ROM of Latin Medieval Poetry (650–1250 A.D.) with a Gateway to Classical and Late Antiquity Texts*, ed. P. Mastandrea and L. Tessarolo (Florence, 2001)
RAC	*Reallexikon für Antike und Christentum*, ed. T. Klauser, E. Dassmann, et al. (Stuttgart, 1950– ; in progress)
RLM	C. Halm, *Rhetores Latini Minores* (Leipzig, 1863)
S	P. H. Sawyer, *Anglo-Saxon Charters: An Annotated List and Bibliography* (London, 1968) [cited by item number]
SASLC	*Sources of Anglo-Saxon Literary Culture*, ed. F. M. Biggs, T. D. Hill, P. E. Szarmach, and E. G. Whatley (Kalamazoo, 2001– ; in progress)
Scribes and Scholars	L. D. Reynolds and N. G. Wilson, *Scribes and Scholars: A Guide to the Transmission of Greek and Latin Literature*, 3rd edn. (Oxford, 1991)
Settimane	*Settimane di studio del Centro italiano di studi sull'alto medioevo* (Spoleto)
SHA	Scriptores [*rectius* Scriptor] Historiae Augustae
TxtTrans	*Texts and Transmission: A Survey of the Latin Classics*, ed. L. D. Reynolds (Oxford, 1983)
UB	Universitätsbibliothek

Introduction

A LIBRARY is simply a collection of books. In the sense in which I shall use the word, however, a library is a collection of books acquired and arranged for the purposes of study and the pursuit of knowledge. (I thus, by this definition, exclude the collections of liturgical books which every Anglo-Saxon church may be assumed to have owned.) Crucial to my definition is the concept of study and the pursuit of knowledge, for it entails the assumption that knowledge is contained in books. The more books, the more knowledge, in theory at least, and again with the corollary that the sum of human knowledge could be contained and represented in a single library, however vast. This seductive notion, of the library as the embodiment of all knowledge, is brilliantly captured in one of the *Ficciones* of the Argentinian writer Jorge Luis Borges (1899–1986), who was Director of the National Library of Argentina, but who was blind when appointed to that post in 1955 (he wrote in one of his poems of 'the skill of God / Who with such magnificent irony / Gave me at the same time darkness and the books').[1] The short story in his *Ficciones* to which I refer is one called 'The Library of Babel' (1941).[2] The library described by Borges 'is composed of an indefinite, perhaps infinite, number of hexagonal galleries . . . From any hexagon one can see the floors above and below—one after another, endlessly. The arrangement of the galleries is always the same: twenty bookshelves, five to each side, line four of the hexagon's six sides.'[3] The layout of the library, with these endless galleries, is obviously that of a labyrinth. And what of the contents? Borges continues: 'In all the Library, there are no two identical books. From those incontrovertible premises, the librarian deduced that the Library is "total"—perfect, complete, and whole.' Borges gives a swift sample of its contents: 'the gnostic gospel of Basilides, the commentary upon that gospel, the commentary on the commentary on that gospel, the translation of every book into every language . . .

---

[1] 'Poema de los dones' (1960): 'la maestría / de Dios, que con magnífica ironía / me dio a la vez los libros y la noche'; Borges, *Obras completas*, ed. Frias, 809.

[2] Ibid. 465–71 ('La biblioteca de Babel'); for English translations, see Borges, *Collected Fictions*, trans. Hurley, 112–18, from which I quote; also in *Labyrinths*, trans. Yates and Irby, 78–86.

[3] *Collected Fictions*, 112.

the treatise Bede could have written . . . on the mythology of the
Saxon people, the lost books of Tacitus.'[4] It is the sort of library
scholars dream about: 'When it was announced that the Library
contained all books, the first reaction was unbounded joy. All men felt
themselves the possessors of an intact and secret treasure. There was
no personal problem, no world problem, whose eloquent solution did
not exist—somewhere in some hexagon.'[5] In short, it is the tantalizing
possibility of acquiring all knowledge that motivates Borges's story.

The conception of a vast and labyrinthine library containing all
existing books, and therefore the sum total of human knowledge, was
given powerful expression in 1980 in Umberto Eco's novel *The Name
of the Rose*, first published in Italian as *Il nome della rosa*.[6] It is clear
that Borges's story was the source and ultimate inspiration of Eco's
novel.[7] The novel concerns the travels of an English monk named
William of Baskerville, an erstwhile student of Roger Bacon and
therefore much given to the spirit of scientific enquiry, to a monastery
called San Michele located somewhere in the Piedmont (north-west
Italy) in 1327. The distinctive feature of the monastery is that it is
built as a fortress, and that its great library, housed in a massive tower
in one corner of the fortress, is laid out as a labyrinth. When William
finally succeeds in penetrating the labyrinth, he is astonished by the
riches of the library's holdings; and indeed they are riches which
would make any student of Anglo-Saxon libraries tremble with
excitement: not only the complete works of Aldhelm and Bede, but
also the *Liber monstrorum*, the *Hisperica famina* (which William
manages to quote inaccurately), and even the works of Virgilius
Maro Grammaticus.[8] On the basis of information given by Eco
concerning the size of the rooms which housed the books, and the
number of shelves in each, John Ward was recently able to calculate
that this vast (but fictional) library contained some 87,000 books.[9]

Now it is preposterous enough that any librarian would wish to
acquire a copy of the *Hisperica famina*; but what is completely
preposterous is the alleged size of the library. No medieval library,

---

[4] *Collected Fictions*, 115.   [5] Ibid.

[6] Eco, *Il nome della rosa*; trans. Weaver as *The Name of the Rose*.

[7] Because of the density and number of its allusions to medieval Latin literature, *The
Name of the Rose* has spawned its own corpus of exegesis, notably Haft, White, and White,
The Key to 'The Name of the Rose'; for the influence of Borges's story on Eco's conception
of his 'labyrinthine library', see pp. 27–8.

[8] *Il nome della rosa*, 313–15; trans. Weaver, 311–12.

[9] Ward, 'Alexandria and its Medieval Legacy', 165.

not even the largest—Clairvaux, say, or the papal library at Avignon—housed more than 2,000 books; and the typical monastic library was much smaller still. *The Name of the Rose* is fiction, of course. But what makes it such compelling reading is the underlying motif that the library functioned to ensure the preservation of all knowledge. As the monastery's senior monk—a blind librarian whose name is Jorge (!)—explains to William:

the work of this monastery . . . is study, and the preservation of knowledge . . . Preservation, I say, and not search, because it is a property of knowledge, as a human thing, that it has been defined and completed over the course of centuries, from the preaching of the prophets to the interpretation of the fathers of the Church. There is no progress, no revolution of ages, in the history of knowledge, but at most a continuous and sublime recapitulation.[10]

These sentiments would apply equally to the work of anonymous Anglo-Saxon librarians, who were concerned with the sublime, but ultimately incomplete, 'recapitulation' of the libraries of late antiquity.

In any case, the imaginative power of Eco's novel, especially its depiction of the vast fictional library, is, I suspect, the source of the renewed enthusiasm for the study of ancient, but lost, libraries which has emerged during the past twenty-five years. There has been so much publication that one might almost speak of the emergence of a new field, a field which might be called 'palaeobibliothecography'. Shortly after Eco's book came Luciano Canfora's study of the lost library of Alexandria, *La biblioteca scomparsa*. Canfora's book is partly a work of fiction (some chapters consist, for example, of imagined dialogue between Demetrius of Phaleron, at whose suggestion the library at Alexandria was probably founded, and Ptolemy I Soter, its royal patron),[11] partly a work of historical reconstruction. It had immediate and immense impact: it was translated into French and English,[12] and inspired in turn a number of independent studies on the Alexandrian library.[13] The spotlight soon shifted to other vanished libraries of the ancient world, and resulted in an important collection of essays on ancient and medieval libraries edited by

[10] *Il nome della rosa*, 402; trans. Weaver, 399.

[11] On the establishment and administration of the library of Alexandria, see below, Ch. 2.

[12] *La Véritable Histoire de la bibliothèque d'Alexandrie*, trans. Manganaro and Dubroca; *The Vanished Library*, trans. Ryle.

[13] El-Abbadi, *The Life and Fate of the Ancient Library of Alexandria*, and MacLeod (ed.), *The Library of Alexandria*.

Guglielmo Cavallo,[14] as well as substantial monographs by Rudolf
Fehrle[15] and Horst Blanck.[16] The English-speaking world is served
by a less weighty but useful book on the subject by Lionel Casson.[17]
The archaeological remains of ancient libraries have been illustrated
in a book edited by Wolfram Hoepfner,[18] and libraries from antiquity
to the Renaissance, both in the Latin West and Byzantine East, are
lavishly illustrated in a massive volume by Konstantinos Staikos.[19]
Byzantine libraries, too, particularly the contents of the vanished
library described and recorded in detail by Photius, patriarch of
Constantinople (858–67, 877–86), have recently attracted scholarly
attention.[20] Nor have publishers been slow to realize the potential of
the burgeoning field of palaeobibliothecography: the Cambridge
University Press has launched a multi-volume project entitled *A
History of Libraries in Britain and Ireland*, of which the first volume,
edited by M. T. J. Webber and E. S. Leedham-Green, extends from
the beginnings to the outbreak of the Civil War.[21]

The present book on the Anglo-Saxon library may similarly be
situated in the context of this burgeoning science of palaeobibliothecography. Before turning to evidence for vanished Anglo-Saxon
libraries, however, it may be helpful briefly to survey what can be
known of the libraries of antiquity, in order to provide some historical
perspective on the nature and contents of Anglo-Saxon libraries.

---

[14] Cavallo (ed.), *Le biblioteche nel mondo antico e medievale*. The volume includes several
reprinted essays (e.g. by Bischoff on the library of Charlemagne), but also important new
essays by Luciano Canfora, 'Le biblioteche ellenistiche' (pp. 3–28) and Paolo Fedeli,
'Biblioteche private e pubbliche a Roma e nel mondo romano' (pp. 29–64).

[15] Fehrle, *Das Bibliothekswesen im alten Rom*.

[16] Blanck, *Das Buch in der Antike*, which includes chapters on 'Die Bibliotheken'
(pp. 133–78), 'Die Architektur und räumliche Einrichtung der Bibliotheken' (pp. 179–
214), and 'Betrieb und Verwaltung der Bibliotheken' (pp. 215–22).

[17] Casson, *Libraries in the Ancient World*.

[18] *Antike Bibliotheken*, ed. Hoepfner.

[19] Staikos, *The Great Libraries*, trans. Cullen. Staikos is an architect with amateur
interest particularly in Byzantine libraries (pp. 137–86); not surprisingly, perhaps, his few
remarks on 'Celtic and Anglo-Saxon libraries' (pp. 197–8) are hopelessly inaccurate.

[20] Wilson, *Photius: The Bibliotheca*. The *Bibliotheca* of Photius was not published until
1601 and only came to be widely known during the course of the 17th c. (even though the
work was known in the 15th c. to both Ambrogio Traversari and Cardinal Bessarion). The
mysterious circumstances which lay behind the publication of the third edition (Rouen,
1653) are explored by Canfora, *La Biblioteca del patriarcha*.

[21] Webber and Leedham-Green (eds.), *A History of Libraries in Britain and Ireland*, i:
From the Beginnings to the Outbreak of the Civil War. The volume is to include a valuable
essay on 'Anglo-Saxon Libraries' by David Ganz. I am extremely grateful to Professor
Ganz for allowing me to read his essay in advance of publication.

Vanished Libraries of Classical Antiquity

BY THE time that the first Anglo-Saxon libraries were assembled, during (presumably) the course of the seventh century AD, libraries both public and private had been a significant feature of Mediterranean civilization for more than a thousand years. Although the largest and most famous of these Mediterranean libraries had been dispersed or destroyed by the time that Pope Gregory's missionaries reached England in 597, some understanding of the organization and contents of the earlier Mediterranean libraries helps to illuminate the severely reduced circumstances in which books were collected and housed in England during the period 600–1100. Before turning to Anglo-Saxon libraries, therefore, I should like briefly to consider Mediterranean libraries, under three headings: Alexandria and the libraries of the Greek world; the libraries of ancient Rome; and Christian libraries of the patristic period.

ALEXANDRIA AND THE LIBRARIES OF THE GREEK WORLD

During the course of the sixth century BC, writing came to be widely used in the Greek world for literary (rather than purely administrative) purposes. Copies of the poems of Homer were made, soon to be followed (in the fifth century) by copies of the plays of the great Athenian playwrights (Aeschylus, Sophocles, Euripides, and Aristophanes), lyric poets such as Pindar, and the historians Herodotus and Thucydides. Inevitably, collections of books—or, properly speaking, papyrus rolls[1]—were assembled, both for private and for public use. Already in the sixth century the tyrant Peisistratus (c.560–527 BC) is said to have assembled a substantial library in Athens,[2] and

---

[1] Turner, *Athenian Books*, and Lewis, *Papyrus in Classical Antiquity*, who notes (pp. 11–13) that papyrus was expensive because it had to be imported from Egypt. See also Lewis, *Papyrus in Classical Antiquity: A Supplement*.

[2] The evidence for Greek libraries is carefully assembled by Platthy, *Sources on the Earliest Greek Libraries*; for Peisistratus, see pp. 97–110 (twenty-seven *testimonia*,

in the following century the playwright Euripides is mocked by
Aristophanes for having acquired a collection of books (*Frogs* 943). By
the end of the century, booksellers are widely attested in Athens and
elsewhere.[3] During the fourth century both Plato and Aristotle are
known to have assembled libraries.[4] It is arguable that the large
personal library of Aristotle served as the inspiration and model for
the great library of Alexandria.[5]

However, all these early attempts to assemble libraries were
eclipsed by the mighty library assembled and funded in Alexandria
by the Ptolemies, the dynasty of kings who succeeded Alexander (d.
323 BC) and who ruled Egypt until it was taken under the direct rule
of Rome following the death of Cleopatra, the last Ptolemy, in 30 BC.
In the attempt to make Alexandria the world's outstanding centre of
learning, the first king of the dynasty, Ptolemy I Soter (367–282 BC),
provided the substantial endowment necessary to establish a Museion
(literally a 'temple of the Muses') in the palace quarter in Alexandria.[6]
This Museion housed, at royal expense, a community of scholars who
were employed, tax-free and all expenses paid, to pursue research and
scientific enquiry.[7] The Museion was established as a result of Soter's
consultation with various advisers, among whom was Demetrius of
Phaleron, sometime tyrant of Athens (317–307 BC) and a Peripatetic
philosopher of the school (called the Lyceum) of Aristotle. Through
the advice of Demetrius, the Ptolemaic Museion was modelled, to
some extent at least, on Aristotle's Lyceum; and it is probable that the
notion of providing a library to sustain the researches of the scholars
attached to the Museion was similarly modelled on the library of
Aristotle. In any event, Soter's son and successor, Ptolemy II
Philadelphus (282–246 BC), is usually credited with establishing the

incl. Isidore, *Etym.* vi. 3. 3: 'apud Graecos autem bibliothecam primus instituisse
Pisistratus creditur'; Isidore's notice is drawn from Aulus Gellius, *Noctes Atticae* vii. 17. 1).

    [3] On the beginnings of the book trade, see Casson, *Libraries in the Ancient World*, 26–8.
    [4] See Platthy, *Sources on the Earliest Greek Libraries*, 121–4 (Plato: eight *testimonia*, incl.
Aulus Gellius, *Noctes Atticae* iii. 17), and 124–9 (Aristotle: eleven *testimonia*, incl. Gellius,
Noctes Atticae iii. 17, and Strabo, *Geogr.* xiii. 1. 54–5, on which see following note).
    [5] Strabo, *Geogr.* xiii. 1. 54: '[Aristotle] was the first to have assembled a collection of
books and to have taught the kings in Egypt how to arrange a library.'
    [6] On the Museion, see Fraser, *Ptolemaic Alexandria*, i. 312–19, and El-Abbadi, *The Life
and Fate*, 84–90.
    [7] An attractive picture of the community is drawn by Pfeiffer, *The History of Classical
Scholarship*, 97: 'They had a carefree life: free meals, high salaries, no taxes to pay, very
pleasant surroundings, good lodgings and servants.' The communal life of the Museion is
inevitably compared with (the popular conception of) scholarly life in Oxford and
Cambridge colleges: cf. Fraser, *Ptolemaic Alexandria*, i. 315–16.

library and appointing a director to supervise its programme of acquisition and accession.[8]

From the time of Philadelphus onwards, the Museion and its library were able to attract the services of some of the most outstanding intellectuals of the Hellenistic world. Among those who held the post of director of the library were (in chronological order): Zenodotus of Ephesus (b. *c*.325 BC), the first director of the library (from *c*.284 BC) and the first great textual critic of Homer;[9] his successor Apollonius of Rhodes (*c*.270–245 BC?), author of the learned and widely influential epic poem *Argonautica*;[10] Eratosthenes of Cyrene (*c*.285–195 BC), director of the library from *c*.245 until his death *c*.195 BC, a scientist skilled in geography, geometry, astronomy, and chronography, who was renowned in antiquity for accurately calculating the circumference of the earth;[11] Aristophanes of Byzantium (*c*.257–180 BC), director of the library until his death, another outstanding (and outstandingly influential) textual critic of the Homeric poems, as well as of Hesiod and Pindar;[12] and finally Aristarchus of Samothrace (*c*.216–144 BC), director from *c*.153 BC, and influential as a textual critic and commentator on early Greek poetry.[13] Towering above all these, in many ways, was the scholar-poet Callimachus of Cyrene, who flourished under Ptolemy II Philadelphus (282–246 BC), and who, although he apparently never held the post of director of the library, was inextricably bound up in its activities.[14] This is not the place to describe the influential corpus of Callimachus' learned poetry; what is important here is that, as scholar-librarian, he compiled a monumental (but now lost) work in 120 rolls called the *Pinakes* ('Tables'), a vast bio-bibliographical catalogue of all the authors represented in the Alexandrian library.[15]

---

[8] On the library itself, see the earlier study by Parsons, *The Alexandrian Library*, and esp. Fraser, *Ptolemaic Alexandria*, i. 320–35, as well as Casson, *Libraries*, 31–47. More recent studies include: El-Abbadi, *The Life and Fate*; Delia, 'From Romance to Rhetoric'; Barnes, 'Cloistered Bookworms'; and there is imaginative (if often fictional and unreliable) treatment in Canfora, *The Vanished Library*, trans. Ryle, on which see above, p. 3. A bracing antidote to much wishful thinking about the size and nature of the library is found in Bagnall, 'Alexandria: Library of Dreams'.

[9] Pfeiffer, *The History of Classical Scholarship*, 105–19.   [10] Ibid. 140–8.

[11] Ibid. 152–70.   [12] Ibid. 171–209.   [13] Ibid. 210–33.

[14] Ibid. 123–40; see also Fraser, *Ptolemaic Alexandria*, i. 330: 'Neither the Suda-*Life* of Callimachus nor the Oxyrhynchus papyrus, nor indeed any ancient source, except one, suggests that he was Librarian.' (The 'Oxyrhynchus papyrus', POxy 1241, is a 2nd-c. AD list of the directors of the Alexandrian library.)

[15] On the *Pinakes*, see Pfeiffer, *The History of Classical Scholarship*, 127–34, and esp. Blum, *Kallimachos: The Alexandrian Library*. On the maximum number of rolls which

It is clear from the scope of a work such as the *Pinakes* that the library at Alexandria was vast by ancient standards. In scale and scope it apparently dwarfed any other library in antiquity.[16] Beginning with Philadelphus, the Ptolemies went to huge expense to acquire books of every kind, on every subject, not only in Greek, but also in Egyptian and Hebrew (it was at the instigation of Philadelphus that a Greek translation of the Old Testament was prepared by seventy or so translators, hence known as the 'Septuagint').[17] Galen (AD 129–99) reports at one point that any ship docking in Alexandria had any books it was carrying confiscated for copying.[18] The size of the library is known from the Byzantine poet and commentator John Tzetzes (*c.*1110–*c.*1185), who in his commentary on Aristophanes—possibly based on an earlier Alexandrian commentary, perhaps by Callimachus—notes that the 'Palace library had 400,000 mixed rolls and 90,000 single, unmixed rolls, as Callimachus, who was a young man at the court, records'.[19] That is to say, 490,000 papyrus rolls in total. Scholars treat this figure with respect. An even larger number— nearly 700,000—is given by Aulus Gellius in the second century AD.[20] Now a number of rolls might be accommodated in a single codex (that is to say, in the form of a modern book). Horst Blanck notes, for example, that the *Histories* of Herodotus would have been accommodated in nine rolls, but that the same work is printed in only two modern codex-form books (as, for example, in the Oxford Classical

could have been described in the *Pinakes* (not in any case more than 100,000), see Bagnall, 'Alexandria', 356 n. 36.

[16] There is salutary and sceptical discussion of the size of the library (as reported in ancient testimonies) by Bagnall, 'Alexandria', 351–4.

[17] According to the *Letter of Aristeas* (probably mid-2nd c. BC), it was Ptolemy II Philadelphus who commissioned a Greek translation of the Jewish Law (Torah) for the royal library of Alexandria; the task of translation was accomplished by seventy-two scholars sent from Jerusalem. The text is ed. Pelletier, *La Lettre d'Aristée à Philocrate*; for discussion, see Schürer, *The History of the Jewish People*, iii. 677–87, as well as Fraser, *Ptolemaic Alexandria*, i. 320–1, 696–704, and Gruen, *Heritage and Hellenism*, 207–22.

[18] Galen, *Comm. in Hippocratis Epidemias*, iii; see Fraser, *Ptolemaic Alexandria*, i. 325, ii. 480–1.

[19] Translation adapted from Barnes, 'Cloistered Bookworms', 64; see discussion by Fraser, *Ptolemaic Alexandria*, i. 329, ii. 485, who notes that 'mixed' rolls are probably 'rolls containing more than one work, whether it be by the same or by different authors', whereas unmixed rolls contain 'single works or parts of a single work' (i. 329). See also Canfora, 'Le biblioteche ellenistiche', 11–13.

[20] *Noctes Atticae* vii. 17. 3: 'ingens postea numerus librorum in Aegypto ab Ptolemaeis regibus uel conquisitus uel confectus est ad milia ferme uoluminum septingenta.' The reading *septingenta* (hence 700,000 volumes) is that of the best witness (V), supported by Ammianus Marcellinus, *Res gestae* xxii. 16. 13; the *recentiores*, contaminated by Isidore, *Etym.* vi. 3. 5, read *septuaginta* (hence 70,000 volumes).

Texts edition); furthermore, rolls of poetry may often have been shorter than rolls of prose. And there is no way of knowing how many duplicates the library contained (probably a substantial number, to judge by the work of collation of copies of Homer carried out by Zenodotus, Aristophanes of Byzantium, and Aristarchus). All in all, Blanck suggests, a figure equivalent to some 80,000 modern volumes is probably in question.[21] By any reckoning this is a vast number. No other ancient library approached it.

The site of the Museion and its library has never been identified through archaeological excavation.[22] The layout of the library and its appurtenances must therefore be a matter of conjecture. Basing himself on the layout of the Ramesseum excavated at Thebes in the late nineteenth century, and the possible identification there of a library, Canfora has conjectured that the library of the Museion was 'not a library but a shelf, or several shelves, running along one side of the covered walk'.[23] According to Canfora's hypothesis, scholars would have been obliged to seek out a particular roll (the rolls were identified by means of tags fastened to one end) and consult it *in situ*, while standing in the colonnade, the implication being that the library was designed for quick scholarly consultation of a reference, not for a leisurely afternoon browsing through the treasures of early Greek literature. However, the very scale of the library casts doubt on such a hypothesis: there will of necessity have been numerous administrative offices and accession rooms in the vicinity of the shelves (or, as we should now say, the 'book-stacks'), and it requires no stretch of imagination to suppose that, in the words of P. M. Fraser, 'there were abundant courtyards and colonnades which could have served as reading-rooms and study-quarters, while the "book-stacks" may have been accommodated in rooms attached to the stoa.'[24] Certainly it will have been impossible to do the sort of detailed textual collation accomplished by Zenodotus, Aristophanes, and Aristarchus while remaining standing.

What happened to the library is unknown. Ancient sources conflict. Many books may accidentally have been destroyed during Caesar's war with Alexandria in 48 BC.[25] It has been suggested that

---

[21] Blanck, *Das Buch in der Antike*, 140.

[22] See Rodziewicz, 'A Review of the Archaeological Evidence'.

[23] *The Vanished Library*, 77; cf. Fraser, *Ptolemaic Alexandria*, i. 323.

[24] *Ptolemaic Alexandria*, i. 325.

[25] The (inconclusive) evidence is examined by Fraser, ibid. i. 334–5, and by Barnes, 'Cloistered Bookworms', 70–3.

the library was probably finally destroyed when the palace quarter was sacked by the Emperor Aurelian (270–5) in AD 273.[26] But the legend of the vast library lived on through antiquity and the Middle Ages, and it has recently been revived under the auspices of UNESCO and the Egyptian government, which have constructed a new Alexandrian library, built in granite in the shape of the moon and covered with hieroglyphs, and ready to house five million books and 100,000 manuscripts.[27] There is already grumbling from Islamic fundamentalists about what kind of books are to be included.

Of course the library at Alexandria was not the only library in the Hellenistic world. Other successors of Alexander attempted to rival what the Ptolemies had accomplished at Alexandria, notably the Seleucids who established a library at Antioch during the reign of Antiochus III (222–187 BC), and the Attalids who established at Pergamum a library which was the only library of the ancient world whose holdings could rival those of Alexandria. The library at Pergamum was apparently founded by Eumenes II (197–160 BC); its layout has been revealed by archaeological excavation, and its ruins may be seen to this day.[28] Some indication of the size of the library at Pergamum derives from a report by Plutarch that Marcus Antonius had offered (presumably in 41 or 40 BC) to hand over to Cleopatra (the last Ptolemy) and the library at Alexandria some 200,000 volumes from the library at Pergamum, the eastern empire having come under his control following the defeat of Cassius and Brutus at Philippi in 42 BC.[29]

THE LIBRARIES OF ANCIENT ROME

Rome derived its cultural orientation from Greece, and it is not surprising that Rome should have attempted to emulate its cultural master in the matter of libraries.[30] The earliest Roman libraries,

---

[26] Canfora, *The Vanished Library*, 87, 195. The source of this suggestion is Ammianus Marcellinus, *Res gestae* xxii. 16. 15, who notes that under Aurelian the area of the palace (the Brucheion) was destroyed by fire when Aurelian went to Alexandria to suppress an Egyptian revolt. But see the sceptical discussion of Bagnall, 'Alexandria', 356–9, who suggests that the books may eventually have rotted away through neglect rather than through destruction in a single cataclysmic event.

[27] For illustration, see *Antike Bibliotheken*, ed. Hoepfner, 39–40.

[28] Casson, *Libraries in the Ancient World*, 49–53; *Antike Bibliotheken*, ed. Hoepfner, 41–52.

[29] Plutarch, *Vita M. Antonii*, c. 58; see Canfora, 'Le biblioteche ellenistiche', 13.

[30] The essential discussions of Roman libraries are: Strocka, 'Römische Bibliotheken'; Fehrle, *Das Bibliothekswesen*, an extended essay based on a dissertation; Fedeli, 'Biblioteche

however, were due not so much to emulation as to spoliation. Several substantial Greek libraries were carried back to Italy as spoils of Roman conquests in the Greek East. Following his victory at Pydna (north-east Greece) in 168 BC, L. Aemilius Paullus confiscated the library of the defeated Macedonian king Perseus and transported it to Rome.[31] The famous library of Aristotle, which had undergone many vicissitudes since Aristotle's death in 322 BC, was confiscated following the capture and sack of Athens by Sulla in 86 BC, and transported to Sulla's villa at Cuma (near Naples).[32] Sulla's sometime colleague, L. Licinius Lucullus, in the aftermath of his expedition against Mithridates, king of Pontus, in 66 BC seized the vast royal library as war spoils, and transported it to his magnificent villa at Tusculum (near modern Frascati), where it was made accessible to interested scholars.[33] The presence of these large libraries on Italian soil encouraged private Roman citizens of the first century BC to assemble libraries of their own.[34]

The most famous private libraries were probably those assembled by T. Pomponius Atticus (110–32 BC) and Cicero (106–43 BC), but the amassing of large private libraries was a feature of civilized Roman life which continued into the days of the later Roman empire. To judge by works quoted in his vast oeuvre (some seventy-five titles in c.600 rolls), the library of the antiquary M. Terentius Varro (116–27 BC), housed at his villa at Cassino, must have been enormous. In the first century AD the poet Persius bequeathed to his mentor L. Annaeus Cornutus a personal library which included some 700 rolls containing the writings of Chrysippus.[35] In the third century AD, before c.235, the poet Serenus Sammonicus is said to have bequeathed to the emperor Gordian (II) the Younger (AD 238) a personal library of some 62,000 rolls.[36] A passage in Ammianus Marcellinus (written c.390)

private e pubbliche'; and Casson, *Libraries in the Ancient World*, 61–123. For bibliography for the period 1935–85, see Bruce, 'Roman Libraries'.

[31] Plutarch, *Vita L. Aemilii Paulli*, c. 25; Isidore, *Etym.* vi. 5. 1: 'Romae primus librorum copiam advexit Aemilius Paulus, Perse Macedonum rege devicto.'

[32] Plutarch, *Vita Sullae*, c. 26.

[33] Plutarch, *Vita Luculli*, c. 42; cf. Isidore, *Etym.* vi. 5. 1.

[34] See, in general, Rawson, *Intellectual Life in the Roman Republic*, 100–14, on public patronage, with brief discussion of the library of Atticus at p. 101, and Caesar's plans for his library at p. 113, as well as Fantham, *Roman Literary Culture*, 34–6, 202–3.

[35] According to the *Vita Persi* (anonymous, but supposedly based on a lost *vita* by M. Valerius Probus), c. 1: 'libros circa septingentos Chrysippi siue bibliothecam suam omnem' (*A. Persi Flacci et D. Iuni Iuvenalis Saturae*, ed. Clausen, 33).

[36] SHA, *Gordiani tres*, c. 18.

complains that private libraries in Rome were 'permanently locked up like tombs', hence inaccessible; but at least his complaint verifies the existence of private libraries in the late fourth century.[37] From a later period still, the evidence of the so-called 'subscriptions' points to the existence of private libraries in the hands of Roman aristocrats during the fifth and early sixth centuries. A subscription is a short statement appended to a work (or a book within that work) stating that the text had been revised and corrected by a named individual, sometimes helpfully supplying the date of the revision. Only one autograph subscription appears to have survived,[38] but numerous others were copied along with their accompanying text into later manuscripts.[39] In sum the subscriptions throw light on scholarly activity in aristocratic circles and attest to the existence of private libraries well into the sixth century, a point confirmed by the fact that Boethius, in his *Consolatio Philosophiae* (*c*.525), alludes to a richly furnished library with walls 'ornamented with ivory and glass'.[40]

The enthusiasm for private libraries soon led to the creation of public libraries. The first Roman to contemplate the construction of a large-scale public library was apparently Julius Caesar, who intended that Varro should be its librarian,[41] but Caesar was assassinated (44 BC) before the project got under way. The project was subsequently brought to completion by Asinius Pollio, the wealthy aristocrat whose consulship in 40 BC is celebrated in Vergil's Fourth Eclogue. This library, which is known through written sources only, was apparently situated near the Forum, and consisted of two parts, one to house Greek books and the other to house those in Latin.[42] The model was

[37] *Res gestae* xiv. 6. 18: 'bibliothecis sepulchrorum ritu in perpetuum clausis'.

[38] The subscription to the *Epistulae* of Fronto, in Vatican City, BAV lat. 5750 (?Italy, s. v²; prov. Bobbio), read 'Caecilius saepe rogatus legi emendaui' (it is no longer legible); see Zetzel, 'The Subscriptions in the Manuscripts of Livy and Fronto', 50–5. (The statement in *Scribes and Scholars*, 39, that the subscription of Caecilius is found in Vatican City, BAV Pal. lat. 24, is erroneous.) On subscriptions, see also below, p. 24 with n. 100.

[39] The standard edition of subscriptions is still (incredibly) that of Jahn, 'Über die Subscriptionen'. For more recent treatment of some of the subscriptions, see Zetzel, *Latin Textual Criticism in Antiquity*, 211–31.

[40] *De consolatione Philosophiae* i, pr. 5: 'nec bibliothecae potius comptos ebore ac vitro parietes . . . requiro'.

[41] Suetonius, *Vita Divi Iulii*, c. 44: 'bibliothecas Graecas Latinasque quas maximas posset publicare data Marco Varroni cura comparandarum ac digerendarum'.

[42] Pliny, *NH* vii. 115: 'in bibliotheca, quae prima in orbe ab Asinio Pollione ex manubiis publicata Romae est', recycled by Isidore, *Etym.* vi. 5. 2: 'primum autem Romae bibliotecas publicavit Pollio, Graecas simul atque Latinas, additis auctorum imaginibus in atrio, quod de manubiis magnificentissimum instruxerat.' On the site of the library, see Platner and Ashby, *A Topographical Dictionary of Rome*, 84.

followed in subsequent Roman libraries.[43] The library built by Augustus on the Palatine after *c*.28 BC, for example, remains of which have been excavated, had two identical chambers situated side by side—one for Greek, one for Latin—with the back wall of each chamber having a large recess (presumably to house a statue), and the side walls having numbers of niches, in which would be placed *armaria* or wooden bookcases lined with shelves and having wooden doors (as in a French *armoire*).[44] The central area is open, presumably to accommodate tables and readers. It is the provision for readers and bookcases which distinguishes the layout of this and later Roman libraries from their Greek predecessors, such as that at Alexandria.[45]

Although both Tiberius and Vespasian are known to have built public libraries,[46] the greatest of the Roman libraries was that constructed by the Emperor Trajan (AD 98–117) as part of his monumental forum, dedicated in AD 112, and known as the Bibliotheca Ulpia. Trajan's Bibliotheca Ulpia is well known from excavation, and has been magnificently reconstructed by James E. Packer and his colleagues.[47] Here, too, there were two chambers

---

[43] Notably by the illiterate millionaire freedman Trimalchio, who in the *Satyrica* of Petronius (*c.* AD 66) boasts of owning two libraries, one in Greek and one in Latin (*Sat.* xlviii. 4). Trimalchio's (fictional) libraries are evidently intended to mimic the imperial libraries of Rome; see Courtney, *A Companion to Petronius*, 101.

[44] The so-called 'Palatine Library' was housed in the Temple of Apollo; see Suetonius, *Vita Divi Augusti*, c. 29 ('templum Apollinis in ea parte Palatinae domus excitavit . . . addidit porticus cum bibliotheca Latina Graecaque'), and the references assembled by Lugli, *I monumenti antichi*, i. 282–3, 299. Remains of the Palatine Library have been identified through excavation: see Platner and Ashby, *A Topographical Dictionary*, 84, as well as Strocka, 'Römische Bibliotheken', 307–9, and Casson, *Libraries in the Ancient World*, 82–3. Augustus subsequently built another library, the Bibliotheca Porticus Octaviae, in the Campus Martius, on which see Platner and Ashby, *A Topographical Dictionary*, 84–5.

[45] Cf. Casson, *Libraries in the Ancient World*: 'With such an arrangement—books along the walls and accommodation for readers in the middle—Roman libraries were like modern reading rooms and not at all like Greek libraries, which . . . consisted of small rooms, where books were stored, opening on a colonnade, where readers consulted them' (p. 82); 'Greek libraries were, in essence, stacks. A Roman library was just the opposite: it was designed primarily for readers, to provide them with spacious, handsome surroundings in which to work. The books themselves were nearby yet out of the way, on shelves within the walls' (p. 88).

[46] Pliny, *NH* xxxiv. 43; Aulus Gellius, *Noctes Atticae* xiii. 20. 1 (Tiberius), xvi. 8. 2 (Vespasian).

[47] The full report of excavation and reconstruction is contained in Packer, *The Forum of Trajan in Rome: A Study of the Monuments*; for the Bibliotheca Ulpia, see i. 120–7, with App. B (i. 450–4), with figs. 71–8 and (in vol. 3) fos. 24, 28–30. More accessible to the student of ancient libraries is Packer, *The Forum of Trajan in Rome: A Study of the Monuments in Brief*, incorporating the brilliant architectural reconstructions of the Bibliotheca Ulpia by J. Burge, J. E. Packer, and K. Sarring: see esp. pp. 78–9 with

or reading rooms, one housing Latin books (the East Library), the other housing Greek (the West Library). The rooms were situated facing each other across a square portico, in the centre of which stood Trajan's Column, to this day one of the great visible monuments of imperial Rome. The two chambers now lie beneath the Via dei Fori Imperiali, but Trajan's Column still stands where it was erected in AD 112. A user of the library who wished to consult (say) a book in Greek after having consulted one in Latin, would be obliged to cross the portico and gaze up at the Column: perhaps the most impressive monument ever to adorn a library! The chambers themselves were large (27.10 × 14.69 metres, together occupying roughly the footprint of the Reading Room in the University Library in Cambridge) and lavishly decorated with imported pavonazzetto marble. The walls had niches to house *armaria* running from floor to ceiling, on two storeys. Each chamber had thirty-six *armaria*, and if these were filled with papyrus rolls, it has been calculated that the two chambers might together have accommodated some 20,000 rolls:[48] perhaps the equivalent of 5,000 volumes (roughly the content of the Reading Room in Cambridge). The central areas in each chamber were presumably furnished with chairs and tables fitted with the ancient equivalent of microfilm readers (winding machines to facilitate the rapid consultation of papyrus rolls).[49]

The Bibliotheca Ulpia remained the largest and most lavish of Rome's libraries, but it was by no means the only one. Libraries were often incorporated into public baths, and formed part (for example) of the baths of Trajan, Caracalla, and probably Diocletian.[50] According to a Late Latin text entitled *Libellus de regionibus urbis Romae*, there were twenty-eight public libraries in Rome in the mid-fourth century, but it is not possible to determine which these were.[51] And many provincial cities and *municipia* imitated the model of Rome in the construction of public libraries, as archaeological and epigraphic

figs. 78 and 167–71. At the time of the opening of the New Getty Museum in Malibu (1997), full-size computer-generated reconstructions of the Forum of Trajan were on view, providing an unforgettable impression of what this magnificent monument might once have looked like.

[48] Casson, *Libraries in the Ancient World*, 88.

[49] One of these 'roll-readers' is on exhibit in the Fitzwilliam Museum, Cambridge (GR 25a-k, 1980). I am grateful to Professor Peter Zahn (Berlin) for drawing my attention to this fascinating piece of ancient technology.

[50] Casson, *Libraries in the Ancient World*, 89–92.

[51] The *Libellus de regionibus urbis Romae* [LLA 520] has been ed. by Nordh, with the relevant reference at p. 97: 'bibliothecae .xxviii.'.

evidence (inscriptions recording the dedications of libraries) makes clear. The Younger Pliny, for example, mentions in one of his Letters that he built at his own expense, and endowed with 100,000 sesterces, a library for the citizens of his home town, Como,[52] and at roughly the same time the heirs of one Tiberius Julius Celsus Polemaeanus endowed a magnificent library in Ephesus, the impressive remains of which are still standing.[53]

CHRISTIAN LIBRARIES OF THE PATRISTIC PERIOD

Christianity was a religion of the book. From the very beginnings, all Christian communities needed collections of liturgical books for public prayer.[54] But the holy scriptures needed to be interpreted accurately; and so Christian libraries of scholarly books, necessary for interpreting Scripture, soon developed.[55] Sometimes these libraries will have originated as the private property of individual scholars: for example, that of Origen at Caesarea in Palestine;[56] or that of Jerome, which he transported with him to Bethlehem;[57] or that of Augustine

---

[52] *Ep.* i. 8 ('petiturus sum enim ut rursus uaces sermoni quem apud municipes meos habui bibliothecam dedicaturus', etc.). The extent of Pliny's endowment is known from an inscription found at the site, printed in *Corpus Inscriptionum Latinarum*, ed. Mommsen et al., v. 568–9 (no. 5262).

[53] See Strocka, 'Römische Bibliotheken', 322–9, and, for illustration, *Antike Bibliotheken*, ed. Hoepfner, 123–6.

[54] There is a concise and useful survey of the very earliest congregational libraries, mostly preserved as papyrus fragments, by Van Elderen, 'Early Christian Libraries'.

[55] For general orientation on Christian libraries, see Leclercq, 'Bibliothèques'; Wendel, 'Bibliothek'; and Gamble, *Books and Readers in the Early Church*, 144–202.

[56] Origen left Alexandria following a dispute with the patriarch, and lived at Caesarea (Maritima) from 231 until his death in 253. On his death his library passed to the church of Caesarea, where it was consulted and expanded by Pamphilus (d. 310) and Eusebius (d. 339). Isidore estimated the holdings of the library at Caesarea to have been 30,000 rolls: 'Apud nos [*scil.* Christianos] quoque Pamphilus martyr . . . Pisistratum in sacrae bibliothecae studio primus adaequare contendit. Hic enim in bibliotheca sua prope triginta voluminum millia habuit' (*Etym.* vi. 6. 1). But a more accurate estimate of the extent of its holdings, based on study of works quoted by Eusebius, has recently been made by Carriker, *The Library of Eusebius at Caesarea*, who has identified 288 works, perhaps implying an upper limit of *c*.400 (p. 299), which might correspond at most to 5,000 rolls (p. 32). It is not known where Isidore derived his inflated figure. See also (briefly) Gamble, *Books and Readers*, 155–61.

[57] Jerome writes in a letter of AD 384 that he could not bear to abandon the library which he had assembled at Rome with so much care and effort (*Ep.* xxii. 30: 'bibliotheca quam mihi Romae summo studio ac labore confeceram'). There is much information about Jerome's library in his *Ep.* lxx to Magnus (written AD 397). For reconstruction of Jerome's library, see Grützmacher, *Hieronymus: Eine biographische Studie*, i. 126–9; and see also, briefly, Kelly, *Jerome*, 20, 28–9, 48–9.

in Hippo Regius.[58] At approximately the same time as Jerome and Augustine, the creation of an institutional library to house the Church's archives and to support Christian scholarship was undertaken by the papacy.[59] Pope Damasus (366–84) rebuilt the basilica of (what is now) San Lorenzo in Prasina in order to house archives and a library; the *titulus* which Damasus composed to stand over the door of the new library survives among early medieval *syllogae*.[60] At a later stage, however, the papal library was apparently moved to the Lateran Palace.[61] The so-called *Capella sancta sanctorum*, excavated beneath the Lateran in 1900 and dating from the sixth century, was clearly a library, to judge from the frescoes which adorned it, including one showing a Christian reader holding a codex.[62] Of the contents of the library, however, we know nothing.

In the early sixth century, Pope Agapetus (535–6), probably on the advice of Cassiodorus (who, as we learn from the preface of his *Institutiones*, wished to make Rome a rival to Alexandria and Nisibis in the pursuit of Christian learning),[63] established a substantial library on his private estate on the Caelian Hill. The building in which the library of Agapetus was housed has been recovered by excavation (it was identified by means of an inscription reading BIBLIOTHECA

---

[58] For Augustine's efforts at creating an ecclesiastical library in Hippo Regius, see Possidius, *Vita S. Augustini*, c. 31: 'ecclesiae bibliothecam omnesque codices diligenter custodiendos semper iubebat . . . ecclesiae dimisit una cum bibliothecis libros et tractatus vel suos vel aliorum scriptos habentibus.' On the extent of Augustine's library at Hippo, see Altaner, 'Die Bibliothek Augustins', and Scheele, 'Buch und Bibliothek bei Augustinus', 62–78 (library), 78–85 (archival materials).

[59] On Christian libraries at Rome, see Leclercq, 'Bibliothèques', cols. 863–73, and Callmer, 'Die ältesten christlichen Bibliotheken in Rom'. There is still much of value in De Rossi, 'De origine, historia, indicibus scrinii et bibliothecae sedis apostolicae commentatio', i, pp. iii–cxxxii, a revised and expanded version of his earlier article, 'La biblioteca della sede apostolica'.

[60] ICVR ii. 1 (1888), p. 151 (no. 23): 'archibis, fateor, uolui noua condere tecta, / addere praeterea dextera levaque columnas'; also in *Epigrammata Damasiana*, ed. Ferrua, 210–12 (no. 57). See also discussion by De Rossi, 'De origine . . . commentatio', pp. xxxviii–xlii, and Scalia, 'Gli "archiva" di papa Damaso'.

[61] On the Lateran library, see Callmer, 'Die ältesten christlichen Bibliotheken', 50–6.

[62] There is a large colour plate of this fresco in Leclercq, 'Bibliothèques', after col. 867 (and reproduced from Leclercq in Gamble, *Books and Readers*, 163). For Leclercq, at least, there was no doubt that the reader in question was St Augustine (col. 870). For the excavations at the Lateran, see Leclercq, ibid., cols. 869–70, and Lauer, 'Les Fouilles du Sancta sanctorum à Rome'.

[63] Cassiodorus, *Institutiones*, praef.: 'nisus sum cum beatissimo papa urbis Romae ut, sicut apud Alexandriam multo tempore fuisse traditur institutum, nunc etiam in Nisibi civitate Syrorum Hebreis sedulo fertur exponi, collatis expensis in urbe Romana professos doctores scholae potius acciperent Christianae . . .'.

AGAPETI I A. DXXXV—DXXXVI).[64] It consisted of a single large room (30 × 22 metres), roughly similar in size to each of the rooms of Trajan's Bibliotheca Ulpia; and like it had niches in the walls to house *armaria*.[65] Later in the sixth century, the property, including presumably the library, came into the ownership of Pope Gregory I—we know from the *Liber pontificalis* that he was of the same family as Agapetus—who established there (between 575 and 581) the monastery dedicated to St Andrew from which came Augustine and the Roman monks who effected the conversion of Anglo-Saxon England. That Gregory took pains to preserve the library of Agapetus seems clear from an inscription or *titulus* preserved in a later *sylloga* which records that Agapetus, 'dwelling in this glorious place / skilfully created a beautiful location for the books':

> Sanctorum veneranda cohors sedet ordine ⟨longo⟩
>   divinae legis mystica dicta docens.
> Hos inter residens Agapetus iure sacerdos
>   codicibus pulchrum condidit arte locum.[66]

The *titulus* is preserved in the *sylloga* of Einsiedeln;[67] that it relates to the period of Gregory's papacy (and was copied from an inscription in the library?) seems clear from the rubric which precedes it: 'in bibliotheca sancti Gregorii quae est in monasterio clitauri [*leg.* Clivi Scauri] ubi ipse dyalogorum ⟨libros⟩ scripsit'.[68] Unfortunately we know nothing of the size or contents (save that they included, perhaps not exclusively, patristic literature) of this lavishly constructed library, nor what became of its books.[69]

The original plan of Agapetus and Cassiodorus, to found a Christian academy of books and scholars to compete with those of

---

[64] See Marrou, 'Autour de la bibliothèque du pape Agapit', and, more recently, Grebe, 'Die Bibliothek Agapets', 27–35.

[65] See Colini, *Storia e topografia del Celio*, 202–5, with pl. XI. A wall of the building may still be seen, across the street (Clivo di Scauro) from the basilica of SS. Giovanni e Paolo.

[66] ICVR ii. 1 (1888), p. 28 (no. 55); also discussed by De Rossi, 'De origine . . . commentatio', pp. lv–lvii, and Callmer, 'Die ältesten christlichen Bibliotheken', 57–8. The *sylloga* apparently described a series of portraits (mosaics?) of holy men—the *veneranda cohors*—including Agapetus himself.

[67] ICVR ii. 1 (1888), pp. 9–35.

[68] Ibid. 28; cf., however, Marrou, 'Autour de la bibliothèque', 127.

[69] Marrou (ibid. 167) hypothesized that the library was moved by Gregory from the Caelian Hill to the Lateran Palace, the refurbishment of which he would attribute to Gregory; but his argument is tenuous at best. Cf. also the hesitations of Gamble, *Books and Readers*, 303–4 (n. 67).

Alexandria and Nisibis, was frustrated by the turmoil and invasions of sixth-century Italy by Vandals and then by the armies of Justinian, culminating in Totila's siege of Rome in 546. Some time after the death of Agapetus, Cassiodorus (c.485–c.580), after a distinguished career in civil government, apparently took his books back to his private estate in Calabria, in the toe of Italy, and established there a private academy of Christian learning, at some point during the decade 546 × 555.[70] The estate, called Vivarium (named for the fish-ponds which Cassiodorus had created there), was located at modern Squillace (near Catanzaro).[71] But unlike other monastic establishments, the scholarly regime instituted by Cassiodorus combined Christian with secular (pagan) learning, and his library evidently reflected this regime. Cassiodorus' brief treatise, the *Institutiones*, is intended as an introduction to the resources of the library.[72] As in the case of the secular and Christian libraries of Rome, the books at Cassiodorus' Vivarium were housed in *armaria*, and the *Institutiones* were intended in some sense as a guide to the contents of the individual *armaria*. For example, Cassiodorus explains that the eighth *armarium* contained manuscripts in Greek.[73] How many Greek manuscripts were in question is unknown; but note that Greek texts, which in Trajan's Bibliotheca Ulpia had occupied a library room of their own, now occupy a single *armarium*. At various points in the *Institutiones*, Cassiodorus names Aristotle, Demosthenes, Dioscorides, Galen, Hippocrates, Homer, and Plato; but some of these, for example Demosthenes, may have been no more than names to Cassiodorus, and some at least of the others were read there in Latin translation.[74] The library evidently contained a number

[70] On Cassiodorus and his library, see the (still valuable) essay by Van de Vyver, 'Cassiodore et son oeuvre'; Courcelle, *Les Lettres grecques en Occident*, 313–41; Teutsche, 'Cassiodorus Senator'; O'Donnell, *Cassiodorus*, 177–255; and Gamble, *Books and Readers*, 198–202.

[71] See Courcelle, 'Le Site du monastère de Cassiodore'; further reflections on the identification of the site, id., 'Nouvelles recherches sur le monastère de Cassiodore'.

[72] *Cassiodori Senatoris Institutiones*, ed. Mynors; trans. Jones, *Cassiodorus: An Introduction to Divine and Human Readings*, and more recently by Halporn, *Cassiodorus: Institutions of Divine and Secular Learning and On the Soul*, 103–233. Mynors includes an 'Index auctorum' (pp. 184–93), which he intended to 'serve as a provisional indication of the contents of the library at Vivarium' (p. 183); note that he marks with an obelus those works whose presence in the library is 'certain, or virtually so'.

[73] *Inst.* viii. 15: 'epistulas Iohanne Chrysostomo expositas Attico sermone in suprascripto octavo armario dereliqui, ubi sunt Graeci codices congregati' (ed. Mynors, 32).

[74] Cassiodorus evidently refers to Latin translations in the case of Aristotle's *Categoriae*, *De interpretatione*, and *Topica*, known in the translations of Boethius (*Inst.* ii. 3; ed. Mynors, 112–13); of Dioscorides, *Herbarium* (i. 31, pp. 78–9), Galen, *Therapeutica ad Glauconem* (ibid. 79), and Hippocrates (ibid.). Cassiodorus certainly had some Greek books

of (secular) Latin texts, notably Cicero, Columella, Ennius, Livy, Palladius, Quintilian, Terence, Varro, and (unsurprisingly) Vergil. But the bulk of the library was made up of grammatical and patristic writings in Latin. In terms of its holdings, then, the library at Vivarium was a forerunner of monastic libraries of the early Middle Ages.

Cassiodorus died well into his nineties, in about 575. What happened to the manuscripts which he had assembled at Vivarium? Evidence of surviving manuscripts suggests that they were dispersed variously rather than that they were transferred *en bloc* to another library.[75] During the past century there has been an understandable scholarly temptation to attribute sixth-century manuscripts of unknown origin to Vivarium,[76] but more recent research treats these attempts with scepticism.[77] We are left with a very small residue of some seven manuscripts which were owned and annotated, arguably by Cassiodorus himself, at Vivarium.[78] The diverse provenance and early medieval ownership of these manuscripts suggests that the library of Vivarium was dispersed piecemeal by the heirs of

at Vivarium (cf. the example of John Chrysostom cited in the previous note), for he commissioned various Latin translations from his monks, not least of the *Historia tripartita* [CPG 7502]. On Greek texts at Vivarium, see discussion by Courcelle, *Les Lettres grecques*, 321–36, 382–8.

[75] The suggestion was once made that the library of Vivarium was transferred *en bloc* to Bobbio: Beer, 'Bemerkungen über den ältesten Hss.-Bestand des Klosters Bobbio', with discussion by Gomoll, 'Zu Cassiodors Bibliothek', and Courcelle, *Les Lettres grecques*, 343–5. It is not, perhaps, impossible that the odd Vivarium book ended up in Bobbio; but it must be borne in mind that Bobbio was not founded (by Columbanus) until 613, and that in the years between Cassiodorus' death *c.*575 and the foundation of Bobbio, Italy had been torn apart by the turmoil of Langobard invasions. It is for these reasons that scholars are no longer prepared to believe that large numbers of manuscripts could have passed directly from Vivarium to Bobbio.

[76] Cf. Weinberger, 'Handschriften von Vivarium', and Courcelle, *Les Lettres grecques*, 342–73.

[77] For a survey of earlier attributions, see Troncarelli, 'I codici di Cassiodoro', 50–2 (n. 6), largely reproduced in id., *Vivarium: I libri, il destino*, 39–40 with n. 1, who gives a list of some fifteen manuscripts formerly thought to be from Vivarium, but now known to have no connection with it. A striking number of these rejected manuscripts contain secular classical texts, such as Cicero, Livy (four MSS), and Lucan; their rejection throws important light on our changing conception of the role played by the library at Vivarium in the preservation of classical Latin literature.

[78] See Troncarelli, 'Decora correctio' [on Vat. lat. 5704]; id., 'Litteras pulcherrimas' [on Vat. lat. 5704 and Paris, BNF lat. 8907]; and id., *Vivarium*, 44–5, with Appendices A (p. 95) and B (p. 96). The manuscripts in question are: Milan, Biblioteca Ambrosiana, H. 78 sup. + Turin, Biblioteca nazionale, G. V. 15 (N. Italy, s. vi, with a Bobbio ex-libris); Oxford, BodL, Auct. T. 2. 26, fos. 33–145 (s. v^{med}) + fos. 146–78 (Italy, s. vi/vii); Paris, BNF, lat. 8907 (N. Italy, s. v^{ex}); St Petersburg, Russian National Library, Q. v. I. 6–10 (Italy, s. vi); Vatican City, Archivio S. Pietro, D. 182 (Cagliari, s. v/vi); Vatican City, BAV, lat. 5704 (s. vi^2); and Verona, Biblioteca capitolare, XXXIX (s. vi/vii).

Cassiodorus; and although some manuscripts may have been acquired by the papal library then at the Lateran Palace, as De Rossi suggested long ago,[79] others seemingly remained at large in Italy and Rome (in the possession of booksellers?), awaiting discovery by acquisitive bibliophiles from remote parts of northern Europe.

The library of Vivarium is famous particularly because it is described in the *Institutiones* of Cassiodorus. But there were other sizeable libraries in sixth-century Italy which had equally extensive holdings. One example is the library principally but not exclusively of the writings of Augustine assembled by Eugippius (*c*.460–535) at the monastery called *castrum Lucullanum* at Naples. Cassiodorus in his *Institutiones* describes Eugippius as 'not well-trained in secular literature, but thoroughly learned in the study of sacred writings'.[80] A number of surviving manuscripts (and apographs of manuscripts now lost) indicate the extent and importance of Eugippius' library, not only in his lifetime, but later in the sixth century and on into the seventh.[81] The library of Eugippius could have been consulted by Hadrian, who arrived in Naples *c*.640 as a refugee from the Arab invasions of North Africa, became abbot of a monastery at nearby Nisida (a few miles from the *castrum Lucullanum*), and was appointed in 667 by Pope Vitalian to accompany Archbishop Theodore to England.[82]

The existence of the papal library of the Lateran Palace is also well attested in the seventh century. In October 649, the ill-fated Pope Martin I (649–55) convened at the Lateran Palace the ecumenical council which formally condemned the (imperially endorsed) mono-thelete doctrine. The *acta* of the Lateran Council of 649 include a substantial dossier of 161 quotations from 87 Greek patristic texts designed to illustrate the fallacies of monothelete doctrine and the veracity of dyothelete doctrine, with its emphasis on the double nature, operation and will in Christ.[83] It has been supposed that the

[79] De Rossi, 'De origine . . . commentatio', pp. lv–lvi, followed by Courcelle, *Les Lettres grecques*, 373–82.

[80] *Inst.* i. 23 (ed. Mynors, p. 62).

[81] On Eugippius and his library at the *castrum Lucullanum*, see *Biblical Commentaries*, 114–20, as well as Van de Vyver, 'Cassiodore et son oeuvre', 281–3, and Gorman, 'Eugippius and the Origins of the Manuscript Tradition', 8–14.

[82] *Biblical Commentaries*, 120.

[83] The patristic texts in question are listed summarily by De Rossi, 'De origine . . . commentatio', pp. lxviii–lxxi, in CPG 9402, and more fully in *Concilium Lateranense a. 649 celebratum*, ed. Riedinger, 258–335. See also the list compiled by Henri Leclercq, cited in the following note.

texts quoted in the dossier were available at the time in the Lateran Palace library.[84] It is unlikely that this supposition is entirely correct, because Greek-speaking monks from Roman monasteries, notably that of St Anastasius *ad aquas Salvias*, assisted in the compilation of the *acta*, and may have drawn on their own (Roman) libraries of Greek patristic literature.[85] It is highly likely that Theodore, the future archbishop of Canterbury, was one of the Cilician monks from St Anastasius who assisted in the drafting of the *acta* of the Lateran Council, and whose name appears as one of its signatories.[86] The implication is that, at the least, Theodore will have been thoroughly familiar with the Greek patristic holdings of Roman libraries before his appointment to Canterbury.

One final late antique library needs to be considered: that of Isidore, bishop of Seville (*c.*560–636). Although no trace of it has survived, it is clear from his writings that Isidore had access to a very substantial (private) library, laid out probably like that of Cassiodorus at Vivarium, with books housed in individual wooden *armaria*. A collection of epigrams or *tituli* composed by Isidore and known collectively as *Versus in bibliotheca*, was evidently intended to provide inscriptions for the individual *armaria*.[87] Depending on how the individual epigrams are distinguished, between fourteen and sixteen *armaria* are in question; and, assuming that each *armarium* held thirty codices, the entire library might have comprised a total of some 420 × 480 books.[88] This number squares tolerably well with the number of

---

[84] Leclercq, 'Bibliothèques', cols. 871–3.

[85] On these libraries, see Mango, 'La Culture grecque', and the earlier study of Batiffol, 'Librairies byzantines à Rome'.

[86] See *Biblical Commentaries*, 74–81.

[87] CPL 1212; ICL 1586o, etc. The *versus* are printed in PL 83: 1107–11; Beeson, *Isidor-Studien*, 133–66 (with discussion of the use of *tituli* in libraries at pp. 152–5 and text at pp. 157–66); and most recently by Sánchez Martín, *Isidorus Hispalensis: Versus*. Sánchez Martín divides the first *titulus* into three, so that in his edition the collection consists of eighteen *tituli*; but he does not at any point discuss the contents of the *armaria* which the *tituli* were designed to accompany. On the sources of Isidore's *Versus*, see ibid. 37–100, as well as Sánchez Martín, 'Ecos de poetas tardíos'.

[88] The calculation was made by James, 'Learning and Literature till the Death of Bede', 491; the figure is quoted and discussed by Thompson, *The Medieval Library*, 28. As Beeson edits the *tituli* (*Isidor-Studien*, 157–66), some fifteen pertain to *armaria*, divided up as follows: I (the library), II (Holy Scripture), III (Origen), IV (Hilary), V (Ambrose), VI (Augustine), VII (Jerome), VIII (John Chrysostom), IX (Cyprian), X (the poets Prudentius, Avitus, Juvencus, and Caelius Sedulius), XI (Eusebius and Orosius), XII (Gregory), XIII (Leander of Seville), XIV (legal works: Theodosius, Paulus, Gaius), and XV (miscellaneous books). Sánchez Martín assigns a slightly different distribution: I (the library), II (florilegia et grammatica), III (Holy Scripture), IV (Origen), V (Hilary), VI (Ambrose), VII (Augustine), VIII (Jerome), IX (John Chrysostom), X (Cyprian), XI (the

authors quoted by Isidore throughout the substantial corpus of his writings. Exact figures are not easily available,[89] but in his large corpus of writings, and most notably in his *Etymologiae*, Isidore quotes from more than 200 authors, entailing a larger still number of works: perhaps as many as 475.[90] Of course many of the authors cited by Isidore were cited at second-hand; but by any reckoning his library was a very substantial one. But what happened to the library (no trace of which remains), and the books which it contained, is unknown.[91]

THE END OF ANCIENT LIBRARIES

Indeed very little is known about what happened to the books from all these late antique libraries. Were they all destroyed? Or were they merely dispersed, with the possibility that stray manuscripts might end up at any Italian, or even European, destination? Would books ransacked from public libraries in time of siege and barbarian invasion have had any commercial value? And were there booksellers or other commercial outlets to receive them? In other words, did the sorts of booksellers (*librarii*) frequented by Aulus Gellius in Rome in the mid-second century exist there in any form in the sixth?[92]

poets Prudentius, Avitus, Juvencus, and Caelius Sedulius), XII (Eusebius and Orosius), XIII (Gregory), XIV (Leander), XV (legal works: Theodosius, Paulus, Gaius), XVI (Cosmas, Damianus, Hippocrates, Galen), XVII (*de medicis aegrotisque*), XVIII (*item*).

[89] The extent of Isidore's learning is treated at great length by Fontaine, *Isidore de Séville et la culture classique*, esp. ii. 735–62. A more concise survey of the sources of the *Etymologiae* is given by Díaz y Díaz, 'Introduccion general', in *San Isidoro de Sevilla: Etimologías*, i. 1–257, esp. 189–200. The index of *loci citati* at the end of Lindsay's edition of the *Etymologiae* gives a brief overview, particularly of secular authors cited by Isidore, but takes no account of which citations derive by way of intermediate sources such as Aulus Gellius and the grammarians.

[90] These estimates are based on Fontaine's 'Index locorum' (*Isidore de Séville*, ii. 927–85), but without making allowance for Latin authors later than Isidore there cited, and omitting Greek authors for whom the evidence cited by Fontaine is exiguous. There has been a substantial amount of work done since 1959 on Isidore's sources (and a number of individual books of the *Etymologiae* have been re-edited, with concomitant source study), and it would be useful to attempt a reappraisal of the authors and books known to Isidore.

[91] Cf. Fontaine, *Isidore de Séville*, ii. 738: 'Les destructions et les reconstructions de la Séville arabe et médiévale nous ont mis dans l'impossibilité d'en retrouver la moindre trace matérielle.'

[92] See *Noctes Atticae* v. 4. 1, xiii. 31. 1, xviii. 4. 1, from which it is clear that scholars might assemble at the stall of a *librarius* and carry on learned conversations with friends. The principal function of such *librarii*, however, was the production of new manuscript copies on commission. I have been unable to discover any evidence that *librarii* handled used books for resale. The date of the *Noctes Atticae* is controversial, but probably fell before AD 159: see Holford-Strevens, *Aulus Gellius*, 16–21.

It is not possible to determine with confidence precisely when the great public libraries in Rome were destroyed or dispersed. At *c.* AD 400 the great Bibliotheca Ulpia was still being consulted by scholars in search of historical materials,[93] and in the mid-fifth century the poet Sidonius Apollinaris records with pride that he has been honoured with a bronze statue located amongst those of other writers 'between the two libraries' in the 'Ulpian *porticus*'— that is to say, in the portico between the East and West libraries of the Bibliotheca Ulpia, under the shadow of Trajan's Column.[94] A century later Cassiodorus could still remark on the glory of Trajan's Forum (though he makes no mention of the Bibliotheca Ulpia).[95] It has been suggested that the libraries of the Palatine and of Trajan's Forum were destroyed during the siege of Rome in 546.[96]

Public libraries in other parts of the western Roman empire may similarly have been destroyed or dispersed at this time; but, again, what happened to their books is unknown. In his study of the oldest manuscripts from Lyon, E. A. Lowe suggested that some books from the public library at Lyon may have found their way into the local cathedral library;[97] and Bernhard Bischoff made a similar suggestion in the case of Verona.[98] One wonders where Bobbio (founded 613) acquired its substantial collection of late antique manuscripts: perhaps from a nearby public library, perhaps at (say) Piacenza? Unfortunately, however, even acquisition by a monastic or cathedral library was no guarantee of preservation. During the seventh and early eighth century substantial numbers of late antique manuscripts were washed down and rewritten (so as to produce so-called 'palimpsests'), and in this way much ancient literature has been lost.[99]

---

[93] The anonymous (pseudonymous) author of the *Historia Augusta* notes in his life of the emperor Tacitus (275–6) that he had consulted an ivory book in the sixth bookcase of the Bibliotheca Ulpia containing a decree of the senate signed by this emperor (SHA, *Tacitus* viii. 1: 'habet in Bibliotheca Ulpia in armario sexto librum elephantinum, in quo hoc senatus consultum perscriptum est'); cf. also SHA, *Aurelianus* i. 7, *Probus* ii. 1. For the dating of SHA to the early 390s, see Syme, *Ammianus and the Historia Augusta*, 72–9.

[94] Cf. *Carm.* viii. 8 ('Vlpia quod rutilat porticus aere meo'), *Ep.* ix. 16. 25–8 ('Cum meis poni statuam perennem / Nerva Traianus titulis videret, / inter auctores utriusque fixam / bybliothecae').

[95] *Variae* vii. 6: 'Traiani forum vel sub assiduitate videre miraculum est'.

[96] The suggestion is that of Thompson, *The Medieval Library*, 37.

[97] Lowe, *Codices Lugdunenses Antiquissimi*, i. 8–9.

[98] Bischoff, 'Biblioteche, scuole e letteratura', 124.

[99] See Lowe, 'Codices rescripti'. Bobbio was far and away the most active centre of palimpsesting (p. 485), but numerous palimpsests also survive from Verona (pp. 485–6) and Lyon (p. 486). Palimpsesting was not limited to the pagan authors of classical

Even less is known about what happened to the private libraries of Roman aristocrats which, as we have seen, are well attested through the so-called subscriptions during the fifth and sixth centuries, and which clearly played an important role in the transmission of secular Latin texts.[100] It has been plausibly suggested that private libraries were the source of the numerous secular Latin texts which emerged during the late eighth and earlier ninth centuries—with the implication that such private libraries, inevitably on a much smaller scale than public libraries and located principally in Rome and Ravenna, may have remained intact during the two hundred years of turmoil between c.550 and c.750.[101]

What emerges from these considerations is that, in spite of the turmoil and the (presumed) attendant destruction and dispersal of libraries, some number of books must have been in circulation, and available for acquisition, at the time when Anglo-Saxon England was first drawn into the orbit of Roman culture. As we have seen, the second wave of monks sent to England from Gregory's monastery of St Andrew on the Caelian Hill took with them, as Bede tells us, 'a number of manuscripts' (*codices plurimos*).[102] Some years ago Armando Petrucci succeeded in identifying the style of script used in the scriptorium of Gregory's monastery, which he named 'Roman uncial', and was then able to point to a small corpus of manuscripts in this script which, according to his criteria, had originated in Gregory's monastery.[103] Among these are several which have an early Anglo-Saxon provenance, and these could conjecturally have formed part of the *codices plurimi* sent to England by Gregory. Pride of place goes to a famous copy of the Vulgate gospels, now Cambridge, CCC 286 (s. vi^ex), known as the 'St Augustine's Gospels' from its presumed association with the Roman

antiquity: there are large numbers of palimpsests of pre-Hieronymian biblical texts, as well as superseded liturgical texts and works deemed heretical.

[100] See above, p. 12 with n. 38. The relevance of the subscriptions to our understanding of the textual transmission of Latin classics has been illuminatingly explored by Oronzo Pecere on several occasions, but notably in: 'La tradizione dei testi latini tra IV e V secolo', esp. 29–69; 'I meccanismi della tradizione testuale', esp. 354–66; and 'Esemplari con "subscriptiones"'.

[101] See Bischoff, 'Biblioteche', 126, and esp. Holtz, 'Vers la création des bibliothèques médiévales en Occident', 1073, 1087–8: 'pourtant c'est l'existence relativement éphémère de ces bibliothèques privées accueillantes, dans les résidences des grands seigneurs, qui a largement conditionné la survie de la littérature classique' (p. 1088).

[102] *HE* i. 29; the second wave of monks sent by Gregory included Mellitus, Iustus, Paulinus, and Rufinianus.

[103] Petrucci, 'L'onciale romana'; for the English dimension, see pp. 121–7, and Gameson, 'The Earliest Books of Christian Kent'.

missionary.[104] Judging from annotations in Anglo-Saxon cursive minuscule, the manuscript was in England no later than the eighth century, and there seems no good reason to doubt the traditional association with Augustine. Another copy of the Vulgate gospels, having some textual relationship to CCC 286 but being of slightly later (Italian if not certainly Roman) origin, is Oxford, BodL, Auct. D. 2. 14 (s. vi/vii); evidence of early Anglo-Saxon provenance suggests that it, too, may be associated with Augustine and the Gregorian missionaries.[105] And an argument has recently been advanced that a fragmentary papyrus codex of Gregory, *Hom. .xl. in Euangelia*, now London, BL, Cotton Titus C. xv, fo. 1 (s. vi/vii) is the remnant of a manuscript brought to England by these missionaries.[106]

No doubt the *codices plurimi* mentioned by Bede will also have included liturgical books such as a sacramentary, but none of these survive (and in any case fall outside the scope of the present enquiry).[107] Somewhat later Anglo-Saxon tradition also records (not improbably) that Augustine brought a copy of Gregory's *Regula pastoralis* to England.[108] The important point to stress is that the manuscripts which served as exemplars for the *codices plurimi* were very probably to be found in the library of Pope Agapetus in Gregory's monastery on the Caelian Hill, and thus provide a direct link between the libraries of late antiquity and Anglo-Saxon England.

During the following century, substantial numbers of books from late antique libraries were transported to England. Following his consecration as archbishop of Canterbury in 668, Theodore and his colleague Hadrian will certainly have brought books with them to England:[109] in Theodore's case, books (or copies of books) that were

---

[104] See Petrucci, 'L'onciale romana', 108, 110–11 and pl. XIII, as well as Marsden, 'The Gospels of St Augustine'.

[105] Thus Lowe, *English Uncial*, 17, and Marsden, 'The Gospels'; cf., however, the (palaeographical) hesitations of Petrucci, 'L'onciale romana', 115 n. 116.

[106] Babcock, 'A Papyrus Codex'.

[107] Cf. Ashworth, 'Did St Augustine Bring the *Gregorianum* to England?' See also the comment of Ecgberht, archbishop of York (732–66), who referred to a sacramentary and antiphonary brought to England by Augustine: 'ut noster didascalus beatus Gregorius, in suo Antiphonario et Missali libro, per pedagogum nostrum beatum Augustinum transmisit' (ed. Haddan and Stubbs, *Councils and Ecclesiastical Documents*, iii. 411).

[108] See the metrical preface to King Alfred's translation of the *Regula pastoralis*: 'þis ærendgewrit Agustinus / ofer sealtne sæ suðan brohte / iegbuendum, swa hit ær fore / adihtode dryhtnes cempa, / Rome papa' (*The Anglo-Saxon Poetic Records*, ed. Krapp and Dobbie, vi. 110): 'Augustine brought this text over the salt sea from the south, as it had previously been composed by the Lord's champion, the pope of Rome [i.e. Gregory].'

[109] See *Biblical Commentaries*, 240–2, and below, pp. 31–3, 175–8.

available in Rome, either in the library of the Lateran Palace or in that of his own monastery of St Anastasius *ad aquas Salvias*; in Hadrian's case, books (or copies of books) which were available in Naples and its vicinity, perhaps in the library assembled there by Eugippius in the *castrum Lucullanum*. Few traces of such books remain, however: of Theodore,[110] perhaps a copy of biblical Acts (in Greek and Latin) now in the Bodleian Library, Oxford;[111] of Hadrian, liturgical books from Campania and the vicinity of Naples, subsequently lost or discarded, which have left traces in later Anglo-Saxon liturgical manuscripts.[112]

At the same time as Theodore and Hadrian were making their way to England, various Englishmen began travelling to Rome, no doubt in search of books as well as spiritual enlightenment. We know that Benedict Biscop, founder and first abbot of Monkwearmouth-Jarrow, made six trips to Rome; and Bede specifically notes that on three of these trips he acquired books in Rome, in one case an *innumerabilis copia* of books of all sorts.[113] In another work, the *Aliquot quaestionum liber* [CPL 1364], Bede refers explicitly (c. ii) to an illustrated manuscript which Cuduini (or Cuthwine, as he would be in more familiar late Old English orthography), an early eighth-century

---

[110] London, BL, Stowe 1061, is a volume of 'specimens of ancient writing' compiled in the late 18th c. by the antiquary Thomas Astle (1735–1803), which contains, on fo. 7ʳ, an illustration of a 'codex MS. Paralipom. qui Theodori archiep. Cant. fuisse fertur. Specimen originale e codice descripsit claris. D. Isaac Newton, ex quo hoc iterum descripsi.' (The manuscript was apparently copied somewhere on the Continent; the Isaac Newton in question is not necessarily the great mathematician of that name.) On Astle's book of specimens, see Keynes, 'The Reconstruction of a Burnt Cottonian Manuscript', 129–31. I am most grateful to Simon Keynes for drawing my attention to this reference to Theodore. Unfortunately, the excerpt reproduced by Astle (from 1 Chron. 10: 1 sqq.) is in Greek minuscule script, indicating that the manuscript on which the handwritten facsimile was based is unlikely to have been written earlier than the 10th c. (a Greek biblical manuscript used by Theodore would almost certainly have been in Greek uncials, as is the Greek manuscript of Acts cited in the following note, not in minuscule). In other words, the conjectural attribution to Theodore is false; cf. the case of the 15th-c. manuscript of Homer now in Cambridge, CCC 81, which was thought by Matthew Parker to have been brought to England by Theodore (see *Biblical Commentaries*, 240–1).

[111] Oxford, BodL, Laud graec. 35 (?Sardinia, ?Rome, s. vi/vii) has often been associated with Archbishop Theodore, but without there being any definite evidence in support of the association: see Batiffol, 'Librairies byzantines à Rome', 306–7; Mango, 'La Culture grecque et l'Occident', 688–90; Cavallo, 'Le tipologie della cultura', 476–8; and *Biblical Commentaries*, 170, 241.

[112] See *Biblical Commentaries*, 155–67.

[113] *Historia abbatum*, cc. 6 ('innumerabilem librorum omnis generis copiam adportauit'), 9 ('magna quidem copia uoluminum sacrorum'), 11 ('bibliothecam quam de Roma nobilissimam copiosissimamque aduexerat'); *Venerabilis Baedae Opera Historica*, ed. Plummer, i. 369, 373, 375 respectively.

bishop of the East Angles, had brought back from Rome with him.[114] Cuduini's Roman manuscript does not survive; but in a lavishly illuminated mid-ninth-century manuscript of Caelius Sedulius, *Carmen paschale*, now Antwerp, Musaeum Plantin-Moretus, M. 17. 4 (126) (Liege, s. ix²/³), the scribe carefully reproduced a colophon from his exemplar: FINIT. FINES. FINES CUDVVINI (fo. 68ᵛ). Ludwig Traube first suggested that the Antwerp manuscript might be an apograph of the manuscript (seen and) described by Bede, and he has been followed by subsequent scholars.[115] There are problems with this identification, however, and in my view it is simpler to hypothesize two illuminated but lost manuscripts belonging to Cuduini: an illuminated copy of the *Carmen paschale* (which subsequently served as the exemplar of the Antwerp manuscript), and an illuminated copy of some *Passio S. Pauli* [e.g. BHL 6570] which Cuduini had brought from Rome and showed to Bede, but which has vanished without leaving an identifiable copy.[116] In any event Bede's statement provides another piece of evidence for the importation of Roman books into early Anglo-Saxon England.

---

[114] PL 93: 456: 'libri, quam [*leg.* quem] reuerendissimus ac doctissimus Cudum, Orientalium Anglorum antistes, ueniens a Roma secum in Britanniam detulit, in quo uidelicet libro omnes pene ipsius apostoli [*sc.* St Paul] passiones siue labores per loca opportuna erant depictae'. It was Ludwig Traube who first recognized that the name *Cudum* disguised, through confusion of minims, the Anglo-Saxon name *Cuduini* ('Paläographische Anzeigen', III', 276–8; repr. version, pp. 239–41). Traube found the passage in a manuscript in Paris, and did not realize that the work in question was by Bede; it fell to Paul Lehmann to identify the work as Bede's (*Erforschung*, iii. 184–97 at 186). Unfortunately, this Cuduini is not attested as bishop of the East Angles in any historical source, so the precise dates of his episcopacy cannot be determined, save that he must be later than Eardred and earlier than Aldberht, who was alive when Bede completed his *Historia ecclesiastica* in 731 (v. 23).

[115] Traube, 'Paläographische Anzeigen', p. 277 (repr. version, p. 240). See also Levison, *England and the Continent in the Eighth Century*, 133–4, and Alexander, *Insular Manuscripts*, 83 (no. 65) and ill. 285–301.

[116] What interested Bede in Cuduini's manuscript was the graphic portrayal of the tortures which St Paul suffered (PL 93: 456): 'ubi ita hic locus depictus est, quasi denudatus iaceret apostolus laceratus flagris, lacrimisque perfusus. Superastaret autem ei tortor quadrifidum habens flagellum in manu, sed unam e fidibus in manu sua retentam; tres vero reliquas solum ad feriendum habens exertas', etc. Any student of Roman *passiones martyrum* is inevitably drawn to wonder what Roman instruments of torture looked like, and how they were used, and Bede found his curiosity answered by the illustrations in Cuduini's manuscript. The *Carmen paschale*, on the other hand, which is mostly concerned with Old Testament figural anticipation of events in the life of Christ, contains no mention whatsoever of St Paul, and certainly no description of his tortures. Cf. Alexander, *Insular Manuscripts*, 83: '[Cuduini] . . . is mentioned by Bede as having brought from Rome an illustrated manuscript of the "Passions and labours of St Paul". Probably, therefore, Cuthwine *also* brought to England a copy of the *Carmen paschale*' (my emphasis).

A similar piece of evidence may be mentioned. In a narrative poem in octosyllables addressed by Aldhelm's student Æthilwald to one Wihtfrid,[117] hence datable approximately to the early eighth century, Æthilwald describes a trip to Rome made by three Anglo-Saxon colleagues, two of whom were brothers, one of whom died there. When the two survivors returned to England, they brought 'numerous books' ('en vehebant volumina / numerosa'), and Æthilwald goes on to specify that the books included monastic rules ('mysticis / elucubrata normulis') and books of the Bible, 'which the prophets and the pronouncements of the eloquent apostle had committed to parchment' ('quae profetae, apostoli / doctiloqui oraculi / indiderunt pergaminae').[118] Again, these were probably not library books in the sense in which I am using the term; but the poem provides a further example of the importation of Roman books to England.

How many of these books have survived? David Dumville has identified eleven manuscripts of Italian origin that date from earlier than the seventh century and have a pre-eighth-century English provenance.[119] As he remarks, 'This is a poor remnant of a body of imported books which must by the end of the seventh century have been numbered in thousands rather than hundreds.'[120] I suspect that these figures are overly optimistic, and should myself incline to say 'hundreds rather than dozens'. But England's debt to Mediterranean libraries is incontestable.

Interestingly, one famous manuscript from a late antique Mediterranean library made its way to England in the late seventh century, only to be lost at some later time. This is a manuscript which formed part of the library of Cassiodorus at Vivarium, and which is described by Cassiodorus in his *Institutiones* as his 'codex grandior', a massive pandect of the Vetus Latina translation of the Bible.[121] That this 'codex grandior' of Cassiodorus was identical with a 'pandect of the old translation' acquired by Ceolfrith and Benedict Biscop at

---

[117] *Aldhelmi Opera*, ed. Ehwald, 528–33.

[118] Ibid. 531.

[119] Dumville, 'The Importation of Mediterranean Manuscripts', 106. Three of these eleven have already been mentioned, two in connection with the Gregorian mission (Cambridge, CCC 286 and Oxford, BodL, Auct. D. 2. 14), one in connection with Theodore (Oxford, BodL, Laud graec. 35).

[120] Ibid. 107.

[121] *Inst.* i. 14. 2: 'in codice grandiore littera clariore conscripto, qui habet quaterniones nonaginta quinque, in quo septuaginta interpretum translatio veteris Testamenti in libris quadraginta quattuor continetur; cui subiuncti sunt novi Testamenti libri viginti sex, fiuntque simul libri septuaginta' (ed. Mynors, p. 40).

Rome,[122] is clear from evidence of many kinds, not least that the layout and contents of the prefatory quire of the great Codex Amiatinus [CLA iii. 299], written at Monkwearmouth-Jarrow in the years before 716, were modelled closely on those of the 'codex grandior' as described by Cassiodorus.[123] (Whereas the text of the 'codex grandior' was Vetus Latina, that of the Codex Amiatinus is Vulgate throughout, so it was only in matters of format and layout that the 'codex grandior' served as a model for the English pandect.) Unfortunately, since Bede and the monks of Monkwearmouth-Jarrow had no access to Cassiodorus' *Institutiones*, they cannot fully have realized what an astonishing treasure Ceolfrith and Benedict Biscop had managed to acquire for them in Rome.

In any case, as the example of the 'codex grandior' shows, Anglo-Saxon libraries were in the first instance stocked with books from Mediterranean libraries. Where and how these books were acquired, in Rome or elsewhere, we cannot say; and it is almost certainly unsafe to assume that the same kind of booksellers described by Aulus Gellius as operating in Rome in the second century AD were still in business in the seventh.[124] But who knows? Various texts of sixth-century date refer to the existence of *antiquarii*, '(professional) scribes'.[125] Cassiodorus, for example, devotes a chapter of his *Institutiones* to scribes and the practice of correct spelling (i. 30), and Gregory the Great in his *Dialogi* expresses the hope that every abbot will find 'scribes at work' (*antiquarios scribentes*) in his monastery (i. 4). A late sixth-century manuscript of Orosius (now Florence, Biblioteca Medicea Laurenziana, Plut. LXV. 1) carries the colophon, 'confectus codex in statione Viliaric antiquarii', 'this book was produced in the shop of Viliaric the scribe', where the term *statio* already suggests the later medieval meaning of 'a stationer's shop', and the name suggests that Viliaric was a Goth.[126] Viliaric's

---

[122] *Historia abbatum*, c. 15: 'ita ut tres pandectes nouae translationis, ad unum uetustae translationis quem de Roma adtulerat [*sc.* Ceolfrith] . . .' (ed. Plummer, i. 379).

[123] There is definitive treatment by Meyvaert, 'Bede, Cassiodorus and the Codex Amiatinus'; but see also the remarks of Marsden, *The Text of the Old Testament in Anglo-Saxon England*, 129–39, and id., 'Job in his Place'.

[124] Cf. Meyvaert, 'Bede, Cassiodorus and the Codex Amiatinus', 832 n. 35: 'There were probably many sources in Rome from which manuscripts could be obtained for a good price, and we know that Benedict Biscop was wealthy.' Like Meyvaert, I doubt that the 'codex grandior' was obtained from the papal library at the Lateran.

[125] See Wattenbach, *Das Schriftwesen im Mittelalter*, 424.

[126] Bischoff (*MS* ii. 316) deduced that Viliaric was a *stationarius* [sic] at Ravenna; see further Tjäder, 'Der Codex Argenteus in Uppsala'.

stationer's shop was located in Ravenna; but other evidence points to similar shops in early sixth-century Rome, such as that of one Gaudiosus who had a shop near S. Pietro in Vincoli.[127] Such *antiquarii* would produce books on commission, and at a price.[128] It is therefore interesting to note that, according to Bede in his *Historia abbatum* [CPL 1378], Benedict Biscop, on his third trip to Rome, purchased no small number of books there for which he either 'paid a fitting price' ('librosque omnis diuinae eruditionis non paucos uel placito praetio emptos') or else acquired them as donations from friends.[129] In the same chapter of the *Historia abbatum* Bede goes on to say that Benedict, on his return journey to England, collected books at Vienne which he had previously purchased there (*empticios ibi*), which implies that there were booksellers in southern France as well as in Rome in the mid-seventh century.

In any case, by ways which can no longer be traced, Anglo-Saxon libraries were stocked to the point where, for several centuries, they could sustain the schools and scholarship which put England in the vanguard of European learning. But the processes by which these libraries were built up, to the point that they could even supply books and scholars to staff new foundations in the area of English missionary activity in Germany, are unknown to us because, in their turn, the Anglo-Saxon libraries have themselves vanished. It is to these vanished Anglo-Saxon libraries that we now must turn.

---

[127] Bruyne, 'Gaudiosus, un vieux libraire romain'.
[128] See Bertelli, 'The Production and Distribution of Books', 55–7.
[129] Bede, *Historia abbatum*, c. 4 (ed. Plummer, i. 367).

2

Vanished Libraries of Anglo-Saxon England

FROM the time of the conversion to Christianity of the Anglo-Saxons, in the wake of the Gregorian mission to England in 597, libraries of various kinds began to be assembled in England.[1] In the first instance, before English scriptoria and scriptorial practice had been established (not before the mid-seventh century: the earliest surviving Anglo-Saxon manuscripts date from the very end of the seventh century), books will have had to be imported from the Continent. As the case of the famous 'codex grandior' of Cassiodorus illustrates, books from late antique Mediterranean libraries clearly formed part of the holdings of the earliest Anglo-Saxon libraries. But the matter cannot be adequately evaluated because the Anglo-Saxon libraries themselves are no longer intact, and have, like the 'codex grandior' itself, subsequently vanished. However, it is possible to ascertain the existence of a significant number of well-stocked libraries in England during the centuries between the seventh and the eleventh, and it is appropriate to begin by giving a brief sketch of what vanished Anglo-Saxon libraries are in question.

CANTERBURY IN THE TIME OF THEODORE AND HADRIAN

Theodore, archbishop of Canterbury (668–90), a Greek monk from Tarsus in Cilicia who had studied at Antioch and Constantinople, and had latterly been a member of the community of Greek-speaking Cilician monks at the monastery of S. Anastasio in Rome, arrived in England in 669,[2] to be followed a year later by his colleague Hadrian (d. 709), a Greek-speaking monk from Libya in Africa, who had

---

[1] For synoptic accounts of Anglo-Saxon libraries, see Dumville, 'English Libraries before 1066'; the essays gathered together in Gneuss, *Books and Libraries in Early England*, esp. 'Anglo-Saxon Libraries from the Conversion to the Benedictine Reform' (no. II), 'King Alfred and the History of Anglo-Saxon Libraries', (no. III), and 'Bücher und Leser in England im zehnten Jahrhundert' (no. IV); and Ganz, 'Anglo-Saxon Libraries'.

[2] On Theodore, see *Biblical Commentaries*, 5–81, and (more briefly) Lapidge, 'The Career of Archbishop Theodore'.

latterly been abbot of the monastery of Nisida in the Bay of Naples, and who on arrival in England became abbot of the monastery of SS Peter and Paul (later St Augustine's) in Canterbury.[3] These two scholars brought to England a vast experience of Mediterranean scholarship, and they promptly established a school in Canterbury, to which (as Bede says), 'they attracted a crowd of students into whose minds they daily poured the streams of wholesome learning'.[4] It is possible to form a clear impression of the scope and nature of their teaching from two sources: first, a corpus of biblical commentaries (principally to the Pentateuch and Gospels) which transmit their exposition of the biblical text as recorded, not always accurately, by their Canterbury students,[5] and secondly, the so-called 'Leiden Glossary', a manuscript now in Leiden copied c.800 at St Gallen from a lost Anglo-Saxon exemplar.[6]

In the biblical commentaries, Theodore and Hadrian quote verbatim and *in extenso* from large numbers of books, in Greek and Latin. Of Greek authors, the following are quoted by name: Basil, Clement of Alexandria, Cosmas Indicopleustes (named as *Christianus historiographus*), Ephrem the Syrian, Epiphanius (3×), Evagrius [Ponticus], Gregory of Nazianzus, John Chrysostom (6×), Josephus, Sophronius, and Theophilus; in addition to these, a substantial number of Greek authors were laid under contribution anonymously.[7] It is particularly striking that the commentators quote from Greek texts which have not come down to us: from what were apparently writings in Greek by John Cassian, Evagrius (Ponticus), and Rufinus, the latter containing a Greek word unattested in any other surviving Greek text.[8] The number of Latin authorities quoted in the biblical commentaries is far smaller, and included works by Augustine, Isidore, and Jerome (six works in total).[9] Occasionally, the commentaries contain reference to patristic works (for example by

[3] On Hadrian, see *Biblical Commentaries*, 82–132.

[4] Bede, *HE* iv. 2 ('congregata discipulorum caterua, scientiae salutaris cotidie flumina irrigandis eorum cordibus emanabant'). On the Canterbury school, see Lapidge, 'The School of Theodore and Hadrian'.

[5] *Biblical Commentaries*, 298–423 (text), 427–532 (commentary).

[6] Leiden, Bibliotheek der Rijksuniversiteit, Voss. Lat. Q. 69, fos. 20ʳ–36ʳ; *A Late Eighth-Century Latin–Anglo-Saxon Glossary*, ed. Hessels.

[7] See *Biblical Commentaries*, 206–33, and Lapidge, 'The Study of Greek at the School of Canterbury', 127. The Greek authors quoted but not named include Cyril of Alexandria, Gregory of Nyssa, John Moschus, Maximus the Confessor, Origen, Procopius of Gaza, Severian of Gabala, Theodore of Mopsuestia, and Theodoret of Cyrrhus.

[8] *Biblical Commentaries*, 289–90 (text), 427–9 (commentary).

[9] See ibid. 201–5, and below, App. E.

Rufinus and John Cassian) which have not survived. The sum of these references, in Greek and Latin, implies a substantial library. However, since both Theodore and Hadrian were trained (in Greek) in Mediterranean schools, one must reckon with the possibility that quotations in the biblical commentaries were made from memory, and hence do not imply the existence of a particular book at Canterbury. On the other hand, some quotations are so extensive and agree so closely with the transmitted text, that the hypothesis of quotation from memory becomes untenable.[10]

No such doubts attend the 'Leiden Glossary', which has been shown to contain the record of classroom teaching of Theodore and Hadrian.[11] The 'Leiden Glossary' consists of forty-eight chapters or batches of what are called *glossae collectae*, that is to say, lemmata in the target text are accompanied by explanatory glosses in Latin (and frequently in Old English), in the same order in which the lemmata occur in the text itself. Of the forty-eight chapters, nineteen consist of lemmata (with glosses) from books of the Bible, and hence fall outside the scope of the present discussion; the remaining batches contain lemmata to twenty-three late antique secular and patristic texts.[12] These batches certainly represent books which were available to Theodore and Hadrian in Canterbury; on occasion it is even possible, by comparing lemmata with the apparatus critici of scholarly editions of the texts in question, to situate the text used at Canterbury within the transmissional history of the work as a whole.[13]

Theodore and Hadrian evidently brought books with them, from Rome and Naples respectively, and assembled at Canterbury a library to serve their teaching purposes. How many books this library may have contained is impossible to say: certainly more than twenty-five, probably more than fifty, perhaps even as many as a hundred. Not a single one of these volumes can safely be identified among surviving manuscripts. The Canterbury library has vanished completely.

---

[10] For discussion of lengthy quotations from Basil, *Ep.* cclx and from the *Prolegomena in Aphthonii Progymnasmata*, see Lapidge, 'The Study of Greek at the School of Canterbury', 128–33.

[11] Lapidge, 'The School of Theodore and Hadrian', 150–8, and *Biblical Commentaries*, 173–9.

[12] See below, App. E.

[13] For the text of the *Regula S. Benedicti* expounded at Canterbury by Theodore and Hadrian, see Lapidge, 'The School of Theodore and Hadrian', 158–60; for the text of Eusebius, *Historia ecclesiastica* in the Latin translation of Rufinus, see Lapidge, 'Rufinus at the School of Canterbury'.

MALMESBURY IN THE TIME OF ALDHELM

Aldhelm (d. 709 or 710), who had been a student of Theodore and Hadrian at Canterbury before being appointed to the abbacy of Malmesbury c.680, was very widely read, in both classical and Christian texts. The corpus of Aldhelm's writings, all of which were apparently composed after his appointment to the abbacy, imply the resources of a substantial library. Rudolf Ehwald, Aldhelm's learned editor, identified some ninety texts which Aldhelm names or from which he quotes;[14] and his list can be amplified in the light of more recent work, particularly on Aldhelm's knowledge of grammatical writings and late antique poetry.[15] As far as I am aware, only one of these volumes has ever been identified, even conjecturally. Working back from a list of books in the Malmesbury library compiled by the antiquary John Leland during the years 1536 × 1540,[16] R. M. Thomson suggested that one such book, a copy of Junillus, *Instituta regularia diuinae legis*, written in Anglo-Saxon minuscule dating from c.700 and now preserved as a mere fragment in the Cottonian collection in the British Library,[17] might have been available to Aldhelm at Malmesbury.[18] In favour of Thomson's conjectural identification are the facts that the *Instituta* of Junillus are an exceptionally rare text, and that Aldhelm quotes from them at several points (unfortunately, his quotations do not overlap with text preserved on the extant fragment). Beyond this one possible exception, however, Aldhelm's library at Malmesbury has completely vanished.

MONKWEARMOUTH-JARROW IN THE TIME OF BEDE

We know from the writings of Bede (d. 735), especially from his *Historia abbatum*, that two abbots of his house, the founder Benedict Biscop and his successor Ceolfrith, devoted considerable energies to the establishment of a library at the twin foundations of Monkwearmouth (founded c.673) and Jarrow (founded c.681).[19] Benedict Biscop

[14] *Aldhelmi Opera*, ed. Ehwald, 544–6.
[15] See below, App. E, where roughly 120 works known to Aldhelm are listed.
[16] Leland's Malmesbury list is printed and discussed in *English Benedictine Libraries: The Shorter Catalogues*, ed. Sharpe et al., 262–6 (no. B54).
[17] London, BL, Cotton Tiberius A. xv, fos. 175–80.
[18] Thomson, 'Identifiable Books', 8–10.
[19] On Benedict Biscop, see Wormald, 'Bede and Benedict Biscop'; on Ceolfrith, see Wood, *The Most Holy Abbot Ceolfrid*.

made no fewer than six trips to Rome for the purpose *inter alia* of acquiring books for the monastic library,[20] and Ceolfrith was able to double the holdings of the very considerable library which Benedict had acquired.[21] But in order to know the number and nature of the books in question, we are obliged to turn to Bede's own writings. Bede was very widely read, especially but not exclusively in Christian literature, and the vast corpus of his writings—didactic, exegetical, historical, scientific, poetic—draws on a very substantial number of secular and ecclesiastical writings. The extensive references and allusions to, and quotations from, earlier writings, secular and ecclesiastical, provide some indication of the nature of the library on which he was able to draw. Basing himself on works quoted by Bede, Wolf Laistner in 1935 compiled a list of some 150 titles of works.[22] Laistner was working in a period when the standard edition of Bede's writings was that by J. A. Giles, an edition by any criterion inadequate for scholarly purposes. During the subsequent seventy years more reliable scholarly editions, provided with *apparatus fontium*, have been published, beginning with Laistner's own magisterial edition of Bede's commentaries on Acts[23] and soon followed by that by his pupil C. W. Jones of Bede's computistical writings.[24] Most of Bede's writings are now available in modern editions in the series Corpus Christianorum, Series Latina (published by Brepols at Turnhout in Belgium).[25] Using the *apparatus fontium* to these

---

[20] *Historia abbatum*, cc. 4, 6, 9, 11, 15 (*Venerabilis Baedae Opera Historica*, ed. Plummer, i. 367, 368–9, 373, 375, 379–80 respectively); on the sixth journey in particular, Benedict had brought back from Rome 'a very distinguished and copious collection of books' ('bibliothecam quam de Roma nobilissimam copiosissimamque aduexerat'). See discussion by Dumville, 'The Importation of Mediterranean Manuscripts', 107–9; see also above, pp. 28–9.

[21] *Historia abbatum*, c. 15: 'bibliothecam utriusque monasterii, quam Benedictus abbas magna coepit instantia, ipse non minori geminauit industria' (ed. Plummer, i. 379).

[22] Laistner, 'The Library of the Venerable Bede'. This essay needs to be read in conjunction with id., 'Bede as a Classical and Patristic Scholar'. And see also Brown, 'Bede and his Monastic Library'.

[23] *Bedae Venerabilis Expositio Actuum Apostolorum et Retractatio*, ed. Laistner.

[24] *Bedae Opera de Temporibus*, ed. Jones. This work is dedicated to M. L. W. Laistner.

[25] CCSL 118A–123A–C (1955–2001; in progress). The CCSL edition does not include Bede's historical writings, which were superbly edited by Charles Plummer (see above, n. 20), nor his metrical *Vita S. Cudbercti*, which was superbly edited by Werner Jaager, *Bedas metrische Vita sancti Cuthberti* (Leipzig, 1935). The CCSL edition includes reprints of Laistner's edition of Bede's treatises on Acts (CCSL 121) and of Jones's edition of the computistical treatises (CCSL 123B–C). It must also be said that the *apparatus fontium* in the various CCSL editions are of varying quality: those by Laistner and by Roger Gryson (*Bedae presbyteri Expositio Apocalypseos* (2001)) are excellent in every respect; those by C. W. Jones are serviceable if sometimes overly credulous concerning sources which might

CCSL editions, it is possible to compile a much more extensive list of the Latin writings known to Bede: as many as 250 titles may be in question.[26] However, caution is necessary. Many of the *fontes* identified in CCSL editions, particularly those of the biblical commentaries by Dom David Hurst, turn out on inspection to be illusory.[27] Furthermore, Bede may often have used manuscript miscellanies containing extracts from numerous works.[28] For example, Bede's knowledge of the writings of Augustine, to judge from his (unprinted) *Collectio ex opusculis beati Augustini in epistulas Pauli apostoli* [CPL 1360], was apparently extensive, exhaustive even;[29] but there is a real possibility that he was not using the works of Augustine themselves, but was quoting from an intermediary source such as the *Excerpta ex operibus S. Augustini* by Eugippius of Naples, in which case the number of library books in question would be reduced drastically from forty-eight to eighteen (roughly, that is, to the number of works of Augustine known to Bede as identified by Laistner in 1935). Furthermore, many of the 250 titles might have been contained in composite volumes. Concerning the overall size of Bede's library, it is not possible to improve on Laistner's careful assessment:

How large the collection at Wearmouth-Jarrow was must remain uncertain; for we cannot assume that all the books consulted by Bede were in that place. He may have borrowed, and probably did borrow, some from elsewhere. Still, when every allowance has been made, it is safe to assume that it was one of the best libraries in England in the eighth century.[30]

have been known to Bede; but those by D. Hurst of the major biblical commentaries are poor and unreliable. The sourcing of the biblical commentaries needs to be redone, using electronic databases, on the model of the excellent *apparatus* compiled by Laistner and Gryson.

[26] See below, App. E, as well as Love, 'The Library of Bede'.

[27] Note, for example, the reservations, particularly regarding Bede's alleged knowledge of the writings of Ambrose, in *Ambrose in Anglo-Saxon England*, ed. Bankert, Wegmann, and Wright, *passim*.

[28] In the case of computistical writings, for example, many of the texts quoted by Bede appear to have been assembled in a single volume, known to scholars as 'Bede's computus': a compilation which does not survive in a manuscript dating from Bede's lifetime, but which is preserved in a later copy, the so-called 'Sirmond Manuscript' (now Oxford, BodL, Bodley 309 (Vendôme, s. xi): see *Bedae Opera de Temporibus*, ed. Jones, 105–10). The 'Sirmond Manuscript' contains *inter alia* a number of excerpts, preserved anonymously, from the *Saturnalia* of Macrobius (item no. 34), and it is probable that Bede knew this work only through the anonymous excerpts in his 'computus'.

[29] A complete list of Augustinian citations in this unprinted *collectaneum* of Bede is given by Fransen, 'Description de la collection de Bède'.

[30] Laistner, *A Hand-List of Bede Manuscripts*, 1.

At a rough guess, the *c*.250 titles in Bede's library might have been contained in somewhat fewer volumes, but in any case more than *c*.200.[31] As far as the evidence permits us to say, the library used by Bede at Monkwearmouth-Jarrow was the largest library ever assembled in Anglo-Saxon England.

But this great library has vanished more or less completely. Two copies of the *carmina* of Paulinus of Nola,[32] both dating from *c*.700, have conjecturally been attributed to the scriptorium at Monkwearmouth-Jarrow by Julian Brown.[33] A small fragment (half a bifolium) of a copy of Gregory's *Moralia in Iob*, written in uncial script imitative of Roman models and characteristic of the scriptorium of Monkwearmouth-Jarrow in the time of Abbot Ceolfrith, came to light recently and is now in the Beinecke Library at Yale University.[34] But these are pathetic remnants of what was once a magnificent library.

NURSLING IN THE TIME OF BONIFACE

Of a monastery at Nursling (Hants.), located on the outskirts of modern Southampton, a place which in Anglo-Saxon times was called Nhutscelle, we have only one significant piece of information: namely that the young Wynfrith, subsequently to be known by the name Boniface (*c*.675–754), went to study there with Abbot Wynberht, having been attracted by 'love of spiritual learning' (*spiritali litterarum diligentia prouocatus*), as we learn from Willibald, the English author of the earliest *Vita S. Bonifatii* [BHL 1400], composed at Mainz *c*.760.[35] Little is known of Abbot Wynberht, save that, according to William of Malmesbury, he attested charters of Kings Cædwalla and Ine of Wessex as *clericus regis*;[36] and William preserves a letter written

---

[31] On the numerical relationship between titles and volumes, see below, pp. 58–60.

[32] Vatican City, BAV, Pal. lat. 235, fos. 4–29 and St Petersburg, Russian National Library, Q. v. XIV. 1.

[33] Bately, Brown, and Roberts (eds.), *A Palaeographer's View*, 212; see also Brown and Mackay, *Codex Palatinus 235*, 16–20.

[34] New Haven, Yale University, Beinecke Library 516 (s. viii^in). See Lutz, 'A Manuscript Fragment from Bede's Monastery', and esp. Parkes, 'The Scriptorium of Wearmouth-Jarrow', 95 and n. 10, where the Yale fragment is listed among five manuscripts in imitative Roman uncial 'and hence produced in Wearmouth-Jarrow during the abbacy of Ceolfrid' (p. 94). The remaining four manuscripts are either biblical or liturgical, and so excluded from consideration here.

[35] *Vitae Sancti Bonifatii archiepiscopi Moguntini*, ed. Levison, 9.

[36] *Willelmi Malmesbiriensis monachi Gesta pontificum Anglorum*, ed. Hamilton, 355 (§210). For the attestations in question, see Keynes, *An Atlas of Attestations*, Table IV. The charters in question are S 231, 239, 243, 1164, and 1170. On these charters, see also Levison, *England and the Continent*, 227–8.

by Aldhelm to this same Wynberht.[37] According to Willibald once again, the young Wynfrith-Boniface studied grammar and metrics at Nursling, and soon became so distinguished in Latin composition that he began to teach others.[38]

It was while at Nursling, and in any case before his final departure for the Continent in 718, that Wynfrith-Boniface composed most of the small corpus of Latin writings which are transmitted under his name: an *Ars grammatica* [CPL 1564*b*],[39] a brief treatise on metre (the *Caesurae uersuum* [CPL 1564*c*]),[40] and a collection of metrical *enigmata* on the virtues and vices [CPL 1564*a*].[41] The sources on which these three works draw, as identified by editors, are as follows. For the *Ars grammatica*:[42] Donatus, *Ars maior*; Priscian, *Institutio de nomine et pronomine et uerbo*; Isidore, *Etymologiae*, book i; and Asporius, *Ars grammatica* (GL viii. 39–61). (These four texts were also used by Tatwine in compiling his *Ars grammatica*: see below.) In addition, Wynfrith-Boniface may have used the grammatical writings of Aldhelm, Audax, Charisius, Diomedes, Phocas, Sergius, and Virgilius Maro Grammaticus.[43] For the *Caesurae uersuum*, principally Isidore, *Etymologiae*, books i, vi, and viii, together with Servius, *De centum metris*. The *Enigmata* contain frequent verbal reminiscences of Vergil (*Aeneis*, *Bucolica*, and *Georgica*),[44] as well as occasional reminiscences of the *Carmen paschale* of Caelius Sedulius, the *Psychomachia* of Prudentius, and the *Metamorphoseis* of Ovid.[45] The poetry of Aldhelm, particularly the *Enigmata* and *Carmen de uirginitate*, was a source of continual inspiration.

Wynfrith abandoned his career as grammarian and teacher in order

---

[37] *Aldhelmi Opera*, ed. Ehwald, 502–3 (*Ep.* x).

[38] *Vitae Sancti Bonifatii*, ed. Levison, 9–10: 'ita ut maxima demum scripturarum eruditione—tam grammaticae artis eloquentia et metrorum medullata facundiae modulatione quam etiam historiae simplici expositione . . . imbutus—dictandique peritia laudabiliter fulsit, ut etiam aliis demum paternarum extitit pedagogus traditionum et auctor magisterii.'

[39] CCSL 133B: 9–99.   [40] Ibid. 109–13.   [41] CCSL 133: 279–343.

[42] See Law, *Grammar*, 106–11, 169–87.   [43] Ibid. 110.

[44] The debts to Vergil are as follows (where Virt. = *Enigmata de uirtutibus*, and Vit. = *Enigmata de uitiis*). Aen. i. 278 (Virt. v.16), i. 600 (Vit. i.3), i. 630 (Vit. i.8), ii. 738 (Virt. ii.14, viii.17, Vit. vii.11), iii. 26 (Vit. iii.1–2), iii. 56 (Vit. iii.4), iii. 224 (Vit. iii.36), iii. 620 (Virt. viii.20), iii. 621 (Vit. iii.2), iv. 177 (Vit. iv.13), iv. 181–2 (Vit. iii.1–2), iv. 243 (Virt. vi.12–13, Vit. iii.62, iv.4, vii.10), v. 289 (Virt. Epil. 1), vi. 134–5 (Vit. iv.4), vi. 273 (Vit. v.11), vi. 649 (Virt. ix.12); *Buc.* iii. 71 (prol. 1, 11), iv. 6 (Virt. vi.2); *Georg.* ii. 458 (Virt. iii.5), ii. 474 (Virt. vi.3), iv. 475 (Vit. vii.12), iv. 476 (Vit. ix.11). Is it significant that the *Enigmata* of Boniface contain no reminiscences of the last six books of the *Aeneid*?

[45] Ovid, *Met.* i. 150 (Virt. i.5, vi.3); Caelius Sedulius, *Carmen Paschale* i. 325 (Virt. x.18, Vit. x.6); Prudentius, *Psychomachia* line 161 (Vit. ii.1).

to work as a missionary among the pagan Germans. After returning home from a first abortive attempt to convert the Frisians in 716, he left England forever in 718. In 719 he took the name Boniface (after the Roman martyr Bonifatius), and in 722 was made bishop and papal legate to Germany, becoming archbishop of Germany (east of the Rhine) in 732.[46] (One suspects that his rapid promotion by the papacy was due in no small measure to his excellent command of Latin.) From the time of his first passage to the Continent, Boniface kept up regular correspondence with supporters in various parts of England,[47] and it was from these supporters that he acquired the books necessary to interpret ecclesiastical legislation and doctrine. On the basis of quotations from, and verbal reminiscences of, patristic works in his correspondence, it is possible to ascertain that Boniface had with him in Germany a small, portable working library consisting of the following texts:[48] Julianus Pomerius, *De uita contemplatiua*; Caesarius of Arles, *Sermones*; Isidore, *De ecclesiasticis officiis*;[49] Gregory, *Regula pastoralis*; Augustine, *De baptismo contra Donatistas*; the Cassiodoran *Historia tripertita*; and various collections of conciliar canons and decretals [CPL 1794, 1885, etc.]. Some of these books may originally have come from Wynberht's library at Nursling. For example, in a letter to Daniel, bishop of Winchester, written during the years 742 × 746, Boniface asked the bishop to locate and send to him a copy of the biblical prophets bound in one codex and written in clear and distinct letters (that is, half uncial rather than set or cursive minuscule)— Boniface's eyesight was clearly failing by this time—which had formerly belonged to Wynberht: 'quem uenerande memoriae Winbertus abbas et magister quondam meus de hac uita ad Dominum migrans dereliquit'.[50] Nursling was just a few miles south of Winchester, and Boniface evidently expected Daniel to go there and retrieve the book from Wynberht's library.

Do any manuscripts survive from the library at Nursling, or have

---

[46] For the career of Boniface, see Levison, *England and the Continent, passim*, but esp. 70–93.

[47] *S. Bonifatii et Lullii epistolae*, ed. Tangl; see also Levison, *England and the Continent*, 280–90.

[48] See Schüling, 'Die Handbibliothek des Bonifatius', esp. 329–30. To the works listed by Schüling should be added those identified by Levison (*England and the Continent*, 282–7) and overlooked by Schüling: Gregory, *Dialogi*; Augustine, *De mendacio*, and Jerome, *Liber interpretationis hebraicorum nominum*.

[49] On the intensive use of this treatise by the Anglo-Saxon missionaries, see Levison, *England and the Continent*, 282–3.

[50] *S. Bonifatii et Lullii epistolae*, ed. Tangl, 131 (*Ep.* lxiii).

they all vanished? In fact there is a small corpus of surviving manuscripts which are thought to contain Boniface's handwriting, and which may on this evidence be assigned to Nursling.[51] The manuscripts, and the texts which they contain, are as follows: Fulda, Hessische Landesbibliothek, Bonifatianus 1, a manuscript originally copied 546–7 for Victor, bishop of Capua (541–54), containing his *Euangelicae harmoniae*, a Latin version of Tatian's *Diatessaron* [CPG 1106], with annotations by Boniface to the Epistle of James on fos. 435^v–441^v;[52] Oxford, BodL, Douce 140, containing Primasius, *Comm. in Apocalypsin*; St Petersburg, Russian National Library, Q. v. I. 15, containing Isidore, *In libros Veteris et Noui Testamenti prooemia*, *De ortu et obitu patrum*, *De ecclesiasticis officiis*, *De differentiis rerum*, *Synonyma de lamentatione animae peccatricis*, Aldhelm, *Enigmata* [CPL 1335], etc.; Marburg, Hessisches Staatsarchiv, 319 Pfarrei Spangenberg Hr no. 1, containing Servius, *Comm. in Aeneidos libros*; Marburg, Hessisches Staatsarchiv, Hr 2, 18, containing Boniface, *Ars grammatica*; and Kassel, Gesamthochschulbibliothek, Fol. theol. 65, containing Josephus, *De bello Iudaico* in the Latin version of Hegesippus. These six manuscripts, therefore, are the possible remnants of the otherwise vanished library of Nursling.

YORK IN THE TIME OF ALCUIN

Alcuin (d. 804) had spent his career as student and teacher at York before leaving England in 782, at the age of about 50, to join the court of Charlemagne as one of the king's advisers on ecclesiastical and educational policy. Alcuin had studied with Ælberht, archbishop of York from 766 until his retirement from the world of administrative duties in 778 (he died in 780); on retirement, Ælberht bequeathed his administrative responsibilities to his student Eanbald, who became archbishop of York (778–96); to his student Alcuin he bequeathed his substantial library. We have a clear impression of the nature of Ælberht's teaching, and of the personal library which sustained it, from Alcuin's famous poem 'On the bishops, kings, and saints of York' (*Carm.* i).[53] This poem includes

[51] Parkes, 'The Handwriting of St Boniface'.

[52] See Ranke, *Specimen codicis Novi Testamenti fuldensis*, 19–31. The Fulda provenance of Bonifatianus 1 implies that it was used by Boniface during his Continental sojourn, rather than that it formed part of the library at Nursling, though it may once have done so.

[53] The poem is listed CSLMA ALC 87 and ICL 2176; it is ed. E. Dümmler, MGH, PLAC i. 169–206.

an impressive list of authors who formed part of Ælberht's library, and the list allows us to make an informed guess about the size of York's library in the late eighth century.[54] The list includes the names of forty authors. Some of the names, such as Jerome or Augustine, might imply multiple volumes; other names (Isidore, for example) were omitted because they could not be fitted into a hexameter. Furthermore, the list can be supplemented by books excerpted by Alcuin in his (unprinted) collectaneum, entitled *De laude Dei*,[55] which on available evidence seems to have been compiled during his years at York. In sum, it would be safe to assume that the library at York during the lifetimes of Ælberht and Alcuin contained some hundred volumes.

A few books from the library at York have conjecturally been identified. Bernhard Bischoff suggested that the 'Moore Bede' (Cambridge, UL, Kk. 5. 16), written somewhere in Northumbria *c*.737, might have come to the Continent from York, since it contains additions on its final leaf in a hand that is strikingly similar to those found in manuscripts associated with Charlemagne's court library, and Alcuin would seem an obvious agent of the transmission from Northumbria to Charlemagne's library.[56] Donald Bullough noted that Alcuin quoted the *Expositio psalmorum* of Cassiodorus in a breviate version identical to that contained in the 'Durham Cassiodorus' (Durham, CL, B. II. 30: Northumbria, s. viii$^{2/4}$), implying perhaps a York origin for this important Northumbrian manuscript.[57] To these one might perhaps add a fragment in eighth-century Anglo-Saxon set minuscule recently identified and described by Julia Crick.[58] The leaf in question is one of several surviving *membra disiecta* of a manuscript [CLA ix. 1370] containing the *Epitome* by Justinus of the (otherwise lost) *Historiae Philippicae* of the first-century Roman historian Pompeius Trogus. If the mention of Pompeius the *historicus uetus* in Alcuin's list[59] corresponds in fact to Pompeius Trogus, and if by 'Pompeius Trogus' we understand the *Epitome* of Justinus, then it is possible that the *membra disiecta* are the remnants of a manuscript from the York library, and that Alcuin once

[54] The list is printed and discussed by Lapidge, 'Booklists', 45–9, and below, App. E.
[55] Listed below, App. E; eighteen titles are in question.
[56] Bischoff, *MS*, iii. 160–1; cf. *TxtTrans*, pp. xx–xxi.
[57] Bullough, 'Alcuin and the Kingdom of Heaven', 18–21; but cf. Bailey, *The Durham Cassiodorus*, who assesses evidence for an origin at Monkwearmouth-Jarrow (pp. 21–4).
[58] Crick, 'An Anglo-Saxon Fragment'.
[59] Below, App. E.

again was the agent of their transmission to the Continent.[60] But these are conjectures, not certain identifications. Leaving these conjectures aside, the library at York has vanished.

SMALLER MONASTIC LIBRARIES IN THE PERIOD BEFORE 835

In addition to the major libraries which had been assembled at Canterbury, Malmesbury, Monkwearmouth-Jarrow, Nursling, and York, a number of minor libraries were assembled in various locations in order to sustain the activities of individual scholars. These minor libraries include the following:

Hexham

Bede's friend and colleague Acca, sometime bishop of Hexham (709–31), had, according to Bede, travelled to Rome in the company of the indefatigable Bishop Wilfrid (*HE* iii. 13), and presumably acquired books during the course of that trip; in any event, Bede elsewhere reports that Acca 'built up a very large and excellent library, assiduously collecting histories of the sufferings of the martyrs as well as other ecclesiastical books'.[61] I have argued elsewhere that, using the resources of this library, Acca composed the (lost) Latin *martyrologium* which served as the base-text for the ninth-century *Old English Martyrology*,[62] a work which draws on some eighty *passiones martyrum* as well as a substantial number of other patristic works.[63] Not a single manuscript from Acca's library has ever been identified, however.

Ripon

Bishop Wilfrid (d. 709) endowed his church at Ripon lavishly, and his endowment included at least one book, a copy of the Gospels written on purple parchment in gilded lettering, according to the *Vita S. Wilfridi* [BHL 8889] of his apologist Stephen.[64] Although this

---

[60] This is the assumption made by Reynolds in *TxtTrans*, 197–8, and in *Scribes and Scholars*, 91.

[61] *HE* v. 20 ('sed et historias passionis eorum [*sc.* martyrum], una cum ceteris ecclesiasticis uoluminibus, summa industria congregans, amplissimam ibi [*sc.* at Hexham] ac nobilissimam bibliothecam fecit'). Bede conceivably consulted his friend Acca's collection of *passiones martyrum* in compiling his own *Martyrologium*.

[62] Lapidge, 'Acca of Hexham'; and see below, pp. 46–8, 233–4.

[63] See below, App. E.

[64] *Vita S. Wilfridi*, c. xvii (in *The Life of Bishop Wilfrid*, ed. Colgrave, 36): 'nam quattuor euangelia de auro purissimo in membranis depurpuratis, coloratis, pro animae suae remedio

vita does not show evidence of extensive learning, Stephen presumably had access to at least a small number of books at Ripon which have left traces in the *Vita S. Wilfridi*. These include copies of the anonymous Lindisfarne *Vita S. Cuthberti* [CPL 1379; BHL 2019]; Isidore, *De ortu et obitu patrum*; Jerome, *Liber quaestionum hebraicarum in Genesim*; and Rufinus' Latin translation of Eusebius, *Historia ecclesiastica*. No book from Ripon has ever been identified.

Lindisfarne

In composing his *Vita S. Cuthberti* [CPL 1379; BHL 2019] during the period 698 × 705, the anonymous monk of Lindisfarne drew on a small number of patristic texts which were presumably available to him in the library at Lindisfarne: Ambrose, *Expositio euangelii secundum Lucam*; Athanasius, *Vita S. Antonii* in the Latin translation of Evagrius; Eusebius, *Historia ecclesiastica* in the Latin translation of Rufinus; Gregory, *Dialogi*; Isidore, *De ecclesiasticis officiis*; Sulpicius Severus, *Epistulae* and *Vita S. Martini*; Victorius of Aquitaine, *Cursus paschalis*; and the anonymous *Gesta S. Siluestri*. Not a single volume from the library of Lindisfarne has ever been identified (I except the 'Lindisfarne Gospels' (London, BL, Cotton Nero D. iv), which is not a library book in my definition of the term).

Whitby

The same is true of Whitby, where the anonymous author of the *Vita S. Gregorii* [BHL 3637] had access to at least some of Gregory's writings, notably the *Dialogi*, *Hom. .xl. in Euangelia*, *Moralia in Iob*, and *Regula pastoralis*, as well as at least one of Jerome's *Epistulae* (no. lx), Sulpicius Severus, *Vita S. Martini*, and the *Liber pontificalis*. No surviving manuscript has ever been attributed to the library of Whitby.

Breedon-on-the-Hill

Before his appointment to the archbishopric of Canterbury in 731, Tatwine (d. 734) had been a priest and teacher at the Mercian minster of Breedon-on-the-Hill (Leics.), where he evidently had at his disposal a respectable library, particularly of grammatical texts. His *Ars grammatica* [CPL 1563] shows heavy but intelligent use of the

---

scribere iussit; necnon et bibliothecam librorum eorum, omnem de auro purissimo et gemmis prestiosissimis fabrefactam, compaginare inclusores gemmarum praecepit'. As the context makes clear, *bibliotheca* here means a jewelled bookcase, not a library.

following grammatical works:[65] Asporius, *Ars grammatica* (GL viii. 39–61), Consentius Gallus, *Ars de nomine et uerbo*; Donatus, *Ars maior*; Eutyches, *Ars de uerbo*; Martianus Capella, *De nuptiis Philologiae et Mercurii*, book iii ('De grammatica'); Isidore, *Etymologiae*; Pompeius, *Comm. in artem Donati*; and Priscian, *Institutio de nomine, pronomine et uerbo*; in addition, Tatwine probably drew on Cledonius, *Ars grammatica*; Phocas, *Ars de nomine et uerbo*; Probus, *Catholica*; and Sergius, *Explanationes in Donatum*. In his collection of forty *Enigmata*, Tatwine reveals knowledge of a number of Latin poets, including Vergil, *Aeneis*, *Bucolica*, and *Georgica* (*Aeneis* is also quoted several times, directly, in Tatwine's *Ars grammatica*); Horace, *Carmina*; Juvencus, *Euangelia*; and Caelius Sedulius, *Carmen paschale*. In sum, the writings of Tatwine imply access to a decent working library. But no manuscript from this library has ever been identified.

ANGLO-SAXON LIBRARIES IN THE NINTH CENTURY

Anglo-Saxon book production reached its apogee during the eighth century, as scriptoria geared up to supply the relentless demands for books by Anglo-Saxon missionaries in Germany. Monkwearmouth-Jarrow in particular had the problem that many works of Bede had become best-sellers, so to speak, and the scriptorium there was obliged to devote huge energy to supplying the seemingly insatiable demand for his writings.[66] By the early ninth century, however, this scriptorial energy had largely been spent. By then, churches in Germany had scriptoria of their own, and the educational policies of Charlemagne and his successors led to the multiplication and circulation of books, and the concomitant growth of libraries. Sources of books other than England, notably Italy, were exploited. The result is that, after *c.*800, there was a declining demand for English books on the Continent. The decline in demand for exportable books seems to have coincided, in England, with a serious decline of monastic life. There is no doubt that this decline was accelerated, if not caused, by

[65] On the sources of Tatwine's *Ars*, see the 'Appendix' to de Marco's edition of *Tatuini Opera Omnia*, 95–141, and Law, *Grammar*, 109–13. On Tatwine's knowledge of Martianus Capella (unusual at any time before the 9th c. in Europe, and the late 10th c. in England), see Shanzer, 'Tatwine: An Independent Witness'.

[66] The effect which the increased popularity of Bede's writings had on the scriptorium at Monkwearmouth-Jarrow during the later 8th c. is well discussed by Parkes, 'The Scriptorium of Wearmouth-Jarrow', esp. 108–12.

Viking activity, first by the advent of Viking raiders at coastal monastic sites (Lindisfarne was attacked in 793, Jarrow in 794), and more significantly by the semi-permanent presence of Viking armies in England during the 860s and later.[67] Scholarly activity and book production virtually ceased in England during the middle years of the ninth century.

A graphic picture of this decline is given by King Alfred (871–99) in the famous prose preface to his English translation of Gregory's *Regula pastoralis*, commenting on the state of learning in England when he acceded to the throne in 871:

> Learning had declined so thoroughly in England that there were very few men on this side of the Humber who could understand their divine services in English, or even translate a single letter from Latin into English: and I suppose that there were not many beyond the Humber either. There were so few of them that I cannot recollect even a single one south of the Thames when I succeeded to the kingdom.[68]

This grim picture is confirmed by evidence of various kinds: scarcely a single manuscript written during the period 835 × 885 survives, and scribes who were employed to copy royal charters during the same period were plainly illiterate, to judge from the substantial number of original, single-sheet charters which have survived.[69]

In these circumstances it would be surprising if the well-stocked libraries of the eighth century had been maintained during the ninth. King Alfred again: 'When I reflected on all this, I recollected how—before everything was ransacked and burned—the churches throughout England stood filled with treasures and books.'[70] And yet it is worth asking if all English libraries had indeed been totally destroyed, 'ransacked and burned', in King Alfred's words. A large area of the West Midlands had remained untouched by Viking armies, and a cathedral library at (say) Worcester or Hereford might well have

---

[67] See Sawyer, *The Age of the Vikings*, 120–47; id., *Kings and Vikings*, 78–97; Brooks, 'England in the Ninth Century'; and Keynes, 'The Vikings in England', 48–82.

[68] Keynes and Lapidge, *Alfred the Great*, trans. Keynes and Lapidge, 125.

[69] Lapidge, 'Latin Learning in Ninth-Century England'. A more optimistic (and, in my opinion, unfounded) view of the situation was taken by Morrish, 'King Alfred's Letter'. Elsewhere Morrish provides a handlist of surviving 9th-c. English manuscripts ('Dated and Datable Manuscripts'); but, with the possible exception of a computistical manuscript (Oxford, BodL, Digby 63, apparently written somewhere in Northumbria between the years 844 or 867 × 892), all the manuscripts in her list were written in either the first or the last quarter of the century, not during the crucial period 835 × 885. See also the important discussion by Gneuss, 'King Alfred and the History of Anglo-Saxon Libraries'.

[70] *Alfred the Great*, trans. Keynes and Lapidge, 125.

remained more or less intact. It is worth recalling, for example, that it was the bishop of Worcester, one Wærferth (869 × 872–915), who provided an English translation of Gregory's *Dialogi*, apparently as part of King Alfred's programme of intellectual renewal.[71] It is also the case that various Anglo-Latin writings of the eighth century, which now survive only in English manuscripts of the tenth century or later, were evidently copied from exemplars which had somehow survived the dark years of the ninth century, only to be lost at a later date.[72]

It has often been thought that the enigmatic *Old English Martyrology* could throw important light on this situation, if only it could be reliably dated or localized.[73] As it survives, the *Old English Martyrology* is a historical martyrology consisting, in its present (incomplete) form, of 238 entries, drawn from a wide range of hagiographical sources. The *terminus post quem* for its composition is provided by its use of Bede's *Historia ecclesiastica* (hence it is later than 731); its *terminus ante quem* is established by the fact that it is preserved *inter alia* in a manuscript of the late ninth century (London, BL, Add. 23211 (Wessex, s. ix² [871 × 899])). The *Old English Martyrology* was evidently composed between 731 and 899, therefore; and Old English scholars are in agreement that the language of the text is datable to the later ninth century, probably to the Alfredian period itself.[74] However, it is difficult to use the *Old English Martyrology* as evidence for the holdings of some (unidentified) ninth-century library because of the possibility that the surviving Old English text is itself simply a translation of an earlier but now lost Latin martyrology, compiled somewhere in northern England after 731 and before it served as the exemplar for the (Alfredian period) English translation.

Upon closer inspection, however, it will be seen that the *Old English Martyrology* contains no commemoration of an English saint who died later than the mid-eighth century. The fact that it omits any commemoration of St Boniface, who was martyred in 754, shows that the Latin exemplar must have been composed before that date; and the further fact that it includes no commemoration of St Willibrord,

[71] *Bischof Wærferths von Worcester Übersetzung der Dialoge Gregors des Grossen*, ed. Hecht. It has to be stated, however, that Bishop Wærferth's Latin training left much to be desired, as can be seen from his numerous errors in understanding Gregory's Latin: see Godden, 'Wærferth and King Alfred', esp. 44–7.

[72] See Lapidge, 'Latin Learning in Ninth-Century England', 424–32.

[73] *Das altenglische Martyrologium*, ed. Kotzor.

[74] Ibid. i. 323*–425*, 445*–446*, 449*.

who died at Echternach in November 739, and whose death could not have been reported in Northumbria before 740, implies that the lost Latin martyrology must have been composed between the years 731 (since it uses Bede's *Historia ecclesiastica* as a source) and 740 (since it includes no commemoration of St Willibrord).[75] We know from Bede that Acca had amassed a huge library of hagiographical texts, including particularly *passiones martyrum* (see above, p. 42). The surviving 238 chapters of the *Old English Martyrology* are drawn from the works of some thirty named authors as well as from an astonishing number of anonymous hagiographical texts;[76] and these texts, some one hundred in total, include *passiones apostolorum* and *uitae sanctorum*, but above all *passiones martyrum* (at least eighty of these).[77] It could be (and has been) argued that many of these texts were available to the compiler in a passional or legendary of some form. But it should be remembered that large-scale legendaries, as we known them from the later Middle Ages, date from a period much later than the years 731–40.[78] The earliest surviving Continental legendaries date from no earlier than the mid-eighth century, and typically contain fewer than forty *passiones*; the earliest surviving English passional (now Paris, BNF, lat. 10861 (?Christ Church, Canterbury, s. ix¹)) contains only eighteen *passiones*.[79] The Continental ancestor of the much larger 'Cotton-Corpus Legendary', which contains some 165 *passiones* and *uitae* and was used by late Anglo-Saxon authors such as Ælfric, was not compiled before the late ninth century.[80] Large-scale passionals can therefore throw no light on the library of the scholar who compiled the Latin exemplar of the *Old English Martyrology*. If, as I have suggested, the scholar in question was Acca, the work of compilation could have been done during the years between 731, when Acca was deposed from the see of Hexham, and 740, when he died: the nine years in question being a sort of enforced early retirement, allowing him to draw on the resources of a library which he had spent a lifetime acquiring. On this hypothesis, the

[75] For the details of this argument, see Lapidge, 'Acca of Hexham'.

[76] There is a valuable synopsis of these sources by Rauer, 'The Sources of the *Old English Martyrology*'; the full listing of sources, also by Rauer, is found in the Fontes Anglo-Saxonici Database at ⟨http://fontes.english.ox.ac.uk⟩ (last accessed 13/12/04).

[77] See below, App. E, a listing based on the Fontes Database cited in the previous note.

[78] Philippart, *Les Légendiers latins*, 30–1. The earliest Continental passional [CLA ix. 1238] contains twenty-four *passiones* and one *uita*; the largest of the early passionals [CLA ix. 1242] contains thirty-nine *passiones*.

[79] Brown, 'Paris, Bibliothèque Nationale, lat. 10861', 122.

[80] Jackson and Lapidge, 'The Contents of the Cotton-Corpus Legendary'.

surviving *Old English Martyrology* is a vernacular version, datable probably to the period of Alfred's reign, of a Latin text that was composed a century and a half earlier by Acca, sometime bishop of Hexham. In any event, the *Old English Martyrology* is a remarkable witness to a library of hagiographical texts which has otherwise vanished completely.

KING ALFRED AND THE RESTOCKING OF ENGLISH LIBRARIES

In many ways the *Old English Martyrology* fits in well with the programme of translation of works 'most necessary for all men to know' sponsored by King Alfred, although there is no certain evidence in support of such a link. In any case, once he had secured the peace of Wessex by his defeat of the Viking army at the battle of Edington (878), Alfred was able to turn his attention to the restoration of the country's depleted intellectual resources.[81] As we have seen, Alfred knew of no Latin scholars in Southumbria when he acceded to the throne in 871. He was therefore obliged to import scholars from elsewhere. From the Continent, he invited Grimbald of Saint-Bertin and John the Old Saxon; and from Wales he invited Asser, the bishop of St David's. With the help of these men, Alfred undertook a programme of translation so as to make available in English those books which were deemed 'most necessary for all men to know'. This programme included four works in the translation of which he was personally involved: Gregory, *Regula pastoralis*; Boethius, *De consolatione Philosophiae*; Augustine, *Soliloquia*; and the first fifty psalms of the Psalter. Several other translations were made by scholars working in collaboration with the court: Gregory, *Dialogi* translated by Wærferth, bishop of Worcester; Orosius, *Historiae aduersum paganos*; and Bede, *Historia ecclesiastica* [CPL 1375], both translated anonymously; and I myself should add to this list of translations the previously mentioned *Old English Martyrology*. The implication of this translation activity is that there was available to scholars a small working library at the royal court,[82] and the sources of two of

[81] For Alfred's role in the reconstitution of English libraries, see Gneuss, 'King Alfred and the History of Anglo-Saxon libraries', and Gameson, 'Alfred the Great and the Destruction'.

[82] See Bately, 'Those Books that are Most Necessary'.

the translations in particular—the Boethius[83] and the Orosius[84]—have attracted modern scholarly attention and may shed some light on the contents of the court library. Some of the books present in this (hypothetical) court library may also be reflected in the range of works quoted or alluded to by Asser in his Life of King Alfred (apparently abandoned, incomplete, in 893).[85]

The scholars associated with Alfred's court presumably brought books to England with them. A substantial number of books, nearly eighty in total, survives which were written at various centres on the Continent during the ninth century and which were brought to England before the Norman Conquest.[86] It is possible that some at least of these manuscripts owe their presence in England to the agency of the scholars working under Alfred's patronage. Thus it is tempting to speculate that those manuscripts which have a pre-Conquest English provenance but which originated in either Reims or Saint-Bertin may have been brought by Grimbald, who had been a monk at Saint-Bertin and a member of Archbishop Fulco's household at Reims before coming to England.[87] Other Continental manuscripts

[83] For works laid under contribution during the translation of Boethius, see Wittig, 'King Alfred's *Boethius*', who argues against the simplistic notion that the Alfredian expansions of the Boethian text depend on a single Carolingian commentary (presumably that of Remigius), and suggests instead that Alfred's translators were familiar with Vergil's *Georgics* iv and *Aeneid* vi (with commentary by Servius), with Isidore, *Etymologiae*, and perhaps with Ovid, *Met.* x (p. 185). It should be noted that Wittig's arguments are based on close analysis of only one of the Boethian *metra* (iii met. xii, on Orpheus and Eurydice); further analysis of other passages of the text might well reveal the use of different, and more numerous, sources.

[84] The sources drawn on by the translator(s) of the Orosius are treated in detail by Bately, 'The Classical Additions', and in *The Old English Orosius*, ed. Bately, pp. lv–lxxii. She concludes: 'It would seem, then, that the classical additions to be found in Or. are to be traced back to a variety of Latin sources, including Livy, Sallust, Pliny the Elder, Quintus Curtius, Frontinus, Valerius Maximus, Servius, Jerome, Bede and (though the evidence is not conclusive) probably also Augustine, Firmianus Lactantius and Suetonius' ('The Classical Additions', 249; repeated nearly verbatim in *The Old English Orosius*, p. lxi). It is worth adding that, for a number of these sources—Livy, Curtius Rufus, and Suetonius—there is no independent evidence of circulation in England before 1066 (see below, Catalogue), which casts serious doubt on the validity of Bately's source identifications.

[85] See Lapidge, 'Asser's Reading', and below, pp. 115–20, and App. E.

[86] See below, App. D.

[87] Manuscripts having an origin at Saint-Bertin or Reims and a later English provenance (hence arguably associable with Grimbald) include: Cambridge, CCC 223 (Prudentius; Saint-Bertin, s. ix$^{3/4}$); CCC 272 (psalter; Reims, *c.*883); Cambridge, Pembroke College 308 (Hrabanus Maurus; Reims, s. ix^{2}); Hereford, CL, O. III. 2 (Jerome, Gennadius, Isidore, Augustine, Cassiodorus; France, s. ix$^{3/4}$); London, BL, Royal 15. A. XXXIII (Martianus Capella; Reims, s. ix/x); Royal 15. B. XIX (Bede, *De*

may carry some association with John the Old Saxon.[88] Manuscripts of ninth-century Welsh or Cornish origin and tenth-century English provenance could conceivably have some association with Asser.[89] In any case, it was the importation of Continental books, a process initiated under King Alfred, which put in train the gradual restocking of Anglo-Saxon libraries during the tenth and eleventh centuries.

LIBRARIES IN THE PERIOD OF THE BENEDICTINE REFORM MOVEMENT

The restocking of monastic and cathedral libraries must have been a long and ongoing process, lasting through the tenth century and beyond. But we are hampered in assessing this process because, although there are substantial numbers of surviving English manuscripts dating from the tenth century, it is possible only in certain cases to assign them to particular centres, and thus to evaluate overall holdings. For example, basing himself on the evidence for provenance assembled by Neil Ker,[90] David Dumville has drawn up lists of surviving books written by $c.1100$ and assignable to specific houses, with the following interesting results:[91] Bury St Edmunds (26 surviving manuscripts), Christ Church, Canterbury (45), St Augustine's, Canterbury (63), Durham Cathedral (47), Exeter Cathedral (36), Salisbury Cathedral (35), Winchester, Old Minster (27), and Worcester Cathedral (45). These figures, as will be seen, pertain principally to cathedral libraries. On the other hand, for monastic libraries such as Glastonbury, Abingdon, and Peterborough, which

---

temporum ratione; Reims, s. ix$^{4/4}$); and Utrecht, Universiteitsbibliotheek, 32 (psalter; vicinity of Reims, s. ix^1).

[88] A 9th-c. manuscript now in Oxford, BodL, Rawlinson C. 697 (Aldhelm, Prudentius; NE France, s. ix$^{3/4}$) contains the unique copy of an acrostic poem by John the Old Saxon, and may have some personal association with that scholar.

[89] A pocket gospelbook which also contains two acrostic poems dedicated to King Alfred, now Bern, Burgerbibliothek 671 (?SW England, ?Cornwall, ?Wales, s. ix^1) may owe its presence in 10th-c. Wiltshire to the agency of Asser. Other manuscripts of 9th-c. Welsh or Cornish origin which made their way to England during the course of the 10th c. include: Cambridge, UL, Add. 4543, computistica; UL, Ff. 4. 42, Juvencus; Cambridge, CCC 153, Martianus Capella; Oxford, BodL, Auct. F. 4. 32, fos. 37–47, Ovid, *Ars amatoria* bk. i; BodL, Bodley 572, fos. 1–25, 41–50, mass for St Germanus, scholastic colloquy; Bern, Burgerbibliothek, C. 219, Themistius, *De decem categoriis*. On all these manuscripts, see Lindsay, *Early Welsh Script*.

[90] Ker, *Medieval Libraries of Great Britain*, together with Watson, *Supplement to the Second Edition*.

[91] Dumville, 'English Libraries before 1066', 178–88, 203–19 (App.).

from the 940s onwards were undoubtedly the most productive centres of scholarship in the country, no more than a handful of manuscripts in each case can be identified as having belonged to the monastic library.[92]

The problems can be illustrated by the case of the fenland monastery of Ramsey, which in the lifetime of Byrhtferth must have had a library extensive enough to support his own idiosyncratic scholarship. Yet very few books from the Ramsey library have ever been identified.[93] One might point to a copy of the Commentary of Macrobius on the *Somnium Scipionis*, a work well known to both Byrhtferth and his mentor Abbo, but not apparently to any other Anglo-Saxon scholar.[94] The manuscript is now Paris, BNF, lat. 7299, written in the distinctive script of tenth-century Fleury, to which has been added a quire in Anglo-Caroline minuscule (fos. 3–12) containing a liturgical calendar of evident Ramsey origin.[95] It is a convenient assumption that the book was brought by Abbo to Ramsey, where it acquired its additional quire, and then taken back (or sent back) to Fleury, perhaps by Abbo once again.[96] Byrhtferth and Abbo were also unique among Anglo-Saxon scholars in their knowledge of the *Astronomica* of Hyginus. Among the eighty or so surviving copies of the work, there is one, now London, BL, Harley 2506, which was evidently written at Fleury, but which was decorated by a late tenth-century English illustrator, either at Fleury or in England.[97] The text of Hyginus carries a number of glosses and

---

[92] Dumville (ibid.) lists the following: Glastonbury (3), Abingdon (8), and Peterborough (2). Cf. the remarks of Gneuss, *Handlist*, p. 3: 'Very few books remain from what must have been well-stocked repositories of learning and literature, like the Benedictine houses in Winchester, in Abingdon, Ely, Glastonbury, Malmesbury, Peterborough and Ramsey, the nunneries at Barking, Shaftesbury and Wilton, the cathedrals of London and York.'

[93] I leave out of consideration several liturgical manuscripts which have a Ramsey origin or provenance: Cambridge, Sidney Sussex College, Δ. 5. 15 (100), pontifical; London, BL, Cotton Vitellius A. vii, fos. 1–112, pontifical; London, BL, Harley 2904, psalterium Gallicanum; and Orleans, BM, 127 (105), sacramentary. On these manuscripts, see Dumville, *Liturgy and the Ecclesiastical History*, 75–6, 79, and Lapidge, *ALL* ii. 388–94, 398–403.

[94] See below, Catalogue, p. 320.

[95] See the description by Ebersperger, *Die angelsächsischen Handschriften*, 71–6, as well as Lapidge, *ALL* ii. 395–6.

[96] The hypothesis of Abbo's use of this manuscript is strengthened by the fact that a number of glosses to the text of Macrobius, in the main part of the manuscript, have close verbal parallels in Abbo's Commentary on the *Calculus* of Victorius of Aquitaine: see Peden, *Abbo of Fleury and Ramsey*, 81[–2] n. 57, 95 n. 111.

[97] See Lapidge, *ALL* ii. 399, and esp. Saxl and Meier, *Catalogue of Astronomical and Mythological Illuminated Manuscripts*, iii: *Manuscripts in English Libraries*, i. 157–60.

corrections in Anglo-Caroline minuscule (datable to *c*.1000), and I have often wondered if in these glosses we might have the hand of Byrhtferth himself. In any case it is probably a Ramsey book. That is to say, out of a library of some hundred volumes,[98] it is possible tentatively to identify two surviving manuscripts. The remainder have vanished.

CONCLUSIONS

It is clear from the preceding survey that, in terms of surviving books, Anglo-Saxon libraries have vanished as completely as have those of classical antiquity. Yet we know that these vanished libraries were able to sustain the research of a number of outstanding Anglo-Saxon scholars, over a period of four centuries or more. It we are to understand the nature of the libraries which have vanished, therefore, we must turn to different kinds of evidence. The following three chapters treat the various sorts of evidence by which vanished Anglo-Saxon libraries can be reconstructed.

[98] See below, App. E (pp. 266–74).

3

Reconstructing Anglo-Saxon Libraries (I): The Evidence of Inventories

THE contents of vanished Anglo-Saxon libraries can be reconstructed from three sorts of evidence: surviving inventories of books pertaining to a particular institution or library; surviving manuscripts attributable to a particular institution; and citations by Anglo-Saxon authors (whether writing in Latin or Old English) who drew on the resources of a particular institutional library. Of these three classes of evidence, I begin in this chapter with Anglo-Saxon inventories; surviving manuscripts and citations form the subjects of the two following chapters.

Some thirteen inventories of books survive from Anglo-Saxon England, varying in length from a few items to (at most) sixty-five.[1] As we shall see, the scale of these inventories is extremely modest in comparison with the inventories which survive from ninth-century Continental libraries. It is also extremely modest in comparison with some of the later English medieval catalogues printed in the Corpus of British Medieval Library Catalogues (CBMLC), being edited under the inspired leadership of Richard Sharpe. In the case of English Benedictine houses—the most relevant for comparison with Anglo-Saxon evidence—the late medieval catalogues may run to more than 600 items (Ramsey, for example, or St Mary's York).[2] Furthermore, unlike many late medieval catalogues, the inventories from Anglo-Saxon England are simple lists; that is to say, they do not include shelf-marks against individual items so as to facilitate retrieval and reshelving (and, one might add, identification by modern scholars). Of the thirteen Anglo-Saxon inventories, two may be eliminated at once from our enquiries, since they pertain solely to collections of liturgical books.[3] Several others are unrepresentative for

---

[1] The thirteen inventories are printed and their contents discussed in Lapidge, 'Booklists'.

[2] *English Benedictine Libraries*, ed. Sharpe et al.; for Ramsey, see pp. 350–415 (no. B68); for St Mary's, York, see pp. 678–748 (no. B120).

[3] Lapidge, 'Booklists', nos. VI–VII.

various reasons, in that they record (for example) a few books among a quantity of ecclesiastical furniture gifted by King Æthelstan (924–39) to the community of St Cuthbert,[4] or among property recorded by Ælfwold, bishop of Crediton (c.997–c.1016) in his will (again, these are liturgical books for the most part).[5] But the remaining six inventories throw valuable light on the nature of Anglo-Saxon libraries, both private and institutional.[6]

One brief list of fourteen items,[7] for example, consists of books which belonged to one Æthelstan who, to judge from the contents of the list, must have been a grammarian at some point in the early tenth century: Donatus, *Ars maior* and *Ars minor*; *De arte metrica* (presumably Bede [CPL 1565]) but also *Excerptiones de metrica arte* (unidentifiable, without further specification), and schooltexts such as Persius, the *Disticha Catonis* with accompanying gloss (presumably that of Remigius), and Caelius Sedulius, *Carmen paschale*. Books were expensive:[8] how could a grammarian have afforded fourteen books on his own account? The question is exacerbated by a fuller list of schooltexts found in a manuscript of the late eleventh century, probably copied at Worcester.[9] This list contains sixty items, the majority of them classroom texts (twelve liturgical books in the list are omitted from discussion here): Sedulius in two copies, Prosper (three copies), Arator (two copies), plus Lucan, Persius, Boethius, and other classical authors. Although the list contains at its end a copy of the Gospels and some liturgical books, the overall impression is of a collection of books intended for classroom use rather than an inventory of the holdings of a cathedral church (such as Worcester, where the manuscript was apparently written): the private library of a grammarian, in other words.

Interesting in a different way is a list of books which Bishop Æthelwold of Winchester (963–84) donated c.970 to his new founda-

---

[4] Lapidge, 'Booklists', no. II; see also discussion by Keynes, 'King Athelstan's Books', 170–85.   [5] Lapidge, 'Booklists', no. V.

[6] These six inventories are printed and discussed below, App. A.

[7] Lapidge, 'Booklists', no. III; App. A, INV(i) **a**.

[8] The only literary evidence we have from Anglo-Saxon England concerning the costs involved in copying manuscripts on commission comes from an early 11th-c. *colloquium* or 'school-dialogue' by Ælfric Bata, in which a customer is depicted haggling with a young monk aspiring to be a professional scribe, about the cost of copying a missal (the monk first suggests a price of £2, but is beaten down to 12 mancuses, or about 1½ pounds of silver). For the text, see *Anglo-Saxon Conversations*, ed. Gwara and Porter, 134–6; for discussion, see Lapidge, 'Artistic and Literary Patronage', 43–5.

[9] Lapidge, 'Booklists', no. XI; App. A, INV(i) **e**.

tion at Peterborough (twenty-one items),[10] a sort of start-up collection, including various hagiographical texts and works of lexicographical interest: *De litteris Grecorum* (presumably a Greek–Latin glossary), Jerome's commentary on Hebrew names [CPL 581], and what was presumably the third book of Abbo of Saint-Germain's impenetrable *Bella Parisiacae urbis* (given in Æthelwold's list as *Descidia Parisiacae polis*, showing Æthelwold's typical flair for pompous Greek synonyms).[11] A century later another inventory of books was compiled at Peterborough, containing sixty-five items (including five liturgical books).[12] A few, but only a few, correspond to items recorded in Æthelwold's list of *c*.970:[13] a fact which may throw light on the rapidity with which the stock of Anglo-Saxon libraries was turned over.

One of the principal problems in interpreting the booklists is that of identifying the individual entries:[14] so that *Descidia Parisiacae polis*, if we were unfamiliar with Æthelwold's penchant for turning plain Latin into pseudo-Greek, might go unidentified.[15] In many cases identification is straightforward, as, in the second Peterborough list, 'Augustinus De ciuitate Dei' (INV(i) f. 1). But even when the author is named, it may not be a straightforward task to identify the book. For example, 'Augustinus de penitentia' (INV(i) f. 19). Augustine wrote no work of that title. What is in question is probably two of his sermons (nos. cccli–ccclii), which often circulated together to form a treatise *De utilitate agendae poenitentiae*;[16] but two of Augustine's letters (*Ep.* xci and cliii) also treat penitence, and one or both of them could conceivably be in question here. Problems are more severe if the author is not named. One simply has to know that the *Collatio*

[10] Lapidge, 'Booklists', no. IV; App. A, INV(i) b.

[11] On Æthelwold's penchant for grecism, see Lapidge, 'Æthelwold as Scholar and Teacher', 94–100 (repr. *ALL* ii. 183–211 at 188–94).

[12] Lapidge, 'Booklists', no. XIII; App. A, INV(i) f.

[13] App. A, INV(i) f. 54, 57.

[14] In the case of post-Conquest inventories, one has the excellent guidance of Sharpe, *List of Identifications*, which was compiled to facilitate work on the CBMLC. See also Sharpe's extensive discussion of the problems of identifying works from medieval inventories in his *Titulus: Identifying Medieval Latin Texts*. Much of this book pertains to post-Conquest (English) authors; but particularly relevant to the pre-Conquest period is his discussion of Augustine (pp. 60–1, 88–9), Hilary (pp. 72–3), and Isidore (pp. 74, 91–3).

[15] For the pre-Conquest period, unfortunately, Sharpe's *List of Identifications* is of limited utility, since much of its content pertains to works composed after 1066. For example, it contains no entry for *Descidia Parisiacae polis*, nor for *Bella Parisiacae urbis* (the normal title of the work), nor even for Abbo of Saint-Germain-des-Prés.

[16] This information is found in Sharpe, *List of Identifications*, 19, s.v. 'Sermones de poenitentia'.

Nesterotis abbatis de spirituali scientia (INV(i) f. 21) is not a work by an unrecorded Abbot Nesteros, but one of the 'conversations with desert monks' (no. xiv) which make up Cassian's *Conlationes* [CPL 512]. Similarly an item in the Peterborough list: *Liber notarum* (INV(i) f. 34). Someone's handy note-book? The item almost certainly represents a scribal error for *Liber rotarum* (a *rota*, or 'wheel', was the medieval Latin term for a 'diagram'), where the reference is probably to Isidore's *De natura rerum*, a work which contains a large number of diagrams.[17] But many of the less specific entries are regrettably unidentifiable: *canones*, for example, or *liber miraculorum*.

On very rare occasions it is possible to identify an item in an inventory with a surviving manuscript. For example, the later Peterborough list contains an item 'Ambrosius De sacramentis et Vita sanctorum Nicolai, Botulfi, Guthlaci' (INV(i) f. 16). This unusual combination of contents is found, in the same order, in a late eleventh-century manuscript in the British Library, Harley 3097, which is therefore presumably the very book recorded in the list. But identifications like this are unusual with Anglo-Saxon inventories. The only general exception occurs in the case of a list of fifty-five books gifted by Bishop Leofric to his cathedral chapter at Exeter between 1069 and 1072 (INV(i) d).[18] Some of these can be identified with confidence among surviving manuscripts because, unusually, Bishop Leofric sometimes took the trouble to write *ex-dono* inscriptions in the books which he gifted to Exeter.[19] (On the whole Anglo-Saxon books rarely have *ex-dono* inscriptions,[20] and more rarely still have ex-libris inscriptions.[21]) Interestingly, only one of the books in

---

[17] A similar *liber notarum* in a 9th-c. inventory from Murbach is improbably interpreted by R. McKitterick as 'a dictionary of tironian notes': *The Carolingians and the Written Word*, 193.

[18] Lapidge, 'Booklists', no. X; App. A, INV(i) d, omitting twenty-two liturgical and vernacular books in Leofric's list.

[19] See Förster, 'The Donations of Leofric to Exeter', 10–32. Of the fifty-five books listed in the inventory, seven contain *ex-dono* inscriptions: Cambridge, UL, Ii. 2. 11; Cambridge, CCC 41; Cambridge, Trinity College B. 11. 2; Oxford, BodL, Auct. D. 2. 16; Auct. F. 1. 15, fos. 1–77; Bodley 579; and Bodley 708.

[20] Excepting the manuscripts donated by Leofric listed in the previous note, *ex-dono* inscriptions are found in the following three manuscripts: Cambridge, CCC 140 + 111, pp. 1–8, 55–6, fo. 45ᵛ ('ego Ælfricus scripsi hunc librum in monasterio Baðþonio et dedi Brihtwoldo preposito'); El Escorial, Real Biblioteca, E. II. 1, fo. 1ʳ ('þas boc syllþ Ælfgyþ Gode into Horetune'); and London, Lambeth Palace Library, 149, fos. 1–139, fo. 138ᵛ ('hunc quoque uolumen Ætheluuardus dux gratia Dei ad monasterium Sancte Marie genetricis saluatoris nostri condonauit').

[21] Two exceptions include: a 5th-c. Italian copy of Jerome, *Comm. in Ecclesiasten* now in Würzburg, UB, M. p. th. q. 2, which was owned in England *c.*700 by one Cuthswith,

question is still in Exeter: the so-called 'Exeter Book of Old English Poetry', now Exeter, CL, 3501. This gives us a useful reminder of the rate of dispersal of Anglo-Saxon books: only one of fifty-five books gifted to Exeter by Bishop Leofric remains there to this day.[22] A similar rate of dispersal should probably not be assumed for other cathedral libraries which have been in existence since pre-Conquest times, but we should not be sanguine about the likelihood of Anglo-Saxon cathedral libraries remaining intact, *in situ*.[23]

What, then, do surviving Anglo-Saxon inventories tell us about the nature of Anglo-Saxon libraries? We have to bear in mind that the evidence is partial at best: whereas we have two lists from Peterborough, two from Worcester, and one from Exeter—none of them earlier than the tenth century, however—other major ecclesiastical institutions are not represented at all. There are no pre-Conquest inventories from Canterbury, Winchester, Ramsey, or Malmesbury, to say nothing of Monkwearmouth-Jarrow. Nevertheless, the evidence of booklists tends to reinforce the impression one gains from other kinds of evidence: that Anglo-Saxon libraries were relatively small in extent, seldom surpassing sixty or so books. (This picture

abbess of a monastery perhaps at Inkberrow, to judge by an ex-libris inscription on fo. 1ʳ: 'Cuthsuuithae. boec. thaerae abbatissan' (see Lowe, *English Uncial*, 17 and pl. I, V, and Sims-Williams, 'Cuthswith, Seventh-Century Abbess of Inkberrow'); and a 10th-c. illustrated copy of Prudentius now in Cambridge, CCC 23, which belonged in the 11th c. to Malmesbury Abbey, to judge from an ex-libris inscription on fo. iiᵛ: 'Hunc quicumque librum Aedhelmo depresseris almo / damnatus semper maneas cum sorte malorum' (see Lapidge, 'Artistic and Literary Patronage', *ALL* i. 47). But on the whole Anglo-Saxon libraries did not systematically mark their property with ex-libris inscriptions in the way that, say, Fleury did from the 10th c. onwards.

[22] In fact Gneuss lists some eight manuscripts and fragments now in the Cathedral Library at Exeter which were arguably there before *c*.1100 [Gneuss 256, 257, 258, 258.3, 258.8, 259, 259.5, and 260]. Not all of these books were the gift of Bishop Leofric, of course.

[23] For evident reasons, cathedral libraries were not confiscated and dispersed at the time that monasteries were being dissolved in the late 1530s. Nevertheless, a significant rate of dispersal can be noted for most cathedral libraries by comparing numbers of manuscripts written before *c*.1100 having a cathedral library provenance with numbers of manuscripts still *in situ* there (evidence based on information helpfully assembled by Dumville, 'English Libraries before 1066', 203–19). Thus, for Christ Church, Canterbury, of forty-five assignable manuscripts, three fragments are still *in situ*; for Durham Cathedral, of forty-seven assignable manuscripts, thirty are still *in situ*; for Exeter Cathedral, of thirty-six assignable manuscripts, two are still *in situ*; for Hereford Cathedral, of four assignable manuscripts, three are still *in situ*; for Salisbury Cathedral, of thirty-five assignable manuscripts, twenty-one are still *in situ*; for Winchester Cathedral, of twenty-seven assignable manuscripts, only one is still *in situ*; for Worcester Cathedral, of forty-five assignable manuscripts, five are still *in situ*; and for York Minster, of two assignable manuscripts, one is still *in situ*.

might be modified somewhat if we had booklists from Canterbury and Winchester, but not, perhaps, significantly.)

CONTINENTAL INVENTORIES OF THE NINTH CENTURY

A more useful perspective on the size of Anglo-Saxon libraries is offered by the holdings of Continental ecclesiastical libraries of the ninth century, for which there is substantial evidence in the form of inventories.[24] Although the Continental evidence is not always as full as one might wish,[25] inventories from several Continental houses give a clear picture of the size which a Continental ecclesiastical library might attain during the ninth century. For Saint-Riquier an inventory compiled in the year 831 is preserved in Hariulf's *Gesta ecclesiae Centulensis* (iii. 3), and includes 256 books (specified as *uolumina*).[26] An inventory of the library of Reichenau compiled by one Reginbert in the second decade of the ninth century includes 415 books (specified here as *codices*).[27] One from St Gallen includes 264 books (specified usually as *uolumina*).[28] For Lorsch there are no fewer than four ninth-century inventories;[29] the earliest of them attests to a library of some 590 books (specified as *codices*).[30] For Murbach there is a catalogue of *c*.840 (but preserved only in a fifteenth-century copy) which lists some 335 titles.[31] The contents of the library of the cathedral at Cologne assembled by Bishop Hildebald (d. 819) are

---

[24] A general survey of this evidence is given in McKitterick, *The Carolingians and the Written Word*, 175–96. Unfortunately the utility of the survey is vitiated by pervasive error in her descriptions of the contents of the libraries: the [*sic*] *Ordo Romanus* (p. 179), Daretus Phrygius (p. 179), Tichonius (p. 183), Isidore's *De officiis* (p. 183), the *Dicta Catonis* (p. 184), Hermas Pastor as 'a classical author' (p. 184), the *Visio Barontii* (p. 184), etc.

[25] No 9th-c. inventories survive from the following centres (which are known on other evidence to have had substantial libraries): Auxerre, Corbie, Fleury, Laon, Lyon, Reims, Saint-Amand, and Saint-Denis.

[26] *Hariulf: Chronique de l'abbaye de Saint-Riquier*, ed. Lot, 88–95, and Becker, *Catalogi*, no. 11, with discussion by Dekker, 'La Bibliothèque de Saint-Riquier', esp. 165–75.

[27] MBKDS i. 240–52; previously printed Becker, *Catalogi*, no. 6.

[28] MBKDS i. 66–82; previously printed Becker, *Catalogi*, no. 22. As edited in MBKDS, the 264 books contained 395 titles.

[29] See Bischoff, *Lorsch*, 8–18.

[30] Becker, *Catalogi*, no. 37, repr. from Mai, *Spicilegium Romanum*, v. 161–200; but see the recent and fully annotated edition of all four inventories by Häse, *Mittelalterliche Bücherverzeichnisse aus Kloster Lorsch*.

[31] Milde, *Die Bibliothekskataloge des Klosters Murbach*, 35–61, with discussion by P. Lehmann in MBKDS i. 224 and by Berschin and Geith, 'Die Bibliothekskataloge des Klosters Murbach', who correct a number of Milde's identifications.

recorded in an inventory which apparently dated from 833, and listed some 107 books.[32] Finally, for Bobbio an inventory dating from *c*.900 lists some 666 books (specified here as *libri*).[33]

On the face of it, these figures seem much larger than those of Anglo-Saxon libraries. However, several factors need to be borne in mind when comparing the numbers of books in these ninth-century Continental libraries with numbers of books known to Anglo-Saxon authors as set out in Appendix E. The Continental inventories frequently include biblical and liturgical books, which are excluded from the lists printed in Appendix E. The numbered items listed in Appendix E pertain to titles of individual works, whereas Continental inventories typically list *uolumina* or *codices* or *libri* (and occasionally *quaterniones*). A single *uolumen* or *codex* or *liber* might contain a number of individual works. The inventory of Bobbio,[34] for example, includes a 'librum sancti Augustini .I. de magistro, in quo habentur eiusdem de ordine et de achademica et uera religione'; that is to say, this one *liber* at Bobbio contained four separate titles as I have listed them in Appendix E: *De magistro*, *De ordine*, *Contra Academicos*, and *De uera religione*. On the other hand, a single title of a very large work such as Gregory, *Moralia in Iob*, would typically be bound in multiple *uolumina* or *codices*, as at Saint-Riquier (five *uolumina*), Reichenau (six *codices*), St Gallen (seven *uolumina*), or Bobbio (seven *libri*). In the case of large works in the lists in Appendix E, a single entry might similarly represent several volumes. In these circumstances, it is difficult to work out a simple formula which would allow accurate comparisons between the title-based lists of Anglo-Saxon libraries printed in Appendix E and the volume-based lists of Continental inventories. Take the example of Saint-Riquier, as inventoried by Hariulf: of the works of Jerome, nineteen volumes containing twenty-nine titles; Augustine, twenty-eight volumes containing forty titles; Gregory, fifteen volumes containing only eight titles; Isidore, nine

---

[32] The manuscript was extant as late as the 18th c., but has subsequently been lost. See Decker, 'Die Hildebald'sche Manuskriptensammlung'; and Lehmann, 'Erzbischof Hildebald und die Dombibliothek von Köln'.

[33] Becker, *Catalogi*, no. 32, repr. from Muratori, *Antiquitates Italicae Medii Aevi*, iii. 817–24 (the original is lost). For discussion, see Esposito, 'The Ancient Bobbio Catalogue', and Mercati, 'Le principali vicende della biblioteca del monastero di S. Colombano di Bobbio', with discussion of Muratori's inventory at pp. 26–32. The manuscripts in Muratori's inventory that are still in existence were identified by Gottlieb, 'Ueber Handschriften aus Bobbio', 447–58; in the opinion of Esposito (ibid.) Gottlieb erred in dating many of the identifiable manuscripts to the 11th c. (hence implying a later date for the inventory).   [34] Becker, *Catalogi*, no. 32, item no. 603.

volumes containing thirteen titles; Bede, eleven volumes containing fifteen titles; and so on. In sum, leaving aside biblical books and the seventy volumes containing church canons, etc. (whose contents would in effect be unquantifiable, even if we had the very books before us), the library at Saint-Riquier had 149 library books containing 146 titles. This suggests that the lists of titles given in Appendix E provide a rough but reliable approximation of the number of books owned by Anglo-Saxon libraries (always excluding biblical and liturgical books): Malmesbury in the time of Aldhelm, *c*.120 books; Monkwearmouth-Jarrow in the time of Bede, *c*.250 books (or perhaps *c*.230 if the many treatises of Augustine cited by Bede in his *Collectio ex opusculis beati Augustini in epistulas Pauli apostoli* [CPL 1360] were available to him only in the collectaneum of Eugippius); the Old Minster, Winchester, in the time of Lantfred, Wulfstan, and Ælfric, *c*.100 books; and Ramsey in the time of Abbo and Byrhtferth, *c*.100 books. (The size of Alcuin's library at York is incalculable, but may well have exceeded 100 books.)

Several observations emerge from these very rough figures, which corroborate the impression created by surviving Anglo-Saxon inventories. In the tenth century, following the disruptions of the ninth, Anglo-Saxon libraries apparently failed to regain the size they had attained during the eighth century. But even at their eighth-century apogee, Anglo-Saxon libraries were of a relatively modest size in comparison with those of the Continent, where ninth-century inventories attest to libraries of many hundreds of volumes, reaching at Bobbio a maximum of more than 600 library books, as I define the term, by the beginning of the tenth century.[35]

THE PHYSICAL ARRANGEMENT OF ANGLO-SAXON LIBRARIES

The relatively modest size of Anglo-Saxon libraries, as implied by the inventories, is confirmed in some sense by consideration of the ways in which these libraries were physically housed. In the first place, it seems unlikely that any Anglo-Saxon cathedral or monastery had a room set aside specifically for library use. The spacious rooms with standing presses such as are preserved at (say) Hereford or Lincoln Cathedral or in the early Oxford and Cambridge colleges are an

[35] Note also that, of the 666 *libri* in the Bobbio inventory (above, n. 33), forty-eight are liturgical books and fifteen are books of the Bible; so a total of *c*.600 'library books', in the sense in which I have defined the term, seems a reasonable deduction.

innovation of the late Middle Ages.[36] There is no evidence for standing presses before the twelfth century.[37] On the other hand, the layout of Roman libraries with *armaria* set in niches in the wall, such as could (probably) have been witnessed by a seventh-century Anglo-Saxon traveller to the library of Pope Agapetus (housed in Gregory the Great's monastery *ad clivum Scauri*), seems not to have inspired English imitations. The only unambiguous reference to an *armarium* in Anglo-Saxon sources is the so-called 'Ezra miniature' in the Codex Amiatinus, which shows Ezra seated before an open *armarium*, and nine volumes of the Bible laid out on sloping shelves.[38] But, as I have already mentioned, this drawing occurs in the preliminary quire of the Codex Amiatinus, and may have been taken over from the lost copy of Cassiodorus' *codex grandior*; it can therefore throw no light on the use of *armaria* in Anglo-Saxon monasteries.

To judge from literary sources, Anglo-Saxon libraries appear simply to have been stored in book-chests. The earliest reference occurs in an *enigma* by Aldhelm, which has the title *arca libraria*. The poem is as follows:

> Nunc mea divinis complentur viscera verbis
> Totaque sacratos gestant praecordia biblos;
> At tamen ex isdem nequeo cognoscere quicquam:
> Infelix fato fraudabor munere tali,
> Dum tollunt dirae librorum lumina Parcae.[39]

I take it that *arca* (whether qualified by the word *libraria* or not) unambiguously means 'chest', that is to say, a wooden chest placed on the floor. Such an arrangement could not comfortably house more than a small collection of books.[40] As we have just seen, there is little

[36] See Clark, *The Care of Books*, esp. 125–64.

[37] Ibid. 92–7. The far larger numbers of books which could be accommodated in standing presses created the need to devise cataloguing systems involving shelf-marks which specified the location of a particular book on a particular shelf of a press: see Derolez, *Les Catalogues de bibliothèques*, 30–5.

[38] See discussion and illustration of this *armarium* in Bruce-Mitford, *The Art of the Codex Amiatinus*, esp. 11–14, with fig. 1 and pl. II, and Marsden, 'Job in his Place', esp. fig. 1 (after Bruce-Mitford) and pl. VI.

[39] *Enigma* lxxxix (ed. Ehwald, p. 138): 'Now my inwards are filled with holy words, and all my entrails support sacred books. And yet I am unable to learn anything from them. Unfortunately, I am deprived by fate of such a gift, since the deadly Parcae [i.e. the Fates] take away the illumination which books provide.'

[40] A later (8th-c.?) imitator of Aldhelm's *enigmata*, the Anglo-Latin poet Eusebius, described a book-satchel (*scetha*) in terms modelled on Aldhelm's *arca libraria*: 'In me multigena sapientia constat habunde, / nec tamen illud scire quid est sapientia possum' (CCSL 133. 243). For *scetha* meaning 'book-satchel', see Sharpe, 'Latin and Irish Words

Anglo-Saxon evidence for the sort of standing cupboard or *armarium* which housed libraries in antiquity. In one of his letters, Alcuin mentions the *armarium imperiale*, but he is referring to books in Charlemagne's library, not in his native York.[41] In the eleventh-century Antwerp–London glossary (written and possibly compiled at Abingdon, s. xi[1]: Antwerp, Plantin-Moretus Museum, M. 16. 2 + London, BL, Add. 32246), the entry *bibliotheca uel armarium uel archiuum* is glossed in Old English as *boochord* ('book-hoard'); but the context here suggests that the compiler was interested principally in nouns having the termination *-arium*, rather than in the furnishing of libraries.[42] The sum of this evidence perhaps suggests that Anglo-Saxon libraries were normally housed in book-chests, and that when an Anglo-Saxon scholar wished to consult a book, he got down on his hands and knees and rummaged around in the chest until he came upon the book he required. It needs hardly to be said that such an arrangement could scarcely accommodate a very large library.

The evidence for the physical arrangement of Anglo-Saxon libraries therefore corroborates that of the Anglo-Saxon inventories. In sum, this evidence suggests that Anglo-Saxon libraries were of a relatively modest size. Their size certainly appears modest in comparison with the Roman libraries of antiquity (discussed in Ch. 2), such as the imperial Bibliotheca Ulpia in Trajan's Forum, and those of late antiquity, such as the library of Cassiodorus at Vivarium or of Isidore at Seville. It was also, as we have just seen, modest in comparison with Continental libraries of the ninth century and with English Benedictine libraries of the late Middle Ages. Nevertheless, these modest Anglo-Saxon libraries often contained remarkable treasures, and were able to sustain the research of scholars such as Aldhelm, Bede, and Alcuin, who were in the vanguard of European learning in the eighth century, and passed this learning on to later centuries. We may now turn in the following two chapters to evidence of the contents of Anglo-Saxon libraries, as these may be reconstructed from surviving manuscripts and citations by Anglo-Saxon authors.

for "Book-satchel" ', with discussion of Eusebius at p. 155. A book-satchel, being portable, would presumably have held even fewer books than an *arca libraria*.

[41] Alcuin, *Ep.* cccix: 'si forte in armario imperiali inveniantur' [*scil.* various works by Augustine] (MGH, Epist. iv. 474).

[42] Wright, *Anglo-Saxon and Old English Vocabularies*, i. 185 (line 33). Similarly, the occurrence of the word *armaria* in the text of Augustine, *Enchiridion* as preserved in Cambridge, Trinity College, O. 1. 18 is rendered by an 11th-c. gloss as *boccysta* ('book-chests'): see Napier, *Old English Glosses*, 196.

4
Reconstructing Anglo-Saxon Libraries (II): The Evidence of Manuscripts

F O R the study of manuscripts which formerly belonged to Anglo-Saxon libraries and which happen to survive to the present day, we have the benefit of a wonderful and comprehensive guide: namely Helmut Gneuss's recent *Handlist of Anglo-Saxon Manuscripts*, published in 2001. This book is an amplification of Gneuss's 'Preliminary List of Manuscripts Written or Owned in England up to 1100', first published as an article in 1981. In the original article Gneuss listed some 947 manuscripts. During the course of twenty years' subsequent research on Anglo-Saxon manuscripts, he has had the opportunity to rethink some of his original criteria for inclusion (his first inclination, rightly, had been to inclusiveness), as a result of which he has removed forty-three items which are now known to have been written after AD 1100 and which are treated in Richard Gameson's survey of manuscripts from early Norman England.[1] Gneuss removed a further six manuscripts because they proved unambiguously to be manuscripts which, although written *before* 1100, had only come to England after that date. On the other hand, his indefatigable research and pursuit of manuscripts and fragments in libraries all over the world enabled him to add 335 new items to his list. The net gain, in other words, was some 285 manuscripts, so that the recent *Handlist* now includes *c.*1,235 manuscripts and fragments written or owned in England before about 1100. This is a very substantial sum, and certainly provides abundant raw material for the student of Anglo-Saxon libraries. Unlike the 'Preliminary list', Gneuss has supplied a complete list of contents for each of the entries. Furthermore, he has provided the *Handlist* with two excellent indexes: the first, of authors and texts; and the second, of first lines of poetry preserved in manuscripts of the Anglo-Saxon period, with references to repertories such as ICL. By consulting these indexes one can see at a glance whether or not any manuscripts of (say) the poet Arator survive from

[1] Gameson, *The Manuscripts of Early Norman England*.

pre-Conquest England. The book is thus an indispensable resource for the student of Anglo-Saxon libraries.

However, various caveats need to be borne in mind before we use the list to write the history of Anglo-Saxon libraries. In the first place, a substantial number of the 1,235 manuscripts and fragments which Gneuss lists are liturgical books, or Bibles, or Gospel books or other individual books of the Bible: I count and exclude some 370 of these, leaving us with 865 'library' books. The most acute problem with the remaining 'library' books is that relatively few of them can be assigned with confidence to a place of origin, or even a provenance. As I mentioned in the previous chapter (above, pp. 56–7), very few Anglo-Saxon books contain ex-libris inscriptions which could help us to ascertain who owned them. By the same token, very few have scribal colophons indicating where and by whom they were written. Sometimes, of course, a group of manuscripts shows such similarities of script and production that, on palaeographical grounds, they can be assigned to the same scriptorium and given the same approximate dating. And if even one of the manuscripts happens to carry some mark of ownership, the remainder are dragged along in a chain-gang to the same scriptorium. It was one of the great achievements of the late Alan Bishop that, in a pioneering series of articles printed in the *Transactions of the Cambridge Bibliographical Society* in the 1950s and 1960s, he was in this way able to assign groups of manuscripts to several Anglo-Saxon scriptoria: Christ Church and St Augustine's, Canterbury, and Exeter, for example.[2] And in the wake of such palaeographical evidence, subsequent scholars are in a position to write library histories, as (for example) Nicholas Brooks has done (well) for eleventh-century Christ Church,[3] and Patrick Conner (less well) for Exeter.[4] Using similar methods, but in a more comprehensive way, Tessa Webber has recently been able to reconstruct the

---

[2] Bishop, 'Notes on Cambridge Manuscripts', 1 (1949–53), 432–41 [Christ Church, Canterbury, and elsewhere]; 2 (1954–8), 185–99 [Christ Church and St Augustine's, Canterbury; Exeter], 323–36 [St Augustine's, Canterbury], 3 (1959–63), 93–5 [St Augustine's, Canterbury], 412–23 [St Augustine's and Christ Church, Canterbury]; see also id., 'Lincoln Cathedral MS 182'. The results of these palaeographical investigations are digested in id., *English Caroline Minuscule.*

[3] Brooks, *The Early History of the Church of Canterbury*, 266–78.

[4] Conner, *Anglo-Saxon Exeter*, esp. 33–47. Much of Conner's discussion concerns the Exeter origins of the so-called 'Exeter Book of Old English Poetry' (Exeter, CL, 3501, fos. 8–130), and this discussion has been vigorously challenged by (e.g.) Gameson, 'The Origin of the Exeter Book of Old English Poetry'.

scriptorium and library of immediately post-Conquest Salisbury.[5]
But this method requires as a starting point that at least one
manuscript be reliably assignable to one centre, so that that manuscript can act as the first link in a subsequent chain of palaeographical evidence. But if the starting point is lacking (or has not yet
been recognized as such), no linking chain can be constructed; and
that is why we have virtually no manuscripts from centres which
undoubtedly did possess libraries: Lindisfarne, Hexham, Ripon,
York, Malmesbury, and others in the early period, and Ely, Glastonbury, Peterborough, and Ramsey (among others) in the later period,
to say nothing of minor houses such as Milton Abbas and Abbots-
bury.[6] Helmut Gneuss emphasizes this problem in the preface to his
Handlist:

Our present-day difficulties with regard to the origin and provenance of
Anglo-Saxon books are well-known: the lack of early library catalogues, as
opposed to booklists [and] the lack of early ex-libris inscriptions . . . [so that]
very few books remain from what must have been well-stocked repositories
of learning and literature, like the Benedictine houses in Winchester, in
Abingdon, Ely, Glastonbury, Malmesbury, Peterborough and Ramsey, the
nunneries at Barking, Shaftesbury and Wilton, the cathedrals of London and
York.[7]

In a word, although there are 800+ library books surviving from
Anglo-Saxon England, they do not throw as much light as might be
wished on the contents of individual libraries.

THE CONTENTS OF SURVIVING ANGLO-SAXON MANUSCRIPTS

The surviving manuscripts, nevertheless, permit a number of
observations: first of all, the generalization that *many* classical and
most patristic writings are preserved in Anglo-Saxon manuscripts,
and hence were available for study at some time or place in pre-
Conquest England. This much may be seen from perusal of the index
to Helmut Gneuss's *Handlist*. In fact it is equally instructive to
consider what classical and patristic works are *not* represented among

---

[5] Webber, *Scribes and Scholars at Salisbury Cathedral*; and see also the earlier study of
Salisbury by Ker, 'The Beginnings of Salisbury Cathedral Library'.

[6] Such evidence as exists for assigning surviving manuscripts to these houses is
conveniently assembled by Dumville, 'English Libraries before 1066', 203–19.

[7] Gneuss, *Handlist*, 3.

Anglo-Saxon manuscripts (and it would also be instructive to compare what is not preserved in Anglo-Saxon manuscripts with what is, or is not, preserved in Carolingian manuscripts on one hand, and in post-Conquest Norman manuscripts on the other; but such comparisons lie well beyond the scope of the present discussion). I shall treat in order: classical grammarians, classical poets and dramatists, classical prose writers, and patristic authors.

Of classical grammarians, there is a substantial number of surviving manuscripts, unsurprisingly, given the Anglo-Saxons' dedicated application to grammatical study, and the concerted attempts by scholars such as Aldhelm, Tatwine, and Boniface to compile elementary Latin grammars for their Latin-less Anglo-Saxon pupils. Thus manuscripts survive of classical writers on orthography (Agroecius, Caper, and Cassiodorus), and of the compendious grammarians Donatus (numerous manuscripts of the *Ars maior*) together with his commentators Pompeius and Sergius, and also Priscian (numerous manuscripts of the *Institutio de nomine, pronomine et uerbo* and of the *Institutiones grammaticae*, and a single manuscript of the *Partitiones*). Minor grammatical works such as the *Ars de uerbo* by Eutyches, a student of Priscian, and the *Ars de nomine et uerbo* by Phocas, are also represented. Those classical grammarians who are *not* represented among surviving manuscripts include: Charisius, Diomedes, Consentius, Probus, Sacerdos, and (from a later period) Julian of Toledo.

Of the major classical poets, there is no Anglo-Saxon manuscript or fragment of: Lucretius, Catullus, Tibullus, Propertius, Manilius, Phaedrus, Lucan, or Claudian. A few major classical poets—Ovid and Martial (one epigram only)—are preserved only in fragments. Set these against those poets who *are* represented in Anglo-Saxon manuscripts: Vergil, Horace, Persius, Juvenal, Statius, Nemesianus (third century), Quintus Serenus (third), Ausonius (fourth), and Avianus. The very names suggest that manuscripts of these poets have survived because they were studied in the classroom.

Of dramatists, there is a single late manuscript of Plautus, fragments only of Terence, and nothing, not even a fragment, of Seneca's *Tragoediae*.

Of prose writers, no manuscript survives of: Caesar, Livy, Curtius Rufus, Seneca, Quintilian, Suetonius, Tacitus, Pliny the Younger, and Aulus Gellius. Sallust is represented by a single fragment. Set against these the classical prose writers who *are* represented: Cicero, Vitruvius, Frontinus, Valerius Maximus, Pliny the Elder, Hyginus,

Justinus, Eutropius (fourth century AD), Vegetius (also fourth), Macrobius (fifth), Martianus Capella (fifth), and Boethius (sixth).

However, the classical authors unrepresented in surviving Anglo-Saxon manuscripts were not necessarily missing from Anglo-Saxon libraries. It may be helpful briefly to review the categories of text mentioned above, in the light of evidence from other sources. The principal source of evidence, that of citations by the major authors of Anglo-Saxon England, is assembled in Appendix E, and is summarized, alongside the evidence of surviving manuscripts, in the 'Catalogue of classical and patristic authors and works composed before AD 700 and known in Anglo-Saxon England'.

Of the grammarians, Charisius and Probus are among the authors listed by Alcuin as forming part of Ælberht's library at York;[8] and Boniface drew on Diomedes, and Tatwine on Consentius, respectively, in compiling their own elementary Latin grammars.[9] So we need not doubt that these grammatical works were available in certain Anglo-Saxon libraries. With respect to classical poets, the absence of Anglo-Saxon manuscripts probably does indicate ignorance of their writings in pre-Conquest England. There is no evidence that Catullus, Tibullus, and Propertius were ever known in Anglo-Saxon England (and the evidence that they were known in Carolingian Europe is likewise slender). The same may be said for Manilius and Phaedrus. The jury is out on Lucretius (there is a single quotation of Lucretius in Aldhelm's metrical treatises, and another one in Bede's *De arte metrica*).[10] But of the classical poets unrepresented by any surviving Anglo-Saxon manuscript, there is no doubt that both Lucan and Claudian were studied in Anglo-Saxon England: Lucan is listed in two Anglo-Saxon inventories (and several poets, notably Bede, are heavily indebted to Lucan's distinctive diction). Claudian is quoted *nominatim* by Aldhelm, and Bede's poetic diction reveals unambiguous debts to Claudian as well.[11] Arguments could also be mounted for Anglo-Saxon poets' knowledge of Ovid (especially the *Metamorphoseis*).

Of the dramatists, the sole manuscript of Plautus listed by Gneuss dates from *c*.1100 (London, BL, Royal 15. C. XI) and comes from Salisbury, which suggests that the text was one brought to England by Norman scholars in the years after 1066.[12] I know of no evidence

---

[8] See App. E (below, p. 231).
[10] See below, pp. 101–5.
[9] See above, pp. 38, 44.
[11] See below, pp. 113–14.
[12] See Thomson, 'British Library Royal 15. C. XI', and Webber, *Scribes and Scholars*, 63–4.

for knowledge of Plautus by pre-Conquest Anglo-Latin authors. On the other hand there is no doubt that certain pre-Conquest authors knew Terence: Aldhelm quotes from both the *Phormio* and the *Adelphoe*; Frithegod, in the preface to his *Breuiloquium Vitae Wilfridi*, which he wrote in Archbishop Oda's name, quotes twice from Terence (once from the *Andria*, once from the *Phormio*); and 'Terence' (without specification) occurs in at least one Anglo-Saxon inventory.[13] In the case of Seneca, Aldhelm quotes *verbatim* and *nominatim* from Seneca's *Agamemnon*, suggesting that he had access to a copy of the *Tragoediae* at Malmesbury in the late seventh century.[14]

As far as prose writers are concerned, citations by Anglo-Saxon authors provide no evidence, to my knowledge, for the historians I named (Caesar, Livy, Tacitus, etc.), or for Quintilian or Pliny the Younger or Aulus Gellius, and in this case the manuscript evidence probably does offer a reliable indicator. But in spite of the manuscript evidence, some at least of Seneca's prose writings were apparently known: the First Old English riddle, with its powerful evocation of the divine cosmic *spiritus* moving over earth and sea and causing volcanoes and earthquakes by being constricted in terrestrial caverns, is drawn unambiguously from Seneca's *Naturales quaestiones*, as I argued a few years ago;[15] and at the very end of the Anglo-Saxon period, Goscelin of Saint-Bertin, writing his *Liber confortatorius* at Peterborough *c*.1080, quotes unambiguously from Seneca's *Epistulae morales* (or *Epistulae ad Lucilium* as they are also called).[16] The late Leighton Reynolds, in his masterly survey of the transmission of the *Epistulae morales*, demonstrated that in the early Middle Ages they were transmitted in two separate batches (Letters 1–88 and Letters 89–124), and it would seem that the two batches were combined to form a single collection only at some point in the earlier twelfth

---

[13] See below, pp. 141 (the inventory in App. A), 334 (Catalogue). For Frithegod/ Fredegaudus, see *Frithegodi monachi Breuiloquium*, ed. Campbell, 2 (*Andria* 176), 3 (*Phormio* 506). On the identity of Frithegod/Fredegaud, see Lapidge, *ALL* ii. 157–81.

[14] See below, pp. 93–5.

[15] Lapidge, 'Stoic Cosmology'. No Anglo-Saxon manuscript of Seneca's *Naturales quaestiones* survives. On the Continental circulation of the work, see *TxtTrans*, 376–8, where it is stated (by H. M. Hine) that 'no manuscript is earlier than the twelfth century'; more recently, however, Hine has pointed to a collection of excerpts of the work in a 9th-c. manuscript from Brittany, now Munich, BSB, Clm. 18961, associated somehow with the circle of Alcuin: 'The Manuscript Tradition of Seneca's *Naturales quaestiones*', 558–61. I am very grateful to Harry Hine for discussion on this point.

[16] See the *apparatus fontium* in Talbot, 'The *Liber confortatorius* of Goscelin of Saint-Bertin', esp. 78–9.

century, perhaps at the Norman abbey of Jumièges.[17] Goscelin quotes only from the earlier batch (Letters 1–88), which possibly indicates that when he was reading Seneca at Peterborough the two batches had yet to be combined. In any event, Anglo-Saxon libraries apparently contained more classical authors and works than might be guessed from manuscript evidence alone.

A similar picture emerges in respect of patristic authors. It would be otiose to give here a list of all the patristic writings which are preserved in manuscripts surviving from the Anglo-Saxon period.[18] Suffice it to say that the major patristic authors are well represented. (It must be stressed, however, that many of the manuscripts in question date only from the last quarter of the eleventh century, suggesting that it was Norman rather than Anglo-Saxon scholars who saw to the provision of extensive holdings of patristic writings.)[19] Ambrose (some thirty works, usually in multiple manuscripts); Augustine (some sixty-five works, usually in multiple manuscripts, and no omission of any of his major writings, as far as I am competent to judge); Jerome (some twenty-five works, including all the principal biblical commentaries and saints' lives); Gregory the Great (all the major writings in multiple copies); as well as a host of lesser figures— Cyprian, Orosius, Cassian, Caesarius, Cassiodorus, Isidore—and most of the principal Late Latin poets: Juvencus, Caelius Sedulius, Arator, Cyprianus Gallus. Nevertheless, there are some striking omissions from Anglo-Saxon manuscripts: the prose writings of Tertullian (but see below); of Lactantius; of Hilary of Poitiers; of Pope Leo the Great; and of Lucifer of Cagliari, to mention only a few. Of major Late Latin poets there is no Anglo-Saxon manuscript of either Alcimus Avitus or of Dracontius. But the manuscripts, once again, present only a partial picture: Lactantius, Hilary, and Leo are among the authors which Alcuin names as having formed part of Ælberht's library at York;[20] Lucifer of Cagliari is named in a late

---

[17] Reynolds, *The Medieval Tradition of Seneca's Letters*, esp. 90–124, and id., in *TxtTrans*, 369–75.

[18] See instead the Catalogue (below, pp. 275–342), and the Index to Gneuss, *Handlist*.

[19] As is argued persuasively by Thomson, 'The Norman Conquest and English Libraries', and Webber, 'The Patristic Content of English Book Collections'; and see also the standard account of Anglo-Saxon book production at this time in Ker, *English Manuscripts in the Century after the Norman Conquest*. Of course at the same time as books were being brought to English libraries and copied by English and Norman scribes, other Anglo-Saxon books were being taken from England to Norman abbeys, as has been demonstrated convincingly by Dumville, 'Anglo-Saxon Books'.

[20] See below, pp. 229–31 (App. E).

Anglo-Saxon inventory, though the work in question is not specified.[21] Alcimus Avitus is named by Alcuin and included among the
inventory of books which Bishop Æthelwold sent to Peterborough
(and that Avitus' poem on Old Testament history was closely studied
by Anglo-Saxon poets is unambiguously clear from the Old English
poem *Exodus*).[22] Although Dracontius is not named in Alcuin's list,
his poem *De laudibus Dei* was certainly known in York, if not
elsewhere, for it was extensively excerpted by Alcuin in his own
(unprinted) collectaneum entitled *De laude Dei*, and was imitated by
the York poet(s), student(s) of Alcuin, who composed the tedious
verse *Miracula S. Nyniae*.[23]

THE SURVIVAL OF ANGLO-SAXON MANUSCRIPTS IN POST-CONQUEST ENGLISH LIBRARIES

Surviving manuscripts provide a sound but not complete index to
what books were owned (and studied) in Anglo-Saxon libraries; and
the index is valuable so long as it is collated with evidence of
inventories and citations by Anglo-Saxon authors. Even so, surviving
manuscripts provide only a partial view of the books which were once
contained in Anglo-Saxon libraries. It goes without saying that many
Anglo-Saxon books may have survived cataclysmic events like the
Norman Conquest only to be destroyed in more recent times, through
neglect during the later Middle Ages, through wilful destruction in
the 1530s when the monasteries were dissolved at the instigation of
Henry VIII, and through ignorance in early modern times.[24] A
complete census of the holdings of Anglo-Saxon libraries would
ideally take account of Anglo-Saxon manuscripts now lost but
recorded in historical sources of various kinds, in medieval library
catalogues (twelfth to fifteenth centuries), in records made by
antiquaries in the sixteenth century, and by more recent scholars
who may have noted the existence of a manuscript which has
subsequently perished. It would be a useful enterprise to compile a

---

[21] See below, p. 141 (App. A).

[22] See below, pp. 135 (App. A), 230 (App. E).

[23] For the citation of Dracontius in Alcuin's *De laude Dei*, see below, p. 232 (App. E);
for the recycling of lines from Dracontius in the *Miracula S. Nyniae* [ICL 14261], see the
apparatus fontium to Karl Strecker's edition of the poem in MGH, PLAC iv. 943–61. On
the attribution of this poem to the circle of Alcuin's students, see Lapidge, *ALL* i. 385–7.

[24] There is an excellent overview of what happened to medieval libraries in post-
medieval times by Ker, 'The Migration of Manuscripts'.

list of all such records. In the absence of such a list, I shall give a few examples of the sort of Anglo-Saxon books which evidently survived the Norman Conquest, but have subsequently been lost.

Historical sources

By reference to historical sources, I have in mind the sort of entry which is found in a late eleventh-century memorandum in the fourteenth-century 'Winchester Cartulary', concerning one Blackman Goldsmith (*Aurifaber*), a monk in the service of Bishop Walkelin (1070–98), who fraudulently tampered with a charter of William I; he also 'stole a book of St Æthelwold written at Glastonbury by his own hand'.[25] Blackman subsequently had his neck wrung by an evil spirit when he was walking by the shore of the river Itchen at Bitterne, but what happened to the Æthelwold manuscript is unknown. Assuming that the attribution is correct, such a manuscript would be a priceless witness to the development of Anglo-Saxon script in the tenth century, not only at Glastonbury, where Æthelwold spent the 940s and early 950s, but also later at Abingdon and Winchester.

Medieval library catalogues

There is a substantial amount of information concerning Anglo-Saxon books contained in (post-Conquest) medieval manuscript catalogues, either in print or awaiting publication, in the Corpus of British Medieval Library Catalogues (CBMLC). The catalogues edited in this series were compiled at different times and places, and according to different criteria; but in sum they offer a reliable indication of the libraries of those religious houses, cathedrals and monasteries, which happened to feel the need to compile records of their holdings. Evidently the religious houses which are most likely to have owned Anglo-Saxon books after the Norman Conquest are those which were in existence before that event: that is to say, Benedictine monasteries. There would be little point in searching for Anglo-Saxon books among the holdings of Cistercian or Franciscan houses. In effect our search needs to be restricted to Benedictine houses which happened to be in existence before 1066; and for catalogues compiled in the late twelfth century, or later, there needs to be some indication that, in the mind of the compiler, the book in question seemed 'ancient' or 'very ancient', or was written in Old English. The point may be illustrated by reference to post-medieval catalogues from Burton-on-Trent, Bury St Edmunds, and Glastonbury.

Burton-on-Trent was founded by Wulfric Spot in 1004; and although its medieval catalogue dates from the late twelfth century (*c*.1175), it is possible that some of the manuscripts then in its possession dated from the eleventh century. This would certainly be the case with the seven volumes in Old English (these include copies of the Old English translations of Bede's *Historia ecclesiastica* [CPL 1375] and the *Historia Apollonii* [LLA 727], as well as several biblical and liturgical books which do not concern us here).[26] Given the specification of two copies of a martyrology as *uetera*, it is interesting to note elsewhere in the list, among titles of Latin works, a 'really ancient homiliary'—'Omeliarium uetustissimum'— the adjective here surely implying a pre-Conquest book.[27]

By the same token, the Tudor antiquary John Leland (*c*.1503–52) includes among his annotations on manuscripts from Bury St Edmunds,[28] immediately preceding a manuscript of Aldhelm's *Carmen de uirginitate* and *Enigmata* (which can be identified as Oxford, BodL, Rawlinson C. 697, a ninth-century manuscript which Leland does not describe as 'ancient'), a copy of Sallust which he describes as 'very ancient': *uetustissimus codex Sallustii*. Could this also have been a pre-Conquest manuscript of Sallust? The problem is that the antiquity of a manuscript will have seemed different to someone writing in the twelfth century from what it might have seemed to Leland four centuries later.[29]

We need to bear this caveat in mind when we consider the terminology used to describe apparently 'ancient' manuscripts by the mid-thirteenth-century compiler (1247–8) of the medieval catalogue from Glastonbury,[30] a house which may be presumed to have had a large library from the time of the abbacy of Dunstan (*c*.940 onwards), but from which a disappointingly small number of pre-Conquest manuscripts can be identified.[31] The compiler seems to

---

[26] *English Benedictine Libraries*, ed. Sharpe et al., 33–42 (cat. no. B11).
[27] Ibid. 41 (item no. 58).   [28] Ibid. 95–8 (cat. no. B16).
[29] Ibid. 97. The editors suggest identification with Cambridge, Pembroke College 114, a 12th-c. manuscript. But it must recalled that such identifications are necessarily conjectural, and that an Anglo-Saxon manuscript could conceivably be in question. The only surviving pre-1100 manuscript of Sallust listed by Gneuss is two flyleaves of Cambridge, CCC 309, datable to s. xi^{ex} or xi/xii.
[30] *English Benedictine Libraries*, ed. Sharpe et al., 167–215 (cat. no. B39).
[31] There have been some excruciating losses, such as the 'Bella Etheltani regis' (B39, item no. 261), apparently an account of the wars of King Æthelstan (924–39).

have worked out a consistent vocabulary to describe the old books in his library: he uses such terms as 'old but can still be read', 'good but old', 'old but useless', and so on. Thus he adds a note following a substantial list of some twenty manuscripts of saints' Lives, 'Memorandum quod hii omnes libri de uitis sanctorum, *licet uetusti sint*, legi tamen possunt' (italics mine).[32] The apparent consistency of his vocabulary encourages us to attach importance to the distinction which he draws between items which are *uetusti* and those which are older still, *uetustissimi*. For example, he describes as *uetustus* a manuscript containing Julian of Toledo's *Prognosticum* alongside Aldhelm's *Enigmata* [CPL 1335]. From this unusual combination of contents it is possible to identify this book as London, BL, Royal 12. C. XXIII, a manuscript written *c*.1000. On the other hand, he describes as *uetustissimus* a copy of Eutyches, *Ars de uerbo*, a manuscript part of which survives as Oxford, BodL, Auct. F. 4. 32, fos. 1–9, and which was written in Brittany in the mid-ninth century and bound up with other books at Glastonbury in the time of Dunstan. Dare we deduce that a manuscript which he describes as *uetustus* was of tenth- or early eleventh-century date, from the time of the Benedictine revival or later, and one which was *uetustissimus*, of a date earlier than the mid-tenth century? The following books are described as *uetustus*: Augustine *Tractatus in Euangelium Ioannis* and *De opere monachorum*, Prosper *De uera innocentia*, and the Hiberno-Latin treatise *De duodecim abusiuis saeculi* [CPL 1189; BCLL 339] ('omnes uetusti set legi possunt'); Bede's *Historia ecclesiastica* [CPL 1375] ('bona set uetusta'), the *Capitularium collectio* of Ansegisus ('uetusta'), the Old English Orosius ('in anglica uetustus set legibilis'), a copy of Junillus, *Instituta regularia diuinae legis* ('uetustus'), and a copy of Vergil ('uetustus'). I take it that these were all Anglo-Saxon books of the tenth century or later. Alongside these are five books which seemed to the compiler to be even older, and which he described as *uetustissimi*: Jerome, *Comm. in Euangelium Matthaei* and *De consonancia euangeliorum* (presumably a copy of Augustine, *De consensu euangelistarum*), two copies of Alcuin, *De uitiis et uirtutibus* [CSLMA ALC 37], variously bound with other works of Alcuin; and a copy of Priscian, *Institutio de nomine, pronomine et uerbo*. It would be possible to challenge the implications for dating which I draw from the distinction between *uetustus* and *uetustissimus*; but there seems no

---

[32] *English Benedictine Libraries*, ed. Sharpe et al., 197.

reason to doubt that the books in question belonged to the pre-Conquest library of Glastonbury.

Without any indication of apparent antiquity, however, or a statement to the effect that the book was written in Old English, it is virtually impossible to identify Anglo-Saxon books in library catalogues of the later Middle Ages. One can often suspect that a manuscript of an obscure pre-Conquest Anglo-Latin author is unlikely to have commended itself to frequent post-Conquest copying, and that the book in question might therefore be of pre-Conquest date. For example, in the fourteenth-century Ramsey catalogue,[33] there is mention of a 'Liber uersificus Osuualdi monachi'—apparently a copy of the poetic works of Oswald the Younger, an eleventh-century monk of Ramsey and nephew of Archbishop Oswald—which might well be of pre-Conquest date,[34] as might the 'Liber Abbonis super quedam euangelia'.[35] But since both these books, and the works they contained, have been lost, it is impossible to verify the conjecture. All that one can say is that in the fourteenth century there was at least one pre-Conquest book still at Ramsey, a psalter which had belonged to Archbishop Oswald (identical with London, BL, Harley 2904),[36] and there may possibly have been others.

Sixteenth-century antiquaries

The researches of the sixteenth-century antiquaries also uncovered numbers of books which belonged to pre-Conquest libraries and have subsequently been lost.[37] But it is well to remember that the Tudor and Elizabethan antiquaries—John Leland (?1503–52), John Bale

---

[33] *English Benedictine Libraries*, ed. Sharpe et al., 350–415 (cat. no. B68).

[34] Ibid. 369 (item no. 173). On this Oswald the Younger, see Lapidge, *ALL* ii. 132–3, 144–5, 374–5.

[35] *English Benedictine Libraries*, 370 (item no. 177), which corresponds to the fuller entry in the earlier Ramsey catalogue, ibid. 349 (cat. no. B67, item no. 180). No work of this title is known to us under Abbo's name.

[36] Ibid. 414, item no. 596, which is the record of a large number of psalters at Ramsey, without counting that which belonged to Archbishop Oswald, which was apparently held in especial veneration and housed separately ('sine Psalterio sancti Oswoldi'). On the association of Harley 2904 with Archbishop Oswald, and the argument that it was written at Ramsey (and not at Winchester, as was earlier believed), see Lapidge, *ALL* ii. 398–403, and Dumville, *English Caroline Script*, 58–65.

[37] There is an ever-accumulating corpus of scholarship on the English antiquaries, much of it indispensable to the study of pre-Conquest manuscripts. See, notably, Wright, 'The Dispersal of the Monastic Libraries'; 'The Dispersal of the Libraries in the Sixteenth Century', and 'The Elizabethan Society of Antiquaries and the Formation of the Cottonian Library'; Graham and Watson, *The Recovery of the Past*.

(1495–1563), Sir John Prise (1502/3–55), Matthew Parker (1504–75), Robert Talbot (*c*.1505–58), and others—were primarily interested in identifying and recovering books relevant to the history of Britain, particularly its church, not (say) to the transmission of classical learning in Anglo-Saxon England.[38] They thus conscientiously made records of works by pre-Conquest authors in monastic libraries, but not of pre-Conquest books in general, even assuming they had the palaeographical expertise to identify a pre-Conquest book. Leland, for example, claims in his *Comm. de Scriptoribus Britannicis* to have seen copies of the poetic works of Oswald the Younger at both Ramsey and Glastonbury, but both copies have subsequently disappeared.[39] Bale recorded briefly the contents of a manuscript containing the works of Frithegod, and his record is an invaluable testimony to Frithegod's poetic production, but the manuscript does not survive, and was presumably lost forever at the time of the Dissolution.[40] Nevertheless, these antiquaries must often have unearthed valuable ancient manuscripts of interest to classical and patristic scholars. Leland, for example, found at Malmesbury an ancient manuscript of Tertullian, said by him to contain the *De spectaculis* and *De ieiunio*,[41] and it has recently been shown that the manuscript, now lost, was purloined by him and passed by way of intermediaries to the German humanist Beatus Rhenanus, who was able to incorporate some of its readings in his third edition of the works of Tertullian (1539).[42] Whether in fact the manuscript was Anglo-Saxon in origin—Leland thought it had been brought from Rome by Aldhelm (!)—cannot unfortunately be established.

Early modern scholars

A few Anglo-Saxon manuscripts survived the Dissolution, only to be lost in more modern times, in spite of the manuscript searches of

[38] See, in general, Kendrick, *British Antiquity*; McKisack, *Medieval History in the Tudor Age*; and Aston, 'English Ruins and English History'.

[39] Leland, *Commentarii de Scriptoribus Britannicis*, ed. Hall, i. 172.

[40] Bale, *Scriptorum Illustrium Maioris Brytanniae . . . Catalogus*, and id., *Index Brittaniae Scriptorum*, ed. Poole and Bateson, 72–3, 483; see also discussion by Lapidge, *ALL* ii. 157–61.

[41] See *English Benedictine Libraries*, ed. Sharpe et al., 265 (B54, no. 23), as well as Thomson, 'Identifiable Books', 11–13, who inferred, from the inclusion of the two treatises, that the manuscript was probably a copy of the so-called 'Corpus Corbeiense' of Tertullian, hence that it contained five further treatises: *De resurrectione mortuorum* [CPL 19], pseudo-Tertullian, *De trinitate* [CPL 71], *De praescriptione haereticorum* [CPL 5], *De pudicitia* [CPL 30], and *De monogamia* [CPL 28].

[42] Carley and Petitmengin, 'Pre-Conquest Manuscripts from Malmesbury Abbey'.

early modern scholars.[43] For example, in 1623 Patrick Young, sometime librarian of James I and Charles I, compiled a list of the
manuscripts of Worcester Cathedral Library; his catalogue only
came to light in 1941 and was edited for the first time by Neil Ker
and Sir Ivor Atkins (1944).[44] The great merit of their edition is that
they were able to identify most (perhaps 98 per cent) of the 343
manuscripts listed by Young, and thus to provide a clear picture of the
ways in which the books of Worcester's library were alienated in later
times. Even in the early seventeenth century the library contained six
books in Old English (these are now in the Bodleian Library, in either
the Hatton or Junius collections). Interestingly, Young described two
further Anglo-Saxon manuscripts which have subsequently disappeared. The first contained a number of Latin sermons of Caesarius of
Arles (*De diligendis inimicis*, *De reddendis decimis*, *De calendis Ianuariis*,
De auguriis, etc.) and was described by Young as being written in
charactere saxonico.[45] He used this description of two other manuscripts
which happen to have survived: Oxford, BodL, Hatton 93 (*Expositio
missae*: first quarter of the ninth century) and London, BL, Royal 5.
F. III (Aldhelm, of the late ninth century). In other words, the (lost)
manuscript of sermons of Caesarius, in *charactere saxonico*, was very
possibly a ninth-century manuscript. If it dated (say) from the reign of
King Alfred, the pervading concern of its contents with pastoral care
and tithes would be interesting indeed. The second manuscript
contained at its beginning two homilies in Old English (*sermones duo
lingua saxonica*), one on the Antichrist, the other on the day of
judgement.[46] This manuscript was listed among lost manuscripts by
Ker in his *Catalogue of Manuscripts Containing Anglo-Saxon*, and he
there suggested that the two homilies might correspond to Napier 40
and 42.[47] The remaining contents were in Latin, and included Alcuin's
De fide trinitatis [CSLMA ALC 28] and some works of Isidore and
pseudo-Isidore. Most interesting for a literary historian is the fact that
as its final item the lost manuscript contained what Young called
'Æsopi fabulae'; but since he helpfully quoted the opening line
('Romulus Tiberino filio', etc.) it is possible to identify the work as
what is called the 'Romulus vulgaris', the prose version of Æsop which

---

[43] There is an excellent survey of the scholars in question—notably George Hickes,
Humfrey Wanley, and Henry Wharton—by Douglas, *English Scholars*.
[44] *Catalogus Librorum Manuscriptorum Bibliothecae Wigorniensis*, ed. Atkins and Ker.
[45] Ibid. 37 (no. 54).   [46] Ibid. 58 (no. 337).
[47] Ker, *Catalogue*, 473–4 (no. 412); Ker's reference is to *Wulfstan: Sammlung*, 182–90,
191–205.

circulated most widely during the early Middle Ages (the verse fables of Phaedrus, on which the 'Romulus vulgaris' is based, barely circulated at all, and certainly not in Anglo-Saxon England).[48] This is of exceptional importance for our understanding of Anglo-Saxon education, for the 'Romulus vulgaris' was widely studied in early medieval schools, and was converted into hexameters by an anonymous Anglo-Latin poet, probably a contemporary of Bishop Æthelwold, in the later tenth century. Without the evidence of Young's lost Worcester manuscript, we would not know that the prose text, on which the Anglo-Latin poem was based, had been available in pre-Conquest England. I mention this by way of stressing that late evidence, even post-Reformation evidence, can often help to illuminate the contents of Anglo-Saxon libraries.

SURVIVING MANUSCRIPTS FROM THE AREA OF THE ANGLO-SAXON MISSION IN GERMANY

I now turn to a different class of evidence which can also help to illuminate the holdings of pre-Conquest Anglo-Saxon libraries. It is well known that, at the time of the Anglo-Saxon mission to Germany in the mid-eighth century, substantial numbers of Anglo-Saxon manuscripts passed to Germany in order to supply the needs of the expanding missionary church.[49] Boniface himself took a small collection of books for his own personal use, some of which still survive in Fulda, the monastery which he founded in 744,[50] but most of the books were supplied from other English monasteries and scriptoria.[51] The corpus of correspondence of Boniface and Lul is filled with statements from English correspondents to the missionaries in Germany, such as 'I couldn't yet get the corpus of *passiones martyrum*

[48] On evidence for the circulation of the 'Romulus uulgaris' in Anglo-Saxon England, and for the hexameter poem (called the 'Hexametrical Romulus') which is based on it, see Lapidge and Mann, 'Reconstructing the Anglo-Latin Aesop', esp. 1–12.

[49] For general orientation, see the classic discussion of Levison, *England and the Continent*, 132–48; for qualifications to the picture drawn by Levison, particularly involving Frankish evidence, see McKitterick, 'Anglo-Saxon Missionaries'.

[50] See Schüling, 'Die Handbibliothek des Bonifatius', esp. cols. 329–30, for an overview of books quoted by Boniface in his correspondence, and above, pp. 38–9. Two manuscripts owned and annotated by Boniface survive to this day in Fulda: Fulda, Hessische Landesbibliothek, Codex Bonifatianus 1 (Victor of Capua) and Codex Bonifatianus 3 (the Cadmug Gospels); and see above, pp. 39–40.

[51] The effect which the repeated requests for books had on the scriptorium at Monkwearmouth-Jarrow in the later 8th c. is well described by Parkes, 'The Scriptorium of Wearmouth-Jarrow'.

which you requested, but I'm still trying' (*Ep*. xv) or 'I have sent you some copies of the letters of Pope Gregory' (*Ep*. lxxv), together with replies from the missionaries thanking their correspondents for books and requesting further titles: 'thank you for the bounties of holy books which you have sent to your German exile' (*Ep*. xxx); 'I should be grateful if you would send me commentaries on the Pauline epistles' (*Ep*. xxxiv); 'please send some works of Aldhelm, either in prose or quantitative verse or in rhythmic verse' (*Ep*. lxxi); and so on.[52] Since the exported books were supplied from Anglo-Saxon libraries, they can provide a fresh perspective on the holdings of Anglo-Saxon libraries in the mid-eighth century.

The initial recipients of the exported books were the ecclesiastical foundations established by Anglo-Saxon missionaries in Germany: principally Fulda, founded by Boniface in 744; Würzburg, established as a bishopric by Boniface and occupied first by the Anglo-Saxon bishop Burghard in 742; Mainz, which was the first archbishopric established in Germany and was first occupied by Boniface, and then by his protégé Lul on Boniface's death in 754; and then a number of monasteries in the territory of Hesse–Thuringia established by Anglo-Saxon missionaries in the mid-eighth century, such as Hersfeld, Amorbach, Weissenburg, Tauberbischofsheim, and others. The important point is this: that Anglo-Saxon books were sent to all these places at the requests of Boniface and Lul; and that scriptoria in these centres were in the first instance staffed by Anglo-Saxon masters who in due course taught their German students to write Anglo-Saxon minuscule script (whether hybrid, set, or cursive) in imitation of the manuscripts which were being imported from England. The career of Anglo-Saxon minuscule script in Germany lasted for approximately half a century, from (say) the foundation of Fulda and Würzburg in the 740s until *c*.800, when Caroline minuscule began to emerge as the normal vehicle for library books (a few centres, notably Fulda, continued to write Anglo-Saxon script into the second and third decades of the ninth century). If we wish to study the manuscripts produced in the area of the Anglo-Saxon mission to Germany, Lowe's *Codices Latini Antiquiores* [CLA] offers a reliable guide.

Books were being exported to Germany; Anglo-Saxon pilgrims were teaching native Germans how to write Anglo-Saxon script; and these native German scribes were in their turn writing manuscripts in the style of script which they had learnt from their Anglo-Saxon

[52] *S. Bonifatii et Lullii Epistolae*, ed. Tangl, 27, 158, 54, 59, 144 respectively.

masters. Any student of the eighth-century manuscripts from the area of the Anglo-Saxon mission in Germany has therefore to be prepared to distinguish the following three categories of books: books written in Anglo-Saxon England but subsequently exported to Germany; books written in Germany by Anglo-Saxons who had migrated there (some of whom we know by name, such as Willibald diaconus, whom we know from a scribal colophon in a copy of Gregory's *Regula pastoralis*, but also as the author of the first *Vita S. Bonifacii* [BHL 1400], written at Mainz *c*.760); and manuscripts written by German students of Anglo-Saxon masters. It is in practice extremely difficult to distinguish between these three categories, in spite of the confidence with which Lowe sometimes describes the manuscripts in question. In drawing up his *Handlist* of Anglo-Saxon manuscripts, Helmut Gneuss cautiously followed Lowe's lead. That is to say, if Lowe in CLA says 'origin probably Northumbria', the manuscript is included by Gneuss in his *Handlist*; but if Lowe says (as, for example, at CLA vii. 853), 'written in a German centre under Anglo-Saxon influence, possibly at Fulda with which its later history is connected', Gneuss omits it. It must be said that Gneuss is not wholly consistent in his treatment of manuscripts which fall in this grey in-between area and he includes a number of manuscripts which he should probably have excluded (e.g. he includes as Gneuss 911 a Vatican manuscript of Gregory's *Hom. in Hiezechihelem*, of which Lowe [CLA i. 90] says unambiguously, 'written in an Anglo-Saxon centre on the Continent'). (There are some ten manuscripts in Gneuss's list which on his own criteria probably do not belong there.) However, my concern is not to quibble with Gneuss's criteria, but to ask whether the books exported to and copied in the area of the Anglo-Saxon mission in Germany, between *c*.750 and *c*.800, can throw any light on the resources of the Anglo-Saxon libraries in England from which they (or at least their exemplars) may be presumed to have come. In compiling my own working list of manuscripts from the area of the Anglo-Saxon mission (see App. C), I have omitted biblical and liturgical manuscripts and have included only manuscripts written in minuscule script and owned in the area of the Anglo-Saxon mission in Germany. I thus exclude, for example, the various manuscripts in English uncial and half-uncial script which were written or owned at monasteries in Francia (e.g. Cambrai); in any case, a manuscript written in one of these higher grades of script is likely to be a biblical manuscript, hence outside the scope of my investigation.

We are left with a substantial corpus of some 112 manuscripts and fragments. They would make a manageable corpus for palaeographical analysis (excepting the work of Paul Lehmann and Bernhard Bischoff, and Herrad Spilling more recently, surprisingly little sustained work has been done in this area); my concern, however, is with the contents, not the script, of these manuscripts, and what indirect light they may shed on the holdings of Anglo-Saxon libraries in the eighth century. The results are somewhat surprising. Half of the manuscripts contain works by only four patristic authors, namely (in order of perceived importance?), Gregory, Isidore, Jerome, and Augustine. Thus there are twenty manuscripts of the works of Gregory, made up of eight copies of the *Hom. in Hiezechihelem* (App. C, nos. 2, 30, 71, 73, 93, 100, 103, 105), three of the *Regula pastoralis* (nos. 12, 40, 62), three of the *Dialogi* (nos. 29, 45, 67), three of the *Moralia in Iob* (nos. 7, 42, 77), and three of the *Hom. .xl. in Euangelia* (nos. 72, 73, 107). Of the works of Isidore, there are sixteen manuscripts, made up of six copies of the *Etymologiae* (nos. 8, 26, 53, 57, 97, 112), five of the *Synonyma* (nos. 19, 76, 82, 84, 96), two of the *De natura rerum* (nos. 16, 21), and one each of *De ecclesiasticis officiis* (no. 79), *De differentiis rerum* (no. 22), and *Quaestiones in Vetus Testamentum* (no. 80). Of Jerome's works, there are ten manuscripts in total, including three of his *Comm. in Esaiam* (nos. 9, 95, 98), three of his *Comm. in Ecclesiasten* (nos. 38, 78, 83), and one each of his commentaries on Daniel (no. 43), Matthew (no. 99), and the Pauline epistles (no. 106), and one copy of his *Epistulae* (no. 6). Finally, of Augustine's works there are eight manuscripts in total, comprising three of the *Enarrationes in psalmos* (nos. 66, 70, 74), two of *De trinitate* (nos. 1, 10), two of the *Tractatus in Euangelium Ioannis* (nos. 27, 47), and one of the *Epistulae* (no. 14). In addition to these, the *Sermones* of Caesarius of Arles are preserved in three copies (nos. 55, 69, 87), and a number of minor patristic authors are represented by one or two manuscripts each. None, however, is an author unrepresented by manuscripts surviving from Anglo-Saxon England. Quite the contrary. The patristic works exported to the Continent were the staple of Anglo-Saxon libraries.

A somewhat different perspective emerges with respect to grammatical manuscripts, however. The numbers of manuscripts in question are much smaller than those of patristic authors: seven manuscripts in total. The provision of grammatical manuscripts is not surprising in view of the elementary Latin teaching which those who sustained the mission would have been required to undertake. What is more surprising is that the grammatical manuscripts include copies of Charisius (no. 31), Diomedes (no. 32), and Consentius (no. 33): authors of which no manuscript written or owned in Anglo-Saxon England survives. The same is true of the *Ars grammatica* of Julian of Toledo (no. 51): no English manuscript of this exceptionally rare work survives, and the evidence for its use by Anglo-Saxon grammarians is open to question, in the opinion of the late Vivien Law.[53] It is also striking that only a very few manuscripts of school-texts survive from the German missionary area: two copies of Caelius Sedulius, *Carmen paschale* (nos. 23, 49), two copies of Aldhelm, prose *De uirginitate* [CPL 1332] (nos. 5, 50), and one copy of Bede, *De arte metrica* [CPL 1565] (no. 104). And nothing more. But of the classical Latin literature which, as we have seen, was moderately well, if not fully, represented by surviving Anglo-Saxon manuscripts, there is not so much as a trace from the scriptoria of the Anglo-Saxon mission in Germany: not a single manuscript, not a single fragment. Was it that the pressures involved in establishing an incipient missionary church, especially at the hands of hard-nosed ecclesiastics like Boniface and Lul, imparted a tone of high seriousness to all reading and study, so that there was simply no time for the frivolities and delights of reading (say) Vergil or Lucan? The manuscript evidence would suggest so.

INVENTORIES FROM THE AREA OF THE ANGLO-SAXON MISSION IN GERMANY

In discussing the manuscripts which have survived from Anglo-Saxon England, I emphasized that the manuscripts themselves can offer only a partial view of the holdings of Anglo-Saxon libraries, and that it was necessary to qualify the picture by recourse to (say) the evidence of inventories. The same is true of the manuscripts exported to, and copied in, the Anglo-Saxon missionary area in eighth-century Germany. Although, as we have seen in a previous chapter (above, pp. 58–60), there are numerous inventories of Carolingian libraries dating from the ninth century,[54] the three

---

[53] Law, *Grammar*, 99–100.

[54] The Carolingian and post-Carolingian inventories (a number of which are printed in Becker, *Catalogi*) frequently contain references to books subsequently lost which were either of English origin or were ultimately descended from English books, such as the reference in one of the 9th-c. Lorsch catalogues to a creed composed by Archbishop Theodore (Becker, *Catalogi*, 86: 'symbolum quod composuit Theodorus archiepiscopus

earliest surviving Continental inventories date from the eighth century and originate in the area of the Anglo-Saxon missions to Germany. These three inventories, which are printed with commentary as Appendix B, illustrate respectively the eighth-century holdings of the libraries of Würzburg, Fulda, and (probably) Echternach.

The inventory from Würzburg (App. B, no. a) was discovered in 1928 by E. A. Lowe in Oxford, BodL, Laud misc. 126, an eighth-century Frankish copy of Augustine's *De trinitate*, to which a scribe writing Anglo-Saxon set minuscule *c*.800 added on the final folio an inventory of thirty-six books, of which one is noted as being at Holzkirchen (a nearby dependency of Würzburg) and a further one (or four?) at Fulda.[55] It was the implied links with Holzkirchen and Fulda which suggested to Lowe, no doubt rightly, that the list was a record of the books of Würzburg. The books included several works by Gregory (*Regula pastoralis*, *Dialogi*, *Moralia in Iob*), Isidore (*Synonyma*, *De ecclesiasticis officiis*), Augustine (*De doctrina christiana*, *De quantitate animae*, *Enchiridion*, *De trinitate*), and Jerome (*Epistulae* and Commentary on Paul's Letter to the Ephesians). The list is rounded out with some other patristic texts (Juvencus, Orosius, etc.), some of which, such as the psalm commentary of Arnobius Iunior and the *Instituta regularia* of Junillus,[56] are genuine rarities.

The second Continental inventory (App. B, no. b) is from Fulda, and was discovered in 1925 by Paul Lehmann in a manuscript now in Basle, UB, F. III. 15a, a copy of Isidore's *De natura rerum* written at Fulda *c*.800, to which a coeval scribe added, on the last and badly abraded folio, a list of twenty books, which Lehmann reasonably interpreted as an inventory, the earliest such inventory in existence, of the library of Fulda.[57] The list contains mostly biblical books,

Britanniae insulae'), or, in the same inventory, to a copy of Bede's (mostly lost) *Liber hymnorum* (ibid. 111: 'eiusdem [*scil.* Bedae] hymni .LXXVII. in uno codice'). A 16th-c. Fulda catalogue contains reference to an *Impnarius Edilwaldi*, perhaps a hymnal compiled by Ædiluald, an early 8th-c. bishop of Lindisfarne: Schrimpf, *Mittelalterliche Bücherverzeichnisse des Klosters Fulda* (Frankfurt, 1992), 141 (no. 443). But it is not possible to identify Anglo-Saxon books in Carolingian inventories unless, as in these three cases, the book in question was composed by an Anglo-Saxon author.

[55] Lowe, 'An Eighth-Century List of Books'. The inventory is also ed. in *Libri sancti Kyliani*, 142–8, and in MBKDS iv. 2 (1979), 977–9.

[56] As we have seen (above, p. 34), Aldhelm had access at Malmesbury to a copy of Iunillus, a fragment of which may survive as London, BL, Cotton Tiberius A. xv, fos. 175–80.

[57] Lehmann, *Fuldaer Studien*, 49–50; the inventory has been re-edited by Schrimpf, *Mittelalterliche Bücherverzeichnisse des Klosters Fulda*, 5–6 [diplomatic transcription], 6–11

saints' lives, an unspecified chronicle, as well as the standard patristic works of Gregory (*Regula pastoralis*, *Moralia in Iob*), and Isidore (*Synonyma*).

The third inventory (App. B, no. c) was also discovered by Paul Lehmann, and printed by him in 1923.[58] It is found as an early eighth-century addition by an Anglo-Saxon scribe to a manuscript now Vatican City, BAV, Pal. lat. 210. In the opinion of Lehmann, followed by Bischoff, the manuscript originated somewhere in the Low Countries; and if my conjectural identification of item no. 4 in the list with Paris, BNF, lat. 9538 is correct, the place in question may well be Echternach, which was founded by the Anglo-Saxon missionary Willibrord (d. 739), who became the first archbishop of Utrecht in 695.[59] Under Willibrord's direction, Echternach in the early eighth century had an active scriptorium and, presumably, a burgeoning library.[60] The inventory in the Vatican manuscript contains seventeen entries, many of them biblical, but also a number of patristic works, including staple authors such as Gregory (*Dialogi*, *Regula pastoralis*), and Isidore (*De natura rerum*), alongside rarities such as Cyprian, *Testimonia ad Quirinum*.

These early inventories, from the area of Anglo-Saxon missionary activity on the Continent, confirm the impression gained from surviving manuscripts, namely that in the first half-century of their existence, the libraries of the principal centres of the mission were stocked solely with (what might be called) the staple patristic authors: Gregory, Isidore, Augustine, and Jerome, in approximately that order. Thus, of the writings of Gregory, there are three entries for the *Dialogi* (a. 3, b. 10, c. 6), three for the *Regula pastoralis* (a. 2, b. 13, c. 14), two for the *Hom. .xl. in Euangelia* (a. 34, b. 9), and one for the *Moralia in Iob* (a. 21). Of Isidore, there are two entries for the *Sententiae* (a. 22, b. 14), two for *De natura rerum* (b. 15, c. 7), and one each for *De ecclesiasticis officiis* (a. 18) and the *Synonyma* (b. 11). Of Augustine, there are two entries for *De trinitate* (a. 27, c. 4), and one each for *De doctrina christiana* (a. 7), *De fide et symbolo* (a. 8), *De quantitate animae* (a. 16), the *Enchiridion* (a. 19), the *Speculum 'quis*

[reconstructed text with commentary]. On the date of the manuscript, see Spilling, 'Angelsächsische Schrift in Fulda', 62–4.

[58] Lehmann, 'Das älteste Bücherverzeichnis der Niederlande'. For the dating of the manuscript, see Bischoff, *Lorsch*, 64; id., *Die Abtei Lorsch*, pp. 118–19.

[59] On Willibrord, see Levison, *England and the Continent*, 53–69.

[60] See Netzer, 'The Early Scriptorium at Echternach' and 'Willibrord's Scriptorium at Echternach'; and Ferrari, *Sancti Willibrordi venerantes memoriam*, esp. 9–23.

ignorat' (a. 33), and the *Sermones* (b. 18). Of Jerome, there is one entry each for *De uiribus inlustribus* (a. 30), the *Epistulae* (a. 6), and the commentaries on Ecclesiastes (a. 4) and on the epistles of Paul (a. 13). This list of patristic writings represented in the early Continental inventories squares almost exactly, in terms of titles and numerical proportion, with the evidence of surviving manuscripts, surveyed earlier. As in the case of the surviving manuscripts, so too in the inventories, there is not so much as a single classical author or text.

The point needs to be stressed because, by the mid-ninth century, Fulda had acquired the reputation of being a depository of classical texts. Lupus of Ferrières, for example, turned to Fulda in his search for copies of Suetonius' *De uita Caesarum*, which he knew to exist as a two-volume set in Fulda's library.[61] A striking number of classical manuscripts, all apparently written at Fulda during the second quarter of the ninth century, survives to the present day. The following list will give some idea of the richness of Fulda's holdings in this domain: a copy of the *Scriptores Historiae Augustae* surviving as Bamberg, Staatsbibliothek, Class. 54;[62] Valerius Flaccus, *Argonautica*, surviving as Vatican City, BAV, lat. 3277;[63] Tacitus, *Agricola* and *Germania* combined with 'Dictys Cretensis', *Bellum Troianum*, now in Rome, Biblioteca Nazionale, VE 1631;[64] Columella, *De re rustica*, now in Milan, Biblioteca Ambrosiana, L. 85 sup.;[65] Pliny, *Epistulae*, in the so-called 'Nine-Book Tradition', surviving in Florence, Biblioteca Laurenziana, Plut. XLVII. 36;[66] Tacitus, *Annales* books i–vi, also in Florence, Biblioteca Laurenziana, Plut. LXVIII. 1;[67] Ammianus Marcellinus, *Res gestae*, now in Vatican City, BAV, Vat. lat. 1873;[68] Nonius Marcellus, *De compendiosa doctrina*, now in Geneva, UB, lat. 84;[69] and the *Aratea* of Germanicus, now in Basle, UB, AN IV. 18.[70] Others have apparently been lost since the sixteenth century: a copy

---

[61] Servatus Lupus, *Ep.* xci [to Abbot Marcward, dated *c.*844]: 'Quaeso praeterea, ut ad sanctum Bonifatium [*sc.* Fulda] sollertem aliquem monachum dirigatis, qui ex vestra parte Hattonem abbatem deposcat, ut vobis Suetonium Tranquillum de Vita Caesarum, qui apud eos in duos nec magnos codices divisus est, ad exscribendum dirigat' (MGH, Epist. vi [= Epistolae Karolini Aevi, iv] (Berlin, 1925), 81).

[62] Bischoff, *Katalog*, no. 216 (Fulda, s. ix$^{2/4}$); *TxtTrans*, 354; and Gugel, *Welche erhaltenen mittelalterlichen Handschriften*, 60.

[63] *TxtTrans*, 426; Gugel, ibid. 57.   [64] *TxtTrans*, 410; Gugel, ibid. 56.

[65] Bischoff, *Katalog*, no. 2643 (Fulda, s. ix$^{2/4}$); *TxtTrans*, 146; Gugel, ibid. 54.

[66] Bischoff, *Katalog*, no. 1229 (Fulda, s. ix$^{2/4}$); *TxtTrans*, 321; Gugel, ibid. 53.

[67] Bischoff, *Katalog*, no. 1237 (Fulda, s. ix$^{2/4}$); *TxtTrans*, 406–7; Gugel, ibid. 53.

[68] *TxtTrans*, 6–7 (Fulda, s. ix$^{2/4}$); Gugel, ibid. 47.

[69] Bischoff, *Katalog*, no. 1352 (Fulda, s. ix$^{2/4}$); *TxtTrans*, 250; Gugel, ibid. 76.

[70] Bischoff, *Katalog*, no. 258 (Fulda, s. ix$^{1/3}$); *TxtTrans*, 21; Gugel, ibid. 30.

of the 'Roman Land Surveyors' (*Agrimensores*) was unearthed at
Fulda by Johannes Sichardt as late as 1526, but has subsequently
disappeared.[71]

During the second quarter of the ninth century, the abbot of Fulda
was Hrabanus Maurus (d. 856), who was a biblical and patristic
scholar of immense energy and learning, but who is not known
particularly as a classical scholar. However, there is at least one
surviving manuscript which seems to reveal Hrabanus' interest in the
acquisition and copying of rare classical texts: a copy of Aulus
Gellius, *Noctes Atticae*, books ix–xx, which survives as Leeuwarden,
Provinciale Bibliotheek van Friesland, B.A. Fr. 55. This manuscript
is thought to have been copied in 836 at the request of Hrabanus from
an exemplar which had been lent to Lupus of Ferrières by Einhard,
then living in retirement at Seligenstadt.[72] If Hrabanus had requested
the copying of this one text, perhaps he was responsible for others as
well. It is not known where Einhard had acquired the copy of Aulus
Gellius in the first place, nor indeed where Fulda's ninth-century
librarians acquired the exemplars for all the other classical texts listed
above. Perhaps, as Louis Holtz has suggested, the source of such
manuscripts was the private libraries of late antique Roman aristocrats, principally in Rome and Ravenna;[73] but it is fair to ask whether
any of these will still have been in existence in the mid-ninth century.
Whatever the source, one thing seems quite certain: judging from the
evidence of inventories and surviving manuscripts from the area of
the Anglo-Saxon mission in Germany during the period *c*.750–*c*.800,
the exemplars of these classical texts did not come from England, and
did not form part of Fulda's library during the first half-century of its
existence. On the contrary, the evidence indicates clearly that it was
uniquely patristic texts which were sent from England to the
missionaries in Germany.

[71] *TxtTrans*, 2.

[72] Bischoff, *Katalog*, no. 2133; *TxtTrans*, 178; Gugel, ibid. 44. See also Lieftinck, 'Le
Manuscrit d'Aulu-Gelle'. The date of the manuscript is deduced from a letter of Lupus
(*Ep*. v) to Einhard, dated 836: 'Agellium misissem, nisi rursus illum abbas [*sc*. Hrabanus?]
retinuisset, questus necdum sibi eum esse descriptum. Scripturum se tamen vobis dixit,
quod praefatum librum vi mihi extorserit. Verum et illum et omnes ceteros, quibus vestra
liberalitate fruor, per me, si Deus vult, vobis ipse restituam' (MGH, Epist. vi [= Epistolae
Karolini Aevi, iv] (Berlin, 1925), 17). The assumption is then made that the Leeuwarden
manuscript, evidently copied at Fulda (to judge from its script), is identical with that
which, according to his letter as quoted above, Lupus had made for him. But it is only an
assumption.

[73] Holtz, 'Vers la création des bibliothèques', 1073, 1087–8; and cf. above, p. 24.

SURVIVING CONTINENTAL MANUSCRIPTS COPIED
FROM LOST ANGLO-SAXON EXEMPLARS

There is one final class of evidence which, although it is intractable and probably limitless, could ultimately be used to throw light on the contents of Anglo-Saxon libraries, namely manuscripts in Caroline minuscule script copied from lost Anglo-Saxon exemplars in Continental scriptoria from approximately 800 onwards. It is well known that numerous Carolingian manuscripts of the ninth and tenth centuries preserve what are called 'Insular symptoms' which betray copying from an Insular exemplar (above all, the symptoms include misunderstanding of Insular compendia, such as those for *autem* and *enim*, and the various suspensions of *qui*, *quae*, *quod*, etc., but also confusion of Insular minuscule letter-forms, such as *r* and *n*). If one finds in a Carolingian manuscript an ungrammatical *hoc* in postpositive position in a sentence, it is almost a certainty that the Continental scribe failed to recognize the Insular compendium for *autem* (which was written as an *h* with a small hook on its shoulder), and copied it as *hoc*: hence that he was copying from an Insular exemplar.[74] It is difficult to imagine how one would go about compiling a list of manuscripts containing such symptoms. Many classical Latin texts, for example, are alleged, on the basis of perceived symptoms such as these, to have had an 'Insular' phase in their transmission. Several years ago David Dumville undertook a thorough and valuable survey of the palaeographical evidence for Insular symptoms in the transmissional histories of classical Latin texts, examining in detail some twenty text histories, and was able to show that much of the alleged evidence for Insular symptoms—much of it published over a century ago—could equally well be explained in terms of the cursive script of the Roman and sub-Roman periods, from which the Insular cursive scripts derive.[75] In other words, the

---

[74] See Heeg and Lehmann, '*Enim* und *autem*', and the article by Dumville cited in the following note, *passim*. An example of a text abounding in such scribal confusion is a copy of a treatise entitled *De diuersis rebus* (in fact an epitome of Isidore, *Etymologiae*), preserved uniquely in Paris, BNF, lat. 1750 (N. France, s. viii/ix), fos. 146^v–152^r; the scribal confusion of compendia, in combination with the equally revealing attempt to represent graphically the most unusual (from a Continental perspective) abbreviations, such as those for *enim*, *est*, and *inter*, indicates unambiguously that the scribe was copying from an exemplar in some compressed grade of Anglo-Saxon minuscule (set or cursive); and the hypothesis is confirmed by the fact that the scribe unwittingly reproduced a number of Old English words: see Lapidge, 'An Isidorian Epitome', 187–9.

[75] Dumville, 'The Early Mediaeval Insular Churches'.

exemplars from which the alleged 'Insular symptoms' derive may well have been late antique books written somewhere within the Roman empire. And it must be stressed that the hypothesis of classical texts having been transmitted via England to ninth-century Continental libraries sits ill with the more solid evidence provided by manuscripts and inventories from the area of the Anglo-Saxon mission in Germany, which attest solely to the transmission of patristic literature from England to Germany.

We are on safer ground with manuscripts copied by Continental scribes writing Caroline minuscule from exemplars containing Old English (usually in the form of glosses or isolated words). The one thing a Continental scribe could hardly ever understand was a word in Old English; and the presence of garbled Old English in a Continental manuscript points unmistakably to a (usually lost) Anglo-Saxon exemplar. In his *Catalogue of Manuscripts containing Anglo-Saxon*, Neil Ker provided by way of appendix a list of thirty-nine Continental manuscripts which, from the Old English which they preserve, mutilated or unmutilated, were obviously copied from Anglo-Saxon exemplars.[76] In order to illustrate this point, I should like to consider one of the manuscripts in Ker's appendix, for the light which it can throw, not only on its exemplar, but on a whole collection of books which were available in the library at Canterbury in the time of Theodore and Hadrian in the late seventh century. The manuscript in question is now Leiden, Bibliotheek der Rijksuniversiteit, Voss. Lat. Q. 69 (Ker's app. 18), the manuscript which contains the famous 'Leiden Glossary'.[77] The manuscript was copied at St Gallen *c*.800; and because the 'Leiden Glossary' contains some 250 Old English words, its exemplar undoubtedly came from England. Furthermore, the fact that Theodore is quoted as an authority at one point in the glossary, and the fact that there are many explanations shared with the biblical commentaries from the Canterbury school of Theodore and Hadrian, indicates that the lost Anglo-Saxon exemplar used by the St Gallen scribe was a product of that school.[78] But there is more. The 'Leiden Glossary' consists of forty-six batches of lemmata plus glosses (sometimes extensive) drawn from a range of biblical, grammatical, and patristic texts: Donatus *Ars maior* and

---

[76] Ker, *Catalogue*, 475–84; a further six Continental manuscripts containing Old English (App., nos. 40–5) are listed in Ker, 'A Supplement'.

[77] *A Late Eighth-Century Latin–Anglo-Saxon Glossary*, ed. Hessels.

[78] Lapidge, 'The School of Theodore and Hadrian', and *Biblical Commentaries*, 173–9.

Phocas, *Ars de nomine et uerbo*; Gregory, *Dialogi* and *Regula pastoralis*; Isidore, *De natura rerum* and *De ecclesiasticis officiis*; Jerome, *Comm. in Matthaeum*, and many others. (It will be noted that many of these are the works which are preserved in manuscripts in Anglo-Saxon minuscule from the missionary area in eighth-century Germany.) Although it is a tedious task, it is possible to identify all the lemmata within a particular batch, and then compare those lemmata, once identified, with the text from which the lemmata are drawn. Provided there is a modern edition of the text with a good apparatus criticus, one can often situate the text (that is, the text used for teaching in the Canterbury school from which the lemmata derive) within the textual transmission of the work as a whole. I attempted to do this with the first two batches—a canon collection and the *Regula S. Benedicti*— when I drew attention to the exceptional importance of the 'Leiden Glossary' in an article first published in 1986.[79]

A more revealing case is that of the Rufinus batches in the 'Leiden Glossary'. There are three separate batches of lemmata plus glosses from Rufinus' Latin translation of the *Historia ecclesiastica* of Eusebius, some 485 lemmata in all ('Leiden Glossary', nos. iv, v, and xxxv). On many occasions, the three batches preserve three separate interpretations of the one lemma: as if they represented the individual responses of three students, of somewhat differing abilities, to the teacher's explanation of the text.[80] The third Rufinus glossator (batch no. xxxv), for example, had a pronounced interest in Greek etymology, an interest which his two companions did not share. Now although there is a substantial number of manuscripts of Rufinus (and one important manuscript came to light only as recently as 1984),[81] Mommsen's early twentieth-century edition is based in effect on four (FNOP); and of these, FNO agree consistently against P.[82] Collation of the three 'Leiden Glossary' Rufinus batches quickly shows that the manuscript which most closely resembles that used in the Canterbury school is P, now Vatican City, BAV, Pal. lat. 822, a manuscript written at Lorsch *c*.800:[83] not only because of shared lemmata when

---

[79] 'The School of Theodore and Hadrian', 62–6, repr. *ALL* i. 158–62.

[80] See Lapidge, 'Rufinus at the School of Canterbury'.

[81] Breen, 'A New Irish Fragment'; but see the severe criticism of this article by Bammel, 'Das neue Rufinfragment'.

[82] *Eusebius Werke II: Die Kirchengeschichte*, ed. Schwartz and Mommsen. The manuscripts in question are: F = Munich, BSB, Clm. 6375 (South Germany, s. ix^med); N = Paris, BNF, lat. 18282 (s. viii/ix); and O = Paris, BNF, lat. 5500 (s. ix/x); for MS P, see below.   [83] See Bischoff, *Lorsch*, 25.

FNO are ranged against it, but especially because P, the Lorsch manuscript, has at many points been provided with marginal annotations; and these marginal annotations correspond verbatim with the glosses of the third Rufinus glossator in the 'Leiden Glossary'.[84] The Lorsch manuscript obviously cannot have been the manuscript on which the Canterbury master based his teaching—it was written more than a century too late—but there is no difficulty in assuming that it is a copy of that lost exemplar, and that the lost exemplar carried marginal annotations of the third Canterbury Rufinus glossator which are carefully reproduced in the Lorsch manuscript.

Who was this third Rufinus glossator? We know from Bede's *Historia ecclesiastica* the names of four scholars who studied at the Canterbury school—Albinus, Hadrian's successor as abbot of the monastery of SS Peter and Paul at Canterbury; Tobias, later bishop of Rochester; Oftfor, later bishop of Worcester; and John of Beverley, later bishop of York.[85] But another student who certainly studied at Canterbury with the two Mediterranean masters was Aldhelm, as we know from his own correspondence (part of a letter from Aldhelm to Hadrian is preserved by William of Malmesbury).[86] And in his prose *De uirginitate* Aldhelm quotes extensively from Rufinus;[87] so there is no difficulty in the supposition that he had studied the text at Canterbury, and that in theory he could even be one of the three Rufinus glossators. Now at one point in book vii Rufinus quotes a passage from 1 Corinthians 4: 13, as follows: 'et effecti sunt eorum, ut dicit apostoli sermo, peripsima'. The Canterbury master (whether Theodore or Hadrian at this point is irrelevant) evidently drew attention to the Greek word *peripsima* ('off-scouring', 'filth') and glossed it in passing, and the third Rufinus glossator rendered his explanation as 'peripsima. purgamentum uel quisquilia'.[88] What is interesting is that Aldhelm, describing in c. 10 of his *De uirginitate* the aggressive attitude to sin which is to be adopted by the model chaste virgin, states that s/he is to reject 'the blandishments of the world like the off-scourings of filth': 'mundi blandimenta velut quisquiliarum peripsima respuens'.[89] Aldhelm has here combined in one expression the Rufinus lemma and its gloss, in such a way as to suggest that he

[84] See Lapidge, 'Rufinus at the School of Canterbury', 125–7.
[85] *Biblical Commentaries*, 267–8.
[86] Ibid. 268; Aldhelm's Letter to Hadrian is printed in MGH, AA xv. 478 (*Ep.* ii).
[87] See below, App. E (p. 181).   [88] 'Leiden Glossary', xxxv. 195.
[89] MGH, AA xv. 238.

himself is very possibly the third Rufinus glossator. If so, we have in the Lorsch manuscript—Vatican Pal. lat. 822—a copy, probably a close copy, of a manuscript annotated by Aldhelm himself. In any event the certain link between the Canterbury glossary and the glosses in the Lorsch manuscript indicates that Rufinus' *Historia ecclesiastica* is one further example of a work which was transmitted from Anglo-Saxon England to the Continent during the course of the eighth century.

CONCLUSIONS

How many more such manuscripts await identification is impossible to say at this stage of our research. Vivien Law drew attention to a late eighth-century manuscript of the grammarian Audax from Freising, now Munich, BSB, Clm. 6434, which shared a number of striking readings with the (lost) manuscript of Audax that Aldhelm evidently used in compiling his *De metris*, enough to suggest that the Freising manuscript could be a Continental copy of Aldhelm's manuscript.[90] No doubt others await discovery. The point is simply that, in reconstructing the contents of pre-Conquest English libraries, surviving manuscripts tell only part of the story, and their witness needs to be augmented by various kinds of evidence, including that of lost manuscripts. However, as the two examples from Aldhelm indicate, the most secure category of evidence for what books existed in Anglo-Saxon libraries is citations of those books by Anglo-Saxon authors, and it is to this category of evidence that we must now turn.

[90] Law, *Grammar*, 94, and esp. 116 n. 19: 'Discrepancies between this manuscript and that used by Aldhelm are so minor that Clm. 6434 could easily be a direct descendant of Aldhelm's lost copy.'

5

Reconstructing Anglo-Saxon Libraries (III): The Evidence of Citations

In previous chapters, when attempting to put into perspective the evidence for Anglo-Saxon libraries drawn from inventories and surviving manuscripts, I have often referred to works known to, or quoted by, pre-Conquest Anglo-Latin authors. In the present chapter I examine more closely this latter class of evidence, for it can frequently illuminate a problem where the other classes of evidence are silent; but it also has to be said at the outset that this is the class of evidence where most work remains to be done (and in the case of certain authors has yet to begin). It is well known to Anglo-Saxonists that the optimistically entitled book by J. D. A. Ogilvy, *Books Known to the English 597–1066*, published in a revised edition in 1967, is simply inadequate for the uses of modern scholarship.[1] It was awareness of the inadequacies of Ogilvy's book that inspired the creation, during the 1980s, of two large, well-organized, and complementary international projects, called respectively *The Sources of Anglo-Saxon Literary Culture*, under the general editorship of Paul Szarmach in America, and *Fontes Anglo-Saxonici*, a vast computer database of sources identified in Anglo-Saxon authors, produced through the collaborative effort of scholars in several British universities and now managed in Oxford.

The first project, referred to by Anglo-Saxonists as SASLC, takes as its point of departure, like Ogilvy's book, the authors who can be shown to have been known in pre-Conquest England, so that (in principle) one would be able to look up Ambrose, Apuleius, or Augustine, and see which of their works were known to the Anglo-Saxons. The first volume of SASLC has recently been published (it follows on the heels of a *Trial Version* published in 1990);[2] this first

---

[1] The book was severely reviewed by Helmut Gneuss, *Anglia*, 89 (1971), 129–34, and L. Wallach, *Journal of English and Germanic Philology*, 68 (1969), 156–61. Ogilvy later issued an extensive set of 'addenda and corrigenda' in *Mediaevalia*, 7 (1984 for 1981), 281–325 (repr. as *Old English Newsletter, Subsidia*, 11 (1985)).

[2] *Sources of Anglo-Saxon Literary Culture*, i, ed. Biggs et al. This volume does not of

volume starts at the beginning of the alphabet and contains entries for two authors named Abbo, one of Fleury, the other of Saint-Germain in Paris, and a lengthy entry (464 pages) of so-called 'acta sanctorum', in effect a complete listing of all saints' *passiones* and *vitae* known in Anglo-Saxon England. These three entries are very thoroughly done; but one has to say, without being unduly pessimistic, that, judging from the fact that it has taken fifteen years to produce this first volume, it may be several centuries before we are able to make use of a complete SASLC.[3]

Fontes Anglo-Saxonici, the Oxford-based project, has made much more tangible progress, and now consists of a database approaching some 30,000 entries pertaining to some 1,200 texts, the result of comprehensive sourcing of most Old English authors and a smaller number of Anglo-Latin authors (notably some works of Bede).[4] One is now in a position to form a synoptic view, for example, of what patristic sources were employed by the authors of Old English homilies. But because the major Anglo-Latin authors are not yet represented in the database—Archbishop Theodore, Aldhelm, the majority of Bede's writings, Alcuin, Byrhtferth, and others—any search of the database can as yet give only a partial answer to questions concerning what Latin authors were read or studied in Anglo-Saxon England. In spite of these two noble enterprises, therefore, one is still left more or less on one's own when it comes to forming an overall picture of what books were available in Anglo-Saxon libraries.

In the discussion of citations by Anglo-Saxon (principally Latin) authors which follows, I shall make a distinction between quotations and verbal reminiscences, because the evidence of each needs to be evaluated differently.[5] A quotation provides the safest sort of

itself supersede *Sources of Anglo-Saxon Literary Culture: A Trial Version*, ed. Biggs, Hill, and Szarmach, which includes a number of entries extending past AC-.

[3] One completed entry, which will form part of a future SASLC volume, has been printed separately: *Ambrose in Anglo-Saxon England*, ed. Bankert, Wegmann, and Wright.

[4] *Fontes Anglo-Saxonici* is accessible on the World Wide Web at <http://fontes.en-glish.ox.ac.uk> (accessed 13/12/04). A CD-ROM version of the database was issued in 2002, but does not incorporate the frequent updatings which have been added to the database since then.

[5] There is helpful orientation in the use of printed concordances and electronic databases in Berlioz et al., *Identifier sources et citations*, 77–92; and for the distinction between quotation and allusion, cf. pp. 5–6, where four categories of verbal debt are distinguished (*emprunt, citation, allusion*, and *démarquage*). The remainder of the book deals with source-identification in such medieval genres as proverbs, liturgy, civil and canon law, hagiography, councils and synods, sermons, and *exempla*.

evidence when an Anglo-Saxon author names his source and then quotes that source verbatim and *in extenso*. A reminiscence consists of a collocation of several words taken, often involuntarily, from an antecedent source. Given that the antecedent source is not named, there is always scope for doubt about the nature of the debt. Some examples will clarify the distinction I am trying to draw;[6] and I begin with quotations.

QUOTATIONS

The writings of Aldhelm provide a useful introduction to the problems. Aldhelm apparently had access to a substantial library at Malmesbury, to judge from the list of quotations in his writings which Rudolf Ehwald, Aldhelm's great editor, was able to compile by way of supplying an index of 'loci classici et ecclesiastici'.[7] Aldhelm's library evidently contained some astonishing rarities. I mentioned in the previous chapter (above, p. 68) that at one point in his treatise *De metris*, Aldhelm had quoted two lines from Seneca's tragedy *Agamemnon*.[8] This fact is interesting enough in itself, for Seneca's *Tragoediae* were otherwise unknown between late antiquity and the late eleventh century.[9] Aldhelm prefaces his quotation with the statement, 'ut Lucius Annaeus Seneca in sexto uolumine': that is to say, 'Seneca, in the sixth roll', where *uolumine* evidently refers to a papyrus roll. Could Aldhelm really have had access to papyrus rolls of Seneca's *Tragoediae*? Papyrus was certainly used for documentary purposes during the early Middle Ages, above all by the papal chancery, but also for private charters in Italy and Merovingian Gaul.[10] A few papyrus manuscripts survive from late antiquity and

---

[6] The following discussion is based on evidence assembled in App. E.

[7] *Aldhelmi Opera*, ed. Ehwald, 544–6. The contents of Ehwald's index have been incorporated and expanded in my App. E.

[8] Ibid. 194. Aldhelm quotes *Agamemnon*, lines 729, 787 (*Seneca: Agamemnon*, ed. Tarrant, 137, 140). Tarrant also reproduced Ehwald's text of the *De metris* concerning the *Agamemnon* (ibid. 101).

[9] *TxtTrans*, 378. On the transmission of Seneca's *Tragoediae*, the essential discussions are Schmidt, 'Rezeption und Überlieferung', 17–31; and *Seneca: Agamemnon*, ed. Tarrant, 23–87. There is one manuscript of Seneca's *Tragoediae* of pre-Aldhelmian date (R = Milan, Biblioteca Ambrosiana, G. 82 sup., of the 5th c.); but since it contains only 117 lines of the *Medea* and 76 of the *Oedipus*, it is of no help in placing Aldhelm's quotations from the *Agamemnon* within the tradition.

[10] See the (still useful) discussion of Wattenbach, *Das Schriftwesen im Mittelalter*, 96–111, as well as Santifaller, *Beiträge zur Geschichte der Beschreibstoffe*, i. 25–76. Needless perhaps to say, papyrus documents were not issued in the form of rolls (Wattenbach, 104:

the early Middle Ages.[11] However, these books are almost invariably in the form of *codices*, not of rolls.[12] In any case, given the damp English climate, it is unlikely that papyrus books, whether in the form of *codices* or rolls, would survive for long,[13] and therefore that Aldhelm is most unlikely to have been quoting Seneca's *Agamemnon* directly from a papyrus roll. This implies that the manuscript which Aldhelm was using, or its ancestor, preserved as rubrics an indication of what *Tragoediae* of Seneca had been copied from what rolls at the time when they were transferred from papyrus roll to parchment codex.[14] The *Agamemnon*, according to Aldhelm's note, had been contained in the sixth such roll. Now the earliest surviving manuscript of Seneca's *Tragoediae*, the so-called 'Codex Etruscus' (a late eleventh-century manuscript now in Florence, Biblioteca Medicea Laurenziana, Plut. XXXVII. 13 (N. Italy [?Pomposa], s. xi^{ex})), the principal representative of what editors call the E-class, transmits nine plays;[15] in the sequence of these plays the *Agamemnon* occurs in seventh position. The apparent discrepancy between Aldhelm's description *in sexto uolumine* and the play's position as number seven in the sequence in the Codex Etruscus led Ehwald to suspect

'der Gebrauch der Rollen scheint früh abgekommen zu sein'). None of the sources discussed by Wattenbach and Santifaller pertains to Anglo-Saxon England.

[11] See, in general, Tjäder, *Die nichtliterarischen lateinischen Papyri*. Surviving examples include: Paris, BNF, lat. 11641, etc., of Luxeuil origin and datable to *c*.700, made up of gatherings of three or four papyrus bifolia, containing Augustine, *Epistulae*; St Gallen, SB, 226 + Zurich, Zentralbibliothek, RP 5 and RP 6, of southern French origin and late 7th-c. date, containing Isidore, *Synonyma*; Geneva, Bibliothèque publique et universitaire, Pap. Lat. VI, a 5th-c. fragment containing unidentified pre-Justinianic legislation; Vienna, ÖNB, lat. 2160, etc. of southern Italian origin and 6th-c. date, containing Hilary, *De trinitate* [CPL 433]; and Paris, BNF, lat. 8913 + 8914, of late 6th-c. date and Burgundian origin, containing Avitus, *Homiliae* [CPL 994] (see Gasnault, 'Fragment retrouvé'). Again, none of these books pertains to Anglo-Saxon England.

[12] The only fragments of papyrus rolls of late antique date, containing Latin texts and surviving from the western empire, are Pommersfelden, Gräflich Schönborn'sche Bibliothek, Lat. pap. 7–13, of Italian origin and datable to *c*.500, containing Evagrius, *Altercatio*; and Lat. pap. 14, of 5th-c. Italian date, containing a text of Nicetas of Remesiana.

[13] In fact the only evidence pertaining to Anglo-Saxon familiarity with papyrus is one of the *Enigmata Tullii* (a text of presumed, if not demonstrable, Anglo-Saxon origin) whose subject is *De papiro* (no. xxvii: CCSL 133A: 753). The possibility has recently been mooted that a papyrus fragment of Gregory's *Hom. .xl. in Euangelia*, now London, BL, Cotton Titus C. xv, fo. 1 (s. vi/vii) derives from a book that 'came to England with the early missionaries from Rome, perhaps even with St Augustine of Canterbury': Babcock, 'A Papyrus Codex'.

[14] There is a splendidly clear account of this process by Roberts and Skeat, *The Birth of the Codex*.

[15] On the 'Codex Etruscus', see *Seneca: Agamemnon*, ed. Tarrant, 24–8.

that Aldhelm's *sexto* should be emended to *septimo*.[16] But his proposed emendation was based on the assumption that each play of Seneca occupied a single papyrus roll. (It should be noted, however, that there is considerable discrepancy in length of the six plays which precede the *Agamemnon* in the 'Codex Etruscus', with the *Phoenissae* at 664 lines being only about half as long as the *Hercules Furens* or the *Phaedra*, both of which are about 1,300 lines long: so that one roll might—in theory—have contained two plays.) It is equally an assumption, unverifiable in the circumstances, that the sequence of the plays in the 'Codex Etruscus' reproduces the sequence of the plays as they were transmitted in rolls. In any event, the two lines of the *Agamemnon* quoted by Aldhelm contain one variant which associates them unambiguously with the text as preserved in the Codex Etruscus, rather than with the other branch of the tradition (the A-class, which was dominant in England and elsewhere in the later Middle Ages).[17] Accordingly, Aldhelm's brief quotation of two lines of Seneca's *Agamemnon* can throw a tiny bit of light on a textual transmission which is otherwise wholly obscure at this period.

There were further riches in Aldhelm's library. At one place in the same treatise (*De metris*) he discusses the word *stamen*, and illustrates it by saying 'unde Lucanus de Orpheo', and then quotes two lines:[18]

> Nunc plenas posuere colos et stamina Parcae
> multaque dilatis haeserunt saecula filis.

We know from the so-called Vacca Life of Lucan,[19] and from Servius (commenting on *Georgics* iv. 492), that Lucan did indeed compose a poem entitled *Orpheus*, but it has not come down to us.[20] With the exception of two verses quoted by Servius, Aldhelm is the only witness to the text of Lucan's lost poem. One of Aldhelm's disciples or colleagues, the anonymous author of the *Liber monstrorum* [CPL 1124], refers explicitly to the *Orpheus* on two occasions, without

---

[16] *Aldhelmi Opera*, ed. Ehwald, 194 [*app. crit.*]: 'in cod. Etrusco Agamemnon septimum locum habet, qui numerus forsitan sit restituendus'.

[17] The variant is in *Agamemnon* 729: *domus* in Aldhelm and the 'Codex Etruscus', against *domos* in the A-class (PCS). On the differences between the E- and A-branches of the tradition, see *Seneca: Agamemnon*, ed. Tarrant, 52–71.

[18] *Aldhelmi Opera*, ed. Ehwald, 159.

[19] The Vacca Life is ed. C. Hosius in *M. Annaei Lucani De bello ciuili*, 334–6 at 335 ('et ex tempore Orphea scriptum in experimentum aduersus complures ediderat poetas').

[20] *The Fragmentary Latin Poets*, ed. Courtney, 352–3.

however quoting the text, but implying that he had access to it, presumably in the same library as Aldhelm.[21]

Another rarity in Aldhelm's library deserves mention, in so far as it was overlooked by Ehwald. At two points in his treatise *De pedum regulis*, Aldhelm quotes opinions on grammatical matters of one *Valerius grammaticus* (or *Grammaticus*).[22] First, on the scansion of the verb *liquor* ('to be fluid'):

For if *liquor* is the verb of the third conjugation [i.e. not the noun *liquor*, 'liquid'], or of the third 'order', as Valerius *grammaticus* liked to call it, it is a trochee, as Vergil scans it in his *Georgics*, 'canis cum montibus umor / liquitur et Zephiro putris se gleba resolvit' (*Georg.* i. 43–4).[23]

The second citation of Valerius *grammaticus* concerns the inceptive verb *lentesco* ('to become viscous'), 'which Valerius says is derived from the first conjugation',[24] that is, from the first-conjugation verb *lento* ('to make flexible, to protract'). Who is this Valerius *grammaticus*? According to Ehwald, he is otherwise unknown.[25] But if we recall that Aldhelm's first quotation from Valerius concerned a verb used in Vergil's *Georgics* (*liquor*), and note that the rare verb *lentesco* is also used by Vergil in the *Georgics* to describe the quality of rich topsoil (*Georg.* ii. 250: 'sed picis in morem ad digitos lentescit habendo'), an intriguing possibility arises: namely the famous scholar and textual critic M. Valerius Probus, who taught at Beirut during the first century AD, and is known to have commented extensively on the transmitted text of Vergil.[26] Ancient testimonies referring to the scholarship of Valerius Probus have been helpfully collected by Josef Aistermann,[27] and it is clear from these testimonies that Probus devoted considerable attention *inter alia* to Vergil's *Georgics*.[28] (It is

---

[21] See Lapidge, '*Beowulf*, Aldhelm', 169 (*ALL* ii. 289). The two explicit references to Lucan's *Orpheus* in the *Liber monstrorum* are found at i. 5 and ii. 7 (ed. Orchard in *Pride and Prodigies*, 260, 292).

[22] On the question of whether *grammaticus* in antiquity was a cognomen (*Grammaticus*) or was simply an occupational title, see Kaster, *Guardians of Language*, 453–4.

[23] *Aldhelmi Opera*, ed. Ehwald, 153.   [24] Ibid. 172.

[25] Ibid. 153 n. 2: 'Valerius grammaticus est ignotus, quem laudat Aldhelmus etiam p. 172.'

[26] See Timpanaro, *Per la storia della filologia virgiliana*, 77–127, and Zetzel, *Latin Textual Criticism*, 41–54 (but see also the acute comments in the review by H. D. Jocelyn in *Gnomon*, 55 (1983), 307–11). It has become conventional to refer to him as Probus (not to be confused with the shadowy 4th-c. grammarian Probus, author of the *Catholica*: LLA 522.3, Kaster 127) rather than Valerius, but Aldhelm was not to know that.

[27] *De M. Valerio Probo Berytio capita quattuor*, ed. Aistermann. The 135 testimonia are printed at the end of the book (following p. 156), and are paginated in roman numerals (pp. i–lxii).   [28] Ibid., pp. ix–x (nos. 5–10).

not surprising that an anonymous commentary on the *Bucolica* and *Georgica*, which first came to light in 1493 and was first printed in 1507, should have been attributed to Valerius Probus; but modern scholarship rejects this attribution.[29]) Certainly Aistermann had no hesitation in identifying Aldhelm's Valerius *grammaticus* with M. Valerius Probus, and he included the two quotations from Aldhelm's *De pedum regulis* among the *testimonia* of the first-century grammarian.[30] If the identification is sound, Aldhelm's library boasted a copy of yet another important ancient text which has subsequently been lost.[31]

Aldhelm certainly had access to other classical texts which have not otherwise survived, as we have seen in the case of Lucan's *Orpheus*. By the same token, Aldhelm on three occasions quotes in his *De metris* from a poem entitled 'Gratiarum actio' ('Thanksgiving') by an otherwise wholly unknown classical poet named Paulus Quaestor.[32] Edward Courtney, who includes Aldhelm's quotations of this poem in his recent edition of fragmentary Latin poets, suggests that Paulus' full title was probably 'quaestor sacri palatii', an office established by Diocletian, with the implication that he was writing no earlier than the late third, and perhaps not before the fourth, century.[33] In any event, beyond Aldhelm's three quotations, we know nothing of the Late Latin poet Paulus Quaestor.

Aldhelm's library was evidently well stocked with classical and late antique texts, to judge not only from these rarities, but also from the

[29] There are two modern editions: by Keil, *M. Valerii Probi in Vergilii Bucolica et Georgica Commentarius*, and by Hagen, in *Appendix Serviana*, 321–90. On the unsatisfactory nature of these editions, and of the need for a new edition based more intelligently on humanist copies of the text, see Gioseffi, *Studi sul commento a Virgilio*, esp. 41–134. In any case, as far as the present discussion is concerned, the commentary contains no discussion of *Georg.* i. 43–4 and ii. 250; and it must be said that the concerns of the anonymous commentator are topographical and mythological rather than strictly philological, as were those of M. Valerius Probus (see *testimonia* nos. 67–125 in *De M. Valerio Probo*, ed. Aistermann, pp. xxvi–lii) and the Valerius *grammaticus* quoted by Aldhelm.

[30] *De M. Valerio Probo*, ed. Aistermann, 56: 'Nam quod Valerium dixit Aldhelmus, quin de Valerio Probo . . . agatur, dubitandum non est.' The Aldhelmian *testimonia* are printed by Aistermann as nos. 64 (corresponding to *Aldhelmi Opera*, ed. Ehwald, 153) and 96 (Ehwald, 96).

[31] It is perhaps worth noting that the (lost) 10th-c. inventory of books from Bobbio (Becker, *Catalogi*, no. 32; see above, p. 59) included an item 'libros Valerii Probi III' (= *De M. Valerio Probo*, ed. Aistermann, p. v (*test.* no. 39)).

[32] *Aldhelmi Opera*, ed. Ehwald, 79, 86, 87.

[33] *The Fragmentary Latin Poets*, ed. Courtney, 428. In *The Prosopography of the Late Roman Empire*, i, ed. Jones, Martindale, and Morris, the sole entry for a *quaestor* (whether of the imperial palace or otherwise) is the Paulus Quaestor cited by Aldhelm: p. 684 (Paulus 7).

standard classical authors, poets mostly, from whom he quotes.[34]
Were other Anglo-Saxon libraries similarly stocked? Anglo–Latin
authors would sometimes like us to think so. Thus Byrhtferth, writing
his *Vita S. Oswaldi* (the earliest Life of Oswald, archbishop of York,
who died in 992) at Ramsey sometime around the year 1000, notes that
(I quote) 'if the comic poet Turpilius, treating the vicissitudes of
letters', had been present, he would not have been able to describe
Oswald's greatness.[35] Sextus Turpilius [LLA 131.7] was a contemporary of Terence (second century BC) who, like Terence, translated a
number of Greek plays of the New Comedy into Latin. All these plays
have perished, except for a handful of fragments. It would beggar the
imagination to think that Byrhtferth at Ramsey, writing *c*. AD 1000,
had access to even one play of Turpilius. He did not. He was simply
quoting from a letter of Jerome (who in the fourth century AD could
conceivably have had access to Turpilius), in which Jerome referred to
Turpilius' comment on the transience of letters.[36] Byrhtferth, characteristically, suppressed the fact that his reference to Turpilius was
drawn at second-hand from Jerome. But at least we now know that
Byrhtferth had read Jerome's Letters, and hence that a manuscript of
the collection was available at Ramsey in the late tenth century (no
such manuscript appears to survive).[37]

Similarly, a contemporary of Byrhtferth, the anonymous Winchester poet who produced a metrical Life of the Breton saint Iudoc
(BHL 4512; ICL 16714), at one point concludes a hexameter by
saying that the saint and his patron embraced each other when Iudoc
returned from Rome, 'both men harmoniously giving dear embraces':
'amplexus karos dantes concorditer ambo' (line 372).[38] The unusual,
indeed unique, hexameter cadence *concorditer ambo*, occurs in only

---

[34] See below, App. E (pp. 178–91). Of classical Latin poets, Aldhelm had first-hand
knowledge of: Claudian, Lucan (ten of the thirteen lines which he quotes from the *Bellum
ciuile* are not found in any grammarian), Juvenal, Persius, Terence, and Vergil. (His
knowledge of these poets is proved by his verbatim citations in his metrical treatises.) He
possibly also knew: Horace, Ovid, and Statius. (His knowledge of these three poets is
suggested by verbal reminiscences in his own verse.)

[35] Byrhtferth, *Vita S. Oswaldi* iii. 9: 'Turpilius comicus, tractans de uicissitudine
literarum, si adesset, non quiuisset egregia ipsius gesta reuoluere' (ed. in Raine, *Historians
of the Church of York*, i. 425–6).

[36] *Ep.* viii. 1 (CSEL 54: 31); see Sheerin, 'Turpilius and St Jerome'.

[37] See below, Catalogue, p. 315.

[38] Lapidge, 'A Metrical *Vita S. Iudoci*', 292, 305 [*comm.*]. This example is properly a
reminiscence, not a quotation: I press it into service here for the possible light which it
might seem to throw on the transmission of a poet who was an older contemporary of
Turpilius.

one poet previous to the tenth century: Q. Ennius, who in book i of his *Annales* (line 110 Skutsch) had written the hexameter 'aeternum seritote diem concorditer ambo' ('join harmoniously together the eternal day').[39] One would be staggered to think that there was a copy of Ennius' *Annales* at Winchester in the late tenth century; and the more likely explanation is that the Winchester poet remembered the Ennian cadence from having read it in the grammarian Charisius, who alone of the Latin grammarians preserves this line.[40] But at least we now know that a copy of Charisius was available at Winchester in the late tenth century: a not unimportant fact, given that no copy of Charisius is found among surviving Anglo-Saxon manuscripts.[41]

In assessing quotations of Latin authors, then, one has always to bear in mind the possibility of intermediary sources. An excellent methodological guide to this problem may be found in Robert Maxwell Ogilvie's study of the classical writings known to Lactantius.[42] Lactantius (*c*.240–*c*.320), particularly in his *Diuinae institutiones* [CPL 85], quotes from a wide range of authors in his defence of Christianity, and in attempting to reconstruct his library, Ogilvie analysed his quotations from these authors, classical, biblical, patristic. In the case of classical poets, for example, Ogilvie analysed Lactantius' quotations from Cicero, Ennius, Horace, Juvenal, Lucan, Lucretius, Naevius, Ovid, Persius, Plautus, Propertius, Terence, and Vergil, in order to determine how many of these he had actually read. Ogilvie demonstrates (convincingly and surprisingly) that Lactantius took at second hand, from intermediary sources, his quotations of Cicero, Ennius, Juvenal, Lucan, Naevius, Plautus, and Propertius. The only poets he can be shown actually to have read are Horace, Lucretius, Ovid, Persius, Terence, and Vergil. It is a sobering thought that, even in the early fourth century—the *Diuinae institutiones* were composed at Rome during the decade 303 × 313—the archaic Latin poets (Cicero, Ennius, Naevius) were known only at second hand, and that the remainder were known presumably because they formed part of the school curriculum. And it was

---

[39] *The Annals of Q. Ennius*, ed. Skutsch, 78, 250 [*comm*.].
[40] Charisius, *Ars grammatica* (GL i. 196).   [41] See below, Catalogue, p. 297.
[42] Ogilvie, *The Library of Lactantius*; cf., however, the severe review by E. Heck, *Gnomon*, 52 (1980), 572–4, whose principal criticism is that Ogilvie derived most of the information in his book from the *apparatus fontium* of Samuel Brandt's edition of the *Diuinae institutiones* (CSEL 19; Vienna, 1890). But I should have thought that the reason why editors such as Brandt provide *apparatus fontium* is to enable subsequent scholars such as Ogilvie to reconstruct the library resources available to the author in question.

principally these same authors—Horace, Ovid, Persius, Terence, and Vergil (leaving aside for the moment the doubtful case of Lucretius)—whose works were transmitted to the Middle Ages and served as the staple of the medieval school curriculum, alongside a corpus of Christian-Latin poets.

If many works of Latin literature were unknown at first hand to Lactantius in the early fourth century, it is hardly surprising that they should not have been known at first hand to Aldhelm nearly four centuries later. Aldhelm evidently derived his knowledge of certain republican authors from intermediate sources, principally Priscian but also other Late Latin grammarians such as Audax. Thus in the space of a brief paragraph of his *De pedum regulis* (c. 134), in which he discussed words which naturally constitute a second paeon,[43] such as *nouacula* and *pecuscula*, Aldhelm drew a sequence of three examples from Cicero's speech *In Pisonem*, from the *Annales* of Ennius, and from Sallust, *Bellum Iugurthinum*. As the context reveals in each case, however, all three examples were taken from the *Institutiones grammaticae* of Priscian, a work which Aldhelm had obviously digested thoroughly.[44] By the same token, Aldhelm evidently derived his knowledge of the obscure grammarian Albinus [Kaster 182] indirectly from Audax, rather than from first-hand acquaintance with a grammarian whose writings are otherwise unknown.[45]

In the case of Juvenal, one might think that the substantial number of named quotations from the *Saturae* was a reliable marker of Aldhelm's knowledge of that poet. He quotes Juvenal on nine occasions.[46] Of the nine quotations, four can be located in Priscian's *Institutiones grammaticae*. Of these four, one shares a striking variant with Priscian against other manuscripts of the tradition. Whereas the text of Juvenal *Sat.* xi. 203, as printed by its most recent editor (Wendell Clausen) reads 'nostra bibat uernum contracta cuticula

---

[43] A paeon is a metrical foot consisting of one long and three short syllables, named 'first', 'second', etc. depending on which syllable was long. Thus a second paeon had the metrical structure ⏑ — ⏑ ⏑.

[44] *Aldhelmi Opera*, ed. Ehwald, 186–7: Cicero, *In Pisonem* xxv. 2, from GL ii. 109; Ennius, *Annales* i. 14 Skutsch, from GL ii. 97; and Sallust, *Bellum Iugurthinum* c. 2, from GL ii. 95. Note, however, that elsewhere Aldhelm quotes a holospondaic line of Ennius (*dubia* 9 Skutsch) as 'hi producuntur legati Minturnenses' (Ehwald, 84), whereas Audax—from whom Aldhelm is thought to have derived the line—gives it as 'introducuntur legati Minturnenses' (GL vii. 338). Is the variant due to Aldhelm's carelessness, or was he drawing on a source other than Audax?

[45] *Aldhelmi Opera*, ed. Ehwald, 82, from GL vii. 339.

[46] Ibid. 79 (*Sat.* x. 133, xiii. 118), 85 (xiii. 19, 23), 164 (ix. 50), 167 (xiv. 129–30), 183 (xi. 203), 184 (iii. 97, xiv. 280).

solem' ('let my wrinkled old skin drink in the spring-time sunshine'), the text as quoted by Aldhelm and Priscian reads 'combibet [Aldhelm: cumbibet] aestivum contracta cuticula solem' ('my wrinkled old skin shall drink up the summer sun'). The shared variant was taken by Manitius and Ehwald to prove that Aldhelm took the line indirectly from Priscian, not directly from the text of Juvenal.[47] But did he? Is it not equally possible that both Aldhelm and Priscian had independent access to a variant text of Juvenal, one that has not otherwise survived? The early transmission of Juvenal is murky, to say the least, and there is little agreement on the extent to which late antique scribes and readers tinkered with the text.[48] Furthermore, there is the problem of where Aldhelm found the remaining five lines of Juvenal, which are found neither in Priscian nor in any other ancient grammarian. It is striking that, when citing Juvenal, Aldhelm always specifies the very books from which his citations are taken (e.g. 'unde Iunius Iuvenalis satiricus libro .III.', 'Iuvenalis satirarum libro .V.', 'unde Iuvenalis libro .V.', etc.).[49] This suggests that he had access to a complete edition of the Satires, divided into the five books in which Juvenal issued them. In any case, the question of whether Aldhelm knew Juvenal only at second hand should be left open until such time as an intermediary source which contains all Aldhelm's quotations can be identified.

More complex still is the question of Aldhelm's knowledge of Lucretius, De rerum natura. When discussing words which naturally constitute dactyls in his De pedum regulis (c. 120), Aldhelm supplies a list of compounds in -ger, such as setiger and aliger, and when he comes to mention laniger, he adds that the word is illustrated in a hexameter which he quotes without naming the author: 'Lanigerae pecudes et equorum duellica proles'.[50] The line is in fact from Lucretius (DRN ii. 661). Because Aldhelm does not name Lucretius, one might suspect that the line was simply lifted from a grammarian.[51] The problem is that the line is not quoted by any of the Late

---

[47] Manitius, 'Zu Aldhelm und Baeda', 566, 593; and Aldhelmi Opera, ed. Ehwald, 183 n. 2, followed by Highet, Juvenal the Satirist, 192: 'it seems that he [sc. Aldhelm] took all his quotations from the master grammarian Priscian'.

[48] TxtTrans, 200–3, esp. p. 200 with n. 6.

[49] Altogether Juvenal composed sixteen Saturae (the last is a mere fragment), which he issued in five books at various times between c. AD 107 and 130, as books I (Sat. i–v), II (Sat. vi), III (Sat. vii–ix), IV (Sat. x–xii), and V (Sat. xiii–xvi).

[50] Aldhelmi Opera, ed. Ehwald, 165.

[51] For example, Bede in his De arte metrica (CCSL 123A: 130) quotes nominatim a line of Lucretius (DRN vi. 868); but the context of the quotation is a discussion of the

Latin grammarians edited in Keil's great *Grammatici Latini*.[52] Nevertheless, Ehwald argued that Aldhelm 'seems to have taken the line, not from Lucretius, but from some grammarian, perhaps Nonius Marcellus'.[53] The *Compendiosa doctrina* by the African grammarian Nonius Marcellus is a vast dictionary of republican (hence archaic) Latin which was composed at an uncertain date, perhaps in the early fourth century.[54] In fact Nonius quotes the relevant line of Lucretius on two occasions, once in book ii when discussing the word *buceriae*, and again in book iii discussing the word *greges*.[55] Could Aldhelm have taken the line of Lucretius from Nonius?

The problem is that no Anglo-Saxon author can be shown unambiguously to have known the *Compendiosa doctrina*. In the *apparatus fontium* to his edition of Bede's *De orthographia*,[56] C. W. Jones adduced no fewer than twenty-one verbal debts to the *Compendiosa doctrina*.[57] Among these, Jones prefaced twelve with the indication 'cf.' On examination, all of the debts prefaced by 'cf.' turn out to be illusory. For example, Bede's discussion of the words *senecta* and *senium* (lines 1089–94) is said by Bede himself to be taken from Augustine—*Haec Augustinus*—and Jones correctly identifies Bede's source in Augustine's *Enarrationes in psalmos*; but nevertheless Jones adds a note, 'cf. . . . Nonius I, 492 (I, pp. 3–5; III,

circumstances in which *u* is treated as a consonant, which shows unambiguously that the discussion was lifted, along with the quotation of Lucretius, from the grammarian Audax (GL vii. 329).

[52] As can be seen from the thorough *Index scriptorum* to GL compiled by F. Boettner (GL vii. 579–668).

[53] *Aldhelmi Opera*, ed. Ehwald, 165 n. 1: 'Hunc versum non ex Lucretio ipso, sed ex grammatico aliquo, fortasse ex Nonio Marcello . . . Aldhelmus desumpsisse videtur.' Ehwald made similar suggestions concerning Nonius elsewhere in his edition of Aldhelm: pp. 164 n. 2, 166 n. 2, and 169 n. 1. Manitius ('Zu Aldhelm und Baeda', 599–600) adds a further three possible debts of Aldhelm to Nonius.

[54] *Nonii Marcelli De compendiosa doctrina*, ed. Lindsay. I cite Lindsay's edition by volume and page number (confusingly, Lindsay's own index is keyed not to his own text but to that of J. Mercerus (Paris, 1614)).

[55] Ibid. 113, 307 respectively.

[56] CCSL 123A: 7–57.

[57] See the 'Index auctorum' to Jones's edition of Bede's *opera didascalica* (CCSL 123C: 782–3). In fact twenty-seven debts are listed, but these include several repetitions. Elsewhere, Jones ('Bede's Place in Medieval Schools', 266) claimed that Bede in his *De orthographia* 'certainly used tracts of seventeen grammarians, and probably ten more'; but the more rigorous examination of Bede's sources by Dionisotti has reduced this number to 'at most seven, probably in fewer volumes: Caper, Agroecius, Virgilius Maro Grammaticus, a grammar of the Charisian group, a collection of *idiomata* and *differentiae*, a *de latinitate* (Caper?) and an [unidentified] orthographical work': 'On Bede, Grammars and Greek', 121.

p. 790)'.[58] Nonius discusses the word *senium*: there is no further link between his discussion and Bede's, who has explicitly taken his information from Augustine. Similarly, Bede draws his discussion of *ordibor* and *ordiar* (line 789) directly from the *De orthographia* of Flavius Caper; in his *apparatus*, Jones correctly identifies Caper as the source, but adds 'cf. Nonius (I, p. 57)', where, under the headword *ordire*, Nonius quotes Accius ('non parvam rem ordibor'). Bede's source, in other words, is Caper, and the reference to Nonius is otiose. Sometimes Jones's references to Nonius only serve to point up differences between his information and Bede's, as when Bede asserts (line 613) that *larba* is to be spelled with *b* (i.e. not with *u*, as in *larua*). Jones refers us to Nonius (I, p. 64), where Nonius quotes a republican expression *cerriti et larvati*—in other words, an example of the very spelling which Bede urges his readers to avoid. In sum, the twelve parallels to Nonius adduced by Jones and marked 'cf.' fail to establish any link between Nonius and Bede, and it is clear that Jones did not regard them as indicators of Bede's debt to Nonius; they merely provide supplementary information for the reader's benefit, and properly have no place in an *apparatus fontium*.

With respect to the remaining nine parallels which are cited by Jones but not marked 'cf.', there is at least the suspicion that Jones regarded them as *possible* sources for information in Bede's *De orthographia*.[59] Unfortunately, none of the parallels is sufficient to establish a certain link between Nonius and Bede. For example, Bede stipulates (line 1221) that the correct spelling of *uerbex* is with an initial *u* (i.e. not *berbex*); as source for this observation, Jones cites Nonius (I, p. 278), who provides a quotation from Varro's treatise *De uita populi Romani* to illustrate the spelling *uerbecem*. But except for their insistence on the spelling with initial *u*, there is no further verbal link between Nonius and Bede, and in his *apparatus fontium* Jones goes on to list further parallels in Charisius and Cassiodorus (the latter of whom was quite clearly drawing on Nonius, as the quotation from Varro demonstrates). Again, Bede at one point discusses the word *contagium* and various related forms (lines 256-7): 'Contagium et contagia neutro genere dicenda; et haec contagio feminino'. Jones

---

[58] Jones's reference is to the pagination of the edition of Nonius by Lindsay, cited above, n. 54.

[59] These nine 'possible' debts to Nonius are listed in App. E, below, p. 220. One might add, for what it is worth, that all the nine parallels from Nonius occur in books i–iii of the *Compendiosa doctrina* (cf. the discussion of the manuscript transmission of Nonius, below, p. 104).

cites the discussion of Nonius (I, p. 292): 'CONTAGIO feminino genere appellatur' (followed by a quotation from Sallust) . . . 'Contagia neutro Lucretius' (followed by a quotation). Bede's information *could*, perhaps, have been derived from Nonius, but the parallel is not close, and Jones goes on to cite (apparently as equally possible sources) Marius Victorinus and Charisius. All the nine parallels to Nonius adduced by Jones (but not marked 'cf.') are of this sort. None of them, in my view, is sufficiently close to establish a certain link between Bede and Nonius. Bede, therefore, cannot be used to prove that the *Compendiosa doctrina* of Nonius circulated in early Anglo-Saxon England.

No surviving Anglo-Saxon manuscript preserves the *Compendiosa doctrina*. Is it possible, nevertheless, that the work could have been known to Aldhelm or Bede in late seventh-century England? Some answer to this question is provided by consideration of the manuscript transmission of the *Compendiosa doctrina*.[60] No manuscript of the work earlier than the ninth century survives. All surviving manuscripts descend from a single (lost) archetype, which was divided into three volumes, one containing books i–iii, another the whole of book iv, and the third books v–xx. Each of these three parts enjoyed a different transmission. Since the quotations of Lucretius with which we are concerned occur in books ii and iii, we may focus our attention on the first part. The principal witness to this first part (books i–iii) is a manuscript now in Leiden, Bibliotheek der Rijksuniversiteit, Voss. Lat. F. 73, known to editors as L, and written at Tours in the early ninth century; in the opinion of Bernhard Bischoff, it could even have been written during Alcuin's lifetime.[61] W. M. Lindsay, whose Teubner edition of Nonius we still use, was able to prove, on the basis of a portion of text of book iv transferred in L to the very beginning of book i, and therefore representing a dislocated leaf in the archetype, that L was copied directly from the archetype itself.[62] Given that L probably dates from the lifetime of Alcuin, the question next arises of whether the lost archetype could have been a manuscript brought to Tours from England by Alcuin. A manuscript written in England before *c*.800 would no doubt have contained Anglo-Saxon symptoms (letter-forms and abbreviations), and one would expect that some of these would be reproduced

[60] See *TxtTrans*, 248–52 (L. D. Reynolds).
[61] Bischoff, *MS*, iii. 67: 'wahrscheinlich noch zu Alkuins Lebzeiten'.
[62] Lindsay, 'A Study of the Leyden MS of Nonius Marcellus', 30.

in L. Yet Lindsay, who knew as much about Insular abbreviations as anyone ever has, noted none.[63] There is, in other words, no evidence that the text of the *Compendiosa doctrina* was ever known in, or transmitted by way of, England. I am therefore unable to accept Ehwald's hypothesis that Aldhelm derived his single quotation of Lucretius from Nonius.

This takes us back to the original question of whether Aldhelm could have read Lucretius at first hand. Lucretius has a very distinctive poetic style, comprising various sorts of archaism and above all his relentless use of so-called 'poetic compounds'.[64] If Aldhelm had indeed read Lucretius, one might expect that these features of his verse would be imitated by the Anglo-Saxon poet. Yet there is very little evidence of Lucretian diction in Aldhelm's verse.[65] But it should be recalled that the distinctive poetic diction of Lucan—whose *Bellum ciuile* Aldhelm had undoubtedly read, since in his metrical treatises he quotes ten lines from it which are not found in any grammarian—also left no trace in Aldhelm's verse.[66] The question of Aldhelm's knowledge of Lucretius should be left open, therefore.

In short, one must beware of assuming too quickly that a quotation in an Anglo-Latin author derives from an intermediary source. Each quotation needs to be evaluated individually. A number of years ago the late Peter Hunter Blair argued that, of the seventy-eight quotations of Vergil to be found in Bede's didactic treatises (*De arte metrica*, *De orthographia*, *De schematibus et tropis*), seventy-one could be found in grammarians (the figures derive from Boettner's *index scriptorum* to Keil's *Grammatici Latini*) and he thought it 'reasonable to suppose that the remaining seven were derived at second hand from similar sources'. He concluded: 'It seems clear beyond all doubt that the seventy-eight Virgilian quotations in the school treatises were all derived directly or indirectly from the grammarians and not from Virgil's own works.'[67] He then noted a few further Vergilian quotations in other works of Bede (mostly the

[63] Ibid. 37, where he suggests that 'the script of the archetype was minuscule', but does not say *Insular* minuscule.

[64] See *Titi Lucreti Cari De Rerum Natura*, ed. Bailey, i. 132–4.

[65] See the discussion of Orchard, *The Poetic Art of Aldhelm*, 130 n. 19, who points to a few hexameter cadences in Aldhelm which might echo Lucretian diction, such as *Carmen de uirginitate* 1552, *belli certamina saeva*, which may be a reminiscence of *DRN* i. 475 (*saevi certamina belli*). On the whole, however, Orchard doubts that Aldhelm knew Lucretius at first hand.

[66] Orchard, ibid. 140–1. [67] Hunter Blair, 'From Bede to Alcuin', 247.

patristic commentaries), and similarly found that they could be located in Keil's index. He concluded by envisaging Bede as saying to an interlocutor: 'All that I knew of Virgil was what I could read in other men's writings.'[68] This poorly thought-out argument was subsequently demolished by Neil Wright, largely on the basis of Hunter Blair's own evidence, by showing that whereas Bede characteristically quoted an entire Vergilian hexameter, the grammarian alleged to be Bede's source usually quoted only the first two or three words: the implication being that, even if Bede was using the grammarian, he knew his Vergil well enough to complete the quoted lines.[69] But what finally makes Hunter Blair's argument wholly untenable is that he nowhere considered Bede's metrical *Vita S. Cudbercti*. As I shall suggest below, the style and diction of this poem are as pervasively Vergilian as any poem composed during the early Middle Ages. Not only had Bede read Vergil; he had seemingly internalized every aspect of Vergil's poetic technique.[70] One must therefore be cautious about alleging the ancient grammarians as intermediary sources for a medieval author's knowledge of classical Latin verse.

VERBAL REMINISCENCES

So much for quotations. I now move on to the more difficult question of verbal reminiscences. Until recently, one's appreciation of the range of an author's reading depended on the resources of a precise memory for verbal collocations, either on the part of the editor or of the reader. Someone like Max Manitius evidently had a prodigious memory for words and phrases borrowed from previous authors.[71] The last decade or so has seen the publication on CD-ROM of a number of corpora of Latin texts, and for those scholars who do not have Manitius's prodigious memory, the use of these CD-ROMs can greatly facilitate the identification of verbal reminiscences. For the study of Anglo-Saxon authors, five such databases are in question: the Chadwyck-Healey database of Migne's *Patrologia Latina* (PLD); the CETEDOC Library (= database) of Christian-Latin Texts

---

[68] Hunter Blair, 'From Bede to Alcuin', 250.   [69] Wright, 'Bede and Vergil'.
[70] See also Lapidge, 'Bede and the Poetic Diction of Vergil'.
[71] A powerful demonstration of Manitius's memory for poetic expressions is seen in an article which, in spite of electronic databases, has yet to be superseded: 'Zu Aldhelm und Baeda'.

(CLCLT), based largely on editions published in the *Corpus Christianorum Series Latina* (Turnhout) and *Corpus Scriptorum Ecclesiasticorum Latinorum* (Vienna);[72] the CEDETOC database of the Bibliotheca Teubneriana Latina (BTL), containing all classical Latin authors before *c.*500, whether in prose or verse, published in Teubner editions from the mid-nineteenth century onwards;[73] the CETEDOC database of the series *Auctores Antiquissimi* of the Monumenta Germaniae Historica (e-MGH2); and, finally, *Poetria Nova*, published in Florence by the Società Internazionale per lo Studio del Medioevo Latino, which includes all Latin poetry, in all metres, from the beginnings up to the thirteenth century.[74] These databases greatly facilitate the identification of verbal reminiscences, but, as with all such tools, the results which they provide have to be interpreted with care. I should like briefly to illustrate some of these problems with reference to three texts, in verse and prose: Bede's metrical Life of St Cuthbert; Asser's Life of King Alfred; and Byrhtferth's Lives of SS Oswald and Ecgwine.

Bede, *Vita metrica S. Cudbercti*

First, Bede. I mentioned in an earlier chapter that what is currently known of the library of Monkwearmouth-Jarrow in Bede's lifetime depends essentially on an article published in 1935 by M. L. W. Laistner.[75] In this article Laistner listed all the works on which Bede is known to have drawn, basing himself on evidence of both quotations and verbal remniscences: some 150 works in total. Laistner's work stands in some need of revision and updating, not least because, within the format of an article, he was obliged simply to list the names of authors and works known to Bede, without any indication of where in Bede's works a debt to that author or work might be found. For example, Laistner's entry for 'Prudentius' does not tell us which poems of Prudentius are in question, or where in Bede's works debts to Prudentius are to be found.[76] But it is

---

[72] The fifth version of this database (CLCLT-5) was issued in 2002.

[73] The third version of this database (BTL-3) was issued in 2004.

[74] *Poetria Nova. A CD-ROM*, ed. Mastandrea and Tessarolo. The merit of *Poetria Nova* is that, in addition to medieval Latin, it includes *all* classical Latin poetry from the beginnings (Ennius) through late antiquity to the 7th c., when medieval Latin poetry is thought to begin. There are of course databases for classical Latin literature, such as PHI Latin and ITER (see discussion in Berlioz et al., *Identifier sources et citations*, 80–1); but for the medievalist, *Poetria Nova* provides a more useful range of examples for each individual phrase.

[75] Laistner, 'The Library of the Venerable Bede' (I quote from the original version).

[76] Ibid. 266.

particularly in the case of Bede's knowledge of classical Latin poets where Laistner's list can be revised by recourse to electronic databases. For example, his list contains the name of only one classical poet (Vergil), but the databases bring to light many further debts.

It is well known that Bede, in his didactic treatises on metre and rhetorical devices, drew his discussion from classical grammarians such as Charisius and Pompeius, but that, in place of the illustrations from classical poets which they used, he substituted examples from Scripture and from Christian-Latin poets.[77] Thus a vast proportion of the examples which he cites in his treatise *De arte metrica* is drawn from Christian-Latin poets (95 citations out of 104), not from the classical poets which were cited by the grammarians on which Bede was drawing. This procedure has given rise to the assumption that, as a Christian writer, Bede had no interest in classical Latin verse (the assumption finds its extreme expression in the arguments of Peter Hunter Blair, cited above): and it is an assumption which has seemed to modern scholars to be confirmed by the absence of references to classical poets in Bede's biblical commentaries and historical writings. However, biblical commentaries are no place to look for evidence of a scholar's response to, and knowledge of, classical Latin poets. If we wish to know the ways in which Bede was indebted to classical poets, we have to look at his own poetry, in particular his metrical Life of St Cuthbert, the *Vita S. Cudbercti* [CPL 1380; hereafter *VCM*].[78] (In what follows, I shall omit reference to Bede's extensive indebtedness to Christian-Latin poets such as Juvencus, Caelius Sedulius, Arator, and others: his knowledge of such poets is not in doubt, in so far as his *De arte metrica* is based almost wholly on quotations from their verse.)

One has only to read a few lines of the metrical *Vita S. Cudbercti* to see that the model which guides Bede's sense of style and hexametrical composition is Vergil.[79] Vergilian diction is pervasive in the poem, and not only in the repeated and sometimes lightly retouched hexameters which occur at crucial points of the narrative—as when, describing the sense of alienation which the Northumbrians felt when, after the death of King Ecgfrith in 685, the kingdom had been inherited by King Aldfrith, who hitherto had shown no interest in the kingdom (while studying at Iona), because he had 'abandoned

---

[77] Palmer, 'Bede as Textbook Writer'; Bolton, *A History of Anglo-Literature*, 161–2; and Brown, *Bede the Venerable*, 33.

[78] *Bedas metrische Vita sancti Cuthberti*, ed. Jaager; I have prepared a new edition of the poem (from which I quote), which will form part of *Bede's Latin Poetry*.

[79] I repeat here some of the evidence set out in 'Bede and the Poetic Diction of Vergil'.

the boundaries and sweet lands of his homeland' (*VCM* 550: 'nam patriae fines et dulcia liquerat arua'; verbatim from *Buc.* i. 3), or when Cuthbert had left behind him a cloak to protect him from 'the rain and the penetrating chill of the north wind' (*VCM* 899: 'ne pluuia aut boreae penetrabile frigus adurens'; cf. *Georg.* i. 92–3: 'ne tenues pluuiae . . . acrior aut Boreae penetrabile frigus adurat'). Vergilian reminiscences like this underpin the diction of the metrical *Vita S. Cudbercti* throughout, as when a phantom *ignis edax*—with its loaded associations with the fire which destroyed Aeneas' Troy (*Aen.* ii. 758)—threatens to destroy the village in which Cuthbert is preaching (*VCM* 322). The narrative of St Cuthbert is carried along by the characteristic speech- and transition-formulae which propel Vergil's narrative: *haec ubi dicta, dixerat et, hinc atque hinc, tempore non alio*; and many of Bede's hexameters close with Vergilian cadences: *ab ictu, ad limina tendit, pectore fatur, ad sidera palmas*, etc. But it is not only at the level of verbal reminiscence that Bede shows his debt to Vergil. His preferred hexameter structures are precisely those of Vergil;[80] his use of elision is uniquely high among poets of the early Middle Ages (nearly 20 per cent of his lines have at least one elision, and many lines have two or more: a figure unparalleled among Paul Klopsch's analyses of early medieval Latin poets), even if this figure does not approach the 50 per cent of Vergil's verse (*no* Latin poet approaches Vergil in this respect!).[81] Like Vergil, but even more so, Bede avoided hiatus (Vergil allows the occasional hiatus, Bede none at all). One can observe that, when Bede went back in the 720s to revise his earlier version of the metrical *Vita S. Cudbercti* (what I call the 'Besançon redaction'),[82] it is clear that much of his revision was aimed at removing metrical peccadilloes which he had recognized during the course of fifteen years' (re-)reading Vergil (by incorporating, for example, synizesis of semivowels in words like *semianimem* (236), a practice which Bede evidently learned from *Aen.* iv. 686).

---

[80] For example, Bede's three favourite hexameter structures are as follows (with the percentages of usage given in parentheses): DDSS (15.4%), DSSS (11.8%), and DSDS (10.1%). Those of Vergil are the same, with the first two in reverse order: DSSS, DDSS, DSDS. The terminology (with D = dactyl, S = spondee) is from Duckworth, *Vergil and Classical Hexameter Poetry*, table 1. Bede's similarity to Vergil stands out starkly when his favourite structures are compared with those of other Anglo-Latin poets: see Orchard, 'After Aldhelm', 128–33.

[81] Klopsch, *Einführung in die mittellateinische Verslehre*, 79–82.

[82] For the 'Besançon redaction', see Lapidge, 'Bede's Metrical *Vita S. Cuthberti*'; see also id., 'Prolegomena to an Edition of Bede's Metrical *Vita S. Cuthberti*', 139–42. An edition of the 'Besançon redaction' forms part of my edition of *Bede's Latin Poetry*.

Vergil was the principal influence on Bede's poetic diction; but he had also learned from other classical poets. Next to Vergil in importance was Lucan. At one point in his *De arte metrica* (i. 11), Bede is discussing the aesthetic merits of positioning an adjective before its corresponding noun, as against those of postponing the adjective. In order to illustrate the latter technique, he cites Lucan, 'a skilled poet, setting out to describe the civil wars of Caesar and Pompey', and then cites six lines from the very beginning of the *Bellum ciuile* (i. 1–3, 10–12):[83]

> Bella per Emathios plus quam ciuilia campos
> iusque datum sceleri canimus populumque potentem
> in sua uictrici conuersum uiscera dextra. . . .
> Cumque superba foret Babilon spolianda tropheis
> Ausoniis umbraque erraret Crassus inulta,
> bella geri placuit nullos habitura triumphos.

These lines evidently struck Bede as noteworthy because of Lucan's cluster of postponed adjectives (*bella . . . ciuilia, populumque . . . potentem, umbra . . . inulta*). The six lines in question do not occur as a group in any grammarian.[84] In any event, in my view at least, it would have been impossible to form an appreciation of the aesthetic effect which Bede describes by reading the lines singly in a grammarian (even if one were to posit the sort of lost grammatical source to which modern editors recur in their refusal to believe that Anglo-Saxon authors could have read classical verse *in extenso*). However, what clinches the case is that Lucan's distinctive diction frequently lodged in Bede's memory, and is reused in his metrical *Vita S. Cudbercti*, as the following reminiscences will illustrate:

VCM 18	sicca euangelicis satias de nubibus **arua**
BC ix. 934	**sicca**que letiferis squalent serpentibus **arua**
VCM 24	**aurato nitid**ae lustrat **fulgore** loquelae
BC ix. 728	serpitis, **aurato nitidi fulgore** dracones
VCM 95	hinc sacra maiori **firmatus robore** corda
BC i. 280	dum trepidant nullo **firmatae robore** partes

---

[83] CCSL 123A: 115–16.
[84] See Boettner's index to GL. Priscian quotes one of the lines (i. 3 = GL ii. 348). Note also that Augustine in *De ciuitate Dei* iii. 13 (CCSL 47: 74) quotes the first line and part of the second ('Bella . . . canimus').

VCM 101	quinque fuere rates, **rapido** quae **gurgite** cunctae
BC ii. 233	artatus **rapido** feruet qua **gurgite** pontus
VCM 110	gaudia nam reprobis sunt **tristia fata** proborum
BC ix. 735	emetitur iter tot **tristia fata** suorum
VCM 122	ignea sidereis fulgescere **castra maniplis**
BC iv. 31	et prope consertis obduxit **castra maniplis**
VCM 289	iamque die quarto laeti **cessantibus austris**
BC iii. 68	ubere uix glaebae superat **cessantibus austris**
VCM 295	'Haec et ego', dixit, '**dubio** sub **pectore** mecum'
BC viii. 186	'nostra iubes?' **dubio** contra cui **pectore** Magnus
VCM 446	cerne uiam corui et caecum **depone furorem**
BC ii. 83	ante suam mortes; uanum **depone furorem**
VCM 678	illoque humanis ablatum **in tempore rebus**
BC iv. 477	consulite extremis angusto **in tempore rebus**

In each of these cases, the collocations occur only in Lucan and Bede, and some are highly distinctive (esp. the unique cadence *cessantibus austris*, for example). The verbal reminiscences, in other words, can in this case confirm the evidence of Bede's citations of Lucan, and suggest that Bede had read not only the opening lines of the *Bellum ciuile*, but had internalized much of the earlier poet's diction. In a word, the evidence that Bede had read Lucan strikes me as conclusive.[85]

A similar situation obtains with respect to Bede's knowledge of Ovid's *Metamorphoseis*. Here, too, Bede in his *Comm. in Genesim* quotes several lines of the poem, first from *Met.* i. 84–6:[86]

> pronaque cum spectant animalia cetera terram,
> os homini sublime dedit caelumque uidere
> iussit et erectos ad sidera tollere uultus.

Later in the same commentary he quotes a single line from *Met.* iv. 58:[87]

> coctilibus muris cinxisse Semiramis urbem.

---

[85] Cf. Laistner, 'Bede as a Classical and a Patristic Scholar', 98: 'The evidence for some acquaintance with Lucan is stronger, though not conclusive.' In fact the evidence of verbal reminiscence, established through the use of databases, enables us to resolve Laistner's hesitation.

[86] CCSL 119: 26.   [87] Ibid. 156.

In this case, the group of lines from book i of the *Metamorphoseis* is also quoted by Isidore (*Etym.* xi. 1. 5), but the line from book iv is not quoted by any grammarian. Can Bede's familiarity with Ovid's poem be demonstrated by recourse to verbal reminiscences in the metrical *Vita S. Cudbercti*? Unfortunately the matter is not as clear-cut in the case of Ovid as it was in that of Lucan. The following reminiscences are noteworthy:

VCM 60	Hunc pia complexum Cudberctus **ad oscula** mulcet
Met. iv. 75	aut, hoc si nimium est, uel **ad oscula** danda pateres
VCM 61	obsecrans **siccare genas** deponere luctus
Met. x. 362	flere vetat **siccatque genas** atque oscula iungit
VCM 67	**fas erit** aut uulgi antistes similabitur actis
Met. ii. 645	**fas erit** idque semel dis indignantibus ausus
VCM 115	**rustica** sed iustis dissentit **turba** suadelis
Met. vi. 348	**rustica turba** vetat; dea sic adfata vetantis
VCM 389	cum decus externum puri sit **pectoris index**
Met. ix. 535	esse quidem laesi poterat tibi **pectoris index**
VCM 554–5	**animo**que magis quam / annis **maturus**
Met. viii. 618	ante omnes Lelex, **animo maturus** et aeuo
VCM 677	deciduum **membris** animam posuisse **solutis**
Met. xi. 612	quo cubat ipse deus **membris** languore **solutis**
VCM 719	quinque dies postquam clausi **feruentibus undis**
Met. viii. 651	exiguam sectamque domat **ferventibus undis**

As in the case of Bede's reminiscences of Lucan, the above-listed collocations occur uniquely in Bede and Ovid; but unlike the examples from Lucan, those from Ovid—with the sole exception of the last example—are not, in my opinion, distinctive enough to establish conclusively that Bede had read the *Metamorphoseis* and internalized its diction.[88]

It emerges from the examples of Lucan and Ovid that, in order to establish a poet's debt to an earlier author, the verbal reminiscence must consist of a striking or unusual collocation of words, employed

---

[88] Cf. Laistner, 'Bede as a Classical and a Patristic Scholar', 97–9: 'yet it seems very doubtful whether Bede had read the poem [*sc.* the *Metamorphoseis*], a doubt which applies to Aldhelm also'.

in the same grammatical case and the same metrical feet. But even the application of this criterion leaves much scope for individual judgement: what may strike one reader as a distinctive collocation might strike another as a commonplace. Only rarely is a verbal reminiscence so striking that it can remove, at a stroke, any doubts as to whether the later poet had read the earlier. One such example is found in line 552 of Bede's metrical *Vita S. Cudbercti*, where he is describing the young Osred who succeeded to the Northumbrian throne on the death of his father Aldfrith in 705:

> huius nunc **Tyrio uenerabile pignus in ostro**.

This line derives almost entirely from line 15 of Claudian's poem on the third consulate of the young Honorius (*Carm.* vii), a brief poem of 211 lines composed in AD 396 for the court of Honorius in Milan:[89]

> excepit **Tyrio uenerabile pignus in ostro**.

It is inconceivable that these lines could have been created independently of each other. Bede, therefore, had read Claudian's poem; and alongside the one unambiguous verbal reminiscence may be set several others which on their own, perhaps, would not be regarded as sufficient proof of Bede's knowledge of this poem of Claudian, but which together help to reinforce our impression of Bede's debt to Claudian.

VCM 31	**Aethereumque decus** signis comitatur apertis
vii. 175	**O decus aetherium** terrarum gloria quondam
VCM 279	suerat ubi **uigiles** supplex iam **ducere noctes**
vii. 48	nec non in clipeo **uigiles** producere **noctes**
VCM 343	uita tremens tantum sub **pectore** feruet **anhelo**
vii. 30	sustulit arridens et **pectore** pressit **anhelo**

Given that Bede undoubtedly did know Claudian's poem, these verbal reminiscences may be regarded as convincing, according to the criterion mentioned above; and Bede's knowledge of this poem of Claudian is supported to some extent by the fact that Aldhelm, too, in his treatise *De pedum regulis*, quoted a line (98) from the same poem.[90] The combined evidence of Aldhelm and Bede probably indicates that Claudian's so-called *Carmina maiora* (of which the

---

[89] See Cameron, *Claudian*, 40–5.
[90] *Aldhelmi Opera*, ed. Ehwald, 172.

poem on Honorius' third consulship forms part)[91] were circulating in eighth-century England,[92] or, at the very least, some part of the collection was.[93]

In the case of Claudian, therefore, the one striking and unambiguous verbal reminiscence was supported by several other very plausible verbal debts, which together establish that Bede had read and internalized the diction of Claudian's poem on the third consulship of Honorius. Occasionally, however, a strikingly individual collocation of words in a classical poet will be unsupported by further reminiscences from that poet, leaving us to decide whether a single verbal debt is sufficient to establish literary dependence. When, for example, at one point in the metrical *Vita S. Cudbercti* a Northumbrian audience listens enraptured to Cuthbert's preaching, Bede says that the audience was accustomed to offer its 'thirsty [or: bibulous] ears' to the teacher: 'consuerat bibulasque aures praebere docenti' (*VCM* 358). The metaphor of 'bibulous ears' is a striking one, and is one which (according to the databases) occurs in only one other Latin poet: Persius, who, speaking as Socrates in his fourth Satire, advises Alcibiades—and anyone else who would run for public office—that it is pointless to 'expose thirsty ears' (i.e. listen in any way) to the populace (*Sat.* iv. 50: 'nequiquam populo bibulas donaveris aures'). Although the words do not occur in the same metrical feet, the conjunction of *bibulas* with *aures* is probably so striking that, unless an intermediary source were suddenly to come to light, we must conclude that Bede had read at least this one Satire of Persius (though what he made of lines 33–41 is a good question). Unfortunately, however, several further verbal reminiscences of Persius in Bede's poetry are not decisive and do little to buttress

[91] The *Carmina maiora et publica* (or: *Claudianus maior*) consist of the panegyrics and invectives, but not the *De raptu Proserpinae* nor the substantial collection of *carmina minora*. The terminology is that of T. Birt, in his edition of Claudian in MGH, AA 10 (Berlin, 1892), pp. lxxxii–cxlvi (*Claudianus maior*), cxlvii–clvii (*Claudianus minor*).

[92] The manuscript circulation of Claudian's *Carmina maiora* in the early Middle Ages is totally obscure, since no manuscript of the collection earlier than the 11th c. survives: see *TxtTrans*, 143–5. For the evidence of citation and reminiscence of Claudian's poems in the early Middle Ages, see Birt, pp. lxxvi–lxxxii, and the cursory discussion by Cameron, *Claudian*, 419–22.

[93] The only other poems in the collection for which there are suggestive verbal reminiscences in Bede's poem are: *Carm.* iii [= *In Rufinum I*], of which lines 145–6 ('aeuique **futuri** / **praescius** ardor inest') may be echoed in *VCM* 293 ('forte uiae comiti sed **praescius** ipse **futuri**'), and xix [= *In Eutropium II*, praef.], of which line 65 ('prospectant Paphiae **celsa de rupe** puellae') is apparently echoed in *VCM* 471 ('me quoties, inquit, **celsa de rupe** nefandi').

the evidence of the one (striking) verbal reminiscence.[94] The *Satirae* of Persius were well known to Aldhelm, who quotes from them on several occasions; furthermore, several manuscripts of Persius survive from the later Anglo-Saxon period.[95] Given this evidence for the circulation of Persius in Anglo-Saxon England,[96] it is not perhaps unreasonable to suppose that a copy of Persius was also available in Bede's library at Monkwearmouth-Jarrow.

Verbal reminiscences thus help to establish that Bede had a respectably wide knowledge of classical Latin poets: Vergil, Lucan, and Claudian (certainly), and Ovid and Persius (probably)—a list[97] far longer than one might deduce from the writings of modern scholars who have occupied themselves principally with Bede's exegesis. In any case, Bede's skill in verse composition implies in itself a wide familiarity with classical Latin poetry; and the verbal reminiscences identified by means of electronic databases can help to define the extent of that familiarity.[98]

Asser's *Vita Ælfredi*

The *Vita Ælfredi* or 'Life of King Alfred', composed by the Welshman Asser in 893, presents a scholarly profile strikingly different from that of Bede. Whereas the books known to Bede (and therefore presumably to hand in his monastery of Monkwearmouth-Jarrow) can be numbered in the hundreds, those apparently known to Asser seem scarcely to exceed a dozen. To begin with, Asser quotes verbatim, and sometimes names, five texts (not counting biblical quotations). Of these, W. H. Stevenson, Asser's exemplary editor,[99] identified three: the *Carmen paschale* of Caelius Sedulius in c. 1,

---

[94] Cf. *VCM* 412 with *Sat*. iv. 16 (the use of the rare word *meracum*; but note that Bede scans it differently from Persius, and erroneously).

[95] See below, pp. 184 (App. E), 324–5 (Catalogue).

[96] See also Pulsiano, 'Persius's *Satires*'.

[97] I suspect that the *Thebais* of Statius should also be added to this list, on the strength of a number of striking, if not *per se* decisive, verbal reminiscences: *VCM* 103 ('aliger undis') and *Theb*. ii. 1 ('aliger umbris'), both expressions used as the cadence of a hexameter; *VCM* 240 ('maestam subito quod **pondere noctem**' and *Theb*. viii. 665 ('**maestamque rependere noctem**'); *VCM* 342 ('ductor et **pectore tristi**') and *Theb*. vii. 148 ('**tristi** turbatus **pectore**'); *VCM* 500 ('**dictisque** illam dum affatur **amicis**') and *Theb*. iii. 294 ('**dictisque** ita mulcet **amicis**'); etc.

[98] The databases help to demonstrate that Bede was also familiar with a number of the minor Latin poems from late antiquity printed in the *Anthologia Latina*, i, ed. Riese, including nos. 493a (*VCM* 463), 686 (*VCM* 577), and 808 (*VCM* 510). Whether these poems arrived at Monkwearmouth-Jarrow singly, or as part of a collection, is unclear.

[99] *Asser's Life of King Alfred*, ed. Stevenson, rev. Whitelock.

Augustine's *Enchiridion* in c. 103, and Gregory's *Regula pastoralis* in c. 102, a fact interesting in itself, given that the *Regula pastoralis* was translated into Old English by King Alfred, who in the preface to the translation acknowledges *inter alia* the help of Asser.[100] A fourth quotation in Asser's text (c. 88) was identified recently by Anton Scharer (apparently using the CLCLT database);[101] the quotation is from a Hiberno-Latin collection of proverbs called the *Prouerbia grecorum*. The fifth (c. 90) is a hexameter—'inuigilant animi quibus est pia cura regendi' ('the minds are alert in those in whom the dutiful concern of government resides')—which Asser introduces as having 'been written by a certain wise man a long time ago' ('a quodam sapiente iamdudum scriptum'). The hexameter has not hitherto been identified. From the *Poetria Nova* database, however, it is clear that the line comes (verbatim) from the poem *In laudem Iustini Augusti minoris* of the sixth-century poet Corippus (iii. 139).[102] Flavius Cresconius Corippus, an African grammarian, is known for two poetic works: the *Iohannis*, an epic account of the African campaigns of the Byzantine general John Troglita, composed after the completion of the campaign in 548; and the poem *In laudem Iustini*, written in 566–7 after the death of Justinian and at the time of the consecration of his successor, Justin II, after Corippus had moved from Africa to Constantinople. The *Iohannis* does not concern us. Our concern is to establish how a Welsh scholar, writing in 893 either in Wales or at King Alfred's court in Wessex, could have known the panegyric to Justin II.

The *In laudem Iustini* survives complete in a single witness,[103] a Spanish manuscript in Visigothic minuscule written *c.*900 now in

---

[100] Alfred states that he learned Gregory's text 'from (*inter alios*) Asser my bishop' ('æt Assere minum biscepe'): *King Alfred's West-Saxon Version of Gregory's Pastoral Care*, ed. Sweet, i. 7; Schreiber, *King Alfred's Old English Translation*, 195.

[101] Scharer, 'The Writing of History', 198. Following the CLCLT database, Scharer attributed the quotation to the *Collectaneum* of Sedulius Scottus (CCCM 67), and attempted to draw historical conclusions about the links between Sedulius' views on rulers and King Alfred's rulership; but in fact the quotation is from an earlier anonymous (Hiberno–Latin) work entitled *Prouerbia grecorum*, which Sedulius was merely excerpting: see Simpson, 'The "Proverbia Grecorum"'; the proverb quoted by Asser is at p. 11. Asser very probably knew the *Prouerbia grecorum* independently of Sedulius, since another proverb from the collection is quoted in a 9th-c.(?) Welsh–Latin colloquy, *De raris fabulis*.

[102] The identification immediately disposes of an observation which I made nearly thirty years ago: 'it may be seriously doubted whether Corippus was ever read in Anglo-Saxon England' (*ALL* i. 401).

[103] Several late medieval manuscripts preserve fragments of book iii; for the ways in which these fragmentary witnesses are related to the tradition as represented by the Madrid manuscript, see Placanica, 'Corippus', 56–61.

Madrid (BN, Matritensis 10029).[104] The existence of another manu-script of the work is known from a detailed description in a booklist from Oviedo,[105] dated 882, but this manuscript (which, judging from its contents, was closely related to the Madrid manuscript) has perished. In addition to the works of Dracontius and Corippus, the Madrid manuscript contains a number of works of unambiguous Spanish origin, notably the *Hexameron* and other poems of Eugenius of Toledo.[106] How did the transmission of Corippus' poem get mixed up with these Spanish works, given that it was composed and presented in Constantinople? Two possibilities have been canvassed. On the one hand, between the years 551 and 624 there were close diplomatic relations between Spain and Byzantium (particularly during the three years when a diplomatic mission from Constan-tinople remained in Spain, 579–82), and Corippus' poem could arguably have been brought directly to Spain in the baggage of this mission.[107] On the other hand, the route of transmission could have passed by way of North Africa (Corippus' homeland), gathering on its journey not only the *Iohannis* of Corippus but also the other North African Latin poems such as those by Dracontius which are represented in the Madrid manuscript, and then brought to Spain by refugees from the Moslem invasions of North Africa.[108] In any event, the presence of Corippus' *In laudem Iustini* in Spain no later than the seventh century is guaranteed by the fact that the poem is quoted in the *acta* of the eighth Council of Toledo (653) and again in the *Ars grammatica* of Julian, bishop of Toledo (680–90).

---

[104] The dating of the manuscript is that of Lowe, *Palaeographical Papers*, i. 49 ('saec. ix/ x ut vid.'). There is a full description of the manuscript by Vendrell Penaranda, 'Estudio del códice de Azagra'. She demonstrates that the codex is a miscellany of at least five separate parts, which she calls 'sectors'; Corippus is contained in Sector A (consisting of quires I–VIII, XI), along with Eugenius' recension of Dracontius and eighty-four other poems of Eugenius, and the hymn 'Cantemus socii' of Caelius Sedulius.

[105] Becker, *Catalogi*, no. 26 (p. 60); there is a more recent edition in Gil, *Corpus Scriptorum Muzarabicorum*, ii. 707–8. Although the manuscript which preserves the booklist (El Escorial, Real Biblioteca de San Lorenzo, R. II. 18) has an ex-libris inscription of the cathedral of Oviedo, the contents indicate that the manuscript, and hence the booklist, pertains rather to Córdoba: see Collins, 'Poetry in Ninth-Century Spain', 188.

[106] The contents of Madrid 10029 were first listed by Ewald, 'Reise nach Spanien', 316–18; Ewald's list is followed by L. Traube in MGH, PLAC 3: 125–6, and Traube's list by Stache, *Flavius Cresconius Corippus In Laudem Iustini Augusti Minoris*, 31 n. 34. These earlier lists are superseded by the article of Vendrell Penaranda, cited above, n. 104.

[107] See Ramírez de Verger, 'Sobre la historia del texto'.

[108] Speck, 'Marginalien zu dem Gedicht', esp. 83 with n. 6. See also *TxtTrans*, p. xix: the manuscript (Madrid 10029) is 'a prime exhibit for the transmission through Spain of the literature of the Vandal kingdom'.

By the late eighth century, *In laudem Iustini* was known to scholars in the court circle of Charlemagne, hence in the late years of the eighth century, as Dieter Schaller has demonstrated.[109] In particular, there are verbal reminiscences in the *carmina* of Theodulf of Orléans and in the anonymous poem *Karolus magnus et Leo papa* (presumptively the work of Einhard). Schaller advanced the attractive hypothesis that it was Theodulf, a Visigoth by birth, who brought a copy of Corippus' poem from Spain to Charlemagne's court, where it was read by other poets resident there.

By what route did the poem come to the notice of Asser, in either Wessex or Wales, in the late ninth century? On the one hand, it could simply have been brought to England from a Carolingian library by one of the Continental scholars at King Alfred's court, either Grimbald or John the Old Saxon. On the other hand, it is possible, in theory at least, that Asser came across a copy of the poem in England. It is worth remembering that in 1886 Max Manitius identified several verbal reminiscences in Aldhelm's verse to the *In laudem Iustini*;[110] these reminiscences were recently re-examined by Andy Orchard, who inclined to find some of Manitius's parallels convincing, and was able to add two of his own.[111] Of the following five examples, the first three were identified by Manitius, the remaining two by Orchard:

CdV 1361	et caput infandum funestos **liquerat artus**
ILI i. 246	in caelum properans securos **linqueret artus**
CdV pr. 11	omnitenens dominus, mundi **formator et auctor**
ILI ii. 12	lux aeterna Deus, rerum **formator et auctor**
Enig. xii. 3	moxque genestarum **frondosa cacumina** scando
ILI ii. 322	ludere coniferae **frondosa cacumina** silvae
Enig. lv. 5	aurea dum **fulvis** flavescit bulla **metallis**
ILI iii. 100	fusca dabant **fulvo** chrysatica vina **metallo**
CdV 2741	Lucifer idcirco deserto **climate caeli**
ILI iii. 197	in modico simulans convexi **climata caeli**

The reader will have to judge whether these reminiscences are distinctive enough to demonstrate Aldhelm's knowledge of Corippus;

---

[109] Schaller, 'Frühkarolingische Corippus-Rezeption'.
[110] Manitius, 'Zu Aldhelm und Baeda', 581.
[111] *The Poetic Art of Aldhelm*, 189–90.

but if he did have access to a copy of the *In laudem Iustini* by *c.*700, that copy could in theory have been available to Asser somewhere in Wessex nearly two hundred years later: possibly, for sake of example, at Sherborne, where Aldhelm was bishop from 705/6 to 709/10, and where Asser was to become bishop two hundred years later (from some point during the decade 890 × 900, until his death in 909). In any event, that a quotation from a Late Latin author otherwise wholly unrepresented in Anglo-Saxon manuscripts should pop up in Asser, shows us how little in fact we know about the holdings of Anglo-Saxon libraries.

The list of Asser's reading as represented by verbatim quotation can be amplified by consideration of verbal reminiscences. In 1983 Simon Keynes and I added the following six titles to the list of Asser's reading:[112] Vergil, Aldhelm's prose *De uirginitate* [CPL 1332], Bede's *Historia ecclesiastica* [CPL 1375], the anonymous *Historia Brittonum* [CPL 1325; BCLL 127–34]; and Einhard's Life of Charlemagne, the *Vita Karoli magni*. The computer databases can now help us to extend our knowledge of the extent of Asser's reading still further.[113] Of classical poets, for example, one can identify several certain debts not only to Vergil but also to Lucan. Of patristic texts, there are in Asser numerous and unambiguous reminiscences of the following: Evagrius' Latin translation of Athanasius' Life of St Anthony; Cassian's *Conlationes*; Cassiodorus' *Expositio psalmorum*; and the *Dialogi* and *Moralia in Iob* of Gregory the Great. Asser's knowledge of the *Dialogi* might square with the fact the *Dialogi* were translated into Old English by a member of Alfred's circle, namely Wærferth, bishop of Worcester. But what is most interesting about Asser's knowledge of patristic authors is the pervasive debt in his Life to the Latin of Orosius' *Historiae aduersum paganos*, particularly its vocabulary for battle and military campaigning. For example, the following distinctive phrases are taken by Asser from Orosius: *inter tantas bellorum clades* (c. 21); *nauali proelio contra paganicas naues in mare congressus est* (c. 64), and *conserto nauali proelio* (c. 67). Many more such reminiscences can be adduced.

This evidence indicates unequivocally that Asser had studied Orosius. Janet Bately, in her edition of the anonymous Old English Orosius (a translation associable with Alfred's court), has suggested, on the basis of recurrent patterns of (mis)spelling of Latin proper

[112] *Alfred the Great: Asser's Life of King Alfred*, 53–5.
[113] See Lapidge, 'Asser's Reading', and below, App. E (pp. 237–9).

names in the Old English text, that such spelling probably derives from dictation by a native Welsh speaker.[114] The production of the Old English Orosius is unambiguously associated with King Alfred, even though (on stylistic grounds) he is unlikely to be its author. Asser's familiarity with the Latin text, as witnessed by his Life of Alfred, helps to confirm the linguistic evidence adduced by Bately, and establish that it may have been Asser himself who dictated the Old English translation of the Latin Orosius.

Byrhtferth of Ramsey

The fenland abbey of Ramsey was founded in 966, through the patronage of Oswald, archbishop of York (971–92) and Æthelwine, ealdorman of East Anglia (d. 992). Oswald had studied monastic discipline at Fleury at some point in the 950s, and Fleury served as an important model for the new fenland abbey. Like Fleury, for example, Ramsey was dedicated to St Benedict. The relationship between the two Benedictine monasteries was consolidated during the 980s, when Abbo of Fleury, one of the most widely learned scholars in Europe at that time, spent two years at Ramsey (985–7) in order to escape uncongenial circumstances at Fleury. (Abbo had been frustrated in his attempt to gain the abbacy of Fleury in 985; but when it became vacant again two years later, Abbo successfully obtained the abbacy, which he then held until he was martyred at La Réole, in Aquitaine, in 1004.) Abbo's principal duty at Ramsey was the instruction of his young English charges. Since Ramsey had been founded scarcely twenty years before his sojourn there, it cannot have acquired a substantial library during that time, certainly not one which could support the research of a scholar such as Abbo. Abbo must necessarily have brought books with him to Ramsey. Some notion of what these books might have been can be gleaned both from the works which Abbo composed in the years immediately preceding his stay at Ramsey (the logical treatise *De syllogismis hypotheticis*, and his commentary on the *Calculus* of Victorius of Aquitaine), and in the two works which he composed while he was there, the *Quaestiones grammaticales* and the *Passio S. Eadmundi* [BHL 2392].[115] In sum these works reveal a deep knowledge of scientific subjects, especially

[114] *The Old English Orosius*, ed. Bately, pp. cx–cxvi.

[115] *Abbo von Fleury, De syllogismis hypotheticis*, ed. Schupp; *Abbo of Fleury and Ramsey: Commentary on the Calculus of Victorius of Aquitaine*, ed. Peden; *Abbon de Fleury: Questions grammaticales*, ed. Guerreau-Jalabert; and *Three Lives of English Saints*, ed. Winterbottom, 67–87 [the *Passio S. Eadmundi*].

astronomy and harmony, which are fundamental to understanding the principles of ecclesiastical computus, as well as an urbane familiarity with classical poets such as Horace, Persius, Juvenal, and Vergil.[116]

The range of Abbo's learning is largely reflected in that of his English pupil, Byrhtferth (c.970–c.1020), as can be seen from the substantial corpus of Byrhtferth's writings, in both Latin and Old English, which embrace hagiography,[117] history,[118] and ecclesiastical computus.[119] In addition to these writings, Byrhtferth compiled, perhaps over many years, a sort of commonplace-book of quotations from various authorities, often very extensive, which he had assembled for the purpose of illustrating the content of two treatises by Bede, the *De natura rerum* [CPL 1343] and the *De temporum ratione* [CPL 2320]. The commonplace-book is known by the title 'glossae Bridferti', that is, 'glosses by Byrhtferth (on Bede's two treatises)'.[120] No manuscript of these 'glossae' has ever been identified; they were first printed by Johann Herwagen in 1563 from a manuscript now unfortunately lost.[121] As a result of some misguided argumentation by C. W. Jones,[122] Byrhtferth's authorship of the glosses was long

---

[116] See below, App. E, pp. 266–74.

[117] Byrhtferth is recognized as the author of two saints' Lives: one of Oswald, archbishop of York (971–92), the *Vita S. Oswaldi* [BHL 6374], the other of Ecgwine, an early 8th-c. bishop of Worcester and founder of the monastery of Evesham, the *Vita S. Ecgwini* [BHL 2432]. I quote both these works from my own forthcoming edition: *Byrhtferth of Ramsey: The Lives of Oswald and Ecgwine* (Oxford Medieval Texts).

[118] Byrhtferth is recognized as the author of the *Historia regum* embedded in the later *Historia regum* of Symeon of Durham (d. c.1130): *Symeonis Monachi Opera Omnia*, ed. Arnold, ii. 3–91. On Byrhtferth's authorship of the *Historia regum*, see Lapidge, *ALL* ii. 317–42.

[119] Byrhtferth first compiled a Latin computus, consisting mostly of diagrams and tables, and drawing heavily on computistical materials brought to England by Abbo; subsequently, some years after Abbo's death at La Réole, Byrhtferth wrote a simplified introduction, in both Latin and English, and which he referred to as his *Enchiridion* or 'handbook', to the earlier Latin computus. For the *Enchiridion*, see *Byrhtferth's Enchiridion*, ed. Baker and Lapidge, 1–250; Byrhtferth's Latin computus is unprinted, but its contents have been reconstructed and partly printed ibid. 373–427.

[120] The best account of the sources of Byrhtferth's *glossae* on Bede is that by Manitius, *Geschichte der lateinischen Literatur*, ii. 699–706.

[121] *Opera Bedae Venerabilis presbyteri anglosaxonis*, ed. Herwagen, i. 165–7, 170, 175–6 bis, 184; ii. 1–49 (Byrhtferth's *glossae* to Bede, *De natura rerum*); ii. 49–173 (Byrhtferth's *glossae* to Bede, *De temporum ratione*). Herwagen's editions of the 'glossae Bridferti' are repr. in PL 90: 187–278 (*glossae* to *De natura rerum*, cc. i–xxxvi; there are no *glossae* for the remaining chapters) and 297–518 (*glossae* to *De temporum ratione*, cc. ii–iii, v–lxiv), 685, 690, 692–5 (*glossae* to Bede, *De temporum ratione*, c. i), 700–2 (*glossae* to Bede, *De temporum ratione*, c. iv).

[122] 'The Byrhtferth Glosses'.

denied; but more recently Michael Gorman has reassessed and reaffirmed the evidence for attributing them to him.[123]

The wide range of sources laid under contribution in these various works by Byrhtferth can provide a valuable indication of what books were available to him in the Ramsey library. More importantly for the present discussion, since none of these texts (with the exception of Byrhtferth's *Enchiridion*) has as yet been carefully sourced,[124] they can provide a test case for the use of CD-ROM databases in the identification of books available to Byrhtferth, and hence an indication of the contents of the library at Ramsey in the early years of the eleventh century.

Byrhtferth was inordinately proud of his learning, and took every possible opportunity to display it (as we have seen in the case of Turpilius).[125] One must therefore be careful about assuming that a work named or cited by Byrhtferth, particularly in the *glossae Bridferti*, indicates first-hand familiarity with that work.[126] For example, among the quotations assembled to illustrate the parts of the firmament as set out c. xxxii of Bede's *De temporum ratione*, we find, a propos of the term *eous* (recte *cohus* or *chous*), the following statement: 'unde et Ennius: "Vix solum complevere Eoum, cum terroribus caeli".'[127] This is a mangled version of a line probably from the *Annales* of Ennius.[128] Byrhtferth, however, did not take it directly from the *Annales*, but rather from Isidore, who in his treatise *De natura rerum* explained the parts of the firmament as follows: 'Partes autem eius: chous, axis, cardines, convexa, poli, sidera. Chous, quod coelum continet. Unde Ennius: "Vix solum complere choum terroribus coeli".'[129] By the same token, in attempting to illustrate Bede's discussion of the term *hebdomada* in c. viii of *De temporum ratione*,

---

[123] 'The Glosses on Bede's *De temporum ratione*'.

[124] Gorman (ibid. 226–31) provided a thorough analysis of the sources of the 'Glossae Bridferti' to one chapter (c. v) of Bede's *De temporum ratione*, by way of illustrating the nature of Byrhtferth's learning.

[125] See above, p. 98.

[126] Gorman, for example, attributes to Byrhtferth knowledge of a number classical Latin authors: 'the compiler [*sc.* of the *glossae Bridferti*] drew on a very large stock of authors and works; from the classical age, we note the names of Varro, Ennius, Lucan, Pliny, Terence, Horace, Virgil and Persius, along with Priscian' ('The Glosses', 219).

[127] PL 90: 441A.

[128] See *The Annals of Q. Ennius*, ed. Skutsch, 123 (sedis incertae fragmenta, no. xcix = no. 558), who prints the line as 'Vix solum complere cohum torroribus caeli', and notes that it is preserved by Isidore, *De natura rerum* xii. 3; see also Skutsch's commentary, pp. 703–4.

[129] PL 83: 983.

Byrhtferth apparently quotes M. Terentius Varro (of Reate), as follows: 'Marcus Varro, homo omnium acutissimus, et sine ulla dubitatione doctissimus, XLI libros scripsit Antiquitatum, inter quos sex de temporibus composuit';[130] but the entire sentence comes not from Varro, but from Augustine, De ciuitate Dei, vi. 6, who devotes several chapters of book vi to Varro's treatise De antiquitatibus as a source for knowledge of pagan religion.

There is no question, therefore, that the library at Ramsey contained copies of the writings of Ennius or Varro, any more than it contained a copy of the comedies of Turpilius. More intriguing, however, is the case of Julianus Pomerius, whose treatise De uita contemplatiua was widely known on the Continent during the early Middle Ages,[131] but does not seem to have been known to any Anglo-Saxon author (although several Anglo-Saxon manuscripts survive).[132] Knowledge of this work by Byrhtferth would therefore fill an important lacuna in our knowledge of Anglo-Saxon scholarship. By way of illustrating c. xxxii of Bede's De temporum ratione, Byrhtferth included the following quotation:

Julianus Pomerius, vir sanae prudentiae, primum coelum dicit esse aerium, a quo et aves coeli vocantur. Secundum sidereum, ubi continentur duodecim signa caeteraque astra praeter septem planetas, quod et firmamentum appellatur. Tertium intelligit spirituale, sive mentale, ubi angeli et animae sanctorum in contemplatione Dei sunt positae, contemplantes super se Deum omnipotentem, qui omni creaturae praesidet, ut praesidendo omnia sustineat, sustinendo circumdet, circumdando impleat.[133]

Unfortunately, however, this quotation is not taken directly from Julianus Pomerius; rather, the entire paragraph is taken from the Expositio in Pauli epistolas of the Carolingian scholar Haymo of Auxerre (d. c.855), as may quickly be established by consultation of the PLD,[134] a work which was well known to Byrhtferth's contemporary Ælfric,[135] and was presumably available at Ramsey as well. In spite of Byrhtferth's seemingly verbatim quotation, there is no evidence that he was familiar with the writings of Julianus Pomerius.

It may be helpful to give a brief synopsis of the Latin writings

[130] PL 90: 326C.
[131] See Laistner, 'The Influence during the Middle Ages of the Treatise De vita contemplativa'.
[132] For the possibility that, during the period of his Continental sojourn, Boniface was familiar with the treatise De uita contemplatiua, see above, p. 39.
[133] PL 90: 442D–414A.
[134] PL 117: 661A.   [135] See App. E (below, p. 259).

known to Byrhtferth, as identified by means of electronic databases,[136] in order to ascertain what library resources were available at Ramsey in the early eleventh century. The general orientation of Byrhtferth's reading is very similar in outline to that of Abbo, his revered master. Of the classical Latin poets, Byrhtferth, like Abbo, certainly knew his Vergil well, since Vergilian diction is pervasive in his hagiographical writings. He seems also to have known Horace (the *Sermones*) and Persius. The distinctive phrase *arridente fortuna* ('smiling Fortune'), which he uses on several occasions, may imply that he had read Juvenal's Sixth Satire.[137] He quotes often from the *Disticha Catonis*. But there the list of classical poets ends. It is striking, however, that Byrhtferth was familiar with the apparatus of commentary necessary for understanding the principal classical poets: Servius on Vergil and Lactantius Placidus on Statius.[138] (Byrhtferth's two extensive quotations from the Lactantius commentary in his *glossae* on Bede may also imply his familiarity with the *Thebaid* of Statius, even though no quotations or verbal reminiscences have as yet been identified.)

Of Christian-Latin poets he knew the standard school-texts intimately: Juvencus, *Euangelia*, Caelius Sedulius, *Carmen paschale*, Arator, *Historia apostolica*, Prudentius (*Liber cathemerinon* and *Psychomachia*), Prosper's *Epigrammata*, as well as Aldhelm (*Carmen de uirginitate* [CPL 1333] and *Enigmata* [CPL 1335]) and Bede (*Versus de die iudicii* [CPL 1370]). This modest range of reading in classical and Christian-Latin poetry does not imply an unusual interest in poetry for its own sake, and is also, perhaps, reflected in the fact that, with the exception of a twelve-line epitaph for Archbishop Oswald (*Vita S. Oswaldi*, v. 19), Byrthferth does not appear to have attempted verse composition.

Byrhtferth's interests, like those of his mentor, lay in the subjects of the (scientific) quadrivium, especially in the domain of ecclesiastical computus, but above all in astronomy and cosmology. Byrhtferth was the first native Anglo-Saxon author to have first-hand knowledge of Macrobius' commentary on the *Somnium Scipionis*, of the *Astro-*

---

[136] The following discussion is based wholly on the information assembled in App. E (below, pp. 266–74).

[137] Juvenal, *Sat.* vi. 605–6 ('Stat Fortuna inproba noctu / adridens nudis infantibus'). Juvenal's image, and the conception of Fortuna which is pervasive in the *Saturae*, are very striking, and one wonders if the formulation *arridente fortuna* was a *façon de parler* devised by Abbo (whose knowledge of Juvenal was thorough) and used by him in his daily conversation, whence Byrhtferth could have picked it up without having read Juvenal for himself.

[138] A debt first noted by Manitius, *Geschichte*, ii. 701.

nomica of Hyginus, and of the so-called *Liber Nemroth* (which, in spite of its name, has nothing to do with the biblical Nimrod, but is rather an astronomical treatise).[139] Byrhtferth also shows comprehensive knowledge of Boethius, *De consolatione Philosophiae*, which he quotes throughout his hagiographical and historical writings.

Byrhtferth also appears to have had access to a respectable collection of patristic texts. These included the major writings of Augustine: *De ciuitate Dei*, *De trinitate*, the *Enarrationes in psalmos*, the *Tractatus* on the Gospel of John, the *De Genesi ad litteram*, as well, perhaps, as the *Confessiones*. He knew the *Epistulae* of Jerome, but of Jerome's biblical commentaries, only the commentary on the Gospel of Matthew. Of the writings of Gregory the Great, Byrhtferth certainly knew the *Dialogi*, the forty Homilies on the Gospels, the *Moralia in Iob*, and the *Regula pastoralis*. Of other standard patristic writings, his hagiography includes frequent verbal reminiscence of the *Expositio psalmorum* of Cassiodorus, as well as the *Etymologiae* of Isidore. We might expect to find more reference to patristic texts if Byrhtferth had composed any biblical commentaries; the list is substantial enough if we remember that his reminiscences of these patristic works simply represent the fruits of his reading; and that the list can be augmented substantially by inclusion of the patristic and computistical texts on which Byrhtferth drew in compiling his *Enchiridion* and excerpted in his *glossae* on Bede. In sum, Ramsey's library in the time of Byrhtferth included somewhat more than 100 volumes. Of these, two can be identified among surviving manuscripts,[140] and more possibly await detection.

CONCLUSIONS

The work of the great pioneers of Anglo-Latin studies—Max Manitius, Rudolf Ehwald, Wolf Laistner, and W. H. Stevenson—succeeded in establishing what books and authors were known in early Anglo-Saxon England to writers such as Aldhelm, Bede, and Asser. Their work was thoroughly, even brilliantly, done, and stands in need of very little correction. But it can now be amplified

---

[139] The *Liber Nemroth* is a Latin translation (of unknown, perhaps 10th-c., date) of a work possibly of Syrian origin. It has not been printed, but excerpts may be read in Haskins, 'Nimrod the Astronomer', and in Dronke, *Dante and Medieval Latin Traditions*, 118–24. See, in general, Livesey and Rouse, 'Nimrod the Astronomer'.

[140] See above, p. 51 n. 93.

substantially by the use of electronic databases of classical and patristic Latin authors. In certain cases, mentioned above, these databases can provide wholly new perspectives on what books and authors were known in early England: Bede's knowledge of Claudian, for example, or Asser's knowledge of Corippus. And as authors of the later Anglo-Saxon period such as Byrhtferth begin to attract more scholarly attention, the role played by Abbo of Fleury in the establishment and redirection of scientific learning will come into clearer focus. In other words, the broad outlines of what books were 'known to the English 597–1066' (to advert to the title of Ogilvy's book mentioned at the outset of this chapter) have been soundly established and are well known, but the use of electronic databases will inevitably continue to provide refinements and additions to those outlines.

Conclusions

I CONCLUDE with some general observations on the nature of Anglo-Saxon libraries. Evidence of various kinds indicates that Anglo-Saxon libraries were not large, at least in comparison with ninth-century Continental libraries, as we know these from surviving inventories, or with later medieval cathedral and monastic libraries in England, as we know these from the catalogues printed in CBMLC. The largest Anglo-Saxon library appears to have been that assembled at Monkwearmouth-Jarrow by Benedict Biscop and Ceolfrith, as we know it from the voluminous writings of Bede. This library may have contained more than 200 volumes. But other Anglo-Saxon libraries were much smaller than this. Aldhelm's library at Malmesbury, Alcuin's at York, the library at tenth-century Winchester used by Lantfred, Wulfstan, and Ælfric, and that at Ramsey used by Abbo and Byrhtferth, may have contained more (but probably not substantially more) than 100 volumes each. Other libraries whose contents we know from surviving inventories—for example those at eleventh-century Worcester and Peterborough—were smaller still. The typical Anglo-Saxon monastic library probably owned fewer than fifty volumes, all of which could be housed in a simple book-chest.

To judge from the combined evidence of inventories, surviving manuscripts, and citations, as set out in the Catalogue below, the typical Anglo-Saxon library housed a small core of staple patristic texts, scarcely exceeding twenty titles: Gregory, *Dialogi, Hom. .xl. in Euangelia, Moralia in Iob*, and *Regula pastoralis*; Isidore, *De ecclesiasticis officiis, De natura rerum, Etymologiae*, and *Synonyma*; Jerome, *Epistulae*, and possibly the *Comm. in Euangelium Matthaei*; and Augustine, *De ciuitate Dei, De trinitate, Enarrationes in Psalmos, Enchiridion*, and the *Epistulae* and *Sermones* in selections. To these works of the four major patristic authors (at least as suggested by the Anglo-Saxon evidence), one may add several individual works: Cassian, *Conlationes* and Eusebius, *Historia ecclesiastica*, as translated by Rufinus, as well as a small corpus of Christian-Latin poets who were read as school-texts: Arator, *Historia apostolica*, Juvencus, *Euangelia*, Prosper, *Epigrammata*, and Caelius Sedulius, *Carmen paschale*. (In the later Anglo-Saxon period, but not necessarily earlier than *c*.900, all libraries probably had copies of Caesarius, *Sermones* and Boethius, *De consolatione Philosophiae* as well.) These are the works which were almost certainly to be found in any Anglo-Saxon library, whether large or small. And when in the mid-eighth century Anglo-Saxon missionaries began to establish monastic and cathedral libraries in Germany, it was these staple works which were exported from English libraries.

Whatever their overall size, these libraries were able to sustain the research of a number of outstanding Anglo-Saxon scholars—Aldhelm, Bede, and Alcuin, to name only the most eminent three. What is striking about the libraries of these scholars is their very functionality. The principal purpose for which libraries were assembled was the interpretation of Scripture and the regulation of the Church. For these purposes Anglo-Saxon libraries could apparently supply all relevant patristic literature. For example, Bede, in compiling his commentary on the Song of Songs [CPL 1353], had before him all available writings on the subject: Aponius, *Explanatio in Canticum canticorum*; Gregory, *Hom. in Canticum canticorum*; Julian of Eclanum, *De amore seu Comm. in Canticum canticorum*, a work which has not survived beyond the few fragments quoted by Bede; and Origen, *Comm. in Cantica canticorum* as translated by Rufinus and *Hom. .ii. in Cantica canticorum* as translated by Jerome. Similarly, in compiling his *Explanatio Apocalypseos* [CPL 1363], Bede had access to all the relevant literature: Caesarius of Arles, *Expositio in Apocalypsim*; Cassiodorus, *Complexiones*; Primasius of Hadrumentum, *Comm. in Apocalypsim*; and Tyconius, *Comm. in Apocalypsim*. From the point of view of a scholar setting out to compile commentaries on the Song of Songs and Revelation, Bede could not have had a better-stocked library. A similar argument could be made about the library at Winchester from which Ælfric compiled the exegetical homilies on the Gospels which form part of his *Catholic Homilies*.

The contents of Anglo-Saxon libraries must therefore reflect choice rather than random acquisition. And if these libraries lacked certain kinds of text, that too is probably the result of choice. Consider the kinds of text which are unrepresented in any Anglo-Saxon library: polite discussions by Roman gentlemen of political, moral, and literary matters (the dialogues of Cicero; the *Noctes Atticae* of Aulus Gellius; the Letters of Pliny the Younger and, from a later period, those of Symmachus and Sidonius Apollinaris);[1] philosophical and cosmo-

---

[1] An exception here is the *Saturnalia* of Macrobius, which was known to Abbo and Byrhtferth. Bede quotes the *Saturnalia* in his *De temporum ratione* without realizing that its

logical literature (treatises of Cicero on the nature of the gods; the dialogues and letters of the younger Seneca); treatises describing the rhetorical training required of a young gentleman (the *Rhetorica ad Herennium*; Cicero, *De oratore*; Quintilian, *Institutio oratoria*, along with the model speeches of the elder Seneca); lyric poetry (Horace, *Odes* and *Epodes*; Statius, *Silvae*); and especially love poetry (Catullus, Tibullus, Propertius, and Ovid of the *Amores*, *Ars amatoria*, and *Heroides*).[2] These works were not acquired by Anglo-Saxon librarians because they were of no use to scholars engaged in interpreting the Bible and explaining the organization of the Church.

The functional bias of Anglo-Saxon libraries needs to be borne in mind when considering the received view of Anglo-Saxon libraries as the preservers and transmitters of classical (and patristic) learning. What I call the received view was formulated authoritatively by Bernhard Bischoff in a paper delivered at Spoleto in 1963: 'It was the Anglo-Saxons who transmitted the idea of a library well stocked for instruction and study, and balanced equally [*sc.* between classical and patristic literature] to Carolingian Europe. The classics formed one part of their libraries; and it is certain that a number of Anglo-Saxon manuscripts became the archetypes of later Carolingian transmission.'[3] As proof of these assertions, Bischoff cited the single surviving leaf of Justinus' *Epitome* of Pompeius Trogus which has been mentioned above in another context:[4] he implied that the single leaf was the mere tip of a vast iceberg of texts which the Anglo-Saxons transmitted to the Continent. In the same spirit, Reynolds and Wilson, in their classic *Scribes and Scholars*, state that 'the [Anglo-Saxons'] practical provision of books . . . must have had an immeasurable effect on the revival—and hence the survival—of Latin literature'.[5] 'Must have': but did it?

author was Macrobius; presumably he took the quotations from some sort of computistical miscellany.

[2] There are minor exceptions in the case of Ovid: book i of the *Ars amatoria* is preserved in Oxford, BodL, Auct. F. 4. 32, fos. 37–47, and two lines of *Amores* iii. 8 are preserved as a distich [lines 3–4: ICL 8093] in two manuscripts, Oxford, BodL, Rawlinson G. 57 + 111 and Paris, Bibliothèque Sainte-Geneviève 2410. The distich in question ('ingenium quondam fuerat pretiosius auro, / at nunc barbaria est grandis habere nihil') has nothing to do with love, and was clearly excerpted as a maxim on the relationship of gold to genius.

[3] 'Scriptoria e manoscritti mediatori', 324: 'Sono stati gli anglosassoni, che hanno trasmesso l'ideale di una biblioteca ben provista per la preparazione e lo studio e ben equilibrata nella sua composizione all'Europa carolingia. Appare nelle loro biblioteche una parte dei classici; ed è certo che alcuni codici anglosassoni sono divenuti capostipiti della tradizione carolingia.'

[4] See above, p. 41, and below, p. 230.   [5] *Scribes and Scholars*, 90.

The evidence on which these suppositions are based is that of three manuscripts (two of them mere fragments) which were written in England by *c*.800 but were preserved in Continental libraries:[6] a copy of part of books ii–vi of the *Naturalis historia* of the Elder Pliny now in Leiden, Bibliotheek der Rijksuniversiteit, Voss. Lat. F. 4, fos. 4–33, written in Anglo-Saxon set minuscule somewhere in Northumbria during the first half of the eighth century; a leaf of the *Epitome* of Justinus now in London, BL, Harley 5915, fo. 10, written *c*.800 in Anglo-Saxon set minuscule, perhaps in Northumbria, perhaps at York;[7] and a fragment of the commentary of Servius on Vergil's *Aeneid* now in Marburg, Hessisches Staatsarchiv, 319 Pfarrei Spangenberg Hr Nr. 1, written in the early eighth century in Anglo-Saxon cursive minuscule, perhaps in Southumbria and perhaps in the circle of Boniface.

The question is whether this one manuscript and these two fragments do indeed represent the tip of an iceberg of classical texts transmitted by way of England to the Continent. Those who believe in the existence of such an iceberg will no doubt point to the remarkable collection of classical Latin texts which were available at Fulda, an Anglo-Saxon foundation, in the mid-ninth century: the assumption being that it was Anglo-Saxon missionaries who brought them there (that is to say, not the manuscripts themselves but their exemplars, or 'archetypes', as Bischoff calls them).[8] In my view, however, there is overwhelming evidence against such an assumption. As we have seen, the manuscripts written during the eighth century in the area of the Anglo-Saxon mission (listed below, App. C), as well as the inventories compiled in that area (printed below, App. B), contain between them not so much as a single classical text.[9] And this evidence squares exactly with the impression we have gained of the contents of Anglo-Saxon libraries, namely that they were assembled with the sole purpose of supporting the interpretation of Scripture and the regulation of the Church. Such a purpose sits ill with the enthusiastic campaign for the acquisition of classical Latin texts as evidently took place at Fulda, and other Carolingian libraries, during

---

[6] *TxtTrans*, p. xxi.

[7] See above, p. 41, with the discussion of Crick, 'An Anglo-Saxon Fragment'. As Crick showed, the Harley fragment is probably from the same manuscript as a (lost) leaf formerly belonging to Ernst Fischer of Weinheim [CLA ix. 1370].

[8] See above, pp. 84–5.

[9] Excepting copies of classical grammarians (including Servius), which were needed for instruction in Latin.

the ninth century. It is not fully clear where ninth-century Caro-lingian librarians found copies of the classical texts which adorned their libraries; but it is fairly certain that the copies in question did not come from England. In the light of the evidence it seems rather that it was only by accident, not by design, that Anglo–Saxon libraries happened to possess unusual classical texts, such as the copies of Lucan's *Orpheus*, the *Gratiarum actio* of Paulus Quaestor, and the commentary by Valerius Probus on Vergil's *Georgics*, which were apparently available to Aldhelm in his library at Malmesbury.

In the end, the study of vanished libraries is a very depressing business: depressing, because it enforces an awareness of how much has been lost. What one sees is that the transmission of knowledge flowed as a kind of stream from the fourth century BC down to the eleventh century AD. Libraries acted as conduits, but also as filters, in this stream of transmission. The flow of Greek books from Alexandria to Roman libraries was inevitably impeded and reduced by the Romans' lack of interest in any but the best-known Greek authors. The holdings of Greek and Roman literature in the Roman double libraries were further reduced when works were transferred from roll to codex at about the same time as the number of Romans able to read Greek declined markedly; and Christian educators effected a further reduction by their disinclination to copy works of pagan tenor. Libraries of the sixth and seventh centuries AD can have held only a tiny fraction of what was available in earlier centuries.[10] It was from this tiny fraction of classical authors, augmented by copies of patristic texts, that Anglo–Saxon libraries were constituted. Yet the modest Anglo–Saxon libraries were evidently able to sustain scholarship of a quality unmatched elsewhere in Europe, and from their modest resources to supply the libraries of the English mission to Germany in the eighth century.

I began the Lowe Lectures by referring to Umberto Eco's *Name of the Rose*, and to the vast (fictional) library of San Michele which is portrayed in it. Readers will know that the novel is narrated many

---

[10] Some impression of the vast amount of Latin literature that has been lost is admirably conveyed by Bardon, *La Littérature latine inconnue*, of which vol. i treats the literature of the Republic, vol. ii that of the Empire down to the early fifth century. Bardon prefaces his discussion with the statistics (taken from A. F. Wert) that, of 772 Latin authors whom we know by name, 276 are merely names and 352 are known only through fragments; of the remaining 144 (20% of the total), we have one or more works, though only rarely their complete output. It is impossible even to guess how many of the 772 authors would have been represented in Roman libraries of late antiquity.

years after the event by Adso of Melk, and that the library itself was
destroyed by fire while Adso and William of Baskerville were visiting
the monastery years earlier. At the end of his life, Adso returns to the
site of San Michele, and finds scraps of manuscripts lying among the
rubble; he collects as many scraps as he can carry (two full travelling
sacks) and sets off home:

Along the return journey and afterward at Melk, I spent many, many hours
trying to decipher those remains. Often from a word or a surviving image I
could recognize what the work had been. When I found, in time, other copies
of those books, I studied them with love . . . At the end of my patient
reconstruction, I had before me a kind of lesser library, a symbol of the
greater, vanished one: a library made up of fragments, quotations, unfinished
sentences, amputated stumps of books.[11]

This, *mutatis mutandis*, is the situation confronting any modern
scholar who would attempt to reconstruct vanished Anglo-Saxon
libraries.

[11] Eco, *Il nome della rosa*, 502; trans. Weaver, *The Name of the Rose*, 500.

Appendix A
Six Inventories of Latin Books from Anglo-Saxon Libraries

On a previous occasion, I have published all the booklists surviving from Anglo-Saxon England, in so far as they were known to me ('Booklists', first printed in 1985); these booklists included a number of inventories of books intended for scholarly purposes, but also a number of lists of liturgical books and ecclesiastical furniture, as well as lists of books written in the vernacular. Since the present discussion is concerned neither with liturgical nor vernacular books, what is reprinted here is simply the inventories of books intended for scholarly purposes. With each inventory I supply in square brackets the number which it was given in 'Booklists' (hence the present inventory (a) corresponds to 'Booklists', no. III); but note that I have removed all liturgical and vernacular items from the individual inventories. Accordingly, the numbering of individual items within the inventories is often different from that which it had in 'Booklists'. Details of which alphanumerical repertories (e.g. CPG, CPL, etc.) contain references to individual authors and works earlier than AD 700 may be found in the Catalogue, below.

a. Books owned by a grammarian named Æthelstan (s. x^2)
['Booklists', no. III]

London, BL, Cotton Domitian i, is a mid-tenth-century English copy of Isidore's *De natura rerum*. On fo. 55^v of this manuscript was added a list of books belonging to one Æthelstan (*þis syndon ða bec þe Æþestanes wæran*). The identity of this Æthelstan is unknown. It is unlikely that the books in question had formerly belonged to King Æthelstan (924–39); the nature of the books in the inventory suggests instead that their owner was an otherwise unattested schoolmaster or grammarian.

1. De natura rerum
2. Persius
3. De arte metrica
4. Donatum minorem
5. Excerptiones de metrica arte
6. Apocalipsin
7. Donatum maiorem
8. Alchuinum
9. Glossam super Catonem

10. Libellum de grammatica arte que sic incipit: 'Terra que pars'
11. Sedulium
12. ond .i. gerim wæs Alfwoldes preostes
13. Glossa super Donatum
14. Dialogorum

1. The first item, Isidore's *De natura rerum*, constitutes the bulk of the manuscript (Cotton Domitian i) into which the inventory has been copied. 2. Persius, *Saturae*. 3. *De arte metrica*: possibly Bede's treatise of that name [CPL 1565]. 4. Donatus, *Ars minor*. 5. *Excerptiones de metrica arte*: unidentifiable without further specification. 6. *Apocalipsin*: might seem most naturally to refer to the biblical Apocalypse (Revelation); but such a book would seem out of place in what is otherwise a collection of schoolbooks, and it is possible that the reference here is to Bede's *Expositio Apocalypseos* [CPL 1363]. 7. Donatus, *Ars maior*. 8. Presumably a grammatical work by Alcuin, perhaps his *Ars grammatica* [CSLMA, ALC 9 [pp. 21–3]; PL 101: 849–902) or *De orthographia* CSLMA, ALC 32 [pp. 152–5]; PL 101: 901–20). 9. *Glossam super Catonem*: a copy of a commentary (presumably also including the text) on the *Disticha Catonis*, presumably that by Remigius of Auxerre, which is preserved in fragmentary state in at least one Anglo-Saxon manuscript, Cambridge, Gonville and Caius College, 144/194. 10. The book in question was a copy of a type of grammar called a 'parsing' grammar (on the type, see Law, *Grammar*, 135–6, and *History*, 148); no copy of a parsing grammar beginning 'Terra que pars' survives from Anglo-Saxon England, however. 11. Caelius Sedulius, *Carmen paschale*. 12. OE *gerim* refers to a computus, which without further specification is impossible to identify, nor is it possible to identify the priest Ælfwold to whom the book had previously belonged. 13. Presumably a copy of one of the Late Latin commentators on Donatus: Cledonius, Pompeius, or Sergius; see Law, *History*, 81–3. 14. *Dialogorum*: presumably the *Dialogi* of Gregory, but just possibly, given the content of the inventory, a volume of school-room *colloquia*, many of which circulated in late Anglo-Saxon England (see *Anglo-Saxon Conversations*, ed. Gwara and Porter, 1–70).

b. Books donated by Æthelwold, bishop of Winchester (963–84), to the monastery at Peterborough ['Booklists', no. IV]

Bishop Æthelwold refounded the abbey of Peterborough *c*.970: on the date and circumstances, see *Wulfstan of Winchester: Life of St Æthelwold*, ed. Lapidge and Winterbottom, 40–1 (c. 24). A record of the endowment, including the inventory of books printed below, is preserved as S 1448, and printed in Robertson, *Anglo-Saxon Charters*, 72–5, and in Friis-Jensen and Willoughby, *Peterborough Abbey*, 3–6 (BP 1). Because later inventories survive from Peterborough, such as that printed below as INV(i) f, but also including one made in the sixteenth century before Dissolution (see

James, *Lists of Manuscripts*, and Friis-Jensen and Willoughby, *Peterborough Abbey*), it is often possible, through comparison of the inventories, to establish the precise identity of a particular book.

1. Beda in Marcum
2. Liber miraculorum
3. Expositio Hebreorum nominum
4. Prouisio futurarum rerum
5. Augustinus de achademicis
6. Vita sancti Felicis metrice
7. Sinonima Isidori
8. Vita Eustachii
9. Descidia Parisiace polis
10. Medicinalis
11. De duodecim abusiuis
12. Sermo super quosdam psalmos
13. Commentum Cantica canticorum
14. De eucharistia
15. Commentum Martiani
16. Alchimi Auiti
17. Liber differentiarum
18. Cilicius Ciprianus
19. De litteris Grecorum
20. Liber bestiarum

1. Bede, *Comm. in Marcum* [CPL 1355]. **2.** *Liber miraculorum*: possibly the work of that title by Gregory of Tours, but equally possibly a miscellaneous collection of hagiographical texts and *miracula*. **3.** Jerome, *Liber interpretationis Hebraicorum nominum*. **4.** Julian of Toledo, *Prognosticum futuri saeculi*. **5.** Augustine, *Contra Academicos*. **6.** *Vita sancti Felicis metrice*: presumably the *Carmina* of Paulinus of Nola, most of which concern celebrations on the recurring feast of St Felix, the patron saint of Paulinus' church at Nola. **7.** Isidore, *Synonyma de lamentatione animae peccatricis*. **9.** *Vita Eustachii*: from comparison with later Peterborough inventories, it is possible to establish that this item refers to a poem on St Eustachius [BHL 2767; ICL 14237] which was composed under the patronage of Bishop Æthelwold, either at Abingdon or Winchester: see Lapidge, 'Æthelwold and the *Vita S. Eustachii*'. **9.** *Descidia Parisiace polis*: an inflated title for Abbo of Saint-Germain-des-Prés, *Bella Parisiace urbis* (MGH, PLAC iv. 72–122); see the entry on Abbo by P. Lendinara in SASLC i. 15–18. **10.** *Medicinalis*: a medical treatise, unidentifiable without further specification. **11.** *De duodecim abusiuis saeculi*, a work which passed during the later Middle Ages under the name of St Cyprian, but which is now known to have been composed in seventh-century Ireland; an OE version is preserved in six pre-Conquest English manuscripts (*Old English Homilies*, ed. Morris, 296–304). **12.** Several patristic authors composed commentaries on a few selected psalms: Ambrose, Origen as translated by Rufinus, and Prosper of Aquitaine. **13**. *Commentum Cantica canticorum*: a number of commentaries on the Song of Songs circulated in the early Middle Ages, including those of Aponius and Gregory's *Hom. .ii. in Canticum canticorum*, but the commentary most likely to be in question here is probably that by Bede, *In Cantica canticorum allegorica expositio* [CPL 1353]. **14**. No patristic work carries precisely this title; the reference is possibly to a work of Ambrose, either *De sacramentis* or *De mysteriis*, or to one of Augustine's Letters (*Ep.* liv, replying to questions by Ianuarius *de sacramentis . . . et eucharistia*); alternatively, Friis-Jensen and Willoughby (*Peterborough Abbey*, 5) suggest Remigius of Auxerre, *Expositio missae* [PL 101: 1246–71]. **15**. *Commentum Martiani*: presumably the commentary on Martianus Capella by Remigius of Auxerre, an Anglo-Saxon fragment of which [Gneuss 127] was identified by Parkes, 'A Fragment of an Early-Tenth-Century Anglo-Saxon Manuscript'. **16**. *Alchimi Auiti*: the *Carmina de spiritalis historiae gestis* by Alcimus Avitus. **17**. *Liber differentiarum*: either Isidore, *De differentiis uerborum* or pseudo-Isidore, *Liber differentiarum seu De proprietate sermonum*. **18**. *Cilicius Ciprianus*: if the work of Cyprian given to Peterborough by Æthelwold is identical with that listed in the late eleventh-century Peterborough inventory (below, INV(i) f. **54**), what is in question here is a copy of the *Epistulae* of Caecilius Cyprianus. **19**. *De litteris Grecorum*: presumably a Greek–Latin glossary, unidentifiable without further specification. **20**. *Liber bestiarum*: presumably a copy of a redaction of the Latin *Physiologus*; for the complex medieval transmission of this work, see Orlandi, 'La tradizione del "Physiologus"', and for its transmission in England, see Frank, *Die Physiologus-Literatur*.

c. Books donated by Sæwold, sometime abbot of Bath, to the church of Saint-Vaast in Arras, *c.*1070 ['Booklists', no. VIII]

In an eleventh-century copy of Augustine, *Tractatus in euangelium Ioannis* now in Arras, BM, 849 (539), the scribe entered on fo. 159ʳ a list of books donated by one Sæwold to Saint-Vaast. The Sæwold in question was at one time abbot of the monastery of St Peter, Bath, but had evidently been forced to flee to Flanders in the aftermath of the Norman Conquest. Because some of the identifiable books in the list were written in England, there is a presumption that Sæwold had owned all the books in the list during his tenure of the abbacy of Bath, but had taken them back with him to Flanders and subsequently donated them to the Flemish monastery which gave him refuge. The inventory, in other words, may be taken as evidence of the personal library of an English ecclesiastic at the time of the Conquest. In reprinting the list, I omit the first three items (a Gospel book, a missal, and a copy of the Heptateuch, as well the reference to a 'Librum uersuum et tractuum totius anni', evidently a gradual containing verses and responsories as well as tracts for the entire liturgical year); and note that I have revised some palaeographical datings and localizations in the light of Bischoff, *Katalog*.

1. Librum Moralium Gregorii .xx.
2. Librum Haimonis usque in Pascha
3. Librum Claudii super Matheum
4. Librum Regule sancti Benedicti et Diadema monachorum
5. Librum Dialogorum Gregorii
6. Librum Vitarum patrum
7. Librum Expositionis Ambrosii de psalmo .cxviii.
8. Librum item De initiandis liber .i. eiusdem [*scil.* Ambrosii], De mysteriis (libri .vi.), Commonitorium Palladii de Bragmanis (liber .i.), Ysidori De officiis (libri .ii.) in uno uolumine
9. Librum Pronosticon
10. Librum Enkiridion
11. Librum Exameron Ambrosii
12. Librum Prosperi ad Iulianum et Ambrosii De officiis
13. Librum Bede super .vii. epistolas canonicas
14. Librum epistolarum Bacharii, Augustini, Eubodii, Macedonii
15. Librum Vitae sancti Richarii
16. Librum Vitae sanctorum confessorum Cutberti, Gutlaci, Aichadri, Filiberti, Dunstani
17. Librum De assumptione sancte Mariae
18. Librum canonum
19. Librum Hystoriae aecclesiastice gentis Anglie
20. Librum Vite sancti Walerici, Mauri, passionum sanctorum martirum Luciani, Maxiani atque Iuliani, in uno uolumine
21. Librum medicinalis
22. Librum Cassiodori De orthographia
23. Librum Parabolarum Salomonis
24. Librum De laude uirginitatis
25. Librum De professione coniugatorum
26. Librum Prudentii
27. Iuuencus, Sedulius in uno uolumine
28. Librum Rabbani super Iudith et Hester
29. Librum Tripartite historie ecclesiastice

1. Gregory, *Moralia in Iob*, which properly consists of thirty-five, not twenty, books. **2.** *Haimonis*: the first part of the Homiliary of Haymo of Auxerre, containing homilies from Advent to Easter; see Barré, *Les Homéliaires carolingiens*, 49–70. **3.** *Claudii super Matheum*: the commentary (in fact a *catena* of quotations from earlier patristic authorities) on Matthew by Claudius of Turin (partly printed PL 104: 833–8). **4.** The *Regula S. Benedicti* [CPL 1852] together with the *Diadema monachorum* of Smar-

agdus of Saint-Mihiel (PL 102: 593–690). **5.** Gregory, *Dialogi*. **6.** *uitarum patrum*: the so-called *Vitas patrum*, a heterogenous collection of lives and sayings principally of the early Egyptian desert fathers [BHL 6524–47]; the manuscript in question survives as Brussels, Bibliothèque Royale, 9850–2 (Soissons, s. vii/viii). **7.** Ambrose, *Expositio de psalmo .CXVIII.*; the manuscript survives as Arras, BM, 899 (590) (NE France, s. ix$^{3/4}$). **8.** A manuscript containing Ambrose, *De mysteriis*; Ambrose, *De sacramentis*; Palladius, *De gentibus Indiae et Bragmanibus*, in Latin translation (PL 17: 1131–46: see Wilmart, 'Les Textes latins de la lettre de Palladius'); and Isidore, *De ecclesiasticis officiis*; the manuscript survives as Arras, BM, 1068 (276) (NE France, s. ix$^{2/3}$). **9.** Julian of Toledo, *Prognosticum futuri saeculi*. **10.** Augustine, *Enchiridion ad Laurentium*. **11.** Ambrose, *Exameron*; the manuscript survives as Arras, BM, 346 (867) (s. x/xi, supplemented s. xi^{med}). **12.** Julianus Pomerius, *De uita contemplatiua*, combined with Ambrose, *De officiis ministrorum*; the manuscript containing the text of Julianus Pomerius survives as Arras, BM, 435 (326), but that part of it containing the Ambrose has subsequently been lost. **13.** Bede, *Comm. in Epistulas catholicas* [CPL 1362]. **14.** A collection of letters: for various letters transmitted under the name of Bachiarius, see LLA 681 and CPL 568–70; the remaining items were probably letters of Augustine to Evodius (*Epp.* clviii, clx, clxi, clxiii, clxxvii) and Macedonius (*Epp.* clii, cliv). **15.** Alcuin, *Vita S. Richarii* [BHL 7223–7; CSLMA ALC 90 (pp. 501–3)]. **16.** A manuscript containing the anonymous *Vita S. Cuthberti* [BHL 2019], Felix's *Vita S. Guthlaci* [BHL 3723], the anonymous *Vita S. Aichardi* [BHL 181], the anonymous *Vita S. Filiberti* [BHL 6806], and the Englishman B.'s *Vita S. Dunstani* [BHL 2342]; the manuscript survives as Arras, BM, 1029 (812) (s. x/xi). **17.** The manuscript in question survives as Arras, BM, 732 (684) (s. xi), and contains Jerome's *Ep.* xlvi [*ad Paulam et Eustochium de assumptione beate virginis*] as well as Cassiodorus, *De anima* and *Institutiones*. **18.** The manuscript in question survives as Arras, BM, 644 (572) (NE France, s. viii/ix), and contains the canon-collection known as the *Collectio canonum Quesnelliana*. **19.** Bede, *Historia ecclesiastica gentis Anglorum* [CPL 1375]; a fragment of the manuscript in question may survive as New York, Pierpont Morgan Library, M. 826 (Northumbria, s. viii^{ex}). **20.** A legendary (apparently now lost) containing the *vitae* of SS. Walaricus [BHL 8762], Maurus [BHL 5783], Lucianus and Marcianus [BHL 5015], and Iulianus [BHL 4544–5]. **21.** *Librum medicinalis*: not identifiable without further specification. **22.** Cassiodorus, *De orthographia*. **23.** *Librum parabolarum Salomonis*: the manuscript survives as Arras, BM, 1079 (235), fos. 28–80 (NE France, s. ix$^{3/3}$), and contains Bede, *Comm. in Parabolas Salomonis* [CPL 1351], and Bede, *Comm. in Ezram et Nehemiam* [CPL 1349], as well as unedited commentaries on Ecclesiastes and the Song of Songs. **24.** A copy (not extant) of Aldhelm, either the *Prosa de uirginitate* [CPL 1332] or *Carmen de uirginitate* [CPL 1333]. **25.** *Librum de professione coniugatorum*: possibly Augustine, *De bono* *coniugali.* **26.** A copy of some or all of Prudentius' *Carmina.* **27.** A manuscript (not extant) containing Juvencus, *Euangelia* and Caelius Sedulius, *Carmen paschale.* **28.** Hrabanus Maurus, *Expositio in librum Iudith* (PL 109: 539–92) and *Expositio in librum Esther* (PL 109: 635–70); the manuscript survives as Arras, BM, 764 (739), fos. 1–93 (NE France, s. ix^ex). **29.** The Greek tripartite history of Socrates, Sozomen, and Theodoretus, translated into Latin by Cassiodorus as *Tripartita historia ecclesiastica.*

d. Inventory of books procured by Bishop Leofric for the church of Exeter (1069 × 1072) ['Booklists', no. X]

A list of books bequeathed to Exeter by Bishop Leofric was copied into a preliminary quire of a Gospel book acquired by him apparently from Landevennec in Brittany, now Oxford, BodL, Auct. D. 2. 16 (the quire in question is fos. iv, 1–6, with the list on fos. 1^r–2^v); another copy of the list is found in the famous 'Exeter Book' (Exeter, Cathedral Library, 3501, fos. o, 1–7, with the list on fos. 1^r–2^v). Because Leofric frequently added ex-libris inscriptions to his books, it is very often possible to identify items in the inventory. Note that the original inventory includes a very substantial number of liturgical and biblical books, and books in the vernacular, which have been omitted here.

1. Liber pastoralis
2. Liber dialogorum
3. Liber Boetii De consolatione
4. Isagoge Porphirii
5. Passionalis
6. Liber Prosperi
7. Liber Prudentii psicomachie
8. Liber Prudentii ymnorum
9. Liber Prudentii de martyribus
10. Liber Isidori Ethimolagiarum
11. Passiones apostolorum
12. Expositio Bede super euuangelium Luce
13. Expositio Bede super apocalipsin
14. Expositio Bede super .vii. epistolas canonicas
15. Liber Isidori De nouo et ueteri testamento
16. Liber Isidori De miraculis Christi
17. Liber Oserii
18. Liber Persii
19. Sedulies boc
20. Liber Aratoris
21. Diadema monachorum
22. Glose Statii
23. Liber officialis Amalarii

1. Gregory, *Regula pastoralis*; the manuscript survives as Oxford, BodL, Bodley 708 (Christ Church, Canterbury, s. x^{ex}; prov. Exeter, with a Leofric ex-libris inscription). 2. Gregory, *Dialogi*. 3. Boethius, *De consolatione Philosophiae*; the book survives as Oxford, BodL, Auct. F. 1. 15, fos. 1–77 (St Augustine's, Canterbury, s. x^2; prov. Exeter, with a Leofric ex-libris inscription). 4. Porphyry's *Isagoge* or 'Introduction' to Aristotle's *Categories*, was, in the Latin translation of Boethius, the standard account of logic in the early Middle Ages; Boethius also wrote a commentary on Porphyry's *Isagoge*, which may be in question here. 5. A 'passional', that is to say, a collection of *passiones* of martyrs. 6. Probably the *Epigrammata ex sententiis S. Augustini* of Prosper of Aquitaine. 7. Prudentius, *Psychomachia*. 8. Prudentius, *Liber cathemerinon*. 9. Prudentius, *Liber peristephanon*; the three works of Prudentius (nos. 7–9) are contained in Oxford, BodL, Auct. F. 3. 6 (Exeter, s. xi^1, with a Leofric ex-libris inscription). 10. Isidore, *Etymologiae*. 11. Either a manuscript 'passional' (cf. above, no. 5), or conceivably a work such as Isidore, *De ortu et obitu patrum*. 12. Bede, *Comm. in Lucam* [CPL 1356]. 13. Bede, *Explanatio apocalypseos* [CPL 1363]; the manuscript possibly survives as London, Lambeth Palace Library, 149, fos. 1–139 (s. x^2). 14. Bede, *Comm. in Epist. catholicas* [CPL 1362]; the manuscript possibly survives as Oxford, BodL, Bodley 849 (Loire region, s. ix^1; prov. Exeter). 15. Possibly Isidore's *Proeemia* to the books of the Old and New Testaments, or to the pseudo-Isidorian *Quaestiones de ueteri et nouo testamento*, a work of Hiberno-Latin origin: see McNally, 'The Pseudo-Isidorian *De ueteri et nouo Testamento Quaestiones*'. 16. Probably Isidore, *De fide catholica contra Iudaeos*; the manuscript possibly survives as Oxford, BodL, Bodley 394, fos. 1–84 (s. x^2; prov. Exeter). 17. A garbled reference either to Asser's *Vita Alfredi* (which might have been rendered as *Liber Asserii*), or to Orosius, *Historiae aduersum paganos*. 18. Persius, *Saturae*; the book in question is possibly Oxford, BodL, Auct. F. 1. 15, fos. 78–93 (St Augustine's, Canterbury, s. x^2; prov. Exeter). 19. Caelius Sedulius, *Carmen paschale*. 20. Arator, *Historia apostolica*. 21. Smaragdus of Saint-Mihiel, *Diadema monachorum* (PL 102: 593–690). 22. Presumably a glossed copy of Statius, *Thebaid*, such as that in Worcester, CL, Q. 8, fos. 165–72 + Add. 7, fos. 1–6 (?France, s. ix/x; prov. England, s. x/xi). 23. Amalarius of Metz, *De ecclesiasticis officiis* (PL 105: 985–1242; also ed. Hanssens); the manuscript survives as Cambridge, Trinity College B. 11. 2 (St Augustine's, Canterbury, s. x^2; prov. Exeter, with a Leofric ex-libris inscription).

e. Inventory from an unidentified centre, possibly Worcester (s. xi^{ex}) ['Booklists', no. XI]

To an early eleventh-century English copy of Gregory's *Dialogi*, now Oxford, BodL, Tanner 3, a list of books and ecclesiastical furniture was added, probably in the late eleventh century, on fos. 189^v–190^r. Because the manuscript was at Worcester from no later than the second half of the twelfth century, there is some presumption that the list of books was added there. Note that the list principally consists of items which would have been employed in a schoolroom; the various biblical and liturgical manuscripts which the inventory contains are here omitted.

1. Orosius
2. Sedulius
3. Dialogus
4. Glosarius
5. Martianus
6. Persius
7. Prosper
8. Terrentium
9. Sedulius
10. Sychomagia
11. Boetius
12. Lucanus
13. Commentum Remigii super Sedulium
14. Isidorus De natura rerum
15. Arator
16. Glosarius
17. Priscianus maior
18. Tractatus grammatice artis
19. Commentum super Iuuenalem
20. Bucholica et Georgica Virgilii
21. Persius
22. Hystoria anglorum
23. Vita Kyerrani
24. Liber pronosticorum Iuliani
25. .xl. omelia
26. Arator
27. Commentum Boetii super Categorias
28. Liber Luciferi
29. Epigrammata Prosperi
30. Beda De temporibus
31. Liber proemiorum ueteris et noui
32. Liber dialogorum
33. Prosper
34. Seruius De uoce et littera
35. Appolonius
36. Ars Sedulii
37. Boetius Super perhiermenias
38. Liber Albini

39. Historia anglorum
40. Glosarius per alfabetum
41. Expositio psalterii
42. Kategorie Aristotili
43. Aeclesiastica istoria
44. Liber soliloquiorum
45. Vita S. Wilfridi episcopi
46. Haimo
47. Omelia .i.
48. Liber magnus de grammatica arte

1. Orosius, *Historiae aduersum paganos*. 2. Caelius Sedulius, *Carmen paschale*. 3. Possibly Gregory, *Dialogi*; but the context and the singular form could equally suggest a volume containing a schoolroom *dialogus* or 'colloquy'. 4. A glossary (unidentifiable). 5. Martianus Capella, *De nuptiis Philologiae et Mercurii*. 6. Persius, *Saturae*. 7. Prosper, *Epigrammata ex sententiis S. Augustini*. 8. Presumably a play (or plays) by Terence. 9. Another copy of Caelius Sedulius, *Carmen paschale*. 10. Prudentius, *Psychomachia*. 11. Presumably (but not necessarily) Boethius, *De consolatione Philosophiae*. 12. Lucan, *Bellum ciuile*. 13. Remigius of Auxerre's unprinted commentary on the *Carmen paschale* of Caelius Sedulius (excerpts are printed by J. Huemer, CSEL 10: 319–59); an Anglo-Saxon copy of this work, which has the rubric *Commentum Remegii super Sedulium*, survives as Salisbury, CL, 134 (s. x/xi). 14. Isidore, *De natura rerum*. 15. Arator, *Historia apostolica*. 16. Another glossary. 17. Priscian, *Institutiones grammaticae*. 18. An unidentifiable grammatical treatise. 19. Possibly the commentary on Juvenal by Remigius, which is not extant but is known from medieval library catalogues; see Sanford, 'Juvenal', 176. 20. Vergil, *Bucolica* ('Eclogues') and *Georgica*. 21. Another copy of Persius, *Saturae*. 22. Bede, *Historia ecclesiastica gentis Anglorum* [CPL 1375]. 23. A copy of a *vita* of St Ciaran, either the saint of Clonmacnois [BHL 4654–5] or of Saigir [BHL 4657–8]. 24. Julian of Toledo, *Prognosticum futuri saeculi*. 25. The specific number of homilies—forty—may suggest that the work in question is Gregory, *Hom. .xl. in euangelia*. 26. Another copy of Arator, *Historia apostolica*. 27. Boethius' Commentary on Aristotle's Categories. 28. Possibly a reference to the patristic writings of Lucifer of Cagliari [CPL 112–18]. 29. Another copy of the *Epigrammata* of Prosper of Aquitaine. 30. Bede, *De temporibus* [CPL 2318]. 31. Isidore, *In libros ueteris ac noui testamenti prooemia*. 32. Presumably Gregory, *Dialogi*; note that the book in which the present inventory is found is itself a copy of Gregory's *Dialogi*. 33. Yet another copy of Prosper's *Epigrammata ex sententiis S. Augustini*. 34. Not Servius but Sergius, *De littera*; the name Sergius was frequently confused with that of Servius in manuscript transmission. 35. The Late Latin romance, *Historia Apollonii regis Tyri* (ed. G. Schmeling (Leipzig, 1988)). 36. One of the grammatical

commentaries by Sedulius Scottus, who wrote commentaries on Donatus [BCLL 681–2], Priscian [BCLL 683], and Eutyches [BCLL 684], all ed. B. Löfstedt in CCCM 40 B–C (Turnhout, 1977). **37**. Boethius's Commentary on Aristotle's *Peri Hermeneias*, also called *De interpretatione*. **38**. A work (unspecified) by Alcuin. **39**. Another copy of Bede, *Historia ecclesiastica gentis Anglorum* [CPL 1375]. **40**. A glossary arranged in a- or ab- order. **41**. The title suggests that the work in question was Cassiodorus, *Expositio psalmorum*. **42**. Presumably Boethius' Latin translation of Aristotle's Categories (rather than the *Categoriae decem*, which in the early Middle Ages were transmitted under the name of Augustine). **43**. Presumably Eusebius, *Historia ecclesiastica*, in the Latin translation by Rufinus. **44**. Augustine, *Soliloquia*. **45**. Stephen of Ripon, *Vita S. Wilfridi* [BHL 8889]. **46**. A work by Haymo of Auxerre, either one of his many biblical commentaries, or his Homiliary. **47**. Presumably a homiliary (unfortunately unspecified). **48**. A collection of grammatical writings (unfortunately unspecified).

f. Inventory possibly from Peterborough (s. xi/xii) ['Booklists', no. XIII]

Oxford, BodL, Bodley 163 is a composite manuscript, of which the third part, fos. 250–1, contains *inter alia* the following inventory. A scribble on fo. 250ᵛ records the obit of a monk of Peterborough who died in 1359, suggesting that the provenance, if not necessarily the origin, of fos. 250–1 is Peterborough. The hypothesis of a Peterborough origin for the inventory is confirmed by the fact that some of the books can be identified in the earlier inventory of books given to Peterborough by Bishop Æthelwold (printed above, INV(i) b), and others with items in the abbey's fifteenth-century *Matricularium* (ed. James, *Lists of Manuscripts*, 30–81, and Friis-Jensen and Willoughby, *Peterborough Abbey*, 49–177 (BP 21)). Note that, as in the case of the previous inventories, I omit biblical and liturgical items, as well as works in the vernacular.

1. Augustinus De ciuitate Dei
2. Augustinus De uerbo Domini
3. Augustinus De bono coniugii et uirginitatis
4. Augustinus Super Iohannem
5. Augustinus Retractionum
6. Augustinus De uidendo Deum et uera religione
7. Ecclesiastica historia Eusebii Cesaris
8. Historia anglorum
9. Tripartita historia
10. Hieronimus Super Iosue
11. Hieronimus Contra Iouinianum
12. Hieronimus Super Isaiam
13. Hieronimus Super prophetas

14. Hieronimus Super Ezechielem (libri duo)
15. Hieronimus Super Danihelem
16. Ambrosius De sacramentis et Vita sanctorum Nicolai, Botulfi, Guðlaci
17. Origenis De singularitate clericorum
18. Dialogus Basilii et Iohannis
19. Augustinus De penitentia
20. Gennadius ecclesiasticorum dogmatum
21. Collatio Nesterotis abbatis de spirituali scientia, Abraham de mortificatione, Cremonis de perfectione
22. Ambrosius De uirginitate
23. Hisidorus Super Genesim
24. Amalarius De diuinis officiis
25. Fredulfus historiographus
26. Iosephus Antiquitatum
27. Isidorus in Hebreis numeris
28. Gregorius Pastoralis cure
29. Gregorii Moralia in Iob
30. Vite patrum
31. Haimo Super epistolas Pauli
32. Haimo In euangeliis
33. Epistolares Hieronimi .iii. (unus maior, duo minores)
34. Liber notarum
35. Questiones in Genesi et diffinitio philosophie et liber differentiarum
36. Item liber differentiarum
37. Vita sancti Felicis uersifice
38. Vita sancti Aðeluuodi
39. Pronosticon futuri secli
40. Vita sancti Wilfridi
41. Vita sancti Giseleni
42. Diadema monachorum
43. Paradisus
44. Glosa in Genesim
45. Super Psalterium
46. Isidorus De summo bono
47. Cronica Prosperi
48. Augustinus De diuersis rebus
49. Vita sancti Fursei et Baronti uisio
50. Gregorii Nazanzeni Apologiticus
51. Historia Romanorum et Africanorum
52. Expositio super .l. psalmos
53. Epistolaris Cipriani
54. Vita beati Gregorii pape
55. Exameron Ambrosii
56. Canones

57. Passio Eustachii Placide uersifice
58. Historia Clementis et Vita beati Martini
59. Rabanus De institutione clericorum
60. Liber miraculorum

1. Augustine, *De ciuitate Dei*. 2. Augustine wrote no work of this title; possibly the reference is to his treatise *De sermone Domini in monte*, but Friis-Jensen and Willoughby (*Peterborough Abbey*, 8) point out that a collection of Augustine's sermons *De uerbis Domini et apostoli* (ninety-nine sermons on the Gospels and epistles: see Verbraken, 'La Collection de sermons') circulated under a similar title. 3. Two works of Augustine are in question: the *De bono coniugali* and *De sancta uirginitate*. 4. Augustine, *Tractatus in euangelium Ioannis*. 5. Augustine, *Retractationes*. 6. The first of these items is in fact one of Augustine's *epistulae* (*Ep.* cxlvii), a letter which often circulated separate from the collection as a treatise entitled *De uidendo Deo*; the other is his treatise *De uera religione*. 7. Eusebius of Caesarea, *Historia ecclesiastica*, in the Latin translation of Rufinus. 8. Presumably Bede, *Historia ecclesiastica gentis Anglorum* [CPL 1375]; the manuscript in question is possibly the first part (fos. 1–227) of Bodley 163 itself (see above). 9. The Greek tripartite history of Socrates, Sozomen, and Theodoretus, translated into Latin by Cassiodorus as *Tripartita historia ecclesiastica* [ed. CSEL 71 (1952)]. 10. Jerome did not write a commentary on Joshua; conceivably the work in question is Rufinus' Latin translation of Origen's twenty-six homilies on Joshua, a work which frequently passed during the Middle Ages under the name of Jerome. 11. Jerome, *Aduersus Iouinianum*. 12. Jerome, *Comm. in Isaiam*. 13. Jerome, *Comm. in prophetas minores*. 14. Jerome, *Comm. in Hiezechielem*. 15. Jerome, *Comm. in Danielem*. 16. Ambrose, *De sacramentis*; the three *uitae* in question are presumably Otloh of St Emmeram, *Vita S. Nicholai* [BHL 6126], Folcard of Saint-Bertin, *Vita S. Botulfi* [BHL 1428], and Felix, *Vita S. Guthlaci* [BHL 3723]; these three works are preserved together in London, BL, Harley 3097, a manuscript which also contains Ambrose, *De sacramentis*, and is thus presumably the book in question here. 17. The work of this title [CPL 62] is not by Origen, but it was frequently transmitted during the Middle Ages under the name of Cyprian (see Schepens, 'L'Epître *De singularitate clericorum*'). 18. The work in question is the Latin translation of John Chrysostom's *De sacerdotio*, a dialogue in six books between John and one Basil; the identity of the Latin translator is unknown, but may have been Anianus of Celeda. 19. A copy of two of Augustine's *sermones* (nos. ccli–cclii) which together form a treatise *De utilitate agendae poenitentiae*, which often circulated separate from the sermon-collection. 20. Gennadius, *Liber siue diffinitio ecclesiasticorum dogmatum*. 21. The three works listed separately here are from the *Conlationes* of Cassian: nos. xiv (*De spirituali scientia*), xxiv (*De mortificatione*), and xi (*De perfectione*), respectively. 22. Ambrose, *De uirginitate*. 23. Isidore did not devote a separate commentary to Genesis; the

work in question is probably his *Mysticorum expositiones sacramentorum seu Quaestiones in Vetus Testamentum*. **24**. Amalarius of Metz, *De ecclesiasticis officiis* (PL 105: 985–1242; also ed. Hanssens). **25**. Presumably Frecuulf of Lisieux, *Historia* (ed. M. I. Allen, 2 vols. CCCM 169–169A (2002)). **26**. The Latin translation by Cassiodorus of Josephus, *Antiquitates*. **27**. Isidore wrote no work of this title; the work in question is probably the pseudo-Isidorian *Liber de numeris*, a Hiberno-Latin compilation of the eighth century (partial ed. PL 83: 1293–1302; see McNally, *Der irische Liber de Numeris*). **28**. Gregory, *Regula pastoralis*. **29**. Gregory, *Moralia in Iob*. **30**. The so-called *Vitas patrum*, an early title used to describe a massive but heterogeneous collection of lives and sayings principally of the early Egyptian Desert Fathers [BHL 6524–7]. **31**. Haymo of Auxerre's Commentary on the Pauline Epistles (PL 117: 361–938). **32**. Haymo of Auxerre is not known to have composed a commentary on the Gospels; possibly the work in question is his *Homiliae de tempore* (PL 118: 11–746). **33**. Jerome's substantial collection of *Epistulae*, preserved in three separate manuscripts (the modern CSEL edition is similarly printed in three separate volumes). **34**. The entry *Liber notarum* represents a scribal error for *Liber rotarum* ('Book of Diagrams'), a title under which Isidore's *De natura rerum* travelled during the Middle Ages. **35**. Assuming that the third of these titles refers to Isidore's treatise *De differentiis uerborum*, it is possible that the first was a copy of Isidore's *Quaestiones in Vetus Testamentum*; alternatively, the *Liber differentiarum* could conceivably be Boethius, *De differentiis topicis*, in which case the *Diffinitio philosophie* might be the treatise *De definitionibus*, a work now known to be by Marius Victorinus, but which passed under Boethius' name during the Middle Ages, and was intended as an introduction to Cicero's *Topica*. **36**. Another copy of the previously listed (and unidentifiable) work. **37**. Presumably Paulinus of Nola's *Carmina* on Felix, the patron saint of Nola. **38**. A copy of a *Vita S. Æthelwoldi*, either that by Wulfstan of Winchester [BHL 2647], or the abbreviated version of Wulfstan's work by Ælfric [BHL 2646]; however, Friis-Jensen and Willoughby (*Peterborough Abbey*, 12) point out that John Leland copied excerpts from Wulfstan's *Vita S. Æthelwoldi* at Peterborough in the 1530s, so that Wulfstan's text rather than Ælfric's abbreviation is probably in question here. **39**. Julian of Toledo, *Prognosticum futuri saeculi*. **40**. Stephen of Ripon, *Vita S. Wilfridi* [BHL 8889]. **41**. Presumably one of the several *uitae* of the Flemish saint Gislenus [BHL 3552–8]. **42**. Smaragdus of Saint-Mihiel, *Diadema monachorum* (PL 102: 593–690). **43**. Presumably the text referred to as *Paradisus Heraclidis* [BHL 6532], ed. PL 74: 243–342), which is a Latin translation of part of the *Historia Lausiaca* of Palladius, which in turn circulated as part of the massive collection of *Vitas patrum* (see above, no. 30). **44**. Unidentifiable without further specification. **45**. Unidentifiable without further specification. **46**. Isidore, *Sententiae*; the title *De summo bono* derives from the first sentence of the treatise ('Summum bonum Deus est . . .'). **47**. Prosper of Aquitaine,

Epitome chronicorum. **48.** Possibly a copy of Augustine, *De diuersis quaestionibus .lxxxiii.*, or perhaps simply a miscellaneous collection of his writings. **49.** The Merovingian *Vita S. Fursei* [BHL 3209] in combination with the *Visio Baronti* [CPL 1313]. **50.** Gregory of Nazianzus, *Oratio* ii (*Liber apologeticus de fuga*), in the Latin translation of Rufinus. **51.** Probably Victor of Vita, *Historia persecutionis Africanae prouinciae.* **52.** Either an incomplete copy of a commentary on all 150 psalms (say, Augustine, *Enarrationes in psalmos* or Cassiodorus, *Expositio psalmorum*), or possibly the commentary attributed to Prosper of Aquitaine on Psalms c–cl alone. **53.** Cyprian, *Epistulae.* **54.** Probably not the Anglo-Latin *Vita S. Gregorii* composed at Whitby in the late seventh century [BHL 3637], but more likely the later Continental Life by John the Deacon [BHL 3641]. **55.** Ambrose, *Exameron.* **56.** An unidentifiable collection of ecclesiastical legislation. **57.** A metrical *Passio S. Eustachii*, possibly identical with one of the books earlier given by Bishop Æthelwold to Peterborough (above, INV(i) **b. 8**), and presumably that listed at ICL 14237, for which a tenth-century origin in the ambit of Æthelwold's Winchester has been argued in Lapidge, *ALL* ii. 213–23. **58.** The pseudo-Clementine *Recognitiones* in the Latin translation of Rufinus, in combination with Sulpicius Severus, *Vita S. Martini.* **59.** Hrabanus Maurus, *De institutione clericorum* (PL 107: 293–420). **60.** *Liber miraculorum*: the title of one of the books earlier given by Bishop Æthelwold to Peterborough (INV(i) **b. 2**), and possibly the work of this title by Gregory of Tours.

Appendix B
Eighth-Century Inventories of Latin Books from the Area of the Anglo-Saxon Mission in Germany

Three inventories of eighth-century date survive from the area of the Anglo-Saxon mission in Germany: one from Würzburg, one from Fulda, and the third from an unidentified centre probably in the Low Countries, presumptively Echternach. These three texts are the earliest inventories which survive from the Middle Ages, and it is perhaps significant that it was Anglo-Saxons who, among medieval peoples, first devised the practice of recording the contents of their libraries: see recent discussion by Berschin, 'An Unpublished Library Catalogue', esp. 202–3, and Gorman, 'The Oldest Lists of Latin Books'. Note that, in the commentary which accompanies each inventory, I do not comment on biblical or liturgical entries.

a. The inventory from Würzburg

The inventory is preserved in Oxford, BodL, Laud misc. 126, a copy of Augustine's *De trinitate*; the inventory was added on a blank page at the end of the manuscript, now fo. 260^r. The handwriting of the inventory was dated by E. A. Lowe to *c*.800; but, as Berschin rightly observed, in spite of the date of the script, there is nothing 'typically Carolingian' about the contents of the list ('An Unpublished Library Catalogue', 203). Rather, the inventory throws light on an earlier period of the Anglo-Saxon mission, and its compilation perhaps dates from soon after the founding of the see of Würzburg in 742. It has been printed by Lowe in 'An Eighth-Century List', and is also ed. in *Libri sancti Kyliani*, 142–8, and in MBKDS iv. 2 (1979), 977–9.

1. Actus apostulorum
2. pastoralem
3. dialogorum
4. commentarium *ad Holzkirihhun*
5. historia anglorum
6. epistola sancti hieronimi
7. liber doctrine christiane
8. sancti augustini de fide
9. sancti ambrosi de fide
10. liber orosi
11. liber arnouii
12. iuuenci super euangelia
13. liber super effeseos

14. episcopal
15. decreta pontificum
16. liber augustini de quantitate anime
17. liber iunili
18. official
19. enceridion
20. liber prosperi
21. moralia in iob libri xxiii
22. summum bonum
23–4. lectionari duo
25. glosa
26. liber althelmi
27. liber de trinitate
28–9. liber esaiae duo
30. catalogus hieronimi presbyteri de auctoribus librorum
31. grammatica sancti augustini et sancti bonifati
32. epistulae sancti pauli
    ad fultu
33. speculum
34. omelia sancti gregorii maiora pars
35. liber prouerbium
36. beatitudines

1. The famous copy of Acts, in Greek and Latin, now Oxford, BodL, Laud Gr. 35. 2. Gregory, *Regula pastoralis*. Lowe draws attention to two copies of this work, one in Oxford, BodL, Laud misc. 263 (Anglo-Saxon script, s. ix^{in}), the other in Würzburg, UB, M. p. th. f. 42 (Caroline minuscule, s. ix), which has a flyleaf in Anglo-Saxon script. Either or both of these manuscripts could be later copies of that listed in the inventory. 3. Gregory, *Dialogi*. Lowe draws attention to an early ninth-century copy of the *Dialogi* from Würzburg, now Würzburg, UB, M. p. th. f. 19, written partially in Anglo-Saxon script. 4. Without further specification, it is impossible to identify this item; but given the Anglo-Saxon connections of many items in the list, Lowe tentatively suggested identification with the fifth-century uncial copy of Jerome, *Comm. in Ecclesiasten*, now Würzburg, UB, M. p. th. q. 2, which was owned in late seventh-century England by Cuthswith, abbess of Inkberrow, and subsequently taken to the Continent; see *Libri Sancti Kyliani*, 159–60, and Sims-Williams, 'Cuthswith, Seventh-Century Abbess of Inkberrow'. The note *ad Holzhirihhum* is added in Caroline minuscule (of a date later than the manuscript), and implies that the manuscript was on loan to Holzkirchen (a dependency of Fulda) at the time the entry was being annotated. 5. Bede, *Historia ecclesiastica gentis Anglorum* [CPL 1375]. 6. Presumably what was intended by the cataloguer was the *Epistulae* (plural) of St Jerome. 7. Augustine, *De doctrina christiana*. Lowe draws attention to a

ninth-century manuscript of the work from Würzburg, now Oxford, BodL, Laud misc. 121, which was evidently copied from an exemplar in Anglo-Saxon script, conceivably the book inventoried here. **8.** Either Augustine's *De fide et symbolo*, or his *De fide et operibus*. **9.** Ambrose, *De fide*. **10.** Orosius, *Historiae aduersum paganos*. **11.** A work of Arnobius Iunior; to judge by the use made of Arnobius by other Anglo-Saxon authors, the work in question is likely to be the *Comm. in psalmos* rather than works which enjoyed only limited circulation, such as the *Conflictus cum Serapione* [CPL 239]. This conjecture is confirmed by the fact that a Würzburg inventory of *c*.1000 lists a copy 'Arnobii in totum psalterium' (MBKDS iv. 978). **12.** Juvencus, *Euangelia*. **13.** A commentary on Paul's Letters to the Ephesians, presumably that of Jerome, *Comm. in .iv. epistulas Paulinas*, which, in addition to Ephesians, also included commentary on the Letters to Galatians, Titus, and Philemon. **14.** The title *episcopal* indicates at the very least that the inventory pertains to an episcopal library (as Würzburg was). **15.** A collection of papal decretals: perhaps the *Codex decretalium* of Dionysius Exiguus; see Wurm, *Studien und Texte zur Decretalensammlung*. Lowe suggests identification with Würzburg, UB, M. p. th. f.72. **16.** Augustine, *De quantitate animae*. **17.** Iunillus, *Instituta regularia diuinae legis*. **18.** Presumably Isidore, *De ecclesiasticis officiis*; Lowe suggests identification with Würzburg, UB, M. p. th. q. 18 (Insular script, s. viii^{ex}). **19.** Augustine, *Enchiridion ad Laurentium*. **20.** A *liber Prosperi* could refer to any of a number of works by Prosper of Aquitaine, but most probably to either the metrical *Epigrammata ex sententiis S. Augustini*, the *Expositio psalmorum a centesimo usque ad centesimum quinquagesimum*, or the (prose) *Sententiae ex operibus S. Augustini*. **21.** Gregory, *Moralia in Iob*, a work which in fact consists of thirty-five books; so either the numeral *.xxiii.* has been mutilated in transmission, or the book in question was an incomplete copy. **22.** Isidore, *Sententiae*. **25.** Perhaps a collection of glosses (biblical and otherwise) like those generated at the school of Canterbury in the late seventh century, and subsequently diffused in Continental manuscripts such as the 'Leiden Glossary' (see Lapidge, 'The School of Theodore and Hadrian'). **26.** A 'liber Althelmi' refers presumably either to Aldhelm's prose *De uirginitate*, which is often transmitted under the title *De laudibus uirginitatis* [CPL 1332], or the verse contrafactum of that work, the *Carmen de uirginitate* [CPL 1333]. Lowe points out that a mid-ninth-century copy of the prose *De uirginitate* is extant as Würzburg, UB, M. p. th. f.21, and that this manuscript shows signs of having been copied from an exemplar in Anglo-Saxon script, arguably identical with the book inventoried here. **27.** Augustine, *De trinitate*; probably the book in question is Laud misc. 126 itself, the manuscript into which the inventory was copied. **30.** Jerome, *De uiris inlustribus*. **31.** The grammatical treatise of Augustine is presumably the *Ars breuiata*, ed. C. F. Weber (1861); see Law, 'St Augustine's *De grammatica*'; that of Boniface, the *Ars grammatica* [CPL 1564b], is ed. in CCSL 133B: 15–99. As Lowe points out, this work of Augustine is transmitted alongside the *Ars grammatica* of Boniface in Vatican City, BAV, Pal. lat. 1746 (Lorsch, s. ix^{in}; see Bischoff, *Lorsch*, 118–19). **32.** The manuscript in question is Würzburg, UB, M. p. th. f. 69. **33–6**: as the rubric indicates, these four books were on loan to Fulda at the time the inventory was being copied. **33.** Augustine, *Speculum 'Quis ignorat'*. **34.** Of the several collections of homilies which Gregory composed, that in question here is possibly the *Hom. .xl. in euangelia*, which, as Lowe observes, is preserved in a late-eighth-century manuscript from Würzburg, UB, M. p. th. f. 45, which may be the book in question here. **36.** Unidentifiable; Lowe suggests Chromatius of Aquileia, the forty-first of whose *Sermones .xliii.* is entitled *Sermo de octo beatitudinibus*.

b. The inventory from Fulda

An inventory of twenty-three books (containing forty-eight titles) is preserved in a manuscript from Fulda, now Basle, UB, F. III. 15a, fos. 17^v–18^r; but these folios are badly abraded and barely legible. The inventory was first discovered and deciphered by Paul Lehmann: *Fuldaer Studien*, 49–50. The manuscript is dated to *c*.800 by Spilling, 'Angelsächsische Schrift in Fulda', 62–4. The inventory has been re-edited recently by Schrimpf, *Mittelalterliche Bücherverzeichnisse*, 5–6 (diplomatic transcription), 6–11 (reconstructed text with commentary). Given the illegibility of the script, it is hardly surprising that these two experienced palaeographers should have read various of the entries in varying ways. Furthermore, whereas Lehmann's edition recorded the entries as books (hence twenty-three items), Schrimpf prints the entries as titles (hence forty-eight items).

On the Fulda inventory, see also Hoffmann, *Buchkunst und Königtum*, i. 141; Berschin, *Biographie*, iii. 38–9; and Gorman, 'The Oldest Lists'.

In reprinting the inventory, I follow the numbering of Lehmann; but note that I have added capitalization and punctuation. Letters in square brackets are supplied by conjecture, either Lehmann's or Schrimpf's. As elsewhere in this volume, I do not comment on biblical or liturgical items (items nos. 1–3, 5–7).

1. [u . . .de u . . .] euangelii scidula sanctus Lucas iste medicus
2. Actus apostulorum
3. Epistulas apostulorum
4. Apocalipsis postuli sancti Pauli
5. Regum
6. Libri Salamonis tres et Sapiencia mos.
7. Thobias, Daniel, Esaias, Ieremias
8. Certamina apostulorum omnium
9. Omilias sancti Gregori super euangelium et commentarium sancti Gregori super Ehiel
10. De alligorum sancti Gregori

11. Sinonima sancti Esidori. Sancti Basillis
12. Liber sancti Effrem
13. Pastoralis sancti Gregori
14. Liber tres sentiarum
15. Sancti Esidori r[..]arum.
16. Liber uitas patrum, miracula patrum
17. Liber de creaturarum sancti Esidori me [a]rte uirginitate sancti [. . .]
18. Liber sermones sancti Augustini
19. Tres libri super uirginitatis et uita sancti Malhi monachi in unum librum
20. Vita sancti Pauli et Antoni et in illum librum passio sancti Ciriaci
21. Omilia [..] [. . .ssio] et sanctae Cirillae [. . . . . .] in unum librum
22. [Erasmi] . . .[Agnes] in unum librum et sancta Eogenia, Cyp[rianus et Iustina] in unum librum
23. Liber uita sanctorum dormientium in Effeso qui dormierunt, et in il[l]um librum sunt cronih, sancti Furseus liber, sententialis liber, liber Alexantri

4. Perhaps an Insular redaction of the *Visio S. Pauli*, or perhaps, as Schrimpf suggests, the eighth-century manuscript of Revelation from Fulda, now Kassel, Gesamthochschulbibliothek, Oct. theol. 5 (s. viii). 8. As Berschin points out ('An Unpublished Library Catalogue', 203 n. 10), the title refers to 'the well known collection of *Passiones apostolorum*', on which see Berschin, *Biographie*, i. 88–93. The present entry possibly pertains to a book similar to, if not identical with, Würzburg, UB, M. p. th. f. 78 (s. viii²). 9. Gregory, *Hom. .xl. in euangelia*, together with his *Hom. in Hiezechielem*. 10. The word *De alligorum* presumably represents a corruption of *Dialogorum*, hence a copy of Gregory's *Dialogi*. 11. Isidore, *Synonyma de lamentatione animae peccatricis*, possibly that preserved in Basle, UB, F. III. 15c, fos. 12–27, in combination with a Latin translation of an unspecified work of Basil, presumptively the *Regula S. Basilii* in the translation of Rufinus, as preserved in a Fulda manuscript of *c*.800, now Basle, UB, F. III. 15c, fos. 28–41. 12. A Latin translation of one of the many works of Ephrem which were transmitted in Greek (*Ephraem Graecus*: CPG 3905–4175); for a list of those six works which circulated in Latin (*Ephraem Latinus*), see CPL 1143: *De die iudicii et de resurrectione* [CPG 4080], *De beatitudine animae* [CPG 3935], *De patientia* [= *De paenitentia*] [CPG 3913], *In luctaminibus* [CPG 3920, 3935], *De die iudicii* [CPG 3940, 4089], and *De compunctione cordis* [CPG 3909, 3968]. A number of spurious writings also circulated in Latin under the name of Ephrem: CPL 1143a–1152. 13. Gregory, *Regula pastoralis*. 14. Isidore, *Sententiarum libri tres*; perhaps identical with Basle, UB, F. III. 15g (Fulda, s. ix^{1/3}). 15. Isidore, *De natura rerum*, which often passed under the title *Liber rotarum*, as here. 16. The *Vitas patrum*, a heterogenous collection of lives and sayings principally of the early Egyptian desert fathers [BHL 6524–47]. 17. Pseudo-Isidore, *De ordine creaturarum*, a work now

known to be of seventh-century Hiberno-Latin composition [BCLL 342]; in combination with a work on virginity, perhaps Augustine's *De sancta virginitate*, or possibly, as Schrimpf suggests, Aldhelm, prose or verse *De virginitate* [CPL 1332–3]. **18.** The *Sermones* of Augustine. **19.** Three unspecified treatises on virginity (perhaps those by Ambrose or Augustine), in combination with Jerome, *Vita S. Malchi*. **20.** Possibly simply Jerome's *Vita S. Pauli primi eremitae*, the central episode of which concerns the meeting of Paul and Antony in the desert; in combination with the *Passio S. Cyriaci* [BHL 7022], which in turn was often transmitted alongside the *Inventio S. Crucis* [BHL 4169]. **21.** An unspecified homily, bound up with a *passio* of St Cyrillus [BHL 2068]; note that there is no surviving *passio* of a St Cyrilla. **22.** A volume containing the *passiones* of St Erasmus [BHL 2578–82], St Agnes [BHL 156], St Eugenia [BHL 2666], and SS. Cyprian and Iustina [BHL 2050–1]. (The manuscript is badly abraded here, and Schrimpf's reconstruction differs significantly from that of Lehmann, which I follow.) **23.** A volume containing the *passio* of the Seven Sleepers of Ephesus (*septem dormientes*) [BHL 2315–19], unspecified *chronica*, the *Vita S. Fursei* [BHL 3209], perhaps Prosper of Aquitaine's (prose) *Sententiae ex operibus S. Augustini* (Schrimpf suggests instead Defensor of Ligugé, *Liber scintillarum*), and a *liber Alexandri*: possibly the *Passio SS. Alexandri, Euentii et Theoduli* [BHL 266], or perhaps the *Epistula Alexandri ad Aristotelem* [LLA 640].

c. Inventory from an unidentified centre in the Low Countries (Echternach?)

A third inventory is found as an early eighth-century addition by an Anglo-Saxon scribe to a manuscript now Vatican City, BAV, Pal. lat. 210, fo. 1ʳ; it was discovered and printed by Lehmann, 'Das älteste Bücherverzeichnis'. The script is dated to the early eighth century by Bischoff, *Lorsch*, 64. The manuscript was thought by Lehmann, followed by Bischoff, to have originated in the Low Countries, but the precise origin of the list is unknown. However, if item 4 in the following list is identical with Paris, BNF, lat. 9538, perhaps the inventory is to be associated with the circle of the Anglo-Saxon missionary Willibrord, hence with Echternach.

The following edition is based on that of Lehmann, but the numeration and punctuation are mine. As elsewhere in the volume, I omit to comment on the biblical and liturgical items in this list: nos. 1–3, 5, 10, 16–17.

1. quatuor e[uan]gelium sancta
2. duo sacramentorium
3. duo homelias
4. quindecim libri Augustini
5. undecem episto[le] Pauli
6. dealogorum

   7. rotarum
   8. regule
   9. liber locorum
  10. liber profetarum
  11. liber Cipriani testimoniali
  12. Sedulius metri [. . .]
  13. de igni purgatorio
  14. pastoralis
  15. uita Pauli et Antonio
  16. .ii. antefonarias
  17. duo libri Pauli

4. Presumably Augustine's *De trinitate*, which is divided into fifteen books; possibly the manuscript in question here is Paris, BNF, lat. 9538, an eighth-century manuscript in Anglo-Saxon script possibly from Echternach; see also below, App. C, no. 10. **6.** Gregory, *Dialogi*. **7.** Isidore, *De natura rerum*. **8.** Presumably a collection of monastic rules, as distinct from Gregory's *Regula pastoralis*, which is listed as no. 14 below. **9.** A *liber locorum* presumably pertains to places in the Holy Land, and might thus refer either to Jerome's Latin translation, under the title *De situ et nominibus locorum Hebraicorum*, of the *Onomasticon* of Eusebius, or to one of the early Holy Land pilgrimages (e.g. Egeria), or to a work such as Adomnán, *De locis sanctis*; Bede's redaction of Adomnán's work of the same title [CPL 2333] is probably too late to be in question here. **11.** Cyprian, *Testimonia ad Quirinum*, a biblical florilegium. **12.** Caelius Sedulius, *Carmen paschale*. **13.** A book containing a dream-vision description of the tortures of hell, such as that of the monk of Much Wenlock recorded by Boniface, *Ep*. x, or Bede's account of the vision of Dryhthelm in *HE* v. 12, or the *Visio Baronti* [CPL 1313]. **14.** Gregory, *Regula pastoralis*. **15.** Jerome, *Vita S. Pauli primi eremitae*, the central episode of which concerns the meeting of SS Paul and Antony in the desert.

Appendix C
Surviving Eighth-Century Manuscripts from the Area of the Anglo-Saxon Mission in Germany

The following list of manuscripts has been compiled directly from CLA (together with its Supplement and two published series of Addenda). In cases where more detailed manuscript catalogues exist (for example that of Hans Thurn for the manuscripts of Würzburg), I have expanded the telegraphic lists of contents given by Lowe; but I have reproduced exactly Lowe's datings and localizations. The appendix is organized according to volumes of CLA; I give in each case the CLA number, the correct shelf-mark of the manuscript, Lowe's palaeographical description and dating, and the contents. If a manuscript listed in CLA is also listed by Gneuss, *Handlist*, the Gneuss number is supplied in square brackets.

It is obvious that there are severe difficulties in distinguishing between manuscripts written in England and subsequently taken to the Continent (either by an Anglo-Saxon missionary or some other agent), and manuscripts written on the Continent either by Anglo-Saxon scribes or by Continental scribes trained by Anglo-Saxons. Gneuss carefully excluded the latter category, but with difficulty of discrimination. I have attempted no such differentiation, and simply repeat Lowe's attributions.

As elsewhere in the volume, I omit biblical and liturgical manuscripts. The numbering of items is my own, and is simply intended to facilitate indexing. Details of which alphanumerical repertories (e.g. CPG, CPL, etc.) contain references to individual authors and works earlier than AD 700 may be found in the Catalogue, below.

CLA i: The Vatican City (1934), nos. 1–117

1. [CLA i. 83] Vatican City, BAV, Pal. lat. 202: 'written in an Anglo-Saxon centre on the Continent', s. viii/ix. Contents: Augustine, *De trinitate*.

2. [CLA i. 90] Vatican City, BAV, Pal. lat. 259: 'written in an Anglo-Saxon centre on the Continent', s. viii. [Gneuss 911]. Contents: Gregory, *Hom. in Hiezechielem*.

3. [CLA i. 95] Vatican City, BAV, Pal. lat. 554, fos. 5–12: 'origin uncertain, but probably an Anglo-Saxon centre on the Continent; in any case the MS. was on the Continent soon after it was written', s. viii/ix. [Gneuss 911.5]. Contents: Ecgbert, *Poenitentiale* [CPL 1887].

4. [CLA i. 97] Vatican City, BAV, Pal. lat. 577: 'written, or perhaps only

rubricated, by Herimundus (fo. 31ᵛ) in a continental centre of Anglo-Saxon tradition. The MS. was certainly at Mainz by 1479', s. viii/ix. (More recent scholars, in particular Bernhard Bischoff, would assign the manuscript to Fulda, and date it to the late eighth century.) Contents: Dionysius Exiguus, *Canones* [First Recension].

CLA ii: Great Britain and Ireland (1935, 2nd edn. 1972), nos. 118–277

5. [CLA ii. *135] Cambridge, UL, Add. 4219: 'Germanic centre with south English connections', s. viii/ix. Contents: Aldhelm, prose *De uirginitate* [CPL 1332] (frg.).

6. [CLA ii. *146] Cheltenham, Phillipps 36185 + Marburg, Hessische Staatsarchiv, Hr 2, 4a–c: 'probably Fulda', s. viii². Contents: Jerome, *Epistulae* (frg.).

7. [CLA ii. *155] Durham, Cathedral Library, C. IV. 8, flyleaf: 'Continental, Anglo-Saxon minuscule', s. viii/ix. Contents: Gregory, *Moralia in Iob* (frg.).

CLA iii: Italy, Ancona—Novara (1938), nos. 278–406: nil

CLA iv: Italy, Perugia—Verona (1947), nos. 407–516: nil

CLA v: France, Paris (1950), nos. 517–703

8. [CLA v. 559] Paris, BNF, lat. 4871, fos. 161–8: 'origin probably Northumbria', s. viii/ix. [Gneuss 885]. Contents: Isidore, *Etymologiae*.

9. [CLA v. 584] Paris, BNF, lat. 9527: 'written either in England or in an Anglo-Saxon centre on the Continent (by the same scribe as produced CLA v. 588)', s. viii. Contents: Jerome, *Comm. in Esaiam*.

10. [CLA v. 588] Paris, BNF, lat. 9538: 'written in England or, more probably, in an Anglo-Saxon centre on the Continent . . . presumably Echternach', s. viii. Contents: Augustine, *De trinitate*.

11. [CLA v. 598] Paris, BNF, lat. 10400, fos. 107–8: 'written in England or in a continental centre under Anglo-Saxon influence, such as Echternach', s. viii/ix. Contents: Bede, *Expositio Apocalypseos* [CPL 1363] (frg.).

12. [CLA v. 651] Paris, BNF, lat. 13089, fos. 49–76: 'written probably in England', s. viiiᵐᵉᵈ [Gneuss 898.5]. Contents: Gregory, *Regula pastoralis*.

13. [CLA v. **4] Paris, BNF, lat. 17177, fos. 5–12 [+ Vatican City, BAV, lat. 304, flyleaf]: 'written presumably in a continental centre with Anglo-Saxon connections', s. viii¹. [Gneuss 900.5]. Contents: Theodore of Mopsuestia, *Comm. in epistulas Pauli minores*, in Latin translation.

CLA vi: France, Abbéville–Valenciennes (1953), nos. 704–841

14. [CLA vi. 737] Boulogne-sur-Mer, BM, 58 (63–4): 'written by Anglo-Saxon scribes, perhaps on the Continent', s. viii². [Gneuss 799. 5]. Contents: Augustine, *Epistulae.*

15. [CLA vi. 740] Cambrai, Médiathèque municipale 470 (441): 'written doubtless in an Anglo-Saxon centre on the Continent. Provenance Cambrai', s. viii¹. [Gneuss 808.5]. Contents: Philippus Presbyter, *Comm. in librum Iob.*

CLA vii: Switzerland (1956), nos. 842–1023

16. [CLA vii. 842] Basle, UB, F. III. 15a, fos. 1–23: 'written in a continental centre with an Anglo-Saxon tradition, most likely at Fulda', s. viii/ix. Contents: Isidore, *De natura rerum.*

17. [CLA vii. 843] Basle, UB, F. III. 15a, fos. 24–32: 'written in an Anglo-Saxon scriptorium, presumably on the Continent and probably at Fulda', s. viii/ix. Contents: pseudo-Isidore, *Liber differentiarum seu De proprietate sermonum.*

18. [CLA vii. 844] Basle, UB, F. III. 15b, fos. 1–19: 'written in England and, to judge by the script, in the North. Reached Fulda at an early date', s. viii¹. [Gneuss 785]. Contents: pseudo-Isidore, *De ordine creaturarum.*

19. [CLA vii. 845] Basle, UB, F. III. 15c, fos. 12–27: 'written in a German centre under Anglo-Saxon influence. Belonged to Fulda', s. viii². Contents: Isidore, *Synonyma de lamentatione animae peccatricis.*

20. [CLA vii. 846] Basle, UB, F. III. 15c, fos. 28–64: 'written in a German centre under Anglo-Saxon influence; belonged to Fulda', s. viii/ix. Contents: *Regula S. Basilii,* trans. Rufinus.

21. [CLA vii. 848] Basle, UB, F. III. 15f: 'written doubtless in England, to judge by script and other palaeographical features. Reached Fulda presumably at an early date', s. viii¹. [Gneuss 786]. Contents: Isidore, *De natura rerum.*

22. [CLA vii. 849] Basle, UB, F. III. 15l: 'written in an Anglo-Saxon centre, probably on the Continent', s. viii¹. [Gneuss 787]. Contents: Isidore, *De differentiis rerum siue Differentiae theologicae uel spiritales,* Gennadius, *De uiris inlustribus.*

23. [CLA vii. 853] Basle, UB, O. IV. 17: 'written in a German centre under Anglo-Saxon influence, possibly at Fulda with which its later history is connected', s. viii/ix. Contents: Sulpicius Severus, *Epistulae,* Caelius Sedulius, *Carmen paschale.*

24. [CLA vii. 976] St Gallen, SB, 913: 'written presumably in Germany by a scribe trained in the Anglo-Saxon tradition', s. viii². Contents: excerpta varia, biblical glosses (ed. Bischoff and Lapidge, *Biblical Commentaries,* 534–41).

25. [CLA vii. 982] St Gallen, SB, 1394, pp. 121–2, 125–6, 127–8: fragment, 'written most likely in a German centre with Anglo-Saxon traditions', s. viii^{ex}. Contents: Aldhelm, *De metris* and *Enigmata* [CPL 1335] (frg.).

26. [CLA vii. 983] St Gallen, SB, 1394, pp. 123–4: 'written most likely in a German centre with Anglo-Saxon traditions', s. viii/ix. Contents: Isidore, *Etymologiae* (frg.).

CLA viii: Germany, Altenburg–Leipzig (1959), nos. 1024–1229

27. [CLA viii. 1055] Berlin, Staatsbibliothek Preußischer Kulturbesitz, Phillipps 1662: 'written in an important Anglo-Saxon centre in the Mainz–Fulda–Hersfeld region', s. viii^{ex}. Contents: Augustine, *Tractatus in Euangelium Ioannis*.

28. [CLA viii. 1068] Berlin, Staatsbibliothek Preußischer Kulturbesitz, Theol. lat. fol. 355: binding fragment, 'written presumably in South England, possibly in an Anglo-Saxon centre on the Continent', s. viii^2. [Gneuss 791.3]. Contents: saints' Lives (frg.).

29. [CLA viii. 1070] Bonn, UB, S 366: two folios, 'written apparently in an Anglo-Saxon centre on the Continent, possibly at Werden itself', s. viii/ix. Contents: Gregory, *Dialogi* (frg.).

30. [CLA viii. 1095] Karlsruhe, Badische Landesbibliothek, Aug. perg. 221, fos. 54–107: 'written presumably in Northumbria or on the Continent in an Anglo-Saxon centre with Northumbrian connexions', s. viii^{med}. [Gneuss 831.6]. Contents: Gregory, *Hom. in Hiezechielem*.

31. [CLA viii. 1124] Karlsruhe, Badische Landesbibliothek, fragm. aug. 116 [+ Vienna, ÖNB, lat. 482 (frg.)]: 'written in an Anglo-Saxon centre presumably on the Continent, and probably the very centre whence came most of the other Karlsruhe Anglo-Saxon grammatical fragments and the Gotha Aldhelm (CLA viii. 1207)', s. viii^{ex}. Contents: Charisius, *Ars grammatica*.

32. [CLA viii. 1125] Karlsruhe, Badische Landesbibliothek, fragm. aug. 117: same origin as CLA viii. 1124. Contents: Diomedes, *Ars grammatica*.

33. [CLA viii. 1126] Karlsruhe, Badische Landesbibliothek, fragm. aug. 118: same origin as CLA viii. 1124. Contents: Consentius Gallus, *Ars de nomine et uerbo*.

34. [CLA viii. 1127] Karlsruhe, Badische Landesbibliothek, fragm. aug. 119 [+ 127 + 128 + 129 + 130 + 131 + 134, + St Paul in Carinthia, Stiftsbibliothek, 979, fos. 5–6], 'written in an Anglo-Saxon scriptorium presumably on the Continent, probably the same one that produced the other grammatical texts' as in CLA viii.1124, s. viii^{ex}. Contents: Bonifatius, *Ep. ad Sigebertum*; Tatwine, *Ars grammatica* [CPL 1563] (frg.).

35. [CLA viii. ** 1009] Karlsruhe, Badische Landesbibliothek, fragm. aug.

122 [+ Zurich, Staatsarchiv A.G. 19, no. xiii, fos. 26–7]: 'written presumably in England and probably in Northumbria, to judge from the script. The fragments came from Reichenau', s. viii^{ex}. [Gneuss 831.7]. Contents: Priscian, *Institutio de nomine et pronomine et uerbo* (frg.).

36. [CLA viii. 1129] Karlsruhe, Badische Landesbibliothek, fragm. aug. 136: 'written in an Anglo-Saxon scriptorium presumably on the Continent, probably the one that produced the other grammatical texts [as CLA viii. 1124]', s. viii^{ex}. Contents: Martianus Capella, *De nuptiis Philologiae et Mercurii*, book iii.

37. [CLA viii. 1133] Kassel, Gesamthochschulbibliothek, Fol. philol. 15 [+ Fritzlar, Stiftskirche St Peter, Schatzkammer s.n.]: 'written most likely in Germany, in one of the Anglo-Saxon missionary centres', s. viii/ix. Contents: Priscian, *Institutiones grammaticae* (frg.).

38. [CLA viii. 1134] Kassel, Gesamthochschulbibliothek, Fol. theol. 21: 'written probably in a Northumbrian centre and doubtless copied in the Ambrose part from an ancient exemplar; belonged later to the monastery of Fulda', s. viii. [Gneuss 832] Contents: Jerome, *Comm. in Ecclesiasten*, Ambrose, *De apologia prophetae David*.

39. [CLA viii. 1136]: Kassel, Gesamthochschulbibliothek, Fol. theol. 24: 'written in an Anglo-Saxon centre in Germany, possibly in Fulda itself, to judge by the script', s. viii. Contents: Primasius, *Comm. in Apocalypsin*.

40. [CLA viii. 1138] Kassel, Gesamthochschulbibliothek, Fol. theol. 32: 'written apparently in a south English centre, perhaps in the same scriptorium as the Corpus Glossary (CLA ii. 122); was in Fulda by the ninth century', s. viii^2. Contents: Gregory, *Regula pastoralis*.

41. [CLA viii. 1143] Kassel, Gesamthochschulbibliothek, Manuskripten-Anhang 18: 'written most likely in England, possibly in an Anglo-Saxon centre on the Continent', s. viii^2. Contents: Cassian, *Conlationes*.

42. [CLA viii. 1144] Kassel, Gesamthochschulbibliothek, Manuskripten-Anhang 19 [+ Hersfeld, Stadtarchiv, lat. iv]: 'written in an Anglo-Saxon centre in Germany, possibly at Hersfeld', s. viii/ix. Contents: Gregory, *Moralia in Iob* (frg.).

43. [CLA viii. 1145] Kassel, Gesamthochschulbibliothek, Manuskripten-Anhang 19, 1a: 'written most probably in an Anglo-Saxon centre on the Continent', s. viii^{ex}. Contents: Jerome, *Prologus in Danielem* (frg.).

44. [CLA viii. 1181] *olim* Dresden, Sächsische Landesbibliothek, R 52um: 'written in an Anglo-Saxon centre in Germany', s. viii^{ex}. Contents: [anonymi Scotti], *Comm. in Matthaeum* (frg.) [destroyed in 1945].

45. [CLA viii. 1186] Düsseldorf, UB, K1: B. 213: 'written either in England or in an Anglo-Saxon centre in Germany, like Werden', s. viii/ix. Contents: Gregory, *Dialogi* (frg.).

46. [CLA viii. 1188] Düsseldorf, UB, K2: E. 32: 'written in an Anglo-Saxon centre, probably on the Continent and possibly at Werden', s. viii^{ex}. Contents: *Collectio canonum Quesnelliana*.

47. [CLA viii. 1202] Göttingen, Niedersächsische Staats- und Universitätsbibliothek, Müller III. 1–2 [+ Hersfeld, Städtisches Museum, C 185]: 'written in an Anglo-Saxon scriptorium on the Continent, and doubtless in Germany', s. viii/ix. Contents: Augustine, *Tractatus in Euangelium Iohannis* (frg.).

48. [CLA viii. 1203] Göttingen, Niedersächsische Staats- und Universitätsbibliothek, Apparat. diplom. I. 1: 'written in an Anglo-Saxon centre doubtless on the Continent', s. viii/ix. Contents: [anonymi] *Comm. in Epistulas Pauli* (frg.).

49. [CLA viii. 1206] Gotha, Landesbibliothek, Mbr. I. 75, fos. 1–22: 'written in South England or possibly in an Anglo-Saxon centre on the Continent; was probably at Murbach and bound up with the Aldhelm part already in the early ninth century', s. viii^{ex}. Contents: Caelius Sedulius, *Carmen paschale*.

50. [CLA viii. 1207] Gotha, Landesbibliothek, Mbr. I. 75, fos. 23–69: 'written probably in the same Anglo-Saxon scriptorium which produced the Reichenau grammatical fragments dealt with in' CLA viii. 1124, s. viii. Contents: Aldhelm, prose *De uirginitate* [CPL 1332].

51. [CLA viii. 1210] Gotha, Landesbibliothek, Mbr. II. 193: 'written in an Anglo-Saxon centre, most likely on the Continent and quite likely in one such as Fulda', s. viii^{ex}. Contents: Julian of Toledo, *Ars grammatica*.

52. [CLA viii. 1224] *olim* Heidelberg, UB, Palat. lat. 921: 'written [in Anglo-Saxon minuscule] in a German scriptorium in the Main region', s. viii/ix. Contents: Jordanes, *De summa temporum uel origine actibusque gentis Romanorum, De origine actibusque Getarum*. [destroyed in 1880].

53. [CLA viii. 1225] Hersfeld, Stadtarchiv, lat. III [+ Stiftspfarrei s.n.]: 'written in an Anglo-Saxon centre in Germany, possibly at Hersfeld', s. viii^{2}. Contents: Isidore, *Etymologiae* (frg.)

CLA ix: Germany, Maria-Laach–Würzburg (1959), nos. 1230–1442

54. [CLA ix. 1234] Münster in Westphalen, Staatsarchiv, Msc. I. 243, fos. 3–10: 'written at Fulda [in Anglo-Saxon minuscule], as text and script suggest; was apparently at Münster or Werden in the first half of the ninth century', s. viii^{ex} [post 779]. Contents: Dionysius Exiguus, *Cyclus magnus Paschae*.

55. [CLA ix. 1264] Munich, Bayerische Staatsbibliothek, Clm. 6298: 'written in a German centre in the Anglo-Saxon tradition, doubtless in the Mainz–Fulda–Würzburg region', s. viii^{ex}. Contents: Caesarius of Arles, *Sermones*.

56. [CLA ix. 1306] Munich, Bayerische Staatsbibliothek, Clm. 14641, fos.

32–47: 'written at Fulda [in Anglo-Saxon minuscule]', s. viii^{ex} [post 779]. Contents: *tabulae paschales.*

57. [CLA ix. 1332] Munich, Bayerische Staatsbibliothek, Clm. 29051a: 'written apparently in some continental centre under Insular influence', s. viii^2. Contents: Isidore, *Etymologiae* (frg.).

58. [CLA ix. 1346] Nürnberg, Germanisches Nationalmuseum, 7152: 'written in an Anglo-Saxon scriptorium, presumably in Germany', s. viii^{ex}. Contents: *homiliarium* [unidentified] (frg.).

59. [CLA ix. 1373] Bad Windsheim, Stadtbibliothek, fragm. s.n.: 'written doubtless in a German centre with Anglo-Saxon traditions, in Hessia or in the Main region', s. viii/ix. Contents: *Passio S. Sebastiani* [CPL 2229; BHL 7543] (frg.).

60. [CLA ix. 1381] Wolfenbüttel, Herzog August Bibliothek, Helmst. 496a: 'written in an Anglo-Saxon centre in Germany, presumably at Fulda', s. viii/ ix. Contents: the Carolingian *Capitularium* of AD 789.

61. [CLA ix. 1397] Würzburg, UB, M. ch. f. 36 (binding): 'written doubtless in a Germanic centre under Anglo-Saxon influence, such as Fulda', s. viii/ix. Contents: [unidentified] *fragmentum argumenti exegetici super Paulum* (frg.).

62. [CLA ix. 1400] Würzburg, UB, M. p. j. f. 7, fo. A + M. p. th. f. 28 (binding) [+ Oxford, BodL, Laud misc. 263]: 'written doubtless in an Anglo-Saxon centre in Germany, most likely at Mainz, by Willibaldus diaconus', s. viii^{ex}. Contents: Gregory, *Regula pastoralis* (frg.).

63. [CLA ix. 1401] Würzburg, UB, M. p. misc. f. 3 + 5a, + M. p. th. f. 5 + 13 + 37 + 38 + 60 + q.2 (binding strips): 'origin uncertain, presumably an Anglo-Saxon centre on the Continent, to judge from the use of parchment instead of vellum', s. viii/ix. Contents: *Decreta pontificum* (*Collectio Dionysiana*) (frg.)

64. [CLA ix. 1402] Würzburg, UB, M. p. misc. f. 5a: 'written doubtless in a German scriptorium with Anglo-Saxon connexions', s. viii/ix. Contents: Cassiodorus, *Institutiones*; Cassiodorus, *Computus paschalis* [cf. CPL 906]; Cassiodorus, *De propositionum modis* [cf. CPL 906]; Julius Severianus, *Praecepta artis rhetoricae* [RLM, pp. 353–70].

65. [CLA ix. 1404] Würzburg, UB, M. p. th. f. 13: 'written in a continental centre under Anglo-Saxon influence, perhaps in the Würzburg region and in the same scriptorium which produced [CLA ix. 1425]', s. viii^2. Contents: Defensor of Ligugé, *Liber scintillarum.*

66. [CLA ix. 1405] Würzburg, UB, M. p. th. f. 17: 'written doubtless in an Anglo-Saxon scriptorium on the Continent, probably in the Würzburg region', s. viii^2. Contents: Augustine, *Enarrationes in psalmos.*

67. [CLA ix. 1406] Würzburg, UB, M. p. th. f. 19: 'written presumably in a

West German scriptorium with Anglo–Saxon connexions, possibly at Lorsch or its vicinity', s. viii/ix. Contents: Gregory, *Dialogi*.

68. [CLA ix. 1407] Würzburg, UB, M. p. th. f. 27: 'written in an Anglo–Saxon scriptorium on the Continent, probably in Germany, but hardly at Würzburg, though the manuscript may have reached this centre by the ninth century', s. viii². Contents: Origen, *In Numeros homiliae .xxviii.*, trans. Rufinus.

69. [CLA ix. 1408] Würzburg, UB, M. p. th. f. 28: 'written in a German centre where Anglo–Saxon influence was still alive, presumably in Bavaria, to judge by the script, textual tradition, and the German glosses', s. viii$^{4/4}$. Contents: Caesarius, *Sermones* (excerpts); *Acta suppositi concilii Caesareae* [CPL 2307]; *Epistula Titi* [CPL 796]; *Epistula Iohannis Constantinopoli ad Eutropium*, trans. Anianus of Celeda [CPG 4392]; *Passio S. Christophori* [BHL 1766]; *Ratio orbis ex quo terra condita est* [cf. CPL 633].

70. [CLA ix. 1410] Würzburg, UB, M. p. th. f. 43, fos. 1–17, 41–53: 'written in England or in an Anglo–Saxon centre on the Continent, presumably in the same scriptorium as Gregory's Homilies on Ezechiel on fos. 18–40 [CLA ix. 1411]', s. viii. [Gneuss 944.5]. Contents: Augustine, *Enarrationes in psalmos*.

71. [CLA ix. 1411] Würzburg, UB, M. p. th. f. 43, fos. 18–40: 'written in England or in an Anglo–Saxon centre on the Continent, presumably in the same scriptorium as Augustine in Psalmos on fos. 1–17 and 41–53 [CLA ix. 1410]', s. viii. [Gneuss 944.5]. Contents: Gregory, *Hom. in Hiezechielem*.

72. [CLA ix. 1412] Würzburg, UB, M. p. th. f. 45: 'written in an Anglo–Saxon centre in Germany, probably in the Würzburg region, and presumably in a nunnery', s. viii². Contents: Gregory, *Hom. .xl. in Euangelia*.

73. [CLA ix. 1414] Würzburg, UB, M. p. th. f. 47: 'written in an Anglo–Saxon centre, probably on the Continent . . . ; but it is not excluded that the manuscript was written in Kent, especially as the biblical glosses sprang from the Canterbury school', s. viii^{ex}. Contents: biblical glosses (ed. Bischoff and Lapidge, *Biblical Commentaries*, 552–9); Gregory, *Hom. .xl. in Euangelia*; Gregory, *Hom. in Hiezechielem*.

74. [CLA ix. 1418] Würzburg, UB, M. p. th. f. 64: 'written in an Anglo–Saxon centre on the Continent, perhaps at Würzburg itself', s. viii/ix. Contents: Augustine, *Enarrationes in psalmos*.

75. [CLA ix. 1425] Würzburg, UB, M. p. th. f. 78: 'written in an Anglo–Saxon centre on the Continent, perhaps in the Würzburg region, and in the same scriptorium which produced [CLA ix. 1404]', s. viii². Contents: *passiones apostolorum*.

76. [CLA ix. 1426] Würzburg, UB, M. p. th. f. 79: 'written in England, probably in the South or in Mercia; was in Germany at latest by the ninth century, to judge by the glosses', s. viii. [Gneuss 946]. Contents: Isidore, *Synonyma de lamentatione animae peccatricis*.

77. [CLA ix. 1427] Würzburg, UB, M. p. th. f. 149a: 'written in an Anglo-Saxon centre on the Continent, to judge by the use of parchment, and probably by a scribe trained in the Northumbrian tradition', s. viii². [Gneuss 946.5]. Contents: Gregory, *Moralia in Iob*.

78. [CLA ix. 1430a] Würzburg, UB, M. p. th. q. 2: 'written in Italy. Came to England, probably in the seventh century . . . reached Würzburg perhaps by the eighth century', s. v. Contents: Jerome, *Comm. in Ecclesiasten*.

79. [CLA ix. 1432] Würzburg, UB, M. p. th. q. 18: 'written doubtless in an Anglo-Saxon scriptorium in Germany', s. viii². Contents: Isidore, *De ecclesiasticis officiis*.

80. [CLA ix. 1433] Würzburg, UB, M. p. th. q. 24: 'written by an Anglo-Saxon scribe, presumably on the Continent and probably in some German centre', s. viii². [Gneuss 944.3]. Contents: Isidore, *Mysticorum expositiones sacramentorum seu Quaestiones in uetus Testamentum*.

81. [CLA ix. 1434] Würzburg, UB, M. p. th. q. 26: 'written doubtless in an Anglo-Saxon centre on the Continent, perhaps at Würzburg itself', s. viii/ix. Contents: Aponius, *In Cantica canticorum expositio*; Jerome, *Vita S. Malchi*; Jerome, *Ep.* xiv; *Passio S. Iohannis* [CPG 1097; BHL 4320] [pseudo-Mellitus]; *Passio S. Euphrosynae* [BHL 2733].

82. [CLA ix. 1435] Würzburg, UB, M. p. th. q. 28a: 'written doubtless in an Anglo-Saxon centre on the Continent, presumably in the Würzburg region, to judge from its palaeographical kinship to [CLA ix. 1405]', s. viii/ix. Contents: Isidore, *Synonyma de lamentatione animae peccatricis*, *Passio S. Eugeniae* [BHL 2666] [pseudo-Rufinus]; *Passio S. Potiti* [BHL 6908] (frg.).

83. [CLA ix. 1436] Würzburg, UB, M. p. th. q. 28b, fos. 1–42: 'written in an Anglo-Saxon centre on the Continent, presumably in the Fulda–Würzburg region', s. viii/ix. Contents: *homiliae variae* (incl. pseudo-Caesarius, *Sermones*); pseudo-Augustine, *Sermo de resurrectione Domini*); *exegetica varia*; *Passio S. Caeciliae* [BHL 1496]; *Passio S. Iulianae* [BHL 4522] *Passio S. Agnae* [BHL 157]; Jerome, *Comm. in Ecclesiasten* (excerpts).

84. [CLA ix. 1437] Würzburg, UB, M. p. th. q. 28b, fos. 43–64: 'written doubtless in an Anglo-Saxon centre on the Continent and presumably in Germany, if not in Würzburg itself', s. viii/ix. Contents: Isidore, *Synonyma de lamentatione animae peccatricis*.

85. [CLA ix. 1438] Würzburg, UB, M. p. th. q. 30: 'written in an Anglo-Saxon centre on the Continent and presumably in Germany', s. viii/ix. Contents: *Verba seniorum* [BHL 6527, 6529].

86. [CLA ix. 1439] Würzburg, UB, M. p. th. q. 31, fos. 1–41, 52–9: 'written

in an Anglo-Saxon centre on the Continent, presumably in Germany', s. viii/ix. Contents: *Collectio canonum Hibernensis*; *Collectio canonum Andegauensis.*

87. [CLA ix. 1442] Würzburg, UB, M. p. th. o. 1: 'written in a south-west German centre such as Murbach; migrated early to the Main region or Hessia, where the last four folios were added in Anglo-Saxon minuscule', s. viii/ix. Caesarius, *Sermones*; Caesarius, *Ep. .ii. ad sanctimoniales*; *Regula magistri.*

CLA x: Austria, Belgium, Czechoslovakia, Denmark, Egypt, and Holland (1963), nos. 1443–1588

88. [CLA x. 1443] Innsbruck, UB, fragm. 72 [+ Vienna, ÖNB, lat. ser. n. 3643]: 'written in an Anglo-Saxon centre, presumably in Germany to judge by the script', s. viii/ix. Contents: Josephus, *Bellum Iudaicum*, trans. and abbrev. Hegesippus (frg.).

89. [CLA x. 1514] Vienna, ÖNB, lat. ser. N. 3642: 'written presumably in an Anglo-Saxon centre on the Continent, to judge by the script', s. viii/ix. Contents: Muirchú moccu Macthéni, *Vita S. Patricii* [CPL 1105; BHL 6497; BCLL 303] (frg.).

90. [CLA x. 1515] Vienna, ÖNB, lat. ser. N. 3644: 'written in England, and presumably in the North, or possibly in an Anglo-Saxon foundation on the Continent', s. viii. Contents: Eusebius, *Historia ecclesiastica*, trans. Rufinus (frg.).

91. [CLA x. 1551] Brussels, Bibliothèque Royale, II. 1069, fos. 59–97: 'written in an Anglo-Saxon centre on the Continent, to judge by the use of parchment', s. viii². Contents: *passiones apostolorum* (palimpsest frg.).

CLA xi: Hungary, Luxembourg, Poland, Russia, Spain, Sweden, the United States, and Yugoslavia (1966), nos. 1589–1811

92. [CLA xi. 1589] Budapest, National Széchenyi Library, Cod. lat. 442 [+ Budapest, UL, fragm. lat. 1 + Berlin, Staatsbibliothek Preußischer Kulturbesitz, Grimm 132, 1 + Munich, Stadtarchiv, Historischer Verein Oberbayern, 733/16]: 'written in South England or in a German scriptorium under Anglo-Saxon influence', s. viii/ix. Contents: Bede, *Vita metrica S. Cuthberti* [CPL 1380; BHL 2020] (frg.).

93. [CLA xi. 1591] Esztergom, Archiepiscopal Library, s.n.: 'written most likely in England, possibly in an Anglo-Saxon centre on the Continent', s. viii². Contents: Gregory, *Hom. in Hiezechielem* (frg.).

94. [CLA xi. 1599] St Petersburg, Public Library, F. v. I. 3, fos. 1–38: 'written probably in Northumbria, possibly by Northumbrian scribes in a

continental centre, and in the same scriptorium that produced the manu-script of Jerome on Isaiah with which it is bound [CLA xi. 1600]', s. viii². [Gneuss 840.5]. Contents: the book of Job, with glosses from Philippus Presbyter, *Comm. in librum Iob.*

95. [CLA xi. 1600] St Petersburg, Russian National Library, F. v. I. 3, fos. 39–108: 'written probably in Northumbria, possibly by Northumbrian scribes in a continental centre, and in the same scriptorium that produced the glossed manuscript of Job with which it is bound [CLA xi. 1599]', s. viii². [Gneuss 840.6]. Contents: Jerome, *Comm. in Esaiam.*

96. [CLA xi. 1655] New York, Columbia UL, Plimpton 129 [+ New York, Pierpont Morgan Library, M. 559]: 'written in an Anglo-Saxon centre, probably in Germany', s. viii/ix. Contents: Isidore, *Synonyma de lamenta-tione animae peccatricis* (frg.).

CLA Supplement (1971), nos. 1589–1811

97. [CLA Supp. 1674] Berlin, Staatsbibliothek, Stiftung Preußischer Kulturbesitz, Lat. fol. 445 [+ Munich, Dr B. Bischoff Collection, s.n.]: 'written in an Anglo-Saxon centre in Germany', s. viii/ix. Contents: Isidore, *Etymologiae* (frg.).

98. [CLA Supp. 1686] Düsseldorf, UB, Fragm. K19: Z. 8/1 (*olim* Staatsarchiv Z. 4 nr 1): 'written in an Anglo-Saxon centre, probably in Germany', s. viii^ex. Contents: Jerome, *Comm. in Esaiam* (frg.).

99. [CLA Supp. 1698] Fulda, Hessische Landesbibliothek, Fragm. s.n. [+ Marburg, Hessisches Staatsarchiv, Hr. 2, 4d]: 'written in an Anglo-Saxon centre in Germany', s. viii^ex. Contents: Jerome, *Comm. in Euangelium Matthaei* (frg.).

100. [CLA Supp. 1730] Marburg, Hessisches Staatsarchiv, Hr. 1, 3: 'Written probably on the Continent, presumably at Fulda', s. viii. Contents: Gregory, *Hom. in Hiezechielem* (frg.).

101. [CLA Supp. 1731] Marburg, Hessisches Staatsarchiv, Hr. 2, 2: 'written in an Anglo-Saxon centre in Germany, presumably at Fulda', s. viii^ex. Contents: Eucherius, *Instructiones* (frg.).

102. [CLA Supp. 1732] Marburg, Hessisches Staatsarchiv, Hr. 2, 6: 'written presumably at Fulda', s. viii^ex. Contents: patristica (frg.).

103. [CLA Supp. 1733] Marburg, Hessisches Staatsarchiv, Hr. 2, 7 a-h: 'written doubtless on the Continent and presumably at Fulda', s. viii^med. Contents: Gregory, *Hom. in Hiezechielem* (frg.).

104. [CLA Supp. 1749] Paris, BNF, lat. 16668: 'written at Lorsch [but one of the scribes writes Anglo-Saxon minuscule]', s. viii^ex. Contents: Bede, *De arte metrica* [CPL 1565]; Aldhelm, *Carmen de uirginitate* [CPL 1333]; Themistius, *De arte dialectica.*

105. [CLA Supp. 1787] Fulda, Priesterseminar, fragm. s.n.: 'written in an Anglo-Saxon centre in Germany, apparently by a German scribe [writing Anglo-Saxon minuscule]', s. viii^2. Contents: Gregory, *Hom. in Hiezechielem* (frg.).

106. [CLA Supp. 1788] Graz, Stieiermärkisches Landesarchiv, fragm. s.n.: 'written presumably in an Anglo-Saxon centre in Germany such as Fulda', s. viii^{ex}. Contents: Jerome, *Comm. in .iv. epistulas Paulinas* [ad Titum] (frg.).

CLA Addenda (1985), nos. 1812–65 [= Add. (i)]

107. [CLA Add. (i). 1820] Kassel, Gesamthochschulbibliothek, Quart. theol. 166 [*olim* Manuskripten-Anhang 19/7, 1]: one leaf, 'written presumably in Germany in a centre with Anglo-Saxon traditions', s. viii^{ex}. Contents: Gregory, *Hom. .xl. in euangelia* (frg.).

108. [CLA Add. (i). 1831] Hersfeld, Stiftskirche, s.n.: one bifolium, 'written in a German centre with Anglo-Saxon traditions, most likely at Hersfeld', s. viii/ix. Contents: Paterius, *Liber testimoniorum ueteris testamenti quem Paterius ex opusculis S. Gregorii excerpi curauit* (frg.).

109. [CLA Add. (i). 1838] Marburg, Hessisches Staatsarchiv, HR nr 2, 10c: two fragmentary folios, 'written presumably in an Anglo-Saxon centre in Germany', s. viii/ix. Contents: Bede, *Homiliae* [CPL 1367] (frg.).

110. [CLA Add. (i). 1848] Münster in Westphalen, UB, Fragmentenkapsel 1, no. 3: one folio, 'written in England, later presumably in a German monastery', s. viii^2. [Gneuss 856.2]. Contents: Bede, *Historia ecclesiastica gentis Anglorum* [CPL 1375] (frg.).

111. [CLA Add. (i). 1850] Nürnberg, Germanisches Nationalmuseum, Kupferstichkabinett, Kapsel 536/SD 285: one bifolium, Anglo-Saxon minuscule, 'written in a German centre with Anglo-Saxon traditions in the Main region or in Hessia', s. viii/ix. Contents: Bede, *De temporum ratione* [CPL 2320] (frg.).

CLA Addenda (1992), nos. 1866–84 [= Add. (ii)]

112. [CLA Add. (ii). 1869] Chicago, Newberry Library 1.5, fragm. 26: one folio, Anglo-Saxon minuscule, 'written probably in an Anglo-Saxon centre in Germany', s. viii/ix. Contents: Isidore, *Etymologiae* (frg.).

Appendix D
Ninth-Century Manuscripts of Continental Origin
Having Pre-Conquest English Provenance

The following list is based principally on Gneuss, *Handlist*, but the information concerning date and origin has been correlated with that given in Bischoff, *Katalog* (in fact there are very few discrepancies, because, until Bischoff's death in 1991, the two scholars collaborated closely, and most of the details concerning ninth-century Continental manuscripts in Gneuss's *Handlist* were either supplied or confirmed by Bischoff personally). I also include additional information contained in Gneuss, 'Addenda and Corrigenda'. It is obviously not possible to be certain that every single item in the following list was in an English library by 1066 (or 1100), but many, certainly the majority, appear to have been so, as will emerge from the following list. Under 'English provenance' I record the place and/or date at which a manuscript is first attested in England; if there is no certain evidence for a pre-Conquest provenance, I state '? unknown', and then in parentheses give the later (that is, post-1100) provenance, if known. In sum the list provides an interesting indication of the sort of books which were imported into England in the years following King Alfred's revival of ecclesiastical life in the 890s. References to relevant entries in Gneuss and Bischoff, *Katalog*, may be found in the Index of Manuscripts.

1. Arras, BM, 764 (739), fos. 1–93: NE France, s. ix^{ex}. English provenance: Bath, s. x. Contents: Hrabanus Maurus, *Comm. in Iudith, Comm. in Hester*.

2. Brockenhurst, Parish Church, Parish register: NE France, s. ix$^{2/4}$. English provenance: ? unknown. Contents: Socrates, Sozomen, and Theodoretus, *Tripartita historia ecclesiastica*, trans. Cassiodorus (frg.).

3. Cambridge, CCC 193: N. France, s. ix$^{2/3}$. English provenance: s. xi? Contents: Ambrose, *Exameron*.

4. Cambridge, CCC 223: Arras, s. ix$^{3/4}$, with additions made at Saint-Bertin, s. ix^{ex}. English provenance: s. x^1. Contents: Prudentius, *Apotheosis, Contra Symmachum, Dittochaeon, Hamartigenia, Liber cathemerinon, Liber peristephanon, Psychomachia*; John Scotus Eriugena, *Carm.* ix [ICL 1417].

5. Cambridge, CCC 272: Rheims, 883 × 884. English provenance: s. xi (later Christ Church, Canterbury). Contents: psalter, with glosses drawn from Cassiodorus, *Expositio psalmorum*.

6. Cambridge, CCC 279: NW France, s. ix/x. English provenance: s. x/xi (later Worcester). Contents: *Synodus episcoporum* [BCLL 599]; *Liber ex lege*

Moysi [BCLL 611]; *Collectio canonum Hibernensis*, 'Recension A' [BCLL 612].

7. Cambridge, CCC 330, pt. ii: France, s. ix^ex^. English provenance: s. x (later Malmesbury). Contents: ?Martin of Laon, *Comm. in Martianum Capellam.*

8. Cambridge, CCC 399: N. France, s. ix^1^. English provenance: s. x^1^. Contents: Julian of Toledo, *Prognosticum futuri saeculi.*

9. Cambridge, CCC 430: Saint-Amand, s. ix^ex^. English provenance: s. x (later St Augustine's, Canterbury). Contents: Martin of Braga, *Formula uitae honestae*; Ferrandus of Carthage, *Ep.* vii *ad Reginum* [CPL 848]; Ambrosius Autpertus, *Sermo de cupiditate.*

10. Cambridge, Fitzwilliam Museum, 45-1980: Brittany (?Dol), s. ix^ex^. English provenance: s. x^med^. Contents: Gospels.

11. Cambridge, Pembroke College 17: Tours, s. ix^1^. English provenance: s. xi (later Bury St Edmunds). Contents: Jerome, *Comm. in Esaiam.*

12. Cambridge, Pembroke College 81: ?S. France, s. ix^2/3^. English provenance: ? unknown (later Bury St Edmunds). Contents: Bede, *De templo Salomonis* [CPL 1348], *In libros Regum quaestiones .xxx.* [CPL 1347], *Super Canticum Abacuc allegorica expositio* [CPL 1354].

13. Cambridge, Pembroke College 83: Saint-Denis, s. ix^1^. English provenance: Bury St Edmunds, s. xi^2^. Contents: Bede, *In Lucae euangelium expositio* [CPL 1355].

14. Cambridge, Pembroke College 91: N. France (Bischoff: Nähe Kanalküste), s. ix^1/3^. Contents: Jerome, *Tractatus .lix. in psalmos.*

15. Cambridge, Pembroke College 108: E. France, s. ix^2/3^. English provenance: ? unknown (later Bury St Edmunds). Contents: Vigilius of Thapsus, *Contra Arianos, Sabellianos, Photinianos dialogus*; Eusebius, *Historia ecclesiastica*, trans. Rufinus; etc.

16. Cambridge, Pembroke College 308: Reims, s. ix^2^ (before 882). English provenance: s. ix^ex^ (later Ely). Contents: Hrabanus Maurus, *Comm. in Epistulas paulinas.*

17. Cambridge, St John's College Ii. 12. 29, flyleaves: France, s. ix^1^. English provenance: ? unknown. Contents: Isidore, *Etymologiae* (frg.).

18. Cambridge, Trinity College B. 14. 3, flyleaves 1–4: Nonantola, s. ix^1^. English provenance: s. xi (later Christ Church, Canterbury). Contents: Ambrose, *Expositio de psalmo .cxviii.* (frg.).

19. Canterbury, CL, Add. 127/19 + Maidstone, Kent County Archives, PRC 19/1 a+b: N. France, s. ix/x. English provenance: probably St Augustine's, Canterbury, date unknown. Contents: Priscian, *Institutiones grammaticae* (frg.).

20. Coburg, Landesbibliothek, 1: Metz, s. ix$^{2/3}$. English provenance: royal court, 923 × 936. Contents: Gospel list, Gospels.

21. Hereford, CL, O. III. 2: ?France, s. ix$^{3/4}$. English provenance: ?Salisbury, s. xi^{ex} (later Hereford, s. xii^{med}). Contents: Jerome, *De uiris inlustribus*; Gennadius of Marseilles, *De uiris illustribus*; Isidore, *De uiris illustribus*; Augustine, *Retractationes*; Cassiodorus, *Institutiones* i; Isidore, *In libros ueteris et noui Testamenti prooemia*; *De ecclesiasticis officiis*; *De ortu et obitu patrum*; *Allegoriae quaedam sacrae scripturae*.

22. London, BL, Add. 23944: N. France (?Paris region, ?Beauvais region), s. ix$^{3/4}$. English provenance: s. xi^{ex} (later Burton-upon-Trent). Contents: Augustine, *De nuptiis et concupiscentia*; Augustine, *Contra Iulianum haeresis Pelagianae defensorem libri sex*.

23. London, BL, Add. 24193, fos. 17–158: ?Orleans, s. ix^1. English provenance: s. x$^{3/4}$. Contents: Venantius Fortunatus, *Carmina*.

24. London, BL, Arundel 125: NE France (?Saint-Bertin), s. ix^1. English provenance: s. x/xi. Contents: biblical (Job and Ezra).

25. London, BL, Cotton Caligula A. xv, fos. 3–38, 42–64, 73–117: N. France, s. ix^1. English provenance: s. ix/x. Contents: Jerome, *De uiris inlustribus*; Jerome, *Vita S. Pauli primi eremitae*; Isidore, *Etymologiae* (exc.); Cyprian, *Ad Quirinum (Testimoniorum libri .iii.)*; etc.

26. London, BL, Cotton Claudius B. v: West Germany, s. ix^1. English provenance: royal court, then Bath, s. x^1. Contents: *Concilium oecumenicum sextum Constantinopolitanum A.D. 680*.

27. London, BL, Cotton Galba A. xviii [+ Oxford, BodL, Rawlinson B. 484, fo. 85]: NE France (vicinity of Reims?), s. ix^1. English provenance: royal court, s. ix^2 or x^{in}. Contents: Psalterium Gallicanum.

28. London, BL, Cotton Otho B. ix: Brittany, s. ix$^{4/4}$. English provenance: royal court, then Chester-le-Street, by 934; Durham, s. x^{ex}. Contents: Gospels (frg.).

29. London, BL, Cotton Otho E. xiii: Brittany, s. ix/x. English provenance: ? unknown (later St Augustine's, Canterbury). Contents: *Liber ex lege Moysi* [BCLL 611]; *Collectio canonum Hibernensis*, 'Recension A'; *Canones Adomnani* [BCLL 609]; *Canones Wallici* [BCLL 995].

30. London, BL, Cotton Tiberius A. ii: Lobbes, s. ix/x. English provenance: royal court, *ante* 939, then Christ Church, Canterbury, s. x^1. Contents: Gospels.

31. London, BL, Cotton Tiberius A. vii, fos. 165–6: W. France, s. ix$^{3/4}$. English provenance: s. xi^1. Contents: Prosper of Aquitaine, *Epigrammata ex sententiis S. Augustini*.

32. London, BL, Cotton Vespasian B. vi, fos. 1–103: Saint-Denis, s. ix$^{2/4}$.

English provenance: s. xi^{in}. Contents: Bede, *De temporum ratione* [CPL 2320].

33. London, BL, Cotton Vespasian D. xiv, fos. 170–224: N. (NE?) France, s. ix$^{1/4}$. English provenance: S. England, *ante* 912. Contents: Isidore, *Synonyma de lamentatione animae peccatricis*.

34. London, BL, Cotton Vitellius C. iii, fos. 86–138: N. France, s. ix$^{3/4}$. English provenance: ? unknown. Contents: Macrobius, *Saturnalia* books i–ii.

35. London, BL, Egerton 874: NE France, s. ix$^{3/4}$. English provenance: s. xi^2. Contents: Caesarius of Arles, *Expositio in Apocalypsim*.

36. London, BL, Harley 208: Saint-Denis, s. ix^1. English provenance: s. x/xi (later York). Contents: Alcuin, *Epistulae* [CSLMA ALC 45].

37. London, BL, Harley 213: France, s. ix$^{3/3}$. English provenance: ? unknown (later Old Minster, Winchester, then York, s. xvi). Contents: Alcuin, *Expositio in Ecclesiasten* [CSLMA ALC 50], *Compendium in Canticum canticorum* [CSLMA ALC 15], Augustine, *Sermo de disciplina Christiana*, Gregory, *Hom. .xl. in Euangelia* (exc.).

38. London, BL, Harley 526, fos. 1–27: NE France, s. ix^{ex}. English provenance: s. x^{med}. Contents: Bede, *Vita metrica S. Cuthberti* [CPL 1380].

39. London, BL, Harley 647: Lotharingia, s. ix$^{2/4}$. English provenance: ?Ramsey, s. x/xi (later St Augustine's, Canterbury). Contents: Cicero, *Aratea*; Hyginus, *Astronomica*; Macrobius, *Comm. in Somnium Scipionis* (exc.); Pliny, *Naturalis historia* (exc.); Martianus Capella, *De nuptiis Philologiae et Mercurii* (exc.).

40. London, BL, Harley 652, fos. 1*–4*: N. France, s. ix^{med}. English provenance: ? unknown (later St Augustine's, Canterbury). Contents: Alan of Farfa, *Homiliarium* (frg.).

41. London, BL, Royal 1. A. XVIII: Brittany, s. ix/x. English provenance: ?royal court, then St Augustine's, Canterbury, 924 × 939. Contents: Gospels.

42. London, BL, Royal 4. B. XIV, fos. 1*–2*: ?Italy, s. ix/x. English provenance: ? unknown (later Worcester). Contents: missal (frg.).

43. London, BL, Royal 5. E. XIII: N. France (Kanalküste?), s. ix^{ex}. English provenance: s. x^{med} (later Worcester). Contents: Cyprian, *Ad Quirinum (Testimoniorum libri .iii.)* [CPL 39] (exc.); *Collectio canonum Hibernensis* (exc.); etc.

44. London, BL, Royal 15. A. XVI: ?N. France, s. ix/x. English provenance: St Augustine's, Canterbury, s. x^2. Contents: Juvencus, *Euangelia*; Aldhelm, *Enigmata* [CPL 1335]; Bede, *De arte metrica* [CPL 1565] (exc.).

45. London, BL, Royal 15. A. XXXIII: Reims, s. ix/x. English provenance:

s. x^2 (later Worcester). Contents: Remigius of Auxerre, *Comm. in Martianum Capellam*; Martin of Laon (?), *Comm. in Martianum Capellam* (exc.).

46. London, BL, Royal 15. B. XIX, fos. 36–78: Reims, s. ix$^{4/4}$. English provenance: s. x? Contents: Bede, *De temporum ratione* [CPL 2320].

47. London, Lambeth Palace Library, 237, fos. 146–208: Arras, s. ix$^{2/4}$. English provenance: ?Glastonbury, s. x^{in}. Contents: Augustine, *Enchiridion ad Laurentium*; Sextus, *Sententiae* trans. Rufinus.

48. London, Lambeth Palace Library, 325, fos. 2–144: N. France, s. ix$^{3/4}$. English provenance: ? unknown (later Durham). Contents: Ennodius, *Epistulae, Dictiones, Carmina*.

49. London, Lambeth Palace Library, 377: Tours, s. ix$^{2/4}$. English provenance: s. x^{med}. Contents: Isidore, *Sententiae*.

50. London, Lambeth Palace Library, 414, fos. 1–80: Saint-Amand, s. ix^{in}. English provenance: ? unknown (later St Augustine's, Canterbury). Contents: patristic excerpts (Ambrose, Augustine, Cassian, Eucherius, Jerome, etc.).

51. London, Lambeth Palace Library, 1231: France (Brittany?), s. ix. English provenance: ? unknown. Contents: *Collectio canonum Hibernensis* (frg.).

52. New York, Public Library 115: Landévennec, s. ix$^{3/3}$. English provenance: SW England, s. x^{med}. Contents: Gospel list, Gospels.

53. Oxford, BodL, Auct. F. 4. 32, fos. 1–9: Brittany, s. ix$^{2/4}$. English provenance: Glastonbury, s. x^2. Contents: Eutyches, *Ars de uerbo*.

54. Oxford, BodL, Barlow 4: NE France, s. ix$^{2/3}$. English provenance: s. xi^2 (later Worcester). Contents: Smaragdus of Saint-Mihiel, *Expositio libri comitis*.

55. Oxford, BodL, Bodley 218: Tours, s. ix^1. English provenance: s. x. Contents: Bede, *In Lucae euangelium expositio* [CPL 1356].

56. Oxford, BodL, Bodley 310, fos. 1–145: E. France, s. ix$^{3/4}$. English provenance: ? unknown. Contents: Gregory, *Moralia in Iob*.

57. Oxford, BodL, Bodley 381, fos. i–ii: NE France, s. ix$^{3/4}$. English provenance: ? unknown (later St Augustine's, Canterbury). Contents: Gospel list (exc.).

58. Oxford, BodL, Bodley 516: NE France, s. ix$^{3/4}$. English provenance: s. xi^1 (later Salisbury). Contents: Augustine, *Ep.* cxlvii; Cassiodorus, *De anima*; Halitgar of Cambrai, *Poenitentiale*; etc.

59. Oxford, BodL, Bodley 572, fos. 51–107: NE France, s. ix^1. English provenance: ? unknown. Contents: *Poenitentiale Cummeani* [CPL 1882; BCLL 601]; other penitential texts.

60. Oxford, BodL, Bodley 579: Arras, s. ix/x. English provenance: Canterbury, s. x$^{1/4}$, then Exeter, s. xi^{med}. Contents: sacramentary.

61. Oxford, BodL, Bodley 849: W. France, AD 818. English provenance: SW England, s. x, later Exeter, s. xi. Contents: Bede, *Super epistulas catholicas expositio* [CPL 1362].

62. Oxford, BodL, Hatton 42, fos. 1–142 (Part I): Brittany, s. ix$^{1/3}$; contents: *Collectio canonum Hibernensis*, recension B, *Canones Wallici* [BCLL 995], *Canones Adamnani* [BCLL 609], Gaius, *Institutiones*; fos. 142–204 (Part II): ?N. France, s. ix^1; contents: *Collectio canonum Dionysio-Hadriana*; Ansegesis, *Capitularium collectio*. English provenance (both parts): ?Glastonbury, s. x^{in}, then Christ Church, Canterbury, s. x/xi, then Worcester, s. xi^{in}.

63. Oxford, BodL, Lat. class. c. 2, fo. 18 [+ Cambridge, CCC EP-0-6 (binding fragment) + Deene Park Library, L. 2. 21 + London, BL, Sloane 1044, fo. 6 + Oxford, All Souls College 330, nos. 54–5]: W. France, s. ix$^{2/3}$. English provenance: s. x^{ex}. Contents: Vergil, *Aeneis* (frg.), *Georgica* (frg.).

64. Oxford, BodL, Rawlinson C. 697: NE France, s. ix$^{3/4}$. English provenance: ?Glastonbury, s. x^{med}. Contents: Aldhelm, *Enigmata* [CPL 1335], *Carmen de uirginitate* [CPL 1333]; Prudentius, *Psychomachia*; etc.

65. Oxford, Merton College 309, fos. 114–201: ?France, s. ix/x. English provenance: ? unknown. Contents: Cicero, *Topica* (frg.), Boethius, *Comm. in Ciceronis Topica*.

66. Oxford, St John's College 194: Brittany, s. ix/x. English provenance: s. x^{med} (later Christ Church, Canterbury). Contents: Gospels, etc.

67. Paris, BNF, lat. 2825, fos. 57–81: NE France, s. ix/x. English provenance: s. x^{med}. Contents: Bede, *Vita metrica S. Cudbercti* [CPL 1380]; etc.

68. Paris, BNF, lat. 7585: NE France, s. ix^2. English provenance: s. x^2. Contents: Isidore, *Etymologiae*.

69. Paris, BNF, lat. 8085, fos. 2–82: France (Loire region?), s. ix^{med}. English provenance: s. x/xi. Contents: Prudentius, *Apotheosis, Contra Symmachum, Dittochaeon, Hamartigenia, Liber cathemerinon, Liber peristephanon, Psychomachia*.

70. Peterborough, CL, H. 3. 40 (endleaf): France, s. ix$^{3/4}$. English provenance: ?Peterborough. Contents: Frecuulf of Lisieux, *Historia* (frg.).

71. Rouen, BM, 26: N. France, s. ix^{med}. English provenance: s. x. Contents: biblical texts; Alcuin, *Expositio in Ecclesiasten* [CSLMA ALC 50] (exc.), *Carm.* lxxviii; Augustine, *Enchiridion ad Laurentium*; Isidore, *Etymologiae* (exc.); etc.

72. Saint-Omer, BM, 202: NE France, s. ix^2. English provenance: ?Exeter, s. xi^{med}. Contents: Gospel of Nicodemus; *Passio S. Margaretae* [BHL 5303]; *Vindicta Saluatoris*; etc.

73. Salisbury, CL, 101: W. France, s. ix^{ex}. English provenance: Christ

Church, Canterbury, s. x. Contents: Isidore, *Mysticorum expositiones sacramentorum seu Quaestiones in uetus Testamentum*; Adalbert of Metz, *Speculum Gregorii*; Augustine, *In Ioannis epistulam ad Parthos tractatus .x..*

74. Salisbury, CL, 133: Tours, s. ix$^{1/4}$. English provenance: ? unknown (later Salisbury). Contents: Alcuin, *Expositio in Ecclesiasten* [CSLMA ALC 50].

75. Salisbury, CL, 158, fos. 9–83: France, s. ix^2 or ix/x. English provenance: Salisbury, s. xi^{ex}. Contents: Bede, *De temporum ratione* [CPL 2320].

76. Utrecht, Universiteitsbibliothek, 32, fos. 1–91: (vicinity of) Reims, s. ix^1. English provenance: Christ Church, Canterbury, s. x/xi. Contents: Psalterium Gallicanum.

77. Vatican City, BAV, Vat. lat. 3363: France (Loire region?), s. ix^1. English provenance: ?Glastonbury, s. x^{med}. Contents: Boethius, *De consolatione Philosophiae*.

78. Windsor Castle, Royal Library, Jackson Collection 16: Saint-Amand, s. ix$^{2/4}$. English provenance: ? unknown (later Longleat House, s. xvii). Contents: Augustine, *De ciuitate Dei* (frg.).

79. Worcester, CL, Q. 8, fos. 164–71 [+ Add. 7, fos. 1–6]: ?France, s. ix/x. English provenance: ? unknown (later Worcester). Contents: Statius, *Thebais* (frg.).

80. Worcester, CL, Q. 28: France, s. ix^2. English provenance: Canterbury, s. xi (later Worcester). Contents: Eusebius, *Historia ecclesiastica*, trans. Rufinus.

Appendix E
Latin Books Cited by the Principal Anglo-Saxon Authors

This Appendix attempts to provide a complete listing of the Latin sources quoted or alluded to by the principal authors of Anglo-Saxon England: Theodore and Hadrian, Aldhelm, Bede, Alcuin, the anonymous author of *The Old English Martyrology*, Asser, Lantfred, Abbo of Fleury, Wulfstan of Winchester, Ælfric, and Byrhtferth. In the case of Aldhelm, I have drawn principally on the *apparatus fontium* of Rudolf Ehwald's edition of Aldhelm, supplemented by more recent research, particularly on his use of grammatical and poetic sources; for Bede, the *apparatus fontium* to the editions of Bede's works in CCSL, supplemented by my own sourcing of Bede's Latin poetry (and helpfully improved by access to Rosalind Love's essay on 'The Library of Bede', to appear in vol. i of *The History of the Book in Britain*); and for the Old English Martyrologist and Ælfric, the excellent compendia of sources available in the *Fontes Anglo-Saxonici Database*. In the case of the remaining authors (Theodore and Hadrian, Alcuin, Asser, Lantfred, Abbo, Wulfstan of Winchester, and Byrhtferth), the sources listed have been identified through my own researches.

For the texts which were used as sources by Anglo-Saxon authors, I have attempted to put references in a consistent format, whereby I typically cite chapter number (if the work in question is a treatise of modest length: e.g. Augustine *De bono coniugali*), but book and chapter for more extensive works (e.g. Augustine *De ciuitate Dei* or *De trinitate*). I have used this form of citation in order to avoid citing page references to specific editions, such that a reference to (e.g.) book and chapter of Augustine's *De ciuitate Dei* can be located regardless of whether one is using the PL, CSEL, or CCSL edition (or any other for that matter). In the case of longer works for which there is no agreed editorial subdivision into books or chapters (e.g. Jerome *Liber quaestionum hebraicarum in Genesim*), no reference to subdivisions of any kind is attempted. Details of which alphanumerical repertories (e.g. CPG, CPL, etc.) contain references to individual authors and works earlier than AD 700 may be found in the Catalogue, below.

In the following lists of citations, note that, in cases where a text is drawn on heavily and frequently by an Anglo-Saxon author, I normally give a maximum of twenty citations from any single work by that Anglo-Saxon author, as being a sufficient number to demonstrate beyond doubt the author's familiarity with the work in question; further citations of the work are signalled by 'etc.'. When a work is drawn on throughout by an

Anglo–Saxon author, I note such usage by the term 'passim' (wherever possible I give the number of citations in question in the form '30×').

It will be realized that, in limiting myself to the 'principal' authors of Anglo–Saxon England, I have perforce omitted a large number of minor authors whose inclusion would greatly extend the list of Latin books given below. The limitation is partly due to considerations of space, but above all because a thorough analysis of the sources of the authors in question has yet to be undertaken. For the sources of Boniface and Tatwine, for example, see the brief discussions above (pp. 37–40, 43–4). The *Breuiloquium Vitae Wilfridi* of Fredegaud (Frithegod) of Canterbury, if properly sourced, would throw light on the circulation of a number of authors otherwise poorly represented (for example, the *Comoediae* of Terence, from which Fredegaud quotes the *Andria* and the *Phormio*), or not represented at all (for example, the *Sermones antiqui* of Fabius Planciades Fulgentius [LLA 710], from which Fredegaud draws a number of obscure lexical items). So, too, would the voluminous writings of Goscelin of Saint-Bertin, which have yet to be edited adequately, let alone sourced: in his *Liber confortatorius*, for example, composed at Peterborough *c.*1080, Goscelin shows first-hand knowledge of the *Epistulae* of Seneca [LLA 335], a work not otherwise attested in Anglo–Saxon England. Nevertheless, the books cited by the 'principal' authors listed below give a representative view of what books were to be found in Anglo–Saxon libraries.

a. Theodore and Hadrian of Canterbury

i. The 'Leiden Glossary'

The so-called 'Leiden Glossary' is preserved in a manuscript now at Leiden, Bibliotheek der Rijksuniversiteit, Voss. lat. Q. 69, fos. 20^r–36^r, but written at St Gallen, *c.*800. Because the glossary incorporates some 250 glosses in Old English, it is clear that the St Gallen scribe had before him an exemplar written in England. Various evidence indicates that the original glossary was compiled in the school of the Mediterranean scholars Theodore and Hadrian at Canterbury, during the years 670 × 690: see Lapidge, 'The School of Theodore and Hadrian'. The 'Leiden Glossary' is ed. Hessels, *A Late Eighth-Century Latin–Anglo-Saxon Glossary*; it is cited, as LdGl, by chapter and line number of Hessels's edition. As elsewhere in this study, I omit the glosses to books of the Bible (LdGl vii–xxv).

Athanasius
[1] *Vita S. Antonii*, trans. Evagrius: LdGl iii.52–65, xxviii.1–17, 22–3

Augustine
[2] *Sermones*: LdGl xxxvii.1–20

Benedict of Nursia
[3] *Regula*: LdGl ii.1–193

Cassian, John
[4] *De institutis coenobiorum*: LdGl xxxiv.1–55, xlviii.1–74

Cassiodorus
[5] *Expositio psalmorum*: LdGl xxviii.18–21, 24–88

Donatus, Aelius
[6] *Ars maior*: LdGl xliii.1–22, 27–48, 51–6

Eucherius of Lyon
[7] *Instructiones*: LdGl xxxiii.1–31

Eusebius of Caesarea
[8] *Historia ecclesiastica*, trans. Rufinus: LdGl iv.1–120, v.1–32, xxxv.1–306

Gildas
[9] *De excidio Britanniae*: LdGl vi.1–31, xl.1–22, xli.17–21

Gregory the Great
[10] *Dialogi*: LdGl xxxix.1–44, 46–8, 54, 72
[11] *Regula pastoralis*: LdGl xxxix.49–53

Isidore of Seville
[12] *De ecclesiasticis officiis*: LdGl xxvi.1–13
[13] *De natura rerum*: LdGl xxvii.1–33, xliv.1–28
[14] *Etymologiae*: LdGl xliii.23–6, 49–50

Jerome (Hieronymus)
[15] *Comm. in Euangelium Matthaei*: LdGl xxix.1–73
[16] *De uiris inlustribus*: LdGl xxx.1–96

Orosius, Paulus
[17] *Historiae aduersum paganos*: LdGl xxxvi.1–22

Phocas [LLA 704; Kaster 121]
[18] *Ars de nomine et uerbo*: LdGl xlv.1–31, xlvi.1–39

Sulpicius Severus
[19] *Dialogi*: LdGl iii.4–51, xli.17–21, xlii.1, 3, 5, 10, 15–19
[20] *Vita S. Martini*: LdGl iii.1–3, xlii.4

ANONYMOUS WRITINGS
[21] *Canones ecclesiastici*: LdGl i.1–133, xxxix.55–71, xli.1–6

[22] passiones martyrum: *Passio S. Eugeniae* [CPL 2184; BHL 2666] [pseudo-Rufinus]: LdGl xlii.21, 23–7

[23] *Recognitiones*, trans. Rufinus [pseudo-Clement]: LdGl xxxviii.1–45

ii. The Canterbury Biblical Commentaries

The 'Canterbury Biblical Commentaries' represent the written record made by anonymous Anglo-Saxon students of the *viva voce* classroom exegesis of the Bible given at the school of Canterbury by the two great Mediterranean masters Theodore and Hadrian during the years 670 × 690; the commentaries are ed. Bischoff and Lapidge, *Biblical Commentaries*. Because both Theodore and Hadrian were native speakers of Greek who had been trained in Greek schools, it is unsurprising that most of the sources for their exegesis are Greek patristic writings, notably Josephus, Clement of Alexandria, Basil of Caesarea, Epiphanius, John Chrysostom, Cosmas Indicopleustes, the corpus of Greek writings which passed under the name of 'Ephraem Graecus'. All of these are cited by name, but the writings of many other Greek exegetes are drawn on without their authors being named (see Bischoff and Lapidge, ibid. 205–33). Many of the quotations from these Greek authors, sometimes but not invariably rendered in Latin, are extensive, too long, and accurate (probably) to be the result of memory, with the implication that a certain number of Greek books must have been available at late seventh-century Canterbury. Unfortunately no such book has survived. By contrast with the extensive list of Greek patristic sources, the number of Latin works cited in the Canterbury biblical commentaries is relatively restricted, limited in effect to works of Augustine, Jerome, and Isidore. In the following list I use the following abbreviations for edited parts of the corpus of Canterbury biblical commentaries (substantial amounts remain unedited):

EvII = the Second Commentary on the Gospels (ed. Bischoff and Lapidge, 396–423, with commentary at 503–32)

Gn-Ex-EvIa = the Supplementary Commentary on Genesis, Exodus, and the Gospels (ed. Bischoff and Lapidge, 386–95, with commentary at 498–502)

PentI = the First Commentary on the Pentateuch (ed. Bischoff and Lapidge, 298–385, with commentary at 427–97)

Augustine

[24] *Quaestiones in Heptateuchum*: i. 4 (Gn-Ex-EvIa 11), ii. 21 (Gn-Ex-EvIa 18), iii. 20 (PentI 376), iv. 18 (PentI 414), iv. 19 (PentI 418), iv. 35 (PentI 433)

Isidore

[25] *De differentiis uerborum*: i. 340 (EvII 136)

[26] *Etymologiae*: i. 36. 6 (PentI 188), vi. 19. 35 (PentI 259), vii. 6. 43 (PentI 124), ix. 6. 18 (PentI 386, 387), x. 1 [+ xi. 1. 4] (PentI 52), x. 249 (PentI

380), xi. 1. 140 (PentI 113), xiv. 3. 2–4 (Gn-Ex-EvIa 9), xix. 21. 5 (PentI 295), xx. 13. 4 (PentI 409)

Jerome (Hieronymus)
[27] *Comm. in Euangelium Matthaei*: i. 10 (EvII 20), ii. 12 (EvII 76)
[28] *Epistulae*: xxxvi (Gn-Ex-EvIa 8)
[29] *Liber quaestionum hebraicarum in Genesim*: PentI 134, 147, 187

b. Aldhelm of Malmesbury

Aldhelm was an author of impressively wide reading in classical and patristic authors. Most of his citations were identified in the monumental edition of Rudolf Ehwald (*Aldhelmi Opera*), and the following list is based principally on Ehwald's index of 'loci classici et ecclesiastici' (pp. 544–6). It will be realized that some of the authors and works listed by Ehwald may have been known to Aldhelm from intermediary sources; on the problems in determining the use of such sources, see above, pp. 93–105. Furthermore, Ehwald's identifications of Aldhelm's sources have been amplified and corrected by subsequent scholarship, notably, in respect of grammatical writings, by Law, 'The Study of Latin Grammar', esp. 46–57 (*Grammar*, 93–101); and, in respect of Aldhelm's verbal reminiscences of earlier poets, by Orchard, *The Poetic Art of Aldhelm*, esp. 126–238. (I do not, however, list the poets for whom Orchard found only 'slight', that is negligible, evidence for Aldhelm's use (pp. 215–18): Ausonius, Claudius Marius Victorius, Eugenius of Toledo, Paulinus of Pella, and Sidonius Apollinaris.) I use the following abbreviations for Aldhelm's writings, as edited by Ehwald, *Aldhelmi Opera*:

CdV = *Carmen de uirginitate*, ed. Ehwald, 350–471, cited by line number
CE = *Carmina ecclesiastica*, ed. Ehwald, 11–32, cited by poem number and line number (note that CE iv itself consists of twelve poems)
CR = *Carmen rhythmicum*, ed. Ehwald, 524–8, cited by line number
Enigm. = *Enigmata*, ed. Ehwald, 97–149, cited by poem number and line number
Ep. = *Epistulae*, ed. Ehwald, 475–503, cited by page number of Ehwald's edition
Metr. = *De metris*, ed. Ehwald, 77–96, cited by page number of Ehwald's edition
Ped.reg. = *De pedum regulis*, ed. Ehwald, 150–204, cited by page number of Ehwald's edition
prDV = the prose *De uirginitate*, ed. Ehwald, 226–323, cited by page number of Ehwald's edition

Andreas Orator
[1] *Carmen de Maria uirgine ad Rusticianam*: Metr. p. 80

Arator
[2] *Historia apostolica*: *Ep. ad Florianum* line 21 (Enigm. xcvi.1), *Ep. ad Vigilium* lines 1 (Metr. p. 80), 6 (Metr. p. 80), i. 59 (Ped.reg. p. 153), i. 62 (Ped.reg. p. 153), i. 70 (CE iv.1.12), i. 100 (CdV 1252), i. 157 [+ ii. 901] (CdV 38), i. 173 (CdV 397), i. 211 (CdV 913), i. 219 (CE iv.2.33), i. 404

(CdV 1129, 1480), i. 455 (CdV 852, 867), i. 456 (CdV 2431), i. 540 (Enigm. xcvi.7), i. 552 (Metr. p. 71), i. 662 (CdV 492), i. 754 (Enigm. c.5), i. 795 (Enigm. xxxv.1), i. 849 (CdV 679), i. 864 (CdV 679), i. 871 (Metr. p. 92), i. 883 (Metr. p. 93), i. 887 (CdV 1316), i. 899 [+ i. 1076] (CE i.6, iv.1.2), ii. 96 (CdV 1365), ii. 100 (Enigm. lxvi.5), ii. 149 (CdV 1677), ii. 160 (CdV 1977), ii. 414 (CdV 2231), ii. 687 (CdV 1365), ii. 779 (CE iv.6.7), ii. 789 (CdV 417), ii. 797 (CE iv.6.7), ii. 901 (CdV 38), ii. 912 (CdV 203), ii. 1072 (CE iv.1.14), ii. 1156–60 (CE iv.2.24–8)

Athanasius
[3] *Vita S. Antonii*, trans. Evagrius: prDV p. 265

Audax
[4] *De Scauri et Palladii libris excerpta per interrogationem et responsionem*: Metr. pp. 82–9

Augustine
[5] *De bono uiduitatis*: cc. vi–viii (prDV p. 243)
[6] *De ciuitate Dei*: i. 18 (prDV p. 319), xxi. 4 (prDV p. 237), xxii. 22 (Ped.reg. p. 198)
[7] *De haeresibus*: c. v (Metr. p. 71)
[8] *De libero arbitrio*: Metr. p. 81
[9] *De magistro*: Metr p. 81
[10] *De musica*: Metr. p. 81
[11] *De sancta uirginitate*: cc. xi (prDV p. 243), xxxi (prDV p. 242), xxxii (prDV p. 242), xxxiii (prDV p. 243), xxxv (prDV p. 242), xli (prDV p. 242), l (prDV p. 242)
[12] *Enarrationes in psalmos*: [ps. clxvii] xix: prDV p. 319
[13] *Epistulae*: cxxxviii (Ped.reg. p. 196)
[14] *Soliloquia*: Metr. p. 81

Avitus, Alcimus
[15] *Carmina de spiritalis historiae gestis*: i. 25 (CdV 1584), ii. 358 (CdV 846), vi. 223 (CE iv.6.7), vi. 512 (CdV 1912)

Cassian, John
[16] *Conlationes*: praef. (prDV p. 242), v. 6 (CdV 2498, 2681; prDV p. 241), v. 16 (CdV 2548, 2574, 2666, 2672), v. 17 (CdV 2487), v. 18 (CdV 2446), v. 22 (CdV 2651), v. 23 (CdV 2631), v. 25 (CdV 2671, 2696, 2752), v. 26 (CdV 2493)
[17] *De institutis coenobiorum*: v. 11 (CdV 2468), vi. 19 (prDV p. 264), vii. 3 (CdV 2663), xi. 1 (CdV 2678), xii. 4 (CdV 2730)

Cicero

[18] *Actio in C. Verrem secunda*: iv. **26**. **57** (Ped.reg. p. 197), v. **72**. **188** (Ped.reg. p. 196)

[19] *In L. Catilinam oratio III*: vi. **14** (Ped.reg. p. 196)

Claudian

[20] *Carmina maiora*: iii [= *In Rufinum* I], lines **219** (CdV 1352), **274** (Enigm. c.8, CdV 259, 1887); vii [= *De .III. consulatu Honorii*], lines **4** (Enigm. xxiv.2), **98** (Ped.reg. p. 172)

[21] *De raptu Proserpinae*: iii. **292** (CdV 310)

Epithalamium Laurentii: see ANONYMOUS WRITINGS

Corippus, Flavius Cresconius

[22] *In laudem Iustini*: i. **246** (CdV 1361), ii. **12** (CdV praef. 11), ii. **322** (Enigm. xii.3), iii. **100** (Enigm. lv.5), iii. **197** (CdV 2741)

[23] *Iohannes*: i. **47** (Enigm. xxix.7), i. **260** (CdV 1146), i. **380** (CdV 314), iii. **238** (CdV 2678), iv. **303** (CE iv.1.6), vi. **564** (CdV 1413, 2243, 2389), viii. **221** (CdV 1311)

Cyprian of Carthage

[24] *De habitu uirginum*: cc. v–vi (prDV p. 315), ix (prDV p. 315), xii (prDV p. 315)

Cyprianus Gallus

[25] *Heptateuchos*: **Gen. 31** (CdV 62), **572** (CdV 1445, 2816); **Exod. 4** (CdV 751), **20** (Enigm. xcii.3), **56** (CdV 1798), **131** (CdV 1775), **201** (CdV 910); **Num. 503** (Ped.reg. p. 189), **749** (CdV 1793); **Iudic. 18** (Metr. p. 92), **185** (CdV 2508), **212** (CdV 1525), **227** (Enigm. lxxii.1), **359** (Enigm. xcvi.4), **395** (Enigm. xlvi.4), **679 + 681** (Ped.reg. p. 158); **Reges IV** (Metr. p. 80)

Damasus

[26] *Epigrammata*: i. **1** (CdV 2712), i. **6** (CE i.15), i. **10** (CE i.13, iv.2.2), i. **20** (CdV 440), i. **24** (CdV 1631), i. **26** (CdV 1916), iii. **3** (Enigm. lxxix.7), iii. **7** (Enigm. xxvii.1), xvi. **9** (CdV 746, 1843), xvii. **4** (CdV 2300), xxxv. **4** (CdV 683), xlvii. **4** (CdV 1317, 2340, 2376)

Donatus, Aelius

[27] *Ars maior*: Metr. pp. 77, 78, Ped.reg. p. 179

[28] *Vita Vergilii*: cc. vii (Ped.reg. p. 157), xvii (Ped.reg. p. 186)

Dracontius

[29] *Laudes Dei*: i. **63** (Enigm. xxxiii.1), i. **149** (CdV praef. 31), i. **580** (CdV 2691), ii. **102** (CdV 2349, 2901), ii. **295** (Enigm. xxxvi.3, CdV 1749), ii. **692** (CdV 2745)

[30] *Satisfactio*: lines 5 (CdV 2784), 9 (CdV 2875), 131 (CdV 354), 151 (CdV 775, 2160)

Ennius, Quintus
[31] *Annales*: i. 14 Skutsch (Ped.reg. p. 186), **dubia** 9 Skutsch (Metr. p. 84)

Eusebius of Caesarea
[32] *Chronicon*, trans. Hieronymus: Metr. p. 88; Ped.reg. pp. 190, 192
[33] *Historia ecclesiastica*, trans. Rufinus: vi. 7 (prDV p. 270), viii. 12 (prDV p. 269), x. 8 [Rufinus] (prDV p. 265), x. 13–18 [Rufinus] (prDV p. 272), xi. 9 [Rufinus] (prDV p. 262)

Gildas
[34] *De excidio Britanniae*: c. iii (prDV p. 301)

Gregory the Great
[35] *Dialogi*: ii. 3 (prDV p. 269), ii. 23 (CdV 858–80), ii. 33 (prDV p. 300; CdV 2034–50), iii. 17 (Ped.reg. p. 191)
[36] *Hom. .xl. in Euangelia*: i. 6 (prDV p. 314)
[37] *Moralia in Iob*: xxxi. 45 (prDV p. 242)
[38] *Regula pastoralis*: c. iv (prDV p. 322)

Horace
[39] *Sermones*: i. 1. 29 (CdV 2796), i. 2. 79 (CdV 758, 2684, 2774), i. 2. 95 (CdV 2508), I. 4. 40 (CDV 50), ii. 2. 56 (Enigm. lviii.1), ii. 5. 12 (CdV 238), ii. 7. 86 (Enigm. c.57)

Isidore of Seville
[40] *De ecclesiasticis officiis*: ii. 25 (prDV p. 295)
[41] *De natura rerum*: c. xxx (CR 97)
[42] *De ortu et obitu patrum*: cc. xxxvi (prDV p. 250), lxxii (prDV p. 254), lxxxii (prDV 256)
[43] *Etymologiae*: i. 4. 10 (Enigm. xxx), xii. 2. 3 (Enigm. xxxix.6), xii. 6. 51 (Enigm. xxxvii.6), xii. 8. 14 (Enigm. xxxvi. 1), xii. 11. 5 (CR 31), xvi. 4. 1 (Enigm. xxv)
[44] *Synonyma de lamentatione animae peccatricis*: Metr. p. 81

Jerome (Hieronymus)
[45] *Aduersus Iouinianum*: c. iii (prDV p. 236)
[46] *Comm. in Danielem*: **prol.** (prDV p. 251), i. 1 (prDV p. 252), ix. 24 (prDV p. 251)
[47] *Comm. in Euangelium Matthaei*: iii. 19 (prDV p. 252)
[48] *Comm. in Prophetas minores*: *Ionam* i. 12 (prDV p. 269)
[49] *Epistulae*: xxii [ad Eustochium] (prDV pp. 236, 246, 247, 303), lxiv (CR 85)

[50] *Liber interpretationis hebraicorum nominum*: prDV p. 250

[51] *Liber quaestionum hebraicarum in Genesim*: Ped.reg. p. 171, prDV p. 256

[52] *Vita S. Hilarionis*: cc. **prol.** (prDV p. 266), **ii** (prDV p. 266), **iii** (prDV p. 266), **v** (prDV p. 266), **xxxix** (prDV p. 266), **xl** (prDV p. 267)

[53] *Vita S. Malchi*: cc. **iii** (prDV p. 270), **iv** (prDV p. 270), **vi** (prDV p. 270)

[54] *Vita S. Pauli primi eremitae*: cc. **iv** (prDV p. 265), **v** (prDV p. 265), **vi** (Ped.reg. p. 155; prDV p. 265), **x** (prDV p. 265)

Junillus Africanus

[55] *Instituta regularia diuinae legis*: **praef.** (Metr. p. 81)

Juvenal [LLA 375]

[56] *Saturae*: **iii. 8** (CdV 995), **iii. 97** (Ped.reg. p. 184), **vi. 87** (CdV 2058), **ix. 50** (Ped.reg. p. 164), **x. 133** (Metr. p. 79), **xi. 203** (Ped.reg. p. 183), **xiii. 19** (Metr. p. 85), **xiii. 23** (Metr. p. 85), **xiii. 118** (Metr. p. 79), **xiv. 129–30** (Ped.reg. p. 167), **xiv. 280** (Ped.reg. p. 184), **xv. 162** (Enigm. xxxix.1), **xvi. 1** (CE iv.3.10), **xvi. 11** (CdV 356)

Juvencus

[57] *Euangelia*: **praef. 13** (CdV 2690), **i. 1** (Metr. p. 85), **i. 8** (Metr. p. 85), **i. 12** (Ped.reg. p. 174), **i. 69** (CdV 1704, 2158; CE ii.26), **i. 85** (CdV 246), **i. 108** (CdV 1905), **i. 117** (CdV 920), **i. 132** (CdV 1263), **i. 140** (CdV 1707; CE ii.29; Enigm. lxxxii.6), **i. 308** (CdV 1744), **i. 356** (CdV 1031), **i. 364** (Enigm. lxv.6), **i. 404** (CdV 1432), **i. 405** (Ped.reg. p. 156), **i. 407** (CdV 2061), **i. 421** (CdV 981), **i. 424** (CE iv.5.6), **i. 436** (CdV 1968), **i. 517** (CdV 1140, 1230), **i. 521** (CdV 1857; Enigm. praef. 28), **i. 534** (CdV 368, 1472, 2124), **i. 730** (CE iv.6.17), **i. 738** (CDv 557, 956), **i. 744** (Enigm. lxxii.2), **i. 748** (Enigm. lxxvi.5), **i. 759** (CdV 2436), **i. 768** (CE iv.2.20), **ii praef. 8** (Ped.reg. p. 194), **ii. 343** (Enigm. lxxvi.5), **ii. 519** (Enigm. xxiv.4), **ii. 575** (CdV 831), **ii. 591–2** (Ped.reg. p. 186), **ii. 719** (CdV 1328, 1545), **ii. 814** (CdV 2750), **iii. 168** (CdV 152), **iii. 225** (Ped.reg. p. 158), **iii. 229** (Ped.reg. p. 154), **iii. 370** (CdV 1178; CE iv.4.8), **iii. 394** (Enigm. xciii.5), **iii. 395** (Enigm. xvii.4), **iii. 397** (CdV 203, 316), **iii. 407** (CdV 2715), **iii. 409** (CdV 2902), **iii. 485** (CdV 88, 1722), **iii. 495** (CdV 2815), **iii. 496** (CdV 109), **iii. 532** (CE i.6, iv.1.2), **iii. 675** (CdV 919), **iii. 687** (CdV 1572), **iii. 697** (Enigm. lxiv.3), **iii. 720** (CdV 297), **iii. 729** (CdV 2635), **iv. 157** (CdV 372), **iv. 197** (CdV 2624), **iv. 224** (Enigm. lxxxix.3), **iv. 242** (Enigm. xx.1), **iv. 307** (CdV 2048), **iv. 324** (CdV 1665), **iv. 366** (CdV 2683), **iv. 406** (Enigm. xciii.4), **iv. 423** (CdV 1486, 2371), **iv. 537** (CE iv.6.12), **iv. 651** (Enigm. lxxvii.1), **iv. 672** (CE iv.6.13; Enigm. lxxvi.7), **iv. 684** (Enigm. x.1), **iv. 697** (CdV 2527), **iv. 757** (CdV 1066)

Lactantius Firmianus

[58] *De opificio Dei*: c. **xv** (Ped.reg. p. 197)

Lucan

[59] *Bellum ciuile*: i. 4 (Enigm. xcvi.3), i. 86 (Enigm. xcvi.3), i. 238 (CdV 1549), i. 605 (CdV 1521, 2690), ii. 11 (CdV 1040), ii. 212 (CdV 2396), iii. 505 (CdV 2480), iii. 579 (Metr. p. 87), iii. 762 (Metr. p. 92), iv. 384 (CdV 2673), iv. 811 (CdV 2155), v. 442 (Metr. p. 89), v. 537 (Enigm. x.1), v. 800 (Metr. p. 86), vi. 24 (Metr. p. 89), vi. 386–7 (Ped.reg. p. 185), vi. 536 (CdV 1828), vii. 492 (CdV 1347), vii. 569 (CdV 297), viii. 282 (Metr. p. 86), viii. 289 (Metr. p. 79), viii. 386 (CdV 869), ix. 6 (Enigm. iv.4), ix. 324 (CdV 2807), ix. 430 (Metr. p. 79), x. 21 (Metr. p. 85), x. 267 (Ped.reg. p. 197), x. 538 (Metr. p. 79)

[60] *Orpheus*: Ped.reg. p. 159

Lucretius

[61] *De natura rerum*: i. 154 (CdV 2324), i. 475 (CdV 1552), i. 866 (Enigm. xiv.2), ii. 661 (Ped.reg. p. 165)

Mallius Theodorus

[62] *De metris*: Ped.reg. p. 200

Orosius, Paulus

[63] *Historiae aduersum paganos*: i. 13 (Ped.reg. p. 167), vii. 10 (Ped.reg. p. 175)

Ovid

[64] *Metamorphoseis*: i. 63 (Enigm. li.3), i. 733 (CdV 1715), ii. 220 (CdV 1771), iii. 164 (CdV 1236, 1753, 2421), iv. 726 (CE iv.6.23), vi. 713 (CdV 1077), vii. 258 (CdV 1521), vii. 414 (CdV 575), vii. 626 (Enigm. xl.1), vii. 792 (Enigm. c.9), viii. 371 (Enigm. c.54), viii. 654 (CE iii.74), ix. 229 (CdV 666), ix. 475 (Enigm. praef.13), x. 10 (CdV 925), xi. 149 (CdV 1718), xi. 551 (CdV 2040), xi. 596 (CdV 1569), xii. 194 (CdV 1287), xiii. 395 (Enigm. xxxiv.2, l.2, lxxviii.3), xiii. 567 (Enigm. xxi.5), xiii. 730–xiv. 74 (Enigm. xcv), xiv. 1–14 (Enigm. xcv), xiv. 50 (Enigm. xxxviii.6), xiv. 58 (Enigm. xcv.3), xiv. 60 (Enigm. xcv.11), xiv. 64 (Enigm. xcv.5), xiv. 752 (Enigm. lxxii.4, CdV 2869), xv. 320 (CdV 478), xv. 359 (Enigm. xxxi.5), xv. 651 (CdV 1569), xv. 879 (CdV 304)

Paulinus of Milan

[65] *Vita S. Ambrosii*: c. iii (prDV p. 260)

Paulinus of Nola

[66] *Carmina*: xv. 1 (Metr. p. 96; CdV 904), xv. 69–70 (CdV 896, 2176), xv. 185 (CdV 1758), xvi. 20 (CdV 1799), xvi. 252 (CdV 269), xvi. 283 (CE iv.8.2), xviii. 231 (CdV 784), xix. 288 (CdV praef. 11), xix. 344 (CdV 700), xix. 726 (CdV 488), xxvii. 39 (CdV 971), xxvii. 89 (CdV 584), xxvii. 411 (CdV 414–15), xxvii. 434 (CdV 1437)

Paulinus of Périgueux

[67] *De uita S. Martini*: i. **231** (CdV 1089), i. **287** (CdV 155, 729, 2378), ii. **154** (CE iv.10.13), ii. **650** (CdV 1792), iii. **370** (CE iv.2.27), iv. **480** (CE ii.10), iv. **500** (CdV 2823), iv. **645** (CdV 131), v. **338** (CdV 2814), v. **450** (CdV 1333, 2504, 2846), v. **476** (CE iv.6.20), vi. **269** (CdV 2236)

Paulus Quaestor

[68] *Gratiarum actio*: Metr. pp. 79, 86, 87

Pelagius

[69] *Epistula ad Demetriadem*: prDV pp. 303–4

Persius

[70] *Saturae*: **prol. 1** (Enigm. praef. 13), **prol. 1–3** (Metr. p. 78), ii. **75** (Ped.reg. p. 168), v. **19–20** (Metr. p. 88; CdV 1188), v. **120** (CdV 1188, 1574, 2265)

Phocas

[71] *Ars de nomine et uerbo*: Metr. pp. 79, 95; Ped.reg. p. 191

Pliny the Elder

[72] *Naturalis historia*: xxxii. **154** (Enigm. xvii), xxxvii. **44** (Ped.reg. p. 165), xxxvii. **48** (Ped.reg. pp. 165, 173), xxxvii. **59** (Enigm. ix), xxxvii. **61** (Enigm. xxv)

Pompeius

[73] *Comm. in artem Donati*: Ped.reg. p. 150

Priscian

[74] *Institutio de nomine et pronomine et uerbo*: Ped.reg. p. 174
[75] *Institutiones grammaticae*: Ped.reg. pp. 156, 171, 175, 176, 177, 179, 181, 183, 185, 187, 188, etc.

Proba

[76] *Cento Vergilianus*: **proem. 1** (Ped.reg. p. 188)

Prosper of Aquitaine

[77] *Carmen de ingratis*: lines **158** (CE iv.8.11), **796** (CdV 300), **928** (CdV 2026)
[78] *Epigrammata ex sententiis S. Augustini*: iii. **5** (Metr. p. 79), vi. **1** (Ped.reg. p. 189), viii. **1** (CdV 1687), xv. **6** (Ped.reg. p. 168), xviii. **3** (CdV 103), xxi. **1** (Ped.reg. p. 162), xxi. **3** (CdV 1809, 2353), xlii. **9** (Ped.reg. p. 162), li (prDV p. 319), lviii. **7** (CdV 2825), lxii. **7** (CdV 38–9), lxiv. **4** (Ped.reg. p. 197), lxvii. **1** (Metr. p. 89), lxviii. **1** (Metr. p. 93), lxxi. **3** (Metr. p. 93), lxxi. **5** (Ped.reg. pp. 158, 178), lxxvi (prDV p. 319), lxxvi. **3** (CdV 129), lxxxviii. **1** (Ped.reg. p. 175; prDV p. 318), lxxxix. **2** (Ped.reg. p. 174),

xciv. 5 (Metr. p. 96), ci. 8 (prDV p. 246), cii. 5 (CdV 103), civ. 5 (CdV 34)

Prudentius

[79] *Apotheosis*: lines 127 (CE iv.6.6), 544 (CE i.10, iv.13.5), 632 (Enigm. praef. 9), 697 (CdV 679), 701 (CE iv.8.6), 910 (CdV 131, 654)
[80] *Contra Symmachum*: i. 141 (CdV 1662), i. 148 (CE iv.1.10), i. 375 (CdV 2659), i. 456 (CdV 2029), i. 577 (CdV 1418), ii. 7 (CdV praef. 34), ii. 155 (CdV 113, 1457), ii. 301 (Enigm. xc.2), ii. 758 (CdV praef. 4), ii. 815 (Enigm. lxxi.4), ii. 896 (CdV 848, 1521), ii. 990 (CdV 329)
[81] *Hamartigenia*: lines 281 (CdV 1; Enigm. c.7), 580 (CdV 1832), 919 (CE iv.7.24)
[82] *Liber cathemerinon*: v. 48 (Enigm. xcvi.1)
[83] *Liber peristephanon*: iii. 5 (CdV 521), v. 287 (CdV 2442), viii. 7 (CE iv.1.10), ix. 79 (CE iv.8.7), xi. 90 (Enigm. lxiii.5), xi. 117 (CdV 7, 263), xi. 191 (CdV 2580), xi. 225 (CdV 2882), xiv. 25 (CdV 1952), xiv. 55 (CdV 1952, 2546)
[84] *Psychomachia*: lines 6 (CdV 2865), 7 (Enigm. lxxii.8), 96 (CdV 2634), 355 (CdV praef. 34), 436 (CdV 2575), 452 (CdV 2547), 716 (CdV 185), 736 (CdV 2882), 752 (CdV 1552)

Sallust

[85] *Bellum Iugurthinum*: c. c (Ped.reg. p. 187)

Sedulius, Caelius

[86] *Carmen paschale*: praef. 13–14 (prDV p. 232; CdV 2772), i. 1 (Metr. p. 85), i. 5 (CdV 70), i. 18 (Ped.reg. p. 184), i. 20 (CdV 2457), i. 23 (CdV 2415), i. 28 (CdV 1543), i. 44 (CdV 1307; CE iv.1.18), i. 47 (CdV 690; CE iv.3.11, iv.9.4), i. 48 (CdV 370), i. 49 (CdV 113, 1457), i. 56 (CE i.20), i. 61 (CdV 514), i. 91 (Enigm. lxxviii.2), i. 95 (CdV 543, 685, 1455), i. 98 (Ped.reg. p. 160), i. 103 (CdV 2348), i. 127 (CdV 1755), i. 129 (CdV 477, 498), i. 130 (Ped.reg. p. 198), i. 135 (Ped.reg. p. 156), i. 136 (Ped.reg. p. 190; CdV 5, 423, 1736; Enigm. xvii.1), i. 140 (Ped.reg. p. 174), i. 146 (CdV 1625), i. 157 (Ped.reg. p. 190), i. 160 (Ped.reg. p. 195), i. 161 (Ped.reg. p. 179), i. 162 (CE iv.12.11), i. 163 (CdV 2733), i. 170 (Ped.reg. p. 156), i. 175 (Enigm. lxiii.7), i. 179–80 (prDV p. 249; CdV 188), i. 183 (prDV p. 250), i. 203 (prDV p. 284; Enigm. liv.4), i. 208 (Ped.reg. p. 181; CdV 2775), i. 219 (CdV 1443), i. 236 (CdV 362, 1241, 1434, 1999), i. 248 (CdV 1198), i. 259 (Ped.reg. p. 158), i. 278 (Enigm. c.15), i. 279 (Ped.reg. p. 188), i. 285 (CdV 1589), i. 301 (CdV praef. 17), i. 305–6 (Ped.reg. p. 189; CdV 2017), i. 311 (CdV 650; CE iv.10.18), i. 313 (CdV praef. 24, 1686; CE ii.5; Enigm. lxxxi.1), i. 341 (CdV 571, 752, 1226, 1503, 2005, 2019, 2027, 2275; Enigm. xci.5), i. 350 (Ped.reg. p. 187), i. 360 (CdV 412), i. 368 (Ped.reg. p. 173), ii. 12 (CdV 793; CE iii.12), ii. 19 (CdV 478), ii. 49

(Ped.reg. p. 160), ii. **51** (CdV 2737), ii. **67** (CdV 898), ii. **72** (CdV 1070), ii. **113** (CdV 1691; CE ii.13), ii. **116** (CE iv.7.23), ii. **139** (CR 12; Ped.reg. p. 154), ii. **149** (CdV 1684), ii. **158** (CdV 2054), ii. **160–1** (Ped.reg. p. 190), ii. **166** (CdV 1532, 1576, 1733), ii. **171** (CdV 436), ii. **176** (CdV praef. 25, 396; CE iv.10.16), ii. **197** (CdV 549), ii. **202** (CE ii.2), ii. **206** (CdV 709, 2273), ii. **209** (CE ii.2), ii. **283** (CdV 2018), iii. **34** (CE iv.2.20), iii. **36** (CE iv.2.21), iii. **71** (CdV 427, 1595), iii. **75** (CdV 381, 1210), iii. **81** (CdV 365), iii. **82** (Ped.reg. p. 161; Enigm. c.17), iii. **110** (CdV 2065), iii. **122** (Ped.reg. p. 160), iii. **126** (CE iv.2.33), iii. **128** (Metr. p. 89), iii. **138** (CdV 1496), iii. **173** (CE iv.10.5), iii. **183** (CdV 1001), iii. **185** (CdV 2423), iii. **190** (CdV 436), iii. **201** (CE iv.1.31), iii. **206** (Enigm. xli.6), iii. **235** (CdV 813; Enigm. lviii.5), iii. **239** (CdV 454), iii. **254** (CdV 1088), iii. **264** (Ped.reg. p. 157), iii. **282** (Enigm. xxxi.1), iii. **295** (CdV 1212), iii. **300** (CdV 929; Enigm. liv.5), iv. **21** (CdV 2756), iv. **36** (CdV 472), iv. **38** (CdV 958, 2869; Enigm. lxxii.4), iv. **49** (CdV 2085), iv. **55** (Enigm. lxix.1), iv. **63** (CdV 1913; CE iv.9.6; Enigm. xcv.2), iv. **75** (CdV 2823), iv. **78** (Ped.reg. p. 153), iv. **89** (CE iv.2.13), iv. **93** (CdV 2718), iv. **142** (Ped.reg. p. 162), iv. **148** (CE iv.6.7), iv. **162** (CE iv.1.10), iv. **171** (CdV 664), iv. **181** (CdV 921), iv. **219** (CE iv.6.11), iv. **221** (CdV 2108; CE iv.2.20), iv. **228** (CdV 2440), iv. **296** (Enigm. xxxix.4), v. **44** (CdV 2594), v. **46** (CdV 260), v. **72** (CdV 1357), v. **79** (CdV 16), v. **86** (CdV 2580), v. **87** (CdV 2576), v. **92** (Ped.reg. p. 153), v. **97** (CdV 2251), v. **131** (CE v.8), v. **165** (Enigm. xcviii.2), v. **182** (CdV 452, 2889; CE iv.2.21), v. **190** (Ped.reg. p. 153), v. **206** (Enigm. xlii.2, lvi.3), v. **219** (CdV 1404), v. **234** (Ped.reg. p. 158), v. **255** (Ped.reg. p. 185), v. **285** (CdV 2889), v. **288** (CdV 2278; CE iv.2.33), v. **291** (CdV 883), v. **328** (CdV 2369), v. **376** (CE iv.6.11), v. **396** (CE iv.3.8), v. **424** (CdV 1763)

Seneca

[87] *Tragoediae: Agamemnon*: lines **729** (Ped.reg. p. 194), **787** (Ped.reg. p. 194)

Sergius

[88] *Comm. de littera, de syllaba, de pedibus, de accentibus, de distinctione*: Ped.reg. pp. 150–2

Servius

[89] *Comm. in Vergilii Bucolica et Georgica*: **ad Buc. iii. 20** (Ped.Reg. p. 155), **ad Georg. i. 109** (Ped.reg. p. 156)

[90] *Comm. in Vergilii Aeneidos libros*: **ad Aen. i. 744** (Metr. pp. 72–3), **ad Aen. iv. 301** (Ped.reg. p. 170)

Sisebutus rex Visigothorum

[91] *Carmen de eclipsibus solis et lunae*: lines **2** (Metr. p. 80), **54** (CdV 181; Enigm. lxxxi.3)

Solinus

[92] *Collectanea rerum memorabilium*: cc. x (Ped.reg. p. 167), xvii (Ped.reg. p. 169), xix (Ped.reg. p. 159), xxii (Ped.reg. p. 198.26–7), xxvii (Ped.reg. p. 198.13–14), xxx (Enigm. xxiv), xxxviii (Ped.reg. p. 198.28)

Statius

[93] *Thebais*: i. 197 (CdV 1306), ii. 176 (CdV 485), iv. 591 (CE i.9, ii.9; CdV 1907), vi. 873 (Enigm. xi.1), vii. 44 (Enigm. lv.9), viii. 56 (CdV 456), ix. 8 (CE iv.3.29)

Sulpicius Severus

[94] *Vita S. Martini*: cc. ii–iii (prDV p. 261), vii (prDV p. 261), xiii (prDV p. 261), xxvi (prDV p. 266)

'Symposius'

[95] *Aenigmata*: praef. 3 (CdV 2221; Enigm. xii.1), xvii. 2 (Metr. p. 95), xxii. 3 (Ped.reg. p. 154), xxiv. 3 (Ped.reg. p. 167), xxviii. 1 (Enigm. lviii.1), xxix. 2 (CE iv.7.26), xxxv. 2 (Enigm. xxxvi.2, lxxiv.8), xxxvi. 2 (Ped.reg. p. 167), xxxix. 1 (Enigm. lxxi.1), xliv. 1 (Enigm. xlvi.1), xlvii. 1 (Metr. p. 93), lii. 2 (Ped.reg. p. 197), liii. 3 (Ped.reg. p. 154), lviii. 1 (Enigm. ii.1), lviii. 3 (Ped.reg. pp. 154, 160), lxvii. 2 (Enigm. xliv.7), lxxii. 1 (Metr. p. 94), lxxiv. 3 (Enigm. l. 3), lxxix. 1 (Enigm. lxvi.1), lxxxiv. 3 (Metr. p. 96), lxxxix. 1 (Enigm. xlix.1), xci. 3 (Metr. p. 96), xcviii. 2 (Metr. p. 94)

Terence

[96] *Comoediae*: Metr. p. 90 [*Andria?*]; *Adelphoe*: iii. 1 [line 289] (Ped.reg. p. 196); *Phormio*: i. 1 [lines 35–6] (Ped.reg. p. 184), ii. 1 [lines 74–5] (Ped.reg. p. 184)

Valerius Probus, Marcus

[97] *Comm. in Vergilii Bucolica et Georgica*: Ped.reg. pp. 153, 172

Venantius Fortunatus

[98] *Carmina*: i. 2. 26 (CdV 731), i. 15. 33 (CdV 898), ii. 14. 16 (CE v.13), ii. 15. 13 (CdV 55, 80, 323, 392, 2886), iii. 9. 12 (CE iv.10.11), iii. 13. 11 (CdV 266), iv. 9. 27 (CdV 566), v. 5. 87 (CE iv.6.11), vi. 1. 108 (Enigm. c.15), vi. 1a. 25 (CdV 2585), vi. 4. 8 (CdV 1975), vii. 1. 23 (CdV 2529), vii. 6. 5 (CE iii.68), vii. 12. 95 (CdV 735), vii. 24g. 1 (Enigm. xxiv.3, CdV 1347), viii. 3. 5 (CE iv.2.36), viii. 3. 7 (CdV 735), viii. 3. 93 (CdV 2543), viii. 3. 155 (CdV 878), viii. 3. 319 (CdV 2543), viii. 4. 4 (CdV 186, 1070), viii. 5. 5 (CdV 2894), viii. 7. 3 (CdV 167), ix. 2. 1122 (Enigm. c.15), ix. 3. 6 (CdV 1669), x. 6. 15 [+ x. 11. 15] (CdV 698), x. 6. 59 (CdV 698), x. 11. 15 (CdV 698), App. i. 59 (CE iv.3.3), App. i. 101 (CdV 1627)

[99] *Vita S. Martini*: i. 2 [+ iv. 238] (CdV 852), i. 111 (CdV 2850; Enigm.

lvi.2), i. **122** (CdV 898), i. **288** (Enigm. c.35), i. **305** (CdV 719), i. **457** (Enigm. lvi.2), ii. **26** (Enigm. c.54), ii. **27** [+ iii. 293] (CdV 384), ii. **42** (CdV 1428), ii. **88** (CdV 1146), ii. **122** [+ ii. 457] (CE iv.2.36), ii. **323** (CdV 709), ii. **328** (Enigm. xcix.5), ii. **457** (CE iv.2.36), iii. **192** (CE v.6), iii. **328** (Enigm. xcix.5), iii. **449** (CE v.6), iv. **96** (CdV 580), iv. **153** (CdV 2208), iv. **238** (CdV 852), iv. **246** (CdV 1325), iv. **275** (Enigm. xcv.8), iv. **292** (CdV 2309), iv. **471** (CdV 2733)

Vergil
[100] *Aeneis*: i. **1** (Ped.reg. pp. 184, 200), i. **2** (Metr. p. 94), i. **8** (Metr. p. 95), i. **67** (Ped.reg. p. 165; Enigm. xcvii.7), i. **95–6** (Ped.reg. p. 196), i. **176** (CdV 2325), i. **211** (Ped.reg. p. 199), i. **239** (CdV 1171; Enigm. liv.2), i. **262** (Metr. p. 89), i. **333** (Enigm. xcii.7), i. **345** (CdV 2064), i. **374** (Metr. p. 73), i. **379** (CdV 712, 744, 774), i. **431** (Enigm. xlvii.5), i. **434** [= *Georg.* iv. 167] (Metr. p. 83), i. **468** (Ped.reg. p. 171), i. **505** (CE iii.53, iv.6.2), i. **587** (Metr. p. 91), i. **655** (CdV 1288), i. **657** (CdV 2739, 2769), i. **728** (CdV 1288), i. **744** [= iii. 516] (Metr. p. 73), ii. **1** (Ped.reg. p. 197), ii. **3** (Metr. p. 93), ii. **111** (Metr. p. 91), ii. **116** (CdV 1835), ii. **119** (Ped.reg. p. 168), ii. **201** (CdV 1065), ii. **204** (CE iv.7.29), ii. **384** (CdV 618), ii. **450** (CdV 817), ii. **492** (Ped.reg. p. 183), ii. **512** (Enigm. lvii.5), ii. **513** (Ped.reg. p. 186), ii. **523** (CE iv.i.18, iv.9.14), ii. **535** (CdV 1841), ii. **715** (Ped.reg. p. 186), ii. **747** (Ped.reg. p. 169), ii. **749** (CdV 2612), ii. **758** (CdV 1429), ii. **790** (Ped.reg. p. 154), iii. **26** (Ped.reg. p. 169), iii. **354** (Enigm. lxxviii.1), iii. **384** (Ped.reg. p. 182), iii. **491** (prDV p. 300; CdV 1263), iii. **511** (CdV 2231), iii. **516** (Metr. p. 73), iii. **550** (Metr. p. 91), iii. **575** (CdV 1774), iii. **599** (Metr. p. 91), iii. **620** (prDV p. 266), iii. **621** (Ped.reg. p. 181), iii. **644** (Enigm. liii.6), iii. **664** (Metr. p. 91), iii. **666** (Metr. p. 91), iv. **1–2** (Metr. p. 93), iv. **47** (Metr. p. 89), iv. **59** (CdV 125), iv. **119** (CdV 1073), iv. **177**, **181–4** (Enigm. xcvii.12–16), iv. **228** (CdV 1729; Enigm. c.6), iv. **248** (CdV 2707), iv. **301–2** (Ped.reg. p. 171), iv. **303** (Ped.reg. p. 171), v. **344** (Ped.reg. p. 163), iv. **359** (CdV 1132, 1277; Enigm. xc.1), iv. **402** (Enigm. lxv.4), iv. **482** (CE iii.73), iv. **563** (CdV 2739, 2769), v. **13** (CdV 582), v. **54** (CE iii.65), v. **58** (CE iii.42), v. **67** (CdV 2740; Enigm. xciii.2), v. **208** (Enigm. lxxiv.7), v. **255** (Enigm. lvii.1), v. **361** (CdV 312), v. **412** (Enigm. x.3), v. **432** [= xii. 905] (Ped.reg. p. 183), v. **489** (CE v.8), v. **511** (Ped.reg. p. 152), v. **617** (Metr. p. 91), v. **673** (Metr. p. 91), v. **708** (CdV 1721), v. **712** (Metr. p. 91), v. **721** (Metr. p. 91), v. **738** (Metr. p. 91), vi. **33** (Metr. p. 89), vi. **48** (CdV 2430), vi. **75** (Ped.reg. p. 181), vi. **120** (Ped.reg. p. 183), vi. **128** (Metr. p. 83), vi. **164** (CdV 776, 2066), vi. **217** (CdV 2612), vi. **232** (CE iv.2.34), vi. **253** (CdV 1384; Enigm. c.42), vi. **258** (CdV 281), vi. **263** (CdV 533), vi. **305** (CdV 2606), vi. **323** (Enigm. liii.8), vi. **369** (Enigm. liii.8), vi. **371** (CdV 1790), vi. **404** (CdV 455), vi. **413–14** (Ped.reg. p. 157), vi. **504** (CdV 2530), vi. **517** (Ped.reg. p. 171), vi. **646** (Metr. p. 73), vi. **675** (CdV 148), vi. **779**

(Enigm. xxvi.5), vi. **797** (CE iii. 73), vi. **828** (CdV 308), vi. **861** (CdV 2612), vii. **26** (Ped.reg. p. 171; CdV 1363), vii. **59** (Metr. p. 83), vii. **74** (CdV 2271; CE iv.11.10), vii. **123** (Metr. p. 80), vii. **165** (CdV 1958; Enigm. lx.3), vii. **213** (Enigm. xcii.7), vii. **338** (CdV 1867), vii. **341** (Ped.reg. p. 184; CdV 1105, 1328, 1811; Enigm. xcvii.7), vii. **368** (Enigm. lxiv.3), vii. **433** (CdV 2302), vii. **446** (CdV 630, 2231), vii. **447** (CdV 2636), vii. **600** (CdV 2103; CE iii.5), vii. **608** (Enigm. lx.1), vii. **623** (Ped.reg. p. 170), vii. **634** (Metr. pp. 83, 90), vii. **641** (CdV 30), viii. **2** (CdV 2460), viii. **28** (Enigm. lvii.5), viii. **67** (Enigm. xli.6), viii. **77** (CdV 1338), viii. **83** (Ped.reg. p. 200), viii. **94** (Ped.reg. p. 168), viii. **369** (CdV 629), viii. **412** (CdV 1294), viii. **429** (Enigm. v.3), viii. **449** (CdV 72), viii. **507** (CdV 2343, 2481), viii. **596** (Ped.reg. p. 186; prDV p. 230), viii. **700** (CdV 1548), ix. **3** (CdV 534), ix. **23** (CdV 410; Enigm. lix.2), ix. **45** (CdV 1286; CE iv.3.9), ix. **93** (Metr. p. 91), ix. **106** (Metr. p. 91), ix. **146** (Metr. p. 90), ix. **226** (Metr. p. 90), ix. **256** (Metr. p. 91), ix. **415** (CdV 2373), ix. **419** (Metr. p. 91), ix. **445** (CdV 1790), ix. **456** (CdV 1313), ix. **470** (CdV 646; Enigm. xcii.9), ix. **503** (Metr. p. 89), ix. **535** (Ped.reg. p. 196), ix. **580** (Ped.reg. p. 193; CdV 2659), ix. **614–16** (prDV p. 316), ix. **616** (Metr. p. 92), ix. **658** (CE iv.2.13), ix. **726** (CdV 2079), ix. **732** (Enigm. xxvi.5), ix. **758** (Metr. p. 92), x. **1** (Metr. p. 92), x. **12** (CdV 556; CE iv.7.21), x. **54** (Metr. p. 91), x. **115** (Ped.reg. p. 195), x. **121** (CdV 646; Enigm. xcii.9), x. **122** (CdV 1650), x. **145** (CdV 2386), x. **146** (CdV 276, 1552), x. **163** (CdV 30), x. **209** (Enigm. xvii.1), x. **216** (CdV 1537), x. **244** (Enigm. xli.1), x. **264** (Ped.reg. p. 198; CdV 2707; CE iv.9.7), x. **265** (Enigm. xlviii.6, lvii.5), x. **333** (Ped.reg. p. 195), x. **386** (CdV 2267; CE iv.4.12), x. **389** (Ped.reg. p. 196), x. **399** (Ped.reg. p. 198), x. **462–3** (Metr. p. 91), x. **511** (CdV 2316), x. **550** (CdV 2612), x. **689–90** (Ped.reg. p. 195), x. **746** (CdV 959; Enigm. lxi.4, c.6), x. **908** (Ped.reg. p. 198), xi. **1** [= iv. **129**] (Metr. p. 80), xi. **75** (Metr. p. 92), xi. **90** (CdV 1907; CE i.9, ii.9), xi. **136** (Enigm. lxxviii.10), xi. **182** (CdV 2693), xi. **188** (CdV 2612), xi. **202** (CE iii.73), xi. **211** (CdV 2606), xi. **384** (CdV 2530), xi. **424** (CdV 630, 2231), xi. **537** (Metr. p. 83), xi. **875** [+ viii. **596**] (Ped.reg. p. 186; prDV p. 230), xii. **167** (CdV 361, 572), xii. **275** (CdV 2612), xii. **351** (CdV 1841), xii. **493** (Enigm. xxvi.5), xii. **607** (CdV 2254), xii. **677** (Enigm. vii.2), xii. **846** (Enigm. xcvii.3–4), xii. **900** (Enigm. xcvii.1), xii. **905** (Ped.reg. p. 183), xii. **906** (Metr. p. 92)

[101] *Bucolica*: i. **3** (Metr. p. 96), i. **8** (Metr. p. 96), i. **59–62** (Metr. p. 73), i. **62** (Metr. p. 94; Ped.reg. p. 188), iii. **106** (Ped.reg. p. 192), iv. **42–5** (prDV p. 316), iv. **46–7** (Metr. p. 73), v. **20** (CdV 1962), v. **56** (CdV 1307), v. **84** (CE iv.10.8), vi. **13** (Metr. p. 87), vi. **52** (Enigm. liii.6), vi. **66** (Metr. p. 93), vii. **31** (Ped.reg. p. 184), vii. **61** (Ped.reg. p. 164), vii. **42** (Enigm. c.26), viii. **41** (Ped.reg. p. 152), viii. **71** (prDV p. 310), ix. **51** (Metr. p. 89), x. **69** (Metr. p. 89), x. **70** (Enigm. vii.1)

[102] *Georgica*: i. **22** (CdV 111), i. **39** (CdV 1381), i. **43–4** (Ped.reg. p. 153), i.

46 (Ped.reg. p. 173), i. **57** (CE iii.81), i. **58** (CdV 2348), i. **139** (CdV 1936), i. **185** (Enigm. lxv.4), i. **212** (Ped.reg. p. 188), i. **256** (Enigm. lxxviii.10), i. **275** (CdV 1423), i. **335** (Ped.reg. p. 163), i. **382** (CdV 2678), i. **399** (Ped.reg. p. 173), i. **406** (Enigm. xvi.3, xlii.3), i. **409** (Enigm. xvi.3, xlii.3) i. **431** (Ped.reg. p. 159), i. **495** (CdV 2767), i. **497** (1769), ii. **13** (Ped.reg. p. 165; Enigm. lxxxiv.6), ii. **31** (Ped.reg. p. 160; CdV 169), ii. **70** (Ped.reg. p. 152), ii. **77** (Ped.reg. p. 197), ii. **90** (CdV 2792), ii. **121** (Ped.reg. pp. 182, 183), ii. **134** (Ped.reg. p. 197), ii. **172** (CdV 556; CE iv.7.21), ii. **176** (Metr. p. 86; Ped.reg. p. 154), ii. **209** (Enigm. lxxxiii.3), ii. **307** (CdV 2733), ii. **381** (Ped.reg. p. 182), ii. **436** (CdV 399), ii. **471** (Enigm. lxv.6), iii. **11–13** (Ped.reg. p. 202), iii. **32** (CdV 2097), iii. **66** (CdV 2693; Enigm. xxiii.4), iii. **201** (Metr. p. 92), iii. **208** (CdV 2306), iii. **231** (Ped.reg. p. 155), iii. **256** (Ped.reg. p. 165), iii. **270** (Ped.reg. p. 198), iii. **292–3** (Ped.reg. p. 202), iii. **297** (CdV 2780), iii. **345** (Ped.reg. p. 184), iii. **354** (CE iii.25), iii. **392** (CdV 1383), iii. **425** (Ped.reg. p. 152), iii. **449** (Metr. p. 89), iii. **480** (CdV 341), iii. **551–3** (CdV 2635–40), iv. **3** (CdV 656; CE iv.2.8), iv. **5** (Ped.reg. p. 164), iv. **102** (Ped.reg. p. 189), iv. **167** (Metr. p. 32), iv. **190** (CdV 630, 2230, 2231), iv. **194** (Ped.reg. p. 168), iv. **203** (Ped.reg. p. 195), iv. **209** (CdV 650; CE iv.10.18), iv. **223** (CdV 341), iv. **269** (CdV 2799), iv. **441** (CdV 919), iv. **511** (Ped.reg. p. 164), iv. **548** (CdV 1286; CE iv.3.9)

Victorinus, Maximus

[103] *De hexametro uersu siue heroico*: Metr. pp. 90–2

Virgilius Maro Grammaticus

[104] *Epistulae*: ii. 1 (Ep. p. 494)

ANONYMOUS WRITINGS

[105] *Carmen de imagine et somno* [pseudo-Ovid]: Ped.reg. p. 169

[106] *Carmen de resurrectione mortuorum*: lines 1 (CdV 23), 8 (CdV 1426), 20 (CdV 1877), 28 (Enigm. iii.1), 83 (CdV 2827), 92 (CdV 816), 96 (CdV 278), 105 (CE i.15), 208 (CdV 171), 219 (CE ii.20; Enigm. lxxxiv.8; CdV 1698), 356 (CdV 1698), 406 (CdV 2027)

[107] *Culex* [pseudo-Vergil]: lines 408 (Enigm. vi.3, xcvi.9), 413–14 (Ped.reg. p. 157)

[108] *Disticha Catonis*: ii prol. (Ep. xi p. 500)

[109] *Epistula S. Hieronimi de nominibus pedum* [unpr.] [pseudo-Jerome]: Ped.reg. pp. 164, 171, 178

[110] *Epithalamium Laurentii* [pseudo-Claudian]: lines 32 (Enigm. c.15), 36 (Enigm. xxxix.6), 38 (CdV 1169), 41 (Enigm. xxxiii.2), 52 (CdV 2126), 63 (CdV 2788), 66 (CdV 1061), 73 (Ped.reg. p. 164), 79 (CdV 1159), 80 (prDV p. 278; Ped.reg. p. 182; CdV 1159)

[111] *Gesta Siluestri*: prDV pp. 257, 258

[112] *Historia monachorum*, trans. Rufinus: cc. i (prDV p. 267), vii (prDV p. 287), xxx (prDV p. 284)

[113] *Paedagogus* [pseudo-Vergil]: Metr. p. 80, Ped.reg. pp. 160, 186 (?)

[114] *passiones apostolorum*: *Passio S. Iohannis* [CPG 1097, BHL 4320] [pseudo-Mellitus]: prDV pp. 254, 255; *Passio S. Thomae* [BHL 8136?]: prDV p. 255

[115] *passiones martyrum*: *Passio SS. Agapes, Chioniae et Irenes* [BHL 118]: prDV pp. 305–7; *Passio S. Agathae* [BHL 133]: prDV p. 293; *Passio S. Agnetis* [BHL 156] [pseudo-Ambrose]: prDV pp. 298–9; *Passio SS. Anatoliae et Victoriae* [cf. BHL 8591]: prDV pp. 308–10; *Passio S. Babylae* [BHL 889]: prDV pp. 274–5; *Passio S. Caeciliae* [BHL 1495]: prDV p. 292; *Passio S. Christinae* [BHL 1751]: prDV pp. 300–1; *Passio SS. Chrysanti et Dariae* [BHL 1787]: prDV pp. 276–80; *Passio S. Constantinae* [BHL 1927–8?]: prDV pp. 302–3; *Passio SS. Cosmae et Damiani* [BHL 1967]: prDV pp. 275–6; *Passio SS. Dorotheae et Theophili* [BHL 2323]: prDV pp. 301–2; *Passio S. Eugeniae* [CPL 2184, BHL 2666] [pseudo-Rufinus]: prDV pp. 296–8; *Passio S. Eulaliae* [BHL 2699–2700?]: prDV pp. 299–300; *Passio S. Felicis ep. Tubzacensis* [BHL 2894]: prDV p. 264; *Passio SS. Iuliani et Basilissae* [BHL 4529]: prDV pp. 280–4; *Passio SS. Iustinae et Cypriani* [BHL 2047]: prDV pp. 295–6; *Passio S. Luciae* [BHL 4992]: prDV pp. 293–4; *Passio SS. Rufinae et Secundae* [BHL 7359]: prDV pp. 307–8; *Passio S. Theclae* [BHL 8021?]: prDV pp. 299–300

[116] *Recognitiones*, trans. Rufinus [pseudo-Clement]: prDV p. 257

[117] *Syllogai titulorum*: *Sylloge Lauteshamensis quarta* [ICVR ii. 95–118]: Metr. p. 80, Ped.reg. p. 153; xxiiA. 1 [ICL 1429] (CdV 173; Enigm. lv.5; CE iii.70); *Sylloge Turonensis* [ICVR ii. 58–71]: Ped.reg. p. 153

[118] *Versus sibyllae de iudicio*: Metr. pp. 79, 93 (*bis*); lines 2 (Enigm. praef. 35), 13 (CE ii. 31), 23 (Enigm. xiii.1), 25 (CdV 1248; CE iv.6.24), 28 (CdV 795, 847; Enigm. lv.7), 30 (CdV 282)

[119] *Voces animantium*: Ped.reg. pp. 179–80

c. Bede of Monkwearmouth-Jarrow

There is no doubt that Bede had access to a very substantial library at Monkwearmouth-Jarrow. In 1896 Charles Plummer (BOH, pp. l–lii) compiled a useful list of authors named by Bede at some point in his writings (the present utility of Plummer's list is, however, reduced by the fact that his references are to the twelve-volume edition of Bede produced by J. A. Giles in 1843–4). More recently, M. L. W. Laistner, the learned editor of Bede's two treatises on Acts, compiled a list of works cited by Bede, 'The Library of the Venerable Bede'. He gives a long list of works cited by Bede (pp. 263–6), but provides no specific page-and-line references which would allow the reader to verify his attributions. Since the work of Plummer and Laistner, scholarship on Bede has made very considerable advances, to the point that most of his writings are now available in the Corpus Christia-norum. In most cases these volumes are provided with useful *apparatus* of sources (excellent, in the case of editions by Laistner, C. W. Jones, or Roger Gryson; poor, in the case of editions by D. Hurst). I use the following abbreviations for Bede's writings:

Coll. = *Collectio ex opusculis beati Augustini in epistulas Pauli apostoli* [CPL 1360]: unpublished, but described in detail by Fransen, 'Description de la collection de Bède'; cited by item number in Fransen's list

Comm.Abacuc = *Super Canticum Abacuc allegorica expositio* [CPL 1354], ed. J. E. Hudson, CCSL 119B (1983), 377–409, cited by page and line number

Comm.Cant.cant. = *In Cantica Canticorum allegorica expositio* [CPL 1353], ed. Hurst, CCSL 119B (1983), 165–375, cited by page and line number

Comm.Epist.cath. = *Super epistulas catholicas expositio* [CPL 1362], ed. Hurst, CCSL 121 (1983), 179–342, cited by page and line number

Comm.Ezr. = *In Ezram et Neemiam prophetas allegorica expositio* [CPL 1349], ed. Hurst, CCSL 119A (1969), 235–393, cited by page and line number

Comm.Gen. = *Comm. in Genesin* [CPL 1344], ed. Jones, CCSL 118 (1967), cited by page and line number

Comm.Luc. = *In Lucae Euangelium expositio* [CPL 1356], ed. Hurst, CCSL 120 (1960), 1–425, cited by page and line number

Comm.Marc. = *In Marci Euangelium expositio* [CPL 1355], ed. Hurst, CCSL 120 (1960), 427–648, cited by page and line number

Comm.Prov. = *Comm. in Parabolas Salomonis* [CPL 1351], ed. Hurst, CCSL 119B (1983), 21–163, cited by page and line number of the relevant chapter of Proverbs (given in square brackets)

Comm.Sam. = *In Samuelem prophetam allegorica expositio* [CPL 1346], ed. Hurst, CCSL 119 (1962), 1–272, cited by page and line number

Comm.Tob. = *In librum beati patris Tobiae allegorica expositio* [CPL 1350], ed. Hurst, CCSL 119B (1983), 1–19, cited by page and line number

DAM = *De arte metrica* [CPL 1565], ed. C. B. Kendall, CCSL 123A (1975), 81–141, cited by chapter and line number

DDI = *Versus de die iudicii* [CPL 1370], ed. J. Fraipont, CCSL 222 (1955), 439–44, cited by line number

DLS = *De locis sanctis* [CPL 2333], ed. Fraipont, CCSL 175 (1965), 245–80, cited by chapter and line number

DNR = *De natura rerum* [CPL 1343], ed. Jones, CCSL 123A (1975), 189–234, cited by chapter and line number

DO = *De orthographia* [CPL 1566], ed. Jones, CCSL 123A (1975), 7–57, cited by line number

DST = *De schematibus et tropis* [CPL 1567], ed. Kendall, CCSL 123A (1975), 142–71, cited by chapter and line number

DTR = *De temporum ratione* [CPL 2320], ed. Jones, CCSL 123B (1977), 263–460

Epist.Ecgbert. = *Epistula ad Ecgbertum* [CPL 1376], ed. C. Plummer, *Venerabilis Baedae Opera Historica*, i. 405–23, cited by chapter number

Epist.Pleg. = *Epistula ad Pleguinam*, ed. Jones, CCSL 123C (1980), 617–26, cited by line number

Exp.Act. = *Expositio Actuum Apostolorum* [CPL 1357], ed. Laistner, CCSL 121 (1983), 1–99, cited by page and line number of the relevant chapter of Acts (given in square brackets)

Exp.Apoc. = *Expositio Apocalypseos* [CPL 1363], ed. Gryson, CCSL 121A (2001); cited by chapter and line number

HAA = *Historia abbatum* [CPL 1378], ed. Plummer, *Venerabilis Baedae Opera Historica*, i. 364–87, cited by book and chapter number

HE = *Historia ecclesiastica gentis Anglorum* [CPL 1375], ed. Plummer, *Venerabilis Baedae Opera Historica*, i. 5–360, cited by book and chapter number

Hom. = *Homiliae* [CPL 1367], ed. Hurst, CCSL 122 (1955), 1–378, cited by book, homily, and line number

Hymn. = *Hymni* [CPL 1372], ed. Fraipont, CCSL 122 (1955), 407–38, cited by hymn and line number

Mart. = *Martyrologium* [CPL 2032], ed. Dubois and Renaud, *Édition pratique des martyrologes de Bède*; a conspectus of sources drawn on by Bede is given by Quentin, *Les Martyrologes historiques*, 57–112, to which reference (by page number) is given here

Nom.loc. = *Nomina locorum ex beati Hieronimi presbiteri et Flavi Iosephi collecta opusculis* [CPL 1346a], ed. Hurst, CCSL 119 (1962), 273–87, cited by line number

Quaest.Reg. = *In libros Regum quaestiones .xxx.* [CPL 1347], ed. Hurst, CCSL 119 (1962), 289–322, cited by *quaestio* and line number

Retract.Act. = *Retractatio in Actus apostolorum* [CPL 1358], ed. Laistner, CCSL 121 (1983), 101–63, cited by page and line number of the relevant chapter of Acts (given in square brackets)

Tabernac. = *De tabernaculo* [CPL 1345], ed. Hurst, CCSL 119A (1969), 1–139, cited by page and line number

Templ. = *De templo* [CPL 1348], ed. Hurst, CCSL 119A (1969), 141–234, cited by page and line number

VCM = *Vita S. Cudbercti metrica* [CPL 1380; BHL 2020], ed. W. Jaager, *Bedas metrische Vita sancti Cuthberti*, cited by line number

VCP = prose *Vita S. Cudbercti* [CPL 1381, BHL 2021], ed. Colgrave, *Two Lives of Saint Cuthbert*, 141–307, cited by chapter number

Adomnán of Iona

[1] *De locis sanctis*: DLS (*passim* [40×]); i. 2 (Hom. ii.10.188–97), i. 5 (Hom. ii.10.208–13), i. 6 (Hom. ii.10.213–17), i. 7 (HE v.16), i. 22–3 (HE v.17), ii. 1–2 (HE v.16), ii. 6 (Hom. i.7.147–9), ii. 7 (Hom. i.10.52–4), ii. 8–10 (HE v.17)

Agroecius of Sens

[2] *Ars de orthographia*: DO (*passim* [84×])

Aldhelm of Malmesbury

[3] *Carmen de uirginitate* [CPL 1333]: lines 31 (VCM 96), 119 (VCM 258), 309 (VCM 146), 382 (DDI 75), 1407 (VCM 131), 1852 (DDI 123), 2070 (DDI 89); and cf. HE v.18

[4] *Carmina ecclesiastica* [CPL 1331]: iv. 8. 5 (VCM 648)

[5] *De metris* [cf. CPL 1335]: Comm.Gen. p. 110.1314–15; DAM x.9–15, iii.115–16, xi.62–3, xii.9–12, 28–30, xv.13–16, xvi.6

[6] *De pedum regulis* [cf. CPL 1335]: DAM iv.28–30, 66–7, 68–9, 70

[7] *Enigmata* [cf. CPL 1335]: **praef. 17** (VCM 1), **praef. 31** (VCM 73), **liii. 7** (DDI 48), **lviii. 7** (VCM 2), **lix. 6** (VCM 378)

[8] *Epistulae* [CPL 1334]: **iv** [ad Geruntium] (HE v.18)

Ambrose

[9] *De Abraham*: **i. 2** (Comm.Gen. p. 172.1081–3), **i. 3** (Comm.Gen. pp. 187.1586–1607, 194.9–13), **i. 4** (Comm.Gen. p. 199.209–25), **i. 6** (Comm.Gen. pp. 219.911–21, 220.956–65), **i. 7** (Comm.Gen. p. 233.1390–1400), **ii. 5** (Comm.Gen. p. 199.209–25), **ii. 11** (Comm.Gen. p. 205.396–417)

[10] *De Cain et Abel*: **ii. 6** (Comm.Gen. p. 74.59), **ii. 9** (Comm.Gen. p. 77.153–9)

[11] *De fide*: **ii. 5** (Comm.Marc. pp. 615.797–812, 634.1537–9), **ii. 7** (Comm.Epist.cath. [1 Petr. 4] p. 251.8–12)

[12] *De fuga saeculi*: **v. 31** (DO line 1226)

[13] *De Isaac uel anima*: **viii. 73** (Comm.Gen. p. 62.1989–90)

[14] *De Noe et arca*: **i. 1–2** (Comm.Gen. p. 98.902–15), **vi. 13** (Comm.Gen. pp. 106–7.1179–1231), **ix. 27** (Comm.Gen. p. 111.1343–6), **xv. 52** (Comm.Gen. p. 119.1636–51), **xvi. 58** (Comm.Gen. p. 120.1676–82), **xvii. 60** (Comm.Gen. p. 115.1517–23; DTR xi. 48–52), **xix. 67** (DO line 232), **xxxiv. 126** (Comm.Gen. p. 150.280–5), **xxxiv. 128** (Comm.Gen. p. 145.133–6)

[15] *De paenitentia*: **i. 3** (Comm.Epist.cath. [1 Ioh. 5] p. 327.317–18)

[16] *De paradiso*: **iii. 15** (Comm.Gen. p. 49.1539–42), **iii. 16** (Comm.Gen. p. 48.1504–7), **iv. 24** (Comm.Gen. p. 45.1432–6), **xi. 50** (Comm.Gen. p. 56.1797–1805), **xiii. 61** (Comm.Gen. p. 61.1939–46), **xiii. 67** (Comm. Gen. p. 62.1995–2001), **xv. 74** (Comm.Gen. pp. 65–6.2084–2105)

[17] *De spiritu sancto*: **i. 3** (Exp.Act. [Act. 10] p. 55.194–205), **ii. 10** (Exp.Act. [Act. 10] p. 51.87–92), **iii. 11** (Comm.Epist.cath. [1 Ioh. 5] p. 322.107–11; Comm.Gen. p. 211.617–18)

[18] *De uirginibus*: **c. ix** (DO line 1210)

[19] *De uirginitate*: **iii. 4** (Epist. Ecgbert. 5)

[20] *Exameron*: **i. 1** (Comm.Gen. p. 39.1226–9), **i. 2** (Comm.Gen. p. 3.1–19), **i. 4** (Comm.Gen. p. 14.386–9), **i. 6** (Comm.Gen. p. 5.89–96), **i. 8** (Comm.Gen. pp. 5.76–84, 6.123–56), **i. 9** (Comm.Gen. p. 7.162–8, 168–80, 185–94; DTR v.69–70), **i. 10** (Comm.Gen. p. 10.230), **ii. 3** (Comm.Gen. pp. 10.252–9, 268–75, 13.333–42, 342–50), **ii. 4** (Comm. Gen. p. 21.628–36), **iii. 4** (DNR iv.9–14), **iii. 5** (Comm.Gen. p. 12. 295–6; DO lines 84–5), **iii. 6** (DO lines 529–30), **iii. 9** (Comm.Cant.cant. p. 335.753–4), **iii. 12** (Comm.Cant.cant. pp. 224.508–14, 353.590–603), **iii. 13** (Comm.Gen. p. 62.1989–95), **iv. 1** (DO lines 1040–1), **iv. 5** (Comm.Gen. p. 16.450), **iv. 7** (DTR xxviii.3–21, xxix.7–11), **v. 12** (Comm.Gen. p. 20.585–9), **vi. 2** (DTR vii.47–51), **vi. 7** (Comm.Gen.

p. 25.746–58), vi. **8** (Comm.Gen. p. 24.715–17), vi. **9** (Comm.Gen.
pp. 45.1406–10, 107.1212–31), etc.

[21] *Explanatio super psalmos .xii.*: ps. xxxvii. **9** (Exp.Apoc. xiii.15–17), ps.
xxxviii. **1** (DTR lxxi.60–2), ps. xlv. **10** (Comm.Gen. p. 96.832–7)

[22] *Expositio euangelii secundum Lucam*: i. **2** (Comm.Luc. pp. 19–20.17–47),
i. **11** (Comm.Luc. p. 20.53–60), i. **16** (Comm.Luc. p. 21.75–9), i. **18**
(Comm.Luc. p. 22. 129–39), i. **20–1** (Comm.Luc. pp. 22–3.140–6), i. **25**
(Comm.Epist.cath. [1 Ioh. 4] p. 314.142–8), i. **36** (Comm.Luc. p. 26.284–
7), ii. **1** (Comm.Luc. p. 31.474–89), ii. **17** (Comm.Luc. p. 33.560–3), ii. **18**
(Comm.Luc. p. 35.635–7), ii. **22** (Comm.Luc. pp. 35–6.654–62), ii. **30**
(Comm.Luc. p. 40.818–22), ii. **31** (Comm.Luc. p. 40.825–44), ii. **34**
(Comm.Luc. p. 43.957–62), ii. **41** (Comm.Luc. p. 49.1212–13), ii. **51**
(Comm.Luc. p. 36.678–87), ii. **53** (Comm.Luc. p. 54.1381–3), ii. **61**
(Comm.Luc. p. 68.1942–3), ii. **62** (Comm.Luc. p. 70.2007–11), ii. **65**
(Comm.Luc. p. 73.2138–42), ii. **77** (Comm.Luc. p. 79.2379–81), iii. **1**
(Comm.Marc. p. 502.540–3), v. **1** (Comm.Marc. p. 450.524–54), v. **8**
(Comm.Marc. p. 451.562–8), v. **16** (Comm.Marc. p. 458.820–3, 840–4), v.
33 (Comm.Marc. pp. 464.1056–60, 478.1600–6), v. **39** (Comm.Marc.
p. 465.1093–1100, 1107–18), v. **41** (Comm.Marc. pp. 495.255–60,
516.1066–80), v. **44–5** (Comm.Marc. pp. 473.1410–18, 493.172–7), vi.
66 (Comm.Marc. p. 506.671–6), vi. **102** (Comm.Marc. pp. 450.503–6,
468. 1241–4), vii. **133** (Comm.Marc. p. 615.815–20), ix. **25** (Comm.Marc.
p. 583.1626–8), x. **56** (Comm.Marc. p. 615.812–15), etc.

[23] *Hymni*: ii. **1** (DAM xxi. 11), iii. **1** (DAM xxi. 10), iv. **1** (DAM xxi. 9), v.
1 (DAM xxi. 8), vi. **19–20** (DAM xxi. 22–3), xv. **1–4** (DAM xxi. 15–18)

Ambrosiaster
[24] *Quaestiones Veteris et Noui Testamenti*: c. **xli** (Comm.Gen. p. 7.132–7)

Aponius
[25] *Explanatio in Canticum canticorum*: i. **21** (Comm.Gen. p. 61.1939–46), i.
23 (Comm.Gen. p. 61.1939–46); iv. **38** (Comm.Cant.cant. p. 223.470–2),
viii. **74** (Comm.Cant.cant. p. 285.534–8)

Aquila Romanus
[26] *De figuris sententiarum et elocutionis*: DST i.115–17, ii.4

Arator
[27] *Historia apostolica*: Ep. ad Vigilium **23** (DAM xxv.30–1), i. **108–10**
(Exp.Act. [Act. 1] p. 14. 145–7), i. **119** (VCM 204, 706), i. **121** (VCM 6), i.
141 (VCM 756), i. **147** (VCM 7; Exp.Apoc. xxxvii.220–1), i. **226–7** (VCM
36–8), i. **407–10** (Exp.Act. [Act. 4] p. 28.99–102), i. **552–6** (DAM xi.14–
18), i. **570–2** (Exp.Act. [Act. 6] p. 32.6–8), i. **593–5** (Exp.Act. [Act. 7]
p. 38.161–3), i. **624–5** (Exp.Act. [Act. 8] p. 39.18–19), i. **801** (VCM 842),
i. **915** (VCM 212), i. **950** (VCM 72), i. **1054–7** (Exp.Act. [Act. 12]

p. 59.46–9), i. **1055** (VCM 129), ii. **249–50** (VCM 978–9), ii. **441–2** (Exp.Act. [Act. 16] p. 69.39–40), ii. **647–50** (Exp.Act. [Act. 19] p. 78.60–3), ii. **656** (VCM 848), ii. **701–2** (DAM ii.15–16), ii. **714–16** (Exp.Act. [Act. 19] p. 80.102–4), ii. **890–1** (Exp.Act. [Act. 20] p. 83.91–2), ii. **909–10** (Exp.Act. [Act. 20] p. 83.93–4), ii. **1069–70** (VCM 152–3), ii. **1075** (VCM 156), ii. **1107–9** (DAM iii.94–6), ii. **1222** (VCM 10)

Arnobius Iunior
[28] *Commentarii in psalmos*: **ps. civ** (DTR lxvi.186–94)

Arusianus Messius
[29] *Exempla elocutionum*: DO lines 34, 51, 52, 83, 320, 370, 390, 392, 450, 537, 543–9, 614, 645, 656, 661, 799, 966, 1010, 1019

Athanasius
[30] *Vita S. Antonii*, trans. Evagrius: cc. **xx** (VCP c. 22), **xxv** (VCP c. 19), **lviii** (VCP cc. 37, 39), **lxxv** (Exp.Act. [Act. 27] p. 97.40–1)

Audax
[31] *De Scauri et Palladii libris excerpta*: DAM i. 8–10, ii. 23–6, xvi. 18–21, xxiv. 10–18

Augustine
[32] *Ad Orosium contra Priscillianistas et Origenistas*: **v. 6** (Coll. 439)
[33] *Confessiones*: **i. 2** (Coll. 127), **viii. 4** (Coll. 396), **ix. 4** (Coll. 326), **ix. 7** (Mart. [Quentin p. 101]), **x. 3** (Coll. 198), **x. 31** (Coll. 164), **xii. 8** (DNR ii. 1), **xii. 17** (Comm.Gen. p. 3.25–9), **xii. 28** (Comm.Gen. p. 6.114–18), **xii. 29** (Comm.Gen. p. 6.107–14), **xiii. 4–9** (Comm.Gen. p. 7.132–7), **xiii. 5** (Comm.Gen. p. 7.151–61), **xiii. 8** (Comm.Gen. p. 3.25–9), **xiii. 22** (Coll. 113), **xiii. 22–3** (Coll. 146), **xiii. 23** (Comm.Gen. p. 27.804–6), **xiii. 25–6** (Comm.Gen. p. 30.899–942), **xiii. 25** (Coll. 437), **xiii. 26** (Coll. 362), **xiii. 34** (DNR i.9–11)
[34] *Contra Adimantum*: **i. 7** (DTR x.1–59), **ii. 1** (Comm.Gen. p. 32.976–7), **iii. 1** (Comm.Gen. p. 56.1780–95), **iv** (Comm.Gen. p. 78.200–22)
[35] *Contra aduersarium Legis et Prophetarum*: **i. 8–11** (Coll. 232), **i. 8** (Comm.Gen. p. 6.114–18), **i. 14** (Comm.Gen. p. 45.1416–29), **i. 15** (Comm.Gen. pp. 70.2258–61, 72.2316–32), **i. 20** (Coll. 385, 453; Comm. Gen. p. 135.2242–6), **i. 24** (Coll. 8, 183; Comm.Luc. p. 99.3173–4; Exp.Apoc. praef.136–7), **ii. 1** (Coll. 397), **ii. 3** (Coll. 104), **ii. 4** (Coll. 440), **ii. 6** (Coll. 227), **ii. 11** (Coll. 181), **ii. 37** (Exp.Apoc. xxxviii.93–4)
[36] *Contra duas epistulas Pelagianorum*: **i. 2–3** (Coll. 48)
[37] *Contra Faustum Manichaeum*: **vi. 2** (Coll. 180, 375), **xi. 7** (Coll. 377, 441), **xi. 8** (Coll. 248, 311), **xii. 8** (Coll. 333), **xii. 9–13** (Comm.Gen. pp. 81–5.294–455), **xii. 10** (Comm.Gen. pp. 77.150–1, 82.352–64), **xii. 11** (Comm.Gen. p. 83.381–8), **xii. 12** (Comm.Gen. p. 84. 409–19), **xii. 13**

(Comm.Gen. p. 84.424–31), xii. **14** (Comm.Gen. p. 87.505–10; DTR lxvi.
152–5), xii. **15** (Comm.Gen. p. 106.1173–6), xii. **16** (Comm.Gen.
p. 108.1244–9), xii. **18** (Comm.Gen. p. 103.1067–9), xii. **19** (Comm.Gen.
pp. 119.1053–64, 121.1718–24, 1731–8), xii. **22** (Comm.Gen. p. 132.2120–
38), xii. **23** (Comm.Gen. pp. 137–8.2304–6, 2309–22, 2342–5), xiv. **4–6**
(Coll. 271), xiv. **5** (Coll. 65), xvi. **22** (Coll. 293), xvi. **29** (Coll. 373;
Comm.Gen. p. 205.396–417), xxi. **2** (Coll. 231), xxii. **30–2** (Comm.Gen.
pp. 199–200.209–25), xxii. **32** (Comm.Gen. p. 207.459–68), xxii. **35**
(Comm.Gen. p. 234.1439–51; DO line 469), xxii. **36** (Comm.Luc.
pp. 97–8.3095–3110), xxii. **38–40** (Comm.Gen. pp. 235–6.1460–1520),
xxii. **41** (Comm.Gen. pp. 179.1308–29, 224.1080–98), xxii. **42–4**
(Comm.Gen. pp. 229–31.1252–1325)

[38] *Contra Gaudentium Donatistam episcopum libri duo*: i. **30** (Coll. 287)

[39] *Contra Iulianum haeresis Pelagianae defensorem libri sex*: ii. **7** (Hom.
i.11.40–7), iii. **26** (Coll. 58, 296), vi. **7** (Hom. i.11.40–7)

[40] *Contra litteras Petiliani libri tres*: ii. **36** (Hom. i.11.37–40), ii. **72** (Hom.
i.11.37–40), ii. **81** (Coll. 341), ii. **103** (Exp.Apoc. xxxviii.93–4)

[41] *Contra Maximinum haereticum*: ii. **25** (Comm.Gen. pp. 211.615–41,
212.664–9), ii. **26** (Comm.Gen. pp. 219.906–11, 220.956–65)

[42] *Contra secundam Iuliani responsionem imperfectum opus*: i. **86** (Coll. 49), i.
94 (Coll. 399), i. **99** (Coll. 59), i. **141** (Coll. 86, 92, 96, 98, 101, 102), ii. **49**
(Coll. 35), ii. **56** (Coll. 36), ii. **63–84** (Coll. 37), ii. **103–35** (Coll. 40), ii.
137 (Coll. 241), ii. **148** (Coll. 38), ii. **153** (Coll. 87), ii. **158** (Coll. 24, 351),
ii. **160** (Coll. 23)

[43] *Contra Secundinum Manichaeum liber*: cc. v–vii (Coll. 364), viii (Coll. 72)

[44] *De adulterinis coniugiis*: cc. xv (Coll. 161), xvii (Coll. 163), xviii (Coll.
162)

[45] *De agone Christiano*: c. xxii (Hom. i.3.16–17)

[46] *De anima et eius origine*: i. **17** (Coll. 188)

[47] *De baptismo contra Donatistas*: iii. **19** (Coll. 427), iv. **4** (Coll. 381), iv. **5**
(Coll. 330, 429), v. **24** (Coll. 277), v. **27** (Coll. 428)

[48] *De bono coniugali*: c. xviii (Coll. 412)

[49] *De ciuitate Dei*: i. **10** (Coll. 414), ix. **20** (Coll. 175), x. **28** (Coll. 129),
xii. **17** (Coll. 438), xiii. **23** (Coll. 219), xiv. **2–3** (Coll. 299), xiv. **3** (Coll.
238), xiv. **4** (Coll. 148), xv. **1** (Comm.Gen. p. 73.27–33), xv. **2** (Coll.
288; Comm.Gen. p. 213.695–715), xv. **7** (Comm.Gen. p. 76.110–27), xv.
8 (Comm.Gen. p. 85.459–94), xv. **10** (Comm.Gen. p. 93.743–53), xv. **11**
(Comm.Gen. p. 94.785–90; DTR lxvi.121), xv. **13** (Comm.Gen.
p. 95.790–5, 795–810; DTR lxvi.135–44), xv. **15** (Comm.Gen.
p. 91.660–2), xv. **17** (Comm.Gen. p. 86.498–501; DTR lxvi.112–13),
xv. **19** (Comm.Gen. p. 86.479–81), xv. **20** (Comm.Gen. pp. 87.508–18,
88–9.570–609, 98.915–19), xv. **21** (Comm.Gen. p. 92.693–711), xv. **23**
(Coll. 270, 443; Comm.Gen. pp. 99.946–7, 100.992–7; Comm.Luc.
p. 184.723–9), xv. **25** (Comm.Gen. p. 101.1010–14, 1030–3), xv. **27**

(Comm.Gen. p. 111.1370–9), xv. 32 (Coll. 84), xv. 35 (Coll. 90), xvi. 1
(Comm.Gen. p. 107.1212–31), xvi. 3 (Comm.Gen. p. 185.1541–5), xvi. 4
(Comm.Gen. pp. 153.414–16, 155.479–82), xvi. 5 (Comm.Gen.
pp. 154.418–34, 155.473–7), xvi. 10 (DTR lxvi.230–4), xvi. 12 (Comm.
Gen. pp. 165.816–33, 166.869–73), xvi. 13 (Comm.Gen. p. 167.891–3),
xvi. 15 (Comm.Gen. p. 168.933–44; Exp.Act. [Act. 7] p. 33.2–6, 9–12),
xvi. 19 (Comm.Gen. p. 175.1165–76; DTR xxxiv.67–73), xvi. 20 (Comm.
Gen. p. 178.1287–8), xvi. 21 (Comm.Gen. p. 180.1347–58), xvi. 23
(Comm.Gen. p. 195.65–9), xvi. 24 (Comm.Gen. pp. 196–8.95–173,
199.181–8, 192–4), xvi. 25 (Comm. Gen. p. 200.212–25), xvi. 26 (Comm.
Gen. pp. 204.357–71, 206.459–68, 207.485–7), xvi. 27 (Comm.Gen.
p. 206.440–54), xvi. 28 (Comm.Gen. p. 216.801–19), xvi. 29 (Comm.Gen.
p. 211.641–55), xvi. 37 (Coll. 457), xvii. 3 (Coll. 455, 456), xvii. 4 (Coll.
243), xviii. 19 (Coll. 410), xix. 9 (Comm.Gen. p. 153.378–9), xx. 8
(Exp.Apoc. xxxv.30–8), xx. 9 (Exp.Apoc. xxiv.53–6), xx. 6 (Coll. 247),
xx. 13 (Coll. 393; DTR lxix.4), xx. 14–16 (Coll. 174), xx. 19 (Exp.Apoc.
xxii.32–40), xx. 20 (Coll. 215, 389), xx. 24 (Coll. 446), xx. 28 (DTR lxix.65–
7), xxi. 24 (Coll. 109), xxi. 26 (Coll. 151), xxii. 2 (Coll. 282), xxii. 15 (Coll.
321), xxii. 16 (Coll. 78), xxii. 18 (Coll. 322), xxii. 29 (Coll. 200, 361), xxii.
30 (Coll. 210), etc.

[50] *De consensu euangelistarum*: i. 2–3 (Comm.Luc. pp. 8–10.135–213), ii. 1
(Comm.Luc. pp. 67–8.1911–18), ii. 4 (Comm.Luc. pp. 88.2732–8,
89.2744–88), ii. 17 (Comm.Luc. p. 116.642–50; Comm.Marc.
p. 446.361–82), ii. 19 (Comm.Marc. p. 450.514–24), ii. 20 (Comm.Luc.
p. 154.2145–55), ii. 24 (Comm.Luc. p. 187.843–9; Comm.Marc.
p. 495.249–55), ii. 30 (Coll. 304; Comm.Luc. pp. 194–5.1116–58;
Comm.Marc. pp. 504–5.608–53), ii. 40 (Comm.Luc. p. 240.376–90), ii.
43 (Comm.Marc. p. 507.715–25), ii. 51 (Comm.Marc. pp. 531.1683–5,
532.1722–3), ii. 65 (Comm.Marc. pp. 566–7.973–85), ii. 73 (Comm.Marc.
p. 591.1936–43), ii. 75 (Comm.Luc. p. 274.1729–35), ii. 79 (Comm.Marc.
p. 607.475–81), iii. 2 (Comm.Marc. pp. 613–14.734–61), iii. 6 (Comm.
Marc. p. 622.1061–4), iii. 7 (Comm.Marc. p. 439.101–23), iii. 9
(Comm.Marc. p. 627.1257–64), iii. 11 (Comm.Marc. pp. 629–30.1352–
9), iii. 13 (DTR iv.64–9), iii. 16 (Comm.Luc. p. 405.1663–76; Comm.
Marc. p. 633.1468–83), iii. 24 (Comm.Marc. p. 642.1830–40), iii. 25
(Coll. 204; Comm.Luc. p. 415.2076–81; Comm.Marc. pp. 644.1900–17,
647–8.2035–77), iv. 2 (Comm.Luc. p. 111.434–9; Comm.Marc.
p. 447.418–22), iv. 4 (Comm.Marc. p. 527.1506–11), iv. 8 (Exp.Act
[Act. 1] p. 6.2–12), etc.

[51] *De correptione et gratia*: cc. xii (Hom. i.12.113–17), xvi (Coll. 413)

[52] *De diuersis quaestionibus ad Simplicianum*: i, quaest. i. 7–8 (Coll. 56), i,
quaest. i. 17 (Coll. 52, 54, 224, 225), i, quaest. ii. 3 (Coll. 88), i, quaest.
ii. 16 (Coll. 93), i, quaest. ii. 18 (Coll. 95), i, quaest. ii. 19 (Coll. 97), ii,
quaest. ii. 5 (Hom. i.12.146–52)

[53] *De diuersis quaestionibus .lxxxiii.*: quaest. lii (Hom. i.12.146–9), lvi
(Comm.Ezr. p. 300.497–500; Hom. ii.1.193–203), lix (Coll. 254), lxvi
(Coll. 51, 63), lxix (Coll. 448), lxxi (Coll. 178, 342), lxxii (Coll. 344)

[54] *De diuinatione daemonum*: c. xiv (Exp.Apoc. xxxviii.93–4)

[55] *De doctrina Christiana*: i. 36 (Comm.Gen. p. 214.713–17), i. 42–3 (Coll.
202), i. 44 (Coll. 398), ii. 10 (Comm.Gen. p. 214.713–17), iii. 8 (Coll.
388), iii. 9 (Coll. 226), iii. 10 (Coll. 274), iii. 40 (DST ii. 44–5), iii. 43
(Exp.Apoc. praef. 38–9), iii. 44 (Exp.Apoc. praef. 40–6), iii. 45 (Exp.
Apoc. praef. 47–55), iii. 46 (Exp.Apoc. praef. 56–60), iii. 47 (Exp.Apoc.
praef. 62–5), iii. 50 (Exp.Apoc. praef. 75–9), iii. 51 (Exp.Apoc. praef. 86–
95), iii. 52 (Exp.Apoc. praef. 96–9), iii. 53 (Exp.Apoc. praef. 100–5), iii.
55 (Exp.Apoc. praef. 106–8), iv. 21 (Comm.Gen. pp. 136–8.2286–2331)

[56] *De dono perseuerantiae*: c. xvii (Coll. 80)

[57] *De Genesi ad litteram*: i. 2 (Comm.Gen. p. 8.168–80), i. 5 (Comm.
Gen. p. 5.93–6), i. 6 (Comm.Gen. p. 7.156–61), i. 10 (Comm.Gen.
p. 9.203–7; DTR v.19–38), i. 12 (Comm.Gen. pp. 6.103–6, 8.191–4,
13.333–42), i. 14 (Comm.Gen. p. 6.109–10), ii. 1–5 (DNR iii.1–2), ii. 1
(Comm.Gen. p. 11.263–8), ii. 6 (Comm.Gen. p. 11.277–89), ii. 16
(Comm.Gen. p. 17.485–9, 496–501), iii. 1 (Comm.Gen. p. 22.638–49),
iii. 7 (Comm.Gen. p. 21.628–36), iii. 8 (DNR ii.7), iii. 10 (Comm.Gen.
p. 23.672–7; DNR xxv.10–13), iii. 11 (Comm.Gen. p. 23.672–7); iii. 20
(Coll. 383; Comm.Gen. p. 25.758–63, 763–81), iii. 22 (Comm.Gen.
p. 28.837–51), iii. 24 (Comm.Gen. p. 31.951–63), iv. 2–4 (Comm.Gen.
p. 32.966–74), iv. 8 (Coll. 283), iv. 9–12 (Comm.Gen. pp. 33–4.1024–
49), iv. 9 (Coll. 328), iv. 12 (Exp.Act. [Act. 17] pp. 72–3.62–70), iv.
13–16 (Comm.Gen. p. 34.1050–77), iv. 18 (Comm.Gen. p. 35.1080–92;
Exp.Act. [Act. 17] p. 73.70–5), iv. 22 (Comm.Gen. p. 8.180–5), v. 6–7
(Comm.Gen. pp. 41–2.1293–1313), v. 10 (Comm.Gen. p. 43.1339–75),
v. 19 (Coll. 314), vii. 17 (Comm.Gen. p. 45.1406–10), vii. 28
(Comm.Gen. p. 26.781–96), viii. 1 (Comm.Gen. p. 46.1438–41,
1442–3), viii. 4–5 (Comm.Gen. p. 46.1463–70), viii. 6 (Comm.Gen.
p. 47.1480–1500), viii. 7 (Comm.Gen. p. 48.1521–6, 1527–34), ix. 1
(Comm.Gen. p. 54.1716–36), ix. 3 (Comm.Gen. p. 53.1676–1703), ix. 6
(Comm.Gen. p. 54.1703–13), ix. 10 (Comm.Gen. p. 52.1648–56), ix. 12
(Comm.Gen. p. 55.1752–66), ix. 14 (Comm.Gen. p. 55.1738–48), ix. 19
(Comm.Gen. pp. 57.1832–42, 58.1845–51), x. 12 (Coll. 297), x. 19–20
(Coll. 452), xi. 1 (Comm.Gen. pp. 58–9.1866–73), xi. 2 (Comm.Gen.
p. 59.1875–86), xi. 4 (Comm.Gen. p. 59.1886–92), xi. 5 (Comm.Gen.
p. 59.1892–7), xi. 6 (Comm.Gen. pp. 59–60.1897–1903), xi. 8 (Coll.
137), xi. 15 (Coll. 416), xi. 42 (Coll. 409), xii. 8–9 (Coll. 203), xii. 28
(Comm.Gen. p. 46.1437–8), etc.

[58] *De Genesi ad litteram imperfectus liber*: iv. 12 (Comm.Gen. p. 5.76–84),
iv. 14 (Comm.Gen. p. 130.2070–5), iv. 16 (Comm.Gen. p. 6.123–32), v. 2
(Comm.Gen. p. 14. 373–7), v. 19 (Comm.Gen. p. 8.168–72), vii. 28

(Comm.Gen. p. 40.1254), **x. 32** (Comm.Gen. pp. 10–13.248–350), **xiv. 44**
(Comm.Gen. p. 22.638–49), **xvi. 56** (Comm.Gen. p. 25.746–58)

[59] *De Genesi contra Manichaeos*: **i. 2** (Comm.Gen. p. 3.25–9), **i. 3**
(Comm.Gen. p. 5.76–84), **i. 5** (Comm.Gen. p. 6.123–32), **i. 8** (Comm.
Gen. p. 14.373–7), **i. 9** (Comm.Gen. p. 9.208–18), **i. 10** (Comm.Gen.
p. 9.225–30), **i. 12** (Comm.Gen. p. 10.248–50), **i. 13** (Comm.Gen.
p. 14.386–97), **i. 15** (Comm.Gen. pp. 20.589–96, 22.638–49), **i. 17**
(Comm.Gen. p. 26.780–1), **i. 19** (Comm.Gen. p. 27.824–51), **i. 23**
(Comm.Gen. p. 39.1218–24), **ii. 8** (Coll. 141), **ii. 11** (Comm.Gen.
p. 56.1769–75), **ii. 11–12** (Comm.Gen. p. 56.1780–95), **ii. 15** (Comm.Gen.
p. 60.1933–8), **ii. 21** (Comm.Gen. p. 69.2218–20), **ii. 23** (Comm.Gen.
pp. 71–2.2305–19), **ii. 25** (Comm.Gen. p. 65.2084–2105), **ii. 28** (Comm.
Gen. p. 66.2109–11)

[60] *De gestis Pelagii*: c. **xiv** (Coll. 85, 289)

[61] *De gratia et libero arbitrio*: **iii. 5** (Coll. 10), **xvii. 33** (Coll. 75), **xxi. 42–3**
(Coll. 7), **xxii. 44** (Coll. 14)

[62] *De haeresibus*: cc. **v** (Exp.Apoc. iv.80–7), **xxv** (Comm.Gen. pp. 24.715–
17, 28.855–60)

[63] *De mendacio*: **xii. 26** (Coll. 264), **xix. 39** (Coll. 329); and cf. Comm.Sam.
p. 194.2460

[64] *De nuptiis et concupiscentia*: **xi. 24** (Coll. 235; Hom. i.11.40–7), **xxvii. 45**
(Coll. 33)

[65] *De opere monachorum*: **iii. 4—xiv. 15** (Coll. 394)

[66] *De perfectione iustitiae hominis*: **viii. 19** (Coll. 357), **xi. 24** (Coll. 392), **xv.
35** (Coll. 332)

[67] *De praedestinatione sanctorum*: **vii. 12** (Coll. 267), **x. 19** (Coll. 77, 313),
xv. 30 (Exp.Apoc. xxxviii.97–8), **xvi. 33** (Coll. 108), **xx. 40** (Coll. 222)

[68] *De sancta uirginitate*: cc. **v–vi** (Comm.Luc. p. 158.2272–6), **xxvii**
(Exp.Apoc. xxiii.52–67)

[69] *De sermone Domini in monte libri .ii.*: **i. 11** (DTR iv.58–63), **i. 14** (Coll.
173), **i. 14–16** (Coll. 172), **i. 17** (Coll. 3, 211), **i. 19** (Coll. 256), **i. 22** (Coll.
436; Comm.Luc. p. 250.765), **ii. 1** (Coll. 185), **ii. 9** (Coll. 182, 285), **ii. 12**
(Comm.Luc. p. 149.1953–64), **ii. 15** (Comm.Luc. p. 252.855–69, 876–95),
ii. 16 (Coll. 176; Comm.Luc. p. 254.923–33), **ii. 17** (Coll. 220), **ii. 18**
(Coll. 121), **ii. 19** (Coll. 295), **ii. 25** (Coll. 191); and cf. Comm.Luc.
p. 302.236

[70] *De trinitate*: **i. 3** (Coll. 359; DTR praef. 48–51; Comm.Luc. p. 5.30–1), **i.
6** (Coll. 111, 348, 420), **i. 7** (Coll. 343), **i. 8** (Coll. 209), **i. 10** (Coll. 208), **i.
13** (Coll. 138), **ii. 5** (Coll. 279), **iii. 7** (Comm.Gen. p. 19.551–4), **iv. 3**
(Coll. 45, 67; Comm.Gen. p. 52.1648–58), **iv. 4** (DTR xxxix.26–59), **vi. 3**
(Coll. 150, 165), **vi. 4** (Coll. 166), **vi. 9** (Coll. 186), **vii. 3** (Coll. 135, 154),
xii. 6 (Coll. 2, Comm.Gen. p. 27.817–23), **xii. 7** (Coll. 187, 275, 382), **xiii.
16** (Coll. 29, 32), **xiv. 12** (Exp.Act. [Act. 17] p. 73.76–81), **xv. 26**
(Exp.Act. [Act. 2] p. 21.191–3, [Act. 10] p. 54.165–74)

[71] *Enarrationes in psalmos*: [ps. ii] 6 (Coll. 442), 8 (Exp.Apoc. iv. 157–9), [ps. iv] 8 (Comm.Luc. p. 357.2463–72; Comm.Marc. p. 588.1808–17), [ps. v] 3 (Comm.Gen. p. 77–170–6), [ps. vii] 9 (Exp.Apoc. iv.127–30, xxxviii.34–5), 15 (Coll. 189), [ps. x] 3 (DTR xxv.15–26), [ps. xiii] 4 (Coll. 15), [ps. xxv] 3 (Coll. 325; Comm.Gen. p. 135.2246–7), [ps. xxix] ii. 9 (Coll. 153), [ps. xxx] ii. 1 (Coll. 334; Exp.Act. [Act. 3] p. 24.41–3), ii. 2 (Coll. 246), ii. 4 (Coll. 194), ii. 6 (Coll. 18), ii. 13 (Coll. 239, 309), [ps. xxxi] ii. 2 (Coll. 21), ii. 9 (Coll. 22), [ps. xxxii] ii. 14 (DO lines 607–8), [ps. xxxiv] i. 2 (Coll. 337), [ps. xxxviii] 6 (Coll. 355), [ps. xl] 10 (Comm.Gen. p. 56.1780–95), [ps. xliv] 19–20 (Coll. 445), [ps. xlix] 9 (Coll. 160), [ps. l] 9 (Coll. 13), [ps. liv] 11 (Comm.Gen. pp. 152–3.370–80), [ps. lvi] 11 (Comm.Gen. p. 56.1780–95), [ps. lviii] i. 5 (Exp.Act. [Act. 6] p. 32.17), [ps. lxii] 15 (Coll. 408), [ps. lxvii] 17 (DST ii.128–72), [ps. lxvii] 32 (Comm.Gen. p. 97.867–70), [ps. lxx] ii. 4 (DO lines 1089–94), [ps. lxxxvi] 4 (Comm.Gen. p. 105.1145–8), [ps. lxxxvi] 7–8 (Comm.Luc. pp. 43–4.969–71), [ps. lxxxix] 3 (Comm.Gen. p. 122.1756–8), [ps. xcvi] 15 (Comm.Gen. p. 93.729–33), [ps. c] 6 (Comm.Marc. p. 616.830–5), [ps. ci] ii. 13 (Comm.Epist.Cath. [2 Petr. 3] p. 277.42–8), [ps. ciii] i. 8 (Comm.Gen. p. 69.2218–20), [ps. cviii] 26 (Exp.Apoc. vi.40–2), [ps. cxviii] xxix. 1 (Comm.Gen. p. 77.170–6), [ps. cxxxvi] 3–4 (Comm.Gen. p. 37.1161), etc.

[72] *Enchiridion ad Laurentium, seu de fide, spe et caritate*: cc. i (VCM praef.), vii (Coll. 103), xxiii (Comm.Cant.cant. praef. p. 179.482–4), xxxi (Coll. 312), xxxiii (Coll. 31), xli (Coll. 251), lii (Coll. 42, 44), lv (Coll. 431), lxii (Coll. 308, 365), lxix (Coll. 152, 284), lxxviii (Coll. 158, 170), lxxx (Comm.Luc. p. 318.890–5), ciii (Coll. 406), cvii (Coll. 50), cx (Coll. 242), cxv (Comm.Luc. p. 227.2393–2428), cxxi (Coll. 56)

[73] *Epistulae*: xl (Coll. 40), lv (Coll. 352; DNR xx.11–13; DTR xi.33–45, xxv.20–6, xxvii.4–19, lxiv.42–5, 102–6; Exp.Act. [Act. 2] p. 16.29; Exp. Apoc. xix.19–23); lxxxii (Coll. 177, 262, 265, 291–2, 298; Exp.Act. [Act. 18] p. 75.34, [Act. 21] p. 85.32–57), xcviii (Coll. 391), cxx (Coll. 136, Comm.Luc. p. 419.2244), cxxx (Coll. 73, 139, 360), cxl (Coll. 315), cxlvii [= *De uidendo Deo*] (Coll. 142, 201, 230; Comm.Epist.Cath. [1 Ioh. 3] p. 302.55–72, [1 Ioh. 4] p. 314.150–77; Comm.Luc. p. 5.40–6), cxlix (Coll. 372, 374, 376), clvii (Coll. 34, 39, 41), clxiv (Comm.Gen. p. 104.1106–13), clxvii (Comm.Epist.Cath. [Iac. 2] pp. 193.19–26, 194.56–69, 195.69–86, 196.122–9, 197.135–43), clxxxvi (Coll. 205, 266), clxxxvii (Coll. 369), cxc (Coll. 207, Exp. Act. [Act. 15] p. 66.24–7), cxciv (Coll. 9, 74, 76, 89, 91, 94, 110, 281), cxcix (DTR v.5–8, ix.2–23, xxvii.31–6, lxviii.8–52), ccv (Coll. 212, 214; DTR iii.44–5), ccxiv (Coll. 157), ccxv (Coll. 43), ccxvii (Coll. 244), ccxxviii (Coll. 257), cclxv (Exp. Act. [Act. 1] p. 7.35–40)

[74] *In Ioannis epistulam ad Parthos tractatus .x.*: i. 1 (Comm.Epist.cath. [1 Ioh. 1] p. 284.14–19), i. 4 (Comm.Epist.cath. [1 Ioh. 1] p. 285.42–4), i. 6

(Comm.Epist.cath. [1 Ioh. 1] pp. 287–8.143–56), i. 8 (Comm.Epist.cath. [1 Ioh. 2] p. 289.15–23), i. 9 (Comm.Epist.cath. [1 Ioh. 2] p. 290.54–71), i. 12 (Comm.Epist.cath. [1 Ioh. 2] p. 291.104–7), ii. 4 (Coll. 128), ii. 7 (Comm.Epist.cath. [1 Ioh. 2] p. 293.143–8), ii. 11 (Coll. 6), ii. 13 (Comm.Epist.cath. [1 Ioh. 2] pp. 293–4.164–90), iii. 1 (Coll. 451), iii. 4 (Comm.Epist.cath. [1 Ioh. 2] p. 295.242–55), iii. 5 (Comm.Epist.cath. [1 Ioh. 2] p. 296.265–8), iii. 6 (Coll. 99, 126; Comm.Epist.cath. [1 Ioh. 2] p. 296.281–5), iv. 2 (Coll. 100), iv. 3 (Comm.Epist.cath. [1 Ioh. 2] p. 300.390–407), iv. 6 (Coll. 356), iv. 11 (Comm.Epist.cath. [1 Ioh. 3] p. 305.168–73), v. 12 (Comm.Epist.cath. [1 Ioh. 3] p. 307.255–62), vi. 3 (Coll. 303), vi. 4 (Comm.Epist.cath. [1 Ioh. 3] pp. 308–9.301–8), vi. 7 (Comm.Epist.cath. [1 Ioh. 3] p. 309.316–26), vii. 4–7 (Comm.Epist.cath. [1 Ioh. 4] p. 313.97–118), vii. 7 (Coll. 269), viii. 2 (Coll. 221), viii. 3–10 (Comm.Epist.cath. [1 Ioh. 4] p. 315.201–10), viii. 6 (Coll. 417), ix. 3 (Comm.Epist.cath. [1 Ioh. 4] p. 317.253–65), x. 1 (Comm.Epist.cath. [1 Ioh. 4] p. 319.314–49), x. 5 (Coll. 252)

[75] *Quaestiones Euangeliorum*: i. 8 (DTR v.129–34), i. 14 (Coll. 131), ii. 1 (Comm.Luc. p. 24.214–21), ii. 2 (Comm.Luc. pp. 114.564–70, 115.612–24), ii. 3 (Comm.Luc. p. 117.698–704; Comm.Marc. p. 451.569–75), ii. 11 (Coll. 122; Comm.Luc. p. 164.2521–35), ii. 13 (Comm.Luc. pp. 183.684–6, 184.708–13, 186.782–804; Comm.Marc. pp. 491.108–9, 492.115–20, 494.195–8, 207–10, 213–18, 495.241–9), ii. 14 (DTR v.15–18), ii. 17 (Comm.Luc. p. 233.110–13), ii. 18 (Comm.Luc. pp. 125–6.1012–34; Comm.Marc. pp. 460–1.931–41, 945–52), ii. 19 (Comm.Luc. pp. 222.2211–16, 223.2238–9, 2263–75, 224.2287–91), ii. 21 (Comm.Luc. p. 228.2433–64), ii. 22 (Comm.Luc. p. 229.2479–93; Comm.Tob. p. 16.52–5), ii. 27 (Comm.Luc. p. 263.1273–7), ii. 29 (Comm.Luc. p. 254.915–20), ii. 33 (Comm.Luc. pp. 288–90.2316–83), ii. 34 (Comm. Luc. pp. 296–300.36–175), ii. 38 (Comm.Luc. p. 303.311–14), ii. 39 (Coll. 4), ii. 40 (Comm.Luc. pp. 312–14.659–763), ii. 41 (Comm.Luc. p. 319.934–8), ii. 43 (Comm.Luc. p. 319.947–53), ii. 44 (Comm.Luc. pp. 320–1.977–1026), ii. 47 (Comm.Luc. p. 328.1296–1321; Comm.Marc. p. 562.789–813)

[76] *Quaestiones in Heptateuchum*: Gen. i (Comm.Gen. pp. 85–6.459–94), Gen. ii (Comm.Gen. pp. 94.782–5, 166.845–55), Gen. iii (Comm.Gen. pp. 99.946–7, 100.992–5), Gen. iv (Comm.Gen. pp. 111–12.1370–9), Gen. vi (Comm.Gen. p. 110.1334), Gen. viii (Comm.Gen. pp. 113–14.1446–55), Gen. xxi (Comm.Gen. p. 199.192–4), Gen. xxiv (Comm. Gen. pp. 148.222–36, 185–6.1541–5), Gen. xxv (Comm.Gen. pp. 164.808–14, 167–8.903–7, 909–16, 939–44), Gen. xxvi (Comm.Gen. p. 175.1165–76), Gen. xxvii (Comm.Gen. pp. 46.1449–50, 50.1504–7), Gen. xxviii (Comm.Gen. p. 169.952–7), Gen. xxxi (Comm.Gen. p. 204.357–71), Gen. xxxiv (Comm.Gen. p. 211.636–9), Gen. xxxv (Comm.Gen. p. 216.801–19), Gen. xxxvi (Comm.Gen. p. 217.833–6),

Gen. xxxix (Comm.Gen. p. 220.940–9), **Gen.** xlii (Comm.Gen.
p. 222.1015–23), **Gen.** xlv (Comm.Gen. p. 179.1323–9), Gen. lxx (DO
lines 1089–94), Gen. cliii (Comm.Gen. p. 27.800–6), Ex. viii (DO line
240), Ex. xxvi (DO line 170), Ex. xlvii (Exp.Act. [Act. 7] p. 34.23–7), Ex.
lxx (DTR xi.33–45), Ex. cviii (Comm.Gen. p. 98.916–18; Exp.Apoc.
xxxi.44–7), Ex. clxxvii (DO line 30), Lev. lxviii (DO line 215), Deut.
xxxv (Comm.Gen. p. 230.1305–7)

[77] *Retractiones*: **i. 20** (Hom. i.16.178–84)

[78] *Sermones*: ii (Coll. 20, 327), iii (Coll. 290), iv (Comm.Gen. p. 135.2246–
7), vii (Retract.Act. [Act. 7] p. 133.52), viii (DO line 170), xxviii (Coll.
11), xxxvii (Coll. 276), xlvii (DO line 940), xlix (Coll. 278), li
(Comm.Gen. p. 146.140–7; Exp.Apoc. xxxi.44–7), lxi (Coll. 259), lxix
(Hom. i.17.214–19), lxxi (Coll. 145, 193, 426; Hom. i.8.46), lxxvi (DO
line 806; Hom. i.16.178), lxxvii (Coll. 390), ci (Coll. 263; Retract.Act.
[Act. 13] p. 145.33–6), lxxviii (Hom. i.24.123–34), lxxxviii (Hom.
ii.9.112–39), lxxxiii (Exp.Apoc. xxxi.44–7), lxxxix (Hom. i.17.214–19),
ciii (Comm.Tob. p. 16.52–5), cv (Comm.Tob. p. 16.52–5), cx (Hom.
i.14.49–53), cxvi (Hom. ii.9.112–39), cxxiii (DO line 469), cxxv (Hom.
ii.16.141), cxxxi (Coll. 346), cxxxvi (Hom. i.5.89–91), cxlix (Exp.Act.
[Act. 10] pp. 49.35–41, 50.45–6, 51.84–5; Hom. i.16.178), cl (Retract.Act.
[Act. 17] p. 152.11–17), cli (Coll. 218), cliii (Coll. 53, 55), cliv (Coll. 57,
61, 258, 301), clv (Coll. 62, 64, 66, 69), clvi (Coll. 70, 273, 400), clx (Coll.
306), clxii (Coll. 168), clxvii (Coll. 195, 338), clxix (Hom. i.11.153–60),
clxx (DO lines 969–70), clxxvi (Coll. 402), clxxvii (Coll. 415, 419, 422),
clxxxiii (Hom. i.8.46), clxxxix (Hom. i.4.78–9, 91–2), cxc (Hom.
ii.20.61), cxci (Hom. ii.7.93–6), cxciv (Hom. ii.20.61), cxcvi (Hom.
i.5.89–91), cxcvii (Coll. 5, 133, 149, 261, 268, 368), ccv (Coll. 300),
ccxviii (Comm.Marc. p. 632.1430–5), ccxxi (Hom. ii.7.43–51), ccxxviii
(Coll. 46), ccxxix (Coll. 184, 430), ccxxxvi (Coll. 27), ccxlii (Hom.
ii.9.162–8), ccxlvii (Hom. ii.7.93–6), cclii (Comm.Gen. p. 36.1127–8;
Hom. ii.16.141), cclix (Hom. i.11.149–53), cclxiii (Retract.Act. [Act. 10]
p. 142.67–94), cclxviii (Coll. 317; Hom. ii.8.141), cclxx (Hom. i.16.178,
i.23.120, ii.17.298), cclxxviii (Coll. 169; Hom. ii.8.141), cclxxxiii (Coll.
144), cclxxxvii (Hom. ii.20.12–16), ccxcii (Comm.Gen. p. 135.2246–7;
Hom. i.5.89–91), ccxciii (Coll. 407; Hom. ii.19.6–12), ccxcv (Hom.
i.16.178), ccxcviii (Coll. 433), ccxcix (Coll. 240, 402, 432, 435), ccci
(DO line 469), cccii (Coll. 119, 120; Comm.Epist.cath. [1 Petr.]
p. 240.269–7), cccvi (Coll. 234; Mart.), cccviii (Hom. ii.23.103–8),
cccxv (Exp.Act. [Act. 7] p. 38.165–70), cccxix (Retract.Act. [Act. 7]
p. 131.11–18), cccxxx (Coll. 268), cccxxxiv (Coll. 82), cccxxxv (DO
lines 539–40, 607–8), cccxlvi (DO line 931), ccclxi (Coll. 132, 331, 366,
387), cccl (Coll. 196), ccclii (DO lines 976–7), cccliv (Coll. 171), ccclxii
(Coll. 213, 216, 378, 380, 424)

[79] *Tractatus in Euangelium Ioannis*: iii. 2 (Coll. 280), vii. 21–4 (Coll. 245),

x. 4 (Comm.Marc. pp. 578–9.1435–49), xxxv. 2 (Comm.Luc. p. 351.2215–
27; Comm.Marc. p. 582.1581–95), xxxvi. 4 (Coll. 345), xxxvi. 5
(Exp.Apoc. v.63–76), xli. 5 (Coll. 250), xli. 8 (Coll. 294), xli. 12 (Coll.
47), xliv. 1 (Coll. 310), xlv. 9 (Coll. 179), xlvi. 5 (Coll. 347), xlvi. 6 (Coll.
340), l. 7 (Coll. 233), li. 1 (Comm.Luc. p. 345.1974–90), li. 2 (Comm.
Marc. p. 574.1278–82), li. 4 (Comm.Luc. p. 345.1974–90), liii. 5–6 (Coll.
106), liii. 7 (Coll. 358), liii. 10 (Coll. 423), lxii. 1 (Coll. 190), lxv. 1 (Coll.
379), lxxi. 1 (Exp.Act. [Act. 5] p. 30.38), lxxiii. 2 (Coll. 305), lxxiv. 1
(Coll. 192), lxxxv. 1–2 (Coll. 339), lxxxv. 3 (Coll. 143), xciv. 4 (Coll.
249), xcviii. 2 (Coll. 147), c. 1 [+ civ. 3, cv. 5] (Retract.Act. [Act. 4]
p. 123.22–5), cviii. 5 (Coll. 272, 367), cxiii. 2 (Comm.Marc. p. 624.1139–
44), cxvii. 4 (Comm.Luc. p. 404.1653–6), cxiii. 2 (Comm.Luc.
p. 391.1125–30), cxviii. 3 (Comm.Luc. p. 403.1604–6), cxviii. 4
(Comm.Marc. p. 630.1364–76), cxviii. 5 (Comm.Luc. pp. 401–2.1546–
68), cxix. 3–4 (Comm.Luc. p. 404.1629–31), cxix. 4 (Comm.Marc.
p. 635.1554–76)

Avitus, Alcimus
[80] *Carmina de spiritalis historiae gestis*: i. 130 (VCM 868), i. 162 (DDI 59),
ii. 35–7 (Comm.Gen. p. 36.1100–3), iii. 76 (VCM 203), iv. 485 (VCM
323), v. 190 (DDI 95), v. 557 (VCM 58), vi. 6 (VCM 798), app. xviii. 6
(VCM 5)

Basil of Caesarea
[81] *Hom. in Hexaemeron*, trans. Eustathius: i. 6 (Comm.Gen. p. 3.6–14), i. 7
(Comm.Gen. p. 5.89–96), ii. 2 (Comm.Gen. p. 8.168–72), ii. 4 (Comm.
Gen. pp. 5–6.96–107), ii. 5 (Comm.Gen. p. 7.151–6), ii. 7 (Comm.Gen.
p. 8.175–8), ii. 8 (Comm.Gen. p. 8.180–5), iii. 2 (Comm.Gen. p. 8.168–
72), iii. 3 (Comm.Gen. p. 10.248–51), iii. 7 (Comm.Gen. p. 11.275–9), iii.
8 (Comm.Gen. pp. 21–2.628–36), iii. 10 (Comm.Gen. p. 12.295–6), iv. 2
(DTR v.70–4), iv. 6 (HE i.1), iv. 10 (Comm.Gen. p. 13.333–42), v. 9–10
(Comm.Gen. p. 41.1280–7), vi. 10–11 (DTR xxviii.38–59), vii. 1–5
(Comm.Gen. p. 20.585–9), ix. 6 (Comm.Gen. p. 25.744–6),

Benedict of Nursia
[82] *Regula*: cc. vii (Comm.Ezr. p. 350.468), liii (Comm.Gen. p. 213.681),
lxiv (Comm.Cant.cant. p. 323.296–7; HAA xi), lxv (DO line 399), lxxiii
(Comm.Gen. p. 1.26–9)

Caesarius of Arles
[83] *Expositio in Apocalypsim*: Exp.Apoc. (*passim* [270×])
[84] *Sermones*: clxvii [= ccvi] (Exp.Apoc. iv.179–81)

Caper, Flavius
[85] *De orthographia*: DO (*passim*); DAM iv.78–80

Cassian, John

[86] *Conlationes*: xii. 13 (Comm.Gen. p. 170.996), xiv. 8 (Comm.Cant. cant. p. 260.618–25; Comm.Gen. p. 213.695–715; DST ii.219–21, 236–9, 246–7, 276–9), xvii. 19 (Comm.Sam. p. 194.2461), xviii. 7 (Exp.Act. [Act. 5] p. 29.20), xxiii. 3 (Comm.Luc. p. 226.2362–4)

[87] *De incarnatione Domini contra Nestorium*: vi. 23 (DTR v.128–9)

Cassiodorus

[88] *Complexiones in Epistulas apostolorum, Actuum Apostolorum et Apocalypsis Iohannis*: Ioh. 1 (Comm.Epist.cath. p. 181.16–19), Apc. 5 (Exp.Apoc. iv.73–5)

[89] *De orthographia*: DO lines 18–21, 90, 121, 161, 411, 416, 442, 613, 628–37, 873, 933, 955, 963, 1241, 1243

[90] *Expositio psalmorum*: i. 2 (DTR vi.4–8), ii. 3 (DST i. 62–3; Retract.Act. [Act. 4] p. 124.33–8), ii. 6 (DST ii. 26), vi. 2 (DST ii. 26), xiv. 5 (DST i. 34–5), xv. 8 (Retract.Act. [Act. 2] p. 113.138–46), xv. 9 (Retract.Act. [Act. 2] p. 113.148–9), xv. 10 (Retract.Act. [Act. 2] p. 114.168–72), xvi. 8 (DST ii. 22), xvii. 11 (DST i. 84–5), xxiii. 5 (DST ii. 112–13), xxvi. 3 (DST i. 71–2), xxxii. 1 (DST i. 81–2), xl. 3 (DST i. 151), liii. 3 (DST i. 144–50), lxvii. 14 (DST ii. 193–8), lxx. 3 (DST ii. 22), lxxiv. 11 (DST ii. 37–8), lxxxii. 2 (DST i. 80–1), lxxxvi. 1 (Tabernac. p. 81.1565, Templ. p. 192.28), xc. 1 (DST ii. 6–8), xcvii. 4 (DST i. 129–30), cv. 6 (DST i. 103–4), cxviii. 23–6 (DAM x.41–3), cxviii. 127 (Exp.Apoc. xxxvii.247–57, 272–3), cxxi. 3 (DST i. 65–6), cxxxii. 3 (DST i. 146), cxlix. 4 (DST ii. 27), cl. 5 (DO line 775)

Cassius Felix

[91] *De medicina*: Retract.Act. [Act. 28] p. 162.6–17

Charisius, Flavius Sosipater

[92] *Ars grammatica*: DO (*passim*); DAM vi.58–9, xiv.99–102; DNR iii. 9; DST i. 4–5, 8–10, 20–4, 71–2, ii. 63–4, 69–73, 99–101

Cicero

[93] *Actio in C. Verrem secunda*: iii. 34. 78 (DO line 887), iii. 80. 185 (DO line 1161)

[94] *De natura deorum*: ii. 20 (DNR xii.1)

[95] *In L. Catilinam oratio IV*: vi. 13 (DO line 892)

Claudian

[96] *Carmina maiora*: iii [= *In Rufinum I*], lines 145–6 (VCM 293); vii [= *De .III. consulatu Honorii*], lines 15 (VCM 552), 30 (VCM 343), 48 (VCM 279), 175 (VCM 31); xix [= *In Eutropium II, praef.*], line 65 (VCM 471)

Claudius Marius Victorius
[97] *Alethia*: praef. 111 (VCM 669), i. 288 (VCM 101), iii. 327 (VCM 30)

Cledonius
[98] *Ars grammatica*: DO lines 680, 829, 918; DAM ii.21–3

Consentius Gallus
[99] *Ars de nomine et uerbo*: DO lines 42, 235, 386, 581; DAM iii.71–2, xiii.4–5

Constantius
[100] *Vita S. Germani*: i. 19 (HE i. 17), i. 20 (HE i. 17), i. 23 (HE i. 17), i. 24 (HE i. 18), i. 25 (HE i. 18), i. 26 (HE i. 19), i. 28 (HE i. 20), ii. 1 (HE i. 21), ii. 2–4 (HE i. 21)

Cyprian of Carthage
[101] *De habitu uirginum*: cc. vi (Comm.Epist.cath. [1 Petr. 3] p. 232.260–9), x (Comm.Epist.cath. [1 Petr. 3] p. 243.12–17)
[102] *De lapsis*: c. xiii (Mart. [Quentin pp. 97–8])
[103] *De opere et eleemosynis*: c. xiv (Exp.Apoc. iv.257–8)
[104] *De zelo et liuore*: cc. ii–iii (Comm.Epist.cath. [1 Petr. 5] p. 258.83–98)
[105] *Epistulae*: lvi (Exp.Apoc. xiii.52–4)
[106] *Testimoniorum libri .iii. [Ad Quirinum]*: iii. 3 (Retract.Act. [Act. 4] p. 126.87–9)

Cyprianus Gallus
[107] *Heptateuchos*: **Gen.** 1–4 (Comm.Gen. p. 7.132–7), **Gen.** 928–9 (VCM 662); **Exod.** 206 (VCM 921), **Exod.** 507–21 (DAM xvii.8–22); **Deut.** 54 (VCM 828); **Iudic.** 469 (VCM 516)

Didymus
[108] *De spiritu sancto*, trans. Jerome: cc. iii (Exp.Act. [Act. 28] pp. 97–8.45–60), xxix (Exp.Act. [Act. 28] pp. 97–8.45–60), lx (Exp.Act. [Act. 5] p. 29.3–12)

Diomedes
[109] *Ars grammatica*: DO (*passim*); DAM i.28–30, 32–3, 57–8, iii.5–7, 14–15, xii.28–30, 40–1, 50–1, xxiv.11–12, xxv.3–22; DST i.4–5, 20–4, 71–2, 76–7, 90–2, 115–17, 129–30

Dionysius Exiguus
[110] *Argumenta titulorum paschalium*: cc. ii (DTR xlviii.2–22, xlix.3–9), iii (DTR xlvii.46–51, lii.218), iv (DTR xlvii.52–8, liv.11–18), v (DTR xlvii.36–42, lviii.8–12), vi (DTR xlvii.42–6, lviii.3–7), viii (DTR liv.5–9)
[111] *Epistula ad Bonifacium primicerium et Bonum secundicerium de ratione paschae*: DTR xlii.47–62, xlv.2–13, 24–32, lvi.21–60

[112] *Libellus de cyclo magno Paschae (Epistula ad Petronium episcopum)*: DTR
xi.62–73, xvi.42–3, xxx.66–9, xxxviii.48–50, xlvii.7–11

Donatus, Aelius
[113] *Ars maior*: DAM i.30–1, 32–3, 57–8; ii.2–3, 21–3; iii.50–1, 65–6, 137–8;
ix.2, 4–5, 5–8, 12–27; xiii.85–6; DO lines 43, 382, 386, 839; DST i.8–10,
20–4, 42–3, 65–6, 71–2, 80–1, 84–5, 108–9, 129–30, 151, 155–6; ii.2–7, 8–
21, 53–6, 63–9, 78–84, 85–90, 91–2, 107–10, 113–14, 115–16, 120–1, 125–
6, 173–5, 177–82, 182–6, etc.

Dracontius
[114] *Laudes Dei*: i. 7 (DDI 133), i. 13 (DDI 134), i. 17 (DDI 115), ii. 232
(DNR xx.4), ii. 419 (DDI 72), ii. 547–8 (VCM 176), ii. 652 (VCM 874),
ii. 674 (DDI 12), ii. 689 (VCM 215), iii. 241 [+ iii. 638] (DDI 159)
[115] *Satisfactio*: line 79 (DDI 133)

Eugippius
[116] *Excerpta ex operibus S. Augustini*: Coll. (*passim*)

Eusebius of Caesarea
[117] *Chronicon*, trans. Jerome: Exp.Act. [Act. 13] p. 62.45; Retract.Act.
[Act. 13] p. 146.60–1; DTR xviii, lxvi (*passim* [390×]), lxvii; Comm.Ezr.
p. 307.786
[118] *Historia ecclesiastica*, trans. Rufinus: i. 5 (DTR lxvi.971–3; Exp.Act.
[Act. 5] p. 31.82; Retract.Act. [Act. 5] p. 129.49–52), i. 7 (Comm.Luc.
pp. 87–8.2694–2724; DTR lxvi.949.52), i. 12 (Retract.Act. [Act. 1]
pp. 107.78–82, 108.110–12, [Act. 4] p. 127.135), ii. 1 (DTR lxvi.1011–
12; Exp.Act. [Act. 8] p. 39.11, Retract.Act. [Act. 1] p. 108.110–12, [Act. 4]
p. 130.22), ii. 4 (Exp.Act. [Act. 12] p. 57.6–7), ii. 9 (Exp.Act. [Act. 12]
p. 58.18–25; Hom. ii.21.189), ii. 10 (Exp.Act. [Act. 12] pp. 59.63, 60.74–7,
78–9; Retract.Act. [Act. 13] p. 144.4), ii. 12 (Exp.Act. [Act. 11] p. 57.40–
4), ii. 16 (Retract.Act. [Act. 20] p. 156.24), ii. 19 (Exp.Act. [Act. 24]
p. 91.32–4), ii. 21 (Exp.Act. [Act. 21] p. 86.75–81), ii. 23 (Templ.
pp. 162.632–4, 218.1036–8; DTR lxvi.1056–8), iii. 5 (Comm.Luc.
p. 367.179–83; Comm.Marc. pp. 597.86–90, 598.121–5), iii. 11
(Exp.Act. [Act. 1] p. 11.153–5), iv. 4 (DTR lxvii.1147–8), iv. 5
(Comm.Sam. p. 241.1221), v. 1 (Mart. [Quentin p. 98]), vi. 11 (DTR
lxvi.1207–11), vi. 41 (DTR lxvi.1270–4), vii. 1 (DTR lxvi.1277–81), vii.
10 (DTR lxvi. 1290–8), vii. 25 (Exp.Apoc. xxxviii.13–17), vii. 27 (DTR
lxvi.1313), vii. 28 (DTR lxvi.1303–4), vii. 32 (DTR xiv.29–33, xvi.42–3,
xxx.78–86, xlii.33–4), viii. 13 (DTR lxvi.1380–1), ix. 6 (DTR lxvi.1387–
90; Mart. [Quentin p. 99]), ix. 9 (DTR lxvi.982–4), x. 14 [Rufinus]
(Exp.Act. [Act. 1] p. 13.207), x. 25 [Rufinus] (Exp.Act. [Act. 21] p. 84.18–
20), xi. 1 [Rufinus] (DTR lxvi.1463–6), xi. 15 [Rufinus] (DTR lxvi.1511–

14), **xi. 26** [Rufinus] (DTR lxvi.1455–8), **xi. 28** [Rufinus] (Comm.Marc.
p. 509.811–25; DTR lxvi.1446–55; Hom. ii.23.225–6)
[119] *Onomasticon*, trans. by Jerome as *De situ et nominibus locorum
Hebraicorum*: Comm.Cant.cant. p. 207.651–3; Comm.Ezr. pp. 345.261–
7, 273.1287; Comm.Gen. pp. 48.1513, 1527–34, 100.992–5, 177.1248–50,
181.1379–95, 183.1477–80, 184.1485, 1489–90, 1493–4, 1499–1500,
185.1536–9, 1525–7, 188.1611–27, 1627–35, 200.231–4, 202.281–2,
232.1368–70; Comm.Luc. pp. 113.522–4, 157.2261–3, 183.663–5,
198.1259–61, 217.2002, 342.1842–6, 408.1792–3, 414.2027–8; Comm.
Marc. pp. 491.93, 515.1043–4, 525.1425–7, 570–1.1127–31, 614.763–4,
637.1633–4; Comm.Sam. pp. 11.11, 39.1162, 1166, 105.1541, 269.2451–
60; Comm.Tob. p. 8.16–17; Templ. pp. 155.334, 159.511; DLS viii.2–3;
Exp.Act. [Act. 8] p. 43.114–17; Nom.loc. (*passim*), Quaest.Reg. quaest.
xxi.10, xxiii.7, xxiv.7, xxvii.5

Eutropius
[120] *Breuiarium historiae Romanae*: **i. 1** (DTR lxvi.508), **i. 2** (Nom.loc. lines
237–8), **i. 8** (DTR lxvi.661–2), **ii. 9** (Nom.loc. lines 54–5), **vi. 17** (DTR
lxvi.922–4), **vi. 19** (DTR lxvi.926–31), **vii. 3** (DTR lxvi.965–6), **vii. 13**
(HE i.3), **vii. 14** (HE i.3), **vii. 19** (HE i.3), **viii. 1** (DTR lxvi.1095), **viii. 2**
(DTR lxvi.1119–21), **viii. 15** (DTR lxvi.1171–2), **viii. 23** (DTR
lxvi.1230–1), **ix. 15** (DTR lxvi.1318–20), **x. 2** (DTR lxvi.1391–3; HE i.
8); **x. 4** (DTR lxvi.1396–7)

Filastrius
[121] *Diuersarum hereseon liber*: cc. **cv** (Comm.Gen. p. 148.222–36), **cviii**
(Comm.Gen. p. 100.983–6), **cxx** (Comm.Gen. p. 24.715–17), **cxxi**
(Comm.Gen. pp. 142–52.1–356), **cxxxii** (Comm.Gen. p. 79.226–7),
cxlviii (Comm.Gen. pp. 189–92.1649–1772)

Fulgentius of Ruspe
[122] *Ad Thrasamundum regem libri .iii.*: **i. 19** (Retract.Act. [Act. 2]
p. 115.146–9)

Gennadius of Marseilles
[123] *De uiris inlustribus*: cc. **vii** (DTR xliii.81–6; Mart. [Quentin p. 101]), **xl**
(DTR lxvi.1553–5), **xlvii** (DTR lxvi.1545–9), **xlviii** (DTR lxvi.1550–2),
lxxxix (DTR lxvi.1660–1), **xc** (DTR lxvi.1653–9)

Gildas
[124] *De excidio Britanniae*: cc. **vii** (DTR xliii.81–6), **x** (DTR lxvi.1377–9;
HE i.7), **xi** (HE i.7), **xi** (HE i. 8), **xii** (HE i.8), **xiv** (DTR lxvi.1521–6; HE
i.12), **xv** (DTR lxvi.1556–64; HE i.12), **xvi** (DTR lxvi.1556–64; HE i.12),
xvii (DTR lxvi.1565–6; HE i.12), **xviii** (DTR lxvi.1566–71; HE i.12), **xix**
(DTR lxvi.1593–7; HE i.12), **xx** (DTR lxvi.1597–1603; HE i.13,14), **xxi**

(DTR lxvi.1603–6; HE i.14), **xxii** (DTR lxvi.1606–10; HE i.14), **xxiii** (DTR lxvi.1619–25; HE i.14,15), **xxiv** (HE i.15), **xxv** (DTR lxvi.1677–80; HE i.15, 16), **xxvi** (DTR lxvi.1680–2; HE i.16, 22), **lxxxv** (DO lines 650–5)

Gregory the Great

[125] *Dialogi*: **i prol.** (HE praef.), i. **6** (HE ii.7), i. **7** (Mart. [Quentin p. 102]), ii. **1** (DO line 406; DTR lxvi.1707; HAA c. 1), ii. **10** (VCP c. 14), ii. **35** (HE iv.21), ii. **37** (HE iv.21), iii. **2** (DTR lxvi.1694–6), iii. **14** (DO line 602), iii. **31** (DTR lxvi.1750–7), iv. **37** (HE v.12), iv. **40** (HE v.13), iv. **47** (DO line 407), iv. **57** (HE iv.30)

[126] *Hom. in Canticum canticorum*: cc. **xii** (Comm.Cant.cant. p. 190.31–43), **xiii** (Comm.Cant.cant. p. 191.47–51), **xiv** (Comm.Cant.cant. p. 192.83–4), **xxii** (Comm.Cant.cant. p. 193.119–20), **xxxiv** (Comm.Cant.cant. p. 197.295–310), **xlii** (Comm.Cant.cant. p. 199.378–80), **xliv** (Comm. Cant.cant. p. 200.408–14)

[127] *Hom. in Hiezechihelem*: i. **1** (Comm.Luc. p. 37.696–703; Exp.Act. [Act. 10] p. 52.117–19), i. **2** (Comm.Cant.cant. p. 270.1011–12; Comm.Luc. p. 85.2616–26), i. **4** (Comm.Luc. p. 213.1865–70; Comm.Prov. p. 104.47–52), i. **5** (Comm.Prov. p. 46.53–4), i. **6** (Tabernac. p. 13.342), i. **7** (Comm.Luc. pp. 308.491–6, 324.1154–64; Comm.Marc. pp. 553–4.465–9; Exp.Apoc. v.42–3), i. **8** (Comm.Cant.cant. pp. 301.89–90, 371.488–508; Comm.Luc. p. 386.931–4), i. **9** (Comm.Prov. pp. 116.194–8, 129.161–6; Exp.Apoc. xiii.82–5), i. **10** (Comm.Marc. pp. 525–6.1447–86), i. **11** (Comm.Cant.cant. pp. 322.293, 373.540–54; Comm.Luc. p. 130.1201–7; Comm.Marc. pp. 465–6.1123–9; Comm.Prov. p. 52.15–21), i. **12** (Comm. Prov. p. 51.117–21), ii. **1** (Comm.Cant.cant. p. 362.137–53), ii. **2** (Comm.Cant.cant. pp. 370.441–7, 374.599–608; Comm.Luc. pp. 225.2320–32, 226.2366–77; Templ. pp. 153.256–7, 224.1267), ii. **3** (Comm.Cant.cant. pp. 215.183–93, 240.373–6, 361.95–108, 366.287–322, 368.350–5, 369–72, 372–7; Comm.Marc. pp. 486.1921–46, 549.288–96; Templ. pp. 160.532, 215.930, 229.1460), ii. **4** (Comm.Cant.cant. pp. 363.212–20, 372.510–20; Templ. p. 205.550; Exp.Apoc. x.88–90), ii. **5** (Comm.Luc. p. 344.1933–41; Comm.Marc. p. 573.1216–43; Templ. p. 225.1325; Exp.Apoc. vii.20), ii. **6** (Comm.Prov. p. 93.143–4; Comm. Luc. p. 174.342–6; Templ. p. 221.1172), ii. **7** (Comm.Cant.cant. pp. 364.212–20, 371.455–61; Templ. p. 190.1715–20; Exp.Act. [Act. 10] p. 48.2–13), ii. **8** (Comm.Ezr. p. 265.953–4; Templ. p. 214.894), ii. **9** (Comm.Prov. pp. 102.131–3, 135.60–6; Templ. pp. 154.304–5, 212.795, 215.930, 216.959), ii. **10** (Comm.Cant.cant. p. 236.221–30; Tabernac. pp. 13.342, 137.1700; Templ. p. 224.1282; Exp.Apoc. xi.34–6); and cf. HE ii. 1

[128] *Hom. .xl. in Euangelia*: i. **2** (Comm.Marc. p. 570.1094–1124), i. **3** (Comm.Marc. p. 479.1629–39), i. **4** (Comm.Luc. p. 194.1107–13; Comm.

Marc. p. 479.1629–39; Exp.Act. [Act. 16] p. 68.19), i. 6 (Comm. Luc.
pp. 160–2.2376–434), i. 7 (Comm.Cant.cant. p. 316.30–1; Comm.Gen.
p. 236.1516–20; Comm.Luc. pp. 48.1153–60, 80.2407–28; Comm.Marc.
pp. 438.66–74, 441.174–93; Tabernac. p. 58.639), i. 8 (Comm.Luc.
p. 50.1213–14; Comm.Sam. p. 138.65; Exp.Apoc. xxxiii.98–102), i. 10
(Comm.Prov. p. 110.75–7; Exp.Apoc. iv.33, xii.37–9), i. 11 (Comm.Cant.
cant. p. 374.581–3), i. 13 (Comm.Luc. pp. 256–7.992–1066; Tabernac.
p. 108.596), i. 14 (Comm.Ezr. p. 334.1847), i. 15 (Comm.Cant.cant.
p. 336.783–5; Comm.Luc. pp. 173.309–12, 176.401–19, 425–35; Comm.
Marc. pp. 482.1786–90, 483.1818–21), i. 16 (Comm.Luc. pp. 93.2939–76,
96.3023–32; Comm.Epist.cath. [Iac. 1] p. 188.192–3), i. 17 (Comm.Cant.
cant. p. 360.60–4; Comm.Luc. pp. 112.481–3, 215–16.1922–68; Comm.
Marc. pp. 444–5.290–314, 504.604–8, 505.659.67, 579.1451–62; Tabernac.
p. 18.544; Templ. p. 18.1320), i. 19 (Comm.Epist.cath. [1 Ioh. 2]
pp. 290.45–6, 295.217–23), i. 20 (Comm.Luc. p. 75.2205–32; Comm.
Marc. pp. 439.76–80, 440.125–35), ii. 21 (Comm.Cant.cant. p. 216.194;
Comm.Marc. pp. 640–2.1761–1827), ii. 22 (Comm.Cant.cant. p. 316.30–
1), ii. 24 (Comm.Cant.cant. p. 260.610–11; Comm.Luc. p. 114.580–3;
Exp.Apoc. xxxiii.87–90), ii. 25 (Comm.Cant.cant. pp. 281.400–4,
364.188–206, 371.463–72), ii. 29 (Comm.Cant.cant. p. 362.128–35;
Comm.Gen. p. 96.828–42; Comm.Luc. p. 104.160–1; Comm.Marc.
pp. 645–6.1943–2011; Exp.Act. [Act. 1] p. 8.92–6, [Act. 7] p. 38.148–
53), ii. 30 (Comm.Epist.cath. [1 Ioh. 2] p. 298.354–8, [1 Ioh. 5] p. 320.32–
5), ii. 31 (Comm.Luc. pp. 265–7.1380–1467), ii. 32 (Comm.Marc.
pp. 538–40.1961–2055), ii. 33 (Comm.Luc. pp. 167–70.55–194), ii. 34
(Comm.Luc. pp. 27.322–8, 30.426–39, 52.1304, 285–7.2169–2263;
Comm.Tob. p. 6.20–1), ii. 35 (Comm.Prov. p. 94.169–72; Exp.Apoc.
xxv.45–7), ii. 36 (Comm.Epist.cath. [1 Petr. 1] p. 238.183–92; Comm.Luc.
pp. 278–81.1902–2023), ii. 37 (Comm.Luc. pp. 281–3.2027–2111; Exp.
Apoc. xxxviii.98–9), ii. 39 (Comm.Marc. p. 580.1486–93; Comm.Prov.
p. 137.36–7), ii. 40 (Comm.Prov. p. 105.113–17; Comm.Tob. p. 8.5–8;
Exp.Apoc. xxiv.43–7); and cf. HE ii. 1

[129] *Moralia in Iob*: prol. 20 [+ xxxv. 25] (Exp.Apoc. vii.92–5), i. 1
(Comm.Cant.cant. p. 211.22–6), ii. 2 (Comm.Gen. pp. 210–11.602–9,
221.978–81; Exp.Apoc. iii.11–15), ii. 7 (Exp.Apoc. vi.78–80), ii. 10
(Comm.Sam. p. 144.311–14), ii. 11 (Exp.Apoc. vii.79–81), ii. 15 (Exp.
Apoc. xx.35–6), ii. 20 (Exp.Apoc. v. 14–16), ii. 52 (Comm.Cant.cant.
p. 368.341–7), ii. 81 (Exp.Apoc. xxviii.39–40), iii. 16 (Comm.Luc.
p. 95.2993–3002), iii. 28 (Comm.Gen. p. 236.1516–20), iii. 31 (Comm.
Gen. p. 221.967–73), iii. 49 [+ xii. 64] (Exp.Apoc. v.42–3), iv. 1
(Exp.Act. [Act. 8] p. 40.28–36), iv. 4 (Comm.Sam. p. 92.1001; Comm.Ezr.
p. 313.1014), iv. 16 (Comm.Luc. p. 412.1960–9), iv. 27 (Comm.Prov.
p. 27.148–51), iv. 32 (Comm.Gen. p. 96.828–42), v. 2 (Comm.Prov.
p. 84.57–64), v. 5 (Comm.Prov. p. 34.33–43), v. 22 (Comm.Cant.cant.

p. 367.335–9), v. 23 (Comm.Prov. p. 64.74–6), v. 45 (Comm.Prov.
p. 72.110–11), vi. 10 (Comm.Prov. p. 146.215–21), vi. 11 (Comm.Luc.
p. 178.495–502), vi. 22 (Comm.Gen. p. 223.1042–50), vi. 25 (Comm.
Cant.cant. p. 361.110–17), vii. 21 (Comm.Cant.cant. p. 365.252–8), viii.
17 (Comm.Prov. p. 95.36–40), viii. 42 (Comm.Prov. p. 63.44–6), ix. 3
(Comm.Marc. p. 568.1043–54), ix. 11 (Comm.Cant.cant. p. 244.15–20),
ix. 36 (Exp.Act. [Act. 1] p. 12.192–5), ix. 66 (Comm.Gen. pp. 215.772–82,
218.882–90), x. 15 (Comm.Prov. p. 124.117–21), xi. 10 (Comm.Prov.
p. 97.10–11), xi. 33 (Comm.Cant.cant. p. 245.84–93), xii. 15 (Comm.Gen.
p. 63.2017), xii. 53 (Comm.Cant.cant. p. 373.556–61), xii. 55 (Comm.
Prov. p. 107.179–81), xiii. 34 (Comm.Tob. p. 9.45–6), xiv. 28 (Comm.
Prov. p. 130.209.14), xv. 10 (Comm.Prov. p. 112.55–65), xv. 11 (Comm.
Cant.cant. p. 369.414–23), xv. 45 (Comm.Luc. p. 260.1165–70), xvi. 55
(Comm.Luc. p. 200.1324–33; Comm.Marc. p. 513.967–76), xvii. 9
(Comm.Marc. p. 602.300–10), xvii. 29 (Comm.Epist.cath. [2 Petr. 3]
p. 281.177–8), xviii. 43 (Comm.Marc. p. 499.430–5), xviii. 50 (Comm.
Gen. pp. 44.1398–9, 221.967–73), xviii. 75 (Exp.Apoc. xxxvii.194), xix.
20 (Exp.Apoc. v.88–92), xix. 23 (Comm.Luc. p. 118.731–41; Comm.
Marc. p. 452.601–12), xix. 25 (Comm.Gen. p. 220.940–9; Comm.Luc.
p. 213.1846–53), xx. 16 (Exp.Act. [Act. 17] p. 73.90–2), xxi. 8 (Exp.Apoc.
xxxviii.93), xxi. 11 (Comm.Luc. p. 95.3012–21), xxii. 14 (Comm.Gen.
p. 74.55–65), xxiii. 1 (DST i.122–5), xxiii. 6 (Comm.Luc. p. 324.1143–
51; Tabernac. p. 137.1700), xxiii. 13 (Comm.Epist.cath. [1 Petr. 3]
p. 246.117), xxiii. 15 (Comm.Gen. p. 44.1398–9), xxiv. 16 (Exp.Apoc.
xxxvi.20–3), xxv. 16 (Tabernac. p. 56.582), xxvi. 37 (Comm.Luc.
p. 153.2081–96; Exp.Apoc. xxxviii.93), xxvi. 53 (Exp.Apoc. iv.272–4),
xxvi. 73 (Exp.Apoc. xxxviii.93), xxvii. 8 (Comm.Sam. p. 92.1006), xxvii.
29 (Exp.Apoc. xxxiii.98–102), xxvii. 43 (Exp.Act. [Act. 11] p. 56.18–19),
xxviii. 1 (Comm.Gen. p. 36.1103–10; Exp.Act. [Act. 2] p. 16.38–45),
xxviii. 8 (Comm.Gen. p. 236.1516–20), xxviii. 13 (Comm.Luc.
p. 119.747–54), xxxii. 3 (Comm.Luc. pp. 63–4.1745–76), xxxii. 15
(Exp.Act. [Act. 1] p. 11.173–4), xxxii. 23 (Exp.Apoc. xxxi.22–5), xxxii.
24 (Exp.Apoc. xxii.42–4), xxxiii. 21 (Exp.Apoc. xxv.11–13), xxxiii. 30
(Exp.Apoc. xxxv.11), xxxiii. 59 (Exp.Apoc. xxii.8–10), xxxiv. 4 (Exp.Act.
[Act. 23] p. 89.15–17), xxxiv.26 (Exp.Apoc. xxvii.20–2), xxxiv. 33
(Exp.Apoc. xvii.71); and cf. HE ii.1

[130] *Regula pastoralis*: i. 11 (Comm.Cant.cant. p. 322.293), ii. 4 (Comm.
Cant.cant. p. 370.425–8; Comm.Marc. p. 557.594–600), iii. 4 (Comm.
Prov. p. 52.8–13, 15–21), iii. 9 (Comm.Prov. pp. 100.58–62, 139.24–6),
iii. 10 (Comm.Prov. p. 86.148–55), iii. 11 (Comm.Prov. p. 44.244–6;
Exp.Apoc. xii.35–6), iii. 14 (Comm.Prov. pp. 95.36–40, 130.220–4), iii. 15
(Comm.Prov. pp. 101.91–8, 103.2–6), iii. 20 (Comm.Prov. p. 106.122–3),
iii. 23 (Comm.Prov. pp. 54.78–86, 87.28–30), iii. 24 (Comm.Prov.
p. 51.112–13, 114–16), iii. 25 (Comm.Prov. pp. 72.119–21, 123–5,

138.51–4; Exp.Act. [Act. 20] p. 83.72–4), iii. 26 (Comm.Cant.cant. p. 362.119–26), iii. 28 (Exp.Apoc. xxiii.44–9), iii. 30 (Comm.Epist.cath. [2 Petr. 2] p. 276.268–78; Comm.Prov. p. 132.61–5; Exp.Act. [Act. 2] p. 22.225–7), iii. 32 (Comm.Cant.cant. pp. 239.330–4, 366.278–83, 322.293), iii. 34 (Comm.Prov. p. 97.21–2; Exp.Act. [Act. 9] p. 44.15–17); and cf. HE ii. 1

Gregory of Nazianzus
[131] *Orationes .xlv.*, trans. Rufinus: *Oratio de pentecoste et de spiritu sancto* [= no. iv]: c. xv (Exp.Act. [Act. 2] p. 17.71–84)

Gregory of Tours
[132] *Historia Francorum*: v. 26 (Retract.Act. [Act. 28] p. 163.18–24), viii. 20 (Comm.Gen. p. 93.716–19)

Hegesippus: see **Josephus**, *Bellum Iudaicum*

Hilary of Poitiers
[133] *Tractatus super psalmos*: c. ii (Retract.Act. [Act. 13] pp. 147.97–114, 152.59–61)

Horace
[134] *Ars poetica* : 65 (DAM vi.38)
[135] *Epistulae*: i. 2. 56 (Comm.Prov. p. 72.117; Hom. ii.4.151), i. 2. 69–70 (Comm.Prov. p. 113.66–7)
[136] *Sermones*: ii. 3. 310 (DO line 1188)

Isidore of Seville
[137] *Chronica maiora*: DTR lxvi.48, 74, 81, 96, 210–11, 215–16, 220–1, 225–6, 1530–1, 1532–3, 1534, 1539–40, 1576, 1580–2, 1663–4, 1684–5, 1703–5, 1710–11, 1714–16, 1725–6, 1785–7, etc.
[138] *De differentiis rerum*: i. 14 (DO line 130), i. 28 (DO line 117), i. 35 (DO line 133), i. 38 (DO line 136), i. 46 (DO line 121), i. 58 (DO line 267), i. 62 (DO line 128), i. 69 (DO line 45), i. 76 (DO line 156), i. 93 (DO line 296), i. 115 (DO line 229), i. 120 (DO line 205), i. 121 (DO lines 197, 227), i. 129 (DO line 300), i. 134 (DO line 128), i. 149 (DO line 321), i. 154 (DO line 126), i. 163 (DO line 337), i. 171 (DO line 321), ii. 18 (Exp.Apoc. xxxiv.28–9), etc.
[139] *De ecclesiasticis officis*: i. 13 (Exp.Apoc. xxxiii.55–60)
[140] *De natura rerum* [*Liber rotarum*]: cc. i (DTR v.107–12, xi.62–73), ii (DO lines 512–24; DTR vii.4–8, 66–78, xxxv.18–21), iii (DTR viii.36–9), iv (DTR xi.55–60, 97–103, xii.17–22), vi (DTR xxxvi.1–10, 44–6, 96–8, xxxvii.29–32), vii (DNR xix.10–11; DTR xxxv.1–10, 37–41), viii (DTR xxx.2–5), ix (DNR iii.9), x (DNR ix.2–12; DTR xxxiii.3–46, 67–73), xi (DNR iv.2–9, 9–14), xii (DNR v.1, 8–12, x.1), xiii (DNR vii.6–7, viii.1),

xiv (DNR viii.1), xvi (DNR xviii.4–6), xvii (DNR xix.4–6, 6–11; DTR
vii.51–9), xviii (DNR xx.1; DTR vi.40–1, 41–4), xix (DTR xvi.86–93),
xxi (DNR xxii.112–16; DTR vii.19–22), xxii (DNR xi.2–4, xii.7, 8–9),
xxiii (DNR xiii.1), xxiv (DNR xi.4–6), xxv (DNR xi.6–8), xxvi (DNR
xxiv.2–4), xxviii (DTR vii.11–25), xxix (DNR xxviii.2–6), xxx (DNR
xxix.2–5), xxxi (DNR xxxi.2–6), xxxii (DNR xxxii.2–7), xxxiii (DNR
xxxii.5–7, xxxiii.2–4), xxxiv (DNR xxxv.2–3), xxxv (DNR xxxiv.2–4),
xxxvi (DNR xxvi.2–6), xxxvii (DNR xxvii.2–9, 11, 13–17, 21–2), xxxviii
(DNR xxxvi.8–11, 12–15; DTR xxv.3–5, 58–61), xxxix (DNR xxxvii.2–
3), xl (DNR xxxix.1; DTR xxix.7–11), xli (DNR xl.2–6), xlii (DNR
xli.2), xliii (DNR xliii.2–8), xlv (DNR xliv.2–8), xlvi (DNR xlix.2–5),
xlvii (DNR l.2–12), xlviii (DNR li.8–11)

[141] *De ortu et obitu patrum*: c. lxxx (Exp.Act. [Act. 1] p. 10.149;
Retract.Act. [Act. 1] p. 107.61)

[142] *Etymologiae*: i. 7. 15 (DO line 1191), i. 23. 1 (DO line 14), i. 27. 1–3
(DO line 140), i. 27. 4 (DO line 1140), i. 27. 19 (DO line 912), i. 34. 3 (DO
line 996), i. 36. 1 (DST i.6–8), i. 36. 2 (DST i.25–6), i. 36. 6 (DST i.56–
61), i. 36. 8 (DST i.71–2, 76–7, 79), i. 36. 11 (DST i. 80–1), i. 36. 12
(DST i. 90–2), i. 36. 15 (DST i.129–30), i. 37. 1 (DST ii.4), i. 37. 6 (DST
ii.38–44), i. 37. 10 (DST ii.61–2), i. 37. 14 (DST ii.92–6), i. 37. 25 (DST
ii. 187–91), i. 37. 27 (DST ii.198–9), i. 39. 9 (DAM x.2–6), i. 39. 9–11
(DAM xxv.22–5), i. 39. 12–13 (DAM x.18–19), i. 39. 14 (DAM x.39–40),
i. 39. 18 (DAM xxv.12–13), ii. 2. 10 (Comm.Gen. p. 139.2397–2400), ii.
18. 1–2 (DAM xii.50–1), iii. 7. 5 (Comm.Gen. p. 121.1723–4), iii. 21. 2
(DO line 775), iii. 44. 1 (DNR ix.2–4), iii. 51. 2 (DNR xix.6–11), iii. 56
(DTR viii.49–56), iii. 71. 16–17 (DNR xxiv.2–24; DTR xvi.55–7), iii. 71.
23–32 (DNR xvii.2–20), iv. 5. 3 (DTR xxxv.21–5), iv. 5. 4 (Comm.Gen.
p. 130.2146–50), v. 25. 20–1 (DO line 371), v. 26. 2 (DO line 468), v. 8. 2–
4 (DO lines 1245–50), v. 30. 4 (DTR v.107–12), v. 31. 1 (DTR vii.2), v.
31. 4–14 (DTR vii.66–78), v. 33. 2 (DTR xi.84–7), v. 33. 3 (DTR xii.66–
70), vi. 6. 19 (Comm.Gen. p. 171.1022–4), vi. 19. 20 (Exp.Apoc.
xxxiii.55–60), vii. 2. 2 (Exp.Act. [Act. 4] p. 27.58; Retract.Act. [Act. 2]
p. 117.257–8), vii. 3. 13 (Comm.Gen. p. 170.996), vii. 6. 4 (Comm.Gen.
p. 80.273), vii. 6. 7 (Comm.Gen. p. 73.9–11), vii. 6. 8 (Comm.Gen.
p. 73.16–17), vii. 6. 15 (Comm.Gen. p. 98.902–15), vii. 6. 16–18
(Comm.Gen. p. 99.928–31), vii. 9. 16 (DO line 345), vii. 9. 18
(Exp.Act. [Act. 1] p. 10.149), vii. 11. 3 (Exp.Act. [Act. 6] p. 32.14–20),
viii. 3. 1 [+ viii. 4. 4] (Exp.Act. [Act. 5] p. 30.42), viii. 5. 44 (Exp.Act.
[Act. 21] p. 84.18–20), viii. 7. 6 (DO line 258), viii. 11. 18–19 (Exp.Apoc.
xxxv.10–11), viii. 11. 45 (Exp.Act. [Act. 14] p. 65.34–5), ix. 2. 1
(Comm.Gen. p. 99. 928–31), ix. 2. 3 (Comm.Gen. p. 146.161–4), ix. 2.
29 (Comm.Gen. p. 142.21–2), ix. 2. 115–16 (DO line 913), ix. 2. 133
(DTR xxxiv.67–73), ix. 4. 37 (DO lines 589–96), ix. 7. 2 (DO line 667),
xi. 1. 2 (Comm.Gen. p. 93.720–1), xi. 1. 5 (Comm.Gen. p. 93.725–6), xi.

1. 122–3 (Comm.Gen. pp. 132–3.2146–50), xii. 1. 15–22 (Comm.Cant.
cant. p. 219.330–3; Comm.Sam. p. 111.1822–3; Exp.Act. [Act. 9] p. 47.94–
104), xii. 1. 60 (Comm.Ezr. p. 258.685–6; Comm.Sam. p. 198.2607–9),
xii. 2. 29 (Comm.Cant.cant. p. 226.607), xii. 6. 50 (Comm.Cant.cant.
p. 240.388–9; Tabernac. p. 46.154), xii. 7. 11 (Comm.Luc. p. 322.1038–
42), xiii. 2. 3 (DNR iii.28–9; DTR iii.28–9), xiii. 3. 2 (DNR iv.9–14), xiii.
5. 3–5 (DNR v.8–12), xiii. 5. 6 (DNR v.3–6), xiii. 5. 7 (DNR xviii.2–4),
xiii. 7. 1 (DNR xxv.10–13), xiii. 8. 2 (DNR xxviii.6–7), xiii. 9. 1 (DNR
xxix.2–5), xiii. 10. 3 (DNR xxxiii.4–6), xiii. 10. 6 (DNR xxxv.2–3), xiii.
18. 6 (Exp.Act. [Act. 27] p. 94.20–2), xiii. 21. 6–10 (Comm.Gen.
p. 49.1534–7), xiii. 27. 2–4 (DNR xlii.2–7), xiv. 1. 1 (Comm.Gen.
p. 13.359–60), xiv. 3. 2–4 (Comm.Gen. p. 46.1443–7), xiv. 3. 10
(Comm.Gen. p. 146.161–4), xiv. 3. 39 (Comm.Epist.cath. [1 Petr. 1]
p. 225.32), xiv. 4. 13 (DNR xxv.8–9), xiv. 6. 4 (DTR xxxi.70–2), xv. 1. 40
(Exp.Act. [Act. 28] p. 97.30–3), xv. 2. 9 (Exp.Act. [Act. 16] p. 69.24–5),
xv. 2. 10 (Exp.Act. [Act. 21] p. 87.101–3), xv. 2. 34–5 (Exp.Act. [Act. 19]
p. 80–98–101), xvi. 2. 3–7 (Comm.Prov. p. 128.146–54), xvi. 4. 6 (DTR
xxviii.33–6, xliii.88–90), xvi. 5. 8 (Comm.Gen. p. 160.661–2), xvi. 7. 1–2
(Exp.Apoc. xxxvii.151–6), xvi. 7. 4 (Comm.Gen. p. 50.1570–1), xvi. 7. 5
(Exp.Apoc. xxxvii.235–6), xvi. 7. 7 (Exp.Apoc. xxxvii.291–2), xvi. 7. 8
(Exp.Apoc. xxxvii.105–9), xvi. 8. 2 (Exp.Apoc. xxxvii. 192–3), xvi. 8. 3
(Comm.Gen. p. 50.1562–6; Exp.Apoc. xxxvii.195–6; Tabernac.
p. 105.481), xvi. 8. 4 (Exp.Apoc. xxxvii.196–7), xvi. 9. 1 (Exp.Apoc.
xxxvii.328–31), xvi. 9. 3 (Comm.Cant.cant. p. 291.747–8; Exp.Apoc.
xxxvii.305–10; Tabernac. p. 45.149), xvi. 10. 7 (DTR xxviii.33–6), xvi.
13. 1 (Exp.Apoc. v. 56–7), xvi. 14. 1 (Comm.Gen. p. 50.1568–9), xvi. 14.
5 (Exp.Apoc. xxxvii.147–8), xvi. 15. 2 (Exp.Apoc. xxxvii.227–8), xvi. 25.
22 (Comm.Ezr. p. 317.1165), xvi. 26. 11 (Comm.Sam. p. 237.1044), xvi.
26. 12 (Comm.Ezr. p. 317.1165; Templ. p. 212.797), xvi. 26. 13
(Comm.Sam. p. 21.409), xvi. 26. 13–17 (Comm.Luc. p. 297.75), xvii.
7. 19 (Comm.Luc. p. 310.576–8), xvii. 7. 20 (Comm.Luc. p. 334.1522–4),
xvii. 7. 33 (Comm.Cant.cant. p. 210.764–6, 776–7; Templ. p. 168.841),
xvii. 7. 52 (Comm.Sam. p. 146.382–7), xvii. 8. 4 (Comm.Cant.cant.
p. 267.898–901), xvii. 8. 6 (Comm.Gen. p. 49.1557–9), xvii. 8. 9
(Comm.Cant.cant. p. 267.919–20), xvii. 8. 10 (Comm.Cant.cant.
p. 266.852–64), xvii. 8. 12 (Comm.Cant.cant. p. 265.839–42), xvii. 9.
30 (Comm.Cant.cant. p. 335.750–64), xix. 1. 3 (Retract.Act. [Act. 27]
p. 161.14–15), xix. 1. 18–21 (Exp.Act. [Act. 27] p. 94.24–6; Retract.Act.
[Act. 27] p. 162.30–1), xix. 3. 3 (Exp.Act. [Act. 27] p. 95.53–4), xix. 22. 11
(Templ. p. 188.1633), xix. 27. 1 (Tabernac. p. 45.135), xix. 28. 1
(Tabernac. p. 46.160; Templ. p. 188.1633), xix. 28. 2 (Comm.Luc.
p. 302.243–6), xix. 28. 2–4 (Comm.Cant.cant. p. 240.388–9), xx. 2. 15
(Comm.Gen. p. 214.717–23)

[143] *Mysticorum expositiones sacramentorum seu Quaestiones in uetus Testa-*

mentum: **Gen. i. 2** (Comm.Gen. p. 3.25–9), **ii. 1** (Comm.Gen. p. 32.966–74), **ii. 2** (Comm.Gen. p. 39.1218–24), **iii. 1** (Comm.Gen. p. 44.1398–9), **iii. 2** (Comm.Gen. p. 46.1347–8), **v. 1** (Comm.Gen. p. 62.1989–95), **v. 2** (Comm.Gen. pp. 36.1103–10, 63.2017), **v. 4** (Comm.Gen. p. 65.2084–2105), **v. 5** (Comm.Gen. p. 66.2112–15), **v. 6** (Comm.Gen. p. 66.2121–6), **vi. 1** (Comm.Gen. p. 73.27–33), **vi. 5** (Comm.Gen. p. 77.153–9), **vi. 19** (Comm.Gen. p. 85.439–55), **vi. 22** (Comm.Gen. pp. 86–7.498–518), **vii. 1** (Comm.Gen. pp. 98.905–6, 103.1089–92), **vii. 3** (Comm.Gen. p. 105.1145–8), **vii. 4** (Comm.Gen. 106.1168–9), **vii. 5** (Comm.Gen. p. 106.1183–8), **vii. 15** (Comm.Gen. p. 115.1501–6), **vii. 16** (Comm.Gen. p. 118.1602–8), etc.

[144] *Sententiae*: **i. 19** (Comm.Gen. p. 42.1319–33)

Jerome (Hieronymus)

[145] *Aduersus Heluidium de Mariae uirginitate perpetua*: cc. **iv** (DO line 24; Hom. i.5.28–30), **viii** (Hom. i.5.122–5), **xiii** (Exp.Act. [Act. 1] p. 10.145–7), **xiv** (Comm.Marc. p. 502.529–37)

[146] *Aduersus Iouinianum*: **i. 3** (Comm.Luc. p. 177.437–47; DTR i.12–24), **i. 26** (DTR lxvi.1092–4; Hom. i.9.125–8), **i. 30** (Comm.Cant.cant. pp. 202.467–9, 223.489–94; Hom. i. 18.58), **i. 31** (Comm.Cant.cant. p. 316.51–4), **i. 32** (Comm.Cant.cant. p. 254.405–7), **ii. 3** (Comm.Epist. cath. [Iac. 1] p. 188.181–90, [2 Petr. 2] p. 275.252–62), **ii. 6** (DO line 1154), **ii. 22** (Hom. i.13.42–7)

[147] *Altercatio Luciferiani et orthodoxi*: c. **xxii** (Comm.Gen. pp. 102–4.1060–1132)

[148] *Apologia aduersus libros Rufini*: **ii. 25** (DTR praef. 21–2)

[149] *Comm. in Danielem*: **ii. 5** (Comm.Ezr. p. 243.96; DO lines 165, 1160; DTR lxvi.640–6), **ii. 6** (Exp.Act. [Act. 2] p. 18.110), **ii. 7** (DTR lxvi.714; Exp.Apoc. xxi.22–4, xxii.79–81, xxv.33–6, xxxi.42–4), **ii. 8** (Comm.Tob. p. 6.20–1; DTR lxvi.784–7), **iii. 9** (Comm.Ezr. p. 342.141; DTR ix.2–9, 105–12, lxvi.638–9, 726–33, 740–2), **iii. 11** (DTR lxvi.675–9, 782–3, 813–15, 819–23, 826–9, 849–52), **iv. 12** (DTR lxix.4, 53–8; Exp.Apoc. x.83–8), **vi. 5** (Comm.Luc. p. 134.1323–5)

[150] *Comm. in Ecclesiasten*: cc. **i** (Comm.Luc. p. 5.20), **iii** (Comm.Epist. cath. [Iac. 1] p. 190.269–72), **x** (Comm.Prov. p. 134.49–52), **xii** (Comm. Cant.cant. p. 320.198–201)

[151] *Comm. in .iv. Epistulas Paulinas*: **Galatas i** (Exp.Act. [Act. 9] p. 45.51–3), **iii** (Exp.Act. [Act. 5] p. 30–42), **vi** (Comm.Gen. p. 24.715–17); **Titum iii** (Exp.Act. [Act. 5] p. 32.84–8); **Philemonem** (Exp.Act. [Act. 13] p. 61.11–12)

[152] *Comm. in Esaiam*: **i. 2** (Retract.Act. [Act. 9] p. 138.42), **i. 63** (Exp.Apoc. xxxvii.227–8), **ii. 3** (Exp.Act. [Act. 19] p. 79.74–5), **ii. 5** (Comm.Ezr. p. 313.1030; DST i.98–102), **iii. 6** (Exp.Act. [praef.] p. 4.30–5), **iv. 10** (Comm.Gen. p. 145.130–2), **iv. 11** (DST ii.223–5; Retract.Act. [praef.]

p. 103.28), v. 14 (Comm.Gen. p. 157.522–8), v. 22 (Nom.loc. lines 336–40), vi. 14 (DTR v.74–86), vii. 2 (Comm.Gen. p. 103.1096–9), vii. 19 (Comm.Gen. p. 186.1545–6), vii. 51 (Exp.Apoc. xxvii.12–13), viii praef. (DST i.127–8), viii. 24 (Retract.Act. [praef.] p. 103.28), viii. 26 (Exp.Act. [Act. 28] p. 96.16–17), ix. 30 (Nom.loc. lines 146–7), x. 11 (Exp.Apoc. iii. 65–7), x. 16 (Exp.Apoc. iii.65–7), xi. 40 (Quaest.Reg. qu. xxv.5), xii. 41 (Tabernac. p. 59.690), xii. 45 (Comm.Ezr. p. 244.134), xiv. 12–13 (Comm.Gen. pp. 4–5.61–7), xiv. 53 (Exp.Act. [Act. 8] p. 42.87–9, 91–4, 97–9, 100–6), xv. 7 (Exp.Apoc. xxxvii.105–7, 113–16, 123–5), xv. 54 (Comm.Gen. p. 103.1096–9), xv. 55 (Exp.Act. [Act. 13] p. 63.72–3), xv. 56 (Exp.Act. [Act. 8] p. 41.67–8), xvi. 57 (Exp.Act. [Act. 7] p. 36.96), xvi. 58 (Comm.Marc. p. 579.1478–80; Comm.Gen. p. 205.410), xvii. 63 (Exp.Act. [Act. 8] p. 43.126–7), xviii. 66 (Comm.Gen. p. 142.22–7; Exp.Act. [Act. 18] p. 75.39–42)

[153] *Comm. in Euangelium Matthaei*: Comm.Luc. (*passim* [131×]); Comm. Marc. (*passim* [127×]; i. 2 (Hom. i.5.28–30, 63–5), i. 3 (Hom. i.10.42–7, 92), i. 4 (Hom. i.12.31–3, 63–5, 135–8), i. 8 (Hom. ii.14.234–5), i. 9 (Hom. i.21.9–15), i. 10 (Exp.Act. [Act. 1] p. 11.155–6, [Act. 8] p. 39.3–4), ii. 11 (Hom. ii.19.10–12), ii. 13 (DTR i.12–24), ii. 14 (Hom. ii.23.37–44, 145–6), ii. 15 (Exp.Act. [Act. 10] p. 51.78–81), iii. 16 (Comm.Gen. pp. 188–9.1639–41; Hom. i.20.16–20, 78, i.22.2–8, 31), iii. 17 (Hom. i.16.151–3, i.24.55–7, 144), iii. 18 (Hom. i.24.251), iii. 21 (Hom. i.9.125–8, ii.3.44–7, 56–7, 156, ii.21.43–4), iii. 22 (Exp.Act. [Act. 5] p. 30.44–9), iii. 27 (Hom. ii.1.60–1), iv. 23 (Hom. i.3.196–200; Tabernac. p. 61.746–50), iv. 24 (Exp.Act. [Act. 1] p. 8.70–3), iv. 26 (Exp.Act. [Act. 14] p. 65.41–5; Hom. ii.4.75–6), iv. 27 (DTR xxvii.31–6)

[154] *Comm. in Ezechielem*: iii. 9 (Comm.Gen. p. 106.1183–8), viii. 27 (Comm.Gen. pp. 143.40–2, 43–7; Nom.loc. lines 431–2), xii. 41 (Comm. Gen. p. 110.1314–15; Tabernac. p. 77.1395–1400), xiii. 44 (Retract.Act. [Act. 15] p. 149.16–25), xiv. 47 (Exp.Act. [Act. 13] p. 61.27–32)

[155] *Comm. in Hieremiam*: ii. 82 (DO line 715)

[156] *Comm. in Prophetas minores*: **Osee** ii. 5 (DO lines 151–2), ii. 6 (Nom.loc. lines 321–4, 479), ii. 8 (Comm.Gen. p. 214.717–23), iii. 14 (Exp.Apoc. iii.65–7); **Ioel** iii. 18 (Tabernac. p. 59.690–3); **Amos praef.** (DO line 672), ii. 4 (DTR xi.4–6), ii. 5 (Exp.Act. [Act. 7] pp. 36.86–92, 37.108–12; Nom.loc. lines 503–4), iii. 9 (Nom.loc. lines 215–17); **Ionam praef.** (Nom.loc. lines 243–50), i. 7 (Exp.Act. [Act. 1] p. 14.251); **Abacuc** ii. 3 (Comm.Abacuc pp. 386.136–8, 388.208); **Sophoniam** iii (Comm. Ezr. p. 345.271–3), **Aggaeum** ii. 19 (DO lines 650–5), **Zachariam** i. 6 (DO line 165), iii praef. (Exp.Apoc. iii.65–7), iii. 12 (DTR lxvi.536–7)

[157] *Commentarioli in psalmos*: i (Exp.Act. [Act. 13] p. 63.64–6), xxxix (Exp.Act. [Act. 26] p. 92.22–3), xlvii (Exp.Apoc. xxxvii.225–7), lxxxviii (Exp.Act. [Act. 1] pp. 7–8.62–6), cvi (DNR x.1), cix (Exp.Act. [Act. 2] p. 21.201–7)

[158] *De uiris inlustribus*: cc. i (Comm.Epist.cath. [1 Petr.] p. 225.12–16), ii (Comm.Luc. p. 135.1372–95; Comm.Marc. p. 472.1383–92; Comm.Sam. p. 72.174–6; DTR lxvi.1056–8; Exp.Act. [Act. 21] p. 85.22–9, 219–21), iv (Comm.Epist.cath. [Iud.] p. 340.219–21), v (DTR lxvi.1052–3, 1054–5; Exp.Act. [Act. 21] p. 87.94–8, [Act. 28] p. 99.79–81, 87–95), viii (Comm.Epist.cath. [1 Petr.] p. 259.120–38; Comm.Marc. p. 431.16–31; Retract.Act. [Act. 20] p. 156.24), ix (Comm.Luc. p. 100.1–25; Comm. Marc. p. 445.332–41; DTR lxvi.1098–1100, 1102–3; Exp.Apoc. iii.6–7), xvi (Exp.Apoc. xxxiii.11–14; Mart. [Quentin p. 100]), xvii (Comm. Epist.cath. [2 Ioh.] p. 330.76–8; Mart. [Quentin p. 100]), xliii (DTR lxvi.1183–6), liv (DTR lxvi.1236), lxi (DTR xliv.2–6, lxvi.1224–8), lxii (DTR lxvi.1207–11), lxv (DTR lxvi.1250–2, 1301–2), lxviii (DTR lxvi.1298–1300), lxxi (DTR lxvi.1310–12, 1313–14), lxxii (DTR lxvi.1341–3), lxxiii (DTR lxvi.1327–31), lxxv (DTR lxvi.1380–1), lxxvi (DTR lxvi.1348–53)

[159] *Dialogi contra Pelagianos*: i. 1–2 (Comm.Cant.cant. p. 175.339–44)

[160] *Epistulae*: xv (Comm.Gen. p. 103.1074–9), xxi (DO line 324), xxii (Comm.Sam. p. 120.2177–9; DO line 324), xxxvi (Comm.Gen. pp. 79.218, 226–7, 233–7, 255–63, 198–9.174–8, etc.), xxxvii (Exp.Apoc. xxxvii.225–7), xlviii (Comm.Gen. pp. 12.303–6, 105.1138–41; DTR i.12–24), li (DO line 324), liii (Comm.Ezr. pp. 237.4–9, 309.878, 339.6; Exp.Act. [praef.] p. 3.23–8, [Act. 8] p. 41.68–9), lvii (Exp.Act. [Act. 26] p. 92.5–10), lx (Retract.Act. [Act. 21] p. 158.48), lxiv (Tabernac. pp. 98.201–4, 104.447–50, 110.662–3, 113.810–14, 116.892–9, 119.1004–11, 123.1164–72), lxxi (Retract.Act. [Act. 28] p. 163.28–30), cvi (DO line 170; Tabernac. p. 43.74–5), cviii (Exp.Act. [Act. 7] p. 34.44–8, [Act. 8] p. 44.129–31; Hom. i.12.31–3; Retract.Act. [Act. 21] p. 157.7–8), cxii (Exp.Act. [Act. 18] p. 75.35–7, [Act. 24] p. 90.4–7; Retract.Act. [Act. 18] p. 154.33–6), cxvii (DO line 165), cxix (DTR iii.34–40, 41–5, 49), cxxi (DTR xiii.25–8), cxxiv (Comm.Gen. p. 134.2209–11), cxxv (Comm.Gen. p. 130.2043–9)

[161] *Liber interpretationis hebraicorum nominum*: 400+ citations, including: Comm.Abacuc (3×), Comm.Cant.cant. (20×), Comm.Ezr. (*passim* [45×]), Comm.Gen. (*passim* [64×]), Comm.Luc. (*passim* [45×]), Comm. Marc. (15×), Comm.Prov. (2×), Comm.Sam. (*passim* [125×]), Comm. Tob. (5×), DTR (1×), Exp.Act. (17×), Exp.Apoc. (3×), Hom. (*passim* [29×]), Quaest.Reg. (4×), Retract.Act. (3×), Tabernac. (14×), Templ. (9×)

[162] *Liber quaestionum hebraicarum in Genesim*: Comm.Gen. (*passim* [68×]); DST (1×), DTR (2×), Hom. (1×), Retract.Act. (1×)

[163] *Vita S. Hilarionis*: Mart. (Quentin p. 99); c. xli (Exp.Act. [Act. 7] p. 36.98–100)

[164] *Vita S. Pauli primi eremitae*: cc. ii (Exp.Apoc. xiii.52–4), iv (Mart. [Quentin p. 99])

John Chrysostom
[165] *Hom. in diem natalem*: Comm.Luc. p. 28.346–9

Josephus, Flavius
[166] *Antiquitates Iudaicae*, trans. Cassiodorus: i. 2 (Comm.Gen. p. 85.443–4), i. 3 (Comm.Gen. p. 90.628; DTR xxxvi.33–4), i. 5–6 (Comm.Gen. pp. 142–52.1–356), i. 8 (DTR vi.87–90), ii. 15 (DTR lxvi.665), iii. 6 (Comm.Gen. p. 112.1403–10; Tabernac. pp. 13.340–1, 43.72–3, 47.224, 63.823, 64.894, 70.1122), iii. 7 (Tabernac. pp. 111.737, 117.949–53, 958–63), iii. 10 (Comm.Luc. p. 128.1132–9; Comm.Marc. p. 464.1060–2; Comm.Sam. p. 197.2588; DTR lxiii.28–31; Tabernac. pp. 28–9.930–7), iv. 7 (Quaest.Reg. qu. xxi, line 11), v. 1 [+ vi. 13–14] (Comm.Sam. p. 69.47–8), vi. 5 (Comm.Sam. p. 102.1413), vi. 6 (Comm.Sam. pp. 105.1562, 115.1972), vi. 8 (Comm.Sam. p. 144.324), vi. 13 (Comm. Sam. p. 250.1631–4; DTR lxvi.384; Quaest.Reg. qu. iv, lines 21–3), vi. 14 (Comm.Sam. p. 253.1765–8; DTR lxvi.388), vii. 3 (Comm.Sam. p. 162.1079), vii. 12 (Quaest.Reg. qu. x, line 2), vii. 14 (Nom.loc. lines 433–4; Quaest.Reg. qu. xviii, line 76), viii. 3 (Comm.Ezr. p. 293.221; Quaest.Reg. qu. xii, line 7, xiii, line 24, xviii, line 57; Templ. pp. 156.382–4, 161.572, 166.789, 192.15–27, 193.69–72), viii. 6 (Nom.loc. lines 414–23), x. 11 (Comm.Ezr. pp. 243.95, 299.469; DTR lxvi.620, 625–31), xi. 4 (Comm.Ezr. pp. 293.203–4, 300.480), xi. 5 (Comm.Ezr. pp. 307.783, 319.1280, 320.1309, 330.1718, 1747), xi. 8 (Comm.Ezr. p. 376.1491), xv. 3 [+ xvii. 6, xviii. 3] (Comm.Sam. p. 247.1473–84), xvii. 13 (Comm.Luc. p. 74.2172–9; DTR lxvi.982–4), xviii. 2 (Comm.Luc. p. 75.2194–2201), xviii. 5 (Comm.Marc. p. 509.809–11)
[167] *Bellum Iudaicum*, transl. and abbrev. Hegesippus: i. 36 (DTR lxvi. 952–7), i. 37 (DTR lxvi.958–9), i. 42 (DTR lxvi.957–8, 960), ii. 1 (DTR lxvi.987–9), ii. 3 (DTR lxvi.987–9, 1012–15), ii. 5 (DTR lxvi.987–9, 1020–1), ii. 6 (Exp.Act. [Act. 21] p. 87.86–93), iii. 7 (Comm.Luc. p. 400.1497), vi. 5 (Comm.Luc. p. 365.102–8)

Julian of Eclanum
[168] *De amore seu Comm. in Canticum canticorum*: Comm.Cant.cant. pp. 167.15–26, 170–1.151–4, 285.539–48; DO line 52
[169] *De bono constantiae*: Comm.Cant.cant. p. 174.277–95

Julian of Toledo
[170] *Ars grammatica*: DST i.6–8, 8–10, 20–4, 42–3, 56–61, 65–6, 71–2, 80–1, 84–5, 108–9, 115–17, 129–30, 151, 155–6; ii.2–7, 8–21, 31–3, 38–44, 44–5, 49–51, 63–9, 78–84, 85–90, 91–2, 92–6, 99–101, 104–6, 107–10, 113–14, 115–16, etc.
[171] *Prognosticum futuri saeculi*: iii. 1–5 (Epist.Pleg. lines 288–93)

Junillus Africanus
[172] *Instituta regularia diuinae legis*: ii. 2 (DNR ii.2–12)

Juvenal
[173] *Saturae*: ii. 83 (Comm.Luc. pp. 270.1552, 309.547; Comm.Marc.
p. 549.286), xiv. 139 (Comm.Marc. p. 483.1807; Comm.Prov. p. 144.117)

Juvencus
[174] *Euangelia*: praef. 1 (DAM xii.6), 17 (DAM xii.15), 18 (VCM 841), i.
26 (DAM xii.38), i. 91 (DAM iii.87), i. 255 (VCM 918), i. 277 (VCM
979), i. 370 (VCM 733), i. 392 (VCM 864), i. 465 (DAM xii.17), i. 578
(VCM 701 + 704), i. 645 (VCM 831), i. 688 (DDI 73), ii. 97 (VCM 775),
ii. 185 (VCM 721), ii. 681 (VCM 749), iii. 100–1 (VCM 780–1), iii. 105
(VCM 663), iii. 296 (VCM 235, 929), iii. 340 (Retract.Act. [Act. 9]
p. 137.5), iii. 499 (DAM iii.114), iii. 522 (DAM iii.112), iii. 527 (VCM
757), iv. 315 (VCM 759), iv. 343 (DDI 18), iv. 426 (DAM xiv.58), iv. 553
(VCM 194), iv. 631 (DLS iii.1), iv. 725 (VCM 795)

Lactantius Firmianus
[175] *De mortibus persecutorum*: c. xlix (DO line 253)

Leo the Great
[176] *Epistulae*: cxxi (DTR xliv.21–7), cxxix (DTR xliv.33–40), cxxxiii
(DTR vi.28–30, xvi.62, xxxv.70–4)
[177] *Sermones*: xxi (Hom. i.5.89–91), xxv (Hom. i.8.220–1), xxvii (Hom.
i.5.89–91), li (Hom. i.24.101–3)

Licentius
[178] *Carmen ad Augustinum*: lines 49 (DDI 15), 81 (DDI 98)

Lucan
[179] *Bellum ciuile*: i. 1–3 (DAM xi.64–6), i. 10–12 (DAM xi.67–9), i. 280
(VCM 95), ii. 34 (VCM 405), ii. 83 (VCM 446), ii. 126 (DDI 129), iii. 68
(VCM 289), iv. 31 (VCM 122), iv. 382 (VCM 125), iv. 477 (VCM 678), v.
233 (VCM 101), vi. 9 (DDI 56), vi. 502 (DDI 94), viii. 186 (VCM 295),
ix. 384 (VCM 18), ix. 728 (VCM 24), ix. 735 (VCM 110), x. 321 (DDI 52)

Lucian
[180] *Epistula de inuentione corporis S. Stephani martyris*, trans. Avitus of
Braga: Retract.Act. [Act. 8] p. 135.40–58; DTR lxvi.1545–9

Lucretius
[181] *De rerum natura*: i. 629 (DTR ii.28–9), ii. 515–18 (DNR xix.10–11), iv.
652 (DTR vi.1), v. 811–12 (Comm.Gen. p. 13.342–50)

Macrobius

[182] *Saturnalia*: i. 12. 4 (DTR xii.49–51), i. 12. 5 (DTR xii.12–14), i. 12. 8–15 (DTR xii.14–17), i. 12. 16–33 (DTR xii.22–32), i. 12. 34–7 (DTR xii.32–42), i. 12. 38 (DTR xii.43–9), i. 12. 39 (DTR xii.51–7), i. 13. 1–3 (DTR xii.57–66), i. 13. 5–11 (DTR xii.82–100), i. 13. 8–10 (DTR ix.99–102, xlvi.11–19), i. 13. 13–16 (DTR xii.111–20, xl.2–7), i. 13. 19 (DTR xl.7–13), i. 14. 3 (DTR xii.102–11), i. 14. 5 (DTR xxxvi.3–6), i. 14. 6 (DTR xii.104–6), i. 15. 1 (DTR xi.97–103), i. 15. 5–6 (DTR xii.4–12), i. 15. 9–13 (DTR xiii.2–25), i. 15. 16 (DTR xiii.24–5), i. 15. 17 (DTR xiii.20–3)

Mallius Theodorus

[183] *De metris*: DAM ii.12, 34; iii.60–4; x.2–6, 6–9, 21–4; xvii.5–7; xviii.2–4; xx.2–5; xxi.19–21; xxii.2–3; xxiii.2–6

Marcellinus Comes

[184] *Chronicon*: Comm.Epist.cath. [Iac. 3] p. 206.147–51; Comm.Marc. p. 512.918–30; DTR lxvi.1496–8, 1499–1500, 1501–2, 1510, 1527–9, 1541–2, 1543–4, 1577–8, 1613–15, 1616–17, 1626–8, 1643–5, 1647–52, 1665–6, 1667–9, 1672–6, 1669–71, 1711–13, 1720–1; HE i.13, 21

Marius of Avenches

[185] *Chronica*: DTR lxvi.1700–2, 1746–8

Martial

[186] *Epigrammata*: **xiii. 94–5** (Exp.Act. [Act. 9] p. 47.103–4)

Martianus Capella

[187] *De nuptiis Philologiae et Mercurii*: **iii. 302** (DO line 202), **iii. 317** (DO line 258), **iii. 325** (DO line 112), **viii. 826** (DNR xviii.1)

Nonius Marcellus

[188] *De compendiosa doctrina*: DO lines 256, 467, 516, 583, 648, 826, 919–20, 1071, 1221

Optatianus Porphyrius

[189] *Carmina*: **v. 1** (VCM 10), **vi. 23** (VCM 126)

Origen

[190] *Comm. in Cantica canticorum*, trans. Rufinus: Comm.Cant.cant. pp. 190.31–43, 191.47–51, 67–70, 201.437–8, 202.469–73, 203.525–49, 205.581–8, 206.613–17, 208.686–9, 212.63–79, 216.194, 218.277–316, 220.367, 226.586–95

[191] *Comm. in Euangelium Matthaei*, in Latin translation: **x. 9** (Comm.Sam. p. 34.964–7)

[192] *Hom. .ii. in Canticum canticorum*, trans. Jerome: Comm.Cant.cant. pp. 190.31–43, 197.295–310, 205.581–8, 213.117–35, 216.194, 230.732–6

[193] *Hom. .xiii. in Exodum*, trans. Rufinus: Tabernac. p. 43.63, 45.138, 150, 60.709, 64.862, 74.1275, 104.453

[194] *Hom. .xvi. in Leuiticum*, trans. Rufinus: ii. 2–4 (Comm.Sam. p. 45.1420–3)

[195] *Hom. in libros Regum*, trans. Rufinus: **hom.** i (Comm.Sam. pp. 11–23.32–506)

Orosius, Paulus

[196] *Historiae aduersum paganos*: i. 2 (Comm.Ezr. p. 320.1294–1302; Comm.Gen. pp. 48.1525–6, 49.1534–7, 143.44–7; HE i.1; Nom.loc. lines 5–7, 10–12, 20–2, 72, 148, 165, 190–3, 196–7, 218, 280–2, 295–303), ii. 6 (Comm.Gen. pp. 145.133–6, 157.528–41), ii. 8 (DTR lxvi.663–5), ii. 9 (DTR lxvi.705–7), ii. 10 (DTR lxvi.707–8), iii. 13 (DTR lxvi.1421–3), vi. 2 (Nom.loc. lines 47, 85), vi. 7 (HE i.2), vi. 10 (HE i.3), vi. 22 (DTR lxvi.974, 976–7), vii. 2 (DTR lxvi.971–3), vii. 3 (DTR lxvi.974), vii. 5 (DTR lxvi.1017–29), vii. 6 (DTR lxvi.1041–6, 1047–8; Exp.Act. [Act. 18] p. 74.3–7; HE i.3), vii. 7 (DTR lxvi.1064–5), vii. 13 (DTR lxvi.1123–7, 1128–31), vii. 14 (DTR lxvi.1140–2), vii. 15 (DTR lxvi.1153–4, 1158–9; HE i. 4), vii. 16 (DTR lxvi.1168–9, 1170–1, 1177–9), vii. 17 (DTR lxvi.1194–6, 1197–1202; HE i.5), vii. 18 (DTR lxvi.1216–17, 1129, 1135), vii. 19 (DTR lxvi.1238–41), vii. 20 (DTR lxvi.1254–8), vii. 22 (DTR lxvi.1293–4), vii. 32 (DTR lxvi.1307–9, 1317–18), vii. 24 (DTR lxvi.1334–5), vii. 25 (DTR lxvi.1366–8, 1369–70, 1372–3, 1391–3; HE i.6, 8), vii. 27 (Exp.Apoc. iv.51–2), vii. 28 (DTR lxvi.1421–3, 1424–5), vii. 29 (DTR lxvi.1426–7), vii. 33 (DTR lxvi.1483–4, 1487–90, 1491–3), vii. 34 (DTR lxvi.1483–4, 1496–8, 1503, 1506–11, 1519–20; HE i.9), vii. 35 (DTR lxvi.1517–18), vii. 36 (HE i.10), vii. 40 (DTR lxvi.1542–3)

Ovid

[197] *Ars amatoria*: i. 249 (DO line 708), ii. 653 (DO line 709)

[198] *Metamorphoseis*: i. 84–6 (Comm.Gen. p. 26.788–90), i. 548 (DDI 120), ii. 645 (VCM 67), iv. 58 (Comm.Gen. p. 156.517), iv. 75 (VCM 60), iv. 467 (DDI 108), vi. 340 (VCM 727), vi. 348 (VCM 115), vi. 650 (DDI 59), vii. 378 (DO line 1217), viii. 651 (VCM 719), ix. 535 (VCM 389), x. 362 (VCM 61), xi. 612 (VCM 677)

Paulinus of Milan

[199] *Vita S. Ambrosii*: cc. xiv–xv (DTR lxvi.1514–18; Mart. [Quentin p. 101])

Paulinus of Nola

[200] *Carmina*: vi. 152 (DO line 537), vi. 169 (VCM 13), xiv. 89 (VCM 687), xv. 299 (DAM iii.105), xvi. 64 (DAM xiv.42), xvi. 125 (DAM xiii.54),

xvi. 181 (DAM xiv.37), xvii. 1–4 (DAM xviii.7–10), xvii. 45–56 (DAM xviii.12–23), xviii. 35 (DAM xiv.50), xviii. 280 (DAM xiv.87), xviii. 348–51 (VCM 198–9), xix. 350 (VCM 871), xx. 207 (VCM 652), xxi. 339 (VCM 181), xxi. 517 (VCM 75), xxvii. 72 (DAM xiii.50), xvii. 385 (DAM xiv.90), xxvii. 415–20 (Comm.Luc. p. 135.1362–7), xxvii. 620 (DAM xiv.25), xxvii. 637 (DAM xv.21), xxvii. 645 (= VCM 974), xxviii. 37 (DAM xv.25), xxviii. 65–6 (DAM xiii.78–9), xxviii. 81 (VCM 948), xxviii. 91 (DAM xiv.62), xxviii. 115 (VCM 91), xxviii. 202 (DAM xiv.60), xxviii. 215 (DAM xiv.29), xxxi. 21–4 (VCM 44). Bede's *Vita S. Felicis* [BHL 2873] is based almost entirely on Paulinus' *carmina natalicia* for St Felix of Nola.

Pelagius

[201] *Epistula ad Demetriadem*: Comm.Cant. cant. p. 175.344–83

Persius

[202] *Saturae*: iv. 50 (VCM 358)

Philippus Presbyter

[203] *Comm. in librum Iob*: c. xxxviii (DTR iv.42–5, xxix.72–4)

Phocas

[204] *Ars de nomine et uerbo*: DAM vi.58–9; DO lines 102, 338, 680, 772, 918, 940, 1160

Pliny the Elder

[205] *Naturalis historia*: DNR (*passim* [86×]), DTR (*passim* [38×]); ii. 6 (Comm.Gen. pp. 17.483–9, 19.537–48), ii. 11 (Comm.Gen. p. 17.472–7), ii. 42 (Comm.Gen. p. 5.89–96), ii. 69–70 (Comm.Gen. p. 16.436–7), ii. 77 (HE i.1), ii. 106 (Comm.Gen. p. 5.93–6), iii. 61 (Nom.loc. lines 235–6), iii. 73 (Nom.loc. lines 295–303), iii. 86 (Nom.loc. lines 248–51, 295–303), iv. 23 (Comm.Gen. p. 143.44–7), iv. 30 (HE i.1), v. 15 (Hom. ii.2.29–33; ii.15.291), v. 16 (Comm.Gen. p. 48.213), v. 17 (Comm.Ezr. p. 273.1288), v. 20 (Comm.Gen. p. 147.195–9), v. 24 (Nom.loc. line 148), v. 27 (Comm.Gen. pp. 147–8.205–7), v. 31 (Nom.loc. lines 74–5), v. 48 (Nom.loc. lines 12–19), v. 69 (Exp.Act. [Act. 12] p. 59.64; Nom.loc. line 93), v. 69–70 (Nom.loc. lines 155–7), v. 75 (Nom.loc. line 233), v. 76 (Exp.Act. [Act. 12] p. 60.70; Nom.loc. lines 271, 307–11), v. 113 (Nom.loc. line 209), v. 115 (Nom.loc. line 121), v. 123 (Nom.loc. line 51), v. 124 (Nom.loc. line 312), v. 132 (Nom.loc. line 241), v. 139–40 (Retract.Act. [Act. 20] p. 156.9–10), v. 140 (Nom.loc. lines 207–8), v. 145 (Nom.loc. lines 123–5, 202–4; Comm.Epist.cath. [1 Petr. 1] p. 225.32), v. 149 (Nom.loc. lines 67–8), vi. 21 (Comm.Gen. p. 49.1550–3), vi. 186 (Exp.Act. [Act. 8] p. 41.74–5), viii. 5 (Comm.Cant.cant. p. 291.766–9),

viii. **25** (Comm.Epist.cath. [Iac. 3] p. 206.147–51), viii. **69** (Comm.Ezr. pp. 256.586–686), viii. **79** (Comm.Sam. p. 224.513), x. **3–5** (Comm.Luc. p. 322.1038–42), x. **52** (Comm.Cant.cant. p. 202.467–9), xii. **9** (Comm. Gen. p. 49.1555–7, 1559), xii. **26** (Comm.Cant.cant. p. 205.588–95), xii. **34** (Comm.Cant.cant. p. 267.989–901), xii. **43** (Comm.Cant.cant. p. 265.839–42), xii. **54** (Comm.Cant.cant. p. 206.644–55; Comm.Sam. p. 223.472), xii. **62** (Comm.Cant.cant. p. 285.553–5), xiii. **2** (Comm. Cant.cant. p. 264.800–1), xiii. **10** (Retract.Act. [Act. 20] p. 156.11), xv. **16** (Tabernac. p. 12.271), xvi. **9** (Retract.Act. [Act. 14] p. 148.3–4), xviii. **23** (DO line 1054), xix. **1** (Tabernac. p. 45.135), xxiv. **11** (Comm.Cant.cant. p. 210.776–7), xxiv. **18** (Comm.Sam. p. 146.382–7), xxv. **94** (Comm. Cant.cant. p. 336.782–3), xxx. **8** (DO line 1175), xxxi. **46** (Comm.Cant. cant. p. 128.146–54), xxxv. **13** (DO line 227), xxxv. **13–15** (Comm.Gen. pp. 158–60.580–662), xxxvi. **12** (Comm.Luc. p. 166.19–23; Comm.Marc. p. 606.434–8), xxxvii. **24** (Comm.Gen. pp. 49–50.1562–6), xxxvii. **25–6** (Comm.Gen. p. 50.1568–9), xxxvii. **34** (Comm.Gen. p. 50.1570–1)

Polemius Silvius
[206] *Laterculus*: DTR xi.22–9, 88–96, xiv.16–22

Pompeius
[207] *Comm. in artem Donati*: DAM i.22–5, ii. 13–14, iii.41–2, xii.42–9, xiv.13–19; DO lines 42, 79, 386, 680, 829, 854; DST i.20–4, 25, 42–3, 51–2, 56–7, 90–2

Possidius
[208] *Vita S. Augustini*: cc. xxii (VCP c. 16), xxviii (DTR lxvi.1580), xxix (DTR lxvi.1584, 1586; VCP c. 38), lii (Comm.Prov. p. 123.98–9)

Primasius of Hadrumentum
[209] *Comm. in Apocalypsin*: Exp. Apoc. (*passim* [488×])

Priscian
[210] *Institutiones grammaticae*: DO (*passim* [80×])
[211] *Partitiones duodecim uersuum Aeneidos principalium*: DO lines 265, 586, 863, 971

Probus
[212] *Catholica*: DO lines 205, 238, 888–92
[213] *Instituta artium*: DO lines 86, 102, 560, 1140

Prosper of Aquitaine
[214] *Epigrammata ex sententiis S. Augustini*: **praef.** 7–8 (DAM iii.74–5), v. **5–6** (DAM vii.40–1), viii. **7** (DAM xiii.15), xv. **4** (DAM xiv.35), xix. **1** (DAM xiii.11), xxix. **1** (DAM xi.58), xxxi. **3–4** (DAM ii.91–2), xl. **3**

(DAM xiii.75), xli. 1–2 (DAM xi.60–1), xliii. 3–4 (DAM xiii.20–1), liii.
5–6 (DAM x.53–4), liii. 7–8 (DAM x.58–9), lxiv. 3 (DAM xiv.44), lxvii.
3–4 (DAM iii.135–6), lxxii. 1–2 (DAM xiii.27–8), xci. 9 (DAM vii.38),
xcii. 1–2 (DAM iii.107–8), cii. 17–18 (DAM xiii.56–7), ciii. 10 (VCM
12), civ. 5 (DAM xii.22)

[215] *Epigrammata in obtrectatorem Augustini*: HE i.10

[216] *Epitome chronicorum*: HE i.17; Ep.Pleg. line 27; DTR lxvi.1203–4,
1390, 1468–70, 1494–5, 1519–20, 1542, 1574–5, 1585, 1591–2

Prudentius

[217] *Apotheosis*: 36 (VCM 180)

[218] *Contra Symmachum*: ii. 707 (VCM 702)

[219] *Liber cathemerinon*: iv. 74 (VCM 970)

[220] *Liber peristephanon*: v. 267 (DO line 145), viii. 7 (VCM 723), xiii. 44
(VCM 702); Mart.

[221] *Psychomachia*: **praef.** 1–4 (DAM xx.9–12), **98** (DAM xiv.64), **594**
(DAM xiv.66), **803** (DDI 22), **876** (VCM 183)

Quoduultdeus

[222] *Sermo contra quinque haereses*: c. v (Coll. 1)

Sallust

[223] *Bellum Iugurthinum*: cc. **xxxi** (DO line 829), lxxviii (Exp.Act. [Act. 27]
p. 94.20–2)

Sedulius, Caelius

[224] *Carmen paschale*: i. **2** (DAM xi.32), i. **16** (DAM xi.34), i. **17** (DAM
xii.27–8), i. **18** (DAM xii.34–5), i. **25** (DAM iii.38), i. **34** (DAM xii.37), i.
121–6 (DAM xi.7–12), i. **132** (DAM xi.52), i. **136** (DAM xi.26; DST
i.121), i. **140** (DAM xi.28), i. **159** (DAM xii.39) i. **162** (DAM xi. 30; VCM
74), i. **170** (DAM xiii.43), i. **179** (VCM 668), i. **184–7** (Quaest.Reg. qu.
xxviii.17–20), i. **232** (VCM 828), i. **290** (DAM iii.57, xiv.33), i. **319–20**
(DAM iii.99–100), i. **321** (DAM xv.46), i. **368** (VCM 715), ii. 24 (DO line
1227), ii. **36** (DAM iii.85), ii. **63–8** (Comm.Luc. p. 237.246–51), ii. **72**
(VCM 666), ii. **74** (DAM iii.82), ii. **77** (DAM xiii.40), ii. **209** (DAM iii.7),
ii. **215** (DO line 202), ii. **249** (DAM iii. 34), iii. **15** (Exp.Apoc. xxxviii.97),
iii. **51–2** (VCM 154–5), iii. **84** (DAM iii.16), iii. **92** (VCM 876–7), iii. **235**
(DO line 385), iii. **296** (DAM iii.18), iv. **46** (DAM iii.59), v. **8** (DAM
xv.53), v. **59** (DAM vii.44), v. **188–95** (Comm.Luc. p. 401.1537–44), v.
191 (DAM iii.83), v. **196** (DAM xv.56), v. **337** (VCM 829)

[225] *Hymni*: i. **1–2** (DAM x.49–50), i. **5** (DAM xiii.52), i. **109** (DAM
xv.38), i. **110** (DAM xv.40), ii. **1–2** (DAM xxi.5–6)

Sergius

[226] *Comm. de littera, de syllaba, de pedibus, de accentibus, de distinctione*:

DAM i.31–2, 40–3, ii.3–5, 9–11, 21–3, 30–1, iii.2, 8–9, 14–15, 17, 27, 30–
3, 77–9, 97–8, 101, 109–11, 113, 119–20, 126, ix.2–4; DO line 382
[227] *Explanationes in artem Donati*: DAM x.26–32; DO lines 42, 790, 1130–2

Servius

[228] *Comm. in artem Donati*: DAM iii.30–3, 52, 56, 58, 65–8, 97–8, 101,
109–11, 113, iv.22, vi.50–4; DO lines 158, 560, 680, 829
[229] *De centum metris*: DAM viii.8, 9–12, 20–7, xxiv.4
[230] *De finalibus metrorum*: DAM iv.17–21, 25, 26–36, 38–9, v.2–22, vi.3–9,
9–13, 21–3, 27–30, 30–45, 49–50, 54–8, 59–69, 70–6, 77–85, vii.12–14,
19–21, 25–8, 30–6, viii.3–4, 4–7

Solinus

[231] *Collectanea rerum memorabilium*: cc. xv (Exp.Apoc. xxxvii.164–5, 167–
8), xxii (DNR ix.1, 15–16; DTR xxxi.70–2, xxxiv.59–60; HE i.1), xxx
(Exp.Apoc. xxxvii.305–10), lii (Exp.Apoc. xxxvii.140–2)

Statius

[232] *Thebais*: ii. 1 (VCM 103), ii. 416 (DDI 68), ii. 672–3 (VCM 343), vii.
108 (VCM 352), viii. 665 (VCM 240), x. 284 (VCM 159), x. 382 (VCM
932)

Terence

[233] *Comoediae*: *Andria*: v. 4 [line 940] (DO line 1030); *Eunuchus*: prol. 41
(Comm.Luc. p. 5.20)

Tyconius

[234] *Comm. in Apocalypsin*: Exp. Apoc. (*passim* [108×])

Vegetius, Flavius Renatus

[235] *Epitome rei militaris*: i. 24 (HE i.5), ii. 25 (Retract.Act. [Act. 27]
p. 162.33–4), iv. 35 (DTR xxviii.22–32), iv. 38 (DNR xxvii.9–11), iv. 40–
1 (DTR xxv.15–26), iv. 41 (DNR xxxvi.1), iv. 42 (DNR xxxix.1; DTR
xxix.4–5; VCP c. 17)

Venantius Fortunatus

[236] *Carmina*: v. 5. 47 (VCM 281), v. 5. 167 (VCM 300), viii. 3. 1 (DAM
x.17), viii. 3. 2 (DAM x.25), viii. 3. 3 (HE i.7), viii. 3. 7 (DAM iii.40),
viii. 3. 25 (DAM xii.20), viii. 3. 35 (DAM xv.28), viii. 3. 67 (VCM 251),
viii. 3. 99–100 (DAM xi.43–4), viii. 3. 127–8 (DAM xi.46–7), viii. 3. 144
(DAM xiv.27), viii. 3. 153 (VCM 19), viii. 3. 154 (DAM xiv.98), viii. 3.
237–8 (DAM xi.40–1), viii. 3. 264 (DAM iii. 32), viii. 3. 279–80 (DAM
xiv.39–40), viii. 3. 296 (Exp.Apoc. iv. 40), viii. 3. 328 (VCM 700–1), viii.
3. 385 (DO line 1229), viii. 5. 5 (VCM 111)
[237] *Vita S. Martini*: iv. 294 (VCM 98)

Vergil

[238] *Aeneis*: i. 119 (DAM ii.28), i. 162 (VCM 804), i. 374 (DTR vii.72), i.
417 (Comm.Gen. pp. 143–4.68–70), i. 453 (DO line 1014), i. 659 (DO line
817), i. 723–4 (Comm.Cant.cant. p. 317.96–7), i. 750 (DO line 999), ii. 16
(DAM xiv.7), ii. 54 (Comm.Marc. p. 502.516), ii. 71–2 (DO lines 1003–
4), ii. 98–9 (DO line 1208), ii. 109 (VCM 724), ii. 153 (VCM 783–4), ii.
244 (VCM 847), ii. 250–1 (DTR vii.7–8), ii. 488 (VCM 28), ii. 492–3
(DAM xiv.9–10), ii. 542 (VCM 892), ii. 687 (VCM 48), iii. 5 (DO line
1016), iii. 121 (DAM xvi.44), iii. 126–7 (Templ. p. 156.378–9), iii. 237
(DO line 620), iii. 270 (DAM ii.39), iii. 435 (DO line 819), iii. 436 (DAM
xvi.35), iii. 467 (Comm.Sam. p. 148.461), iii. 659 (VCM 76), iv. 99–100
(VCM 428), iv. 228 (DDI 45), v. 186 (DAM xiii.65), v. 189 (DAM iii.45),
v. 374 (VCM 228), v. 381 (VCM 228), v. 546 (DO line 891), v. 547 (VCM
918), v. 629 (DAM xv.12), v. 723 (VCM 848), vi. 179 (DAM iv.23–4), vi.
302 (DO line 1024), vi. 408 (VCM 282), vi. 560–1 (DO line 1241), vi. 597
(DO line 1239), vi. 676 (DO line 562), vi. 731–2 (Tabernac. p. 12.304–5),
vi. 732 (VCM 934–5), vi. 791 (DAM iii.102), vi. 794–5 (DO line 1010),
vi. 796–800 (Comm.Gen. p. 48.1525–6), vii. 277 (DO line 1186), vii. 298
(DO line 1121), vii. 378 (DO lines 1190, 1217), vii. 478 (VCM 730), vii.
634 (DAM xvi.8), viii. 97 (Comm.Gen. p. 16.435), viii. 251 (DO line
1008), ix. 168 (DO line 1006), ix. 325 (DO line 1183), ix. 358 (DO line
1187), ix. 411 (VCM 2), ix. 430 (DAM v.17–18), ix. 503 (DAM xvi.6), ix.
610 (DAM iii.22), x. 42 (DO line 1001), x. 530 (VCM 81), x. 608 (VCM
901), x. 640 (Comm.Epist.cath. [2 Petr. 1] p. 268.266), x. 777 (DO lines
881–2), xi. 5 (DDI 2), xi. 507 (DO line 491), xi. 721 (DO line 138), xi. 733
(VCM 260), xi. 774–5 (DO line 208), xii. 84 (Quaest.Reg. qu. viii.19), xii.
208 (DO line 1127), xii. 287–8 (DO line 1012), xii. 661 (DO line 814), xii.
899–900 (Comm.Gen. p. 100.986), xii. 931 (DO line 875)

[239] *Bucolica*: i. 60 (VCM 885), ii. 11 (DO line 101), ii. 22 (Comm.Prov.
p. 136.102), ii. 65 (DAM iii.80), iii. 63 (Comm.Cant.cant. p. 291.756), iii.
69 (DO line 906), iii. 79 (DAM xvi.39), iii. 92–3 (Comm.Cant.cant.
p. 167.8–9), iii. 96 (DAM xiv.46), v. 82 (DO line 1115), viii. 108 (DAM
xvi.41), ix. 1 (DAM xxv.11), ix. 18 (VCM 59), ix. 23 (DO line 379), ix.
51–2 (DO line 1069), x. 12 (DAM xvi.43), x. 69 (DAM iii.25)

[240] *Georgica*: i. 4 (DAM xvi.37), i. 85 (VCM 333), i. 92–3 (VCM 899), i.
173 (DO line 236), i. 224 (VCM 415), i. 231–2 (DTR xvi.71–2), i. 233–4
(DTR xxxiv.50–1), i. 235–6 (DTR xxxiv.58–9), i. 237–8 (DTR xxxiv.61–
2), i. 260 (VCM 417), i. 330 (DDI 51), i. 351 (VCM 711), i. 352 (DAM
xvi.25), i. 371 (DAM xvi.32), i. 397 (DAM xiv.12), i. 482 (DAM xiv.20),
ii. 117–19 (Comm.Gen. p. 1434.68–70), ii. 349–53 (Comm.Gen.
p. 117.1589–94), ii. 480 (DTR xxix.29–30), iii. 357 (VCM 268), iii.
384–5 (DAM xvi.27–8), iii. 389 (DAM viii.24, xiv.48), iii. 414–15
(Comm.Cant.cant. p. 210.771–2), iii. 449 (DO line 1029), iii. 450 (DO
line 1243), iii. 537 (Comm.Gen. p. 30.904–5), iii. 548 (DAM viii.22), iv.

34 (DAM xv.19), iv. **88** (DO line 105), iv. **125** (DO line 694), iv. **392-3** (DDI 67)

Victorinus, C. Marius

[241] *Ars grammatica*: DAM iii.14–15, 55–6, 115–16; x.16, 26–32, 44–59; xii.28–30; DO lines 140, 256, 273, 333, 382, 680, 739, 918, 1140

[242] *Explanationes in Ciceronis Rhetoricam*: i. **4** (Comm.Gen. p. 216.800–1)

Virgilius Maro Grammaticus

[243] *Epitomae*: v. **13** (DO line 283), vii. **8** (DO lines 290–3), viii. **4** (DO lines 284–9)

ANONYMOUS WRITINGS

[244] *Adhortationes sanctorum patrum (Verba seniorum)*: iii. **1** (*Mart.* [Quentin p. 99])

[245] *Ars Asperi grammatici*: DO lines 190, 563, 680, 1074

[246] *Carmen de resurrectione mortuorum*: lines **143** (DDI 65), **253** (VCM 12)

[247] *Gesta Siluestri*: Mart. (Quentin p. 92)

[248] *Liber de ordine creaturarum* [pseudo-Isidore]: ii. **9** (DNR xxv.3–7), iii. **4** (DNR xxv.16–17), iii. **5** (DNR vii.6–7), iv. **5–6** (DNR iv.2–9), iv. **8** (DNR viii.8–9), vi. **7** (DNR xxv.3–7), vii. **4** (DNR xxv.10–13), vii. **5** (DNR xxxiii.2–4), vii. **6** (DNR xxxiv.2–4, xxxv.2–3), ix. **1–4** (DNR xxxviii.2–10), ix. **7** (DNR xxxix.12–13), xi. **1** (DNR xlv.6–9), xi. **2** (Comm.Gen. p. 93.729–33)

[249] *Liber pontificalis*: DTR lxvi.1109–11, 1144–6, 1164–5, 1180–2, 1232–2, 1242–3, 1266–8, 1284–9, 1374–6, 1399–1402, 1403–4, 1404–7, 1407–8, 1412–14, 1414–16, 1417, 1893–5, 1895–7, etc.; HE i.4, i.23, ii.1, ii.4; Mart. (Quentin pp. 102–4); Comm.Marc. p. 638.1676–8.

[250] *Martyrologium Hieronymianum* [pseudo-Jerome]: Comm.Marc. p. 512.911–13; Mart. (Quentin pp. 109–12); Retract.Act. [Act. 1] pp. 106–7.57–60

[251] *passiones apostolorum*: Passio S. Marci euangelistae [BHL 5276]: Mart. (Quentin pp. 85–6)

[252] *passiones martyrum*: Passio S. Agathae [BHL 133]: Mart. (Quentin p. 57); Passio S. Agnetis [BHL 156]: Mart. (Quentin pp. 57–8); Passio S. Albani [cf. BHL 210d]: HE i.7; Passio SS. Alexandri papae, Euentii et Theoduli [BHL 266]: Mart. (Quentin p. 58); Passio S. Anastasiae [BHL 1795 + 118 + 8093 + 401]: Mart. (Quentin pp. 58–60); Passio S. Anastasii Persae [BHL 410b]: revised by Bede (see HE v.24) as BHL 408; Passio SS. Andochii, Thyrsi et Felicis [BHL 424]: Mart. (Quentin pp. 60–2), Passio S. Apollinaris [BHL 623]: Mart. (Quentin pp. 63–4); Passio S. Benigni [BHL 1153]: Mart. (Quentin pp. 61–2); Passio S. Caeciliae [BHL 1495]: Mart. (Quentin p. 64); Passio S. Caesarii [BHL 1511]: Mart. (Quentin pp. 64–6); Passio S. Callisti papae [BHL 1523]: Mart. (Quentin pp. 66–7);

Passio S. Cassiani [BHL 1626]: Mart. (Quentin p. 68); *Passio S. Clementis papae* [BHL 1848]: Mart. (Quentin pp. 68–9); *Passio S. Cornelii papae* [BHL 1958]: Mart. (Quentin p. 69); *Passio SS. Cosmae et Damiani* [BHL 1967]: Mart. (Quentin p. 70); *Passio S. Eulaliae* [BHL 2696]: Mart. (Quentin p. 71); *Passio S. Euphemiae* [BHL 2708]: Mart. (Quentin pp. 71–2); *Passio S. Eupli* [BHL 2729]: Mart. (Quentin p. 72); *Passio SS. Faustae et Euilasii* [BHL 2833]: Mart. (Quentin pp. 72–3); *Passio S. Felicis ep. Tubzacensis* [BHL 2894]: Mart. (Quentin p. 74); *Passio S. Felicitatis* [BHL 2853]: Mart. (Quentin pp. 73–4); *Passio SS. Ferreoli et Ferrutionis* [BHL 2903]: Mart. (Quentin pp. 74–5); *Passio SS. Gallicani, Iohannis et Pauli* [BHL 3236, 3238]: Mart. (Quentin p. 75); *Acta S. Ianuarii* [BHL 4132]: Mart. (Quentin pp. 75–7); *Passio S. Iulianae* [BHL 4522]: Mart. (Quentin p. 77); *Passio S. Luciae* [BHL 4992]: Mart. (Quentin p. 81); *Passio S. Marcelli papae* [BHL 5234–5]: Mart. (Quentin pp. 82–5); *Passio SS. Marcellini et Petri* [BHL 5231]: Mart. (Quentin p. 82); *Passio SS. Marii et Marthae* [BHL 5543], which includes the *Passio S. Valentini* [BHL 8460]: Mart. (Quentin pp. 86–7); *Passio S. Pancratii* [BHL 6420]: Mart. (Quentin p. 87); *Passio SS. Perpetuae et Felicitatis* [BHL 6633]: Mart. (Quentin pp. 87–8); *Passio S. Phocae* [BHL 6838]: Mart. (Quentin p. 88); the *Passio S. Polochronii* [BHL 6884], which includes the *Passio SS. Abdon et Sennen* [BHL 6], the *Passio S. Laurentii* [BHL 4753], etc.: Mart. (Quentin pp. 77–81); *Passio S. Procopii* [BHL 6949]: Mart. (Quentin p. 89); *Passio SS. Quadraginta martyrum Sebastenorum* [BHL 7539]: Mart. (Quentin pp. 90–1); *Passio S. Quintini* [BHL 6999–7000]: Mart. (Quentin p. 89); *Passio SS. Scillitanorum* [BHL 7531]: Mart. (Quentin pp. 89–90); *Passio S. Sebastiani* [BHL 7543]: Mart. (Quentin pp. 91–2); *Passio SS. Speusippi, Eleusippi et Meleusippi* [BHL 7829]: Mart. (Quentin pp. 62–3); *Passio S. Symphorosae* [BHL 7971]: Mart. (Quentin pp. 92–3); *Passio SS. Victoriae et Anatholiae* [BHL 8591 + 418]: Mart. (Quentin pp. 95–7); *Passio SS. Victoris et Coronae* [BHL 8559]: Mart. (Quentin pp. 94–5)

[253] *Pastor Hermae*: Exp.Act. [Act. 12] p. 59.55–7

[254] *Recognitiones*, trans. Rufinus [pseudo–Clement]: i. 27 (Comm.Gen. p. 12.309–22), i. 65 (Exp.Act. [Act. 5] p. 31.71–4; Retract.Act. [Act. 5] p. 129.38–40); vi. 7 (DTR v.61–9), viii. 23 (DNR xxvi.4–6, xliii.1), viii. 24 (DNR xxxviii.2–10), viii. 42 (DNR xxxi.2–6), viii. 45 (DTR vii.51–9)

[255] *uitae sanctorum*: *Vita S. Lupi Trecensis* [BHL 5087]: HE i.21

d. Alcuin of York

Like Bede before him, Alcuin (d. 804) was a scholar of immense erudition. However, the difficulty with using Alcuin as evidence for books known in Anglo-Saxon England is that, although he was trained at York, he spent the greater part of his documented career on the Continent, at the (largely peripatetic) court of the emperor Charlemagne, from approximately 782 to

790, and again from 793 until his death in 804. (He spent the years 790–3 in Northumbria.) Only a tiny proportion of his vast literary output is thought to have been composed in England, but it is on this tiny proportion that any assessment of the books available to Alcuin at York must be based. Two works are in question: his poem on 'the saints of York', the *Versus de patribus, regibus et sanctis Euboricensis ecclesiae* [CSLMA ALC 87 (pp. 495–7); ICL 2176] and his collectaneum entitled *De laude Dei* [CSLMA ALC 30 (pp. 140–1)]. Of these, the York poem appears to have been composed before Alcuin's departure for the Continent in 782, and was supplemented in 790–3 (lines 1596–1657 are evidently a later addition to the poem). It is not possible to establish the date of *De laude Dei*: it was probably compiled at various times during his career at York, and then, to judge by its manuscript transmission, sent to him by his York students when he had returned to the Continent.

i. Alcuin's poem on the saints of York

Alcuin was trained at York by Ælberht, who subsequently became archbishop of York (in 766). When, in old age, Ælberht withdrew from the world in 778 to spend the last years of his life in prayer, he bequeathed his substantial library to his former pupil Alcuin. In his discussion of Ælberht in his poem on the saints of York, Alcuin gives an impressionistic record of these books (lines 1540–56). The list should not be treated as an exhaustive inventory of authors represented in Ælberht's library (a number of names would not have fitted into a hexameter), but it gives us a useful indication of what authors (if not what texts) were available at York in the third quarter of the eighth century. (Alcuin subsequently had the books shipped to him on the Continent, whence the library was dispersed.) Alcuin lists the names of forty authors whose works were represented in Ælberht's library. In cases where an author is known to have composed only one work, identification is straightforward; but in cases of voluminous authors such as Ambrose, Augustine, Gregory, or Jerome, it is simply not possible to determine what works may have been in question. I have arranged the authors' names in a numerical list (following the order in which they occur in the poem) for purposes of indexing; the names are followed by the line numbers in which they occur. Anyone wishing to read the names as they are preserved in Alcuin's hexameters can consult MGH, PLAC i. 203–4, or 'Booklists', 45–9.

[1] **Hieronymus** (1540): CPL 580–621.
[2] **Hilarius** (1540): CPL 427–64.
[3] **Ambrosius praesul** (1541): CPL 123–65.
[4] **Augustinus** (1541): CPL 250–359.
[5] **Athanasius** (1542): presumably the *Vita S. Antonii*, trans. Evagrius.
[6] **Orosius** (1542): the *Historiae aduersum paganos*.
[7] **Gregorius summus** (1543): Gregory the Great [CPL 1708–14].

[8] **Leo papa** (1543): either the *Epistulae* or the *Sermones*, both of which were apparently known to Bede.

[9] **Basilius** (1544): of the works of Basil which were available and widely circulated in Latin translation, the *Hom. in Hexaemeron*, trans. Eustathius, a work frequently used by Bede, or perhaps the *Asceticon paruum* or *Regula S. Basilii*, trans. Rufinus or *Sermo* xii (*De ascetica disciplina*), both of which circulated in Latin translation.

[10] **Fulgentius** (1544): presumably Fulgentius of Ruspe, either the treatise *Ad Thrasamundum*, a work apparently known to Bede, or (less likely) the *De fide ad Petrum*.

[11] **Cassiodorus** (1545): probably the *Expositio psalmorum*, the most widely circulated of Cassiodorus' writings; less likely the *De anima* or *Institutiones*.

[12] **Chrysostomus . . . Iohannes** (1545): there is no evidence for the transmission of the Greek writings of John Chrysostom in Alcuin's York; possibly what is in question is the Latin translation of the *Hom. in Matthaeum* [CPG 4424], but other of his works were available in Latin translation as well [see CPG 4305, 4308, 4309, 4316, etc.].

[13] **Althelmus** (1546): Aldhelm of Malmesbury [CPL 1331–5].

[14] **Beda magister** (1546): Bede of Monkwearmouth-Jarrow [CPL 1343–82, 2318–23].

[15] **Victorinus** (1547): given the context of logical writings, the author is presumably C. Marius Victorinus and the work in question possibly his *De definitionibus*.

[16] **Boetius** (1547): again, judging from context, the reference is to (some of) Boethius' logical writings [CPL 881–9], rather than to *De consolatione Philosophiae*.

[17] **Pompeius** (1548): Pompeius Trogus, whose *Historiae Philippicae* is not extant, but is known through the *Epitome* of Iustinus.

[18] **Plinius** (1548): presumably Pliny the Elder, whose *Naturalis historia* is listed inappropriately by Alcuin among *historici ueteres*. Various properly historical works by Pliny, such as a *Bellum Germanicum* and *Historiae* (from Claudius to Titus) did not survive into the Middle Ages, and therefore cannot be in question here.

[19] **Aristoteles** (1549): presumably the Latin translation either of the *Categoriae* or the *De interpretatione*.

[20] **rhetor . . . Tullius** (1549): i.e. Cicero (M. Tullius Cicero); given the context, the reference is to (some of) Cicero's rhetorical writings, perhaps the *De inuentione* or the *De oratore*.

[21] **Sedulius** (1550): i.e. Caelius Sedulius, presumably (given the context) the *Carmen paschale*, which Alcuin excerpted in *De laude Dei* (below, no. 55).

[22] **Iuuencus** (1550): the *Euangelia*, which Alcuin excerpted in *De laude Dei* (below, no. 52).

[23] **Alcimus** (1551): i.e. Avitus (Alcimus Ecdicius Avitus), presumably the *Carmina de spiritalis historiae gestis*.

[24] **Clemens** (1551): i.e. Prudentius (Aurelius Prudentius Clemens) [CPL 1437–45].

[25] **Prosper** (1551): i.e. Prosper of Aquitaine, presumably his *Epigrammata ex sententiis S. Augustini*, which Alcuin excerpted in *De laude Dei* (below, no. 53).

[26] **Paulinus** (1551): i.e. Paulinus of Nola, presumably his *Carmina*.

[27] **Arator** (1551): the *Historia apostolica*, which Alcuin excerpted in *De laude Dei* (below, no. 42).

[28] **Fortunatus** (1552): presumably the *Carmina* of Venantius Fortunatus, which Alcuin excerpted in *De laude Dei* (below, no. 56).

[29] **Lactantius** (1552): given the context, presumably the poem *De aue Phoenice* of Lactantius Firmianus.

[30] **Maro Virgilius** (1553): Vergil.

[31] **Statius** (1553): at this date probably the *Thebais* (the *Siluae* seem from other evidence to have been unknown in Anglo-Saxon England, and the *Achilleis* only makes an entrance during the eleventh century).

[32] **Lucanus** (1553): presumably Lucan's *Bellum ciuile*.

[33] **Probus** (1555): possibly the *Catholica* or the *Instituta artium*, both of which may have been known to Bede.

[34] **Focas** (1555): Phocas, *Ars de nomine et uerbo*.

[35] **Donatus** (1555): presumably the *Ars maior*.

[36] **Priscianus** (1555): Priscian, possibly the extensive *Institutiones grammaticae*, or the much more compact *Institutio de nomine, pronomine et uerbo*.

[37] **Seruius** (1556): possibly a genuine work of Servius, but equally possibly one of the several grammatical treatises which travelled under the name of Sergius.

[38] **Euticius** (1556): presumably Eutyches, *Ars de uerbo*.

[39] **Pompeius** (1556): *Comm. in artem Donati*.

[40] **Comminianus** (1556): a late Latin grammarian whose writings are not extant, and are known only through Charisius, *Ars grammatica*.

ii. Alcuin's collectaneum *De laude Dei*

This collectaneum, the title of which is given in manuscript as *De laude Dei et de confessione orationibusque sanctorum collecti ab Alchonio* [leg. *Alcuino*] *leuita libri IV*, is preserved in two manuscripts: Bamberg, Staatsbibliothek, Misc. patr. 17 (s. x), fos. 133–62; and El Escorial, Real Biblioteca de San Lorenzo, B. IV. 17 (southern France, s. ix^{med}), fos. 93–108. The collectaneum, which has exceptional interest for the study of Alcuin and of the church in early Northumbria, is unfortunately unprinted (thus it is welcome news that an edition is in preparation by David Ganz and Susan Rankin); what follows relies on the description of the contents of the Bamberg manuscript by Constantinescu, 'Alcuin et les "Libelli precum"'. (The Escorial manuscript has not been described accurately in print; the following folio references pertain solely to the Bamberg manuscript.) Basically, the collectaneum is divided into four books, of which Books I and II consist of biblical extracts: Book I (fos. 133ᵛ–137ʳ: Genesis to Habacuc); II (fos. 137ʳ–142ʳ: Psalms to Maccabees). Book III (fos. 142ᵛ–145ᵛ) begins with New Testament extracts (Matthew to Revelation), but at fo. 145ᵛ the biblical excerpts end, and a series of hagiographical excerpts, entitled *De martirologio*, for the most part consisting of prayers, begins. It is the contents of the latter part of Book III, and of the entirety of Book IV, which provide evidence of the library from which Alcuin, working at York *c.*790, was able to draw the materials which constitute his collectaneum *De laude Dei*. Because *De laude Dei* has not been printed, I instead give references to page numbers of Constantinescu's article, where the excerpts are identified and discussed and folio references to the Bamberg manuscript are given (Constantinescu was unaware of the existence of the Escorial manuscript).

Aldhelm of Malmesbury
[41] *Carmen de uirginitate* [CPL 1333]: praef. 11–18; 1–16, 32–44, 2813–28, 2871–2904 (p. 56)

Arator
[42] *Historia apostolica*: *Epist. ad Vigilium* 11–26, i. 481–4, 1007–9, 1012–17, ii. 579–83 (p. 55)

Augustine
[43] *Confessiones*: i. 6, i. 9, ii. 15, iii. 19, iv. 1, iv. 4, iv. 14, iv. 31, v. 1, v. 14, v. 17, vi. 4. vi. 9, vii. 8, vii. 12, vii. 16 (p. 31)
[44] *De trinitate*: xv. 28 (p. 32)
[45] *Soliloquia*: i. 2. 2–6 (pp. 31, 33–4)

Bede
[46] *Soliloquium de psalmo .xli.* [CPL 1371a; ICL 2131] (p. 56)
[47] *Carmen de psalmo .cxii.* [CPL 1371c; ICL 8705] (p. 56)

Dracontius
[48] *Laudes Dei*: ii. 1–46, 66–97, 101–6, 115–46, 208–24; iii. 1–23, 25–6, 125–7, 530–46, 548–57, 564–98, 613–19, 625–30, 632–49, 662–4, 666–77, 720–6 (p. 56)

Eusebius of Caesarea
[49] *Historia ecclesiastica*, trans. Rufinus: iv. 15 (p. 24), x. 3 [Rufinus] (p. 25)

Gregory the Great
[50] *Hom. in Hiezechielem*: i. 2 (p. 27), ii. 10 (p. 27)

Isidore
[51] *Synonyma*: i. 29, 44, 55, 58–60, 63–7, 69–72, 74, ii. 60 (pp. 30–1)

Juvencus
[52] *Euangelia*: **praef.** 1–27 (p. 55)

Prosper of Aquitaine
[53] *Epigrammata ex sententiis S. Augustini*: **praef.** 1, 3–4, 7; iii. 1–14, viii. 1–
6, xii. 3–6, xxii. 5–6, xxx. 5–6, xxxvii. 1–6, xxxix. 5–6, xli. 1–6, lv. 1–6,
lvi. 1–4, lvii. 1–4, lviii. 1–2, lxv. 1–6, lxix. 1–2, lxxxii. 1–2, xcvii. 1–2,
xcix. 5–6, ciii. 1–6, civ. 1–8, cv. 1–8 (p. 55)
[54] *Poema coniugis ad uxorem*: 79–90, 97–9, 113–14 (p. 56)

Sedulius, Caelius
[55] *Carmen paschale*: i. 60–101, 282–90, 343–63 (p. 55)

Venantius Fortunatus
[56] *Carmina*: viii. 3. 1–22, 25, 28, 129–278, 394–400 (p. 55)

ANONYMOUS WRITINGS
[57] *Adhortationes sanctorum patrum (Verba seniorum)*: v. 5 (pp. 27–30)
[58] *passiones martyrum* (pp. 26–7): *Passio S. Agathae* [BHL 133], *Passio
S. Agnetis* [BHL 156], *Passio SS. Cosmae et Damiani* [BHL 1967], *Passio
S. Iulianae* [BHL 4522], *Passio SS. Marii et Marthae* [BHL 5543], which
includes the *Passio S. Valentini* [BHL 8460], and the *Passio S. Polochronii*
[BHL 6884], which includes the *Passio SS. Abdon et Sennen* [BHL 6], the
Passio S. Laurentii [BHL 4753], etc.

e. The Old English Martyrology

The so-called *Old English Martyrology* is a narrative or historical martyrology
consisting of 238 chapters, each devoted to the commemoration of a
particular saint's day (arranged in calendar order). The language of the
text as it is preserved has suggeseted to students of Old English an origin in
the ninth century, perhaps during the reign of King Alfred (871–99). The
essential question is whether the text was compiled by the ninth-century
author writing in English but basing himself on disparate and numerous
Latin sources (principally *passiones* of martyrs and Lives of saints), or
whether it is simply an Old English translation of a pre-existing Latin
martyrology. I have stated above (pp. 42, 46–8) and argued elsewhere my
conviction that the work is an English translation of a martyrology compiled
by Bede's colleague Bishop Acca of Hexham during the years 731–40
(Lapidge, 'Acca of Hexham'). In any event, the work draws on a large
number of Latin sources, and thus throws light on the resources of a well-
stocked Anglo-Saxon library, whether at Hexham or elsewhere. The sources
used by this author, in the main hagiographical, have been carefully analysed
by Cross, 'On the Library of the Old English Martyrologist'. More recently,
the sources have been exhaustively studied by Christine Rauer as part of the

work of the project Fontes Anglo-Saxonici; there is a full listing of sources at ⟨http://fontes.english.ox.ac.uk⟩ (accessed 13 Dec. 2004), and a helpful overview in Rauer, 'The Sources of the *Old English Martyrology*'. The list which follows is closely based on the work of Cross and Rauer, but has been presented in the format used elsewhere in this Appendix, whereby references are given to the individual chapters of *The Old English Martyrology* (in the numbering of Kotzor's edition).

Adomnán of Iona
[1] *De locis sanctis*: i. 2 (c. 58), i. 11 (c. 111a), i. 23 (c. 79), ii. 2 (c. 1), ii. 3 (c. 1), ii. 4 (c. 200), ii. 5 (c. 200), ii. 6 (c. 1), ii. 9 (c. 53), ii. 26 (c. 56), iii. 3 (c. 56), iii. 4 (c. 67)

Aldhelm of Malmesbury
[2] *Carmen de uirginitate* [CPL 1333]: lines 460–78 (c. 5), 710–29 (c. 47), 790–1; (c. 16), 971–93 (c. 75), 1840–1 (c. 235), 1925–74 (c. 30), 2222–44 (c. 59), 2331–7 (c. 125), 2426–45 (c. 124)
[3] *De uirginitate* (prose) [CPL 1332]: cc. xxiii (c. 5), xxviii (c. 16), xxxii (c. 75), xxxv (c. 232), xxxvii (c. 47), xl (c. 156), xliii (c. 197), xlv (c. 30), xlvii (c. 130), l (c. 59), lii (c. 124)

Athanasius
[4] *Vita S. Antonii*, trans. Evagrius: cc. ii (c. 22), iv (c. 22), vi (c. 22), vii (c.22), viii (c. 22), x (c. 22), xi (c. 22), xiii (c. 22), xx (c. 22), lvi (c. 22), lix (c. 22), lxi (c. 22)

Augustine
[5] *Sermones*: cclxxxi (c. 39), cccix (c. 184)

Bede of Monkwearmouth-Jarrow
[6] *De temporum ratione* [CPL 1320]: cc. xii (cc. 36b, 58b, 73b, 94b, 116b, 139b, 171b, 200b, 217b), xv (cc. 8a, 58b, 73b, 94b, 116b, 139b, 171b, 200b, 217b, 233b), lxvi [= *Chronica maiora*] (cc. 22, 32, 39, 167, 218)
[7] *Historia abbatum* [CPL 1378]: cc. i (c. 17), ii (c. 17), iii (c. 17), iv (c. 17), vi (c. 17), vii (c. 40), viii (c. 40), xiv (c. 17), xv (c. 196), xvi (c. 196), xvii (c. 196), xxi (c. 196), xxii (c. 196), xxiii (c. 196)
[8] *Historia ecclesiastica gentis Anglorum* [CPL 1375]: i. 7 (c. 109), i. 17 (c. 141), ii. 2 (c. 92), ii. 3 (c. 92), iii. 3 (c. 171), iii. 4 (c. 100), iii. 6 (cc. 100, 146), iii. 9 (c. 146), iii. 11 (c. 146), iii. 12 (c. 146), iii. 13 (c. 146), iii. 15 (c. 171), iii. 17 (c. 171), iii. 19 (c. 21), iii. 23 (c. 214), iv. 3 (cc. 37, 214, 237), iv. 6 (c. 204), iv. 9 (c. 204), iv. 17 (c. 110), iv. 21 (c. 226), v. 2 (c. 81), v. 3 (c. 81), v. 4 (c. 81), v. 5 (c. 81), v. 9 (c. 100), v. 10 (c. 201)
[9] *Martyrologium* [CPL 2032]: cc. 16, 19, 126, 155, *et passim*
[10] *Vita S. Cudbercti* (prose) [CPL 1379; BHL 2021]: cc. iv (c. 171), vii

(c. 49), xvi (c. 14), xxxiv (c. 49), xxxv (c. 49), xl (c. 80), xlii (c. 80), xliii (c. 80), xlvi (c. 66)

[11] *Vita S. Felicis* [BHL 2873]: c. 19

Caesarius of Arles

[12] *Sermones*: ccvii (c. 78), ccviii (c. 78), ccxvi (c. 111)

Eucherius of Lyon

[13] *Passio Acaunensium martyrum*: c. 191

Eusebius of Caesarea

[14] *Historia ecclesiastica*, trans. Rufinus: i. 8 (c. 6), ii. 23 (c. 108), iii. 39 (c. 101), vi. 29 (c. 28), x. 15 [Rufinus] (c. 75)

Felix

[15] *Vita S. Guthlaci* [CPL 2150; BHL 3723]: cc. v (c. 63), vi (c. 63), vii (c. 63), x (c. 63), l (c. 63), liii (c. 15)

Gregory the Great

[16] *Dialogi*: ii prol. (c. 51), ii. 3 (c. 51), ii. 4 (c. 51), ii. 37 (c. 51), iii. 2 (c. 89), iv. 31 (c. 89)

[17] *Hom. .xl. in Euangelia*: i. 3 (c. 229), i. 10 (c. 56), ii. 32 (c. 117), ii. 37 (c. 115), ii. 38 (c. 11)

[18] *Moralia in Iob*: iii. 7 (c. 168)

Isidore of Seville

[19] *De ortu et obitu patrum*: cc. lxviii (c. 114), lxx (c. 233), lxxi (c. 135), lxxii (c. 5), lxxiv (c. 238), lxxvii (c. 108), lxxx (c. 215), lxxxii (c. 207)

Jerome

[20] *Vita S. Hilarionis*: cc. ii (cc. 173, 211), v (c. 211), xxi (c. 211), xliv (c. 211)

[21] *Vita S. Pauli primi eremitae*: cc. iv (c. 16), vi (c. 16), vii (c. 16), ix (c. 16), x (c. 16), xiv (c. 16), xvi (c. 16), xvii (c. 16)

Orosius, Paulus

[22] *Historiae aduersum paganos*: i. 1. 5–6 (c. 1), iv. 5. 2 (c. 1), v. 6. 3 (c. 1), v. 18. 4–5 (c. 1)

Paulinus of Milan

[23] *Vita S. Ambrosii*: cc. xlvii (c. 60), li (c. 60)

Petrus Chrysologus of Ravenna

[24] *Sermones*: xci (c. 111), clii (c. 6), clx (c. 12)

Stephen of Ripon

[25] *Vita S. Wilfridi* [CPL 2151; BHL 8889]: cc. i (c. 68), lvi (c. 68), lxv (c. 68)

Sulpicius Severus

[26] *Dialogi*: iii. 14 (c. 223)

[27] *Vita S. Martini*: cc. iii (c. 223), vii (c. 223), viii (c. 223), xviii (c. 223)

ANONYMOUS WRITINGS

[28] *Adhortationes sanctorum patrum (Verba seniorum)*: iii. 5 (c. 131), iv. 2 (c. 131)

[29] *Gesta Siluestri*: cc. 7, 161

[30] *Liber de ordine creaturarum* [pseudo-Isidore]: cc. 45, 46, 47, 50, 52, 53

[31] *Liber pontificalis*: cc. 10, 14, 20, 28, 86, 89, 91, 143, 147, 202, 205, 228

[32] *passiones apostolorum*: *Inuentio S. Crucis* [BHL 4169] (c. 77), *Inuentio capitis S. Iohannis baptistae* [BHL 4290] (c. 36), *Passio S. Andreae* [BHL 428] (c. 233); *Passio S. Bartholomaei* [BHL 1002] (c. 162), *Passio S. Iacobi minoris* [BHL 4093] (c. 108), *Passio S. Marci euangelistae* [BHL 5276] (c. 70), *Passio S. Matthaei* [BHL 5690] (c. 190), *Passio S. Philippi apostoli* [BHL 6814] (c. 74), *Passio SS. Simonis et Iudae* [BHL 7749–50] (c. 215), *Passio S. Thomae* [BHL 8136] (c. 238), *Reuelatio S. Stephani* [BHL 7851] (cc. 4, 145)

[33] *passiones martyrum*: *Passio SS. Abdon et Sennen* [BHL 6] (c. 139), *Passio S. Adriani* [BHL 3744] (c. 38), *Passio S. Afrae* [BHL 108–9, 111] (c. 149), *Passio SS. Agapes, Chioniae et Irenes* [BHL 118] (c. 59), *Passio S. Agnetis* [BHL 156] (cc. 30, 33), *Passio S. Alexandri papae* [BHL 266] (cc. 76, 166), *Passio S. Ananiae* [BHL 397] (c. 26), *Passio S. Anastasiae* [BHL 401] (cc. 2, 61, 144, 230), *Passio SS. Anatoliae et Audacis* [BHL 418] (c. 124), *Passio S. Andochii* [BHL 424] (cc. 160, 195), *Passio S. Antonini* [BHL 568] (c. 173), *Passio S. Apollinaris ep.* [BHL 623] (c. 134), *Passio S. Babylae* [BHL 890] (c. 34), *Passio S. Benigni* [BHL 1153] (c. 220), *Passio S. Caeciliae* [BHL 1495] (cc. 64, 227), *Passio S. Caesarii* [BHL 1511] (c. 219), *Passio S. Cassiani* [BHL 1626] (c. 155), *Passio S. Christinae* [BHL 1748b] (c. 130), *Passio S. Christophori* [BHL 1764] (c. 73), *Passio SS. Claudii, Nicostrati et soc.* [BHL 1836] (c. 222), *Passio S. Clementis papae* [BHL 1848] (c. 228), *Passio S. Columbae* [BHL 1892] (c. 8), *Passio S. Cornelii papae* [BHL 1958] (c. 183), *Passio SS. Cosmae et Damiani* [BHL 1970] (c. 198), *Passio S. Cypriani* [BHL 2038] (c. 184), *Passio SS. Cyriaci et Iulittae* [BHL 1802–8] (c. 127), *Passio SS. Dionysii, Rustici et Eleutherii* [BHL 2171] (c. 203), *Passio SS. Donati et Hilarini* [BHL 2289–92] (c. 148), *Passio S. Eleutherii* [BHL 2451] (c. 65), *Passio S. Erasmi* [BHL 2582] (c. 97), *Passio S. Eugeniae* [BHL 2666] (cc. 3, 90, 182), *Passio S. Eulaliae* [BHL 2696] (c. 234), *Passio S. Euphemiae* [BHL 2708] (c. 187), *Passio S. Eupli* [BHL 2729] (c. 153), *Passio S. Eusebii* [BHL 2748–9] (c. 142), *Passio SS.*

Faustae et Euilasii [BHL 2833] (c. 189), *Passio S. Felicis ep. Tubzacensis* [BHL 2895b] (c. 170), *Passio S. Felicitatis* [BHL 2853] (c. 123), *Passio SS. Ferreoli et Ferrutionis* [BHL 2903] (c. 103), *Passio S. Genesii notarii* [BHL 3304] (c. 212), *Passio S. Genesii mimi* [BHL 3320] (c. 163), *Passio S. Georgii* [BHL 3363] (cc. 67, 71), *Passio SS. Geruasii et Protasii* [BHL 3514] (cc. 72, 107, 236), *Passio S. Ianuarii* [BHL 4132] (cc. 188, 192), *Passio SS. Iohannis et Pauli* [BHL 3236, 3238] (c. 113), *Passio S. Irenaei* [BHL 4464] (c. 164), *Passio SS. Iuliani et Basilissae* [BHL 4529] (c. 13), *Passio S. Iusti* [BHL 4590] (c. 209), *Passio SS. Iustinae et Cypriani* [BHL 2047, 2050] (c. 197), *Passio S. Laurentii* [BHL 4753] (cc. 147, 150, 151, 154, 208, 213, 216), *Passio SS. Luceiae et Auceiae* [BHL 4980] (c. 112), *Passio S. Luciae* [BHL 4992] (c. 235), *Passio S. Mametis* [BHL 5194] (c. 157), *Passio S. Marcelli Cabillonensis* [BHL 5245] (c. 176), *Passio SS. Marcellini et Petri* [BHL 5231] (cc. 98, 99), *Passio S. Margaretae* [BHL 5303] (c. 122), *Passio S. Mennae* [BHL 5921] (c. 224), *Passio SS. Nazarii et Celsi* [BHL 6039] (c. 137), *Passio S. Pancratii* [BHL 6421] (c. 86), *Passio S. Perpetuae* [BHL 6633] (c. 39), *Passio S. Phocae* [BHL 6838] (c. 126), *Passio S. Procopii* [BHL 6949] (c. 121), *Passio SS. Quadraginta martyrum Sebastenorum* [BHL 7539] (c. 41), *Passio S. Quintini* [BHL 6999–7000] (c. 217), *Passio S. Saturnini* [BHL 7495–6] (c. 231), *Passio SS. martyrum Scillitanorum* [BHL 7531] (c. 128), *Passio S. Sebastiani* [BHL 7543] (cc. 27, 106, 118, 120, 152), *Passio S. Speusippi* [BHL 7828] (c. 23), *Passio S. Symphoriani* [BHL 7967–8] (c. 160), *Passio S. Symphorosae* [BHL 7971] (c. 129), *Passio S. Theclae* [BHL 8020n] (c. 193), *Passio S. Theodoreti* [BHL 8074] (c. 54), *Passio S. Valeriani* [BHL 8488] (c. 185), *Passio S. Victoris Mauri* [BHL 8580] (c. 83), *Passio S. Victoris Massiliensis* [BHL 8570] (c. 132), *Passio SS. Victoris et Coronae* [BHL 8559] (c. 87), *Passio S. Vincentii* [BHL 8627–33] (c. 31), *Passio SS. Viti et Modesti* [BHL 8714] (c. 102)

[34] *uitae sanctorum*: *Vita S. Audomari* [BHL 763] (c. 181), *Vita S. Bertini* [BHL 763] (c. 178), *Vita S. Ceolfridi* [BHL 1726] (c. 196), *Vita S. Fursae* [BHL 3213a] (c. 21), *Vita S. Goaris* [BHL 3565] (c. 186), *Vita S. Lupi* [BHL 5087] (c. 138), *Vita S. Mariae Magdalenae* [BHL 5453] (c. 133), *Vita S. Martialis* [BHL 5551] (c. 116), *Vita S. Pelagiae* [BHL 6609] (c. 210), *Vita S. Petronillae* [BHL 6061] (c. 94), *Vita S. Symeonis Stylitae* [BHL 7957–8] (c. 136), *Vita S. Winnoci* [BHL 8952] (c. 221)

f. Asser of St David's

Asser, sometime bishop of St David's in Wales, came to the attention of King Alfred (871–99) and was invited to join Alfred's court circle, probably in 885. From that time onwards, he spent part of every year in England, and oversaw the king's efforts to learn Latin. As a result, Asser was given the monasteries of Congresbury and Banwell in Somerset (886), and subsequently was appointed bishop of Sherborne (at some point during the decade 890 ×

899), a see which he apparently held until his death in 909. Because of his involvement in the king's education from the late 880s onwards, Asser had the opportunity of observing the king on a daily basis, and on the strength of this knowledge (as well as for the purpose of explaining the king's personality to a Welsh audience), Asser composed his *Vita Alfredi*, a work which he apparently abandoned incomplete in 893. The *Vita Alfredi* reveals a biographer of perspicacity and learning; and it is the Latin reading reflected in the *Vita Alfredi* which probably represents works accessible to Asser in England, and which helps to illuminate the books—one hesitates to say or imply 'royal library'—which were available in the king's entourage in the early 890s: see Lapidge, 'Asser's Reading'. In what follows, reference is to chapter numbers in the standard edition of Stevenson, *Asser's Life of King Alfred*.

Aldhelm of Malmesbury
[1] *De uirginitate* (prose) [CPL 1332]: cc. i (c. 88), iv (c. 22), xxxvii (c. 89)

Arnobius Iunior
[2] *Comm. in psalmos*: ps. cxlviii (c. 96)

Athanasius
[3] *Vita S. Antonii*, trans. Evagrius: cc. iii (c. 76), xl (c. 92)

Augustine
[4] *Enchiridion ad Laurentium, seu de fide, spe et caritate*: c. xx (c. 103)

Bede of Monkwearmouth-Jarrow
[5] *De temporum ratione* [CPL 2320]: cc. ii (c. 24), vi (c. 99)
[6] *Historia ecclesiastica gentis Anglorum* [CPL 1375]: i. 33 (c. 91), iv. 1 (c. 76), iv. 24 (c. 22)

Cassian, John
[7] *Conlationes*: ii. 6 (c. 87), ii. 24 (c. 84), iii. 9 (c. 15), ix. 22 (c. 12), x. 8 (c. 73), xi. 1 (c. 81), xi. 4 (c. 25)

Cassiodorus
[8] *Expositio psalmorum*: ps. xxii (c. 103), ps. xxx (c. 101), ps. lxi (c. 99), ps. cii (cc. 25, 27, 36, 69)

Corippus, Flavius Cresconius
[9] *In laudem Iustini*: iii. 139 (c. 90)

Einhard
[10] *Vita Karoli magni*: prol. 3–9 (c. 73), prol. 7–8 (c. 21)

Eutropius
[11] *Breuiarium historiae Romanae*: ii. 12 (c. 11), iii. 10 (c. 5)

Gregory the Great

[12] *Dialogi*: i prol. 2 (c. 16), iv. 31 (c. 16)

[13] *Moralia in Iob*: v. 7 (c. 13), xvii. 16 (cc. 69, 92), xxvi. 45 (c. 53), xxxi. 47 (c. 93)

[14] *Regula pastoralis*: iii. 20 (c. 102)

Justinus

[15] *Epitome*: i. 8. 14 (c. 81), xxiv. 1. 1 (c. 38)

Lucan

[16] *Bellum ciuile*: iii. 474 (c. 56), iv. 732 (c. 20)

Orosius, Paulus

[17] *Historiae aduersum paganos*: ii. 5. 6 (c. 21), ii. 7. 1 (c. 81), ii. 7. 2 (c. 39), ii. 11. 3 (c. 91), iv. 8. 4 (c. 48), iv. 8. 6 (c. 67)

Paulus Diaconus

[18] *Historia Langobardorum* [CPL 1179]: i. 24 (c. 67), iii. 29 (c. 6), iv. 37 (c. 18), v. 36 (c. 83)

Sedulius, Caelius

[19] *Carmen paschale*: i. 17–26 (c. 1)

Vergil

[20] *Aeneis*: ix. 514 (c. 56)

ANONYMOUS WRITINGS

[21] *Historia Brittonum* [CPL 1325; BCLL 127–34]: cc. 1, 9, 18

[22] *Prouerbia grecorum*: c. 88

[24] *Vita Alcuini* [BHL 242; CSLMA ALC 2]: cc. 79, 81

g. Lantfred of Winchester

On 15 July 971, the bishop of Winchester, Æthelwold (963–84), translated the remains of St Swithun, an obscure ninth-century bishop of Winchester (852–63), from a prominent burial site outside the west door of the Old Minster into the cathedral itself, thus initiating what was to become one of the most extensive relic cults in medieval England. The miracles which heralded the translation, the translation itself, and the many more miracles which followed the translation, were recorded within a year or two of the event by a Continental monk then living among the community of the Old Minster, one Lantfred, a monk originally from Fleury. Lantfred's *Translatio et miracula S. Swithuni* (ed. Lapidge, *The Cult of St Swithun*, 252–333) is perhaps the most ambitious Latin prose work to survive from the period of the Benedictine reform movement in England. Although Lantfred only names one source (Priscian) throughout the text, his prose style shows him to be an author of immensely wide reading in patristic sources; furthermore, in his attempt to elevate his prose style, he very frequently uses poetic expressions drawn from his wide familiarity with classical and Christian Latin verse. References to the *Translatio* are to chapter (in roman numerals) and line number of the Lapidge edition; Epist. refers to the prefatory *Epistola Lantfredi* (ed. Lapidge, 252–4), cited by line number, and Praef. refers to Lantfred's *Praefatio* (ed. ibid. 254–8), also cited by line number.

Aldhelm of Malmesbury
[1] *Carmen de uirginitate* [CPL 1333]: line 89 (ii.36–7)
[2] *Enigmata* [cf. CPL 1335]. iv. 3 (iii.102), c. 13–16 (xxxv.16)

Arator
[3] *Historia apostolica*: i. 37 [+ ii. 1117] (Epist. 25), i. 404 (i.67)

Arnobius Iunior
[4] *Comm. in psalmos*: ps. cxviii (i.54)

Augustine
[5] *De ciuitate Dei*: i. 22 (Epist. 13), ii. 7 (xxxv.20), x. 29 (iii.3), xii. 4 (i.75), xxi. 23 (iii.128–9)
[6] *Enarrationes in psalmos*: ps. xxvi, enarr. ii. 12 (Epist. 2), ps. xxx, enarr. ii, serm. iii. 7 (xxxv.37), serm. iii. 11 (i.78), ps. xli, c. vii (iii.5), ps. xliv, c. iv (Praef. 4), ps. lxvii, c. xxx (Praef. 46), ps. lxxii, c. xxxi (iii.4), ps. lxxxiii, c. viii (Epist. 3), ps. cxlv, c. vi (iii.3–4)
[7] *Epistulae*: clxxxv (Praef. 22, xx.18–19)
[8] *Quaestiones in heptateuchum*: Exod. quaest. xviii (ii.109)
[9] *Sermones*: xxviii (xxiv.5), ccciv (Praef. 10)
[10] *Tractatus in Euangelium Ioannis*: civ. 3 (Praef. 10)

Bede of Monkwearmouth-Jarrow
[11] *De temporum ratione* [CPL 2320] cc. iii (xx.18), viii (ii.53)
[12] *Expositio Apocalypseos* [CPL 1363]: iii. 22 (iii.133–4)
[13] *Historia ecclesiastica gentis Anglorum* [CPL 1375]: i. 1 (Praef. 54)
[14] *Homiliae* [CPL 1367]: i. 8 (xxxv.55)

Boethius
[15] *De consolatione Philosophiae*: ii, pr. i (xxiv.7), iii, pr. ix (xxxi.2), v, pr. iii (xviii.8), v, pr. vi (vii.10)

Calcidius
[16] *Comm. in Platonis Timaeum*: c. clxxxviii (Praef. 66)

Cassian, John
[17] *Conlationes*: i. 13 (iii.83), xii. 6 (xviii.9–10), xv. 5 (Praef. 61), xv. 7 (Epist. 23), xvii. 5 (xxiv.7), xix. 12 (xxxv.37), xxii. 1 (iii.70)

[18] *De institutis coenobiorum*: iv. **30** (i.35)

Cassiodorus
[19] *Expositio psalmorum*: xviii. **14** (Praef. 15), li.**5** (i.56), lxv. **12** (xxv.23), lxxxix. **4** (iii.81–2), cvi.praef (iii.62), cxviii. **54** (i.35), cxlv. **3** (iii.64), cxlvii. **15** (Praef. 29)

Eusebius of Caesarea
[20] *Historia ecclesiastica*, trans. Rufinus: iii. **6** (xviii.18), iii. **23** (xx.36), vi. **3** (xxviii.6), x. **8** [Rufinus] (vi.9–10)

Gregory the Great
[21] *Hom. .xl. in Euangelia*: i. **10** (Praef. 66), i. **11** (i.39), ii. **30** (Praef. 18)
[22] *In librum primum Regum expositiones*: iii. **121** (Praef. 48)
[23] *Moralia in Iob*: ii. **3** (i.24), ii. **6** (ii.83), v. **32** [+ v. **37**, xii. **33**, xxiv. **11**] (iii.128), vi. **36** (xx.18–19), vi. **37** (Epist. 13), xiv. **65** (ix.2), xxiii. **19** (Praef. 4), xxviii. **13** (Praef. 66), xxx. **26** (i.34), xxxi. **44** (iii.54), xxxi. **47** (Epist. 8), xxxiv. **7** (iii.25)

Isidore
[24] *De differentiis rerum*: c. **clxviii** (Epist. 22)
[25] *De ecclesiasticis officiis*: ii. **16** (xxix.23)
[26] *Etymologiae*: x. **70** (xxvii.29), xviii. **6** (ii.39), xix. **7** (xxv.36)

Jerome (Hieronymus)
[27] *Comm. in Danielem*: Praef. 20
[28] *Comm. in .iv. epistulas Paulinas*: [ad Titum] (i.45)
[29] *Comm. in Esaiam*: ix. **30** (iii.20–1)
[30] *Epistulae*: i (xxvii.6), xxxviii (iii.70), cxxii (Praef. 61), cxxxiii (xxxv.37)
[31] *Liber quaestionum hebraicarum in Genesim*: iv.9
[32] *Vita S. Hilarionis*: c. xiii (xxxi.2)

Juvencus
[33] *Euangelia*: ii. **625** (i.43)

Lactantius Firmianus
[34] *De opificio Dei*: viii. **9** (xxvi.17)

Lucretius
[35] *De natura rerum*: ii. **1153–4** (iii.103)

Martianus Capella
[36] *De nuptiis Philologiae et Mercurii*: i. **17** (iii.9), i. **37** (xxxv.27)

Orosius
[37] *Historiae aduersum paganos*: vii. **35. 20** (Praef. 7)

Paulinus of Nola
[38] *Carmina*: xviii. 21 (iv.14–15), xix. 22–3 (ii.59–60), xxv. 208 (i.8)

Priscian
[39] *Institutiones grammaticae*: **Ep. ad Iulianum** (Epist. 15)

Prudentius
[40] *Apotheosis*: lines **213** (ii.88), **386** (i.18)
[41] *Psychomachia*: lines **666** (xxxv.6), **746** (iii.75)

Sedulius, Caelius
[42] *Carmen paschale*: ii. **66** (xviii.24)

Statius
[43] *Thebais*: x. **84–99** (xl.4)

Vergil
[44] *Aeneis*: iii. **121** [+ vii. **392**, viii. **554**] (xxiv.4), iv. **522–32** (iii.63–4), vi.
    145–8 (i.30–2), vi. **570–2** (iii.15)

h. Abbo of Fleury and Ramsey

Abbo of Fleury (d. 1004), sometime abbot of Fleury and one of the greatest
scholars of the tenth century, spent two years of his life (985–7) teaching,
apparently at the invitation of Archbishops Dunstan and Oswald (whom he
knew personally from the latter's period of study at Fleury during the 950s),
at the fenland abbey of Ramsey, on a sort of sabbatical leave and as a means of
escaping from an awkward situation involving his frustrated hopes of
obtaining appointment to the abbacy of Fleury. Ramsey had been founded
a mere twenty years earlier, in 966, and cannot have acquired during that
time a very substantial library, certainly not one which could sustain the
researches of a scholar such as Abbo. It goes without saying that Abbo, if he
wished to communicate to his English students his own scientific and
scholarly interests, must have brought a number of books, perhaps a large
number, with him to Ramsey. Only a tiny number of such books appears to
have survived (or have yet been identified). It is nevertheless possible to form
some impression of what these books may have been by considering two
kinds of evidence: the books on which Abbo drew most heavily in the
scientific writings which he composed at Fleury in the years immediately
preceding his sojourn at Ramsey (notably the *Explanatio in Calculo Victorii*
and the treatise *De syllogismis hypotheticis*, both probably composed in the
early 980s); and writings quoted or alluded to in the two works which he
composed during his years in England (the *Quaestiones grammaticales* and the
Passio S. Eadmundi). I use the following abbreviations for these various works
(and note that I do not list works composed by Abbo after his return to

Fleury, since these are unlikely to shed any light on the holdings of Anglo-Saxon libraries):

Expl. = *Explanatio in Calculo Victorii*, in *Abbo of Fleury and Ramsey: Commentary on the Calculus of Victorius of Aquitaine*, ed. Peden, 63–131, cited by book and chapter number

Quaest.gramm. = *Quaestiones grammaticales*, in *Abbon de Fleury: Questions grammaticales*, ed. Guerreau-Jalabert, 205–75, cited by chapter number

Pass.Ead. = *Passio S. Eadmundi* [BHL 2392], in *Three Lives of English Saints*, ed. Winterbottom, 67–87, cited by chapter number

Syll.hyp. = *De syllogismis hypotheticis*, in *Abbo von Fleury, De syllogismis hypotheticis*, ed. Schupp, cited by chapter number

Unc.min. = *De unciarum minutiis*, in *Abbo of Fleury and Ramsey*, ed. Peden, 134

The list of works derived from these sources may be augmented by other kinds of evidence, notably English manuscript copies of works dating from a period later than Abbo's Ramsey sojourn but which may convincingly be associated with Abbo, such as Helperic's *Liber de computo* (on which see McGurk, 'Computus Helperici'). Finally, the list of works known to Abbo from these various sources is confirmed in interesting ways by the list of works known to his English pupil, Byrhtferth (see below, pp. 266–74).

Aldhelm of Malmesbury

[1] *De uirginitate* (prose) [CPL 1332]: c. cxxiv (Quaest.gramm. c. 43)

Ambrose

[2] *Hymni*: ii [ICL 15627], line 12 (Quaest.gram. c. 16); xxvii [ICL 410; pseudo-Ambrose], line 18 (Quaest.gramm. c. 15)

Augustine

[3] *De doctrina Christiana*: ii. 16 (Expl. iii.17)

Bede of Monkwearmouth-Jarrow

[4] *De temporum ratione* [CPL 1320]: cc. i (Expl. iii.51, 67), iii (Expl. iii.16, 37), iv (Expl. iii.47), v (Expl. iii.36), xvii (Expl. iii.37)

[5] *Historia ecclesiastica gentis Anglorum* [CPL 1375]: i. 15 (Pass.Ead. c. 1)

Benedict of Nursia

[6] *Regula S. Benedicti*: c. vi (Expl. iii.50)

Boethius

[7] *Comm. in Ciceronis Topica*: cc. i (Expl. iii.20, 41), v (Expl. iii.40), xiii (Syll.hyp. c. 9), xiv (Syll.hyp. c. 9)

[8] *De consolatione Philosophiae*: iii, met. ix. 2 (Expl. ii.10), iii, met. ix. 10 (Expl. iii.5)

[9] *De institutione arithmetica*: praef. (Expl. iii. 24), i. 1 (Expl. iii.7), i. 16 (Expl. iii.5, 8, 9), i. 19 (Expl. iii.17), i. 20 (Expl. iii.18), i. 21 (Expl. iii.73),

i. 24 (Expl. iii.74, 78), i. 26 (Expl. iii.60), i. 28 (Expl. iii.75), i. 32 (Expl. iii.20), ii. 1 (Expl. iii.24), ii. 26–7 (Expl. iii.58), ii. 40 (Expl. iii.48)

[10] *De institutione musica*: i. 2 (Expl. iii.11)

[11] *De syllogismo hypothetico*: Syll.hyp. cc. 1–8

[12] *In librum Aristotelis Perihermeneias commentarii editio duplex*: ii. 1. 2 (Expl. iii.20)

[13] *In Porphyrii Isagogen commentorum editio duplex*: i. 8 (Expl. iii.34), ii. 7 (Expl. iii.6), iv. 9 (Expl. iii.30)

[14] *Opuscula sacra*: iii [= *De hebdomadibus*]: Expl. iii.32

Calcidius

[15] *Comm. in Platonis Timaeum*: cc. xxxii (Expl. iii.2, 3), xxxviii (Expl. iii.30), xxxix (Expl. iii.2)

Cassiodorus

[16] *Expositio psalmorum*: xvii. 31 (Expl. iii.35), xxi. 6 (Expl. iii.40), xxii. 6 (Expl. iii.15), li. 5 (Expl. iii.51)

Charisius, Flavius Sosipater

[17] *Ars grammatica*: c. 39

Cicero

[18] *De inuentione*: i. 15. 20 (Expl. iii.41), i. 26. 39 (Expl. iii.37), ii. 154 (Quaest.gramm. c. 3)

Claudianus Mamertus

[19] *De statu animae*: i. 6 (Expl. iii.43), i. 22 (Expl. iii.83), i. 23 (Expl. iii.44), i. 25 (Expl. iii.31), ii. 4 (Expl. ii.12, 13, 15; iii.1), ii. 5 (Expl. ii.16), ii. 6 (Expl. ii.16), iii. 11 (Expl. iii.45)

Donatus, Aelius

[20] *Ars maior*: Quaest.gramm. c. 5

Eutyches

[21] *Ars de uerbo*: Quaest.gramm. cc. 16, 17

Horace

[22] *Ars poetica*: lines 231 (Quaest.gramm. c. 36), 325–30 (Expl. iii.48)

[23] *Carmen saeculare*: line 49 (Quaest.gramm. c. 37)

[24] *Carmina*: i. 1. 1 (Pass.Ead. c. 3), i. 3. 8 (Pass.Ead. c. 8), i. 13. 21 (Quaest.gramm. c. 18), i. 22. 1 (Pass.Ead. c. 11), iii. 2. 13 (Pass.Ead. c. 8), iii. 16. 13–14 (Quaest.gramm. c. 18)

[25] *Epistulae*: i. 5. 19 (Quaest.gramm. c. 29), i. 6. 38 (Expl. iii.48), ii. 1. 10 (Quaest.gramm. c. 31)

[26] *Epodon liber*: ii. 3 (Quaest.gramm. c. 3)

[27] *Sermones*: i. 2. 45–6 (Quaest.gramm. c. 17), i. 10. 34 (Quaest.gramm. c. 4), ii. 3. 156 (Expl. iii.57)

Isidore of Seville

[28] *Etymologiae*: i. 34. 13 (Expl. iii.13), i. 37. 13 (Expl. iii. 37), ii. 9. 6–7 (Expl. iii.40), ii. 28. 23 (Syll.hyp. c. 9), iii. 18. 1–2 (Expl. iii.11), v. 31. 5 (Quaest.gramm. c. 5), v. 37. 1 (Quaest.gramm. c. 43), v. 37. 2 (Quaest. gramm. c. 43), v. 29. 2 (Expl. iii. 37), v. 30. 1 (Expl. iii.36), ix. 2. 132 (Pass.Ead. c. 5), x. 66 (Expl. iii.13), xii. 1. 58 (Expl. iii.81), xiv. 8. 7 (Pass.Ead. c. 5), xvi. 19. 3 (Expl. iii.91), xvi. 25. 3 (Expl. iii.57), xvi. 25. 8 (Expl. iii.41, 52), xvi. 25. 10 (Expl. iii.54), xvi. 25. 14 (Expl. iii.54), xvi. 25. 16 (Expl. iii.54), xvi. 25. 18 (Expl. iii.54), xvi. 25. 20 (Expl. iii.55), xvi. 26. 3 (Expl. iii.95), xvi. 26. 4 (Expl. iii.95), xvi. 26. 3–6 (Expl. iii.95), xvi. 26. 10 (Expl. iii.96), xviii. 9. 1 (Quaest.gramm. c. 5), xx. 2. 14 (Quaest.gramm. c. 25), xx. 10. 7 (Quaest.gramm. c. 5), xx. 14. 2 (Quaest.gramm. c. 5), xx. 14. 10 (Quaest.gramm. c. 5)

Juvenal

[29] *Saturae*: i. 40 (Unc.min.), vi. 372–3 (Quaest.gramm. c. 37)

Lucan

[30] *Bellum ciuile*: iii. 626 (Quaest.gramm. c. 42), iv. 65 (Quaest.gramm. c. 18), iv. 678 (Quaest.gramm. c. 18), iv. 698 (Quaest.gramm. c. 18)

Macrobius, Ambrosius Theodosius

[31] *Comm. in Somnium Scipionis*: i. 6. 11 (Expl. iii.17), i. 6. 24–8 (Expl. iii.19), i. 6. 45–6 (Expl. iii.3), i. 6. 48–53 (Expl. iii.16), i. 6. 54–6 (Expl. iii.19), i. 6. 74–6 (Expl. iii.16), i. 8. 11 (Expl. iii.44), i. 15. 2 (Expl. iii.45), i. 15. 9 (Expl. iii.45), i. 15. 12–13 (Expl. iii.45), i. 21. 9–21 (Expl. iii.37)
[32] *Saturnalia*: vii. 7. 8 (Expl. iii.92), vii. 9. 16 (Expl. iii.44), vii. 12. 8–9 (Expl. iii.93), vii. 12. 11–12 (Expl. iii.93), vii. 12. 13 (Expl. iii.93), vii. 16. 23 (Expl. iii.91)

Martianus Capella

[33] *De nuptiis Philologiae et Mercurii*: i. 6 (Quaest.gramm. c. 41), iii. 253–5 (Quaest.gramm. c. 25), iii. 261 (Quaest.gramm. c. 22), iii. 271 (Quaest. gramm. c. 7), iii. 314 (Quaest.gramm. c. 9), iv. 416 (Syll.hyp. c. 9), v. 524 (Expl. iii.48), vii. 738 (Quaest.gramm. c. 49), vii. 739 (Expl. iii.16), vii. 746 (Expl. iii.69), viii. 862–4 (Expl. iii.19)

Ovid

[34] *Remedia amoris*: line 704 (Quaest.gramm. c. 8)

Persius
[35] *Saturae*: i. 109 (Quaest.gramm. c. 20), ii. 1 (Expl. iii.41), iii. 80 (Pass.Ead. c. 8), v. 12 (Quaest.gramm. c. 15), v. 191 (Expl. iii.57)

Phocas
[36] *Ars de nomine et uerbo*: Quaest.gramm. cc. 15, 34

Pliny the Elder
[37] *Naturalis historia*: vii. 17. 77 (Expl. iii.92), viii. 69. 173 (Expl. iii.81), xxxiii. 19. 60 (Expl. iii.91), xxxiii. 30. 94 (Expl. iii.91), xxxiv. 1. 166 (Expl. iii.91)

Priscian
[38] *De figuris numerorum*: Expl. iii.54, 57
[39] *Institutiones grammaticae*: Quaest.gramm. cc. 8, 9, 10, 11, 13, 14, 15, 17, 18, 19, 20, 21, 22, 25, 26, 29, 30, 31, 33, 34, etc.

Probus
[40] *Catholica*: Quaest.gramm. cc. 26, 39

Prudentius
[41] *Liber peristephanon*: xi. 147 (Quaest.gramm. c. 9)
[42] *Psychomachia*: line 165 (Quaest.gramm. c. 14)

Remius Favinus: see ANONYMOUS WRITINGS, *Carmen de ponderibus*

Sallust
[43] *Bellum Iugurthinum*: vi. 1 (Expl. iii.30)

Sedulius, Caelius
[44] *Carmen paschale*: v. 177 (Quaest.gramm. c. 3)

Servius
[45] *Comm. in Vergilii Aeneidos libros*: ad ix. 769 (Quaest.gramm. c. 24)

Sulpicius Severus
[46] *Dialogi*: ii. 14 (Pass.Ead. c. 5)
[47] *Vita S. Martini*: x. 1 (Pass.Ead. c. 4), x. 4 (Pass.Ead. c. 2)

Terence
[48] *Comoediae*: *Adelphoe* iii [lines 376–7] (Expl. iii.30); *Andria* ii [line 334] (Expl. iii.41); *Phormio* i [lines 36–8] (Expl. iii.40)

Vergil
[49] *Aeneis*: i. 209 (Pass.Ead. c. 8), i. 511 (Quaest.gramm. c. 3), i. 531 (Pass.Ead. c. 2), i. 573 (Quaest.gramm. c. 40), i. 678 (Quaest.gramm. c. 34), iii. 55 (Quaest.gramm. c. 37), iii. 175 (Quaest.gramm. c. 18), iv. 178

(Quaest.gramm. c. 14), v. 28 (Quaest.gramm. c. 17), v. 442 (Quaest. gramm. c. 14), v. 449 (Quaest.gramm. c. 15), vi. 853 (Pass.Ead. c. 7), vii. 733 (Expl. iii.44), viii. 27 (Quaest.gramm. c. 39), ix. 266 (Quaest.gramm. c. 34), x. 331 (Quaest.gramm. c. 14), x. 644 (Quaest.gramm. c. 14), xi. 175 (Quaest.gramm. c. 17), xii. 709 (Quaest.gramm. c. 20)

[50] *Bucolica*: i. 3 (Pass.Ead. c. 8), i. 9 (Quaest.gramm. c. 38), i. 23 (Expl. iii.28), i. 70 (Pass.Ead. c. 5), i. 74 (Pass.Ead. c. 8), ii. 49 (Expl. iii.30), viii. 75 (Quaest.gramm. c. 48), ix. 2–5 (Pass.Ead. c. 8), ix. 28 (Pass.Ead. c. 5)

[51] *Georgica*: i. 37 (Pass.Ead. c. 9), i. 74 (Expl. iii.54), i. 299 (Quaest.gramm. c. 17), i. 350 (Expl. iii.32), iv. 452 (Pass.Ead. c. 8)

ANONYMOUS WRITINGS

[52] *Carmen de ponderibus*: lines 11–12 (Expl. iii.52)

[53] *passiones martyrum*: Passio S. Sebastiani [BHL 7543]: Pass.Ead. c. 10

i. Wulfstan of Winchester

As the cult of St Swithun developed in the years following the translation of the saint's remains in 971, and as a result of the growing fame of the relics' efficacy as publicized by Lantfred's *Translatio*, a member of the Winchester community, one Wulfstan, who was the precentor there in the last decades of the tenth century (hence he is known in contemporary sources as Wulfstan *Cantor*), undertook to recast Lantfred's prose *Translatio* into Latin hexameters. Wulfstan's *Narratio metrica de S. Swithuno* was composed during the years 992–4 at Winchester and put into final form in 996. It is the longest surviving pre-Conquest Anglo-Latin poem, and shows its author to have had deep knowledge of classical and Christian Latin poetry. The text of the *Narratio* is ed. in Lapidge, *The Cult of St Swithun*, 371–551. In what follows I use the following abbreviations for the various parts of the poem (accompanied by line numbers):

Ep.spec. = the *Epistola specialis* addressed to Bishop Ælfheah (ed. Lapidge, 371–97), with line numbers

Ep.gen. = the *Epistola generalis* addressed to the monks of Winchester (ed. Lapidge, 398–401), with line numbers

Praef. = the *Praefatio* (ed. Lapidge, 400–11), with line numbers

i, ii = books i (ed. Lapidge, 410–91), ii (490–551), with line numbers

Aldhelm of Malmesbury

[1] *Carmen de uirginitate* [CPL 1332]: lines 2 [+ 1445, 2816] (i.1125), 16 (Praef. 68), 180 [+ 1528, 1689] (Ep.spec. 136), 207 (Ep.spec. 187), 394 (i.198), 458 (Ep.spec. 227), 484 (ii.99), 490 (Praef. 24), 541 (Ep.spec. 2), 624 (i.338), 651 (ii.64), 681 (i.7), 731 (i.1033), 763 (i.925), 798 (Ep.spec. 310), 958 (i.1500), 984 (Praef. 111), 1089 (i.1216), 1146 (i.10), 1190 (i.274, i.1232), 1288 (i.1341), 1324 (Ep.spec. 177), 1426 (ii.998), 1449 (ii.1097), 1543 (i.984), 1586 (Ep.spec. 159), 1742 (i.1354), 1776 (i.668), 1198

(i.1370), **2005** (Praef. 170), **2059** (Praef. 162), **2173** (ii.821), **2236** (Ep.spec. 255, i.70, i.1106), **2268** (i.92), **2369** (i.944), **2609** (i.40)

[2] *Carmina ecclesiastica* [CPL 1331]: iii. **26** (i.970), iii. **50** (ii.1168), iv. 1. **3** (i.260), iv. 1. **31** (ii.775), iv. 6. **19** (Praef. 99), iv. 7. **11** (i.10), iv. 12. **7** (i.1386)

[3] *Enigmata* [cf. CPL 1335]: iv. **4** (i.392), xi. **1–2** (Ep.spec. 149), xiv. 1 (i.430), lxiii. **1** (Praef. 138), lxxxi. **9** (i.197), xcvi. **1** (Praef. 128), c. **3** (Praef. 140), c. **5** (i.648), c. **25** (Ep.spec. 187)

Arator

[4] *Historia apostolica*: **Epist. ad Vigilium 19** (Praef. 185), **27** (Ep.spec. 15–16), **28** (Ep.spec. 324); i. **8** (i.917), i. **14** (Praef. 43), i. **23** (ii.442), i. **38** (i.1382), i. **54** (i.524), i. **69–70** (Praef. 77), i. **119–20** (Praef. 61–2), i. **144** (Ep.spec. 13), i. **170** (ii.747), i. **221** (Ep.gen. 30), i. **244–5** (i.200–1), i. **260** (Ep.spec. 37), i. **404** (i.151), i. **522–30** (ii.630–9), i. **524** (i.914), i. **545** (i.785–6), i. **709** (Praef. 64), i. **849** (Praef. 7), i. **897** (ii.397); ii. **98** (Praef. 135), ii. **145** (ii.327), ii. **404–6** (ii.544–6), ii. **422** (ii.646), ii. **432** (ii.541), ii. **556** (Praef. 22), ii. **752** (i.1162), ii. **756** (ii.512), ii. **1208** (i.1519), ii. **1217–18** (i.1504–5)

Bede of Monkwearmouth-Jarrow

[5] *Historia ecclesiastica gentis Anglorum* [CPL 1375]: ii. **16** (ii.462–5)
[6] *Versus de die iudicii* [CPL 1370]: line **24** (ii.1146)
[7] *Vita metrica S. Cudbercti* [CPL 1380]: lines **152** (ii.608), **653** (i.1477)

Dracontius

[8] *Laudes Dei*: i. **21** [+ ii. **81**] (Ep.spec. 9)
[9] *Satisfactio*: line **28** (Ep.spec. 6)

Horace

[10] *Epistulae*: i. **5** (Ep.spec. 97)

Juvenal

[11] *Saturae*: vi. **327** (ii.280)

Juvencus

[12] *Euangelia*: i. **404** (Praef. 146), ii. **177** (Ep.spec. 135), iv. **353** (i.1262)

Lucan

[13] *Bellum ciuile*: iii. **64** (Praef. 102), iv. **278** [+ vi. **310**] (Praef. 116), vi. **424** (ii.280), ix. **528** (i.612)

Ovid

[14] *Ars amatoria*: iii. **571** (Praef. 92)
[15] *Fasti*: i. **78** (Ep.spec. 138), iii. **864** (Ep.spec. 60), iv. **432** (Ep.spec. 154)
[16] *Metamorphoseis*: xi. **20** (Ep.spec. 227), xi. **611** (i.507)

[17] *Remedia amoris*: line 450 (Ep.spec. 218)

Prudentius

[18] *Hamartigenia*: lines 410–11 (Ep.spec. 100)

Sedulius, Caelius

[19] *Carmen paschale*: i. praef. 10 (Ep.spec. 122), i. 20 (i.746), i. 26 (ii. 363), i. 39 (Ep.gen. 37), i. 40 (Ep.spec. 56), i. 48 (Praef. 110), i. 70 (Praef. 28), i. 78 (Praef. 4), i. 99 (Ep.spec. 167), i. 102 (i.1126), i. 162 (i.1376), i. 176 (Ep.spec. 224), i. 185 (i.165), i. 270 (ii.447), i. 285 (Ep.spec. 183), i. 287 (ii.53), i. 341 (i.489), i. 342 (Ep.spec. 211); ii. 3–4 (ii.1165–6), ii. 43 (ii.2), ii. 64–5 (ii.755–6), ii. 65 (i.1568), ii. 73 (i.199), ii. 206 (i.83), ii. 141–2 (Praef. 31–2), ii. 143 (i.219), ii. 175 (Praef. 44), ii. 176 (Ep.spec. 115), ii. 245 (Ep.spec. 28), ii. 252 (Ep.spec. 5), ii. 268 (ii.1005); iii. 1 (Praef. 19), iii. 25 (Praef. 175), iii. 38 (ii.109), iii. 44 (i.233), iii. 45 (i.1062), iii. 54 (ii.460), iii. 56 (i.707), iii. 61 (i.1144), iii. 74–5 (i.1174–5), iii. 107 (i.1212), iii. 108 (i.1048), iii. 116 (ii.883), iii. 117 (i.1456), iii. 129 (i.588), iii. 145–6 (ii.758–9), iii. 151 (ii.704), iii. 153 (i.202), iii. 183 (i.1547), iii. 196–8 (i.1163–5), iii. 214 (i.1417), iii. 221 (i.923), iii. 225–6 (i.374–5), iii. 229 (ii.779), iii. 252 (i.892), iii. 256 (i.714), iii. 258 (i.671); iv. 3 (Ep.gen. 20), iv. 5–6 (ii.410–11), iv. 23 (i.653), iv. 24 (Ep.spec. 319), iv. 33 (i.1598), iv. 38 (i.1532), iv. 40 (Ep.spec. 231, i.1097), iv. 41 (i.1116–17), iv. 104 (Praef. 71), iv. 215 (Ep.spec. 295), iv. 219 (ii.658), iv. 221 (i.109, 143), iv. 256 (i.1501), iv. 261–3 (i.1586–8), iv. 282 (i.1120); v. 1 (ii.1), v. 30 (Ep.spec. 144), v. 105 (Ep.gen. 22), v. 197 (Ep.gen. 15), v. 261 (ii.12), v. 316–17 (i.406–7), v. 324 (ii.949), v. 328 (i.9), v. 423–6 (Praef. 45–9)

Statius

[20] *Thebais*: vi. 894 [+ x. 392] (i.544)

Venantius Fortunatus

[21] *Carmina*: i. 1. 12 (= Ep.spec. 178), i. 2. 5–6 (Ep.spec. 65–6), i. 2. 8 (Ep.spec. 254), i. 6. 13 (Ep.spec. 193 + 195), i. 6. 17–20 (Ep.spec. 207–10), i. 12. 4 (Ep.spec. 120), i. 12. 5 (Ep.spec. 125), i. 12. 6 (Ep.spec. 126), i. 15. 102 (Ep.spec. 220), i. 17. 1 (Ep.spec. 323), ii. 3. 2 (Ep.spec. 14), ii. 9. 57–8 (Ep.spec. 243–4), ii. 9. 69 (Ep.spec. 245), iii. 6. 1 (Ep.spec. 213), iii. 6. 2 (Ep.spec. 216), iii. 6. 3 (Ep.spec. 233), iii. 6. 21 (Ep.spec. 241), iii. 6. 28 (Ep.spec. 224, 226, 270), iii. 6. 29–32 (= Ep.spec. 235–8), iii. 6. 45–6 (Ep.spec. 239–40), iii. 6. 48 (Ep.spec. 242), iii. 6. 52 (Ep.spec. 246), iii. 7. 28 (Ep.spec. 252), iii. 7. 43–6 (= Ep.spec. 189–92), iii. 22a. 7–8 (Ep.spec. 271–2), v. 3. 33–4 (Ep.spec. 321–2), v. 3. 41 (Ep.spec. 315), v. 4. 5 (Ep.spec. 317), vii. 5. 30 (Ep.spec. 274), vii. 7. 71 (Ep.spec. 271), vii. 12. 44 (Ep.spec. 284), viii. 3. 141 (i.407)

Vergil

[22] *Aeneis*: i. **14** (i.1025), i. **67** (i.1503), i. **172** (ii.1057), i. **223** (i.859), i. **724** [= vii. **146**] (= Ep.spec. 95), i. **738** (Ep.spec. 97), i. **739** (Ep.spec. 99), ii. **1** (ii.415), ii. **132** (i.936), i. **416–17** (i.945), ii. **265** (i.1186), ii. **268–9** (i.560–1), ii. **488** (Praef. 47, i.414), ii. **752** (ii.53), iii. **90** (ii.502), iii. **94** (i.1496), iii. **95** (ii.516), iii. **130** (ii.1055), iii. **290** [= v. **778**] (Ep.spec. 152, ii.1056), iii. **356** (i.883), iii. **508** (Ep.spec. 140), iii. **589** [+ iv. **7**] (i.1159), iv. **134–6** (i.1271–4), v. **154** (Praef. 103), v. **172** (i.616), v. **481** (i.394), v. **512** (i.1598), vi. **267** (Ep.spec. 283), vi. **573–4** (ii.615), vi. **626** (Ep.spec. 167), vi. **646** (Ep.spec. 165), vi. **676** (i.1137), viii. **554** (i.409), ix. **39** (i.851), ix. **183** (ii.1151), ix. **473–4** (i.774), xi. **340** (Praef. 147), xi. **139** (Ep.spec. 174), xii. **468** (i.147), xii. **558** (ii.952), xii. **592** (ii.452), xii. **897–8** (ii.531–2), xii. **946** (i.1194)

[23] *Bucolica*: viii. **49** (ii.739)

[24] *Georgica*: i. **49** (ii.517), i. **204** (Praef. 164), i. **301** (ii.241), ii. **6** (ii.519), ii. **43–4** (ii.189), iv. **79** (i.582), iv. **179** (Ep.spec. 56), iv. **190** (ii.561), iv. **466** (i.1157)

j. Ælfric of Winchester

Ælfric (*c*.960–*c*.1010) was the author of a substantial corpus of writings (much of it didactic and homiletic in nature) in Old English, as well as a smaller corpus of Latin writings. These writings in sum reveal him as an author of very wide reading, particularly in patristic sources, and imply that he had access to a substantial library. Although from 987 onwards he served as a priest at the minster church of Cerne Abbas (Dorset), before that time he had been a student of Bishop Æthelwold at the Old Minster, Winchester, and the wide range of patristic sources quoted and translated in Ælfric's writings are almost certainly to be seen as a reflection of the resources of the library at the Old Minster during the later tenth century (the writings of Lantfred and Wulfstan *Cantor* help to illuminate the holdings of this same library). We are in an excellent position to evaluate the range of Ælfric's reading largely through the availability of the database of the project *Fontes Anglo-Saxonici* (issued as a CD-ROM (Version 1.1) in 2002; and available in a slightly updated version on the World Wide Web at ⟨http://fontes.en-glish.ox.ac.uk⟩. The *Fontes* database is a superb scholarly tool for the study of books known in Anglo-Saxon England, and it is particularly valuable for authors such as Ælfric, whose writings have been thoroughly sourced. What follows is based essentially on the *Fontes* database, although I have arranged the information provided to conform to the conventions used elsewhere in this Appendix.

I use the following abbreviations for the writings of Ælfric:

Assmann = *Angelsächsische Homilien und Heiligenleben*, ed. Assmann [cited by homily and line number; note that only nos. iii, iv, v, and vi are by Ælfric]

CH i = *Ælfric's Catholic Homilies: The First Series. Text*, ed. Clemoes [cited by homily and line number]

CH ii = *Ælfric's Catholic Homilies: The Second Series. Text*, ed. Godden [cited by homily and line number]

DTA = *Ælfric's De Temporibus Anni*, ed. Henel [cited by chapter and subsection]

Hom.supp. = *Homilies of Ælfric*, ed. Pope [cited by homily and line number]

Interrog.Sig. = 'Ælfric's Version of Alcuin's *Interrogationes Sigeuulfi in Genesin*', ed. MacLean [cited by line number]

Irvine = *Old English Homilies from MS Bodley 343*, ed. Irvine [cited by homily and line number]

LS = *Ælfric's Lives of Saints*, ed. Skeat [cited by Life and line number]

Pref.Gen. = 'Ælfric's Preface to Genesis', ed. Crawford [cited by line number]

Abbo of Fleury

[1] *Passio S. Eadmundi* [BHL 2392]: LS xxxii (*passim*)

Adso of Montier-en-Der

[2] *De ortu et tempore antichristi* (CCCM 45: 20–30): Hom.supp. xviii.304–6

Alcuin

[3] *De animae ratione* [CSLMA ALC 17] (PL 101: 639–50): cc. i (LS i.79–81, 88–96), ii (LS i.195–6, 200–5), iii (LS i.96–100, 155–62, 164–7), iv (LS i.100–9, 155–8, 164–71), v (LS i.167–71), vi (CH i.20, 190–212; Interrog.Sig. 176–7; LS i.112–22), vii (LS i.122–3, 126–31, 224–5), viii (LS i.123–6, 121–41), ix (CH i.1, 161–6; i.10, 125–34; LS i.141–9, 150–3), x (LS i.171–80, 220–4), xi (LS i.180–95), xii (LS i.153–5, 195–6, 205–8, 216–20), xiii (LS i.84–8), xiv (LS i.225–39)

[4] *De uirtutibus et uitiis* [CSLMA ALC 37] (PL 101: 613–38): cc. xxvii (CH ii.12, 531–41; Hom.supp. iv.250–1), xxviii (CH ii.12, 493–500), xxix (CH ii.12, 500–5), xxx (CH ii.12, 505–10), xxxi (CH ii.12, 510–13), xxxii (CH ii.12, 514–24), xxxiv (CH ii.12, 488–92, 524–31, 548–59)

[5] *Expositio Apocalypsis* [CSLMA ALC 49] (PL 100: 1087–1156): v. 11 (CH i.40, 140–7)

[6] *Expositio in Iohannis Euangelium* [CSLMA ALC 51] (PL 100: 737–1008): i. 1 (Hom.supp. i.65–9), ii. 7 (Hom.supp. v.118–22, 143–8), iii praef. (Hom.supp. ii.62, 115–16), iii. 9 (Hom.supp. ii.14–16, 63–7, 76–81, 130–3, 146–50, 184–201, 206–10, 213–31, 256–62, 276–86; Interrog.Sig. 22–4), iii. 19 (Hom.supp. ii.68–75), iv. 21 (LS i.11–16), v. 30 (CH ii.16, 186–99; Irvine iv.328–38, 340–7, 366–8), v. 31 (Irvine iv.349–51, 353–7, 360–5), vi. 37 (Hom.supp. vii.32–8, 40–3, 47–51, 53–7, 62–72, 76–84, 86–9, 164–9, 173–6, 181–6, 196–200, 208–11, 216–18, 221–4), vii. 43 (CH ii.16, 186–99)

[7] *Quaestiones in Genesim* [CSLMA ALC 76] (PL 100: 516–66): Int. 4 (CH i.13, 12–17), Int. 37 (Pref.Gen. 64–9), Int. 38 (CH i.20, 190–212), Int. 40 (Pref.Gen. 64–9), Int. 87 (Pref.Gen. 70–2) Int. 106 (CH i.35, 259–73);

Ælfric's Old English version of the *Interrogationes Sigeuulfi* is translated directly from this work of Alcuin.

[8] *Vita S. Martini* [BHL 5625; CSLMA ALC 89] (PL 101: 657–64): cc. iii (CH ii.34, 59–62), v (CH ii.34, 146–54), vi (LS xxxi.294–7), vii (CH ii.34, 154–60, 178–228), viii (CH ii.34, 239–68), xi (LS xxxi.1485–8), xv (CH ii.34, 296–313)

Aldhelm of Malmesbury

[9] *De uirginitate* (prose) [CPL 1332]: c. xix (CH ii, praef.)

Amalarius of Metz

[10] *De ecclesiasticis seu diuinis officiis (Liber officialis)* [CSLMA AMAL 14]: i. 1 (CH ii.5, 240–69, 272–82), i. 24 (CH ii.3, 262–72), i. 37 (CH i.18, 5–11), i. 39 (CH i.22, 228–33), iv. 20 (CH ii.13, 1–9), iv. 23 (CH ii.16, 208–12)

Ambrose

[11] *Exameron*: v. 77 (CH i.16, AppB.8–24), v. 79–80 (CH i.16, AppB.25–34), vi. 14 (Assmann iv.277–81), vi. 26 (Assmann iv.282–4), vi. 31 (LS xxv.564–73), vi. 37 (Assmann iv.285–8)

Ambrosiaster

[12] *Quaestiones Veteris et Noui Testamenti*: xxvii. 1 (Hom.supp. xxix.51–4, 106–9), xxvii. 2 (Hom.supp. xxix.97–104, 110–12), xxvii. 3 (Hom.supp. xxix.51–9, 66–9, 75–82), xxvii. 4 (Hom.supp. xxix.70–4)

Augustine

[13] *De bono coniugali*: cc. vii (Hom.supp. xix.106–8), ix (Assmann iii.306–18), xxii (Assmann iii.325–9), xxiii (Assmann iii.367–71, 396–420)

[14] *De catechizandis rudibus*: cc. xx (CH ii.4, 239–46), xxi (CH ii.4, 239–67)

[15] *De ciuitate Dei*: xi. 9 (Pref.Gen. 46–7), xv. 16 (Pref.Gen. 17–18), xx. 20 (CH i.40, 140–7); xxii. 8 (CH ii.2, 8–87, 98–113, 124–76)

[16] *De correptione et gratia*: c. x (CH i.7, 156–8)

[17] *De doctrina Christiana*: ii. 29 (CH i.31, 319–21), iii. 19 (Pref.Gen. 19)

[18] *De Genesi ad litteram*: viii. 6 (CH i.1, 74–83)

[19] *De quantitate animae*: c. xvi (LS i.110–12)

[20] *De sancta uirginitate*: cc. ii (Assmann iii.136–47, 153–73), iii (Assmann iii.174–84), iv (Assmann iii.189–206, 232–7), v (Assmann iii.207–20), vi (Assmann iii.131–5, 221–3), xxiv (Assmann iii.421–33), xxvi (Assmann iii. 486–95, 505–25), xxviii (Assmann iii.526–72), xxix (Assmann iii.243–52), xxxi (Assmann iii.383–92), xxxix (Assmann iii.393–5, 434–50), xliv (Assmann iii.372–8)

[21] *De sermone Domini in monte libri .ii.*: i. 1 (CH i.36, 167–79, 181–3), i. 2 (CH i.36, 200–10, 212–18, 220–1, 228–35), i. 5 (CH i.36, 262–6), i. 10 (CH i.3, 160–1, 164–5; Hom.supp. xv.203–13), i. 20 (LS xxxvi.4–10), ii. 2 (Hom.supp. xxx.57–65, 69–74), ii. 5 (CH i.19, 57–70, 74–9), ii. 6 (CH

i.19, 96–105), ii. 7 (CH i.19, 108–26), ii. 9 (CH i.19, 146–7, 149–51), ii. 10 (CH i.19, 186–212)

[22] *De trinitate*: i. 8 (CH i.20, 132–3), iii. 7–9 (Hom.supp. i.258–74), vi. 8 (CH i. 20, 111–12), x. 11 (CH i.20, 190–212)

[23] *Enarrationes in psalmos*: [ps. lxiii] 14 (Hom.supp. vii.97–102), 15 (Hom.supp. vii.116–20), [ps. lxxi] 1 (CH ii.40, 74–85)

[24] *Enchiridion ad Laurentium, seu de fide, spe et caritate*: c. ix (CH ii.5, 227–32)

[25] *Sermones*: v (CH ii.14, 319–27), xlvi (CH i.17AppB3, 38–46, 48–57, 62–71, 79–92, 100–3, 106–15, 127–31, 197–208), lvi (CH i.19, 142–5), lvii (CH i.19, 147–8), lviii (CH i.19, 81, 87), lix (CH i.19, 40–52, 194–212), lxi (CH i.18, 142–5, 153–204), lxiv (Hom.supp. xvi.235–57), lxxi (CH i.33, 129–35; Hom.supp. vi. 221–3, 228–42, 247–9, 269–77; Pref.Gen. 62–3), lxxii (CH ii.26, 63–7, 70–133), lxxvi (CH ii.24, 155–88, 194–207, 213–29), lxxxiii (CH i.31, 267–74; Irvine ii.60–73, 75–90, 96–118, 121–6, 132–60, etc.), xc (CH i.35, 277–80), xciii (CH ii.39, 40–64, 78–86, 92–103, 107–26, 128–31, 136–8, 144–6, etc.), ciii (CH ii.29, 26–35, 86–92), civ (CH ii.29, 36–41, 46–58, 60–73, 83–92, 97–109), cv (CH i.18, 61–9, 71–5, 79–87, 99–104, 109–13, 122–4, 126–39), cxii (CH ii.23, 44–62), cxv (CH ii.28, 28–37), cxvii (CH i.20, 57–72, 164–73), cxviii (CH i.20, 57–72; LS i.16–18), cxx (CH i.20, 177–85; Irvine i.78–88), clxxxvi (CH i.2, 175–81; i.30, 270–2), ccii (CH i.7, 37, 47–51, 57–70, 83–91), cciv (CH i.7, 102–4), ccvi (CH ii.7, 1–9, 28–33, 38–41), ccxlviii (Hom.supp. xiv.85–90), cclxxii (CH ii.15, 138–42, 225–44), cclxxix (CH i.2;7, 80–2, 84–7, 90), cclxxxviii (CH i.25, 135–8), cccxxii (CH ii.2, 98–123), cccl (CH ii.19, 12–16), cccliv (Assmann iii.322–5, 396–420; Hom.supp. xxx.11–12), ccclxx (CH i.9, 38–55, 124–30, 198–203), ccclxxxii (CH i.3, 109–14, 125–9; CH ii.2, 208–13)

[26] *Tractatus in Euangelium Ioannis*: i. 5 (CH i.4, 175–93), i. 13 (Hom.sup. i.171–94), i. 15 (CH ii.12, 55–64; Hom.supp. i.222–46), i. 16 (Hom.supp. i.277–9), i. 17 (Hom.supp. i.280–5), i. 19 (Hom.supp. i.194–8), ii. 6 (Hom.supp. i.311–16, 324–6), iii. 8 (Hom.supp. i.467–9), iv. 14 (CH ii.3, 106–7), v. 5 (CH ii.3, 192–205), vi. 3 (CH ii.3, 179–81), vi. 4 (CH ii.3, 168–78, 182–7), vi. 8 (CH ii.3, 219–28), vi. 11 (Assmann iii.101–3), xii. 5 (Hom.supp. xii.156–7), xii. 8 (CH ii.24, 113–15), xii. 11 (CH ii.13, 241–3, 257–9, 264–88), xv. 4 (Hom.supp. vii.177–80), xv. 6 (Hom.supp. v.102–7, 109), xv. 8 (Hom.supp. v.108), xv. 9 (Hom.supp. v.110–12), xv. 10 (Hom.supp. v.115–17), xv. 11 (Hom.supp. v.118–26), xv. 12 (Hom.supp. v.130–1), xv. 17 (Hom.supp. v.151–8), xv. 25 (Hom.supp. v.174–9, 182–4), xv. 26 (Hom.supp. v.198–202), xv. 27 (Hom.supp. v.208–9), xv. 30 (Hom.supp. v.216–22), xv. 31 (Hom.supp. v.242–6), xv. 32 (Hom.supp. v.256–71), xvi. 5 (CH i.8, 127–38), xvii. 1 (Hom.supp. ii. 91–4, 98–114, 134–8), xvii. 2 (Hom.supp. ii.63–7), xvii. 3 (Hom.supp. ii.117–29), xvii. 4 (Hom.supp. ii.151–62, 167–75, 177–83), xvii. 5 (Hom.supp. ii.177–83),

xvii. 6 (Hom.supp. ii.139–50), xvii. 7 (Hom.supp. ii.184–91), xvii. 9
(Hom.supp. ii.206–10), xvii. 13 (CH ii.12, 277–311), xvii. 15 (Hom.supp.
ii.213–19, 247–50), xx. 3 (Hom.supp. viii.190–9), xxiv. 1 (CH i.12, 54–
63), xxiv. 2 (CH i.12, 64–73), xxiv. 3 (CH i.12, 44–6, 49–54), xxiv. 5 (CH
i.12, 74–96, 98–101), xxiv. 6 (CH i.12, 96–8, 136–40), xxiv. 7 (CH i.12,
131–5), xxvi. 11 (CH ii.15, 199–208), xxxvi. 8 (Hom.supp. viii.200–2),
xxxvi. 9 (Hom.supp. viii.190–9), xxxvii. 6 (Hom.supp. viii.190–9),
xxxvii. 7 (Hom.supp. viii.200–2), xlii. 2 (CH ii.13, 99–107), xlii. 10
(CH i.1, 56–61; ii.13, 66–9), xlii. 12 (CH ii.13, 59–65), xlii. 15 (CH ii.13,
50–9), xliii. 3 (CH ii.13, 119–22), xliii. 9 (CH ii.13, 123–43), xliii. 11
(CH ii.13, 152–68), xliii. 13 (CH ii.13, 152–68), xliii. 14 (CH ii.13, 172–
4), xliii.15 (CH ii.13, 177–83), xliii. 16 (CH ii.13, 190–204), xliii. 17 (CH
ii.13, 208–20), xliv. 1 (Irvine iii.106–31, 145–50), xliv. 2 (Irvine iii. 151–
65), xliv. 3 (Irvine iii.172–6), xliv. 4 (Irvine iii.178–87), xliv. 5 (Irvine
iii.191–4, 197–221), xliv. 6 (Irvine iii. 222–42, 245–50, 254–65), xliv. 9
(CH ii.12, 277–311; Irvine iii.278–84, 289–94), xliv. 11 (Irvine iii. 299–
300), xliv. 12 (Irvine iii.316–18, 321–4), xliv. 13 (Irvine iii.326–34, 340–
3), xliv. 17 (Irvine iii.359–63), xlvi. 6 (CH i.17, 70–3), xlvi. 7 (CH i.17,
18–22), xlvii. 3 (CH i.17, 79–81), xlix. 1 (Hom.supp. vi.111–36, 319–21),
xlix. 2 (Hom.supp. vi.143–51, 170–1), xlix. 3 (Hom.supp. vi.162–9, 173–
4, 176–94, 196–206, 292–300), xlix. 5 (Hom.supp. vi.332–3), xlix. 8
(Hom.supp. vi.338–42, 349–54), xlix. 15 (Hom.supp. vi.359–66), xlix. 26
(Assmann v.40–4), xlix. 27 (Assmann v.106–29, 148–52), xlix. 28
(Assmann v.168–9, 173–6), l. 2 (Assmann v.60–4), l. 3 (Assmann v.54–
9), l. 14 (Assmann v.34–9), li. 7 (Hom.supp. xxv.c1–8), li. 9 (Irvine
iv.304–12), li. 10 (Irvine iv.323–34), li. 11 (Irvine iv.349–51, 353–7, 360–
8; Hom.supp. xxv.a3–7), li. 12 (Hom.supp. xxv.a7–9), li. 13 (Irvine iv.340–
7; Hom.supp. xxv.a15–19), lv. 1 (CH ii.15, 324–35), lxxviii. 3 (Hom.supp.
x.151–8), lxxxv. 3 (CH ii.35, 45–6), xcviii. 8 (CH ii.20, 14–16), civ. 2
(CH ii.22, 35–9), civ. 3 (CH ii.22, 39–49), cv. 1 (CH ii.22, 39–58), cv. 2
(CH ii.22, 61–7), cv. 3 (CH ii.22, 70–88), cv. 4 (CH ii.22, 90–8), cv. 7
(CH ii.22, 101–17), cv. 8 (CH ii.22, 101–17), cvi. 1 (CH ii.22, 119–22),
cvi. 2 (CH ii.22, 150–3), cvi. 5 (CH ii.22, 123–7, 132–6), cvii. 1 (CH ii.22,
147–50), cvii. 2 (CH ii.22, 165–79), cxvi. 1 (CH ii.14, 208–10), cxix. 1
(CH ii.14, 266–7), cxix. 4 (CH ii.14, 284–7), cxx. 2 (CH ii.14, 319–27),
cxx. 5 (CH ii.14, 346–8)

Augustinus Hibernicus
[27] *De mirabilibus sacrae scripturae*: i. 3 (Interrog.Sig. 78–84)

Bede of Monkwearmouth-Jarrow
[28] *Comm. in Genesin* [CPL 1344]: i (CH i.1, 74–83, 110–14, 136–8, 149–50;
ii.12, 277–311; DTA i.6–7, 26, 31–2; iii.2; v.7–9; Interrog.Sig. 87–91, 250,
291–6; Pref.Gen. 64–9), ii (Assmann iv.221–5; Interrog.Sig. 298–300,

350–6, 360–7; Pref.Gen. 70–2), iii (Interrog.Sig. 395–400, 408–9), iv (Interrog.Sig. 423–30)

[29] *De natura rerum* [CPL 1343]: cc. i (Interrog.Sig. 94), ii (DTA i.10), iii (DTA v.1, 3, 6, x.1–3, 6), iv (DTA x.9–10, xi.7–9), v (DTA i.4–6, v.4–5, ix.9), ix (DTA vi.23–6), xi (DTA i.23, 31), xii (DTA ix.4; Hom.supp. xxi.181–6; Interrog.Sig. 109–12, 115–20, 135–42), xiii (Interrog.Sig. 121–7), xx (DTA iii.8), xxii (CH i.40, 39–42; DTA iii.15–17), xxiv (CH i.40, 42–4; DTA ix.13), xxv (DTA x.4, 13), xxvii (DTA x.17–20, 23), xxix (DTA xiv.1), xxxii (DTA xi.1–2, 7–9), xxxiii (DTA xi.1–2, 7–9), xxxiv (DTA xii.1), xxxvi (DTA xiii.1), xliii (DTA iv.54)

[30] *De tabernaculo* [CPL 1345]: i. 3 (Pref.Gen. 83–5, 260–2), ii. 1 (Pref.-Gen. 77–80)

[31] *De temporum ratione* [CPL 2320]: cc. v (DTA i.17–21, 24, vi.21–2), vi (CH i.6, 148–58; DTA i.11, 35–40, ii.1–4), vii (CH i.40, 39–42; DTA i.25, iii.3–4, 6–7, 14), viii (Hom.supp. xxi.181–6; Interrog.Sig. 127–31, 133), xi (DTA iv.33), xvi (DTA iv.1–16, 25–6), xvii (DTA iii.10), xxiv (DTA iii.9), xxv (DTA iii.7, 12–13, viii.9–12), xxvi (DTA iv.50–1; Interrog.Sig. 133), xxvii (DTA iii.5), xxviii (CH i.6, 191–5; DTA viii.13–14), xxix (CH i.6, 196–9; DTA viii.15), xxx (DTA iv.44–6, vi.1–6), xxxi (DTA vi.7–8, 11–12, 14–21), xxxii (DTA vi.9–10, ix.6–7), xxxiv (DTA vi.9), xxxv (DTA iv.36–43, 53), xxxvi (CH i.6, 132–5; DTA iv.16–20, 22–3, 29–32; Interrog.Sig. 134–5), xxxviii (DTA vii.1–9, viii.1), xxxix (DTA vii.1–9), xl (DTA vii.1–9), xliii (DTA viii.1–5, 8), lxx (CH i.40, 147–65)

[32] *Historia ecclesiastica gentis Anglorum* [CPL 1375]: i. 6 (LS xix.1–12), i. 7 (LS xix.13–14, 16–40 *et passim*), i. 23 (CH ii.9, 175–87), i. 25 (CH ii.9, 188–204), i. 26 (CH ii.9, 205–25), i. 27 (CH i.11, 138–50; ii.9, 226–32), i. 29 (CH ii.9, 247–51), i. 31 (CH ii.9, 239–46), i. 32 (CH ii.9, 235–6), ii. 1 (CH ii.9, 3–6, 53–80), ii. 9 (LS xxvi.279–82), ii. 14 (LS xxvi.109–10), ii. 20 (LS xxvi.7–16, 109–10), iii. 1 (LS xxvi.2–29), iii. 2 (LS xxvi.17–41), iii. 3 (LS xxvi.45–69, 85–6), iii. 5 (LS xxvi.45–59, 70–82), iii. 6 (LS xxvi.83–4, 97–108, 169–75), iii. 7 (LS xxvi.119–43), iii. 9 (LS xxvi.144–55, 200–20, 273–6), iii. 10 (LS xxvi.221–38), iii. 11 (LS xxvi. 176–99), iii. 12 (LS xxvi.111–18, 156–68, 192–9, 273–6), iii. 13 (LS xxvi.239–68), iii. 19 (LS xx.7), iv. 14 (LS xxvi.277–8), iv. 17 (LS xx.5–6, 13–23, 25–40 *et passim*), iv. 20 (CH ii.21, 143–76), iv. 25 (CH ii.10, 131–6), iv. 26 (CH ii.10, 176–83, 239–52, 259–66), v. 12 (CH ii.21, 3–20, 22–111), v. 13 (Hom.supp. xix.138–207), v. 14 (Hom.supp. xix.208–41)

[33] *Homeliarum euangelii libri .ii.* [CPL 1367]: i. 3 (Assmann vi.40–55; CH i.13, 65–85, 98–102, 104–6, 108–10, 112–21, 126–8, 133–5, 137–41, 143–5, 149–51), i. 4 (CH i.13, 178–9, 195–9, 202–3, 206–21), i. 6 (CH i.2, 45–52, 62–5, 76–83, 88–97, 102–4, 111–15, 118–28; ii.40, 74–85), i. 7 (CH i.2, 165–74, 199–202, 204–12, 218–19; i.7, 55–7), i. 8 (Hom.supp. i.1–19, 151–60, 169–70, 277–9, 294–8, 317–23, 330–5, 338–49, 352–5, 386–90, 393–402, 404–9, 429–36, 457–60), i. 9 (CH i.4, 3–20, 23–36; i.37, 245–7), i. 10

(CH i.5, 117–22), i. 11 (CH i.6, 3–5, 33–50, 53–78, 106–19, 121–8), i. 12
(CH ii.3, 91–6, 98–106, 109–14, 118–21, 158–61, 168–78), i. 13 (CH i.27,
176–7), i. 14 (Assmann iii.86–8; CH ii.4, 25–35, 37–55, 58–67, 92–9, 104–
22, 161–78, 200–9, 277–91, 308–11, 320–3), i. 18 (CH i.9, 4–12, 59–64,
75–85, 110–22), i. 20 (CH i.26, 17–22, 24–6, 29–30, 35–42, 52–5, 58–66,
73–7, 83–96), i. 21 (CH ii.32, 20–33, 35–40, 44–8, 53–4, 68–73; LS
xv.131–8), i. 25 (Hom.supp. xiii.208–11), ii. 2 (CH i.12, 40–4, 84–91, 102–
4, 107–11, 117–20, 131–5, 141–7), ii. 3 (CH i.14, 34–43, 45–6, 94–5, 98–
103, 122–7, 133–45), ii. 4 (Assmann v.34–9), ii. 5 (CH ii.15, 324–35), ii. 6
(Hom.supp. xvii.67–75, 85–93, 99–102, 106–12, 115–29, 131–4, 138–67,
171–9, 187–202), ii. 7 (CH i.15, 85–9), ii. 9 (CH i.21, 41–7, 86–93), ii. 12
(Hom.supp. viii.66, 159–62, 164–6, 180–2, 208–12, 221–4, 244–9), ii. 13
(Assmann vi.65–76, 84–6, 93–4, 99–104, 116–23, 135–48), ii. 16 (CH i.22,
228–33), ii. 18 (CH ii.24, 100–6, 109–13, 116–25; Hom.supp. xii.59–65,
69–73, 78–90, 118–38, 150–2, 159–64, 168–72, 189–96, 200–15, 227–38),
ii. 19 (CH i.25, 80–3), ii. 20 (Assmann iii.36–42; CH i.25, 57–66, 93–6,
108–14, 118–34), ii. 21 (CH ii.27, 3–5; ii.37, 129–52), ii. 23 (CH i.32, 33–
6, 43–54, 87–102, 110–52, 156–71; Irvine i.48–56), ii. 25 (CH ii.40, 85–8)

[34] *In Cantica canticorum allegorica expositio* [CPL 1353]: iii. 5 (CH ii.14,
298–301)

[35] *In Lucae Euangelium expositio* [CPL 1356]: i (CH i.2, 55–7, i.9, 65–9,
80–5, 135–7, 224–32; i.11, 76–85, 131–7; i.13, 79–85), ii (CH i.33, 17–27,
28–51, 55–8, 60–1, *et passim*; Hom.supp. ii.82–90; xiii.91–2, 104–5, 113–
16, 128–33, 136–40, 154–61; xiv. 41–8, 51–2, 58–64, 66–74, 81–4, 91–7,
111–14, 119–25 *et passim*), iii (CH i.33, 87–116, *et passim*; ii.6, 53–76, 85–
9, 115–35; Irvine ii.208–10), iv (Assmann iv.84–9, 95–8, 101–4, 129–32,
159–67; CH ii.31, 51–8, 63–6, 70–6, 93–8; Hom.supp. iv.59–62, 64–71,
139–46, 150–72, 188–96, 200–4, 209–11, 220–34, 242–5, 255–66, 273–81,
298–94), v (CH i.14, 69–74; ii.28, 17–28, 64–82; ii.31, 24–34, 38–47;
Hom.supp. xvi.103–20, 146–58, 173–82, 207–9, 262–78; xviii.60–1, 89–
102, 112–25, 143–52, 200, 206–21), vi (CH i.21, 38–41; i.40, 129–31, 157–
65; ii.5, 140–2; ii.14, 241–4, 301–9; ii.16, 50–2, 55–63)

[36] *In Marci Euangelium expositio* [CPL 1355]: ii (CH ii.23, 131–46, 179–94;
ii.24, 87–92; ii.25, 19–30, 32–66, 72–9, 97–127, 135–7; Hom.supp.
xvii.78–81, 215–19, 252–7, 260–71), iii (CH i.34, 211–16, 225–37;
Hom.supp. viii.101–2, 106–18), iv (Assmann iv.48–50, 67–83; CH ii.14,
120–18; Hom.supp. xviii.328–44, 347–65)

[37] *Super Acta Apostolorum expositio* [CPL 1357]: [**Act. 1**] (CH i.20, 227–8;
i.21, 68–71, 74–81, 86–93; ii.14, 154–5, 159–62, 164–6), [**Act. 12**] (CH
ii.24, 42–6)

[38] *Super epistulas catholicas expositio* [CPL 1362]: [**1 Petr. 2**] (Assmann
v.153–4; CH ii.40, 108–17, 125–31)

[39] *Vita S. Cudbercti metrica* [CPL 1380; BHL 2020]: lines **46–9** (CH ii.10,
7–27), **75–81** (CH ii.10, 28–35), **81–5** (CH ii.10, 35–9), **86–91** (CH ii.10,

39–43), **165–78** (CH ii.10, 51–8), **180–4** (CH ii.10, 59–63), **220–47** (CH
ii.10, 74–94), **291–308** (CH ii.10, 97–112), **313–32** (CH ii.10, 112–27),
333–9 (CH ii.10, 127–31), **347–8** (CH ii.10, 137–57), **369–72** (CH ii.10,
137–57), **373–6** (CH ii.10, 159–62), **406–12** (CH ii.10, 171–6), **431–4** (CH
ii.10, 190–200), **462–70** (CH ii.10, 210–12), **492–517** (CH ii.10, 212–25),
518–35 (CH ii.10, 226–38), **565–70** (CH ii.10, 272–5), **571–4** (CH ii.10,
275–7), **575–82** (CH ii.10, 277–81), **591–6** (CH ii.10, 286–91), **664–79** (CH
ii.10, 294–303), **597–609** (CH ii.10, 304–7), **680–705** (CH ii.10, 324–31)
[40] *Vita S. Cudbercti prosa* [CPL 1381; BHL 2021]: cc. i (CH ii.10, 7–27), ii
(CH ii.10, 28–35, 44–7), vi (CH ii.10, 59–63), vii (CH ii.10, 63–3), ix (CH
ii.10, 131–6), x (CH ii.10, 74–94), xii (CH ii.10, 97–112), xiii (CH ii.10,
112–27), xv (CH ii.10, 137–57), xvii (CH ii.10, 162–70), xviii (CH ii.10,
171–6), xix (CH ii.10, 176–90), xxi (CH ii.10, 201–9), xxii (CH ii.10,
210–12), xxiv (CH ii.10, 239–58), xxvi (CH ii.10, 259–66), xxxii (CH
ii.10, 282–6), xxxiv (CH ii.10, 292–4), xxviii (CH ii.10, 308–21), xxxix–
xl (CH ii.10, 324–31), xlii (CH ii.10, 333–8)

Benedict of Nursia
[41] *Regula*: cc. ii (CH ii.19, 123–7), xxviii (CH i.8, 82–3), li (CH ii.11, 222–
5)

Caesarius of Arles
[42] *Sermones*: xvi (Hom.supp. xxx.75–81, 85–90, 99–103), xxv (CH i.18,
208–10), xliii (Hom.supp. xix.102–4), l (LS xvii.124–8), liv (LS xvii.68–
83, 88–94, 96–9, 108–9, 129–42, 166–76 etc.), cliv (Hom.supp. xviii.320–
5), clxxix (CH ii.40, 258–75, 279–87), clxxxix (Assmann iii.302–5), ccxix
(CH i.3, 60–72, 81–90, 98–107, 131–49, 151–60, 167–85), ccxxii (CH i.5,
102–7)

Candidus of Fulda
[43] *Opusculum de passione Domini* (PL 106: 57–104): cc. vii (CH ii.14, 139–
47), ix (CH ii.14, 101–3), xii (CH ii.14, 139–47), xiv (CH ii.14, 103–5),
xvi (CH ii.14, 301–9), xix (CH ii.14, 319–27)

Cassian, John
[44] *Conlationes*: praef. (Hom.supp. iv.250–1), v. 2 (CH ii.12, 483–6), v. 15
(CH ii.12, 477–83), v. 16 (CH ii.12, 488–92, 531–41)

Cassiodorus
[45] *De anima*: cc. iii (CH i.1, 108–10), vii (LS i.110–12)
Tripartita historia ecclesiastica: see **Socrates, Sozomen, and Theodoretus**

Eusebius of Caesarea
[46] *Chronicon*, trans. Jerome: CH i.40, 36–7
[47] *Historia ecclesiastica*, trans. Rufinus: **i. 8** (CH i.5, 123–30, 132–41, 162–6;

i.32, 40–1), i. 11 (CH i.32, 43–54, 57–61, 189–95), i. 13 (LS xxiv.82–112, 125–34, 135–88), ii. 5 (Assmann iv.239–48), ii. 6 (CH ii.24, 46–7), ii. 23 (CH ii.17, 64–104), iii. 1 (CH i.21, 236–9), iii. 5 (Assmann v.67–71; CH i.28, 25–33, 39–41), iii. 6 (Assmann v.71–81; CH i.28, 41–9), iii. 7 (Assmann v.88–92; CH i.28, 23–5, 55–7), iii. 8 (CH ii.17, 105–24), ix. 9 (CH ii.18, 23–37), x. 1–14 [Rufinus] (Assmann iv.195–202), x. 7 [Rufinus] (CH ii.18, 38–51; LS xxvii.4–7), x. 8 [Rufinus] (CH ii.18, 38–51; LS xxvii.8–13), xi. 23 [Rufinus] (Hom.supp. xxi.521–41, 546–50, 556–60; xxvi.18–27), xi. 24 [Rufinus] (Hom.supp. xxi.565–71)

Fulgentius of Ruspe
[48] *Sermones .viii.*: iii (CH i.3, 29–31, 114–29, 187–201), iv (CH i.7, 57–70)

Gregory the Great
[49] *Dialogi*: i. 4 (CH i.33, 52–3), ii prol. (CH ii.11, 3–7), ii. 1 (CH ii.11, 8–41), ii. 2 (CH ii.11, 45–60), ii. 3 (CH ii.11, 61–94), ii. 4 (CH ii.11, 109–17), ii. 5 (CH ii.11, 118–34), ii. 6 (CH ii.11, 135–9), ii. 7 (CH ii.11, 94–108), ii. 8 (CH ii.11, 140–86), ii. 9 (CH ii.11, 187–93), ii. 10 (CH ii.11, 193–204), ii. 11 (CH ii.11, 205–22), ii. 12 (CH ii.11, 222–33), ii. 14 (CH ii.11, 234–7), ii. 15 (CH ii.11, 247–61), ii. 16 (CH ii.11, 262–73), ii. 18 (CH ii.11, 274–82), ii. 20 (CH ii.11, 286–91), ii. 21 (CH ii.11, 292–301), ii. 22 (CH ii.11, 302–33), ii. 23 (CH ii.11, 334–61), ii. 24 (CH ii.11, 362–75), ii. 25 (CH ii.11, 376–92), ii. 26 (CH ii.11, 393–5), ii. 27 (CH ii.11, 396–412), ii. 28 (CH ii.11, 413–29), ii. 29 (CH ii.11, 429–33), ii. 30 (CH ii.11, 434–42), ii. 32 (CH ii.11, 470–85), ii. 33 (CH ii.11, 486–512), ii. 34 (CH ii.11, 512–21), ii. 35 (CH ii.11, 522–46), ii. 36 (CH ii.11, 547–50), ii. 37 (CH ii.11, 554–72), ii. 38 (CH ii.11, 577–84), iv. 18 (CH ii.19, 204–11), iv. 34 (CH i.16, 140–2), iv. 36 (CH i.35, 122–32), iv. 37 (CH ii.21, 116–30), iv. 38 (CH ii.21, 116–30)
[50] *Hom. .xl. in Euangelia*: i. 1 (CH i.40, 21–35, 37–9, 51–64, 69–104, 108–29, 165–79), i. 2 (CH i.10, 30–67, 69–75, 87–125, 134–45, 156–64), i. 5 (CH i.38, 45–79, 107–16, 119–50), i. 6 (CH i.32, 64–8, 75–8), i. 7 (CH i.25, 115–18, 189–97), i. 8 (CH i.2, 80–3, 141–62), i. 9 (CH ii.38, 39–111, 118–29, 132–49, 152–75, 179–89), i. 10 (CH i.7, 52–5, 75–8, 92–102, 116–24, 128–32, 205–31, 233–43, 247–61; i.15, 171–82), i. 12 (CH i.28, 194–222; ii.39, 27–40, 47–8, 64–71, 134–6, 138–44, 146–53, 208–12), i. 13 (Assmann iv.67–89, 95–8, 101–4), i. 14 (CH i.17, 13–15, 17–18, 34–59, 74–7, 79–81, 84–7), i. 15 (CH ii.6, 33–52, 91–105, 167–205), i. 16 (CH i.11, 30–6, 127–50, 154–99; ii.7, 10–25), i. 17 (CH ii.36, 16–22, 26–56, 58–68, 70–7, 80–90, 93–9, 101–37), i. 18 (CH ii.13, 43–8, 81–94, 107–17, 145–9, 185–90, 208–20 *et passim*; Pref.Gen. 69–70), i. 19 (CH i.35, 208–11, 214–18; ii.5, 34–6, 39–133, 137–84, 187–227), i. 20 (CH i.25, 50–6, 189–211, 213–17; ii.3, 23–5, 30–2), ii. 21 (CH i.15, 75–84, 89–111, 116–35, 139–70; ii.12, 195–205), ii. 22 (CH ii.15, 269–84, 287–317), ii. 23 (CH

ii.16, 41–50, 52–5, 64–96), ii. **24** (CH ii.16, 130–207; Hom.supp. xiv.152–
71), ii. **25** (CH i.14, 171–8; Pref.Gen. 89–92), ii. **26** (CH i.16, 27–33, 38–
43, 47–72, 75–98, 101–24; i.22, 214–27), ii. **27** (CH i.35, 280–4; i.36, 82–4;
ii.19, 18–21, 47–54, 73–85; ii.35, 51–4, 58–62, 97–105, 110–16; Hom.supp.
viii.69–72), ii. **28** (CH i.8, 127–38; i.40, 110–20), ii. **29** (CH i.3, 74–80;
i.21, 74–86, 110–17, 122–35, 137–9, 155–81, 183–93, 195–218, 224–33), ii.
30 (CH i.22, 111–30, 132–40, 145–55, 156–72, 175–210, 214–27; ii.3, 150–
1, 153–8, 164–78; ii.19, 25–42; Hom.supp. x.59–64, 67–71, 83–6, 109–15,
122–6), ii. **31** (CH ii.26, 101–6), ii. **34** (CH i.2, 58–62; i.24, 17–23, 25–45,
48–59, 63–75, 77–186, 193–6, 207–8; Interrog.Sig. 290–1), ii. **35** (CH
ii.37, 22–33, 37–65, 85–8, 91–4, 110–12, 115–18, 123–54, 164–75), ii. **36**
(CH ii.23, 24–30, 33–7, 39–42, 44–73, 80–94, 96–110, 113–22), ii. **38** (CH
i.17 AppB3, 217–22; i.35, 27–41, 46–50, 54–78, 84–93, 98–114, 117–20,
122–41, 143–93, 211–13, 219–30 *et passim*), ii. **39** (Assmann v.82–7; CH
i.23, 135–63; i.28, 17–18, 58–9, 62–6, 69–74, 97–102, 105–10, 114–30,
136–50, 152–61, 164–5, 180–91), ii. **40** (CH i.23, 30–59, 61, 64–71, 73–89,
94–114, 120–31; ii.37, 176–201)

[51] *Hom. in Hiezechihelem*: i. **4** (LS xv.197–214)
[52] *Moralia in Iob*: praef. **3** (CH ii.30, 51–2, 140–2), praef. **5** (CH i.31,
250–4), ii. **4** (CH ii.30, 26–30), iii. **8** (CH ii.30, 125–7), iii. **10** (CH ii.30,
97–101), xvii. **12** (CH i.34, 266–9), xviii. **9** (CH i.40, 157–65), xxxi. **47**
(Hom.supp. i.10–16), xxxii. **19** (Interrog.Sig. 258–9), xxxv. **16** (CH ii.30,
210–17)
[53] *Regula pastoralis*: iii. **16** (CH i.5, 50–61; ii.36, 131–7)

Gregory of Tours
[54] *Historia Francorum*: i. **48** (CH ii.34, 314–27; LS xxxi.1371–7, 1441–84,
1489–92), ii. **34** (CH i.18, 5–11)

Haymo of Auxerre
[55] *Expositio in Pauli epistolas* (PL 117: 359–938): [**Rom. xiii**] (CH i.39, 26–
7, 34–5, 42–4, 50–1, 63–5, 95–6); [**1 Cor. iii**] (CH ii.40, 103–4, 239–50)
[56] *Historiae sacrae epitome* (PL 118: 817–74): ii. **26** (CH ii.17, 64–73), iii. **2**
(CH i.21, 236–9), ix. **1–6** (CH i.20, 213–27), ix. **10** (CH i.20, 231–4)
[57] *Hom. aliquot de sanctis* (PL 118: 747–804): i (CH i.38, 12–14, 24–31, 34–
9, 156–9), ii (CH i.25, 90–4), iv (Irvine iv.304–19, 340–7, 353–7), viii (CH
i.36, 183–97, 205–10, 212–18, 237–41, 245–8, 266–74), x (Assmann iv.67–
83, 95–8)
[58] *Hom. de tempore* (PL 118: 11–746): ii (CH i.40, 65–8, 129–31, 157–65),
ix (Hom.supp. i.10–16, 20–6, 183–94, 461–3), xi (CH i.4, 175–93), xii
(CH i.5, 40–53, 71–81, 130–66, 178–82), xiii (CH i.9, 155–63, 170–80,
186–203), xiv (CH i.6, 12–13, 102–7; i.9, 65–73, 85–92, 110–17, 132–7),
xv (CH i.5, 62–9, 71–81; i.7, 52–5, 71–3, 79–82, 92–102, 105–15, 133–6,
247–58), xvi (CH ii.7, 10–25), xviii (CH i.4, 3–20; ii.4, 37–44, 55–7, 79–

91, 161–78, 230–9, 268–76, 295–305), **xix** (CH i.7, 15–24, 29–35, 40–4, 49–58, 65–75, 105–15, 127–46, 152–3, 159–65, *et passim*; i.35, 98–109), **xx** (CH ii.23, 24–8, 30–3, 142–6; Hom.supp. xvii.215–19), **xxiii** (CH i.10, 23–9, 51–9, 75–87, 105–16), **xxv** (CH ii.8, 34–7, 45–57), **xxviii** (CH i.11, 27–30, 42–6, 62–7, 154–89, 199–213, 218–23; ii.7, 10–25), **xxxii** (CH i.1, 56–61), **xlii** (Hom.supp. iv.27–30, 76–89, 92–6, 101–6, 120–3, 126–9, 135–8, 139–46, 150–62, 175–7, 188–96, 205–11, 216–19, 273–86), **xlix** (CH i.12, 26–83, 112–17, 122–8), **lvi** (CH ii.13, 66–9, 81–94, 96–9, 190–204, 221–3, 228–36, 288–90), **lxiv** (CH i.14, 61–3, 69–74, 86–9, 128–45, 149–56; ii.14, 58–63, 205–8, 219–21, 238–40, 327–33), **lxxxi** (CH i.16, 27–33, 47–53, 65–72, 98–100), **lxxxiii** (CH i.17, 13–15, 49–54, 74–7), **lxxxv** (Assmann vi.71–6, 93–8, 116–23), **lxxxvii** (Hom.supp. vii.32–8), **lxxxix** (Hom.supp. vii.59–62, 164–6, 170–3, 183–6, 208–12, 225–7), **xcii** (CH i.18, 79–87, 104–9, 113–14, 137–9, 145–52), **xcvi** (CH i.21, 155–81), **xcviii** (Hom.supp. ix.158–71, 174–86), **c** (Hom.supp. x.38–43, 49–56, 75–9, 83–6, 109–15, 122–6, 131–8, 142–69, 186–7, 190–200, 207–10), **cviii** (CH ii.3, 55–60, 219–28; ii.13, 259–64; ii.24, 106–8; Hom.supp. xii.47–55, 91–4, 150–2, 178–82), **cxiv** (CH i.24, 41–5, 77–84, 196–7), **cxv** (Hom. supp. xiii.43–5, 141–5, 154–61), **cxvii** (Hom.supp. xiv.53–7, 147–51, 190–4, 217–25), **cxviii** (Assmann iii.86–8; Hom.supp. xv.26–35, 80–98, 102–6, 109–21, 131–3, 144–8, 152–5, 188–90, 214–21), **cxix** (CH ii.25, 78, 129–34), **cxx** (CH ii.26, 52–4), **cxxi** (Hom.supp. xvi.39–46, 49–56, 94–8, 146–58, 173–82, 218–29, 284–92), **cxxii** (Assmann v.77–87; CH i.28, 20–3, 52–5, 60–1, 80–4, 91–3, 161–2, 166–75; CH ii.28, 93–8), **cxxiv** (Hom.supp. xvii.106–12, 115–19, 187–202), **cxxvii** (CH ii.31, 47–8), **cxxxv** (CH i.35, 98–109), **cxxxvi** (CH i.8, 127–38)

Heiric of Auxerre

[59] *Hom. per circulum anni* (CCCM 116–116B): **i. 15** (CH i.6, 12–13, 66–78), **i. 28** (CH i.11, 37–42, 52–7), **i. 40** (Hom.supp. iii.176–87), **i. 47** (Hom.supp. v.208–9), **ii. 20** (Hom.supp. xiii.43–5, 113–16, 175–7), **ii. 23** (CH i.26, 17–22, 60–6, 73–7, 78–81), **ii. 30** (CH ii.28, 1–16, 42–4, 83–9)

Hilduin of Saint-Denis

[60] *Passio S. Dionysii* [BHL 2175] (PL 106: 23–50): cc. **ii** (LS xxix.1–5), **v** (LS xxix.6–16), **vi** (LS xxix.20–45), **vii–viii** (LS xxix.46–92), **xiv** (LS xxix.46–92), **xvi** (LS xxix.93–101), **xvii** (LS xxix.93–125), **xviii** (CH i.37, 33–8), **xix** (CH i.37, 39–43; LS xxix.126–57), **xx** (LS xxix.126–57, 162–3), **xxi** (LS xxix.126–57), **xxii** (CH i.37, 43–7; LS xxix.158–61), **xxiii** (LS xxix.166–202), **xxiv–xxv** (LS xxix.203–16), **xxvi** (LS xxix.217–29), **xxvii** (LS xxix.230–43), **xxviii** (LS xxix.244–55), **xxix** (LS xxix.256–74), **xxx** (LS xxix.276–9), **xxxi** (LS xxix.280–317), **xxxiii–xxxiv** (LS xxix.318–39), **xxxvi** (LS xxix.318–39)

Hrabanus Maurus

[61] *Comm. in Librum Iudicum et Ruth* (PL 108: 1107–1224): i. 10 (Hom.supp. xiv.172–5), ii. 16 (Hom.supp. xiv.172–5)

[62] *Comm. in Matthaeum* (PL 107: 727–1156): v. 15 (CH ii.25, 111–13), viii. 27 (LS x.97–108)

[63] *Hom. de festis praecipuis* (PL 110: 9–468): xx (CH i.19, 179), cii (CH i.25, 4–27)

Isidore of Seville

[64] *Chronica maiora*: Assmann iv.203–12; Hom.supp. x.170–6

[65] *De ecclesiasticis officiis*: i. 26 (CH i.1, 1–5; i.2, 42–5, 174–5; ii.1, 41–3)

[66] *De natura rerum [Liber rotarum]*: cc. xii (DTA ix.9), xiii (DTA i.7–9), xv (DTA i.33–4), xxv (DTA ix.1–3), xxvi (DTA ix.6–8, 10–12), xxx (DTA x.10)

[67] *De ortu et obitu patrum*: cc. lxvii [lxviii] (CH i.26, 100–4, 274–5; LS x.5–15), lxxi [lxxii] (LS xv.159–73), lxxxii [lxxxiii] (LS xv.141–9)

[68] *Etymologiae*: iii. 63. 1 (Interrog.Sig. 120–1), vii. 2. 12 (Interrog.Sig. 537–40), vii. 4. 1–8 (Interrog.Sig. 512–37), vii. 6. 65 (CH ii.40, 74–85), viii. 11. 5 (Hom.supp. xxi.197–201), ix. 3. 16 (CH i.2, 52–3), xii. 2. 14–16 (LS xxv.564–73), xii. 8. 2 (Hom.supp. i.258–74), xviii. 1. 2–4 (LS xxv.705–14)

[69] *In libros Veteris et Noui Testamenti prooemia*: c. lxxxvi (LS xv.176–7)

[70] *Mysticorum expositiones sacramentorum seu Quaestiones in Vetus Testamentum*: Gen. i. 2 (Pref.Gen. 48–55), v. 4 (Interrog.Sig. 249–50), v. 14 (Interrog.Sig. 290–6), x. 2 (Interrog.Sig. 392–5), xv. 3 (Interrog.Sig. 472–5), xv. 5 (Interrog.Sig. 475–86); Ex. i. 2 (CH ii.12, 178), i. 3 (CH ii.12, 179–80), xv. 1 (CH ii.15, 38–43, 50–9, 317–20), xix. 1 (CH ii.12, 186–91), xx. 3 (CH ii.12, 186–95), xxiii. 3 (CH ii.12, 208–12; Hom.supp. xx.128–39), xxiv. 1 (CH ii.12, 215–19), xxviii. 1 (CH ii.12, 221–5), xxviii. 2 (CH ii.12, 226–43), xxix. 2 (CH ii.12, 260–1), xxix. 3 (CH ii.12, 267–73), xxix. 9 (CH ii.12, 312–17), xxix. 10 (CH ii.12, 320–5), xxix. 11 (CH ii.12, 317–20), xxix. 12 (CH ii.12, 325–6), xxix. 13 (CH ii.12, 326–8), xxix. 14 (CH ii.12, 328–31), xxix. 15 (CH ii.12, 331–3), xxix. 16 (CH ii.12, 334–7), xxx. 1 (CH ii.12, 255–60), xxxi. 1 (CH ii.12, 250–4), xliv. 1 (CH ii.12, 337–43), l. 1 (CH ii.12, 337–43); Leuit. i. 1 (CH ii.12, 344–56), i. 3 (CH ii.12, 357–66), i. 3–5 (CH ii.12, 366–73); Ios. i. 2 (CH ii.12, 416–24), vii. 1–3 (CH ii.12, 425–38), xii. 2 (CH ii.12, 565–71), xv. 1 (CH ii.12, 571–9), xviii. 1 (CH ii.12, 560–5)

Jerome (Hieronymus)

[71] *Aduersus Iouinianum*: i. 26 (Pref.Gen. 29–36), ii. 9 (CH i.27, 142–50)

[72] *Comm. in .iv. Epistulas Pauli*: Ephesios iii (CH i.11, 110–11)

[73] *Comm. in Euangelium Matthaei*: praef. (LS xv.111–18, 127–9, 131–8, 141–56, 159–73, 178–81, 192–4, 197–214, 219–24), i. 4 (CH i.11, 37–42,

89–91, 110–11, 131–7), i. 7 (CH ii.26, 14–22; Hom.supp. xiii.162–71), iii.
18 (CH i.34, 167–72, 247–9), iv. 24 (Hom.supp. xviii.328–44), iv. 25 (CH
ii.38, 118–29), iv. 26 (CH ii.14, 54–8, 98–101), iv. 27 (CH ii.14, 159–64,
208–10, 225–7, 258–62, 289–98)

[74] *De uiris inlustribus*: cc. i (CH i.26, 103–5; LS x.5–15), iii (LS xv.127–9),
vii (LS xv.154–6), viii (LS xv.141–9), ix (LS xv.159–73)

[75] *Epistulae*: liii (Pref.Gen. 73–4), cxxi (Hom.supp. xvi.284–92; xxviii.8–
13), cxxiii (Pref.Gen. 19)

[76] *Liber interpretationis hebraicorum nominum*: CH i.2 (1×), i.13 (2×), i.14
(2×)

[77] *Tractatus .lix. in psalmos*: cc. xcv (Assmann iii.288–93), cxv (Assmann
iii.294–7)

Julian of Toledo

[78] *Prognosticum futuri saeculi*: i. 1 (Hom.supp. xi.103–10), i. 2 (Hom.supp.
xi.94–102), i. 5 (Hom.supp. xi.111–17), i. 7 (Hom.supp. xi.200–7), i. 10
(Hom.supp. xi.181–3), i. 11 (Hom.supp. xi.118–28), i. 12 (Hom.supp.
xi.129–38), i. 13 (Hom.supp. xi.129–38), i. 15 (CH ii.35, 105–8; Hom.
supp. xi.139–59), i. 18 (Hom.supp. xi.163–7), i. 22 (Hom.supp. xi.208–
13), ii. 9 (Hom.supp. xi.185–94), ii. 10 (Hom.supp. xi.185–94), ii. 11
(Hom.supp. xi.243–53), ii. 13 (Hom.supp. xi.185–94), ii. 14 (Hom.supp.
xi.208–13), ii. 15 (Hom.supp. xi.216–19), ii. 16 (Hom.supp. xi.216–19), ii.
19 (Hom.supp. xi.220–8), ii. 22 (Hom.supp. xi.229–31), ii. 24 (Hom.supp.
xi.232–5), ii. 25 (Hom.supp. xi.236–42), ii. 26 (Hom.supp. xi.236–42), ii.
27 (Hom.supp. xi.271–2), ii. 31 (Hom.supp. xi.261–70), ii. 32 (Hom.supp.
xi.261–7, 504–7), ii. 35 (Hom.supp. xi.243–53), ii. 37 (Hom.supp. xi.254–
8), iii. 1 (Hom.supp. xi.273–5), iii. 2 (CH i.40, 150–3), iii. 5 (CH i.40, 47–
51; Hom.supp. xi.285–95), iii. 7 (CH i.21, 86–93; Hom.supp. xi.347–9),
iii. 8 (Hom.supp. xi.350–3), iii. 11 (Hom.supp. xi.354–9), iii. 15
(Hom.supp. xi.297–301), iii. 20 (CH i.5, 112–16; i.16, 126–30; Hom.supp.
xi.305–11, 325), iii. 22 (CH i.16, 130–3; Hom.supp. xi.320–4), iii. 23 (CH
i.16, 133–5; Hom.supp. xi.326–31), iii. 24 (CH i.16, 138–40; Hom.supp.
xi.312–19), iii. 26 (Hom.supp. xi.339–42), iii. 29 (Hom.supp. xi.332–8),
iii. 33 (CH i.27, 177–92; Hom.supp. xi.360–90), iii. 36 (Hom.supp.
xi.345–6; Hom.supp. xi.405–12, 414–17, 451–4), iii. 38 (Hom.supp.
xi.459–65), iii. 39 (Hom.supp. xi.466–72), iii. 40 (Hom.supp. xi.473–7),
iii. 41 (Hom.supp. xi.478–92), iii. 42 (Hom.supp. xi.493–503), iii. 44
(Hom.supp. xi.455–8), iii. 45 (Hom.supp. xi.519–25), iii. 46 (Hom.supp.
xi.508–18), iii. 47 (Hom.supp. xi.508–18), iii. 51 (Hom.supp. xi.504–7),
iii. 52 (Hom.supp. xi.526–41), iii. 55 (Hom.supp. xi.533–41), iii. 58
(Hom.supp. xi.548–57), iii. 60 (Hom.supp. xi.562–5), iii. 61 (Hom.supp.
xi.558–61, 566–74), iii. 62 (Hom.supp. xi.566–74); Ælfric also produced
an epitome of this work by Julian: ed. in Gatch, *Preaching and Theology*,
134–46

Martin of Braga

[79] *De correctione rusticorum*: cc. v (Hom.supp. xxi.72–81), vi (Hom.supp. xxi.72–92), vii (Hom.supp. xxi.101–3, 105–7, 113–17, 126–7, 133–8, 150–3, 159–80), x (CH i.6, 129–32, 141–3), xii (LS xvii.105–7), xvi (LS xvii.100–4, 129–35, 143–7)

Origen

[80] *Comm. in Euangelium Matthaei*, in Latin translation: iv (CH ii.26, 30–41, 48–52, 61–3, 67–9, 136–47)

[81] *In Lucam homiliae .xxxix.*, trans. Jerome: xvii (CH i.9, 163–8, 186–97)

Paschasius Radbertus of Corbie

[82] *De assumptione S. Mariae uirginis* [pseudo-Jerome] (CCCM 56C: 97–162): i. 1 (CH i.30, 20–64, 66–107, 110–55 *et passim*), vii. 38 (CH i.36, 124–7)

[83] *De corpore et sanguine Domini* (CCCM 16: 1–131): c. xiv (CH ii.15, 159–73)

Paulus Diaconus

[84] *Vita S. Gregorii Magni* [BHL 3639]: CH i.9, 12–173; ii.19, 54–5

Pelagius

[85] *Expositiones .xiii. epistularum Pauli*: [Rom. xiii. 11] (CH i.39, 34–5, 37–9, 44–6), [Rom. xiii. 12] (CH i.39, 56–9, 68), [Rom. xiii. 13] (CH i.39, 70–9, 88–9)

Petrus Chrysologus of Ravenna

[86] *Sermones*: clii (CH i.5, 93–6, 107–12)

Prosper of Aquitaine

[87] *Epitome chronicorum*: CH i.40, 36–7

Quoduultdeus of Carthage

[88] *Sermo (quartus) contra Iudaeos, paganos et Arianos*: cc. i (Hom.supp. i.410–12), iii (Hom.supp. i.113–44), v (Hom.supp. i.413–26), xi (CH ii.1, 134–7, 140–3), xiii (CH ii.1, 205–7, 214–15), xv (CH ii.1, 217–18, 247–66), xvi (CH ii.1, 219–21)

Ratramnus of Corbie

[89] *De corpore et sanguine Domini* (PL 121: 103–70): cc. vi (CH ii.15, 90–9), vii (CH ii.15, 90–9), viii (CH ii.15, 90–9), ix (CH ii.15, 100–7), x (CH ii.15, 100–7), xvii (CH ii.15, 111–16), xviii (CH ii.15, 117–24), xix (CH ii.15, 117–24), xx (CH ii.15, 174–80), xxii (CH ii.15, 184–90), xxv (CH ii.15, 153–7), xxvii (CH ii.15, 191–8), xxviii (CH ii.15, 191–8), xxix (CH ii.15, 210–14), xxxix (CH ii.15, 220–2), xlix (CH ii.15, 124–8), lx (CH ii.15, 153–7), lxix (CH ii.15, 128–30), lxxii (CH ii.15, 130–8), lxxiii (CH

ii.15, 225–44), lxxiv (CH ii.15, 130–8), lxxv (CH ii.15, 249–54), lxxvi
(CH ii.15, 143–7), lxxvii (CH ii.15, 143–7), lxxviii (CH ii.15, 199–208),
lxxxviii (CH ii.15, 153–7), xciii (CH ii.15, 138–42), xcv (CH ii.15, 249–
54), xcix (CH ii.15, 217–20)

Remigius of Auxerre

[90] *Comm. in Apocalypsin* [pseudo-Haymo] (PL 117: 937–1220): iii. 11 (CH
i.40, 140–7)

Sedulius, Caelius

[91] *Carmen paschale*: v. 188–95 (CH ii.14, 291–4)

Sedulius Scottus

[92] *Liber de rectoribus christianis* [BCLL 685]: cc. xv (Hom.supp. ix.46–54),
xix (Hom.supp. ix.46–54)

Smaragdus of Saint-Mihiel

[93] *Diadema monachorum* (PL 102: 593–690): c. lxxxix (CH i.6, 180–1)
[94] *Collectiones epistularum et euangeliorum de tempore et de sanctis seu Expositio
libri comitis* (PL 102: 13–552): CH i.2, 55–7; i.3, 91–8; i.7, 73–5, 79–81, 105–
15; i.8, 167–8; i.9, 124–30; i.12, 105; i.14, 69–74; i.16, 44–6; i.27, 80–2, 87–9,
134–8, 142–52, 155–63, 165–73; i.33, 16–17; i.34, 167–72, 247–9; i.39, 50–1;
i.40, 157–65; ii.4, 29–35, 70–8, 100–4; ii.6, 53–76, 85–9, 115–35; ii.8, 22–8,
30–3, 45–51, 68–79, 81–7, 89–98, 101–19, 122–7; ii.14, 63–8, 298–301; ii.15,
258–69; ii.16, 50–2, 55–63, 186–99; ii.26, 14–22; Hom.supp. xvii.249;
Irvine i.63–77, 102–7, 121–6, 139–42, 149–52, 160–7

Socrates, Sozomen, and Theodoretus

[95] *Tripartita historia ecclesiastica*, trans. Cassiodorus: i. 1 (Hom.supp.
xxvi.23–7), i. 9 (Hom.supp. xxvi.7–15), ix. 2 (Hom.supp. xxii.59–60),
ix. 4 (Hom.supp. xxii.62–7; xxvi.15–17), ix. 6 (Hom.supp. xxvi.4–6), ix.
27 (Hom.supp. xxi.516–20; xxvi.18–22), ix. 28 (Hom.supp. xxi.536–41,
546–54, 556–60), ix. 30 (Hom.supp. xxvi.28–139), xi. 9 (Hom.supp.
xxii.73–8), xi. 15 (Hom.supp. xxii.73–8), xi. 17 (Hom.supp. xxii.73–8),
xi. 18 (Hom.supp. xxii.73–8)

Sulpicius Severus

[96] *Dialogi*: ii. 1 (CH ii.34, 239–68; LS xxxi.901–33), ii. 2 (LS xxxi.934–64),
ii. 3 (LS xxxi.965–1010), ii. 4 (LS xxxi.1011–37, 1300–4), ii. 5 (LS
xxxi.650–81), ii. 8 (CH ii.34, 239–68), ii. 9 (CH ii.34, 239–68; LS
xxxi.1038–65), ii. 11 (LS xxxi.1066–1102), ii. 13 (LS xxxi.684–709), iii.
2 (LS xxxi.1103–17), iii. 3 (LS xxxi.1119–34), iii. 4 (LS xxxi.1161–77),
iii. 6 (LS xxxi.1198–1214), iii. 7 (LS xxxi.1215–16, 1219–28), iii. 8 (LS
xxxi. 1178–97, 1229–44), iii. 9 (LS xxxi.1245–66), iii. 10 (LS xxxi.1267–
76), iii. 14 (LS xxxi.1135–42, 1277–1304)

[97] *Epistulae .iii.*: i. 10–15 (LS xxxi.845–97), iii. **6** (LS xxxi.1306–12), iii. **7**–
8 (LS xxxi.1313–27), iii. **9**–10 (LS xxxi.1328–48), iii. **11**–12 (LS
xxxi.1328–48), iii. **6**–12 (CH ii.34, 270–95), iii. **13** (CH ii.34, 270–95;
LS xxxi.1328–48), iii. **14**–17 (CH ii.34, 296–313; LS xxxi.1349–70), iii. **17**
(LS xxxi.1378–81), iii. **18** (LS xxxi.1382–4)

[98] *Vita S. Martini*: cc. **prol.** (LS xxxi.1–7), **i** (LS xxxi.1–7, 9), **ii** (CH ii.34,
1–6, 7–18, 20–6; LS xxxi.10–57), **iii** (CH ii.34, 27–44; LS xxxi. 58–93), **iv**
(CH ii.34, 45–58; LS xxxi.94–130), **v** (CH ii.34, 59–74; LS xxxi.94–141,
143–69), **vi** (CH ii.34, 74–82, 86–9; LS xxxi.170–302), **vii** (CH ii.34, 90–
103; LS xxxi.204–38), **viii** (CH ii.34, 105–9; LS xxxi.239–53), **ix** (CH
ii.34, 110–16; LS xxxi.254–62, 264–85), **x** (CH ii.34, 116–32; LS
xxxi.286–93, 310–40), **xi** (CH ii.34, 133–46; LS xxxi.341–65), **xii** (CH
ii.34, 154–60; LS xxxi.366–87), **xiii** (CH ii.34, 161–77; LS xxxi.388–426),
xiv (CH ii.34, 178–89; LS xxxi.427–63), **xv** (LS xxxi.464–83), **xvi** (CH
ii.34, 196–8; LS xxxi.484–505), **xvii** (CH ii.34, 204–11; LS xxxi.506–47),
xviii (LS xxxi.548–71), **xix** (LS xxxi.574–91, 601–9), **xx** (LS xxxi.610–
27, 629–49), **xxi** (LS xxxi.682–3, 705–9, 775–90), **xxii** (LS xxxi.710–48),
xxiii (LS xxxi.792–830), **xxiv** (CH ii.34, 229–38; LS xxxi.749–74, 831–
44), **xxv** (LS xxxi.1–7, 298–301, 592–8), **xxvi** (LS xxxi.298–305), **xxvii**
(LS xxxi.306–9)

Theodulf of Orleans

[99] *De ordine baptismi* (PL 105: 223–40): c. **i** (CH ii.3, 247–61)

ANONYMOUS WRITINGS

[100] *Comm. in Pentateuchum* [pseudo-Bede]: **Gen. i** (Pref.Gen. 48–59, 64–
9), **xli** (Pref.Gen. 74–7)

[101] *De duodecim abusiuis saeculi* [pseudo-Cyprian]: Hom.supp. ix.46–54

[102] *Historia monachorum*, trans. Rufinus: cc. **vii** (LS xxv.812–62), **xvi** (LS
xx.123–30), **xxviii** (Hom.supp. xxix.13–34)

[103] *Liber de ordine creaturarum* [pseudo-Isidore]: cc. **xxxii** (CH ii.19, 100–
4), **lii** (CH ii.19, 96–9), **liii** (CH ii.19, 100–4), **liv** (CH ii.19, 100–4)

[104] *Liber pontificalis*: LS x.5–15

[105] *passiones apostolorum*: *Passio S. Andreae* [BHL 428]: CH i.38 (*passim*);
Passio S. Bartholomaei [BHL 1002]: CH i.31 (*passim*); *Passio S. Iacobi
maioris* [BHL 4057]: CH ii.1 (*passim*), ii.27 (*passim*); *Passio S. Iohannis*
[CPG 1097; BHL 4320] [pseudo-Mellitus]: CH i.4 (*passim*), i.37, 247–9;
Passio S. Marci [BHL 5276]: LS xv (*passim*); *Passio S. Matthaei* [BHL
5690]: CH ii.32 (*passim*); *Passio SS. Petri et Pauli* [BHL 6657]: CH i.26,
160–272, 275–97; ii.19 (*passim*); LS xvii (*passim*); *Passio S. Philippi* [BHL
6814]: CH ii.17 (*passim*); *Passio SS. Simonis et Iudae* [BHL 7750]: CH ii.33
(*passim*); *Passio S. Thomae* [BHL 8136]: LS xxxvi (*passim*)

[106] *passiones martyrum*: *Passio S. Agathae* [BHL 134]: LS viii (*passim*);
Passio S. Agnetis [BHL 156]: LS vii (*passim*); *Passio S. Alexandri papae*

[BHL 266]: CH ii.18 (*passim*), Hom.supp. xxiii (*passim*); *Passio S. Apollinaris ep.* [BHL 623]: LS xxii (*passim*); *Passio S. Caeciliae* [BHL 1495]: LS xxxiv (*passim*); *Passio SS. Chrysanthi et Dariae* [BHL 1787]: LS xxxv (*passim*); *Passio S. Clementis papae* [BHL 1848]: CH i.37 (*passim*); *Passio SS. Septem Dormientium* [BHL 2316]: CH ii.27, 184–230; *Passio S. Eugeniae* [BHL 2666] [pseudo-Rufinus]: LS ii (*passim*); *Passio SS. Gallicani, Iohannis et Pauli* [BHL 3236, 3238]: LS vii (*passim*); *Passio S. Georgii* [BHL 3373]: LS xiv (*passim*); *Passio SS. Iuliani et Basilissae* [BHL 4532]: LS iv (*passim*); *Passio S. Longini* [BHL 4965]: LS xxvii (*passim*); *Passio S. Luciae* [BHL 4992]: LS ix (*passim*); *Passio S. Mauritii* [BHL 5743] [pseudo-Eucherius]: LS xxviii (*passim*); *Passio SS. Polochronii et al.* [BHL 6884]: CH i.29 (*passim*), LS xxiv (*passim*); *Passio SS. Quadraginta martyrum Sebastenorum* [BHL 7539]: LS xi (*passim*); *Passio S. Sebastiani* [BHL 7543]: LS v (*passim*); *Passio S. Vincentii* [BHL 8693]: Irvine iv (*passim*)

[107] *uitae sanctorum*: *Vita S. Basilii* [BHL 1023]: CH i.30, 207–57, LS iii (*passim*); *Vita S. Cuthberti* [BHL 2019]: CH ii.10 (*passim*); *Vita S. Fursei* [BHL 3210]: CH ii.20 (*passim*); *Vita S. Mauri* [BHL 5773]: LS vi (*passim*)

k. Byrhtferth of Ramsey

Byrhtferth was a monk at the fenland monastery of Ramsey from a time shortly after its foundation (966) until his death in *c.*1020. Few details of his life are known, save for the important fact that he had the opportunity of studying with the great scholar Abbo of Fleury during the latter's sojourn at Ramsey during the years 985–7. Although a recent foundation, Ramsey soon acquired a substantial library, probably *inter alia* as a result of books brought to England by Abbo. Although very few surviving manuscripts from Ramsey's library have been identified, some notion of its holdings can be gleaned from the very substantial corpus of Byrhtferth's writings (see above, pp. 121–5). I use the following abbreviations for the writings of Byrhtferth.

Comp. = Byrhtferth's *Computus*, reconstructed and ed. Baker and Lapidge in *Byrhtferth's Enchiridion*, 373–427 [cited by page number]

Ench. = *Byrhtferth's Enchiridion*, ed. Baker and Lapidge, 1–250 [cited by part, sub-chapter and line number]

HR = *Historia regum*, in *Symeonis Monachi Opera Omnia*, ed. Arnold, ii. 3–91 [cited by part and sub-chapter]

Glossae DNR = the 'glossae Bridferti' to Bede's *De natura rerum*, cc. i–xxxvi, pr. PL 90: 187–278 [cited by column number and location (A, B, C, D) of PL]

Glossae DTR = the 'glossae Bridferti' to Bede's *De temporum ratione*, cc. i–lxiv, pr. PL 90: 297–548 [cited by column number and location (A, B, C, D) of PL]

Glossae Loq.digit. = the 'glossae Bridferti' to Bede's so-called treatise *De loquela per gestum digitorum* [= properly c. i of his *De temporum ratione*], pr. PL 90: 685C, 690B, 692C–695A [cited by column number and location (A, B, C, D) of PL]

Glossae Rat.unc. = the 'glossae Bridferti' to Bede's so-called treatise *De ratione unciarum* [= properly c. iv of his *De temporum ratione*], pr. PL 90: 700D–702B [cited by column number and location (A, B, C, D) of PL]

VSE = *Vita S. Ecgwini*, in *Byrhtferth of Ramsey: The Lives of Oswald and Ecgwine*, ed. Lapidge [cited by part and sub-chapter; Epil. = Byrhtferth's Epilogus or 'preface' to the work]

VSO = *Vita S. Oswaldi*, in *Byrhtferth of Ramsey: The Lives of Oswald and Ecgwine*, ed. Lapidge [cited by part and sub-chapter; Prol. = Byrhtferth's prologue to the work]

Abbo of Fleury

[1] *Passio S. Eadmundi* [BHL 2392]: cc. iii (VSO iv.13), v (VSO i.4)

Adrevald of Fleury

[2] *Historia translationis S. Benedicti* [BHL 1117]: cc. iii (VSO iii.6), xxii (VSE iv.9)

Aldhelm of Malmesbury

[3] *Carmen de uirginitate* [CPL 1333]: lines 2–3 (VSO v.1), 4 (VSO v.1), 5 (VSO v.1), 24–7 (Ench. ii.1.204–5), 1071 (VSE i.7), 1625 (Comp. p. 376), 2903 (VSE Epil.)

[4] *De uirginitate* (prose) [CPL 1332]: cc. i (VSE i.1), ii (VSO i.4, ii.4; VSE Epil., ii.4), iii (Comp. p. 375; VSO ii.2, v.11; VSE iv.8), iv (Comp. p. 375), v (Comp. p. 375), vi (Comp. p. 375), vii (VSO iii.6), x (Ench. i.3.6–7; VSO ii.8), xi (Comp. p. 376; VSO ii.8, iv.2), xii (VSO v.4), xiii (Comp. p. 376; VSE iv.6, 8), xv (VSE ii.1), xviii (VSO iii.6; VSE Epil.), xx (VSO iii.14), xxiii (VSE Epil.), xxviii (Comp. p. 376), xxxiv (VSE iv.6), xl (Ench. ii.1.205–14), xlviii (VSO iii.14), liii (Ench. iv.2.14), etc.

[5] *Enigmata* [cf. CPL 1335]: praef. (VSE iv.10), vi (HR iii.22), xlvi. 1–5 (VSO iii.1), lix (VSO ii.9)

Ambrose

[6] *Exameron*: i. 10 (Glossae DTR 312D–313B)

Ansegis of Fontenelle

[7] *Capitularium collectio*: VSO ii. 5, iii. 7

Arator

[8] *Historia apostolica*: i. 226–7 (HR ii.20; Ench. ii.3.265–6, iii.2.3–4; VSE Epil.), i. 899 (VSE i.13)

Asser

[9] *Vita Ælfredi*: cc. i (HR iv. 3), ii (HR iv. 3), iv (HR iv. 3), xiv (HR iv. 1), xv (HR iv. 1), *et passim*

Augustine

[10] *Confessiones*: i. 4 (VSO iii.15), xiii. 18 (VSO v.1)

[11] *De ciuitate Dei*: vi. 2 (Glossae DTR 326), vi. 6 (Glossae DTR 326C), xi.

5 (Glossae DTR 311D–312C), xi. 7 (Glossae DTR 313D), xi. 30 (Glossae Loq.digit. 693C), xi. 31 (Glossae Loq.digit. 694C), xv. 12 (Glossae DTR 465B), xvi. 3 (VSE iv. 1), xvi. 9 (Glossae DTR 453D–454A), xix. 23 (VSO iii.20), xxii. 22 (VSO iii.20), xxii. 30 (Ench. ii.1.281–8)

[12] *De Genesi ad litteram*: vi. 9 (VSO v.1)

[13] *De trinitate*: ii. 18 (VSE iv.2), iii. 4 (Glossae DTR 311D), iv. 2 (VSO iv.11), iv. 4 (Ench. iv.1.111–18), iv. 6 (Glossae DTR 315C)

[14] *Enarrationes in psalmos*: ps. xxxii, narr. ii (VSO ii.8), ps. xxxv (VSO iii.9), ps. lviii, narr. i. 10 (VSO iv.11), ps. lxi (VSO v.1), ps. cxxxix (VSO iv.12)

[15] *Tractatus in Euangelium Ioannis*: xvii. 5 (Glossae DNR 186C), xliii. 7 (VSO ii.9)

B⟨yrhthelm?⟩

[16] *Vita S. Dunstani* [BHL 2342]: cc. ii (VSO iii.1), xii (VSO v.7), xvi–xvii (VSO v.6), xxi (VSO i.1), xxxvi (VSO v.7)

Bede of Monkwearmouth-Jarrow

[17] *Comm. in Genesim* [CPL 1344]: Glossae DTR 309C, VSO iii. 20

[18] *Comm. in Lucam* [CPL 1356]: Comp. p. 376; VSE Epil., ii. 8

[19] *De arte metrica* [CPL 1565]: Ench. ii.1.436, 447–8, 470–3, 473–89, 491–6, 496–502; VSO prol., ii. 8

[20] *De natura rerum* [CPL 1343]: c. xxxix (HR iii.22; Ench. iii.2.131–8); cc. i–xxxvi of the work are glossed entire in Glossae DNR

[21] *De orthographia* [CPL 1566]: VSO iv.6

[22] *De temporum ratione* [CPL 1320]: cc. xix (Comp. p. 417), xx (Comp. p. 378), xxx (Comp. p. 378), xli (Ench. ii.1.121–36), xlii (Ench. ii.1.179–88), liii (Ench. i.2.45–62), lxvi (Ench. iv.2 *passim*); cc. i–lxiv of the work are glossed entire in Glossae DTR

[23] *De schematibus et tropis* [CPL 1567]: Ench. ii.3.22–127; VSO prol.

[24] *Expositio in Canticum Abacuc* [CPL 1354]: VSO ii.2

[25] *Historia abbatum* [CPL 1378]: cc. i (HR ii.3), iv (HR ii.6), vi (HR ii.7–8), vii (HR ii.9), viii (HR ii.10), ix (VSE i.11), etc.

[26] *Historia ecclesiastica gentis Anglorum* [CPL 1375]: i. 15 (Glossae DTR 356D), iii. 1–6 (VSE iv.11), v. 19 (VSE iii.3), v. 23 (HR ii.19), v. 24 (Comp. p. 377; HR ii.20)

[27] *Homiliae* [CPL 1367]: i. 12 (VSO v.1), i. 13 (VSO v.3), i. 16 (VSO v.16), ii. 23 (VSE ii.8)

[28] *Versus de die iudicii* [CPL 1370]: quoted entire at HR ii.16; lines 18 (VSO iv.17), 6–9, 10, 49, 50–5, 57–61, 66–7, 79–80, 124–7 (VSE i.11), 59–71 (Ench. iv.2.98–102)

[29] *Vita S. Cudbercti* (prose) [CPL 1379; BHL 2019]: cc. vi (VSO ii.8, iv.18), xi (VSO ii.4), xxxiv (VSO iv.21), xli (VSO v.2), xliii (VSO v.2)

Boethius

[30] *De consolatione Philosophiae*: i, pr. ii (VSO iv.1); i, met. ii. 1–3 (VSE iv.10), 3, 25, 27 (HR ii.1); i, met. iii. 7–8 (VSO i.4, iv.1); i, met. v. 29–36 (HR iii.22), 46–8 (HR iv.7); i, pr. vi (VSO i.1); ii, pr. i (VSO ii.3); ii, met. iii. 5 (VSO i.4); ii, met. iv. 1–4, 17–22 (HR iv. 15), 4, 7, 22 (VSO i.1); ii, pr. v (VSO i.1); ii, met. vii. 12–14 (HR ii.1); iii, met. i. 7–10 (HR iii.29); iii, met. iv. 1–3, 7–8 (HR iv.9); iii, pr. vi (VSO v.15); iii, met. ix. 10–12 (HR iii.29); iv, met. v. 21–2 (HR iii.27, iv.1); iv, met. vi. 27–9 (HR iv.1)

Boniface (Wynfrith)

[31] *Epistulae* (ed. Tangl): lxxiii (VSE i.14)

Cassiodorus

[32] *Expositio psalmorum*: i. 1 (VSO iv.12), vii. 18 (VSO v.11), xxxviii. 16 (VSO ii.2), l. praef. (VSO iii.5), lxvi. praef. (VSO ii.9), lxvii. 7 (VSO iv.21), xcix. 1 (VSO ii.4), ci. 1 (VSO iv.18)

Cuthbert of Monkwearmouth-Jarrow

[33] *Epistula de obitu Bedae* [CPL 1383; BHL 1068]: VSO v.17

Dionysius Exiguus

[34] *Argumenta titulorum paschalium*: Glossae DTR 344C
[35] *Epistula ad Bonifacium primicerium et Bonum secundicerium de ratione paschae*: VSO v.3

Donatus

[36] *Ars maior*: Ench. iii.1.462–6

Donatus Ortigraphus

[37] *Ars grammatica* [BCLL 667]: VSO iii.18

Eucherius of Lyon

[38] *Formulae spiritalis intelligentiae*: i. 11 (Glossae Loq.digit. 693C)

Eugenius of Toledo

[39] *Carmina*: xxxvii ('Heptametron de primordio mundi'): Glossae DTR 341C

Eusebius of Caesarea

[40] *Historia ecclesiastica*, trans. Rufinus: i. 7 (Glossae DTR 338C), iii. 28 (VSE iv.3), vii. 6 (VSE iv.3), vii. 28 (Glossae DTR 427D), x. 1–2 [Rufinus] (Glossae DTR 480B), x. 6 [Rufinus] (Glossae DTR 484D)

Eutropius

[41] *Breuiarium historiae Romanae*: i. 12 (VSO iii.14)

Gregory the Great

[42] *Dialogi*: iii. **5** (VSO iii.6), iv. **20** (VSO v.20), iv. **31** (VSO iii.14), iv. **36** (VSO v.1, 16), iv. **47** (VSO v.13)

[43] *Hom. .xl. in Euangelia*: i. **3** (Glossae DTR 500C), i. **6** (VSO iv.9), i. **10** (Glossae DTR 302C), ii. **22** (Ench. iii.1.59–112, iv.1.10), ii. **40** (VSO i.1)

[44] *Hom. in Hiezechielem*: ii. **5** (Glossae Loq.digit. 694A)

[45] *Moralia in Iob*: i. **14** (Glossae Loq.digit. 694B), iv. **16** (VSO iv.1), vii. **30** (VSO i.4), ix. **21** (VSO ii.6), xi. **45** (VSO Prol.), xii. **34** (VSO iv.20), xiii. **18** (VSO v.6), xvi. **31** (Ench. iv.1.15–18), xvii. **24** (Glossae DTR 453B), xxviii. **1** (Glossae DTR 478C), xxx. **10** (VSO v.1), xxxi. **33** (VSO ii.7), xxxv. **8** (Ench. iv.1.158–9)

[46] *Regula pastoralis*: iii. **17** (VSO ii.2), iii. **35** (VSO iii.7)

Haymo of Auxerre

[47] *Comm. in Cantica canticorum* (PL 117: 295–358): c. **v** (Glossae DTR 420D)

[48] *Comm. in Genesin* [pseudo-Remigius] (PL 121: 51–134): [Gen. ii. 8] (Glossae DTR 478D), [Gen. ii.12] (Glossae DTR 478D–479B)

[49] *Expositio in Apocalypsin* (PL 117: 937–1220): iii. **10** (Glossae DTR 415C), iii. **12** (Glossae DTR 492B)

[50] *Expositio in Pauli epistolas* (PL 117: 359–938): [2 Cor.] **xii** (Glossae DTR 443A)

[51] *Homiliae de tempore* [PL 118: 11–746]: **xviii** (Ench. iv.1.123–54), **xxii** (Ench. iv.1.296–305, 310–22), **xxviii** (Ench. iv.1.377–84), **xxxi** (Glossae DTR 315B), **lxx** (Glossae DTR 312D, 314D—315A), **cxix** (Glossae Loq.digit. 693D)

Heiric of Auxerre

[52] *Glossae in Bedae Temporum rationem ex codice Melk 412* (unprinted): Glossae DTR 299A, 299C–D, 300 C–D, 303C, 323C–D, 329C, 333D, 336C–337C, 345B–D *et passim*; Glossae Loq.digit. 686D–687C; Glossae Rat.unc. 700D–702B

Helperic of Auxerre

[53] *Liber de computo* (PL 137: 17–48): cc. **i** (Ench. i.1.13–14, 22–4, 26–35), **v** (Ench. i.2.140–57), **vi** (Ench. i.2.63–5, 68–9), **vii** (Ench. i.2.204–9), **x** (Ench. 1.2.259–62, 267–78), **xi** (Ench. i.2.295–303), **xiv** (Ench. i.2.306–16)

Horace

[54] *Carmina*: iii. **3**. 4–5 (VSE ii.12)

[55] *Sermones*: ii. **3**. 117–18 (Glossae DTR 343B)

Hrabanus Maurus

[56] *De computo* (CCCM 44: 163–331): cc. **xi** (Ench. ii.3.69–89, 89–92), xiii

(Glossae DTR 315D; Ench. ii.3.58–61), xv (Glossae DTR 315D; Ench. ii.3.30–1), xvi (Glossae DTR 315D), xix (Glossae DTR 315D–316A, Ench. ii.3.17–18, 56–8, 64–9), xxi (Ench. ii.3.131–3), xxii (Ench. ii.3.148– 50), xxvii (Glossae DTR 316A), xxxiii (Glossae DTR 316A), xlix (Glossae DTR 438C–439A)

Hyginus astronomus
[57] *Astronomica*: ii. 2 (VSO Prol.), iv. 14 (Glossae DTR 406B)

Isidore of Seville
[58] *De natura rerum*: cc. iv (Comp. p. 425), x (Comp. p. 426), x. 1–2 (Glossae DTR 449D–452B), xi (Comp. p. 426), xii. 2 (Glossae DTR 439D–440A–C), xii. 3 (Glossae DTR 440D–441A), xii. 6 (Glossae DTR 442B–C), xiii. 1 (Glossae DTR 442C–D), xvi. 1–3 (Glossae DTR 414D– 415A), xix. 1 (Glossae DTR 406B), xxiii (Comp. p. 426), xxviii. 1–2 (Glossae DTR 322B–C), xxxvii (Comp. p. 426)
[59] *Etymologiae*: i. 19. 1–10 (Ench. iii.3.156–85), i. 21. 2–27 (Ench. iii.3.187–232), i. 22 (VSO iv.1), iii. 6. 4–5 (Ench. iv.1.94–8), iii. 12. 6 (Glossae DTR 325C), iii. 12. 4 (Glossae DTR 326C–D), iii. 44. 1–3 (Glossae DTR 452B–C), v. 30. 5–8 (Ench. ii.3.213–24), v. 34. 3 (Ench. ii.1.411–17), v. 35. 5 (Ench. ii.1.401–7), vii. 1. 6 (Comp. p. 379), vii. 8–9 (Glossae DTR 315C; VSE iv.2), ix. 2 (Glossae DTR 313D–314C), xi. 1. 70–1 (Glossae Loq.digit. 692D–693A), xiii. 6. 7 (Glossae DNR 231D– 232C), xv. 1. 5 (Comp. p. 379), xviii. 1 (VSE iv.2), etc.

Jerome (Hieronymus)
[60] *Comm. in Euangelium Matthaei*: ii (Ench. iv.1.236–40), ii. 13 (Glossae Loq.digit. 690B), iii (Ench. iv.1.242–5), iv. 26 (Glossae DTR 511D), iv. 30 (Glossae DTR 479B)
[61] *Epistulae*: viii (VSO iii.10), xxiii (VSO v.16), lx (VSO iii.9), lxxxii (VSO iii.7), xcvi (VSO iv.3), cxii (VSE iv.3), cxix (Glossae DTR 302C)
[62] *Liber quaestionum hebraicarum in Genesim*: Ench. iii.1.30–1, Glossae DTR 320D, 343D

Juvenal
[63] *Saturae*: ii. 161 (Glossae DNR 205C), vi. 605–6 (VSO i.2, v.11; VSE iii.3, HR iv.4)

Juvencus
[64] *Euangelia*: i. 304 (VSO i.4), iv. 7 (VSO ii.1)

Lactantius Placidus
[65] *Scholia in Statii Thebaidem* (ed. Sweeney): [ad iii. 476] (Glossae DNR 233B), [ad vi. 401] (Glossae DNR 234A—B)

Lantfred of Winchester
[66] *Translatio et miracula S. Swithuni*: cc. i (VSO i.7), vi (VSO iv.18)

Macrobius, Ambrosius Theodosius
[67] *Comm. in Somnium Scipionis*: i. **6. 51** (Glossae DTR 362B), i. **11. 6** (VSO i.1), i. **12. 1** (Glossae DNR 234D; Glossae DTR 363B), i. **17. 3** (VSO Prol.), i. **17. 16** (VSO Prol.; Glossae DTR 363B), i. **20. 3–4** (Ench. i. 1. 176–81, VSO Prol.), i. **20. 9–32** (Glossae DTR 417D–420B), i. **20. 32** (Glossae DTR 324C), i. **21. 1–23** (Glossae DTR 365A–368A), i. **21. 22** (Glossae DNR 232C), i. **22. 10–12** (Glossae DTR 440B–C), i. **22. 11–13** (Comp. p. 426), ii. **2. 13–14** (Glossae DTR 443C–444C), ii. **5. 13–17** (Glossae DTR 443C–444C), ii. **7. 17–21** (Glossae DTR 444C)
[68] *Saturnalia*: i. **16. 36** (Glossae DTR 299D)

Martianus Capella
[69] *De nuptiis Philologiae et Mercurii*: viii. **859** (Glossae DNR 241B), viii. **860** (Glossae DNR 241C; Glossae DTR 412C–D), viii. **863** (Glossae DNR 236B; Glossae DTR 403D), viii. **876–7** (Glossae DNR 241B; Glossae DTR 417A)

Martin of Laon
[70] *Glossae in Bedae Naturam rerum* (CCSL 123A: 192–234 *in calce*): Glossae DNR 190B, 190C, 190D, 192D–193B, 195B, 196B, 200B–D, 202C–D, 205C–D, 207C, 209B, 210A, 211D, 212B–C, 215B–C, 215D, 233C–D, 234D, 235C, etc.
[71] *Glossae in Bedae Temporum rationem* (CCSL 123B: 263–440 *in calce*): Glossae DTR 298D, 314C—D, 319C, 321B, 322D—323C, 324C, 413B—C, etc.

Orosius, Paulus
[72] *Historiae aduersum paganos*: ii. **2. 4** (VSE iv.1), ii. **3. 1** (VSE iv.1), ii. **6. 9** (VSE iv.1)

Paulus Diaconus
[73] *Historia Langobardorum* [CPL 1179]: i. **26** (VSO iii.2, v.19), ii. **28** (VSO v.5)

Persius
[74] *Saturae*: ii. **1** (Glossae DTR 302D), iii. **84** (Ench. iii.3.103)

Pliny the Elder
[75] *Naturalis historia*: ii. **47** (Glossae DTR 416D), ii. **56** (HR iii.8), ii. **58** (Glossae DTR 382A–B, 383B)

Priscian
[76] *De figuris numerorum*: Glossae DTR 343B

[77] *Institutiones grammaticae*: Ench. ii.1.445–7

Prosper of Aquitaine

[78] *Epigrammata ex sententiis S. Augustini*: civ (HR iii.26), cv (HR iii.26)
[79] *Poema coniugis ad uxorem*: line 14 (VSO Prol.)
[80] *Sententiae ex operibus S. Augustini*: c. lvii (Glossae DTR 311D)

Prudentius

[81] *Liber cathemerinon*: iii. 18 (Glossae DTR 418B), v. 1 (VSE iii.3)
[82] *Psychomachia*: lines 285 (VSE i.10), 286–90 (VSO i.7), 355 (VSO ii.2), 769–71 (VSO ii.7), 785–6 (VSO ii.7)

Remigius of Auxerre

[83] *Comm. in Bedae Artem metricam* (CCSL 123A: 81–141 *in calce*): Ench. iii.3.14–20
[84] *Comm. in Bedae Schemata et tropos* (CCSL 123A: 142–71 *in calce*): Ench. iii.3.53–8, 64–74, 90–1, 104–9
[85] *Comm. in Boethii Consolationem Philosophiae* (unprinted): Comp. p. 426; Ench. i.1.105–13; VSO iv.1, iv.10
[86] *Comm. in Martianum Capellam* (ed. Lutz): Glossae DNR 195B–196A; Glossae DTR 299A
[87] *Enarrationes in psalmos* (PL 131: 133–844): VSO iii.13, iv.11

Sedulius, Caelius

[88] *Carmen paschale*: Ep. ad Macedonium (VSO iii.1), i. 62 (VSO ii.4), i. 62–3 (VSO v.1), i. 197–205 (VSE Epil.), iii. 236 (VSO v.7)
[89] *Hymni*: i. 1–4 (VSO v.7), i. 109–10 (VSO v.7)

Sergius

[90] *Comm. de littera, de syllaba, de pedibus, de accentibus, de distinctione*: Ench. ii.3.242

Servius

[91] *Comm. in Vergilii Bucolica et Georgica* [ed. Thilo]: [**ad Buc. v. 14**] (VSO iv.18)
[92] *Comm. in Vergilii Aeneidos libros* [ed. Thilo and Hagen]: [**ad Aen. ii. 777**] (Glossae DTR 302C)

Terence

[93] *Comoediae*: Heauton timorumenos: iii [line 460] (Glossae DTR 418B)

Uranius

[94] *Epistula de obitu Paulini*: cc. viii (VSO iii.10), ix (VSO v.2)

Vergil

[95] *Aeneis*: ii. 1 (VSO v.12), ii. 268–9 (VSO i.7), iv. 359 (VSE ii.13), vi. 625

(VSO ii.3), ix. 769 (VSO i.1, VSE i.10, iv.3, 10), x. 1 (Glossae DNR 204D)

[96] *Bucolica*: viii. 63 (VSO v.14)

[97] *Georgica*: i. 232 (VSO i.4), iii. 347 (VSO i.4)

Wulfstan of Winchester

[98] *Vita S. Æthelwoldi* [BHL 2647]: c. xviii (VSO iii.11, iv.8)

ANONYMOUS WRITINGS

[99] *Annales Eboracenses saeculi octaui*: HR iii.3–21; VSO v.9

[100] *Comm. in Pentateuchum* [pseudo-Bede]: Gen. i (Glossae DTR 309C), Ex. ii (VSO Prol.)

[101] *Disticha Catonis*: i. 9 (VSO iv.2), ii. 3 (VSO iv.9); and cf. Ench. ii.3.242–3

[102] *Kalendarium metricum Rameseiense*: lines 32–3 (VSO v.17), 91 (VSO iii.17), 93–4 (HR iii.24), 112 (VSO v.11)

[103] *Liber de ordine creaturarum* [pseudo-Isidore]: c. v (Glossae DTR 479C)

[104] *Liber Nemroth* (unprinted): VSE Epil.

[105] *Martyrologium Hieronymianum* [pseudo-Jerome]: Glossae DTR 493D–494C

[106] *Voces animantium*: VSO ii.8

Catalogue of Classical and Patristic Authors and Works Composed before AD 700 and Known in Anglo-Saxon England

The following Catalogue is based on the information assembled in Appendices A, B, C, and E. Its contents will (in theory at least) eventually be superseded by the *Fontes Anglo-Saxonici* database, and by SASLC. For the time being, my intention is to provide within the covers of a single volume a concise list of 'books known to the English' in a form more reliable than that currently available in J. D. A. Ogilvy's work of 1967, *Books Known to the English 597–1066*. In order to reduce the Catalogue to a manageable size, I have omitted all works composed and authors active after AD 700: thus the writings of Aldhelm and Bede are not included here, nor are the Carolingian authors who were assiduously studied in late Anglo-Saxon England, such as Abbo of Saint-Germain-des-Prés and Remigius of Auxerre. The evidence for the Anglo-Saxons' knowledge of each work is given under five headings:

INV(i) = reference to the six Anglo-Saxon inventories of books printed above in Appendix A; thus, under INV(i), the reference a. 1 refers to the first numbered item in the inventory labelled (a); and so on.

INV(ii) = reference to the three inventories of books from the area of the Anglo-Saxon mission in Germany, printed above in Appendix B. Thus, under INV(ii), the reference a. 1 refers to the first numbered item in the inventory labelled (a); and so on.

MSS(i) = reference to manuscripts of Anglo-Saxon origin or provenance listed by Gneuss, *Handlist*, together with supplementary items listed in Gneuss, 'Addenda and Corrigenda'. The manuscripts are here listed according to their present location; in each case the relevant Gneuss no. may be found in the Index of Manuscripts. Note that I have on certain occasions simplified the often very complex information given by Gneuss concerning the origin and provenance of a manuscript; users of the present Catalogue are advised to control data given here with that given by Gneuss.

MSS(ii) = reference to manuscripts written before *c*.800 in Anglo-Saxon script from the area of the Anglo-Saxon mission in Germany, and listed in Lowe, CLA and above, Appendix C. Reference is to numbered items in the list given in Appendix C.

CIT = reference to citations by Anglo-Saxon authors of works composed before AD 700, as listed above, Appendix E; references are given in the following short forms:

Theodore/Hadrian
Aldhelm
Bede
Alcuin
OEM [= the Old English Martyrology]
Asser
Lantfred
Abbo
Wulfstan
Ælfric
Byrhtferth

The numbers which accompany each such reference refer to the number assigned to that work in Appendix E. To facilitate consultation, I supply for each author and work the reference to an alphanumerical bibliography, such as CPG, CPL, LLA, Kaster, etc.

Adomnán of Iona
De locis sanctis [CPL 2332; BCLL 304]
   CIT: Bede 1; OEM 1

Agroecius of Sens [LLA 705; Kaster 181]
Ars de orthographia [CPL 1545]
   MSS(i): Cambridge, CCC 221, fos. 25–64 (England, s. x)
   CIT: Bede 2

Ambrose [LLA 655]
De Abraham [CPL 127]
   MSS(i): Durham, CL, B. II. 6 (s. xi^{ex})
   CIT: Bede 9
De apologia prophetae Dauid [CPL 135]
   MSS(i):
      Boulogne-sur-Mer, BM, 32 (37) (Italy, s. vi^1; prov. England, s. viii)
      Durham, CL, B. IV. 12, fos. 39–120 (Durham, s. xi/xii)
      Kassel, Gesamthochschulbibliothek, Fol. theol. 21 (?Northumbria, s. viii)
      Oxford, BodL, Bodley 137 (?Exeter, s. xi^{ex})
   MSS(ii): no. 38
De bono mortis [CPL 129]
   MSS(i):
      Durham, CL, B. II. 6 (s. xi^{ex})
      Oxford, BodL, Bodley 94 (England, s. xi/xii)

De Cain et Abel [CPL 125]
   CIT: Bede 10
De excessu fratris [CPL 157]
   MSS(i):
      Boulogne-sur-Mer, BM, 32 (37) (Italy, s. vi^{I}; prov. England, s. viii)
      Durham, CL, B. II. 6 (s. xi^{ex})
      Oxford, BodL, Bodley 137 (?Exeter, s. xi^{ex})
      Oxford, BodL, Bodley 835 (Salisbury, s. xi^{ex})
De fide [CPL 150]
   INV(ii): a. 9
   MSS(i):
      Oxford, BodL, Bodley 739 (?Exeter, s. xi/xii)
      Oxford, BodL, Bodley 762, fos. 149–226 (s. xi^{ex}; prov. Ely)
      Oxford, BodL, Bodley 827 (Christ Church, Canterbury, s. xi^{ex})
      Salisbury, CL, 140 (Salisbury, s. xi^{ex})
   CIT: Bede 11
De fuga saeculi [CPL 133]
   MSS(i): Oxford, BodL, Bodley 94 (England, s. xi/xii)
   CIT: Bede 12
De Isaac uel anima [CPL 128]
   MSS(i): Oxford, BodL, Bodley 94 (England, s. xi/xii)
   CIT: Bede 13
De incarnationis dominicae sacramento [CPL 152]
   MSS(i):
      Oxford, BodL, Bodley 739 (?Exeter, s. xi/xii)
      Oxford, BodL, Bodley 827 (Christ Church, Canterbury, s. xi^{ex})
      Salisbury, CL, 140 (Salisbury, s. xi^{ex})
De institutione uirginis [CPL 148]
   INV(ii): b. 19 (?)
De Iacob et uita beata [CPL 130]
   MSS(i): Oxford, BodL, Bodley 94 (England, s. xi/xii)
De Ioseph patriarcha [CPL 131]
   MSS(i):
      Boulogne-sur-Mer, BM, 32 (37) (Italy, s. vi^{I}; prov. England, s. viii)
      Durham, CL, B. II. 6 (s. xi^{ex})
      Oxford, BodL, Bodley 137 (?Exeter, s. xi^{ex})
      Oxford, BodL, Bodley 835 (Salisbury, s. xi^{ex})
De mysteriis [CPL 155]
   INV(i): b. 14 (?), c. 8
   MSS(i):
      Durham, CL, B. IV. 12, fos. 39–120 (Durham, s. xi/xii)
      London, BL, Harley 865 (s. xi^{ex}; prov. St Albans)
      London, BL, Harley 3097 (?Peterborough, s. xi/xii)
      Oxford, BodL, Bodley 768 (Salisbury, s. xi^{ex})

Paris, BNF, lat. 1751 (?St Augustine's, Canterbury, s. xi²)

De Nabuthae [CPL 138]
MSS(i):
    Durham, CL, B. II. 6 (s. xi^ex)
    London, BL, Royal 5. F. XIII (s. xi^ex; prov. Salisbury)

De Noe et arca [CPL 126]
CIT: Bede 14

De obitu Theodosii [CPL 159]
MSS(i): London, BL, Royal 5. F. XIII (s. xi^ex; prov. Salisbury)

De obitu Valentiniani [CPL 158]
MSS(i):
    Durham, CL, B. II. 6 (s. xi^ex)
    Oxford, BodL, Bodley 94 (England, s. xi/xii)

De officiis ministrorum [CPL 144]
INV(i): c. 12
MSS(i): Oxford, BodL, Bodley 92 (s. xi/xii; prov. Exeter)

De paenitentia [CPL 156]
MSS(i):
    Boulogne-sur-Mer, BM, 32 (37) (Italy, s. vi¹; prov. England, s. viii)
    Cambridge, UL, Kk. 1. 23, fos. 67–135 (Christ Church, Canterbury, s. xi^ex)
    Durham, CL, B. II. 6 (s. xi^ex)
    Oxford, BodL, Bodley 137 (?Exeter, s. xi^ex)
    Oxford, BodL, Bodley 835 (Salisbury, s. xi^ex)
CIT: Bede 15

De paradiso [CPL 124]
MSS(i):
    Durham, CL, B. II. 6 (s. xi^ex)
    Oxford, BodL, Bodley 94 (England, s. xi/xii)
CIT: Bede 16

De patriarchis [CPL 132]
MSS(i):
    Boulogne-sur-Mer, BM, 32 (37) (Italy, s. vi¹; prov. England, s. viii)
    Durham, CL, B. II. 6 (s. xi^ex)
    Oxford, BodL, Bodley 137 (?Exeter, s. xi^ex)
    Oxford, BodL, Bodley 835 (Salisbury, s. xi^ex)

De sacramentis [CPL 154]
INV(i): b. 14 (?), c. 8, f. 16
MSS(i):
    London, BL, Harley 865 (s. xi^ex; prov. St Albans)
    London, BL, Harley 3097 (?Peterborough, s. xi/xii)
    Oxford, BodL, Bodley 768 (Salisbury, s. xi^ex)
    Paris, BNF, lat. 1751 (?St Augustine's, Canterbury, s. xi²)

De spiritu sancto [CPL 151]
  MSS(i):
    Durham, CL, B. IV. 12, fos. 39–120 (Durham, s. xi/xii)
    Oxford, BodL, Bodley 739 (Exeter, s. xi/xii)
    Oxford, BodL, Bodley 762, fos. 149–226 (s. xi^{ex}; prov. Ely)
    Oxford, BodL, Bodley 827 (Christ Church, Canterbury, s. xi^{ex})
    Salisbury, CL, 140 (Salisbury, s. xi^{ex})
  CIT: Bede 17
De uiduis [CPL 146]
  MSS(i):
    Cambridge, Trinity College, B. 14. 30, fos. 58–129 (s. xi^{ex}; prov.
      Exeter)
    Oxford, BodL, Bodley 768 (Salisbury, s. xi^{ex})
    Oxford, BodL, Bodley 792 (s. xi/xii; prov. Exeter)
    Paris, BNF, lat. 1751 (?St Augustine's, Canterbury, s. xi^2)
De uirginibus [CPL 145]
  INV(ii): b. 19 (?)
  MSS(i):
    Cambridge, Trinity College, B. 14. 30, fos. 58–129 (s. xi^{ex}; prov.
      Exeter)
    Oxford, BodL, Bodley 768 (Salisbury, s. xi^{ex})
    Oxford, BodL, Bodley 792 (s. xi/xii; prov. Exeter)
    Paris, BNF, lat. 1751 (?St Augustine's, Canterbury, s. xi^2)
  CIT: Bede 18
De uirginitate [CPL 147]
  INV(i): f. 22
  INV(ii): b. 19 (?)
  MSS(i):
    Cambridge, Trinity College, B. 14. 30, fos. 58–129 (s. xi^{ex}; prov.
      Exeter)
    Oxford, BodL, Bodley 768 (Salisbury, s. xi^{ex})
    Oxford, BodL, Bodley 792 (s. xi/xii; prov. Exeter)
    Paris, BNF, lat. 1751 (?St Augustine's, Canterbury, s. xi^2)
  CIT: Bede 19
Epistulae [CPL 160]
  MSS(i):
    Boulogne-sur-Mer, BM, 32 (37) (Italy, s. vi^1; prov. England, s. viii)
    London, BL, Royal 5. F. XIII (s. xi^{ex}; prov. Salisbury)
    Oxford, BodL, Bodley 137 (?Exeter, s. xi^{ex})
Exameron [CPL 123]
  INV(i): c. 11, f. 55
  MSS(i):
    Arras, BM, 346 (867) (?Abingdon, s. x/xi; prov. Bath, prov. Saint-
      Vaast)

Cambridge, UL, Kk. 1. 23, fos. 1–66 (Christ Church, Canterbury, s. xi/xii)

Cambridge, CCC 193 (N. France, s. ix²; prov. England, s. xi)

Cambridge, Trinity College O. 3. 35 (s. xi/xii; prov. Chichester)

CIT: Bede 20; Ælfric 11; Byrhtferth 6

Exhortatio uirginitatis [CPL 149]

INV(ii): b. 19 (?)

MSS(i):

Cambridge, Trinity College, B. 14. 30, fos. 58–129 (s. xi^ex; prov. Exeter)

Oxford, BodL, Bodley 768 (Salisbury, s. xi^ex)

Oxford, BodL, Bodley 792 (s. xi/xii; prov. Exeter)

Paris, BNF, lat. 1751 (?St Augustine's, Canterbury, s. xi²)

Explanatio super psalmos .xii. [CPL 140]

INV(i): b. 12 (?)

CIT: Bede 21

Expositio de Psalmo .cxviii. [CPL 141]

INV(i): c. 7

MSS(i):

Cambridge, Trinity College, B. 14. 3, flyleaves 1–4 (Nonantola, s. ix¹; prov. England, s. xi) (frg.)

Oxford, BodL, Lat. theol. d. 34 (?Durham, s. xi/xii)

Expositio euangelii secundum Lucam [CPL 143]

MSS(i):

Cambridge, Trinity College, B. 3. 9 (Christ Church, Canterbury, s. xi/xii)

London, Lambeth Palace Library, 414, fos. 1–80 (Saint-Amand, s. ix¹; provenance Canterbury)

CIT: Bede 22

Hymni [CPL 163]

CIT: Bede 23; Abbo 2

Ambrosiaster [LLA 643]

Comm. in .xiii. epistulas Paulinas [CPL 184]

MSS(i): Oxford, BodL, Bodley 756 (Salisbury, s. xi^ex)

Quaestiones Veteris et Noui Testamenti [CPL 185]

MSS(i):

Salisbury, CL, 37, flyleaves, fos. 1–4 (England, s. xi; prov. Salisbury) (frg.)

Salisbury, CL 129 (Salisbury, s. xi^ex)

CIT: Bede 24; Ælfric 12

Andreas Orator

Carmen de Maria uirgine ad Rusticianam [CPL 1485b; ICL 17345]

CIT: Aldhelm 1

Aponius
In Canticum canticorum expositio [CPL 194]
  INV(i): b. 13 (?)
  MSS(i): Boulogne-sur-Mer, BM, 74 (82) (England [?Bath], s. viii¹)
  MSS(ii): no. 81
  CIT: Bede 25

Aquila Romanus [LLA 448.2]
De figuris sententiarum et elocutionis (RLM pp. 22–37)
  CIT: Bede 26

Arator [LLA 794]
Historia apostolica [CPL 1504]
  INV(i): d. 20, e. 15, e. 26
  MSS(i):
    Cambridge, UL, Gg. 5. 35 (St Augustine's, Canterbury, s. xi^med)
    Cambridge, Trinity College B. 14. 3 (Christ Church, Canterbury,
      s. x/xi)
    London, BL, Add. 11034 (?England, s. x)
    London, BL, Royal 15. A. V, fos. 30–85 (s. xi^ex)
    London, Westminster Abbey Library, 17 (England, s. xi/xii) (frg.)
    Oxford, BodL, e Mus. 66 [offsets] (?N. Italy, s. vi or vii)
    Oxford, BodL, Rawlinson C. 570 (St Augustine's, Canterbury, s. x²)
    Paris, BNF, lat. 8092 (England, s. xi¹)
  CIT: Aldhelm 2; Bede 27; Alcuin 27, 42; Lantfred 3; Wulfstan 4;
    Byrhtferth 8

Arnobius Iunior [LLA 744]
Comm. in psalmos [CPL 242]
  INV(ii): a. 11
  CIT: Bede 28; Asser 2; Lantfred 4

Arusianus Messius [LLA 614]
Exempla elocutionum (GL vii. 437–514)
  CIT: Bede 29

Athanasius
Epistulae .ii. ad Luciferum Calaritanum [CPG 2232; cf. CPL 117] [pseudo-
      Athanasius]
  MSS(i): Oxford, BodL, Bodley 147 (?Exeter, s. xi^ex)
Vita S. Antonii, trans. Evagrius [CPG 2101; BHL 609]
  MSS(i): Worcester, CL, F. 48, fos. 1–48 (s. xi^ex; prov. Worcester)
  CIT: Theodore/Hadrian 1; Aldhelm 3; Bede 30; Alcuin 5; OEM 4;
    Asser 3

Audax [LLA 522.1; Kaster 190]
De Scauri et Palladii libris excerpta per interrogationem et responsionem (GL
   vii. 320–62)
   MSS(i): Columbia (Mo.), University of Missouri, Ellis Library,
      Fragmenta manuscripta 2 (?Wales, s. ix; prov. Winchester, s. x^{in})
   CIT: Aldhelm 4; Bede 31

Augustine [LLA 691]
Ad Orosium contra Priscillianistas et Origenistas [CPL 327]
   CIT: Bede 32
Ars breuiata [CPL 1557]
   INV(ii): a. 31
Confessiones [CPL 251]
   MSS(i):
      Cambridge, Trinity College B. 3. 25 (Christ Church, Canterbury,
         s. xi^{ex})
      London, BL, Harley 3080 (W. England, s. xi/xii)
   CIT: Bede 33; Alcuin 43; Byrhtferth 10
Contra Academicos [CPL 253]
   INV(i): b. 5
Contra Adimantum [CPL 319]
   CIT: Bede 34
Contra aduersarium Legis et Prophetarum [CPL 326]
   MSS(i):
      Cambridge, Trinity College B. 3. 33 (Christ Church, Canterbury,
         s. xi/xii)
      Salisbury, CL, 128, fos. 5–116 (Salisbury, s. xi^{ex})
   CIT: Bede 35
Contra duas epistulas Pelagianorum [CPL 346]
   CIT: Bede 36
Contra Faustum Manichaeum [CPL 321]
   MSS(i): Oxford, BodL, Bodley 135 (?England, s. x/xii; prov. Exeter)
   CIT: Bede 37
Contra Gaudentium Donatistam episcopum libri duo [CPL 341]
   CIT: Bede 38
Contra Iulianum haeresis Pelagianae defensorem libri sex [CPL 351]
   MSS(i):
      Cambridge, Trinity College B. 3. 33 (Christ Church, Canterbury,
         s. xi/xii)
      Oxford, BodL, Bodley 145 (s. xi^2)
      Salisbury, CL, 138 (Salisbury, s. xi^{ex})
   CIT: Bede 39
Contra litteras Petiliani libri tres [CPL 333]
   CIT: Bede 40

Contra Maximinum haereticum [CPL 700]
  CIT: Bede 41
Contra mendacium [CPL 304]
  MSS(i):
    Cambridge, Trinity College B. 3. 33 (Christ Church, Canterbury,
      s. xi/xii)
    London, BL, Harley 5915, fo. 12 (Christ Church, Canterbury, s. xi^{ex})
      (frg.)
    Oxford, BodL, Bodley 765, fos. 10–77 (Salisbury, s. xi^{ex})
    Oxford, BodL, Bodley 804 (s. xi/xii; prov. Exeter)
Contra secundam Iuliani responsionem imperfectum opus [CPL 356]
  CIT: Bede 42
Contra Secundinum Manichaeum liber [CPL 325]
  CIT: Bede 43
Contra sermonem Arianorum [CPL 702]
  MSS(i):
    Cambridge, Trinity College B. 3. 33 (Christ Church, Canterbury,
      s. xi/xii)
    Salisbury, CL, 128, fos. 5–116 (Salisbury, s. xi^{ex})
De adulterinis coniugiis [CPL 302]
  MSS(i):
    Cambridge, Trinity College B. 3. 33 (Christ Church, Canterbury,
      s. xi/xii)
    London, Lambeth Palace Library, 149, fos. 1–139 (s. x^2; prov.
      Exeter)
    Salisbury, CL, 128, fos. 5–116 (Salisbury, s. xi^{ex})
  CIT: Bede 44
De agone Christiano [CPL 296]
  MSS(i):
    Oxford, Trinity College 4 (?Angers, ?Tours, s. x/xi; prov.
      Canterbury)
    Salisbury, CL, 63 (Salisbury, s. xi^{ex})
  CIT: Bede 45
De anima et eius origine [CPL 345]
  MSS(i):
    Cambridge, Trinity College B. 3. 33 (Christ Church, Canterbury,
      s. xi/xii)
    Oxford, BodL, Bodley 804 (s. xi/xii; prov. Exeter)
    Salisbury, CL, 128, fos. 5–116 (Salisbury, s. xi^{ex})
  CIT: Bede 46
De baptismo contra Donatistas [CPL 352]
  MSS(i): London, BL, Royal 5. B. II (s. xi/xii; prov. Bath)
  CIT: Bede 47

De bono coniugali [CPL 299]
    INV(i): c. 25, f. 3
    CIT: Bede 48; Ælfric 13
De bono uiduitatis [CPL 301]
    CIT: Aldhelm 5
De catechizandis rudibus [CPL 297]
    CIT: Ælfric 14
De ciuitate Dei [CPL 313]
    INV(i): f. 1
    MSS(i):
        Cambridge, CCC 173, fos. 57–83 (S. England, s. viii²) (exc.)
        Durham, CL, B. II. 22, fos. 27–231 (?Durham, s. xi^{ex})
        Oxford, BodL, Bodley 691 (?England, s. xi/xii; prov. Exeter)
        Windsor Castle, Royal Library, Jackson Collection 16 (Saint-Amand,
            s. ix$^{2/4}$; prov. England?)
    CIT: Aldhelm 6; Bede 49; Lantfred 5; Ælfric 15; Byrhtferth 11
De consensu euangelistarum [CPL 273]
    MSS(i):
        London, BL, Cotton Cleopatra A. iii* (?Northumbria, ?S. England,
            s. viii²) (frg.)
        Oxford, BodL, Bodley 148 (?England, s. xi/xii; prov. Exeter)
    CIT: Bede 50
De correptione et gratia [CPL 353]
    MSS(i):
        Brussels, Bibliothèque royale, 444–52 (St Augustine's, Canterbury,
            s. xi/xii)
        Salisbury, CL, 117 (?Continent, s. x; prov. Salisbury)
    CIT: Bede 51; Ælfric 16
De cura pro mortuis gerenda [CPL 307]
    MSS(i):
        Cambridge, Trinity College B. 3. 33 (Christ Church, Canterbury,
            s. xi/xii)
        London, BL, Harley 5915, fo. 12 (Christ Church, Canterbury, s. xi^{ex})
            (frg.)
        Oxford, BodL, Bodley 765, fos. 10–77 (Salisbury, s. xi^{ex})
De disciplina Christiana [CPL 310]
    MSS(i):
        Salisbury, CL, 63 (Salisbury, s. xi^{ex})
        Salisbury, CL, 106 (Salisbury, s. xi^{ex})
        Salisbury, CL, 169, fos. 1–77 (Salisbury, s. xi^{ex})
De diuersis quaestionibus ad Simplicianum [CPL 290]
    CIT: Bede 52
De diuersis quaestionibus .lxxxiii. [CPL 289]
    INV(i): f. 48

MSS(i):

Cambridge, Trinity College B. 1. 40 (St Augustine's, Canterbury, s. xi^ex)

Salisbury, CL, 168 (Salisbury, s. xi^ex)

CIT: Bede 53

De diuinatione daemonum [CPL 306]

CIT: Bede 54

De doctrina Christiana [CPL 263]

INV(ii): a. 7

MSS(i): Salisbury, CL, 106 (Salisbury, s. xi^ex)

CIT: Bede 55; Abbo 3; Ælfric 17

De dono perseuerantiae [CPL 355]

MSS(i):

Brussels, Bibliothèque royale, 444–52 (St Augustine's, Canterbury, s. xi/xii)

Salisbury, CL, 117 (?Continent, s. x; prov. Salisbury)

CIT: Bede 56

De excidio urbis Romae [CPL 312]

MSS(i): Cambridge, UL, Kk. 1. 23, fos. 67–135 (Christ Church, Canterbury, s. xi^ex)

De fide ac symbolo [CPL 293]

INV(ii): a. 8 (?)

MSS(i): Cambridge, UL, Kk. 1. 23, fos. 67–135 (Christ Church, Canterbury, s. xi^ex)

De fide et operibus [CPL 294]

INV(ii): a. 8 (?)

De Genesi ad litteram [CPL 266]

MSS(i):

Lincoln, CL, 13 (A. 1. 26) (s. xi^ex; prov. Lincoln)

Salisbury, CL, 114, fos. 6–122 (Salisbury, s. xi^ex)

Salisbury, CL, 128, fos. 1–4 (Salisbury, s. xi^ex) (frg.)

CIT: Bede 57; Ælfric 18; Byrhtferth 12

De Genesi ad litteram imperfectus liber [CPL 268]

CIT: Bede 58

De Genesi contra Manichaeos [CPL 265]

MSS(i): Lincoln, CL, 13 (A. 1. 26) (s. xi^ex; prov. Lincoln)

CIT: Bede 59

De gestis Pelagii [CPL 348]

CIT: Bede 60

De gratia et libero arbitrio [CPL 352]

MSS(i):

Brussels, Bibliothèque royale, 444–52 (St Augustine's, Canterbury, s. xi/xii)

Salisbury, CL, 117 (?Continent, s. x; prov. Salisbury)

CIT: Bede 61

De haeresibus [CPL 314]

MSS(i):

Cambridge, Trinity College B. 3. 25 (Christ Church, Canterbury, s. xi^{ex})

London, BL, Harley 3859 (?England, s. xi/xii) (frg.)

CIT: Aldhelm 7; Bede 62

De libero arbitrio [CPL 260]

MSS(i):

Oxford, Trinity College 4 (?Angers, ?Tours, s. x/xi; prov. Canterbury)

Salisbury, CL, 106 (Salisbury, s. xi^{ex})

CIT: Aldhelm 8

De magistro [CPL 259]

MSS(i): London, BL, Royal 8. C. III (St Augustine's, Canterbury, s. x^{ex})

CIT: Aldhelm 9

De mendacio [CPL 303]

MSS(i):

Cambridge, Trinity College B. 3. 33 (Christ Church, Canterbury, s. xi/xii)

Oxford, BodL, Bodley 765, fos. 10–77 (Salisbury, s. xi^{ex})

CIT: Bede 63

De musica [CPL 258]

CIT: Aldhelm 10

De natura boni [CPL 323]

MSS(i):

Salisbury, CL, 63 (Salisbury, s. xi^{ex})

Salisbury, CL, 106 (Salisbury, s. xi^{ex})

De natura et gratia [CPL 344]

MSS(i):

Brussels, Bibliothèque royale, 444–52 (St Augustine's, Canterbury, s. xi/xii)

Salisbury, CL, 117 (?Continent, s. x; prov. Salisbury)

De nuptiis et concupiscentia [CPL 350]

MSS(i):

London, BL, Add. 23944 (Paris–Beauvais region, s. ix^2; prov. England, s. xi^{ex})

Oxford, BodL, Bodley 145 (s. xi^2)

Salisbury, CL, 138 (Salisbury, s. xi^{ex})

CIT: Bede 64

De octo Dulcitii quaestionibus [CPL 291]

MSS(i):

Durham, CL, B. IV. 12, fos. 39–120 (Durham, s. xi/xii)

Hereford, CL, P. I. 10 (W. England, s. xi/xii)

Salisbury, CL, 106 (Salisbury, s. xi^ex)

Salisbury, CL, 169, fos. 1–77 (Salisbury, s. xi^ex)

De opere monachorum [CPL 305]

CIT: Bede 65

De ordine [CPL 255]

MSS(i): New York, Pierpont Morgan Library, M. 926, fos. 74–8 (s. xi²; prov. St Albans) (frg.)

De peccatorum meritis et remissione et de baptismo paruulorum [CPL 342]

MSS(i): London, BL, Royal 5. B. II (s. xi/xii; prov. Bath)

De perfectione iustitiae hominis [CPL 347]

MSS(i):

Brussels, Bibliothèque royale, 444–52 (St Augustine's, Canterbury, s. xi/xii)

Salisbury, CL, 117 (?Continent, s. x; prov. Salisbury)

CIT: Bede 66

De praedestinatione sanctorum [CPL 354]

MSS(i):

Brussels, Bibliothèque royale, 444–52 (St Augustine's, Canterbury, s. xi/xii)

Salisbury, CL, 117 (?Continent, s. x; prov. Salisbury)

CIT: Bede 67

De quantitate animae [CPL 257]

INV(ii): a. 16

MSS(i): Salisbury, CL, 106 (Salisbury, s. xi^ex)

CIT: Ælfric 19

De sancta uirginitate [CPL 300]

INV(i): f. 3

INV(ii): b. 17 (?), b. 19 (?)

CIT: Aldhelm 11; Bede 68; Ælfric 20

De sermone Domini in monte libri .ii. [CPL 274]

CIT: Bede 69; Ælfric 21

De spiritu et littera [CPL 343]

MSS(i): London, BL, Royal 5. B. II (s. xi/xii; prov. Bath)

De trinitate [CPL 329]

INV(ii): a. 27, c. 1

MSS(i):

Cambridge, UL, Add. 6220 no. 14 (England, s. xi¹) (frg.)

Cambridge, Trinity College B. 3. 31 (Christ Church, Canterbury, s. xi/xii)

Edinburgh, NLS, Advocates 18. 7. 8, fos. 1?, 4, 5, 8?, 9, 16, 28, 31 (s. viii) (palimpsest, lower script, frg.)

MSS(ii): nos. 1, 10

CIT: Bede 70; Alcuin 44; Ælfric 22; Byrhtferth 13

De unico baptismo [CPL 336]
  MSS(i): London, BL, Royal 5. B. II (s. xi/xii; prov. Bath)
De utilitate credendi [CPL 316]
  MSS(i):
    Cambridge, UL, Kk. 1. 23, fos. 67–135 (Christ Church, Canterbury,
      s. xi^{ex})
    Salisbury, CL, 63 (Salisbury, s. xi^{ex})
De uera religione [CPL 264]
  INV(i): f. 6
  MSS(i):
    Cambridge, Trinity College B. 3. 33 (Christ Church, Canterbury,
      s. xi/xii)
    Salisbury, CL, 106 (Salisbury, s. xi^{ex})
Enarrationes in Psalmos [CPL 283]
  INV(i): f. 52 (?)
  MSS(i):
    Berlin, Staatsbibliothek Preußischer Kulturbesitz, Grimm 132,2
      (?England, ?Germany, s. viii^{med}) (frg.)
    Cambridge, Trinity College B. 5. 26 (Christ Church, Canterbury,
      s. xi^{ex})
    Cambridge, Trinity College B. 5. 28 (Christ Church, Canterbury,
      s. xi^{ex})
    Canterbury, CL, U3/162/28/1 (St Augustine's, Canterbury, s. xi/xii)
    Durham, CL, B. II. 13 (Normandy, s. xi^{ex}; prov. Durham)
    Durham, CL, B. II. 14 (Normandy, s. xi^{ex}; prov. Durham)
    London, BL, Add. 19835 (Normandy or England, s. xi/xii) (exc.)
    London, BL, Royal 5. D. I + 5. D. II (s. xi/xii; prov. Rochester)
    Oxford, BodL, e Mus. 7 (?Bury St Edmunds, s. xi^{ex})
    Oxford, BodL, e Mus. 8 (?Bury St Edmunds, s. xi^{ex})
    Oxford, Trinity College 54 (s. x^{med})
    Tokyo, Collection of Professor Toshiyuki Takamiya 55 (Christ
      Church, Canterbury, s. xi/xii) (frg.)
    Würzburg, UB, M. p. th. f. 43 (s. viii^{med}; prov. Würzburg) (frg.)
  MSS(ii): nos. 66, 70, 74
  CIT: Aldhelm 12; Bede 71; Lantfred 6; Ælfric 23; Byrhtferth 14
Enchiridion ad Laurentium seu de fide, spe et caritate [CPL 295]
  INV(i): c. 10
  INV(ii): a. 19
  MSS(i):
    Bern, Burgerbibliothek, 680 (s. x^{ex})
    Cambridge, Pembroke College 41 (Christ Church, Canterbury, s. xi^{in})
    Cambridge, Trinity College O. 1. 18 (St Augustine's, Canterbury,
      s. x/xi)

London, Lambeth Palace Library, 237, fos. 146–208 (Arras, s. ix^{med}; prov. England, s. x^{in})

Oxford, BodL, Lat. th. d. 33 [+ Hatton 48, fo. 77 + Oxford, St John's College Ss. 7. 2, pastedown] (Worcester, s. xi^{ex}) (frg.)

Salisbury, CL, 157 (?England, s. xi^{ex})

Salisbury, CL, 172 (?Canterbury, s. x^2)

Rouen, BM, A. 292 (26) (England, s. x; prov. Jumièges, s. xi)

CIT: Bede 72; Asser 4; Ælfric 24

Epistulae [CPL 262]

INV(i): b. 14 [*Ep.* liv] (?), c. 14 [*Ep.* cliii, cliv, clviii, clx, clxi, clxiii, clxxvii], f. 6 [*Ep.* cxlvii]

MSS(i):

Boulogne-sur-Mer, BM, 58 (?England, s. viii^2; prov. Saint-Bertin) [*Ep.* liv, clxxxvii]

Boulogne-sur-Mer, BM, 63, fos. 35–86 (France, s. x; prov. S. England, s. x^{med}) [*Ep.* clxvi, ccv]

Cambridge, UL, Kk. 1. 23, fos. 67–135 (Christ Church, Canterbury, s. xi^{ex}) [*Ep.* cxxvii]

Cambridge, Trinity College B. 4. 26 (Christ Church, Canterbury, s. xi^{ex})

Durham, CL, B. II. 21, fos. 9–158 (Durham, s. xi^{ex})

Hereford, CL, P. I. 10 (W. England, s. xi/xii) [*Ep.* cxxx]

Oxford, BodL, Bodley 94 (?England, s. xi/xii) [*Ep.* liv, ccix, ccl]

Oxford, BodL, Bodley 145 (s. xi^2) [*Ep.* cc, ccvii]

Oxford, BodL, Bodley 516 (NE France, s. ix$^{3/4}$; prov. Brittany or Wales, s. x; prov. Salisbury) [*Ep.* cxlvii]

Oxford, BodL, Bodley 572, fos. 1–50 (Cornwall or Wales, s. x) [*Ep.* cxxx]

Salisbury, CL, 63 (Salisbury, s. xi^{ex}) [*Ep.* cxl]

Salisbury, CL, 117 (?Continent, s. x; prov. Salisbury) [*Ep.* ccxiv, ccxv, ccxxv, ccxxvi]

Salisbury, CL 138 (Salisbury, s. xi ex) [*Ep.* cc, ccvii]

Salisbury, CL, 157 (?England, s. xi^{ex}) [*Ep.* cxxx]

Salisbury, CL, 169, fos. 1–77 (Salisbury, s. xi^{ex}) [*Ep.* cxxx]

MSS(ii): no. 14

CIT: Aldhelm 13; Bede 73; Lantfred 7 [*Ep.* clxxxv]

In Ioannis epistulam ad Parthos tractatus .x. [CPL 279]

MSS(i):

Avranches, BM, 81 (?England, ?NW France, s. xi^2; prov. Mont Saint-Michel)

Cambridge, Trinity College B. 4. 26 (Christ Church, Canterbury, s. xi^{ex})

London, BL, Harley 5915, fo. 2 (s. xi^{med}) (frg.)

London, BL, Royal 5. B. VI (s. xi/xii; prov. Rochester)

Oxford, BodL, Bodley 813 (?Exeter, s. xi^{ex})
Salisbury, CL, 101 (W. France, s. ix^{ex}; prov. Canterbury, s. x)
CIT: Bede 74
Quaestiones Euangeliorum [CPL 275]
MSS(i): Cambridge, UL, Kk. 5. 34 (Winchester, s. x^{ex}) (exc.)
CIT: Bede 75
Quaestiones in Heptateuchum [CPL 270]
CIT: Theodore/Hadrian 24; Bede 76; Lantfred 8
Retractationes [CPL 250]
INV(i): f. 5
MSS(i):
Cambridge, Trinity College B. 3. 25 (Christ Church, Canterbury, s. xi^{ex}) (exc.)
Durham, CL, B. II. 22, fos. 27–231 (?Durham, s. xi^{ex}) (exc.)
Hereford, CL, O. III. 2 (France, s. ix$^{3/4}$)
Lincoln, CL, 13 (A. 1. 26) (s. xi^{ex}; prov. Lincoln) (exc.)
London, BL, Harley 3080 (W. England, s. xi^{ex}) (exc.)
London, BL, Royal 5. B. XIV (?Gloucester, s. xi/xii; prov. Bath) (exc.)
Oxford, BodL, Bodley 148 (?England, ?Normandy, s. xi/xii; prov. Exeter) (exc.)
Oxford, BodL, Bodley 391 (St Augustine's, Canterbury, s. xi^{ex})
Oxford, BodL, Bodley 691 (?England, ?Normandy, s. xi/xii; prov. Exeter) (exc.)
Oxford, BodL, Bodley 815 (s. xi^{ex}; prov. Exeter) (exc.)
Salisbury, CL, 6 (Salisbury, s. xi^{ex}) (exc.)
Salisbury, CL, 63 (Salisbury, s. xi^{ex}) (exc.)
Salisbury, CL, 88 (Salisbury, s. xi^{ex})
CIT: Bede 77
Sermones [CPL 284]
INV(i): f. 2 (?), f. 19 [*Serm.* cccli–ccclii]
INV(ii): b. 18
MSS(i):
Avranches, BM, 81 (?England, NW France, s. xi^2; prov. Mont Saint-Michel) [*Serm.* lxviii, lxxiv, lxxix, lxxxv]
Cambridge, UL, Kk. 1. 23, fos. 67–135 (Christ Church, Canterbury, s. xi^{ex}) [*Serm.* clxxx, cclix, cccxlviii, cccl, cccli, ccclxxxix]
Canterbury, CL, Lit. A. 8 (St Augustine's, Canterbury, s. xi/xii)
Dublin, Trinity College 174 (B. 4. 3), fos. 1–44, 52–6, 95–103 (Salisbury, s. xi^{ex}) [*Serm.* cclxxvi, cccxvi, ccclxxxii, app. ccxvii]
Durham, CL, B. II. 6 (s. xi^{ex}; prov. Durham) [*Serm.* ix]
Durham, CL, B. III. 16, fos. 159–60 (Normandy, s. xi^{ex}; prov. Durham) (frg.)

Durham, CL, B. IV. 12, fos. 1–120 (Durham, s. xi/xii) [*Serm.* cc, cccli, cccxciii, app. cxxi, cxxviii, cxxxviii]

Edinburgh, NLS, Advocates 18. 4. 3, fos. 1–122 (s. xi^ex; prov. Durham) [*Serm.* lii]

Hereford, CL, P. I. 10 (W. England, s. xi/xii) [*Serm.* xxxvii]

London, BL, Royal 5. B. II (s. xi/xii; prov. Bath) [*Serm.* xlvi, xlvii]

Oxford, BodL, Bodley 94 (?Normandy, s. xi/xii; prov. Exeter) [*Serm.* ccclv, ccclvi]

Oxford, BodL, Bodley 229 (France, s. x/xi; prov. Exeter)

Oxford, BodL, Bodley 765, fos. 1–9 (Salisbury, s. xi^ex) [*Serm.* ccli, cccxciii]

Salisbury, CL, 106 (Salisbury, s. xi^ex) [*Serm.* xxxvii]

Salisbury, CL, 169, fos. 1–77 (Salisbury, s. xi^ex) [*Serm.* xxxvii, cccli, cccxciii]

Stockholm, Riksarkivet, Fragm. 194 + 195 (Normandy, s. xi^ex; prov. England) (frg.)

CIT: Theodore/Hadrian 2; Bede 78; OEM 5; Lantfred 9; Ælfric 25

Soliloquia [CPL 252]

INV(i): e. 44

MSS(i):

Brussels, Bibliothèque royale, 8558–63, fos. 1–79 (?S. England, ?Mercia, s. x^1)

Salisbury, CL, 173 (Continent, s. x^ex; prov. Salisbury)

CIT: Aldhelm 14; Alcuin 45

Speculum 'Quis ignorat' [CPL 272]

INV(ii): a. 33

Tractatus in Euangelium Ioannis [CPL 278]

INV(i): f. 4

MSS(i):

Cambridge, Trinity College B. 4. 2 (Christ Church, Canterbury, s. xi^ex)

Durham, CL, B. II. 16 (St Augustine's, Canterbury, s. xi^ex; prov. Durham)

Durham, CL, B. II. 17 (Normandy, s. xi^ex; prov. Durham)

London, BL, Royal 3. C. X (s. xi/xii; prov. Rochester)

Oxford, BodL, Bodley 301 (s. xi/xii; prov. Exeter)

Oxford, BodL, e Mus. 6 (Bury St Edmunds, s. xi^ex)

Oxford, BodL, Lat. theol. c. 10, fos. 100–100a (s. xi/xii)

Salisbury, CL, 67 (Salisbury, s. xi^ex)

MSS(ii): nos. 27, 47

CIT: Bede 79; Lantfred 10; Ælfric 26; Byrhtferth 15

Augustinus Hibernicus
De mirabilibus sacrae scripturae [CPL 1123; BCLL 291]
  CIT: Ælfric 27

Ausonius [LLA 554]
Eclogae
  MSS(i):
    Aberystwyth, NLW, 735C (France, s. xi^1; prov. England) [ICL 4582]
    Exeter, CL, 3507 (S. England, s. x^2; prov. Exeter) [ICL 12559]
Ephemeris
  MSS(i): Cambridge, UL, Kk. 5. 34 (Winchester, s. x^{ex}) [*Eph.* iii]
Technopaegnion
  MSS(i): Cambridge, UL, Kk. 5. 34 (Winchester, s. x^{ex}) [*Techn.* vi–xiv]

Avianus [LLA 622]
Fabulae
  MSS(i):
    Edinburgh, NLA, Advocates 18. 6. 12 (s. xi^{ex}; prov. Thorney)
    Oxford, BodL, Auct. F. 2. 14 (s. xi^2; prov. Sherborne)
    Oxford, BodL, Rawlinson G. 57 + 111 (s. xi^{ex})

Avitus, Alcimus [LLA 794]
Carmina de spiritalis historiae gestis [CPL 995]
  INV(i): b. 16
  CIT: Aldhelm 15; Bede 80; Alcuin 23

Basil of Caesarea
Asceticon paruum (*Regula S. Basilii*), trans. Rufinus [CPG 2876]
  INV(ii): b. 11
  MSS(ii): no. 20
  CIT: Alcuin 9 (?)
Hom. in Hexaemeron, trans. Eustathius [CPG 2835]
  CIT: Bede 81; Alcuin 9 (?)
Hom. super psalmos, trans. Rufinus [CPG 2836]
  MSS(i): Winchester, Winchester College 40A (?France, s. viii^2) (frg.)

Benedict of Nursia [LLA 743]
Regula S. Benedicti [CPL 1852]
  INV(i): c. 4
  MSS(i):
    Cambridge, UL, Ll. 1. 14, fos. 70–108 (s. xi^2)
    Cambridge, CCC 57 (Abingdon, s. x/xi)
    Cambridge, CCC 178, pp. 287–457 (Worcester, s. xi^1)
    Cambridge, CCC 368 (s. x/xi)
    Cambridge, Trinity College O. 2. 30, fos. 129–72 (St Augustine's,
      Canterbury, s. x^{med})

London, BL, Cotton Tiberius A. iii, fos. 2–173 (Christ Church, Canterbury, s. xi^med)

London, BL, Cotton Titus A. iv (?Winchester, ?St Augustine's, Canterbury, s. xi^med)

London, BL, Harley 5431, fos. 4–126 (St Augustine's, Canterbury, s. x/xi)

Oxford, BodL, Hatton 48 (?S. England, ?Mercia, s. viii^in)

Oxford, CCC 197 (?Worcester, s. x^{4/4}; prov. Bury St Edmunds, s. xi^med)

Wells, CL, 7 (s. xi^med) (frg.)

CIT: Theodore/Hadrian 3; Bede 82; Abbo 6; Ælfric 41

Boethius [LLA 711]

Comm. in Categorias Aristotelis [CPL 882]

INV(i): e. 27, e. 42

MSS(i): Lichfield, CL, 1a (?France, s. x²)

Comm. in Ciceronis Topica [CPL 888]

MSS(i): Oxford, Merton College 309, fos. 114–201 (?France, s. ix/x)

CIT: Abbo 7

De consolatione Philosophiae [CPL 878]

INV(i): d. 3, e. 11

MSS(i):

Antwerp, Plantin-Moretus Museum, M. 16. 2 (Abingdon, s. xi¹)

Cambridge, UL, Gg. 5. 35 (St Augustine's, Canterbury, s. xi^med) (exc.)

Cambridge, UL, Kk. 3. 21 (?Abingdon, s. xi¹)

Cambridge, CCC 214 (?Canterbury, s. x/xi)

El Escorial, Real Biblioteca, E. II. 1 (?Continent, ?England, s. x/xi; prov. Horton)

Geneva, Bibliotheca Bodmeriana, 175 (?Canterbury, s. x/xi)

London, BL, Vespasian D. xiv, fos. 170–224 (England, s. x^in; prov. Christ Church, Canterbury) (exc.)

London, BL, Egerton 267, fo. 37 (Abingdon, s. x^ex) (frg.)

Oxford, BodL, Auct. F. 1. 15, fos. 1–77 (St Augustine's, Canterbury, s. x²; prov. Exeter, s. xi²)

Oxford, BodL, Digby 174, fo. iii (s. ix; prov. England) (frg.)

Oxford, CCC 74 (s. xi²)

Oxford, Merton College E. 3. 12 (s. x/xi) (frg.)

Paris, BNF, lat. 6401 (?England, s. x/xi; prov. Fleury)

Paris, BNF, lat. 6401A (Christ Church, Canterbury, s. x/xi; prov. France)

Paris, BNF, lat. 14380, fos. 1–65 (Christ Church, Canterbury, s. x^ex)

Paris, BNF, lat. 17814 (?Christ Church, Canterbury, s. x^ex)

Vatican City, BAV, lat. 3363 (Loire region, s. ix¹; prov. England)

CIT: Lantfred 15; Abbo 8; Byrhtferth 30
De institutione arithmetica [CPL 879]
  MSS(i):
      Berlin, Staatsbibliothek Preußischer Kulturbesitz, Lat. fol. 601, fos.
        1–67 (England, s. x/xi)
      Cambridge, CCC 352 (?St Augustine's, Canterbury, s. x²)
      Oxford, Balliol College 306, fos. 5–41 (?France, s. x; prov. England)
      Paris, BNF, lat. 6401 (?England, s. x/xi; prov. Fleury)
  CIT: Abbo 9
De institutione musica [CPL 880]
  MSS(i):
      Avranches, BM, 236 (s. x/xi; prov. Mont Saint-Michel, s. xi^{ex})
      Cambridge, CCC 260 (Christ Church, Canterbury, s. x²) (exc.)
  CIT: Abbo 10
De syllogismo hypothetico [CPL 886]
  CIT: Abbo 11
De topicis differentiis [CPL 889]
  INV(i): f. 35 (?)
In Porphyrii Isagogen commentorum editio duplex [CPL 881]
  INV(i): d. 4
  MSS(i): Cambridge, CCC 206 (?England, s. x¹)
  CIT: Abbo 13
In librum Aristotelis Perihermeneias commentarii editio duplex [CPL 883]
  INV(i): e. 37
  CIT: Abbo 12
Opuscula sacra [CPL 890–4]
  MSS(i): Cambridge, CCC 206 (?England, s. x¹)
  CIT: Abbo 14

Caelius Sedulius: *see* **Sedulius, Caelius**

Caesarius of Arles [LLA 771]
Ad sanctimoniales epistulae .ii. [CPL 1010]
  MSS(ii): no. 87
Expositio in Apocalypsin [CPL 1016]
  MSS(i):
      Boulogne-sur-Mer, BM, 63, fos. 35–86 (France, s. x; prov.
        S. England, s. x^{med})
      London, BL, Egerton 874 (NE France, s. ix²; prov. St Augustine's,
        Canterbury, s. xi²)
      Oxford, BodL, Hatton 30 (Glastonbury, s. x²)
  CIT: Bede 83
Sermones [CPL 1008]
  MSS(i):
      Boulogne-sur-Mer, BM, 63, fos. 1–34 (England, s. xi¹) (exc.)

Brussels, Bibliothèque royale, 8558–63, fos. 1–79 (S. England or
Mercia, s. x[1]) (exc.)

Brussels, Bibliothèque royale, 9850–2, fos. 4–139, 144–76 (Soissons,
s. vii/viii; prov. Bath?) (exc.)

Copenhagen, Kongelige Bibliotek, G.K.S. 1595 (Worcester, s. xi[1];
prov. Denmark) (exc.)

Dublin, Trinity College 174, fos. 1–44, 52–6, 95–103 (Salisbury,
s. xi[ex]) (exc.)

Oxford, BodL, Bodley 163, fos. 1–227, 250–1 (s. xi[in]; prov.
Peterborough) (exc.)

Oxford, BodL, Bodley 229 (France, s. x/xi; prov. Exeter) (exc.)

Oxford, BodL, Bodley 392 (Salisbury, s. xi[ex]) (exc.)

Oxford, BodL, Bodley 572, fos. 1–50 (Wales, s. x[ex]; prov.
Winchester, s. xi, St Augustine's, Canterbury, s. xi[ex]) (exc.)

Oxford, Trinity College 28 (s. xi; prov. Old Minster, Winchester)
(exc.)

Salisbury, CL, 63 (Salisbury, s. xi[ex]) (exc.)

Vatican City, BAV, Reg. lat. 338, fos. 64–126 (N. France or
Germany, s. x/xi; prov. England, s. xi[1]?) (exc.)

MSS(ii): nos. 55, 69, 87

CIT: Bede 84; OEM 12; Ælfric 42

Calcidius [LLA 566]
Comm. in Platonis Timaeum
CIT: Lantfred 16; Abbo 15

Caper, Flavius [LLA 438]
De orthographia (GL vii. 92–112)
MSS(i): Cambridge, CCC 221, fos. 1–24 (England, s. x)
CIT: Bede 85

Cassian, John [LLA 673]
Conlationes [CPL 512]
INV(i): f. 21
MSS(i):
London, Lambeth Palace Library, 414, fos. 1–80 (Saint-Amand, s. ix[1];
prov. St Augustine's, Canterbury, s. xi/xii) (exc.)
Oxford, BodL, Hatton 23 (Worcester, s. xi[2]) (exc.)
Salisbury, CL, 10 (Salisbury, s. xi[ex])
MSS(ii): no. 41
CIT: Aldhelm 16; Bede 86; Asser 7; Lantfred 17; Ælfric 44
De incarnatione Domini contra Nestorium [CPL 514]
CIT: Bede 87
De institutis coenobiorum [CPL 513]
MSS(i):

Cambridge, St John's College 101, fos. 1–14 (St Augustine's, Canterbury, s. x²)

Oxford, BodL, Auct. D. infra 2. 9, fos. 1–110 (St Augustine's, Canterbury, s. x²)

CIT: Theodore/Hadrian 4; Aldhelm 17; Lantfred 18

Cassiodorus

Complexiones in Epistulas apostolorum, Actuum Apostolorum et Apocalypsis Iohannis [CPL 903]

CIT: Bede 88

Computus paschalis [cf. CPL 906]

MSS(ii): no. 906

De anima [CPL 897]

INV(i): c. 17

MSS(i): Oxford, BodL, Bodley 516 (? N. Italy, ?NE France, s. ix²; prov. England, s. xi¹)

CIT: Ælfric 45

De orthographia [CPL 907]

INV(i): c. 22

MSS(i): Cambridge, CCC 221, fos. 1–24 (England, s. x)

CIT: Bede 89

De propositionum modis [cf. CPL 906]

MSS(ii): no. 64

Expositio psalmorum [CPL 900]

INV(i): e. 41, f. 52 (?)

MSS(i):

Cambridge, CCC 272 (Reims, s. ix²; prov. England, s. xi) (exc.)

Cambridge, St John's College, Aa. 5. 1, fo. 67 (S. England, s. viii¹; prov. Ramsey) (frg.)

Durham, CL, B. II. 30 (Northumbria [?York], s. viii¹) (breviate version)

Düsseldorf, UB, Fragm. K16: Z.3/1 (Northumbria, s. viii¹) (frg.)

CIT: Theodore/Hadrian 5; Bede 90; Alcuin 11 (?); Asser 8; Lantfred 19; Abbo 16; Byrhtferth 32

Historia tripartita: see **Socrates, Sozomen, and Theodoretus**

Institutiones [CPL 906]

INV(i): c. 17

MSS(i):

Cambridge, Trinity College, R. 15. 14, pt. i (?N. France, ? Flanders, s. x¹; prov. St Augustine's, Canterbury)

Hereford, CL, O. III. 2 (France, s. ix³ᐟ⁴; prov. England, s. xiˣ)

Oxford, BodL, Bodley 391 (St Augustine's, Canterbury, s. xiˣ)

Salisbury, CL, 88 (Salisbury, s. xiˣ)

MSS(ii): no. 64

Cassius Felix
De medicina
   CIT: Bede 91

Charisius, Flavius Sosipater [LLA 523.2; Kaster 200]
Ars grammatica (GL i. 1–296)
   MSS(ii): no. 31
   CIT: Bede 92; Alcuin 40; Abbo 17

Chromatius of Aquileia [LLA 660]
Sermones [CPL 217]
   INV(ii): a. 36 (?)

Cicero [LLA 268]
Actio in C. Verrem secunda
   CIT: Aldhelm 18; Bede 93
Aratea
MSS(i):
     Cambridge, Trinity College R. 15. 32 (New Minster, Winchester, s. xi¹)
     London, BL, Cotton Tiberius B. v, fos. 2–73, 77–88 (?Christ Church, Canterbury, s. xi²ᐟ⁴)
     London, BL, Harley 647 (Lotharingia, s. ix²ᐟ⁴; prov. England [?Ramsey])
     London, BL, Harley 2506 (Fleury, s. x/xi; prov. England, s. xi¹)
De natura deorum
   CIT: Bede 94
De inuentione
   MSS(i): Dublin, Trinity College 927 (?France, ?England, s. xi²)
   CIT: Alcuin 20 (?); Abbo 18
In L. Catilinam orationes .iv.
   MSS(i): Edinburgh, NLS, Advocates 18. 7. 8 (s. xiᵉˣ; prov. Thorney)
   CIT: Aldhelm 19 [*oratio III*]; Bede 95 [*oratio IV*]
Orationes Philippicae
   MSS(i): Vatican City, BAV, lat. 3228 (?England, s. x²)
Somnium Scipionis: see **Macrobius**

Claudian [LLA 623]
Carmina maiora
   CIT: Aldhelm 20 [*Carm.* iii, vii]; Bede 96 [*Carm.* iii, vii, xix]
De raptu Proserpinae
   CIT: Aldhelm 21
Epithalamium Laurentii: see ANONYMOUS WRITINGS

Claudianus Mamertus [LLA 767]
De statu animae [CPL 983]
  CIT: Abbo 19

Claudius Marius Victorius
Alethia [CPL 1455]
  CIT: Bede 97

Cledonius [LLA 702; Kaster 31]
Ars grammatica (GL v. 9–79)
  INV(i): a. 13 (?)
  CIT: Bede 98

Consentius Gallus [LLA 702; Kaster 203]
Ars de nomine et uerbo (GL v. 338–404)
  MSS(ii): no. 33
  CIT: Bede 99

Constantius
Vita S. Germani [BHL 3453]
  CIT: Bede 100

Corippus, Flavius Cresconius [LLA 790]
In laudem Iustini [CPL 1516]
  CIT: Aldhelm 22; Asser 9
Iohannes [CPL 1515]
  CIT: Aldhelm 23

Cornutus, L. Annaeus [LLA 334]
Comm. in Persii Saturas
  MSS(i):
    Cambridge, Trinity College O. 4. 10 (St Augustine's, Canterbury, s. x$^{2/4}$)
    London, BL, Royal 15. B. XIX, fos. 79–199 (Reims, s. x; prov. England)

Cyprian of Carthage [LLA 478]
De bono patientiae [CPL 48]
  MSS(i): Salisbury, CL, 9, fos. 1–60 (Salisbury, s. xi^{ex})
De catholicae ecclesiae unitate [CPL 41]
  MSS(i): Salisbury, CL, 9, fos. 1–60 (Salisbury, s. xi^{ex})
De dominica oratione [CPL 43]
  MSS(i):
    Oxford, BodL, Bodley 765, fos. 10–77 (Salisbury, s. xi^{ex})
    Salisbury, CL, 9, fos. 1–60 (Salisbury, s. xi^{ex})
De habitu uirginum [CPL 40]
  CIT: Aldhelm 24; Bede 101

De lapsis [CPL 42]
 CIT: Bede 102
De mortalitate [CPL 44]
 MSS(i): Salisbury, CL, 9, fos. 1–60 (Salisbury, s. xi^{ex})
De opere et eleemosynis [CPL 47]
 MSS(i): Salisbury, CL, 9, fos. 1–60 (Salisbury, s. xi^{ex})
 CIT: Bede 103
De zelo et liuore [CPL 49]
 CIT: Bede 104
Epistulae [CPL 50]
 INV(i): b. 18, f. 53
 MSS(i): London, BL, Add. 40165 A.1 (?Africa, s. iv^{ex}) (frg.)
 CIT: Bede 105
Testimoniorum libri .iii. [*Ad Quirinum*] [CPL 39]
 INV(ii): c. 11
 MSS(i):
  London, BL, Cotton Caligula A. xv, fos. 3–117 (NE France, s. viii^2; prov. England, s. ix/x)
  London, BL, Royal 5. E. XIII (N. France or Brittany, s. ix^{ex}; prov. England, s. x^{med})
 CIT: Bede 106

Cyprianus Gallus [LLA 630]
Heptateuchos [CPL 1423]
 MSS(i): Cambridge, Trinity College B. 1. 42 (St Augustine's, Canterbury, s. x^2)
 CIT: Aldhelm 25; Bede 107

Damasus [LLA 641]
Epigrammata [CPL 1635]
 MSS(i):
  Cambridge, CCC 23 (S. England, s. x^2) (exc.)
  Cambridge, CCC 173, fos. 57–83 (S. England, s. viii^2)
  Oxford, Oriel College 3 (Christ Church, Canterbury, s. x^{ex})
 CIT: Aldhelm 26

Defensor of Ligugé
Liber scintillarum [CPL 1302]
 MSS(i):
  Cambridge, Clare College 30, pt. ii (Worcester, s. xi^2)
  Cambridge, CCC 190, pp. iii–xii, 1–294 (Exeter, s. xi$^{3/4}$) (exc.)
  London, BL, Royal 7. C. IV (Christ Church, Canterbury, s. xi^1)
 MSS(ii): no. 65

Didymus
De spiritu sancto, trans. Jerome [CPG 2544]
  MSS(i): Hereford, CL, P. 1. 10 (W. England, s. xi/xii)
  CIT: Bede 108

Diomedes [LLA 524; Kaster 47]
Ars grammatica (GL i. 299–529)
  MSS(ii): no. 32
  CIT: Bede 109

Dionysius Exiguus
Argumenta titulorum paschalium [CPL 2285]
  MSS(i):
    Cambridge, UL, Kk. 5. 32, fos. 61–72, 76 (W. England, s. xi/xii)
    Münster in Westfalen, Staatsarchiv, Msc. I. 243, fos. 1, 2, 11–12
      (?Northumbria, s. viii¹)
  CIT: Bede 110; Byrhtferth 34
Codex canonum [cf. CPL 1765]
  MSS(ii): no. 4
Codex decretalium [cf. CPL 652c]
  INV(ii): a. 15 (?)
  MSS(ii): no. 63
*Epistula ad Bonifacium primicerium et Bonum secundicerium de ratione
    paschae* [CPL 2286]
  MSS(i):
    London, BL, Cotton Domitian ix, fo. 8 (?England, s. viii²) (frg.)
    Oxford, BodL, Digby 63 (Northumbria, s. ix²)
  CIT: Bede 111; Byrhtferth 35
Libellus de cyclo magno Paschae (Epistula ad Petronium episcopum) [CPL
    2284]
  MSS(ii): no. 54
  CIT: Bede 112

Donatus, Aelius [LLA 527; Kaster 52]
Ars maior (GL iv. 367–402)
  INV(i): a. 7
  MSS(i):
    Geneva, Bibliotheca Bodmeriana, 175 (?Canterbury, s. x/xi)
    London, BL, Cotton Cleopatra A. vi, fos. 2–53 (?W. England,
      ?Wales, s. x^med)
  CIT: Theodore/Hadrian 6; Aldhelm 27; Bede 113; Alcuin 35; Abbo 20;
    Byrhtferth 36
Ars minor (GL iv. 355–66)
  INV(i): a. 4

Vita Vergilii
  CIT: Aldhelm 28

Dracontius [LLA 787]
Laudes Dei [CPL 1509]
  CIT: Aldhelm 29; Bede 114; Alcuin 48; Wulfstan 8
Satisfactio [CPL 1511]
  CIT: Aldhelm 30; Bede 115; Wulfstan 9

Ennius, Quintus [LLA 117]
Annales
  CIT: Aldhelm 31

Ennodius [LLA 785]
Carmina [CPL 1490]
  MSS(i): London, Lambeth Palace Library, 325 (N. France, s. ix²; prov. Durham)
Dictiones [CPL 1489]
  MSS(i): London, Lambeth Palace Library, 325 (N. France, s. ix²; prov. Durham)
Epistulae [CPL 1487]
  MSS(i): London, Lambeth Palace Library, 325 (N. France, s. ix²; prov. Durham)

Ephraem (Latinus) [CPL 1143]
  INV(ii): b. 12

Epiphanius of Salamis
De mensuris et ponderibus, in Latin translation [CPG 3746]
  MSS(i): London, BL, Royal 13. A. XI (?NW France, s. xi/xii; prov. England)

Eucherius of Lyon
Formulae spiritalis intelligentiae [CPL 488]
  MSS(i):
    London, Lambeth Palace Library, 414, fos. 1–80 (Saint-Amand, s. ix¹; prov. St Augustine's, Canterbury)
    Zurich, Zentralbibliothek, Z. XIV. 30, Nr. 11 (s. viii^med)
  CIT: Byrhtferth 38
Instructiones [CPL 489]
  MSS(ii): no. 101
  CIT: Theodore/Hadrian 7
Passio Acaunensium martyrum [CPL 490; BHL 5737–9]
  CIT: OEM 13

Eugenius of Toledo
Carmina [CPL 1236]
  CIT: Byrhtferth 39

Eugippius
Excerpta ex operibus S. Augustini [CPL 676]
  CIT: Bede 116

Eusebius of Caesarea
Chronicon, trans. Hieronymus [CPG 3494]
  CIT: Aldhelm 32; Bede 117; Ælfric 46
Historia ecclesiastica, trans. Rufinus [CPG 3495]
  INV(i): e. 43, f. 7
  MSS(i):
    Cambridge, CCC 187 (Christ Church, Canterbury, s. xi/xii)
    Cambridge, CCC 192 (Landevennec, s. x^{med}; prov. England, s. x^2)
      (exc.)
    Cambridge, Pembroke College 108 (E. France, s. ix$^{2/3}$; prov. Bury St
      Edmunds) (exc.)
    Worcester, CL, Q. 28 (France, s. ix^2; prov. England, s. xi)
    Wormsley (Bucks), The Wormsley Library, s.n. (?Ireland,
      ?Northumbria, s. vii; prov. England)
  MSS(ii): no. 90
  CIT: Theodore/Hadrian 8; Aldhelm 33; Bede 118; Alcuin 49; OEM 14;
    Lantfred 20; Ælfric 47; Byrhtferth 40
Onomasticon, trans. by Jerome as *De situ et nominibus locorum Hebraicorum*
  [CPG 3466]
  INV(ii): c. 9 (?)
  MSS(i):
    Durham, CL, B. II. 11, fos. 1–108 (Normandy, s. xi^{ex}; prov.
      Durham)
    Oxford, BodL, Bodley 808 (?Normandy, ?England, s. xi/xii)
  CIT: Bede 119

Eutropius [LLA 538]
Breuiarium historiae Romanae
  MSS(i): London, BL, Harley 2729 (Durham, s. xi^{ex})
  CIT: Bede 120; Asser 11; Byrhtferth 41

Eutyches [LLA 704; Kaster 57]
Ars de uerbo (GL v. 447–89)
  MSS(i): Oxford, BodL, Auct. F. 4. 32, fos. 1–9 (Brittany, s. ix$^{2/4}$; prov.
    Glastonbury, s. x^1)
  CIT: Alcuin 38; Abbo 21

Filastrius
Diuersarum hereseon liber [CPL 121]
    CIT: Bede 121

Frontinus, Sextus Iulius [LLA 398]
Strategemata
    MSS(i): London, BL, Harley 2729 (Durham, s. xi^{ex})

Fulgentius of Ruspe [LLA 754]
Ad Thrasamundum regem libri .iii. [CPL 816]
    CIT: Bede 122; Alcuin 10 (?)
De fide ad Petrum [CPL 826]
    MSS(i): Durham, CL, B. IV. 12, fos. 1–120 (Durham, s. xi/xii)
Epistulae [CPL 817]
    MSS(i): Durham, CL, B. IV. 12, fos. 1–120 (Durham, s. xi/xii) (exc.)
Sermones .viii. [CPL 828–35]
    CIT: Ælfric 48

Gaius iurisconsultus [LLA 426.9]
Institutiones
    MSS(i): Oxford, BodL, Hatton 42, fos. 1–142 (Brittany, s. ix$^{1/3}$; prov.
    England, s. x/xi)

Galen
Therapeutica (de medendi methodo ad Glauconem), in Latin translation
    MSS(i): Cambridge, Peterhouse 251, fos. 106–91 (St Augustine's,
    Canterbury, s. xi^{ex})
Epistula de febribus, in Latin translation
    MSS(i): London, BL, Sloane 475, fos. 125–231 (s. xi^{ex})

Gaudentius of Brescia
Tractatus .xxi. [CPL 215]
    MSS(i): Oxford, All Souls College, SR.80.g.8 (s. xi^{ex}) (frg.)

Gennadius of Marseilles
De uiris illustribus [CPL 957]
    MSS(i):
        Cambridge, CCC 23 (S. England, s. x^{ex}) (exc.)
        Cambridge, CCC 223 (Arras, s. ix$^{3/4}$; prov. England, s. x^1) (exc.)
        Durham, CL, B. IV. 9 (s. x^{med}; prov. Durham) (exc.)
        Hereford, CL, O. III. 2 (France, s. ix$^{3/4}$; prov. England, s. xi^{ex})
        Oxford, BodL, Bodley 391 (St Augustine's, Canterbury, s. xi^{ex})
        Salisbury, CL, 88 (Salisbury, s. xi^{ex})
    MSS(ii): no. 22
    CIT: Bede 123
Liber siue diffinitio ecclesiasticorum dogmatum [CPL 958]
    INV(i): f. 20

MSS(i):
Basle, UB, F. III. 15l (England, s. viii^I; prov. Fulda)
Durham, CL, B. IV. 12, fos. 1–120 (Durham, s. xi/xii)
London, BL, Royal 8. C. III (St Augustine's, Canterbury, s. x^{ex}) (exc.)
Salisbury, CL, 165, fos. 122–78 (Salisbury, s. xi^{ex})

Germanicus [LLA 346]
Aratea [ICL 41]
MSS(i): Aberystwyth, NLW, 735C, fos. 1–26 (France, s. xi^I; prov. England or Wales, s. xi)

Gildas
De excidio Britanniae [CPL 1319; BCLL 27]
MSS(i): London, BL, Cotton Vitellius A. vi (St Augustine's, Canterbury, s. x^{med})
CIT: Theodore/Hadrian 9; Aldhelm 34; Bede 124

Gregory the Great
Dialogi [CPL 1713]
INV(i): a. 14 (?), c. 5, d. 2, e. 3 (?), e. 32
INV(ii): a. 3, b. 10, c. 6
MSS(i):
Cambridge, Clare College 30, pt. i (Worcester, s. xi^2)
Canterbury, CL, Add. 32 (s. xi^{in}) (frg.)
London, Lambeth Palace Library 204 (Christ Church, Canterbury, s. xi^I)
Münster in Westfalen, UB, Fragmentenkapsel 1 no. 2 (s. viii^2)
Oxford, BodL, Tanner 3 (s. xi^{in}; prov. Worcester)
Rouen, BM, A. 337 (?Christ Church, Canterbury, s. x^{ex}) (exc.)
Salisbury, CL, 96 (?England, s. x; prov. Salisbury)
Stuttgart, Württembergische Landesbibliothek, Theol. et Philos. Q. 628 (?Northumbria, s. vii/viii)
Wrocław, Biblioteka Uniwersytecka, Akc. 1955/2 + 1969/430 (?Northumbria, s. viii^I) (frg.)
MSS(ii): nos. 29, 45, 67
CIT: Theodore/Hadrian 10; Aldhelm 35; Bede 125; OEM 16; Asser 12; Ælfric 49; Byrhtferth 42
Hom. .ii. in Canticum canticorum [CPL 1709]
INV(i): b. 13 (?)
CIT: Bede 126
Hom. .xl. in Euangelia [CPL 1711]
INV(i): e. 25
INV(ii): a. 34 (?), b. 9
MSS(i):

Boulogne-sur-Mer, BM, 106, binding strip (?England, s. viii/ix) (frg.)

Cambridge, CCC 69 (S. England, s. viii/ix) (exc.)

Durham, CL, B. III. 11, fos. 1–135 (?Liege, s. xi^{ex}; prov. Durham)

Edinburgh, NLS, Advocates 18. 7. 8, fos. 26, 33 (s. viii^{ex}) (frg.)

London, BL, Cotton Titus C. xv, fo. 1 (s. vi/vii) (frg.)

Oxford, BodL, Bodley 314 (Exeter, s. xi/xii)

Salisbury, CL, 132 (s. xi^2; prov. Salisbury)

Worcester, CL, Q. 21 (France, s. x/xi; prov. Worcester, s. xi/xii)

MSS(ii): nos. 72, 73, 107

CIT: Aldhelm 36; Bede 128; OEM 17; Lantfred 21; Ælfric 50; Byrhtferth 43

Hom. in Hiezechihelem [CPL 1710]

MSS(i):

Cambridge, UL, Ff. 3. 9 (Christ Church, Canterbury, s. xi^{ex})

Cambridge, St John's College 35 (s. xi^{ex}; prov. Bury St Edmunds)

Durham, CL, B. IV. 13 (s. xi^{ex}; prov. Durham)

Karlsruhe, Badische Landesbibliothek, Aug. perg. 221, fos. 54–107 (?Northumbria, s. viii^{med})

London, BL, Royal 6. A. VII, fos. 1, 162 (Worcester, s. xi^{ex})

London, Lambeth Palace Library, 96, fos. 2–112 (s. xi^{ex})

Oxford, BodL, Bodley 223 (s. xi^2; prov. Worcester)

Oxford, BodL, Bodley 707 (?Normandy, s. xi^{ex}; prov. Exeter)

Windsor, St George's Chapel, 5 (s. xi/xii; prov. Christ Church, Canterbury, s. xii)

Vatican City, BAV, Pal. lat. 259 (?England, s. viii/ix)

Würzburg, UB, M. p. th. f. 43, fos. 18–40 (s. viii^{med}; prov. Würzburg) (exc.)

MSS(ii): nos. 2, 30, 71, 73, 93, 100, 103, 105

CIT: Bede 127; Alcuin 50; Ælfric 51; Byrhtferth 44

In librum primum Regum expositiones [CPL 1719]

CIT: Lantfred 22

Moralia in Iob [CPL 1708]

INV(i): c. 1, f. 29

INV(ii): a. 21

MSS(i):

Cambridge, Trinity College B. 4. 9 (Christ Church, Canterbury, s. xi/xii) (exc.)

Durham, CL, B. III. 10 (Normandy, s. xi^{ex}; prov. Durham) (exc.)

London, BL, Royal 3. C. IV + 6. C. VI (s. xi/xii; prov. Rochester)

New Haven, Yale University, Beinecke Library 516 (Northumbria, s. viii^1) (frg.)

New York, Pierpont Morgan Library, G. 30 (?Northumbria, s. vii^{ex}) (frg.)

Oxford, BodL, Bodley 310, fos. 1–145 (E. France, s. ix²; prov. England)

Oxford, BodL, G. 1. 7 Med. + G. 1. 9 Med., binding fragments (s. xi^in) (frg.)

Oxford, Magdalen College lat. 267, fos. 60–1 (?England, ?Continent, s. xi/xii) (frg.)

Oxford, Trinity College 39 (Normandy, s. xi^ex; prov. England) (exc.)

St Petersburg, Russian National Library, F. v. 1. 3, fos. 1–38 (?Northumbria, s. viii¹)

Salisbury, CL, 33 (Salisbury, s. xi^ex)

Würzburg, UB, M. p. th. f. 149a (Southumbria, s. viii²) (exc.)

York, Minster Library, XVI. Q. 1 + XVI. Q. 2 (s. xi^ex; prov. York)

MSS(ii): nos. 7, 42, 77

CIT: Aldhelm 37; Bede 129; OEM 18; Asser 13; Lantfred 23; Ælfric 52; Byrhtferth 45

Registrum epistularum [CPL 1714]

MSS(i):

Cambridge, UL, Ii. 3. 33, fos. 1–194 (Christ Church, Canterbury, s. xi/xii)

Cambridge, CCC 223 (Arras, s. ix^{3/4}; prov. England, s. x¹; addition of s. x/xi) (frg.)

Durham, CL, B. III. 9 (s. xi^ex; prov. Durham)

Lincoln, CL, 106 (?Normandy, ?England, s. xi^ex) (exc.)

London, BL, Royal 6. C. X (s. xi/xii; prov. Rochester)

Oxford, BodL, Bodley 193 (?England, ?Normandy, s. xi/xii; prov. Exeter)

Regula pastoralis [CPL 1712]

INV(i): d. 1, f. 28

INV(ii): a. 2, b. 13, c. 14

MSS(i):

Boulogne-sur-Mer 63, fos. 1–34 (England, s. xi¹; prov. Saint-Bertin) (exc.)

Cambridge, CCC 361 (?Malmesbury, s. xi^med)

Glasgow, UL, Hunterian 431, fos. 1–102 (s. x/xi; prov. Worcester)

Kassel, Gesamthochschulbibliothek, Fol. theol. 32 (S. England, s. viii; prov. Fulda)

London, BL, Cotton Otho A. i (Southumbria, s. viii²) (frg.)

London, Harley 5228, fo. 140 (?Wales, s. ix; prov. Worcester) (frg.)

Oxford, BodL, Bodley 708 (Christ Church, Canterbury, s. x^ex)

Oxford, BodL, Bodley 783 (Normandy, s. xi^ex; prov. Exeter)

Oxford, St John's College 28 (St Augustine's, Canterbury, s. x²)

Paris, BNF, lat. 9561 (Southumbria, s. viii¹)

Paris, BNF, lat. 13089, fos. 49–76 (Northumbria, s. viii^med)

Salisbury, CL, 157 (?England, s. xi^ex)

Shrewsbury, Shrewsbury School 21 (Normandy, s. xi/xii; prov.
Durham)
Worcester, CL, Add. 3 (s. viii) (frg.)
MSS(ii): nos. 12, 40, 62
CIT: Theodore/Hadrian 11; Aldhelm 38; Bede 130; Asser 14; Ælfric
53; Byrhtferth 46

Gregory of Nazianzus
Orationes .xlv., trans. Rufinus [CPG 3010]
INV(i): f. 50 [*Oratio* ii]
MSS(i):
Oxford, Trinity College 4 (?Angers, ?Tours, s. x/xi; prov. St
Augustine's, Cantebury, s. xi^ex) (*Oratio* ii)
Salisbury, CL, 9, fos. 1–60 (Salisbury, s. xi^ex) (*Oratio* xvii)
Salisbury, CL, 89 (Fécamp, s. xi^med; prov. Salisbury)
CIT: Bede 131 [*Oratio* iv]

Gregory of Tours
De uirtutibus S. Martini [BHL 5618]
MSS(i):
Hereford, CL, O. VI. 11 (s. xi^ex; prov. Hereford) (exc.)
London, Collection of R. A. Linenthal, s.n. (s. xi^1) (frg.)
Oxford, Trinity College 4 (?Angers, ?Tours, s. x/xi; prov. St
Augustine's, Canterbury, s. xi^ex) (exc.)
Vatican City, BAV, Reg. lat. 489, fos. 61–124 (s. xi^1) (exc.)
Historia Francorum [CPL 1023]
MSS(i):
Avranches, BM, 29 (Southumbria, s. x/xi) (exc.)
Hereford, CL, O. VI. 11 (s. xi^ex; prov. Hereford) (exc.)
Vatican City, BAV, Reg. lat. 489, fos. 61–124 (s. xi^1) (exc.)
CIT: Bede 132; Ælfric 54
Libri miraculorum [CPL 1024]
INV(i): b. 2 (?), f. 60 (?)
MSS(i): Cambridge, Trinity College O. 10. 23 (s. xi^ex; prov. Exeter)
(exc.)

Hegesippus: *see* **Josephus**, *Bellum Iudaicum*

Hilary of Poitiers [LLA 582]
Tractatus super psalmos [CPL 428]
CIT: Bede 133

Horace [LLA 234]
Ars poetica
MSS(i):

Cambridge, Trinity College R. 3. 57 (Christ Church, Canterbury, s. xi/xii)

Oxford, Queen's College 202 (s. xi/xii)

CIT: Bede 134; Abbo 22

Carmen saeculare

CIT: Abbo 23

Carmina

MSS(i):

Cambridge, UL, Gg. 5. 35 (St Augustine's, Canterbury, s. xi^med) (exc.)

Cambridge, Trinity College R. 3. 57 (Christ Church, Canterbury, s. xi/xii)

Oxford, Queen's College 202 (s. xi/xii)

CIT: Abbo 24; Byrhtferth 54

Epistulae

MSS(i):

Edinburgh, NLS, Advocates 18. 6. 12 (s. xi^ex; prov. Thorney) (exc.)

Oxford, Queen's College 202 (s. xi/xii)

CIT: Bede 135; Abbo 25; Wulfstan 10

Epodon liber

MSS(i):

Cambridge, Trinity College R. 3. 57 (Christ Church, Canterbury, s. xi/xii)

Oxford, Queen's College 202 (s. xi/xii)

CIT: Abbo 26

Sermones

MSS(i):

Cambridge, Trinity College R. 3. 57 (Christ Church, Canterbury, s. xi/xii)

Oxford, Queen's College 202 (s. xi/xii)

CIT: Aldhelm 39; Bede 136; Abbo 27; Byrhtferth 55

Hyginus astronomus [LLA 265]

Astronomica

MSS(i):

Aberystwyth, NLW, 735C, fos. 27–47 (?England, ?Wales, s. xi)

Cambridge, Trinity College R. 15. 32 (New Minster, Winchester, s. xi^1)

London, BL, Harley 647 (Lotharingia, s. ix^2/4; prov. Ramsey, s. x/xi) (exc.)

London, BL, Harley 2506 (Fleury, s. x/xi; prov. England, s. xi^1)

London, BL, Royal 13. A. XI (Normandy, s. xi/xii) (exc.)

CIT: Byrhtferth 57

Hyginus minor gromaticus [LLA 397]
Constitutio limitum
    MSS(i): Cambridge, Trinity College R. 15. 14, pt. 1 (N. France, s. x¹; prov. St Augustine's, Canterbury)

Isidore of Seville
Allegoriae quaedam sacrae scripturae [CPL 1190]
    MSS(i):
        Arras, BM, 764, fos. 134–81 (?Winchester, s. ix/x; prov. Bath, s. xi; prov. Saint-Vaast, Arras)
        Düsseldorf, UB, Fragm. K1: B. 210 (?England, ?Werden, s. viii²) (frg.)
        Hereford, CL, O. III. 2 (France, s. ix³ᐟ⁴; prov. England, s. xiᵉˣ)
        Munich, BSB, Clm. 14096, fos. 1–99 (?Wales, ?Cornwall, ?Brittany, s. viii/ix; prov. Regensburg)
        Oxford, BodL, Bodley 391 (St Augustine's, Canterbury, s. xiᵉˣ)
        Oxford, BodL, Bodley 444, fos. 1–27 (Salisbury, s. xiᵉˣ)
        Salisbury, CL, 88 (Salisbury, s. xiᵉˣ)
        Salisbury, CL, 157 (?England, s. xiᵉˣ)
Chronica maiora [CPL 1205]
    CIT: Bede 137; Ælfric 64
De differentiis rerum siue Differentiae theologicae uel spiritales [CPL 1202]
    MSS(ii): no. 22
    CIT: Bede 138; Lantfred 24
De differentiis uerborum [CPL 1187]
    INV(i): b. 17 (?), f. 35
    MSS(i):
        Basle, UB, F. III. 15l (England, s. viii¹; prov. Fulda)
        Cambridge, Trinity College O. 2. 30, fos. 1–70 (s. xi/xii; prov. Southwark) (exc.)
        London, BL, Royal 5. E. XVI (Salisbury, s. xiᵉˣ) (exc.)
        Saint-Omer, BM, 279, fos. 1–2 (?England, s. viii; prov. Saint-Bertin) (frg.)
        St Petersburg, Russian National Library, Q. v. I. 15 (SW England, s. viii²) (exc.)
    CIT: Theodore/Hadrian 25
De ecclesiasticis officiis [CPL 1207]
    INV(i): c. 8
    INV(ii): a. 18
    MSS(i):
        Hereford, CL, O. III. 2 (France, s. ix³ᐟ⁴; prov. England, s. xiᵉˣ) (exc.)
        London, BL, Cotton Vespasian D. xii (Christ Church, Canterbury, s. xiᵐᵉᵈ) (exc.)

Salisbury, CL, 88 (Salisbury, s. xi^{ex}) (exc.)
St Petersburg, Russian National Library, Q. v. I. 15 (SW England,
s. viii^2)
MSS(ii): no. 79
CIT: Theodore/Hadrian 12; Aldhelm 40; Bede 139; Lantfred 25;
Ælfric 65
De fide catholica contra Iudaeos [CPL 1198]
INV(i): d. 16
MSS(i):
Cambridge, Trinity College O. 2. 30, fos. 1–70 (s. xi/xii; prov.
Southwark)
London, BL, Royal 5. E. XVI (Salisbury, s. xi^{ex})
London, BL, Royal 6. B. VIII, fos. 1–57 (?St Augustine's,
Canterbury, s. xi) (exc.)
Oxford, BodL, Bodley 319 (SW England, s. x^2; prov. Exeter) (exc.)
Oxford, BodL, Bodley 394, fos. 1–84 (?France, ?England, s. x^2; prov.
Exeter)
De natura rerum [*Liber rotarum*] [CPL 1188]
INV(i): a.1, e. 14, f. 34
INV(ii): b. 15, c. 7
MSS(i):
Basle, UB, F. III. 15f (England, s. viii^1; prov. Fulda)
Cambridge, CCC 291 (St Augustine's, Canterbury, s. xi/xii) (exc.)
Exeter, CL, 3507 (Southumbria, s. x^2; prov. Exeter, s. xi^2)
London, BL, Cotton Domitian i, fos. 2–55 (St Augustine's,
Canterbury, s. x^2)
London, BL, Cotton Vitellius A. xii, fos. 4–77 (Salisbury, s. xi^{ex})
Oxford, BodL, Auct. F. 2. 20 (s. xi^{ex}; prov. Exeter?)
Weimar, Landesbibliothek, Fol. 414a (?England, s. viii^2) (frg.)
MSS(ii): nos. 16, 21
CIT: Theodore/Hadrian 13; Aldhelm 41; Bede 140; Ælfric 66;
Byrhtferth 58
De ortu et obitu patrum [CPL 1191]
INV(i): d. 11 (?)
MSS(i):
Arras, BM, 764, fos. 134–81 (?Winchester, s. ix/x; prov. Bath, s. xi;
prov. Saint-Vaast, Arras)
Düsseldorf, UB, Fragm. K1: B. 210 (?England, ?Werden, s. viii^2)
(frg.)
Hereford, CL, O. III. 2 (France, s. ix$^{3/4}$; prov. England, s. xi^{ex})
Munich, BSB, Clm. 14096, fos. 1–99 (?Wales, ?Cornwall, ?Brittany,
s. viii/ix; prov. Regensburg)
Oxford, BodL, Bodley 391 (St Augustine's, Canterbury, s. xi^{ex})
Oxford, BodL, Bodley 444, fos. 1–27 (Salisbury, s. xi^{ex})

Salisbury, CL, 88 (Salisbury, s. xi^{ex})
Salisbury, CL, 157 (?England, s. xi^{ex})
CIT: Aldhelm 42; Bede 141; OEM 19; Ælfric 67
De uiris illustribus [CPL 1206]
MSS(i):
Hereford, CL, O. III. 2 (France, s. ix$^{3/4}$; prov. England, s. xi^{ex})
Oxford, BodL, Bodley 391 (St Augustine's, Canterbury, s. xi^{ex})
Salisbury, CL, 88 (Salisbury, s. xi^{ex})
Etymologiae [CPL 1186]
INV(i): d. 10
MSS(i):
Bamberg, Staatsbibliothek, Misc. phil. 1 (?Brittany, ?England, s. x) (exc.)
Cambridge, St John's College Ii. 12. 29, flyleaves (France, s. ix^{1}) (frg.)
Cambridge, Trinity College B. 15. 33 (S. England, s. x^{in}) (exc.)
Cambridge, Trinity College R. 15. 14, pt. i (N. France or Flanders, s. x^{1}; prov. St Augustine's, Canterbury) (exc.)
Cambridge, Trinity College O. 2. 30, fos. 1–70 (s. xi/xii) (exc.)
Düsseldorf, UB, Fragm. K 15: O17 + K 19: Z.8/7b (?Northumbria, s. viii^{2}) (frg.)
London, BL, Cotton Caligula A. xv, fos. 3–117 (NE France, s. viii^{2}; prov. England, s. ix/x) (exc.)
London, BL, Harley 5977 nos. 64 and 71 (?Continent, s. x/xi; prov. England?) (exc.)
London, BL, Royal 5. E. XVI (Salisbury, s. xi^{ex}) (exc.)
London, BL, Royal 6. C. I (St Augustine's, Canterbury, s. xi)
London, BL, Royal 15. C. XI, fos. 113–94 (Salisbury, s. xi/xii) (exc.)
London, BL, Sloane 475, fos. 125–231 (s. xi^{ex}) (exc.)
Longleat House (Wilts.), Library of the Marquess of Bath, NMR 10589, flyleaves (Ireland, s. vii/viii; prov. Glastonbury) (frg.)
Oxford, BodL, Bodley 239 (?Normandy, s. xi/xii; prov. Exeter)
Oxford, Queen's College 320 (?Canterbury, s. x^{med})
Oxford, Trinity College 28 (s. xi; prov. Old Minster, Winchester) (exc.)
Paris, BNF, lat. 4871, fos. 161–8 (?Northumbria, s. viii/ix) (frg.)
Paris, BNF, lat. 7585 (France, s. ix$^{2/4}$; prov. St Augustine's, Canterbury, s. x^{2})
Rouen, BM, A. 292 (N. France, s. ix^{1}; prov. England, s. x) (exc.)
MSS(ii): nos. 8, 26, 53, 57, 97, 112
CIT: Theodore/Hadrian 14, 26; Aldhelm 43; Bede 142; Lantfred 26; Abbo 28; Ælfric 68; Byrhtferth 59
In libros Veteris et Noui Testamenti prooemia [CPL 1192]
INV(i): d. 15 (?), e. 31

MSS(i):

Arras, BM, 764, fos. 134–81 (?Winchester, s. ix/x; prov. Bath s. xi)

Hereford, CL, O. III. 2 (France, s. ix$^{3/4}$; prov. England, s. xi^{ex})

Munich, BSB, Clm. 14096, fos. 1–99 (?Wales, ?Cornwall, ?Brittany, s. viii/ix; prov. Regensburg)

Oxford, BodL, Bodley 391 (St Augustine's, Canterbury, s. xi^{ex})

Oxford, BodL, Bodley 444, fos. 1–27 (Salisbury, s. xi^{ex})

St Petersburg, Russian National Library, Q. v. I. 15 (SW England, s. viii^{2}; prov. Corbie)

Salisbury, CL, 88 (Salisbury, s. xi^{ex})

Salisbury, CL, 157 (?England, s. xi^{ex}; prov. Normandy)

CIT: Ælfric 69

Mysticorum expositiones sacramentorum seu Quaestiones in Vetus Testamentum [CPL 1195]

INV(i): f. 23, f. 35 (?)

MSS(i):

Cambridge, Trinity College B. 4. 27 (Christ Church, Canterbury, s. x^{ex})

London, BL, Royal 3. B. I (s. xi/xii; prov. Rochester)

Salisbury, CL, 101 (W. France, s. ix^{ex}; prov. Christ Church, Canterbury, s. x)

Salisbury, CL, 135 (Salisbury, s. xi^{ex})

Würzburg, UB, M. p. th. q.24 (?England, ?Germany, s. viii^{2})

MSS(ii): no. 80

CIT: Bede 143; Ælfric 70

Sententiae [CPL 1199]

INV(i): f. 46

INV(ii): a. 22, b. 14

MSS(i):

London, BL, Royal 7. C. IV (?Christ Church, Canterbury, s. xi^{1}) (exc.)

London, Lambeth Palace Library, 377 (Tours, s. ix^{1}; prov. England, s. x^{med})

Luzern, Staatsarchiv, Fragm. PA 1034/21007 (Northumbria, s. viii^{1}) (frg.)

Worcester, CL, Add. 5 (s. viii^{2}) (frg.)

CIT: Bede 144

Synonyma de lamentatione animae peccatricis [CPL 1203]

INV(i): b. 7

INV(ii): b. 11

MSS(i):

Cambridge, CCC 448 (?Worcester, s. x^{1})

London, BL, Cotton Vespasian D. xiv, fos. 170–224 (England, s. x^{in})

London, BL, Harley 110 (Christ Church, Canterbury, s. x^{ex})

London, BL, Royal 5. E. XIX (Salisbury, s. xi^ex)
St Petersbury, Russian National Library, Q. v. I. 15 (SW England, s. viii²; prov. Corbie)
Salisbury, CL, 173 (Continent, s. x^ex; prov. Salisbury)
Würzburg, UB, M. p. th. f. 79 (Southumbria, s. viii¹)
MSS(ii): nos. 19, 76, 82, 84, 96
CIT: Aldhelm 44; Alcuin 51

Jerome (Hieronymus) [LLA 647]

Aduersus Heluidium de Mariae uirginitate perpetua [CPL 609]
MSS(i): Durham, CL, B. II. 10, fos. 1–183 (Christ Church, Canterbury, s. xi^ex; prov. Durham)
CIT: Bede 145

Aduersus Iouinianum [CPL 610]
INV(i): f. 11
MSS(i):
Brussels, Bibliothèque royale, 444–52 (St Augustine's, Canterbury, s. xi/xii)
London, BL, Harley 865 (s. xi^ex; prov. St Albans)
Oxford, BodL, Bodley 94 (?England, ?Normandy, s. xi/xii; prov. Exeter)
CIT: Aldhelm 45; Bede 146; Ælfric 71

Altercatio Luciferani et orthodoxi [CPL 608]
MSS(i): Kassel, Gesamthochschulbibliothek, Fol. theol. 21 (Northumbria, s. viii; prov. Fulda, s. ix)
CIT: Bede 147

Apologia aduersus libros Rufini [CPL 613]
CIT: Bede 148

Comm. in Danielem [CPL 588]
INV(i): f. 15
MSS(i):
Cambridge, Trinity College B. 3. 5 (Christ Church, Canterbury, s. xi^ex)
London, BL, Harley 3097 (s. xi/xii; prov. Peterborough)
Marburg, Hessisches Staatsarchiv Hr 2, 17 + Kassel, Gesamthochschulbibliothek Fol. theol. 265 (s. viii) (frg.)
Oxford, BodL, Bodley 385 (Continent, s. xi/xii; prov. Canterbury)
CIT: Aldhelm 46; Bede 149; Lantfred 27

Comm. in Ecclesiasten [CPL 583]
INV(ii): a. 4 (?)
MSS(i):
Kassel, Gesamthochschulbibliothek, Fol. theol. 21 (Northumbria, s. viii; prov. Fulda, s. ix)

Würzburg, UB, M. p. th. q.2 (Italy, s. v; prov. England, s. vii; prov.
Würzburg, s. vii)

MSS(ii): nos. 38, 78, 83

CIT: Bede 150

Comm. in .iv. Epistulas Pauli [CPL 591]

INV(ii): a. 13

MSS(i):

London, BL, Royal 3. B. I (s. xi/xii; prov. Rochester) (exc.)

Gerleve, Abteibibliothek, s.n. (s. viii²) (frg.)

MSS(ii): no. 106

CIT: Bede 151; Lantfred 28; Ælfric 72

Comm. in Esaiam [CPL 584]

INV(i): f. 12

MSS(ii): nos. 9, 95, 98

CIT: Bede 152; Lantfred 29

Comm. in Euangelium Matthaei [CPL 590]

MSS(i):

Cambridge, Trinity College B. 1. 17 (Christ Church, Canterbury,
s. xi/xii)

Shrewsbury, Shropshire Record Office, 1052/1 (?Northumbria,
s. viii²) (frg.)

Worcester, CL, Add. 2 (?Spain, s. vii; prov. Worcester, s. viii) (frg.)

MSS(ii): no. 99

CIT: Theodore/Hadrian 15, 27; Aldhelm 47; Bede 153; Ælfric 73;
Byrhtferth 60

Comm. in Ezechielem [CPL 587]

INV(i): f. 14

MSS(i): Oxford, BodL, Rawlinson C. 723 (Salisbury, s. xi^{ex})

CIT: Bede 154

Comm. in Hieremiam [CPL 586]

MSS(i):

London, BL, Royal 3. B. XVI (s. xi/xii; prov. Bath)

Salisbury, CL, 24 (Salisbury, s. xi^{ex})

CIT: Bede 155

Comm. in Prophetas minores [CPL 589]

INV(i): f. 13

MSS(i):

Cambridge, UL, Gg. 4. 28 (s. xi/xii)

Cambridge, Trinity College B. 3. 5 (Christ Church, Canterbury,
s. xi^{ex})

Durham, CL, B. II. 9 (Normandy, s. xi^{ex}; prov. Durham)

Oxford, BodL, e Mus. 26 (s. xi/xii; prov. Bury St Edmunds)

CIT: Aldhelm 48; Bede 156

Commentarioli in psalmos [CPL 582]
  CIT: Bede 157
Contra Vigilantium [CPL 611]
  MSS(i): Durham, CL, B. II. 10, fos. 1–183 (Christ Church,
    Canterbury, s. xi^{ex})
De uiris inlustribus [CPL 616]
  INV(ii): a. 30
  MSS(i):
    Hereford, CL, O. III. 2 (France, s. ix^{3/4}; prov. England)
    London, BL, Cotton Caligula A. xv, fos. 3–117 (NE France, s. viii²,
      prov. England, s. ix/x)
    Oxford, BodL, Bodley 391 (St Augustine's, Canterbury, s. xi^{ex})
    Salisbury, CL, 88 (Salisbury, s. xi^{ex})
  CIT: Theodore/Hadrian 16; Bede 158; Ælfric 74
Dialogi contra Pelagianos [CPL 615]
  CIT: Bede 159
Epistulae [CPL 620]
  INV(i): c. 17 [*Ep*. xlvi], f. 33
  INV(ii): a. 6
  MSS(i):
    Cambridge, UL, Dd. 2. 7 (Christ Church, Canterbury, s. xi^{ex})
    Cambridge, Trinity College B. 3. 33 (England, s. xi^{ex})
    Durham, CL, B. II. 10, fos. 1–183 (Christ Church, Canterbury,
      s. xi^{ex})
    Durham, CL, B. II. 11, fos. 1–108 (Normandy, s. xi^{ex}; prov.
      Durham)
    Hereford, CL, O. VI. 11 (England, s. xi^{ex})
    Kassel, Gesamthochschulbibliothek, Fol. theol. 21 (Northumbria,
      s. viii) (exc.)
    St Petersburg, Russian National Library, Q. v. I. 15 (SW England,
      s. viii²; prov. Corbie) (exc.)
  MSS(ii): nos. 6, 81 [*Ep*. xiv]
  CIT: Theodore/Hadrian 28; Aldhelm 49; Bede 160; Lantfred 30;
    Ælfric 75; Byrhtferth 61
Liber interpretationis hebraicorum nominum [CPL 581]
  INV(i): b. 3
  MSS(i):
    Durham, CL, B. II. 11, fos. 1–108 (Normandy, s. xi^{ex}; prov.
      Durham)
    Oxford, BodL, Bodley 808 (?England, ?Normandy, s. xi/xii; prov.
      Exeter)
    Oxford, BodL, Marshall 19 (?E. France, s. xi^i; prov. Canterbury)
  CIT: Aldhelm 50; Bede 161; Ælfric 76

Liber quaestionum hebraicarum in Genesim [CPL 580]
  MSS(i):
    Durham, CL, B. II. 11, fos. 1–108 (Normandy, s. xi^{ex}; prov.
    Durham)
    Oxford, BodL, Bodley 808 (England, s. xi/xii; prov. Exeter)
  CIT: Theodore/Hadrian 29; Aldhelm 51; Bede 162; Lantfred 31;
    Byrhtferth 62

Tractatus .lix. in psalmos [CPL 592]
  MSS(i):
    Cambridge, Pembroke College 91 (N. France, s. ix$^{1/3}$; prov. Bury St
    Edmunds)
    London, BL, Royal 4. A. XIV, fos. 1–106 (?Winchester, s. x^{med};
    prov. Worcester)
    Wrisbergholzen, Archiv des Grafen von Goertz-Wrisberg, HS Nr. 3
    (?England, ?Germany, s. ix$^{1/3}$) (frg.)
  CIT: Ælfric 77

Vita S. Hilarionis [CPL 618; BHL 3879]
  MSS(i): Worcester, CL, F. 48, fos. 1–48 (s. xi^{ex}; prov. Worcester)
  CIT: Aldhelm 52; Bede 163; OEM 20; Lantfred 32

Vita S. Malchi [CPL 619; BHL 5190]
  INV(ii): b. 19
  MSS(i): London, BL, Cotton Otho C. i, vol. ii (?Worcester, s. xi^{med})
  MSS(ii): no. 81
  CIT: Aldhelm 53

Vita S. Pauli primi eremitae [CPL 617; BHL 6596]
  INV(ii): b. 29, c. 15
  MSS(i):
    Cambridge, CCC 389 (St Augustine's, Canterbury, s. x^2)
    London, BL, Cotton Caligula A. xv, fos. 3–117 (NE France, s. viii^2;
    prov. England, s. ix/x)
    Worcester, CL, F. 48, fos. 1–48 (s. xi^{ex}; prov. Worcester)
  CIT: Aldhelm 54; Bede 164; OEM 21

John Chrysostom

De compunctione cordis, trans. Anianus of Celeda [CPG 4308–9?]
  MSS(i): Düsseldorf, UB, Fragm. K1: B215 + K2: C118 + K15: oo
    (?Northumbria, s. viii^{med}) (frg.)

De muliere Cananaea [CPG 4529; cf. CPL 645]
  MSS(i):
    London, BL, Royal 5. B. XV, fos. 57–64 (St Augustine's,
    Canterbury, s. xi^{ex})
    Oxford, BodL, Bodley 516 (?N. Italy, ?NE France, s. ix^2; prov.
    England) (exc.)

De reparatione lapsi, trans. Anianus of Celeda (?) [CPG 4305?]
  MSS(i): Düsseldorf, UB, Fragm. K1: B215 + K2: C118 + K15: oo
    (?Northumbria, s. viii^{med}) (frg.)
De sacerdotio, trans. Anianus of Celeda (?) [CPG 4316]
  INV(i): f. 18
Hom. in diem natalem [CPG 4334?; BHGa 1892]
  CIT: Bede 165

Jordanes [LLA 725]
De origine actibusque Getarum [CPL 913]
  MSS(ii): no. 52
De summa temporum uel origine actibusque gentis Romanorum [CPL 912]
  MSS(ii): no. 52

Josephus, Flavius
Antiquitates Iudaicae, trans. Cassiodorus
  INV(i): f. 26
  MSS(i):
    Durham, B. II. 1 (s. xi/xii; prov. Durham)
    London, BL, Royal 13. A. XXII (Mont Saint-Michel, s. xi²; prov. St
      Augustine's, Canterbury) (exc.)
  CIT: Bede 166
Bellum Iudaicum, trans. and abbrev. Hegesippus
  MSS(i):
    Durham, B. II. 1 (s. xi/xii; prov. Durham)
    Kassel, Gesamthochschulbibliothek, Fol. Theol. 65 (Italy, s. vi; prov.
      England, s. viii; prov. Fulda, s. viii?)
    London, BL, Royal 14. C. VIII (s. xi^{ex})
    London, Lambeth Palace Library, 173, fos. 1–156 (s. xi/xii)
  MSS(ii): no. 88
  CIT: Bede 167

Julian of Eclanum
De amore seu Comm. in Canticum canticorum [CPL 751]
  CIT: Bede 168
De bono constantiae [CPL 752]
  CIT: Bede 169

Julian of Toledo
Ars grammatica [CPL 1266]
  MSS(ii): no. 51
  CIT: Bede 170
Prognosticum futuri saeculi [CPL 1258]
  INV(i): b. 4, c. 9, e. 24, f. 39

MSS(i):
    Boulogne-sur-Mer, BM, 63, fos. 1–34 (England, s. xi^1; prov. Saint-Bertin) (exc.)
    Cambridge, Clare College 30 pt. ii (Worcester, s. xi^2)
    Cambridge, CCC 399 (N. France, s. ix^1; prov. England, s. x^1)
    London, BL, Royal 12. C. XXIII (Christ Church, Canterbury, s. x/xi)
    Oxford, BodL, Bodley 792 (?England, ?Normandy, s. xi/xii; prov. Exeter)
    Oxford, BodL, Laud misc. 546 (Normandy, s. xi^{ex}; prov. Durham)
    Oxford, University College 104 (s. xi^{ex})
  CIT: Bede 171; Ælfric 78

Julianus Pomerius
De uita contemplatiua [CPL 998]
  INV(i): c. 12
  MSS(i):
    London, BL, Royal 5. E. X (s. xi/xii; prov. Rochester)
    Oxford, BodL, Bodley 126 (Old Minster, Winchester, s. xi/xii)

Julius Honorius
Cosmographia
  MSS(i): Cambridge, Trinity College O. 4. 34 (Christ Church, Canterbury, s. xi/xii) (frg.)

Junillus Africanus
Instituta regularia diuinae legis [CPL 872]
  INV(ii): a. 17
  MSS(i): London, BL, Cotton Tiberius A. xv, fos. 175–80 (S. England, s. vii/viii; prov. Malmesbury) (frg.)
  CIT: Aldhelm 55; Bede 172

Justinus [LLA 637]
Epitome
  MSS(i):
    Cambridge, Clare College 18 (?St Albans, s. xi/xii)
    London, BL, Harley 5915, fo. 10 (Northumbria, s. viii^{med}) (frg.)
  CIT: Alcuin 17; Asser 15

Juvenal [LLA 375]
Saturae
  MSS(i):
    Cambridge, Trinity College O. 4. 10 (St Augustine's, Canterbury, s. x$^{2/4}$)
    Cambridge, Trinity College O. 4. 11 (N. France, s. x^2; prov. England, s. xi/xii)
  CIT: Aldhelm 56; Bede 173; Abbo 29; Wulfstan 11; Byrhtferth 63

Juvencus [LLA 561]
Euangelia [CPL 1385]
   INV(i): c. 27
   INV(ii): a. 12
   MSS(i):
      Cambridge, UL, Ff. 4. 42 (Wales, s. ix^2; prov. England, s. x/xi)
      Cambridge, UL, Gg. 5. 35 (St Augustine's, Canterbury, s. xi^{med})
      Cambridge, CCC 304 (Italy, s. viii^1; prov. England, s. ix/x)
      London, BL, Royal 15. A. XVI (N. France, s. ix/x; prov.
        Canterbury, s. x^2)
      Oxford, BodL, Barlow 25 (?England, s. x)
      Paris, Bibliothèque Sainte-Geneviève 2410 (Christ Church,
        Canterbury, s. x/xi)
   CIT: Aldhelm 57; Bede 174; Alcuin 22, 52; Lantfred 33; Wulfstan 12;
      Byrhtferth 64

Lactantius Firmianus [LLA 570]
Carmen de aue phoenice [CPL 90; ICL 4500]
   MSS(i):
      Cambridge, UL, Gg. 5. 35 (St Augustine's, Canterbury, s. xi^{med})
      Oxford, BodL, Auct. F. 2. 14 (?Sherborne, s. xi^2)
   CIT: Alcuin 29
De mortibus persecutorum [CPL 91]
   CIT: Bede 175
De opificio Dei [CPL 87]
   CIT: Aldhelm 58; Lantfred 34

Lactantius Placidus [LLA 614]
Scholia in Statii Thebaidem (ed. Sweeney)
   CIT: Byrhtferth 65

Leo the Great
Epistulae [CPL 1656]
   CIT: Bede 176; Alcuin 8 (?)
Sermones [CPL 1657]
   CIT: Bede 177; Alcuin 8 (?)

Licentius
Carmen ad Augustinum [CPL 262°; ICL 983]
   CIT: Bede 178

Lucan [LLA 342]
Bellum ciuile
   INV(i): e. 12
   CIT: Aldhelm 59; Bede 179; Alcuin 32; Asser 16; Abbo 30; Wulfstan 13
Orpheus
   CIT: Aldhelm 60

Lucian
Epistula de inuentione corporis S. Stephani martyris, trans. Avitus of Braga
[CPL 575; BHL 7850]
  CIT: Bede 180

Lucifer of Cagliari [LLA 535]
  INV(i): e. 28 (?)

Lucretius [LLA 218]
De natura rerum
  CIT: Aldhelm 61; Bede 181; Lantfred 35

Macrobius, Ambrosius Theodosius [LLA 636]
Comm. in Somnium Scipionis
  MSS(i):
    Aberystwyth, NLW, 735C, fos. 1–26 (France, s. xi^1; prov. England
      or Wales, s. xi) (frg.)
    London, BL, Cotton Tiberius B. v, fos. 2–73, 77–88 (?Canterbury,
      ?Winchester, s. xi^1) (exc.)
    London, BL, Harley 647 (Lotharingia, s. ix$^{2/4}$; prov. Fleury, prov.
      Ramsey, s. x/xi) (exc.)
    London, BL, Harley 2506 (Fleury, s. x/xi; prov. England, s. xi^1)
      (exc.)
    Oxford, BodL, Auct. F. 2. 20 (s. xi^{ex}; prov. Exeter?)
  CIT: Abbo 31; Byrhtferth 67
Saturnalia
  MSS (i):
    London, BL, Cotton Vitellius c. iii, fos. 86–138 (N. France, s. ix$^{3/4}$;
      prov. England)
    London, BL, Harley 3859 (?England, ?France, s. xi/xii)
  CIT: Bede 182; Abbo 32; Byrhtferth 68

Mallius Theodorus [LLA 613]
De metris (GL vi. 585–601)
  CIT: Aldhelm 62; Bede 183

Marcellinus Comes [LLA 726]
Chronicon [CPL 2270]
  CIT: Bede 184

Marius of Avenches
Chronica [CPL 2268]
  CIT: Bede 185

Marius Victorinus: *see* **Victorinus, Marius**

Martial [LLA 373]
Epigrammata
  MSS(i): Cambridge, Trinity College O. 4. 10 (St Augustine's,
    Canterbury, s. x$^{2/4}$) (exc.)
  CIT: Bede 186

Martianus Capella [LLA 710]
De nuptiis Philologiae et Mercurii
  INV(i): e. 5
  MSS(i):
    Cambridge, CCC 153 (Wales, s. ix^{ex}; prov. England, s. x^1)
    Cambridge, CCC 206 (England, s. x^1) (exc.)
    Cambridge, CCC 330 pt. i (?Normandy, ?Malmesbury, s. xi/xii)
    Cambridge, Trinity College R. 15. 32 (New Minster, Winchester,
      s. xi^1) (exc.)
    London, BL, Cotton Tiberius B. v, fos. 2–73, 77–88 (?Canterbury,
      ?Winchester, s. xi^1) (exc.)
    London, BL, Harley 2506 (Fleury, s. x/xi; prov. England, s. xi^1)
      (exc.)
    London, BL, Harley 3826 (Abingdon, s. x/xi) (exc.)
  MSS(ii): no. 36 [bk iii]
  CIT: Bede 187; Lantfred 36; Abbo 33; Byrhtferth 69

Martin of Braga [LLA 777]
De correctione rusticorum [CPL 1086]
  CIT: Ælfric 79
Formula uitae honestae [CPL 1080]
  MSS(i): Cambridge, CCC 430 (Saint-Amand, s. ix/x; prov. England,
    s. x)

Nemesianus, Marcus Aurelius Olympius [LLA 555.1]
Cynegetica [ICL 17029]
  MSS(i): Paris, BNF, lat. 4839 (England, s. x/xi)

Nonius Marcellus [LLA 615; Kaster 237]
De compendiosa doctrina
  CIT: Bede 188

Optatianus Porphyrius [LLA 544]
Carmina [CPL 1386a]
  MSS(i):
    Boulogne-sur-Mer, BM, 189 (Christ Church, Canterbury, s. x/xi)
      (exc.)
    Durham, CL, B. IV. 9 (s. x^{med}; prov. Durham) (exc.)
  CIT: Bede 189

Origen

Comm. in Cantica canticorum, trans. Rufinus [CPG 1433]
  CIT: Bede 190

Comm. in Euangelium Matthaei, in Latin translation [CPG 1450]
  CIT: Bede 191; Ælfric 80

Hom. .xvi. in Genesim, trans. Rufinus [CPG 1411]
  MSS(i): Durham, CL, B. III. 1 (Normandy, s. xi^{ex}; prov. Durham)

Hom. .xiii. in Exodum, trans. Rufinus [CPG 1414]
  MSS(i):
    Durham, CL, B. III. 1 (Normandy, s. xi^{ex}; prov. Durham)
    Salisbury, CL, 159 (s. xi^{ex}; prov. Salisbury)
  CIT: Bede 193

Hom. .xvi. in Leuiticum, trans. Rufinus [CPG 1416]
  MSS(i):
    Durham, CL, B. III. 1 (Normandy, s. xi^{ex}; prov. Durham)
    Oxford, All Souls College SR. 80. g. 8 (s. xi^{ex}) (frg.)
    Salisbury, CL, 159 (s. xi^{ex}; prov. Salisbury)
  CIT: Bede 194

Hom. .xxviii. in Numeros, trans. Rufinus [CPG 1418]
  MSS(i): London, BL, Royal 4. A. XIV, fos. 1–106 (?Winchester, s. x^{med})
    (exc.)
  MSS(ii): no. 68

Hom. .xxvi. in Iosue, trans. Rufinus [CPG 1420]
  INV(i): f. 10 (?)
  MSS(i): Durham, CL, B. III. 1 (Normandy, s. xi^{ex}; prov. Durham)

Hom. .ix. in Iudices, trans. Rufinus [CPG 1421]
  MSS(i): Durham, CL, B. III. 1 (Normandy, s. xi^{ex}; prov. Durham)

Hom. in libros Regum, trans. Rufinus [CPG 1423]
  MSS(i): Durham, CL, B. III. 1 (Normandy, s. xi^{ex}; prov. Durham)
  CIT: Bede 195

Hom. de psalmis, trans. Rufinus [CPG 1428; cf. CPL 198f]
  INV(i): b. 12 (?)

Hom. .ii. in Canticum canticorum, trans. Jerome [CPG 1432]
  MSS(i):
    Durham, CL, B. II. 10, fos. 1–183 (Christ Church, Canterbury,
      s. xi^{ex}; prov. Durham)
    Durham, CL, B. III. 1 (Normandy, s. xi^{ex}; prov. Durham)
  CIT: Bede 192

Hom. .xxxii. in Isaiam, trans. Jerome [CPG 1437]
  MSS(i): Durham, CL, B. III. 1 (Normandy, s. xi^{ex}; prov. Durham)

Hom. .ii. in Hieremiam, trans. Jerome [CPG 1438]
  MSS(i): Durham, CL, B. III. 1 (Normandy, s. xi^{ex}; prov. Durham)

Hom. .xiv. in Hiezechielem, trans. Jerome [CPG 1441]
  MSS(i): Durham, CL, B. III. 1 (Normandy, s. xi^{ex}; prov. Durham)

In Lucam homiliae .xxxix., trans. Jerome [CPG 1451]
    CIT: Ælfric 81

Orosius, Paulus [LLA 682]
Historiae aduersum paganos [CPL 571]
    INV(i): d. 17 (?), e. 1
    INV(ii): a. 10
    MSS(i):
        Cambridge, Clare College 18 (?St Albans, s. xi/xii)
        Cambridge, Trinity College O. 4. 34 (Christ Church, Canterbury,
            s. xi/xii)
        Düsseldorf, Nordrhein-Westfälisches Hauptstaatsarchiv Z 11/1
            (?Northumbria, s. viii²) (frg.)
        Exeter, CL, FMS/ 1, 2, 2a (?N. France, s. x¹) (frg.)
        London, BL, Add. 19835 (?Normandy, ?England, s. xi/xii) (exc.)
        Oxford, BodL, Bodley 163, fos. 1–227, 250–1 (?Peterborough,
            s. xi^med) (exc.)
    CIT: Theodore/Hadrian 17; Aldhelm 63; Bede 196; Alcuin 6; OEM 22;
        Asser 17; Lantfred 37; Byrhtferth 72

Ovid [LLA 230]
Amores
    MSS(i):
        Oxford, BodL, Rawlinson G. 57 + 111 (s. xi^ex) (exc.)
        Paris, Bibliothèque Sainte-Geneviève 2410 (Christ Church,
            Canterbury, s. x/xi) (exc.)
Ars amatoria
    MSS(i):
        Oxford, BodL, Auct. F. 4. 32, fos. 37–47 (Wales, s. ix/x; prov.
            Glastonbury, s. x²) (exc.)
        Paris, Bibliothèque Sainte-Geneviève 2410 (Christ Church,
            Canterbury, s. x/xi) (exc.)
    CIT: Bede 197; Wulfstan 14
Fasti
    CIT: Wulfstan 15
Metamorphoseis
    MSS(i): Vatican City, BAV, Reg. lat. 1671 (Worcester, s. x/xi) (exc.)
    CIT: Aldhelm 64; Bede 198; Wulfstan 16
Remedia amoris
    CIT: Abbo 34; Wulfstan 17

Palladius of Helenopolis
De gentibus Indiae et Bragmanibus [CPG 6038]
    INV(i): c. 8

Historia Lausiaca [CPG 6036]
INV(i): f. 43 [*Paradisus Heraclidis*]

Paterius
*Liber testimoniorum ueteris Testamenti quem Paterius ex opusculis S. Gregorii
excerpi curauit* [CPL 1718]
MSS(i): Worcester, CL, Add. 4 (s.viii) (frg.)
MSS(ii): no. 108

Paulinus of Milan [LLA 657]
Vita S. Ambrosii [CPL 169; BHL 377]
MSS(i): London, BL, Cotton Claudius A. i, fos. 41–156 (?Winchester,
s. xi/xii)
CIT: Aldhelm 65; Bede 199; OEM 23

Paulinus of Nola [LLA 627]
Carmina [CPL 203]
INV(i): b. 6, f. 37
MSS(i):
St Petersburg, Russian National Library, Q. v. XIV. 1
(?Northumbria, s. viii^1) (exc.)
Vatican City, BAV, Pal. lat. 235, fos. 4–29 (Northumbria, s. viii^{in})
CIT: Aldhelm 66; Bede 200; Alcuin 26; Lantfred 38

Paulinus of Périgueux [LLA 797]
De uita S. Martini [CPL 1474; BHL 5617]
CIT: Aldhelm 67

Paulus Quaestor [LLA 546.5]
Gratiarum actio
CIT: Aldhelm 68

Pelagius [LLA 651]
Epistula ad Demetriadem [CPL 737]
CIT: Aldhelm 69; Bede 201
Expositiones .xiii. epistularum Pauli [CPL 728]
MSS(i): Berlin, Staatsbibliothek Preußischer Kulturbesitz, Grimm 139,
1 (Northumbria, s. viii^1) (frg.)
CIT: Ælfric 85

Persius [LLA 362]
Saturae
INV(i): a. 2, d. 18, e. 6, e. 21
MSS(i):
Cambridge, Trinity College O. 4. 10 (St Augustine's, Canterbury,
s. x$^{2/4}$)
Edinburgh, NLS, Advocates 18. 6. 12 (s. xi^{ex}; prov. Thorney)

London, BL, Royal 15. B. XIX, fos. 79–199 (Reims, s. x; prov. England)

Oxford, BodL, Auct. F. 1. 15, fos. 78–93 (St Augustine's, Canterbury, s. x²)

Oxford, BodL, Auct. F. 2. 14 (?Sherborne, s. xi²)

CIT: Aldhelm 70; Bede 202; Abbo 35; Byrhtferth 74

Petrus Chrysologus of Ravenna

Sermones [CPL 227]

CIT: OEM 24; Ælfric 86

Philippus Presbyter

Comm. in librum Iob [CPL 643]

MSS(i):

Cambrai, BM, 470 (?English, s. viii¹)

Oxford, BodL, Bodley 426, fos. 1–118 (Wessex, s. ix¹)

St Petersburg, Russian National Library, F. v. I. 3, fos. 1–38 (?Northumbria, s. viii²)

MSS(ii): nos. 15, 94

CIT: Bede 203

Phocas [LLA 704; Kaster 121]

Ars de nomine et uerbo (GL v. 410–39)

MSS(i): Oxford, BodL, Auct. F. 2. 14 (?Sherborne, s. xi²)

CIT: Theodore/Hadrian 18; Aldhelm 71; Bede 204; Alcuin 34; Abbo 36

Plautus [LLA 127]

Comoediae

MSS(i): London, BL, Royal 15. C. XI, fos. 113–94 (Salisbury, s. xi/xii)

Pliny the Elder [LLA 399]

Naturalis historia

MSS(i):

Leiden, Bibliotheek der Rijksuniversiteit, Voss. Lat. F. 4, fos. 4–33 (Northumbria, s. viii¹) (exc.)

London, BL, Cotton Tiberius B. v, fos. 2–73, 77–88 (?Christ Church, Canterbury, s. xi²ᐟ⁴) (exc.)

London, BL, Harley 647 (Lotharingia, s. ix²ᐟ⁴; prov. Fleury, prov. Ramsey, s. x/xi) (exc.)

London, BL, Harley 2506 (Fleury, s. x/xi; prov. England, s. xi¹) (exc.)

CIT: Aldhelm 72; Bede 205; Alcuin 18; Abbo 37; Byrhtferth 75

Polemius Silvius [LLA 732]

Laterculus [CPL 2256]

CIT: Bede 206

Pompeius [LLA 702; Kaster 125]
Comm. in artem Donati (GL v. 95–312)
   INV(i): a. 13 (?)
   MSS(i): St Paul in Carinthia, Stiftsbibliothek, 2/1 (25.2.16), fos. 1–20
     (s. viii[1])
   CIT: Aldhelm 73; Bede 207; Alcuin 39

Possidius [LLA 692]
Vita S. Augustini [CPL 358; BHL 785]
   CIT: Bede 208

Primasius of Hadrumetum
Comm. in Apocalypsin [CPL 873]
   MSS(i): Oxford, BodL, Douce 140 (S. England, s. vii/viii)
   MSS(ii): no. 39
   CIT: Bede 209

Priscian [LLA 703; Kaster 126]
De figuris numerorum (GL iii. 406–17)
   CIT: Abbo 38; Byrhtferth 76
Institutio de nomine, pronomine et uerbo [CPL 1550] (GL iii. 443–56)
   MSS(i):
     Columbia, Mo., University of Missouri, Ellis Library, Fragmenta
      manuscripta 2 (?Wales, s. ix; prov. Winchester, s. x[in])
     Karlsruhe, Badische Landesbibliothek, Fragm. aug. 122
      (Northumbria, s. viii[ex]) (frg.)
     London, BL, Cotton Domitian i, fos. 2–55 (St Augustine's,
      Canterbury, s. x[2])
     St Petersburg, Russian National Library, O. v. XVI. 1, fos. 1–16 (s.
      x[1])
     Worcester, CL, Q. 5 (Christ Church, Canterbury, s. x[ex]; prov.
      Worcester)
   MSS(ii): no. 35
   CIT: Aldhelm 74; Alcuin 36 (?)
Institutiones grammaticae [CPL 1546] (GL ii. 1–597, iii. 1–377)
   INV(i): e. 17
   MSS(i):
     Cambridge, UL, Ii. 2. 1 (Christ Church, Canterbury, s. xi/xii)
     Cambridge, UL, Add. 4406 no. 74 (England, s. xi[2]) (frg.)
     Cambridge, Jesus College 28 (France, s. xi[ex]; prov. Durham)
     Cambridge, Magdalene College, Pepys 2981 (7) (?England, s. xi[2])
     Cambridge, Trinity College O. 2. 51, pt. ii (Canterbury, s. xi/xii)
     Canterbury, CL, Add. 127/19 (?N. France, s. ix/x; prov. St
      Augustine's, Canterbury?) (frg.)
     Columbia, Mo., University of Missouri, Ellis Library, Fragmenta
      manuscripta 2 (?Wales, s. ix; prov. Winchester, s. x[in]) (exc.)

MSS(ii): no. 37
CIT: Aldhelm 75; Bede 210; Alcuin 36 (?); Lantfred 39; Abbo 39;
Byrhtferth 77
Partitiones duodecim uersuum Aeneidos principalium [CPL 1551] (GL iii.
459–515)
CIT: Bede 211
Periegesis [CPL 1554; ICL 10028]
MSS(i):
Karlsruhe, Badische Landesbibliothek, Fragm. aug. 212 (?England,
?France, s. x¹)
London, BL, Cotton Tiberius B. v, fos. 2–73, 77–88 (?Christ
Church, Canterbury, s. xi²/⁴)
Paris, BNF, lat. 4839 (England, s. x/xi)

Proba [LLA 562]
Cento Vergilianus [CPL 1480]
MSS(i): Evreux, BM, 43 (?England, s. x) (exc.)
CIT: Aldhelm 76

Probus [LLA 522.3; Kaster 127]
Catholica (GL iv. 1–43)
CIT: Bede 212; Alcuin 33 (?); Abbo 40
Instituta artium (GL iv. 47–192)
CIT: Bede 213; Alcuin 33 (?)

Prosper of Aquitaine [LLA 762]
Carmen de ingratis [CPL 517]
CIT: Aldhelm 77
Epigrammata ex sententiis S. Augustini [CPL 526]
INV(i): d. 6, e. 7, e. 29, e. 33
INV(ii): a. 20 (?)
MSS(i):
Cambridge, UL, Gg. 5. 35 (St Augustine's, Canterbury, s. xi^med)
Cambridge, CCC 448 (S. England, s. x¹)
Cambridge, Trinity College O. 2. 31 (Christ Church, Canterbury,
s. x/xi)
London, BL, Cotton Tiberius A. vii, fos. 165–6 (W. France, s. ix³/⁴;
prov. England, s. xi) (frg.)
London, BL, Harley 110 (Christ Church, Canterbury, s. x^ex)
CIT: Aldhelm 78; Bede 214; Alcuin 25, 53; Byrhtferth 78
Epigrammata in obtrectatorem Augustini [CPL 518; ICL 2728]
CIT: Bede 215
Epistula ad Rufinum de gratia Dei et libero arbitrio [CPL 516]
MSS(i): Durham, CL, B. IV. 12, fos. 39–120 (Durham, s. xi/xii)

Epitome chronicorum [CPL 2257]
INV(i): f. 47
CIT: Bede 216; Ælfric 87
Expositio psalmorum a centesimo usque ad centesimum quinquagesimum [CPL 524]
INV(i): b. 12 (?), f. 52 (?)
INV(ii): a. 20 (?)
Poema coniugis ad uxorem [CPL 531; ICL 458]
MSS(i):
Cambridge, UL, Gg. 5. 35 (St Augustine's, Canterbury, s. xi^med)
Cambridge, CCC 448 (S. England, s. x^I)
Cambridge, Trinity College O. 2. 31 (Christ Church, Canterbury, s. x/xi)
London, BL, Cotton Tiberius A. vii, fos. 165–6 (W. France, s. ix^3/4; prov. England, s. xi) (frg.)
London, BL, Harley 110 (Christ Church, Canterbury, s. x^ex)
CIT: Alcuin 54; Byrhtferth 79
Pro Augustino responsiones ad capitula obiectionum Gallorum calumniantium [CPL 520]
MSS(i):
Brussels, Bibliothèque royale, 444–52 (St Augustine's, Canterbury, s. xi/xii)
Durham, CL, B. IV. 12, fos. 39–120 (Durham, s. xi/xii)
Pro Augustino responsiones ad capitula obiectionum Vincentianarum [CPL 521]
MSS(i): Durham, CL, B. IV. 12, fos. 39–120 (Durham, s. xi/xii)
Pro Augustino responsiones ad excerpta Genuensium [CPL 522]
MSS(i): Durham, CL, B. IV. 12, fos. 39–120 (Durham, s. xi/xii)
Sententiae ex operibus S. Augustini [CPL 525]
INV(ii): a. 20 (?), b. 23 (?)
MSS: Cambridge, CCC 448, fos. 87–103 (S. England, s. xi/xii) (exc.)
CIT: Byrhtferth 80

Prudentius [LLA 629]
Apotheosis [CPL 1439]
MSS(i):
Cambridge, CCC 223 (Saint-Vaast, Arras, s. ix^3/4; prov. England, s. x^I)
Durham, CL, B. IV. 9 (s. x^med; prov. Durham)
Oxford, BodL, Auct. F. 3. 6 (s. xi^I; prov. Exeter)
Paris, BNF, lat. 8085, fos. 2–82 (?Loire region, s. ix^med; prov. England, s. x/xi)
CIT: Aldhelm 79; Bede 217; Lantfred 40

Contra Symmachum [CPL 1442]

  MSS(i):

    Boulogne-sur-Mer, BM, 189 (Christ Church, Canterbury, s. x/xi)

    Cambridge, CCC 23 (S. England, s. x/xi) (frg.)

    Cambridge, CCC 223 (Saint-Vaast, Arras, s. ix$^{3/4}$; prov. England, s. x^{1})

    Christchurch, New Zealand, private collection, s.n. (Canterbury, s. x/xi) (frg.)

    Durham, CL, B. IV. 9 (s. x^{med}; prov. Durham)

    Oxford, BodL, Auct. F. 3. 6 (s. xi^{1}; prov. Exeter)

    Oxford, Oriel College 3 (Christ Church, Canterbury, s. x^{ex})

    Paris, BNF, lat. 8085, fos. 2–82 (?Loire region, s. ix^{med}; prov. England, s. x/xi)

  CIT: Aldhelm 80; Bede 218

Dittochaeon [CPL 1444]

  MSS(i):

    Cambridge, UL, Gg. 5. 35 (St Augustine's, Canterbury, s. xi^{med})

    Cambridge, CCC 223 (Saint-Vaast, Arras, s. ix$^{3/4}$; prov. England, s. x^{1})

    Cambridge, CCC 448, fos. 87–103 (S. England, s. xi/xii)

    Cambridge, Gonville and Caius College 144/194 (?England, s. x^{1}; prov. St Augustine's, Canterbury) (exc.)

    Cambridge, Trinity College O. 2. 31 (Christ Church, Canterbury, s. x/xi)

    Durham, CL, B. IV. 9 (s. x^{med}; prov. Durham)

    Oxford, BodL, Auct. F. 2. 14 (?Sherborne, s. xi^{2})

    Oxford, BodL, Auct. F. 3. 6 (s. xi^{1}; prov. Exeter)

    Oxford, Oriel College 3 (Christ Church, Canterbury, s. x^{ex})

    Paris, BNF, lat. 8085, fos. 2–82 (?Loire region, s. ix^{med}; prov. England, s. x/xi)

Hamartigenia [CPL 1440]

  MSS(i):

    Cambridge, UL, Gg. 5. 35 (St Augustine's, Canterbury, s. xi^{med}) (exc.)

    Cambridge, CCC 223 (Saint-Vaast, Arras, s. ix$^{3/4}$; prov. England, s. x^{1})

    Cambridge, Gonville and Caius College 144/194 (?England, s. x^{1}; prov. St Augustine's, Canterbury) (exc.)

    Durham, CL, B. IV. 9 (s. x^{med}; prov. Durham)

    Oxford, BodL, Auct. F. 3. 6 (s. xi^{1}; prov. Exeter)

    Paris, BNF, lat. 8085, fos. 2–82 (?Loire region, s. ix^{med}; prov. England, s. x/xi)

  CIT: Aldhelm 81; Wulfstan 18

Liber cathemerinon [CPL 1438]

  INV(i): d. 8

  MSS(i):

    Boulogne-sur-Mer, BM, 189 (Christ Church, Canterbury, s. x/xi)

    Cambridge, CCC 223 (Saint-Vaast, Arras, s. ix$^{3/4}$; prov. England, s. x^1)

    Durham, CL, B. IV. 9 (s. x^{med}; prov. Durham)

    Oxford, BodL, Auct. F. 3. 6 (s. xi^1; prov. Exeter)

    Oxford, Oriel College 3 (Christ Church, Canterbury, s. x^{ex})

    Paris, BNF, lat. 8085, fos. 2–82 (?Loire region, s. ix^{med}; prov. England, s. x/xi)

  CIT: Aldhelm 82; Bede 219; Byrhtferth 81

Liber peristephanon [CPL 1443]

  INV(i): d. 9

  MSS(i):

    Boulogne-sur-Mer, BM, 189 (Christ Church, Canterbury, s. x/xi)

    Cambridge, CCC 23 (S. England, s. x/xi)

    Cambridge, CCC 223 (Saint-Vaast, Arras, s. ix$^{3/4}$; prov. England, s. x^1)

    Cambridge, CCC 448, fos. 87–103 (S. England, s. xi/xii) (exc.)

    Durham, CL, B. IV. 9 (s. x^{med}; prov. Durham)

    Oxford, BodL, Auct. F. 3. 6 (s. xi^1; prov. Exeter)

    Oxford, Oriel College 3 (Christ Church, Canterbury, s. x^{ex})

    Paris, BNF, lat. 8085, fos. 2–82 (?Loire region, s. ix^{med}; prov. England, s. x/xi)

  CIT: Aldhelm 83; Bede 220; Abbo 41

Psychomachia [CPL 1441]

  INV(i): d. 7, e. 10

  MSS(i):

    Cambridge, UL, Gg. 5. 35 (St Augustine's, Canterbury, s. xi^{med})

    Cambridge, CCC 23 (S. England, s. x/xi)

    Cambridge, CCC 223 (Saint-Vaast, Arras, s. ix$^{3/4}$; prov. England, s. x^1)

    Cambridge, Trinity College O. 2. 51, pt. i (s. x^2)

    Durham, CL, B. IV. 9 (s. x^{med}; prov. Durham)

    London, BL, Add. 24199, fos. 2–38 (s. xi^2; prov. Bury St Edmunds)

    London, BL, Cotton Cleopatra C. viii, fos. 4–37 (Christ Church, Canterbury, s. x/xi)

    London, BL, Cotton Titus D. xvi, fos. 2–35 (St Albans, s. xi/xii)

    Munich, Bayerische Staatsbibliothek, Clm. 29336 (s. x/xi) (frg.)

    Oxford, BodL, Auct. F. 3. 6 (s. xi^1; prov. Exeter)

    Oxford, BodL, Rawlinson C. 697 (NE France, s. ix$^{3/4}$; prov. England, s. x^{med})

Paris, BNF, lat. 8085, fos. 2–82 (?Loire region, s. ix^med; prov.
England, s. x/xi)
CIT: Aldhelm 84; Bede 221; Lantfred 41; Abbo 42; Byrhtferth 82

Quoduultdeus of Carthage [LLA 751]
Sermo (quartus) contra Iudaeos, paganos et Arianos [CPL 404]
CIT: Ælfric 88
Sermo (decimus) aduersus quinque haereses [CPL 410]
MSS(i): Salisbury, CL, 63 (Salisbury, s. xi^ex)
CIT: Bede 222

Remius Favinus: *see* ANONYMOUS WRITINGS, *Carmen de ponderibus*

Sallust [LLA 254]
Bellum Iugurthinum
MSS(i): Cambridge, CCC 309, flyleaves (?England, ?Continent, s. xi/xii;
prov. England) (frg.)
CIT: Aldhelm 85; Bede 223; Abbo 43

Sedulius, Caelius [LLA 793]
Carmen paschale [CPL 1447]
INV(i): a. 11, c. 27, d. 19, e. 2, e. 9
INV(ii): c. 12
MSS(i):
Cambridge, UL, Gg. 5. 35 (St Augustine's, Canterbury, s. xi^med)
Cambridge, CCC 173, fos. 57–83 (S. England, s. viii²; prov.
Winchester, Canterbury)
Edinburgh, NLS, Advocates 18. 7. 7 (s. x^ex; prov. Thorney)
Evreux, BM, 43 (?England, s. x)
London, BL, 15. B. XIX, fos. 1–35 (Christ Church, Canterbury,
s. x²)
Oxford, BodL, Lat. theol. c. 4 (?Worcester, s. x²) (frg.)
Paris, BNF, lat. 8092 (England, s. xi^{2/4})
Paris, Bibliothèque Sainte-Geneviève 2410 (Christ Church,
Canterbury, s. x/xi)
MSS(ii): nos. 23, 49
CIT: Aldhelm 86; Bede 224; Alcuin 21, 55; Asser 18; Lantfred 42;
Abbo 44; Wulfstan 19; Ælfric 91; Byrhtferth 88
Hymni [CPL 1449]
MSS(i):
Cambridge, UL, Gg. 5. 35 (St Augustine's, Canterbury, s. xi^med)
Cambridge, CCC 173, fos. 57–83 (S. England, s. viii²; prov.
Winchester, Canterbury)
Edinburgh, NLS, Advocates 18. 7. 7 (s. x^ex; prov. Thorney)
Evreux, BM, 43 (?England, s. x)

London, BL, 15. B. XIX, fos. 1–35 (Christ Church, Canterbury, s. x²)

Paris, BNF, lat. 8092 (England, s. xi²ᐟ⁴)

Paris, Bibliothèque Sainte-Geneviève 2410 (Christ Church, Canterbury, s. x/xi)

CIT: Bede 225; Byrhtferth 89

Seneca [LLA 335]
Tragoediae
CIT: Aldhelm 87 [*Agamemnon*]

Serenus (Sammonicus), Quintus [LLA 556]
Liber medicinalis [ICL 11975]
MSS(i): Paris, BNF, lat. 4839 (England, s. x/xi)

Sergius [LLA 705; Kaster 255]
Comm. de littera, de syllaba, de pedibus, de accentibus, de distinctione (GL iv. 475–85)
INV(i): e. 34
CIT: Aldhelm 88; Bede 226; Byrhtferth 90
Explanationes in artem Donati (GL iv. 486–565)
INV(i): a. 13 (?)
MSS(i): St Paul in Carinthia, Stiftsbibliothek, 2/1 (25.2.16), fos. 43–75 (s. viii¹)
CIT: Bede 227

Servius [LLA 612; Kaster 136]
Comm. in artem Donati (GL iv. 405–48)
CIT: Bede 228
Comm. in Vergilii Bucolica et Georgica
CIT: Aldhelm 89; Byrhtferth 91
Comm. in Vergilii Aeneidos libros
MSS(i): Marburg, Hessisches Staatsarchiv, 319 Pfarrei Spangenberg Hr Nr. 1 (SW England, s. viii¹; prov. Fulda) (frg.)
CIT: Aldhelm 90; Abbo 45; Byrhtferth 92
De centum metris (GL iv. 456–67)
CIT: Bede 229
De finalibus metrorum (GL iv. 449–55)
CIT: Bede 230

Sextus
Sententiae, trans. Rufinus [CPG 1115]
MSS (i): London, Lambeth Palace Library, 237, fos. 146–208 (Arras, s. ixᵐᵉᵈ; prov. England, s. xⁱⁿ)

Sextus Placitus
Liber medicinae ex animalibus
  MSS(i):
    Oxford, BodL, Bodley 130 (?Bury St Edmunds, s. xi^{ex})
    Herrnstein near Siegburg, Bibliothek der Grafen Nesselrode, 192,
      fos. 1–20 (S. England, s. ix/x) [destroyed]

Sisebutus rex Visigothorum
Carmen de eclipsibus solis et lunae [CPL 1300; ICL 16513]
  CIT: Aldhelm 91

Socrates, Sozomen, and Theodoretus
Historia tripartita ecclesiastica, trans. Cassiodorus [CPG 7502]
  INV(i): c. 29, f. 9
  CIT: Ælfric 95

Solinus [LLA 409]
Collectanea rerum memorabilium
  MSS(i):
    Cambridge, Clare College, s.n. (pastedown) (Bury St Edmunds,
      s. xi^{ex}) (frg.)
    London, BL, Harley 3859 (?England, ?France, s. xi/xii)
  CIT: Aldhelm 92; Bede 231

Statius [LLA 369]
Achilleis
  MSS(i): Oxford, BodL, Auct. F. 2. 14 (?Sherborne, s. xi²)
Thebais
  INV(i): d. 22
  MSS(i):
    Cambridge, UL, Gg. 5. 35 (St Augustine's, Canterbury, s. xi^{med})
      (exc.)
    Cambridge, St John's College 87, fos. 1–50 (France, s. xi²; prov.
      England, s. xi/xii?)
    London, BL, Royal 15. C. X (?St Augustine's, Canterbury, s. x²)
    Worcester, CL, Q. 8, fos. 165–72 + Add. 7, fos. 1–6 (?France, s. ix/x;
      prov. England, s. x/xi) (frg.)
  CIT: Aldhelm 93; Bede 232; Alcuin 31; Lantfred 43; Wulfstan 20

Sulpicius Severus [LLA 672]
Dialogi [CPL 477]
  MSS(i):
    Hereford, CL, O. VI. 11 (s. xi^{ex})
    London, BL, Add. 40074 (Christ Church, Canterbury, s. x/xi)
    Vatican City, BAV, Reg. lat. 489, fos. 61–124 (s. xi¹)
  CIT: Theodore/Hadrian 19; OEM 26; Abbo 46; Ælfric 96

Epistulae .iii. [CPL 476]
  MSS(i):
    Avranches, BM, 29 (S. England, s. x/xi) (exc.)
    Hereford, CL, O. VI. 11 (s. xi^ex)
    London, BL, Add. 40074 (Christ Church, Canterbury, s. x/xi)
    Vatican City, BAV, Reg. lat. 489, fos. 61–124 (s. xi^1)
  MSS(ii): no. 23
  CIT: Ælfric 97
Vita S. Martini [CPL 475; BHL 5610]
  INV(i): f. 58
  MSS(i):
    Avranches, BM, 29 (S. England, s. x/xi)
    Hereford, CL, O. VI. 11 (s. xi^ex)
    London, BL, Add. 40074 (Christ Church, Canterbury, s. x/xi)
    Vatican City, BAV, Reg. lat. 489, fos. 61–124 (s. xi^1)
  CIT: Theodore/Hadrian 20; Aldhelm 94; OEM 27; Abbo 47; Ælfric 98

'Symposius' [LLA 548]
Aenigmata
  MSS(i):
    Cambridge, UL, Gg. 5. 35 (St Augustine's, Canterbury, s. xi^med)
    Edinburgh, NLS, 18. 6. 12 (s. xi^ex; prov. Thorney) (exc.)
    London, BL, Royal 12. C. XXIII (Christ Church, Canterbury, s. x^2)
    London, BL, Royal 15. B. XIX, fos. 79–199 (Reims, s. x; prov.
      England)
  CIT: Aldhelm 95

Terence [LLA 129]
Comoediae
  INV(i): e. 8
  MSS(i): Oxford, Brasenose College 18 (?England, s. xi?)
  CIT: Aldhelm 96 [*Adelphoe, Phormio*]; Bede 233 [*Andria, Eunuchus*],
    Abbo 48 [*Adelphoe, Andria, Phormio*], Byrhtferth 93 [*Heauton
    timorumenos*]

Tertullian [LLA 474]
Apologeticum
  MSS(i): Oxford, BodL, Lat. theol. d. 34 (?Durham, s. xi/xii)

Themistius
De decem categoriis
  MSS(i):
    Bern, Burgerbibliothek, C. 219 (4) (?Wales, ?SW England, s. ix^ex)
    Cambridge, CCC 206 (?England, s. x^1)
    Cambridge, Trinity College O. 11a. 5 (NE France, s. ix/x; prov.
      England?) (frg.)

Theodore of Mopsuestia
Comm. in epistulas Pauli minores, in Latin translation [CPG 3845]
MSS(ii): no. 13

Tyconius [LLA 687]
Comm. in Apocalypsin [CPL 710]
CIT: Bede 234

Uranius
Epistula de obitu Paulini [CPL 207; BHL 6558]
CIT: Byrhtferth 94

Valerius Maximus [LLA 314]
Facta et dicta memorabilia
MSS(i): London, BL, Add. 19835 (?Normandy, ?England, s. xi/xii)
(exc.)

Valerius Probus, Marcus [LLA 393]
Comm. in Vergilii Georgica
CIT: Aldhelm 97

Vegetius, Flavius Renatus [LLA 604]
Epitome rei militaris
MSS(i):
London, BL, Cotton Cleopatra D. i, fos. 83–128 (?Continent, s. xi$^\mathrm{I}$;
prov. Canterbury)
London, BL, Harley 3859 (?England, s. xi/xii)
CIT: Bede 235

Venantius Fortunatus
Carmina [CPL 1033]
MSS(i):
Badminton (Glos.), Duke of Beaufort Muniments, 704. 1. 16
(?Canterbury, s. x^2) (exc.)
Cambridge, Gonville and Caius College 144/194 (?England, s. x$^\mathrm{I}$;
prov. St Augustine's, Canterbury) (exc.)
Cambridge, Pembroke College 312C, no. 5 (s. x/xi) (frg.)
London, BL, Add. 24193 (France, s. ix$^\mathrm{I}$; prov. England, s. x^2)
CIT: Aldhelm 98; Bede 236; Alcuin 28, 56; Wulfstan 21
Vita S. Martini [CPL 1037; BHL 5624]
CIT: Aldhelm 99; Bede 237

Vergil [LLA 224]
Aeneis
MSS(i):
Cambridge, UL, Gg. 5. 35 (St Augustine's, Canterbury, s. xi$^\mathrm{med}$)
(exc.)

London, BL, Royal 8. F. XIV, fos. 3–4 (?Continent, s. xi^{in}; prov.
Bury St Edmunds) (frg.)
London, College of Arms, Arundel 30, fos. 5–10, 208 [palimpsest,
lower script] (s. x^1; prov. Bury St Edmunds) (frg.)
Oxford, BodL, Lat. class. c. 2, fo. 18 [+ Deene Park Library, L. 2.
21 + London, BL, Sloane 1044, fo. 6 + Oxford, All Souls College
330, nos. 54–5] (W. France, s. ix$^{2/3}$; prov. England, s. x^{ex}) (frg.)
Vatican City, BAV, Reg. lat. 1671 (Worcester, s. x^2)
CIT: Aldhelm 100; Bede 238; Asser 20; Lantfred 44; Abbo 49;
Wulfstan 22; Byrhtferth 95
Bucolica
INV(i): e. 20
MSS(i): Vatican City, BAV, Reg. lat. 1671 (Worcester, s. x^2)
CIT: Aldhelm 101; Bede 239; Abbo 50; Wulfstan 23; Byrhtferth 96
Georgica
INV(i): e. 20
MSS(i):
Exeter, CL, 3507 (S. England, s. x^2; prov. Exeter, s. xi^2) (exc.)
Oxford, BodL, Lat. class. c. 2, fo. 18 [+ Deene Park Library, L. 2.
21 + London, BL, Sloane 1044, fo. 6 + Oxford, All Souls College
330, nos. 54–5] (W. France, s. ix$^{2/3}$; prov. England, s. x^{ex}) (frg.)
Vatican City, BAV, Reg. lat. 1671 (Worcester, s. x^2)
CIT: Aldhelm 102; Bede 240; Abbo 51; Wulfstan 24; Byrhtferth 97

Victor of Vita
Historia persecutionis Africanae prouinciae [CPL 798]
INV(i): f. 51
MSS(i):
Cambridge, Trinity College O. 10. 31 (Christ Church, Canterbury,
s. xi/xii)
Edinburgh, NLS, Advocates 18. 4. 3, fos. 1–122 (s. xi^{ex}; prov.
Durham)

Victorinus, C. Marius [LLA 564; Kaster 273]
Ars grammatica [CPL 1543]
CIT: Bede 241
De definitionibus [CPL 94]
INV(i): f. 35 (?)
CIT: Alcuin 15
Explanationes in Ciceronis rhetoricam [CPL 1544] (RLM pp. 153–304)
CIT: Bede 242

Victorinus, Maximus [Kaster 274]
De hexametro uersu siue heroico (GL vi. 206–15)
CIT: Aldhelm 103

Victorinus of Pettau
Comm. in Apocalypsin [recensio Hieronymiana] [CPL 80]
  MSS(i): Aberdeen, UL, 216 (Salisbury, s. xi^{ex})
Tractatus de fabrica mundi [CPL 79]
  MSS(i); London, Lambeth Palace Library, 414, fos. 1–80 (Saint-
    Amand, s. ix^{1}; prov. St Augustine's, Canterbury)

Vigilius of Thapsus
Contra Arianos, Sabellianos, Photinianos dialogus [CPL 807]
  MSS(i):
    Cambridge, Pembroke College 108 (E. France, s. ix^{2/3}; prov. Bury St
      Edmunds)
    Oxford, BodL, Bodley 147 (England, s. xi^{ex}; prov. Exeter)

Virgilius Maro Grammaticus
Epistulae [BCLL 296]
  CIT: Aldhelm 104
Epitomae [BCLL 295]
  CIT: Bede 243

Vitruvius [LLA 299]
De architectura
  MSS(i):
    London, BL, Cotton Cleopatra D. i, fos. 1–82 (s. xi^{1}; prov. St
      Augustine's, Canterbury)
    London, BL, Harley 3859 (?England, s. xi/xii)

ANONYMOUS WRITINGS

Adhortationes sanctorum patrum (Verba seniorum) [CPG 5570; BHL 6527]
  INV(i): c. 6, f. 30
  MSS(i):
    Brussels, Bibliothèque royale, 9850–2 (Soissons, s. vii/viii; prov.
      Bath?) (exc.)
    London, BL, Add. 15350, fos. 1, 121 (Italy, s. vii/viii; prov. Old
      Minster, Winchester) (exc.)
    London, BL, Cotton Otho C. i, vol. ii (Worcester, s. xi^{med}) (exc.)
    London, BL, Cotton Vespasian D. vi, fos. 2–77 (St Augustine's,
      Canterbury, s. x^{med}) (exc.)
    Worcester, CL, F. 48, fos. 49–104 (Worcester or York, s. xi^{in}) (exc.)
  MSS(ii): no. 85
  CIT: Bede 244; Alcuin 57; OEM 28

Aetna [LLA 348] [pseudo-Vergil]
  MSS(i): Cambridge, UL, Kk. 5. 34 (Old Minster, Winchester, s. x^{ex})

Ars Asperi grammatici [CPL 1554a] (GL viii. 39–61)
   CIT: Bede 245

Carmen de imagine et somno [ICL 12755] [pseudo-Ovid]
   CIT: Aldhelm 105

Carmen de ponderibus [LLA 619; ICL 12104]
   MSS(i): Cambridge, UL, Kk. 5. 34 (Old Minster, Winchester, s. x^ex)
   CIT: Abbo 52

Carmen de resurrectione mortuorum [CPL 1463]
   CIT: Aldhelm 106; Bede 246

Collectio canonum Andegauensis [CPL 1778]
   MSS(ii): no. 86

Collectio canonum Hibernensis [CPL 1794; BCLL 612–13]
   MSS(ii): no. 86

Collectio canonum Quesnelliana [CPL 1770]
   INV(i): c. 18
   MSS(ii): no. 46

Collectio canonum Sanblasiana
   MSS(i): Köln, Dombibliothek, 213 (Northumbria, s. viii^in)

Comm. in Pentateuchum [pseudo-Bede] (PL 91: 189–394)
   CIT: Ælfric 100; Byrhtferth 99

Culex [LLA 340] [pseudo-Vergil]
   MSS(i): Cambridge, UL, Kk. 5. 34 (Old Minster, Winchester, s. x^ex)
   CIT: Aldhelm 107

De duodecim abusiuis saeculi [CPL 1189; BCLL 339] [pseudo-Cyprian]
   INV(i): b. 11
   MSS(i): Salisbury, CL, 168 (Salisbury, s. xi^ex)
   CIT: Ælfric 101

De ordine creaturarum: see *Liber de ordine creaturarum*

De singularitate clericorum [CPL 62] [pseudo-Cyprian]
   INV(i): f. 17

Decretum de libris recipiendis et non recipiendis [CPL 1676] [pseudo-
      Gelasius]
   MSS(i):
      Boulogne-sur-Mer, BM, 63, fos. 1–34 (England, s. xi^1)
      Brussels, Bibliothèque royale, 9850–2 (Soissons, s. vii/viii; prov.
         Bath?, prov. Arras, s. xi^2)
      Hereford, CL, O. III. 2 (France, s. ix^3/4; prov. England, s. xi^ex)

Oxford, BodL, Bodley 391 (St Augustine's, Canterbury, s. xi^ex)
Salisbury, CL, 88 (Salisbury, s. xi^ex)
Salisbury, CL, 165, fos. 122–78 (Salisbury, s. xi^ex)

Disticha Catonis [LLA 488]
  INV(i): a. 9
  MSS(i):
    Cambridge, UL, Gg. 5. 35 (St Augustine's, Canterbury, s. xi^med)
    Cambridge, Trinity College, O. 2. 31 (Christ Church, Canterbury, s. x/xi)
    London, BL, Cotton Vespasian D. vi, fos. 2–77 (?St Augustine's, Canterbury, s. x^med)
    Oxford, BodL, Rawlinson G. 57 + 111 (s. xi^ex)
  CIT: Aldhelm 108; Byrhtferth 101

Epistula Alexandri ad Aristotelem [LLA 640]
  MSS(i): London, BL, Royal 13. A. I (s. xi^ex)

Epistula S. Hieronimi de nominibus pedum
  CIT: Aldhelm 109

Epithalamium Laurentii [ICL 7904] [pseudo-Claudian]
  CIT: Aldhelm 110

Gesta Siluestri [CPL 2235; BHL 7725]
  CIT: Aldhelm 111; Bede 247; OEM 29

Historia Alexandri [LLA 540.1] [pseudo-Callisthenes]
  MSS(i): London, BL, Royal 13. A. I (s. xi^ex)

Historia Apollonii regis Tyri [LLA 727]
  INV(i): e. 35

Historia monachorum, trans. Rufinus [CPG 5620; BHL 6524]
  MSS(i): Worcester, CL, 48, fos. 49–104 (?Continent, s. xi^1; prov. Worcester)
  CIT: Aldhelm 112; Ælfric 102

Ilias latina [ICL 8372]
  MSS(i):
    Oxford, BodL, Auct. F. 2. 14 (?Sherborne, s. xi²)
    Oxford, BodL, Rawlinson G. 57 + G. 111 (s. xi^ex)

Libellus de dignitate sacerdotali [CPL 171a] [pseudo-Ambrose]
  MSS(i):
    London, BL, Harley 3097 (?Peterborough, s. xi/xii)
    Oxford, BodL, Lat. theol. d. 34 (?Durham, s. xi/xii)

Liber de numeris [BCLL 778] [pseudo-Isidore]
    INV(i): f. 27

Liber de ordine creaturarum [CPL 1189; BCLL 342] [pseudo-Isidore]
    INV(ii): b. 17
    MSS(i):
        Basle, UB, F. III. 15b, fos. 1–19 (?Northumbria, s. viii^1; prov. Fulda)
        Paris, BNF, lat. 9561 (Southumbria, s. viii^1; prov. Saint-Bertin)
    MSS(ii): no. 18
    CIT: Bede 248; OEM 30; Ælfric 103; Byrhtferth 103

Liber differentiarum seu De proprietate sermonum [CPL 1226] [pseudo-
    Isidore]
    INV(i): b. 17 (?)
    MSS(ii): no. 17

Liber medicinae ex herbis femininis [pseudo-Dioscorides]
    MSS(i):
        Oxford, BodL, Ashmole 1431 (St Augustine's, Canterbury, s. xi/xii)
        Oxford, BodL, Bodley 130 (?Bury St Edmunds, s. xi^{ex})

Liber Nemroth
    CIT: Byrhtferth 103

Liber pontificalis [CPL 1568]
    MSS(i): Durham, CL, B. II. 11 (Normandy, s. xi^{ex}; prov. Durham)
        (exc.)
    CIT: Bede 249; OEM 31; Ælfric 104

Martyrologium Hieronymianum [CPL 2031]
    CIT: Bede 250; Byrhtferth 105

Medicina de quadrupedibus
    MSS(i): Oxford, BodL, Bodley 130 (Bury St Edmunds, s. xi^{ex})

Paedagogus [ICL 1969] [pseudo-Vergil]
    CIT: Aldhelm 113

passiones apostolorum
    MSS(i):
        Cambridge, CCC 9 + London, BL, Cotton Nero E. i (Worcester,
          s. xi$^{3/4}$)
        Cambridge, Pembroke College 91 (N. France, s. ix$^{1/3}$; prov. Bury St
          Edmunds)
        Paris, BNF, lat. 10861 (s. ix$^{1/4}$)
        Salisbury, CL, 221 + 222 (Salisbury, s. xi^{ex})
    CIT: Aldhelm 114; Bede 251; OEM 32; Ælfric 105

passiones martyrum
  INV(i): d. 5, d. 11 (?)
  INV(ii): b. 22
  MSS(i):
    Cambridge, CCC 9 + London, BL, Cotton Nero E. i (Worcester, s. xi³⁄⁴)
    Cambridge, CCC 361 (?England, s. xi^med)
    Edinburgh, NLS, Advocates 18. 7. 8, fos. 19, 22 (s. viii¹)
    Exeter, CL, FMS/3 (England, s. x¹) (frg.)
    London, BL, Cotton Otho A. xiii (s. xi^in)
    London, BL, Harley 3020, fos. 95–132 (?Winchester, s. x/xi)
    Orleans, BM, 342 (290) (?England, ?Fleury, s. x/xi)
    Paris, BNF, lat. 5574, fos. 1–39 (s. ix/x)
    Paris, BNF, lat. 5575, fos. 1–41 (s. x²)
    Paris, BNF, lat. 10861 (s. ix¹⁄⁴)
    St Petersburg, Russian National Library, O. v. XVI. 1, fos. 1–16 (s. x¹)
    Saint-Omer, BM, 202 (NE France, s. ix²; prov. Exeter, s. xi^med)
    Salisbury, CL, 221 + 222 (Salisbury, s. xi^ex)
  MSS(ii): nos. 28, 59, 75, 81, 82, 83, 91
  CIT: Theodore/Hadrian 22; Aldhelm 115; Bede 252; Alcuin 58; OEM 33; Abbo 53; Ælfric 106

Pastor Hermae [CPG 1052]
  MSS(i): Düsseldorf, UB, Fragm. K1: B 215 + K2: C 118 + K15: 00 (?Northumbria, s. viii^med)
  CIT: Bede 253

Physiologus
  INV(i): b. 20
  MSS(i): Cambridge, CCC 448 (S. England, s. x¹) (exc.)

Prouerbia grecorum [BCLL 344]
  CIT: Asser 22

Quaestiones de Veteri et Nouo Testamento [BCLL 779]
  INV(i): d. 15

Recognitiones, trans. Rufinus [CPG 1015(5); BHL 6644–5] [pseudo–Clement]
  INV(i): f. 58
  MSS(i): Oxford, Trinity College 60 (s. xi^ex)
  CIT: Theodore/Hadrian 23; Aldhelm 116; Bede 254

Regula magistri [CPL 1858]
  MSS(ii): 87

Syllogai titulorum
> CIT: Aldhelm 117 (*Sylloge Laureshamensis quarta*; *Sylloge Turonensis*)

Versus sibyllae de iudicio [ICL 8497]
> CIT: Aldhelm 118

Visio Baronti [CPL 1313; BHL 997]
> INV(i): f. 49
> MSS(i): London, BL, Cotton Otho A. xiii, pt. 1 (s. xi^1)

uitae sanctorum
> MSS(i):
>> Cambridge, CCC 9 + London, BL, Cotton Nero E. i (Worcester, s. xi$^{3/4}$)
>> Dublin, Trinity College 174 (B. 4. 3), fos. 1–44, 52–6, 95–103 (Salisbury, s. xi^{ex})
>> London, BL, Cotton Otho A. xiii, pt 1 (s. xi^1)
>> London, BL, Cotton Tiberius D. iv, fos. 1–105 (?N. France, ?England, s. x/xi; prov. Winchester)
>> London, BL, Harley 3020, fos. 36–94 (Christ Church, Canterbury, s. x/xi)
>> Orleans, BM, 342 (290) (?England, ?Fleury, s. x/xi)
> CIT: Bede 255; OEM 34; Ælfric 107

Voces animantium
> CIT: Aldhelm 119; Byrhtferth 106

Bibliography

ABBO OF FLEURY: *Abbo von Fleury, De syllogismis hypotheticis*, ed. F. Schupp (Leiden and New York, 1997).

——*Abbon de Fleury: Questions grammaticales*, ed. A. Guerreau-Jalabert (Paris, 1982).

——*Abbo of Fleury and Ramsey: Commentary on the Calculus of Victorius of Aquitaine*, ed. A. M. Peden (Auctores Britannici Medii Aevi, 15; London, 2003).

ÆLFRIC: *Ælfric's Catholic Homilies: The First Series. Text*, ed. P. Clemoes (EETS s.s. 17; Oxford, 1997).

——*Ælfric's Catholic Homilies: The Second Series. Text*, ed. M. Godden (EETS s.s. 5; Oxford, 1979).

——*Ælfric's De Temporibus Anni*, ed. H. Henel (EETS o.s. 213; Oxford, 1942).

——*Ælfric's Lives of Saints*, ed. W. W. Skeat, 4 vols. (EETS o.s. 76, 82, 94, 114; Oxford, 1881–1900; repr. as 2 vols., 1966).

——'Ælfric's Preface to Genesis', in *The Old English Version of the Heptateuch*, ed. S. J. Crawford (EETS o.s. 160; Oxford, 1922), 76–80.

——'Ælfric's Version of Alcuin's *Interrogationes Sigeuulfi in Genesin*', ed. G. E. MacLean, *Anglia*, 7 (1884), 1–59.

——*Homilies of Ælfric: A Supplementary Collection*, ed. J. C. Pope, 2 vols. (EETS o.s. 259–60; Oxford, 1967–8).

ALDHELM: *Aldhelmi Opera*, ed. R. Ehwald (MGH AA 15; Berlin, 1919).

ALEXANDER, J. J. G., *Insular Manuscripts 6th to the 9th Century* (London, 1978).

Alfred the Great: Asser's Life of King Alfred and Other Contemporary Sources, trans. S. Keynes and M. Lapidge (Harmondsworth, 1983).

ALTANER, B., 'Die Bibliothek Augustins', *Theologische Revue*, 44 (1948), 73–8.

Das altenglische Martyrologium, ed. G. Kotzor, 2 vols. (Bayerische Akademie der Wissenschaften, phil.-hist. Klasse: Abhandlungen, 88; Munich, 1981).

AMALARIUS OF METZ: *De ecclesiasticis officiis*, ed. J. M. Hanssens, 3 vols. (Studi e testi, 138–40; Rome, 1948–50), ii. 13–543.

Ambrose in Anglo-Saxon England, with Pseudo-Ambrose and Ambrosiaster, ed. D. A. Bankert, J. Wegmann, and C. D. Wright, *Old English Newsletter, Subsidia*, 25 (1997).

Angelsächsische Homilien und Heiligenleben, ed. B. Assmann, repr. with a supplementary introduction by P. Clemoes (Darmstadt, 1964).

Anglo-Saxon Conversations: The Colloquies of Ælfric Bata, ed. S. Gwara and D. W. Porter (Woodbridge, 1997).

The Anglo-Saxon Poetic Records, ed. G. P. Krapp and E. V. K. Dobbie, 6 vols. (New York, 1931–42).

Anthologia Latina, i: *Carmina in Codicibus Scripta*, ed. A. Riese, 2 vols. (Leipzig, 1894–1906).

Antike Bibliotheken, ed. W. Hoepfner (Mainz, 2002).

Appendix Serviana, ceteros praeter Servium et Scholia Bernensia Virgilii commentatores continens, ed. H. Hagen (Leipzig, 1902).

ASHWORTH, H., 'Did St Augustine Bring the *Gregorianum* to England?', *Ephemerides Liturgicae*, 72 (1958), 39–43.

ASSER: *Asser's Life of King Alfred*, ed. W. H. Stevenson, rev. D. Whitelock (Oxford, 1959).

ASTON, M., 'English Ruins and English History: The Dissolution and the Sense of the Past', *Journal of the Warburg and Courtauld Institutes*, 36 (1973), 231–55.

BABCOCK, R. G., 'A Papyrus Codex of Gregory the Great's *Forty Homilies on the Gospels* (London, Cotton Titus C. XV)', *Scriptorium*, 54 (2000), 280–9.

BAGNALL, R. S., 'Alexandria: Library of Dreams', *Proceedings of the American Philosophical Society*, 146 (2002), 348–62.

BAILEY, R. N., *The Durham Cassiodorus* (Jarrow Lecture, 1978).

BALE, J., *Index Brittaniae Scriptorum: John Bale's Index of British and Other Writers*, ed. R. L. Poole and M. Bateson, with intro. by C. Brett and J. P. Carley (Cambridge, 1990).

—— *Scriptorum Illustrium Maioris Brytanniae quam nunc Angliam & Scotiam uocant Catalogus*, 2 vols. (Basle, 1557–9).

BAMMEL, C. P. H., 'Das neue Rufinfragment in irischer Schrift und die Überlieferung der Rufin'schen Übersetzung der Kirchengeschichte Eusebs', in R. Gryson (ed.), *Philologia Sacra: Biblische und patristische Studien für Hermann J. Frede und Walter Thiele zu ihrem siebzigsten Geburtstag*, 2 vols. (Freiburg, 1993), ii. 483–513.

BARDON, H., *La Littérature latine inconnue*, 2 vols. (Paris, 1952–6).

BARNES, R., 'Cloistered Bookworms in the Chicken-Coop of the Muses: The Ancient Library of Alexandria', in MacLeod (ed.), *The Library of Alexandria*, 61–77.

BARRÉ, H., *Les Homéliaires carolingiens de l'école d'Auxerre* (Studi e testi, 225; Rome, 1962), 49–70.

BATELY, J., 'The Classical Additions in the Old English Orosius', in P. Clemoes and K. Hughes (eds.), *England before the Conquest: Studies in Primary Sources Presented to Dorothy Whitelock* (Cambridge, 1971), 237–51.

—— 'Those Books that are Most Necessary for All Men to Know: The Classics and Late Ninth-Century England, a Reappraisal', in A. S. Bernardo and S. Levin (eds.), *The Classics in the Middle Ages* (Binghamton, NY, 1990), 45–78.

——BROWN, M. P., and ROBERTS, J. (eds.), *A Palaeographer's View: The Selected Writings of Julian Brown* (London, 1993).

BATIFFOL, P., 'Librairies byzantines à Rome', *Mélanges d'archéologie et d'histoire [de l'École française de Rome]*, 8 (1888), 297–308.

BECKER, G., *Catalogi Bibliothecarum Antiqui* (Bonn, 1885).

BEDE: *Bedae Opera de Temporibus*, ed. C. W. Jones (Cambridge, Mass., 1943).

——*Bedae presbyteri Expositio Apocalypseos*, ed. Roger Gryson (Turnhout, 2001).

——*Bedae Venerabilis Expositio Actuum Apostolorum et Retractatio*, ed. M. L. W. Laistner (Cambridge, Mass., 1939).

——*Bedas metrische Vita sancti Cuthberti*, ed. W. Jaager (Palaestra, 198; Leipzig, 1935).

——*Opera Bedae Venerabilis presbyteri anglosaxonis*, ed. J. Herwagen, 8 vols. (Basle 1563).

——*Venerabilis Baedae Opera Historica*, ed. C. Plummer, 2 vols. (Oxford, 1896).

BEER, R., 'Bemerkungen über den ältesten Hss.-Bestand des Klosters Bobbio', in *Monumenta Palaeographica Vindobonensia*, ii (Leipzig, 1913), 17–26.

BEESON, C. H., *Isidor-Studien* (Munich, 1913).

BERLIOZ, J., et al., *Identifier sources et citations* (Turnhout, 1994).

BERSCHIN, W., *Biographie und Epochenstil im lateinischen Mittelalter*, 4 vols. in 5 (Stuttgart, 1986–2001).

——'An Unpublished Library Catalogue from Eighth-Century Lombard Italy', *Journal of Medieval Latin*, 11 (2001), 201–9.

——and Geith, K. E., 'Die Bibliothekskataloge des Klosters Murbach aus dem IX. Jahrhundert', *Zeitschrift für Kirchengeschichte*, 83 (1972), 61–87.

BERTELLI, C., 'The Production and Distribution of Books in Late Antiquity', in R. Hodges and W. Bowden (eds.), *The Sixth Century: Production, Distribution and Demand* (Leiden, Boston, and Cologne, 1998), 41–60.

Bischof Wærferths von Worcester Übersetzung der Dialoge Gregors des Grossen, ed. H. Hecht, 2 vols. (Leipzig, 1900–7).

BISCHOFF, B., *Die Abtei Lorsch im Spiegel ihrer Handschriften* (2nd edn., Lorsch, 1989).

——'Biblioteche, scuole e letteratura nelle città dell'alto medio evo', in his *MS*, i. 122–33.

——*Katalog der festländischen Handschriften des neunten Jahrhunderts* (Wiesbaden, 1998– ; in progress) [cited by item number].

——*Lorsch im Spiegel seiner Handschriften* (Munich, 1974).

——'Scriptoria e manoscritti mediatori di civiltà dal sesto secolo alla riforma di Carlo Magno', in his *MS*, ii. 312–27.

BISHOP, T. A. M., *English Caroline Minuscule* (Oxford, 1971).

——'Lincoln Cathedral MS 182', *Lincolnshire History and Archaeology*, 2 (1967), 73–6.

BISHOP, T. A. M., 'Notes on Cambridge Manuscripts', *Transactions of the Cambridge Bibliographical Society*, 1 (1949–53), 432–41; 2 (1954–8), 185–99, 323–36; 3 (1959–63), 93–5, 412–23.

BLANCK, H., *Das Buch in der Antike* (Munich, 1992).

BLUM, R., *Kallimachos: The Alexandrian Library and the Origins of Bibliography*, trans. H. H. Wellisch (Madison, 1991).

BOLTON, W. F., *A History of Anglo-Literature*, i: *597–740* (Princeton, 1967).

S. Bonifatii et Lullii epistolae, ed. M. Tangl (MGH, Epistolae selectae, 1; Berlin, 1916).

BONNER, G. (ed.), *Famulus Christi: Essays in Commemoration of the Thirteenth Centenary of the Birth of the Venerable Bede* (London, 1976).

BORGES, JORGE LUIS, *Collected Fictions*, trans. A. Hurley (Harmondsworth, 1998).

—— *Labyrinths*, trans. D. A. Yates and J. E. Irby (Harmondsworth, 1970).

—— *Obras completas*, ed. C. V. Frias (Buenos Aires, 1974).

BREEN, A., 'A New Irish Fragment of the Continuatio to Rufinus-Eusebius Historia ecclesiastica', *Scriptorium*, 41 (1987), 185–204.

BROOKS, N., *The Early History of the Church of Canterbury: Christ Church from 597 to 1066* (Leicester, 1984).

—— 'England in the Ninth Century: The Crucible of Defeat', *Transactions of the Royal Historical Society*, 5th ser., 29 (1979), 1–20.

BROWN, G. H., 'Bede and his Monastic Library', *Ex libris*, 11 (1999–2000), 12–17.

—— *Bede the Venerable* (Boston, Mass., 1987).

BROWN, M. P., 'Paris, Bibliothèque Nationale, lat. 10861 and the Scriptorium of Christ Church, Canterbury', *Anglo-Saxon England*, 15 (1986), 119–37.

BROWN, T. J., and MACKAY, T. W., *Codex Palatinus 235* (Armarium Codicum Insignium, 4; Turnhout, 1988).

BRUCE, L., 'Roman Libraries: A Review Bibliography', *Libri*, 35/2 (1985), 89–106.

BRUCE-MITFORD, R. L. S., *The Art of the Codex Amiatinus* (Jarrow Lecture 1967).

BRUYNE, D. DE, 'Gaudiosus, un vieux libraire romain', *Revue Bénédictine*, 30 (1913), 343–5.

BYRHTFERTH: *Byrhtferth's Enchiridion*, ed. P. S. Baker and M. Lapidge (EETS s.s. 15; Oxford, 1995).

—— *Byrhtferth of Ramsey: The Lives of Oswald and Ecgwine*, ed. M. Lapidge (Oxford Medieval Texts, forthcoming).

BULLOUGH, D., 'Alcuin and the Kingdom of Heaven: Liturgy, Theology, and the Carolingian Age', in U.-R. Blumenthal (ed.), *Carolingian Essays* (Washington, DC, 1983), 1–69.

CALLMER, C., 'Die ältesten christlichen Bibliotheken in Rom', *Eranos*, 83 (1985), 48–60.

CAMERON, A., *Claudian: Poetry and Propaganda at the Court of Honorius* (Oxford, 1970).

CANFORA, L., *La Biblioteca del patriarca: Fozio censurato nella Francia di Mazzarino* (Rome, 1998).

——*La biblioteca scomparsa* (Palermo, 1987); trans. as *La Véritable Histoire de la bibliothèque d'Alexandrie*, trans. J.-P. Manganaro and D. Dubroca (Paris, 1988); *The Vanished Library*, trans. M. Ryle (London, 1989).

——'Le biblioteche ellenistiche', in Cavallo (ed.), *Le biblioteche nel mondo antico*, 3–28.

CARLEY, J. P., and PETITMENGIN, P., 'Pre-Conquest Manuscripts from Malmesbury Abbey and John Leland's Letter to Beatus Rhenanus concerning a Lost Copy of Tertullian's Works', *Anglo-Saxon England*, 33 (2004), 129–223.

CARRIKER, A., *The Library of Eusebius at Caesarea* (Leiden, 2003).

CASSIODORUS: *Cassiodori Senatoris Institutiones*, ed. R. A. B. Mynors (Oxford, 1937); trans. L.W. Jones, *Cassiodorus: An Introduction to Divine and Human Readings* (New York, 1946); trans. J. W. Halporn, *Cassiodorus: Institutions of Divine and Secular Learning and On the Soul*, with intro. by M. Vessey (Translated Texts for Historians, 42; Liverpool, 2004).

CASSON, L., *Libraries in the Ancient World* (New Haven, 2001).

Catalogus Librorum Manuscriptorum Bibliothecae Wigorniensis Made in 1622–1623 by Patrick Young, ed. I. Atkins and N. R. Ker (Cambridge, 1944).

CAVALLO, G., 'Le tipologie della cultura nel riflesso delle testimonianze scritte', *Settimane*, 34 (1988), 467–516.

——(ed.), *Le biblioteche nel mondo antico e medievale* (2nd edn., Bari, 1989).

CLARK, J. W., *The Care of Books* (Cambridge, 1902).

COLINI, A. M., *Storia e topografia del Celio nell'antichità. Con rilievi, piante e riconstruzioni archetettoniche di I. Gismondi* (Atti della Pontificia Accademia romana di archeologia, 3rd ser., 7; Rome, 1944).

COLLINS, R., 'Poetry in Ninth-Century Spain', *Papers of the Liverpool Latin Seminar*, 4 (1981), 181–95.

Concilium Lateranense a. 649 celebratum, ed. R. Riedinger (Acta Conciliorum Oecumenicorum, 2nd ser., 1; Berlin, 1984).

CONNER, P. W., *Anglo-Saxon Exeter: A Tenth-Century Cultural History* (Studies in Anglo-Saxon History, 4; Woodbridge, 1993).

CONSTANTINESCU, R., 'Alcuin et les "Libelli precum" de l'époque carolingienne', *Revue de l'histoire de la spiritualité*, 50 (1974), 17–56.

Corpus Inscriptionum Latinarum, ed. T. Mommsen et al., 15 vols. in 73 parts (Berlin, 1863– ; in progress).

COURCELLE, P., *Les Lettres grecques en Occident, de Macrobe à Cassiodore* (Paris, 1948).

——'Nouvelles recherches sur le monastère de Cassiodore', in *Actes du Ve Congrès international d'archéologie chrétienne* (Rome, 1957), 511–28.

COURCELLE, P., 'Le Site du monastère de Cassiodore', *Mélanges d'archéologie et d'histoire de l'École française de Rome*, 55 (1938), 259–307.

COURTNEY, E., *A Companion to Petronius* (Oxford, 2001).

CRICK, J., 'An Anglo-Saxon Fragment of Justinus's *Epitome*', *Anglo-Saxon England*, 16 (1987), 181–96.

CROSS, J. E., 'On the Library of the Old English Martyrologist', in Lapidge and Gneuss (eds.), *Learning and Literature in Anglo-Saxon England*, 227–49.

DAMASUS: *Epigrammata Damasiana*, ed. A. Ferrua (Rome, 1942).

DECKER, A., 'Die Hildebald'sche Manuskriptensammlung des Kölner Domes', in *Festschrift der 43. Versammlung deutscher Philologen und Schulmänner dargeboten von den höheren Lehranstalten Kölns* (Bonn, 1895), 215–51.

DEKKER, E., 'La Bibliothèque de Saint-Riquier au moyen âge', trans. J. Godard, *Bulletin de la Société des Antiquaires de Picardie*, 46 (1955–6), 157–97.

DELIA, D., 'From Romance to Rhetoric: The Alexandrian Library in Classical and Islamic Traditions', *American Historical Review*, 97 (1992), 1449–67.

DEROLEZ, A., *Les Catalogues de bibliothèques* (Typologie des sources du moyen âge occidental, 31; Turnhout, 1979).

DE ROSSI, G. B., 'La biblioteca della sede apostolica', *Studi e documenti di storia e diritto*, 5 (1884), 317–80.

—— 'De origine, historia, indicibus scrinii et bibliothecae sedis apostolicae commentatio', in *Codices Palatini Latini Bibliothecae Vaticanae*, i (Vatican City, 1886).

DÍAZ Y DÍAZ, M. C., 'Introduccion general', in *San Isidoro de Sevilla: Etimologías*, ed. J. Oroz Reta and M. A. Marcos Casquero, 2 vols. (Madrid, 1982), i. 1–257.

DIONISOTTI, A. C., 'On Bede, Grammars and Greek', *Revue Bénédictine*, 92 (1982), 111–41.

DOUGLAS, D. C., *English Scholars* (London, 1939).

DRONKE, P., *Dante and Medieval Latin Traditions* (Cambridge, 1986).

DUBOIS, J., and RENAUD, G., *Édition pratique des martyrologes de Bède, de l'anonyme lyonnais et de Florus* (Paris, 1976).

DUCKWORTH, G. E., *Vergil and Classical Hexameter Poetry: A Study in Metrical Variety* (Ann Arbor, 1969).

DUMVILLE, D. N., 'Anglo-Saxon Books: Treasure in Norman Hands?', *Anglo-Norman Studies*, 16 (1993), 83–99.

—— 'The Early Mediaeval Insular Churches and the Preservation of Roman Literature: Towards a Historical and Palaeographical Re-evaluation', in O. Pecere and M. D. Reeve (eds.), *Formative Stages of Classical Traditions: Latin Texts from Antiquity to the Renaissance* (Spoleto, 1995), 197–237.

—— *English Caroline Script and Monastic History: Studies in Benedictinism, A.D. 950—1030* (Studies in Anglo-Saxon History, 6; Woodbridge, 1993).

—— 'English Libraries before 1066: Use and Abuse of the Manuscript Evidence', in M. P. Richards (ed.), *Anglo-Saxon Manuscripts: Basic Readings* (New York and London, 1994), 169–219.

—— 'The Importation of Mediterranean Manuscripts into Theodore's England', in Lapidge (ed.), *Archbishop Theodore*, 96–119.

—— *Liturgy and the Ecclesiastical History of Late Anglo-Saxon England* (Woodbridge, 1992).

EBERSPERGER, B., *Die angelsächsischen Handschriften in den Pariser Bibliotheken* (Heidelberg, 1999).

ECO, U., *Il nome della rosa* (Milan, 1980); trans. W. Weaver, as *The Name of the Rose* (London, 1983).

EL-ABBADI, MOSTAFA, *The Life and Fate of the Ancient Library of Alexandria* (Paris, 1990).

English Benedictine Libraries: The Shorter Catalogues, ed. R. Sharpe, J. P. Carley, R. M. Thomson, and A. G. Watson (CBMLC 4; London, 1996).

ENNIUS: *The Annals of Q. Ennius*, ed. O. Skutsch (Oxford, 1985).

ESPOSITO, M., 'The Ancient Bobbio Catalogue', *Journal of Theological Studies*, 32 (1931), 337–43.

EUSEBIUS: *Eusebius Werke II: Die Kirchengeschichte*, ed. E. Schwartz and T. Mommsen (Die griechischen christlichen Schriftsteller, 9; Leipzig, 1903–9).

EWALD, P., 'Reise nach Spanien im Winter von 1878 auf 1879', *Neues Archiv*, 6 (1881), 219–398.

FANTHAM, E., *Roman Literary Culture from Cicero to Apuleius* (Baltimore and London, 1996).

FEDELI, P., 'Biblioteche private e pubbliche a Roma e nel mondo romano', in Cavallo (ed.), *Le biblioteche nel mondo antico*, 29–64.

FEHRLE, R., *Das Bibliothekswesen im alten Rom: Voraussetzungen, Bedingungen, Anfänge* (Wiesbaden, 1986).

FERRARI, M. C., *Sancti Willibrordi venerantes memoriam: Echternacher Schreiber und Schriftsteller von den Angelsachsen bis Johann Bertels* (Luxembourg, 1994).

FONTAINE, J., *Isidore de Séville et la culture classique dans l'Espagne wisigothique*, 2nd edn., 3 vols. (Paris, 1983 [vols. i–ii are an anastatic reprint of the first edition of 1959; vol. iii contains supplementary notes, bibliography, and indices]).

FÖRSTER, M., 'The Donations of Leofric to Exeter', in *The Exeter Book of Old English Poetry*, ed. R. W. Chambers, M. Förster, and R. Flower (London, 1933).

The Fragmentary Latin Poets, ed. E. Courtney (Oxford, 1993).

FRANK, L., *Die Physiologus-Literatur des englischen Mittelalters und die Tradition* (Tübingen, 1971).

FRANSEN, I., 'Description de la collection de Bède le Vénérable sur l'Apôtre', *Revue Bénédictine*, 71 (1961), 22–70.

FRASER, P. M., *Ptolemaic Alexandria*, 2 vols. (Oxford, 1972).

FRIIS-JENSEN, K., and WILLOUGHBY, J. M. W., *Peterborough Abbey* (CBMLC 8; London, 2001).

Frithegodi monachi Breuiloquium Vitae beati Wilfredi et Wulfstani Cantoris Narratio metrica de sancto Swithuno, ed. A. Campbell (Zurich, 1950).

GAMBLE, H. Y., *Books and Readers in the Early Church: A History of Early Christian Texts* (New Haven, 1995).

GAMESON, R., 'Alfred the Great and the Destruction and Production of Christian Books', *Scriptorium*, 49 (1995), 180–210.

—— 'The Earliest Books of Christian Kent', in id. (ed.), *St Augustine*, 313–73.

—— *The Manuscripts of Early Norman England (c.1066–1130)* (Oxford, 1999).

—— 'The Origin of the Exeter Book of Old English Poetry', *Anglo-Saxon England*, 25 (1996), 135–85.

—— (ed.), *St Augustine and the Conversion of England* (Stroud, 1999).

GANZ, D., 'Anglo-Saxon Libraries', in Webber and Leedham-Green (eds.), *A History of Libraries in Britain and Ireland*, i (forthcoming).

GASNAULT, P., 'Fragment retrouvé du manuscrit sur papyrus des Homélies de saint Avit', *Comtes-rendus de l'Académie des inscriptions et belles-lettres* (1994), 315–23.

GATCH, M. McC., *Preaching and Theology in Anglo-Saxon England: Ælfric and Wulfstan* (Toronto, 1977).

GIL, J., *Corpus Scriptorum Muzarabicorum*, 2 vols. (Madrid, 1973).

GIOSEFFI, M., *Studi sul commento a Virgilio dello pseudo-Probo* (Florence, 1991).

GNEUSS, H., 'Addenda and Corrigenda to the *Handlist of Anglo-Saxon Manuscripts*', *Anglo-Saxon England*, 32 (2003), 293–305.

—— *Books and Libraries in Early England* (Aldershot, 1996).

—— *Handlist of Anglo-Saxon Manuscripts: A List of Manuscripts and Manuscript Fragments Written or Owned in England up to 1100* (Medieval and Renaissance Texts and Studies, 241; Tempe, Ariz., 2001).

—— 'King Alfred and the History of Anglo-Saxon Libraries', in id., *Books and Libraries*, no. III.

—— 'Preliminary List of Manuscripts Written or Owned in England up to 1100', *Anglo-Saxon England*, 9 (1981), 1–60.

GODDEN, M., 'Wærferth and King Alfred: The Fate of the Old English *Dialogues*', in J. Roberts, J. L. Nelson, and M. Godden (eds.), *Alfred the Wise: Studies in Honour of Janet Bately* (Cambridge, 1997), 35–51.

GOMOLL, H., 'Zu Cassiodors Bibliothek und ihrem Verhältnis zu Bobbio', *Zentralblatt für Bibliothekswesen*, 53 (1936), 185–9.

GOODMAN, A. W., *Chartulary of Winchester Cathedral* (Winchester, 1927).

GORMAN, M. M., 'Eugippius and the Origins of the Manuscript Tradition of Saint Augustine's *De Genesi ad litteram*', *Revue Bénédictine*, 93 (1983), 7–30.

—— 'The Glosses on Bede's *De temporum ratione* Attributed to Byrhtferth of Ramsey', *Anglo-Saxon England*, 25 (1996), 209–32.

—— 'The Oldest Lists of Latin Books', *Scriptorium*, 58 (2004), 48–63.

GOTTLIEB, T., 'Ueber Handschriften aus Bobbio', *Zentralblatt für Bibliothekswesen*, 4 (1887), 442–63.

GRAHAM, T., and WATSON, A. G., *The Recovery of the Past in Early Elizabethan England* (Cambridge, 1998).

GREBE, S., 'Die Bibliothek Agapets im Vergleich mit ausgewählten Bibliotheken der Zeit der alten Kirche und des Frühmittelalters', *Bibliothek und Wissenschaft*, 25 (1991), 15–60.

GRUEN, E. S., *Heritage and Hellenism: the Reinvention of Jewish Tradition* (Berkeley, 1998).

GRÜTZMACHER, G., *Hieronymus: Eine biographische Studie zur alten Kirchengeschichte*, 3 vols. (Leipzig, 1901–8).

GUGEL, K., *Welche erhaltenen mittelalterlichen Handschriften dürfen der Bibliothek des Klosters Fulda zugerechnet werden? 1. Die Handschriften* (Fuldaer Hochschulschriften, 23a; Frankfurt, 1995).

HADDAN, A. W., and STUBBS, W. (eds.), *Councils and Ecclesiastical Documents relating to Great Britain and Ireland*, 3 vols. (Oxford, 1869–71).

HAFT, A. J., WHITE, J. G., and WHITE, P. J., *The Key to 'The Name of the Rose'* (Ann Arbor, 1999).

HARIULF: *Hariulf: Chronique de l'abbaye de Saint-Riquier*, ed. F. Lot (Paris, 1894).

HÄSE, A., *Mittelalterliche Bücherverzeichnisse aus Kloster Lorsch: Einleitung, Edition und Kommentar* (Beiträge zum Buch- und Bibliothekswesen, 42; Wiesbaden, 2002).

HASKINS, C. H., 'Nimrod the Astronomer', in his *Studies in the History of Mediaeval Science* (Cambridge, Mass., 1927), 336–45.

HEEG, J., and LEHMANN, P., '*Enim* und *autem* in mittelalterlichen lateinischen Handschriften', *Philologus*, 73 (1914–16), 536–48.

HIGHET, G., *Juvenal the Satirist: A Study* (New York, 1954).

HINE, H. M., 'The Manuscript Tradition of Seneca's *Naturales quaestiones*: Addenda', *Classical Quarterly*, 42 (1992), 558–62.

HOFFMANN, H., *Buchkunst und Königtum im ottonischen und frühsalischen Reich*, 2 vols. (Schriften der MGH, 30; Stuttgart, 1986).

HOLFORD-STREVENS, L., *Aulus Gellius: An Antonine Scholar and his Achievement*, rev. edn. (Oxford, 2003).

HOLTZ, L., 'Vers la création des bibliothèques médiévales en Occident', *Settimane*, 45 (1998), 1059–103.

HUNTER BLAIR, P., 'From Bede to Alcuin', in Bonner (ed.), *Famulus Christi*, 239–60.

ISIDORE OF SEVILLE, *Etymologiae*, ed. W. M. Lindsay (Oxford, 1911).

—— *Isidorus Hispalensis: Versus*, ed. J. M. Sánchez Martín (CCSL 123A; Turnhout, 2000).

JACKSON, P., and LAPIDGE, M., 'The Contents of the Cotton-Corpus Legendary', in P. E. Szarmach (ed.), *Holy Men and Holy Women: Old English Prose Saints' Lives and their Contexts* (Albany, NY, 1996), 131–46.

JAHN, [OTTO], 'Über die Subscriptionen in den Handschriften römischer Classiker', in *Berichte über die Verhandlungen der königlich sächsischen Gesellschaft der Wissenschaften zu Leipzig*, phil.-hist. Klasse, 3 (1851), 327–83.

JAMES, M. R., 'Learning and Literature till the Death of Bede', *Cambridge Medieval History*, iii (Cambridge, 1922), 485–513.

—— *Lists of Manuscripts formerly in Peterborough Abbey* (Oxford, 1926).

JONES, C. W., 'Bede's Place in Medieval Schools', in Bonner (ed.), *Famulus Christi*, 261–85.

—— 'The Byrhtferth Glosses', *Medium Ævum*, 7 (1938), 81–97.

KASTER, R. A., *Guardians of Language: The Grammarian and Society in Late Antiquity* (Berkeley, Los Angeles, and London, 1988).

KELLY, J. N. D., *Jerome: His Life, Writings and Controversies* (London, 1975).

KENDRICK, T. D., *British Antiquity* (London, 1950).

KER, N. R., 'The Beginnings of Salisbury Cathedral Library', in J. J. G. Alexander and M. T. Gibson (eds.), *Medieval Learning and Literature: Essays presented to R. W. Hunt* (Oxford, 1976), 23–49, repr. in his *Books, Collectors and Libraries*, 143–73.

—— *Books, Collectors and Libraries: Studies in the Medieval Heritage*, ed. A. G. Watson (London and Ronceverte, W. Va., 1985).

—— *Catalogue of Manuscripts containing Anglo-Saxon* (Oxford, 1957).

—— *English Manuscripts in the Century after the Norman Conquest* (Oxford, 1960).

—— *Medieval Libraries of Great Britain: A List of Surviving Books* (2nd edn., London, 1964).

—— 'The Migration of Manuscripts from the English Medieval Libraries', *The Library*, 4th ser., 23 (1942–3), 1–11, repr. in his *Books, Collectors and Libraries*, 459–70.

—— 'A Supplement to *Catalogue of Manuscripts Containing Anglo-Saxon*', *Anglo-Saxon England*, 5 (1976), 121–31.

KEYNES, S., *An Atlas of Attestations in Anglo-Saxon Charters, c.670–1066* (Cambridge, 1998).

—— 'King Athelstan's Books', in Lapidge and Gneuss (eds.), *Learning and Literature in Anglo-Saxon England*, 143–201.

—— 'The Reconstruction of a Burnt Cottonian Manuscript: The Case of Cotton MS. Otho A. i', *British Library Journal*, 22 (1996), 113–60.

—— 'The Vikings in England c.790–1016', in P. Sawyer (ed.), *The Oxford Illustrated History of the Vikings* (Oxford, 1997), 48–82.

King Alfred's West-Saxon Version of Gregory's Pastoral Care, ed. H. Sweet, 2 vols. (EETS o.s. 45, 50; London, 1871).

KLOPSCH, K., *Einführung in die mittellateinische Verslehre* (Darmstadt, 1972).

LAISTNER, M. L. W., 'Bede as a Classical and Patristic Scholar', *Transactions of the Royal Historical Society*, 4th ser., 16 (1933), 69–94, repr. in id., *The Intellectual Heritage*, 93–116.

——*A Hand-List of Bede Manuscripts* (Ithaca, NY, 1943).

——'The Influence during the Middle Ages of the Treatise *De vita contemplativa* and its Surviving Manuscripts', in his *The Intellectual Heritage*, ed. Starr, 40–56.

——*The Intellectual Heritage of the Early Middle Ages: Selected Essays by M. L. W. Laistner*, ed. C. G. Starr (Ithaca, NY, 1957).

——'The Library of the Venerable Bede', in A. H. Thompson (ed.), *Bede: His Life, Times, and Writings* (Oxford, 1935), 237–66, repr. in id., *The Intellectual Heritage*, ed. Starr, 117–49.

LAPIDGE, M., 'Acca of Hexham and the Origin of the *Old English Martyrology*', *Analecta Bollandiana*, 123 (2005), 29–78.

——'Æthelwold and the *Vita S. Eustachii*', in Lapidge, *ALL* ii. 213–23.

——'Æthelwold as Scholar and Teacher', in B. Yorke (ed.), *Bishop Æthelwold: His Career and Influence* (Woodbridge, 1988), 89–117.

——'Artistic and Literary Patronage in Anglo-Saxon England', in Lapidge, *ALL* i. 37–91.

——'Asser's Reading', in T. Reuter (ed.), *Alfred the Great: Papers from the Eleventh-Centenary Conferences* (Aldershot, 2003), 27–47.

——'Bede and the Poetic Diction of Vergil', in *Poesía latina medieval (siglos V–XV): Actas del IV Congreso del Internationales Mittellateinerkomitee (Santiago de Compostela, 12–15 septiembre 2002)*, ed. M. C. Díaz y Díaz and J. M. Díaz de Bustamante (Florence, 2005), 739–48.

——*Bede's Latin Poetry* (Oxford Medieval Texts, forthcoming).

——'Bede's Metrical *Vita S. Cuthberti*', in G. Bonner, D. Rollason, and C. Stancliffe (eds.), *St Cuthbert: His Life, Cult and Community to A.D. 1200* (Woodbridge, 1989), 77–93, repr. in Lapidge, *ALL* i. 339–55.

——'*Beowulf*, Aldhelm, the *Liber monstrorum* and Wessex', *Studi medievali*, 3rd ser., 23 (1982), 151–92, repr. in Lapidge, *ALL* ii. 271–312.

——'The Career of Archbishop Theodore', in id. (ed.), *Archbishop Theodore*, 1–29.

——*The Cult of St Swithun* (Oxford, 2003).

——'An Isidorian Epitome from Early Anglo-Saxon England', in Lapidge, *ALL* i. 183–223.

——'Latin Learning in Ninth-Century England', in Lapidge, *ALL* i. 409–54.

——'A Metrical *Vita S. Iudoci* from Tenth-Century Winchester', *Journal of Medieval Latin*, 10 (2000), 255–306.

LAPIDGE, M., 'Prolegomena to an Edition of Bede's Metrical *Vita S. Cuthberti*', *Filologia mediolatina*, 22 (1995), 127–63.

—— 'Rufinus at the School of Canterbury', in P. Lardet (ed.), *La Tradition vive: Mélanges d'histoire des textes en l'honneur de Louis Holtz* (Bibliologia, 20; Turnhout, 2003), 119–29.

—— 'The School of Theodore and Hadrian', *Anglo-Saxon England*, 15 (1986), 45–72, repr. in Lapidge, *ALL* i. 141–68.

—— 'Stoic Cosmology and the Source of the First Old English Riddle', *Anglia*, 112 (1994), 1–25.

—— 'The Study of Greek at the School of Canterbury in the Seventh Century', in Lapidge, *ALL* i. 123–39.

—— 'Surviving Booklists from Anglo-Saxon England', in Lapidge and Gneuss (eds.), *Learning and Literature in Anglo-Saxon England*, 33–89; repr. in *Anglo-Saxon Manuscripts: Basic Readings*, ed. M. P. Richards (New York and London, 1994), 87–167.

—— and GNEUSS, H. (eds.), *Learning and Literature in Anglo-Saxon England: Studies Presented to Peter Clemoes* (Cambridge, 1985).

—— and MANN, J., 'Reconstructing the Anglo-Latin Aesop: The Literary Tradition of the "Hexametrical Romulus"', in *Latin Culture in the Eleventh Century. Proceedings of the Third International Conference on Medieval Latin Studies, Cambridge, September 9–12, 1998*, ed. M. W. Herren, C. J. McDonough, and R. G. Arthur, 2 vols. (Turnhout, 2002), ii. 1–33.

A Late Eighth-Century Latin–Anglo-Saxon Glossary Preserved in the Library of the Leiden University, ed. J. H. Hessels (Cambridge, 1906).

LAUER, P., 'Les Fouilles du Sancta sanctorum à Rome', *Mélanges d'archéologie et d'histoire de l'École française de Rome*, 20 (1900), 251–87.

LAW, V., 'St Augustine's *De grammatica*: Lost or Found?', *Recherches Augustiniennes*, 19 (1984), 155–83.

—— *Grammar and Grammarians in the Early Middle Ages* (London, 1997).

—— *The History of Linguistics in Europe from Plato to 1600* (Cambridge, 2003).

—— 'The Study of Latin Grammar in Eighth-Century Southumbria', *Anglo-Saxon England*, 12 (1983), 43–71, repr. in her *Grammar*, 91–123.

LECLERCQ, H., 'Bibliothèques', *DACL* ii/2 (1925), cols. 842–904.

LEHMANN, P., 'Das älteste Bücherverzeichnis der Niederlände', *Het Boek*, 12 (1923), 207–13, repr. in his *Erforschung*, i. 207–13.

—— *Erforschung des Mittelalters: Ausgewälte Abhandlungen und Aufsätze*, 5 vols. (Leipzig and Stuttgart, 1941–62).

—— 'Erzbischof Hildebald und die Dombibliothek von Köln', *Zentralblatt für Bibliothekswesen*, 25 (1908), 153–9, repr. in his *Erforschung*, ii. 139–44.

—— *Fuldaer Studien: Sitzungsberichte der Bayerischen Akademie der Wissenschaften*, phil.-hist. Klasse (1925), Abt. iii.

LELAND, J., *Commentarii de Scriptoribus Britannicis*, ed. A. Hall, 2 vols. (Oxford, 1709).

LEVISON, W., *England and the Continent in the Eighth Century* (Oxford, 1946).

LEWIS, N., *Papyrus in Classical Antiquity* (Oxford, 1974).

——*Papyrus in Classical Antiquity: A Supplement* (Papyrologica Bruxellensia, 23; Brussels, 1989).

Libellus de regionibus urbis Romae, ed. A. Nordh (Skrifter utgivna av svenska Instituted i Rom, 3rd ser. 8; Lund, 1949).

LIEFTINCK, G. I., 'Le Manuscrit d'Aulu-Gelle à Leeuwarden exécuté à Fulda en 836', *Bullettino dell''Archivio paleografico italiano'*, 1 (1955), 11–17 [+ 9 pls.].

The Life of Bishop Wilfrid by Eddius Stephanus, ed. B. Colgrave (Cambridge, 1927).

LINDSAY, W. M., *Early Welsh Script* (Oxford, 1912).

——'A Study of the Leyden MS of Nonius Marcellus', *American Journal of Philology*, 22 (1901), 29–38.

LIVESEY, S. S., and ROUSE, R. H., 'Nimrod the Astronomer', *Traditio*, 37 (1981), 203–66.

LOVE, ROSALIND C., 'The Library of Bede', in Gameson (ed.), *History of the Book in Britain*, i (forthcoming).

LOWE, E. A., *Codices Lugdunenses Antiquissimi: Le scriptorium de Lyon, la plus ancienne école calligraphique de France*, 2 vols. (Lyon, 1924).

——'Codices rescripti: A List of the Oldest Latin Palimpsests with Stray Observations on their Origin', in his *Palaeographical Papers*, ii. 480–519.

——'An Eighth-Century List of Books in a Bodleian Manuscript from Würzburg and its Probable Relation to the Laudian Acts', *Speculum*, 3 (1928), 3–15; repr. in his *Palaeographical Papers*, i. 239–50.

——*English Uncial* (Oxford, 1960).

——*Palaeographical Papers 1907–1965*, ed. L. Bieler, 2 vols. (Oxford, 1972).

LUCAN: *M. Annaei Lucani De bello ciuili*, ed. C. Hosius (Leipzig, 1905).

LUCRETIUS: *Titi Lucreti Cari De Rerum Natura Libri Sex*, ed. C. Bailey, 3 vols. (Oxford, 1947).

LUGLI, G., *I monumenti antichi di Roma e suburbio*, 3 vols. (Rome, 1930–8).

LUTZ, C. E., 'A Manuscript Fragment from Bede's Monastery', *Yale University Library Gazette*, 48 (1973), 135–8.

MCGURK, P., 'Computus Helperici: Its Transmission in England in the Eleventh and Twelfth Centuries', *Medium Aevum*, 43 (1974), 1–5.

MCKISACK, M., *Medieval History in the Tudor Age* (Oxford, 1971).

MCKITTERICK, R., 'Anglo-Saxon Missionaries in Germany: Reflections on the Manuscript Evidence', *Transactions of the Cambridge Bibliographical Society*, 9 (1986–90), 291–329.

——*The Carolingians and the Written Word* (Cambridge, 1989).

MACLEOD, R. (ed.), *The Library of Alexandria: Centre of Learning in the Ancient World* (London, 2000).

MCNALLY, R. E., *Der irische Liber de Numeris* (Munich, 1957).

—— 'The Pseudo-Isidorian *De ueteri et nouo Testamento Quaestiones*', *Traditio*, 19 (1963), 37–50.

MAI, A., *Spicilegium Romanum*, 10 vols. (Rome, 1838–44).

MANGO, C., 'La Culture grecque et l'Occident au VIIIe siècle', *Settimane*, 20 (1973), 603–58.

MANITIUS, M., *Geschichte der lateinischen Literatur des Mittelalters*, 3 vols. (Munich, 1911–31).

—— 'Zu Aldhelm und Baeda', *Sitzungsberichte der phil.-hist. Classe der kaiserlichen Akademie der Wissenschaften zu Wien*, 112 (1886), 535–634.

MARROU, H.-I., 'Autour de la bibliothèque du pape Agapit', *Mélanges d'archéologie et d'histoire de l'École française de Rome*, 48 (1931), 124–69.

MARSDEN, R., 'The Gospels of St Augustine', in Gameson (ed.), *St Augustine*, 285–312.

—— 'Job in his Place: The Ezra Miniature in the Codex Amiatinus', *Scriptorium*, 49 (1995), 3–15.

—— *The Text of the Old Testament in Anglo-Saxon England* (CSASE, 15; Cambridge, 1995).

MERCATI, G., 'Le principali vicende della biblioteca del monastero di S. Colombano di Bobbio', in his *M. Tulli Ciceronis De re publica libri e codice rescripto Vaticano latino 5757 phototypice expressi*, 2 vols. (Vatican City, 1934), i. 1–171.

MEYVAERT, P., 'Bede, Cassiodorus and the Codex Amiatinus', *Speculum*, 71 (1996), 827–83.

MILDE, W., *Die Bibliothekskataloge des Klosters Murbach aus dem 9. Jahrhundert* (Beihefte zum Euphorion, 4; Heidelberg, 1968).

MORRISH, J., 'Dated and Datable Manuscripts Copied in England during the Ninth Century: A Preliminary List', *Mediaeval Studies*, 50 (1988), 512–58.

—— 'King Alfred's Letter as a Source on Learning in England', in P. E. Szarmach (ed.), *Studies in Earlier Old English Prose* (Albany, NY, 1986), 87–107.

MURATORI, L. A., *Antiquitates Italicae Medii Aevi*, 25 vols. and index (Milan, 1723–1896).

NAPIER, A. S., *Old English Glosses, chiefly Unpublished* (Oxford, 1900).

NETZER, N., 'The Early Scriptorium at Echternach: the State of the Question', in G. Kiesel and J. Schroeder (eds.), *Willibrord, Apostel der Niederlande* (Luxembourg, 1989), 127–34.

—— 'Willibrord's Scriptorium at Echternach and its Relationship to Ireland and Lindisfarne', in G. Bonner, D. Rollason, and C. Stancliffe (eds.), *St Cuthbert, his Cult and his Community to AD 1200* (Woodbridge, 1989), 203–12.

NONIUS MARCELLUS: *Nonii Marcelli De compendiosa doctrina libri XX*, ed. W. M. Lindsay, 3 vols. (Leipzig, 1903).

O'DONNELL, J. J., *Cassiodorus* (Berkeley and Los Angeles, 1979).

OGILVIE, R. M., *The Library of Lactantius* (Oxford, 1978).

OGILVY, J. D. A., *Books Known to the English, 597–1066* (Cambridge, Mass., 1967).

Old English Homilies, First Series, ed. R. Morris (EETS o.s. 29, 34; London, 1868).

Old English Homilies from MS Bodley 343, ed. S. Irvine (EETS o.s. 302; Oxford, 1993).

The Old English Martyrology: see *Das altenglische Martyrologium*, ed. Kotzor.

The Old English Orosius, ed. J. Bately (EETS s.s. 6; Oxford, 1980).

ORCHARD, A., 'After Aldhelm: The Teaching and Transmission of the Anglo-Latin Hexameter', *Journal of Medieval Latin*, 2 (1992), 96–133.

—— *The Poetic Art of Aldhelm* (CSASE 8; Cambridge, 1994).

—— *Pride and Prodigies: Studies in the Beowulf-Manuscript* (Cambridge, 1995).

ORLANDI, G., 'La tradizione del "Physiologus" e i prodromi del bestiario latino', *Settimane*, 31 (1984), 1057–1106.

PACKER, J. E., *The Forum of Trajan in Rome: A Study of the Monuments*, 3 vols. (Berkeley and Los Angeles, 1997).

—— *The Forum of Trajan in Rome: A Study of the Monuments in Brief* (Berkeley and Los Angeles, 2001).

PALMER, R. B., 'Bede as Textbook Writer: A Study of his *De arte metrica*', *Speculum*, 34 (1959), 573–84.

PARKES, M. B., 'A Fragment of an Early-Tenth-Century Anglo-Saxon Manuscript and its Significance', *Anglo-Saxon England*, 12 (1983), 129–40.

—— 'The Handwriting of St Boniface: A Reassessment of the Problems', *Beiträge zur Geschichte der deutschen Sprache und Literatur*, 98 (1976), 161–79, repr. in his *Scribes, Scripts and Readers: Studies in the Communication, Presentation and Dissemination of Medieval Texts* (London and Rio Grande, Ohio, 1991), 121–42.

—— 'The Scriptorium of Wearmouth-Jarrow' (Jarrow Lecture 1982), repr. in his *Scribes, Scripts and Readers: Studies in the Communication, Presentation and Dissemination of Medieval Texts* (London and Rio Grande, Ohio, 1991), 93–120.

PARSONS, E. A., *The Alexandrian Library, Glory of the Hellenic World* (London, 1952).

PECERE, O., 'Esemplari con "subscriptiones" e tradizione dei testi latini: L'Apuleio Laur. 68.2', in *Il libro e il testo: Atti del Convegno internazionale di Urbino, 20–23 settembre 1982*, ed. C. Questa and R. Raffaelli (Urbino, 1984), 111–37, with 11 pls.

—— 'I meccanismi della tradizione testuale', in G. Cavallo, P. Fedeli, and A. Giardina (eds.), *Lo spazio letterario di Roma antica*, iii: *La circolazione del testo* (Rome, 1990), 297–386

—— 'La tradizione dei testi latini tra IV e V secolo attraverso i libri sottoscritti', in A. Giardina (ed.), *Società romana ed impero tardoantico* (Rome, 1986), 19–81.

PELLETIER, A. (ed.), *La Lettre d'Aristée à Philocrate* (Paris, 1962).

A. Persi Flacci et D. Iuni Iuvenalis Saturae, ed. W. V. Clausen (Oxford, 1959).

PETRUCCI, A., 'L'onciale romana: Origini, sviluppo e diffusione di una stilazazzione grafica altomedievale (sec. VI–IX)', *Studi medievali*, 3rd ser., 12 (1971), 75–134.

PFEIFFER, R., *The History of Classical Scholarship from the Beginnings to the End of the Hellenistic Age* (Oxford, 1968).

PHILIPPART, G., *Les Légendiers latins et autres manuscrits hagiographiques* (Typologie des sources du moyen âge occidental, 24–5; Turnhout, 1977).

PLACANICA, A., 'Corippus', in P. Chiesa and L. Castaldi (eds.), *La trasmissione dei testi latini del medioevo—Mediaeval Latin Texts and their Transmission (Te.tra, 1; Florence, 2004), 53–61.

PLATNER, S. B., and ASHBY, T., *A Topographical Dictionary of Rome* (Oxford, 1926).

PLATTHY, J., *Sources on the Earliest Greek Libraries with the Testimonia* (Amsterdam, 1968).

The Prosopography of the Late Roman Empire, i: *A.D. 260–395*, ed. A. H. M. Jones, J. R. Martindale, and J. Morris (Cambridge, 1971).

PULSIANO, P., 'Persius's *Satires* in Anglo-Saxon England', *Journal of Medieval Latin*, 11 (2001), 142–55.

QUENTIN, H., *Les Martyrologes historiques du moyen âge* (Paris, 1908).

RAINE, J., *Historians of the Church of York and its Archbishops*, 3 vols. (Rolls Series; London, 1879–94).

RAMÍREZ DE VERGER, A., 'Sobre la historia del texto del *Panegírico de Justino II* de Coripo (568–882 d.C.)', *Revue d'histoire des textes*, 18 (1988), 229–32.

RANKE, E., *Specimen codicis Novi Testamenti fuldensis* (Marburg, 1860).

RAUER, C., 'The Sources of the *Old English Martyrology*', *Anglo-Saxon England*, 32 (2003), 89–109.

RAWSON, E., *Intellectual Life in the Roman Republic* (Baltimore, 1985).

REYNOLDS, L. D., *The Medieval Tradition of Seneca's Letters* (Oxford, 1965).

ROBERTS, C. H., and SKEAT, T. C., *The Birth of the Codex* (London, 1983).

ROBERTSON, A. J., *Anglo-Saxon Charters* (Cambridge, 1939).

RODZIEWICZ, M., 'A Review of the Archaeological Evidence concerning the Cultural Institutions in Ancient Alexandria', *Graeco-Arabica*, 6 (1995), 317–32.

SÁNCHEZ MARTÍN, J. M., 'Ecos de poetas tardíos en los "Versus" de Isidoro de Sevilla', in *Actas del II Congreso Hispánico de Latín Medieval*, ed. M. Pérez González, 2 vols. (Leon, 1998), ii. 793–802.

SANFORD, E. M., 'Juvenal', *Catalogus Translationum et Commentariorum: Medieval and Renaissance Latin Translations and Commentaries*, ed.

P. O. Kristeller et al., 4 vols. (Washington, DC, 1960– ; in progress), i. 175–238.

SANTIFALLER, L., *Beiträge zur Geschichte der Beschreibstoffe im Mittelalter*, i: *Untersuchungen* (Graz and Cologne, 1953).

SAWYER, P. H., *The Age of the Vikings* (2nd edn., London, 1971).

—— *Kings and Vikings: Scandinavia and Europe A.D. 700–1100* (London, 1982).

SAXL, F., and MEIER, H., *Catalogue of Astronomical and Mythological Illuminated Manuscripts of the later Middle Ages*, iii: *Manuscripts in English Libraries*, i, ed. H. Bober (London, 1953).

SCALIA, G., 'Gli "archiva" di papa Damaso e le biblioteche di papa Ilaro', *Studi medievali*, 3rd ser., 18 (1977), 39–63.

SCHALLER, D., 'Frühkarolingische Corippus-Rezeption', *Wiener Studien*, 105 (1992), 173–87, repr. in his *Studien zur lateinischen Dichten des Frühmittelalters* (Stuttgart, 1995), 346–60 (with a Nachtrag at p. 431).

SCHARER, A., 'The Writing of History at King Alfred's Court', *Early Medieval Europe*, 5 (1996), 177–206.

SCHEELE, J., 'Buch und Bibliothek bei Augustinus', *Bibliothek und Wissenschaft*, 12 (1978), 14–114.

SCHEPENS, P., 'L'Epître *De singularitate clericorum* du ps.-Cyprien', *Recherches de science religieuse*, 13 (1922), 178–210, 297–327, and 14 (1923), 47–65.

SCHMIDT, P. L., 'Rezeption und Überlieferung der Tragödien Senecas bis zum Ausgang des Mittelalters', in E. Lefèvre (ed.), *Der Einfluss Senecas auf das europäische Drama* (Darmstadt, 1978), 12–73.

SCHREIBER, C., *King Alfred's Old English Translation of Pope Gregory the Great's Regula Pastoralis and its Cultural Context* (Frankfurt, 2003).

SCHRIMPF, G., *Mittelalterliche Bücherverzeichnisse des Klosters Fulda* (Frankfurt, 1992).

SCHÜLING, H., 'Die Handbibliothek des Bonifatius: Ein Beitrag zur Geistesgeschichte des ersten Hälfte des 8. Jahrhunderts', *Archiv für Geschichte des Buchwesens*, 4 (1961–3), cols. 285–348.

SCHÜRER, E., *The History of the Jewish People in the Age of Jesus Christ*, rev. G. Vermes et al., 3 vols. in 4 parts (Edinburgh, 1973–87).

Seneca: Agamemnon, ed. R. J. Tarrant (Cambridge Classical Texts and Commentaries, 17; Cambridge, 1976).

SHANZER, D., 'Tatwine: An Independent Witness to Martianus Capella's *De grammatica*?', *Rivista di filologia italiana classica*, 112 (1984), 292–313.

SHARPE, R., *Corpus of British Medieval Library Catalogues: List of Identifications* (London, 1993).

—— 'Latin and Irish Words for "Book-satchel"', *Peritia*, 4 (1985), 152–6.

—— *Titulus: Identifying Medieval Latin Texts. An Evidence-Based Approach* (Turnhout, 2003).

SHEERIN, D. J., 'Turpilius and St Jerome in Anglo-Saxon England', *Classical World*, 70 (1976), 183–5.

SIMPSON, D., 'The "Proverbia Grecorum"', *Traditio*, 43 (1987), 1–22.

SIMS-WILLIAMS, P., 'Cuthswith, Seventh-Century Abbess of Inkberrow, near Worcester, and the Würzburg Manuscript of Jerome on Ecclesiastes', *Anglo-Saxon England*, 5 (1976), 1–21.

Sources of Anglo-Saxon Literary Culture: A Trial Version, ed. F. M. Biggs, T. D. Hill, and P. E. Szarmach (Binghamton, NY, 1990).

Sources of Anglo-Saxon Literary Culture, i: *Abbo of Fleury, Abbo of Saint-Germain-des-Prés, and Acta Sanctorum*, ed. F. M. Biggs, T. D. Hill, P. E. Szarmach, and E. G. Whatley (Kalamazoo, 2001).

SPECK, P., 'Marginalien zu dem Gedicht *In Laudem Iustini Augusti Minoris* des Corippus', *Philologus*, 134 (1990), 82–92.

SPILLING, H., 'Angelsächsische Schrift in Fulda', in A. Brall (ed.), *Von der Klosterbibliothek zur Landesbibliothek: Beiträge zum zweihundertjährigen Bestehen der Hessischen Landesbibliothek Fulda* (Stuttgart, 1978), 47–98.

STACHE, U. J., *Flavius Cresconius Corippus In Laudem Iustini Augusti Minoris: Ein Kommentar* (Berlin, 1976).

STAIKOS, K. S., *The Great Libraries, from Antiquity to the Renaissance (3000 B.C. to A.D. 1600)*, trans. T. Cullen (London, 2000).

STROCKA, V., 'Römische Bibliotheken', *Gymnasium*, 88 (1981), 298–329.

SYME, R., *Ammianus and the Historia Augusta* (Oxford, 1968).

SYMEON OF DURHAM: *Symeonis Monachi Opera Omnia*, ed. T. Arnold, 2 vols. (Rolls Series; London, 1885).

TALBOT, C. H., 'The *Liber confortatorius* of Goscelin of Saint-Bertin', *Studia Anselmiana*, 37 (1955), 1–117.

TATWINE: *Tatuini Opera Omnia*, ed. M. de Marco (CCSL 133; Turnhout, 1968).

TEUTSCHE, L., 'Cassiodorus Senator, Gründer der Klosterbibliothek von Vivarium: Ein Beitrag zur Würdigung seiner wissenschaftlich-bibliothekarischen Leistung', *Libri*, 9 (1959), 215–39.

THOMPSON, J. W., *The Medieval Library*, 3rd edn., with addenda by B. B. Boyer (New York, 1967).

THOMSON, R. M., 'British Library Royal 15. C. XI: A Manuscript of Plautus' Plays from Salisbury Cathedral (*c*.1100)', *Scriptorium*, 40 (1986), 82–7.

—— 'Identifiable Books from the Pre-Conquest Library of Malmesbury Abbey', *Anglo-Saxon England*, 10 (1981), 1–19.

—— 'The Norman Conquest and English Libraries', in P. Ganz (ed.), *The Role of the Book in Medieval Culture*, 2 vols. (Turnhout, 1986), ii. 27–40.

Three Lives of English Saints, ed. M. Winterbottom (Toronto, 1972).

TIMPANARO, S., *Per la storia della filologia virgiliana antica* (Rome, 1986).

TJÄDER, J.-O., 'Der Codex Argenteus in Uppsala und der Buchmeister

Viliaric in Ravenna', in U. E. Hagberg (ed.), *Studia Gothica* (Stockholm, 1972), 144–64.

—— *Die nichtliterarischen lateinischen Papyri Italiens aus der Zeit 445–700* (Lund, 1955).

TRAUBE, L., 'Paläographische Anzeigen, III', *Neues Archiv*, 17 (1901), 264–85, repr. in his *Vorlesungen und Abhandlungen*, ed. F. Boll, 3 vols. (Munich, 1909–20), iii. 229–46.

TRONCARELLI, F., 'I codici di Cassiodoro: Le testimonianze più antiche', *Scrittura e civiltà*, 12 (1988), 47–99.

—— 'Decora correctio: Un codice emendato da Cassiodoro?', *Scrittura e civiltà*, 9 (1985), 147–68

—— 'Litteras pulcherrimas: Correzioni di Cassiodoro nei codici di Vivarium', *Scrittura e civiltà*, 20 (1996), 89–109.

—— *Vivarium: I libri, il destino* (Turnhout, 1998).

TURNER, E., *Athenian Books in the Fifth and Fourth Centuries B.C.* (London, 1952).

Two Lives of Saint Cuthbert, ed. B. Colgrave (Cambridge, 1940).

VALERIUS PROBUS: *De M. Valerio Probo Berytio capita quattuor. Accedit reliquiarum conlectio*, ed. J. Aistermann (Bonn, 1910).

—— *M. Valerii Probi in Vergilii Bucolica et Georgica Commentarius*, ed. H. Keil (Halle, 1848).

VAN DE VYVER, A., 'Cassiodore et son oeuvre', *Speculum*, 6 (1931), 244–92.

VAN ELDEREN, B., 'Early Christian Libraries', in J. L. Sharpe and K. Van Kampen (eds.), *The Bible as Book: The Manuscript Tradition* (London, 1998), 45–59.

VENDRELL PEÑARANDA, M., 'Estudio del códice de Azagra, Biblioteca Nacional de Madrid, Ms. 10029', *Revista de archivos, bibliotecas y museos*, 82 (1979), 655–705 with 6 pls.

VERBRAKEN, P. P., 'La Collection de sermons de saint Augustin "De uerbis Domini et apostoli" ', *Revue Bénédictine*, 77 (1967), 27–46.

Vitae Sancti Bonifatii archiepiscopi Moguntini, ed. W. Levison (MGH, Scriptores rerum Germanicarum in usum scholarum; Hannover and Leipzig, 1905).

WARD, J. O., 'Alexandria and its Medieval Legacy: The Book, the Monk, and the Rose', in MacLeod (ed.), *The Library of Alexandria*, 163–79.

WATSON, A. G., *Medieval Libraries of Great Britain: A List of Surviving Books edited by N. R. Ker. Supplement to the Second Edition* (London, 1987).

WATTENBACH, W., *Das Schriftwesen im Mittelalter* (4th edn., Leipzig, 1896).

WEBBER, T., 'The Patristic Content of English Book Collections in the Eleventh Century: Towards a Continental Perspective', in P. R. Robinson and R. Zim (eds.), *Of the Making of Books: Medieval Manuscripts, their Scribes and Readers: Essays Presented to M. B. Parkes* (Aldershot, 1997), 191–205.

—— Scribes and Scholars at Salisbury Cathedral, c.1075—c.1125 (Oxford, 1992).

—— and LEEDHAM-GREEN, E. S. (eds.), A History of Libraries in Britain and Ireland, i: From the Beginnings to the Outbreak of the Civil War (Cambridge, forthcoming).

WEINBERGER, W., 'Handschriften von Vivarium', in Miscellanea Francesco Ehrle IV (Studi e testi, 40; Vatican City, 1924), 75–88.

WENDEL, C., 'Bibliothek', RAC ii (1954), cols. 231–74.

WILLIAM OF MALMESBURY: Willelmi Malmesbiriensis monachi Gesta pontificum Anglorum, ed. N. E. S. A. Hamilton (Rolls Series, London, 1870).

WILMART, A., 'Les Textes latins de la lettre de Palladius sur les moeurs des Brahmanes', Revue Bénédictine, 45 (1933), 29–42.

WILSON, N. G., Photius: The Bibliotheca (London, 1994).

WITTIG, J., 'King Alfred's Boethius and its Latin Sources: A Reconsideration', Anglo-Saxon England, 11 (1983), 157–98.

WOOD, I., The Most Holy Abbot Ceolfrid (Jarrow Lecture, 1995).

WORMALD, P., 'Bede and Benedict Biscop', in Bonner (ed.), Famulus Christi, 141–69.

WRIGHT, C. E., 'The Dispersal of the Libraries in the Sixteenth Century', in F. Wormald and C. E. Wright (eds.), The English Library before 1700 (London, 1958), 148–75.

—— 'The Dispersal of the Monastic Libraries and the Beginnings of Anglo-Saxon Studies', Transactions of the Cambridge Bibliographical Society, 1 (1949–53), 208–37.

—— 'The Elizabethan Society of Antiquaries and the Formation of the Cottonian Library', Transactions of the Cambridge Bibliographical Society, 1 (1949–54), 176–212.

WRIGHT, N., 'Bede and Vergil', Romanobarbarica, 6 (1981–2), 361–79, repr. in his History and Literature in Late Antiquity and the Early Medieval West (Aldershot, 1995), no. XI.

WRIGHT, T., Anglo-Saxon and Old English Vocabularies, 2nd edn. rev. R. P. Wülcker (London, 1884).

WULFSTAN OF WINCHESTER: Wulfstan of Winchester: Life of St Æthelwold, ed. M. Lapidge and M. Winterbottom (Oxford, 1991).

WULFSTAN OF WORCESTER: Wulfstan: Sammlung der ihm zugeschriebenen Homilien nebst Untersuchungen über ihre Echtheit, ed. A. S. Napier, with addenda by K. Ostheeren (Dublin and Zurich, 1967; originally publ. 1883).

WURM, H., Studien und Texte zur Decretalensammlung des Dionysius Exiguus (Bonn, 1939).

ZETZEL, J. E. G., Latin Textual Criticism in Antiquity (New York, 1981; repr. Salem, NH, 1984).

—— 'The Subscriptions in the Manuscripts of Livy and Fronto and the Meaning of Emendatio', Classical Philology, 75 (1980), 38–59.

Electronic resources

Archive of Celtic-Latin Literature (ACLL-1), ed. A. Harvey, K. Devine, and F. J. Smith (Turnhout, 1994).

Bibliotheca Teubneriana Latina (BTL-3), ed. Centre Traditio Litterarum Occidentalium [dir. P. Tombeur] (Munich and Turnhout, 2004).

Cetedoc Library of Christian Latin Texts (CLCLT-5), ed. P. Tombeur (Turnhout, 2002).

Fontes Anglo-Saxonici: A Register of Written Sources Used by Anglo-Saxon Authors (CD-ROM Version 1.1), ed. D. Miles, R. Jayatilaka, and M. Godden (Oxford, 2002).

The Electronic Monumenta Germaniae Historica (eMGH-2), ed. MGH (Munich and Turnhout, 2000).

Patrologia Latina Database, ed. Chadwyck-Healey Ltd. (Cambridge, 1995).

Poetria Nova: A CD-ROM of Latin Medieval Poetry (650–1250 A.D.), with a Gateway to Classical and Late Antiquity Texts, ed. P. Mastandrea and L. Tessarolo (Florence, 2001).

Index of Manuscripts

Note that in the Index of Manuscripts the abbreviation 'Bischoff' refers to the work which elsewhere in the volume is cited as 'Bischoff, *Katalog*'; the abbreviations 'CLA' and 'Gneuss' are as elsewhere in the volume.

B. III. 11, fos. 1–135 [Gneuss 242]
305

B. III. 16, fos. 159–60 [Gneuss
243.5] 290

B. IV. 9 [Gneuss 246] 303, 321, 328,
329, 330

B. IV. 12, fos. 1–120 [Gneuss 246.8]
276, 277, 279, 286, 291, 303, 304,
327, 328

B. IV. 13 [Gneuss 247] 305

C. IV. 8, flyleaf [CLA ii. *155] 156

Düsseldorf
Nordrhein-Westfälisches
Hauptstaatsarchiv
Z 11/1 (*olim* Z.4 nr 2) [CLA Supp.
1687; Gneuss 820] 323
Universitätsbibliothek
K1: B.210 [CLA viii. 1184; Gneuss
818.5] 309, 310
K1: B. 213 [CLA viii. 1186] 159
K1: B.215 + K2: C.118 + K15: 00
[CLA viii. 1187; Gneuss 819] 316,
317, 341
K2: E. 32 [CLA viii. 1188] 160
Fragm. K15: O17 + K19: Z.8/7b
(*olim* Staatsarchiv Z.4 nr 3/1 +
Fragm. 28) [CLA viii. **1189, and
cf. Supp. p. 6; Gneuss 821] 311
Fragm. K16: Z.3/1 (*olim*
Staatsarchiv Fragm. s.n.) [CLA
Supp. 1786; Gneuss 822] 296
Fragm. K19: Z.8/1 (*olim*
Staatsarchiv Z.4 nr 1) [CLA Supp.
1686] 165

Edinburgh
National Library of Scotland
Advocates 18. 4. 3, fos. 1–122
[Gneuss 251.5] 291, 336
Advocates 18. 6. 12 [Gneuss 252]
292, 308, 324, 334
Advocates 18. 7. 7 [Gneuss 253] 331
Advocates 18. 7. 8 [Gneuss 254] 297
Advocates 18. 7. 8, fos. 1?, 4, 5, 8?,
9, 16, 28, 31 [CLA Supp. 1689;
Gneuss 255] 287
Advocates 18. 7. 8, fos. 19, 22 [CLA
Supp. 1690; Gneuss 255] 341

Advocates 18. 7. 8, fos. 26, 33 [CLA
Supp. 1691; Gneuss 255] 304

El Escorial
Real Biblioteca de San Lorenzo
B. IV. 17 [Bischoff 1193] 231
E. II. 1 [Gneuss 823] 56 n. 20, 293
R. II. 18 117 n. 105

Esztergom
Archiepiscopal Library
s.n. [CLA xi. 1591] 164

Evreux
Bibliothèque municipale
43 [Gneuss 824.5] 327, 331

Exeter
Cathedral Library
3501, fos. 0–7 + Cambridge, UL, Ii.
2. 11 [Gneuss 15] 139
3501, fos. 8–130 [Gneuss 257] 64 n. 4
3507 [Gneuss 258] 292, 310, 336
FMS/ 1, 2, 2a [Gneuss 259.5] 323
FMS/ 3 [Gneuss 260] 341

Florence
Biblioteca Medicea Laurenziana
Amiatino 1 [CLA iii. 299; Gneuss
825] 29, 61
Plut. XXXVII. 13 94
Plut. XLVII. 36 [Bischoff 1229] 84
Plut. LXV. 1 [CLA iii. 298] 29
Plut. LXVIII. 1 [Bischoff 1237] 84

Fulda
Hessische Landesbibliothek
Bonifatianus 1 [CLA viii. 1196;
Gneuss 827.6] 40 with n. 52,
77 n. 50
Bonifatianus 3 [CLA viii. 1198;
Gneuss 827.7] 77 n. 50
Fragm. s.n. + Marburg, Hessisches
Staatsarchiv, Hr. 2, 4d [CLA
Supp. 1698] 165
Priesterseminar
fragm. s.n. [CLA Supp. 1787] 166

Geneva
Bibliothèque publique et universitaire
Lat. 84 [Bischoff 1352] 84
Pap. lat. VI [CLA vii. 886] 94 n. 11

General Index

Sophocles, Greek dramatist, 5

Sophronius, patriarch of Jerusalem, 32

Statius (P. Papinius Statius), Roman
poet [LLA 369] 66, 98 n. 34, 124,
231; writings of: *Achilleis* 231, 333;
Thebais 115 n. 97, 140, 173, 187,
225, 231, 242, 249, 333; *Siluae* 129,
231

Stephen of Ripon, *Vita S. Wilfridi*
[BHL 8889] 42–3, 143, 146, 236

subscriptions 12 with n. 38, 24 with
n. 100

Suetonius (C. Suetonius Tranquillus),
Roman historian [LLA 404]
49 n. 84, 66; *Vita Caesarum* 84

Sulla, L. Cornelius Felix, Roman
dictator (*c.*138–79 B.C.), 11

Sulpicius Severus [LLA 672], writings
of: *Dialogi* [CPL 477] 176, 236,
246, 264, 333; *Epistulae .iii.* [CPL
476] 43, 157, 265, 333; *Vita S.
Martini* [CPL 475; BHL 5610] 43,
147, 176, 187, 236, 246, 265, 334

Swithun, St, patron saint of
Winchester, 239, 247

syllogae of Latin inscriptions 16, 17,
342; *Sylloge Laureshamensis quarta*,
191; *Sylloge Turonensis*, 191; *Sylloge*
of Einsiedeln, 17

Symeon of Durham, *Historia regum*
121 n. 118

Symmachus (Q. Aurelius Symmachus),
Roman statesman [LLA 633] 128

'Symposius', Roman poet [LLA 548],
Aenigmata 187, 334

Synodus episcoporum [BCLL 599] 167

Tacitus (P. Cornelius Tacitus), Roman
historian [LLA 382] 66, 68;
writings of: *Agricola* 84; *Annales* 84;
Germania 84; lost writings of, 2

Talbot, Robert (*c.*1503–58), antiquary,
75

Tatian, *Diatessaron* [CPG 1106] 40

Tatwine, archbishop of Canterbury
(731–4), 38, 43–4, 66, 67, 175;
writings of: *Ars grammatica* [CPL

1563] 43, 158; *Enigmata* [CPL
1564] 44

Tauberbischofsheim 78

Terence (P. Terentius Afer), Roman
dramatist [LLA 129], *Comoediae* of,
19, 66, 68, 98 with n. 34, 99, 100,
122 n. 126, 142, 175, 187, 225, 246,
273, 334

Tertullian (Q. Septimius Florens
Tertullianus) [LLA 474], 69;
writings of: *Apologeticum* [CPL 3]
334; 'Corpus Corbeiense' (incl. *De
resurrectione mortuorum* [CPL 19],
De trinitate [CPL 71], *De
praescriptione haereticorum* [CPL 5],
De pudicitia [CPL 30], *De
monogamia* [CPL 28]) 75 n. 41; *De
spectaculis* [CPL 6] 75; *De ieiunio*
[CPL 29] 75)

Thebes (Egypt), Ramesseum at, 9

Themistius (d. 388), Greek rhetorician,
writings of transmitted in Latin
translation: *De arte dialectica* 165;
De decem categoriis 50 n. 89, 334

Theodore, archbishop of Canterbury
(668–90) 21, 25–6, 31–4, 87, 89, 92,
174, 175–8; as teacher of Aldhelm,
34, 89; biblical commentaries [CPL
1125a] 32; creed (lost) composed
by, 81 n. 5

Theodore of Mopsuestia 32 n. 7; *Comm.
in epistulas Pauli minores*, in Latin
translation [CPG 3845] 156, 335

Theodoret of Cyrrhus 32 n. 7; *and see
also* Socrates, Sozomen, and
Theodoretus

Theodulf of Orléans (d. 821) 118; *De
ordine baptismi* (PL 105: 223–40) of,
265

Theophilus (of Antioch?) 32

Thucydides, Greek historian, 5

Tiberius (Tiberius Iulius Caesar
Augustus), Roman emperor (14–37
A.D.) 13

Tiberius Iulius Celsus Polemaeanus 15

Tibullus (Albius Tibullus), Roman poet
[LLA 228] 66, 67, 129

Tobias, bishop of Rochester (d. 726) 89